KU-739-611

THE DARK HISTORY OF THE

BAY CITY ROLLERS

WHEN THE SCREAMING STOPS

Also by Simon Spence

The Stone Roses: War and Peace
Happy Mondays: Excess All Areas
Still Breathing: True Adventures of the Donnelly Brothers
(with Anthony and Christopher Donnelly)
Just Can't Get Enough: The Making of Depeche Mode
Mr Big: Don Arden (Interviews and Research)
Immediate: The Little Bastard
Stoned: Andrew Loog Oldham (Interviews and Research)
2Stoned: Andrew Loog Oldham (Interviews and Research)

THE DARK HISTORY OF THE

BAY CITY ROLLERS

SIMON SPENCE

OMNIBUS PRESS

London / New York / Paris / Sydney / Copenhagen / Berlin / Madrid / Tokyo

Glasgow Life	
Glasgow Libraries	
IB	
C 006176235	
Askews & Holts	05-Oct-2016
782.421660922 H	£25.00

Copyright © 2016 Simon Spence
This edition copyright © 2016 Omnibus Press
(A Division of Music Sales Limited)

Cover designed by Fresh Lemon
Picture research by Sarah Patblygu

ISBN: 978.1.78305.937.9
Order No: OP56397

The Author hereby asserts his right to be identified as the author of this work in accordance with Sections 77 to 78 of the Copyright, Designs and Patents Act 1988.

All rights reserved. No part of this book may be reproduced in any form or by any electronic or mechanical means, including information storage or retrieval systems, without permission in writing from the publisher, except by a reviewer who may quote brief passages.

Exclusive Distributors
Music Sales Limited,
14/15 Berners Street,
London, W1T 3LJ.

Music Sales Corporation
180 Madison Avenue, 24th
Floor, New York,
NY 10016,
USA.

Music Sales Pty Ltd
Level 4, 30–32 Carrington Street,
Sydney,
NSW 2000,
Australia.

Every effort has been made to trace the copyright holders of the photographs in this book but one or two were unreachable. We would be grateful if the photographers concerned would contact us.

Printed in Malta

A catalogue record for this book is available from the British Library.

Visit Omnibus Press on the web at www.omnibuspress.com

Contents

Contents

To the BPI (British Recorded Music Industry)

'By perseverance, study and eternal desire, any man can become great'
General George S. Patton

Foreword

by Doctor Sarah Nelson

I was always very surprised, when Tam Paton was alive, that police action was not taken against him for sexual abuse or sexual exploitation. Surveillance operations on his house in East Lothian and of the flats [he owned] in the West End of Edinburgh for collection of evidence would have seemed an obvious and productive course to take on many occasions, especially given the numbers of rumours and allegations which circulated, and which certainly I was aware of from the early 1990s onwards. These were among voluntary/charitable sector organisations working with vulnerable young people, among journalists, criminal justice people and others.

Among homeless organisations, probation, drug & alcohol support organisations and youth organisations working with 'difficult' or vulnerable teenagers, it was widely discussed that:

- The boys and young men placed in the flats were troubled and vulnerable with a difficult and often traumatic past e.g. from care
- That prostitution or renting took place in these setting
- That there was a great deal of fear about speaking out and high levels of intimidation and it was alleged there had been at least one murder and other disappearances of young men who had tried to break away

or speak out; that this atmosphere also affected some voluntary sector organisations in their willingness to come forward

- That many of the young men involved with Paton and his circle were involved by them in crime so that it was harder for them to come forward to police
- That probation services found them among the most damaged, fearful and distrustful of all their clients

In retrospect and given my experience of working with both abused women and men, and current revelations of widespread sexual exploitation in England, I think it's possible some of the attitudes that left them exposed were a mixture of:

- Police collusion at high level: I do not have evidence I can offer nor am I suggesting most police were involved. But how could all this take place in plain sight for so long otherwise
- These are throwaway young people that few care about, blamed for their own situations and their reactions to trauma; they were probably a 'nuisance' to police and authorities just like the girls in Rotherham or Rochdale were
- Somebody was giving them a home – a relief of the burden
- Mistaken beliefs among some professionals about genuine choices being made by these boys and young men – that they were freely choosing who to associate with without taking account of the severe damage to their self-esteem of their lives to date, their neediness and vulnerability plus any intimidation they faced. Particular reluctance to be seen to argue against the free choices gay young men were making about their sexuality

I believe that these great injustices to the victims now need to be put right as far as they can, that the perpetrators will have extended beyond Tam Paton himself, that police inquiries and a historical inquiry must actively recognise fears, intimidation and reluctance to come forward through victims' inveiglement into other crimes. This will mean offering at least limited immunity from prosecution, confidential phone lines and other confidential access and the use of skilled staff that have worked with very damaged and distrustful people in the past.

Doctor Sarah Nelson is a Research Associate at the University of Edinburgh (Centre for Research on Families & Relationships) and was joint lead professional adviser to the Scottish Government's National Strategy for Survivors of Childhood Sexual Abuse. She is one of Scotland's leading commentators on sexual abuse and exploitation.

Author's Note

All historic cash figures quoted in this book have been updated to represent the sum the money would have been worth in 2016. For UK currency the author used the prices and inflation calculator at thisismoney.co.uk and for the dollar, www.measuringworth.com

A paedophile is defined as someone sexually attracted to pre-pubescent children, generally 11 and under. A pederast is an adult male who desires or engages in sexual activity with pubescent or adolescent males, broadly aged between 12 and 18.

Everything in this book is based on extensive author interviews conducted in 2015 and comprehensively noted research material. Three confidential informants are quoted.

All information has been corroborated by at least two separate and independent sources. The work has no malicious intent.

The reader is urged to consult the source notes for a detailed explanation of the author's modus operandi and delineation of his sources.

PROLOGUE

Fun Day

Sunday May 18, 1975. Tam Paton, the manager of The Bay City Rollers, is soaking wet. His long brown hair, which is thinning on top, his slacks, casual shirt and black shoes with two-inch heels, which raise him to 6ft tall, are all drenched. He is a little heavy but still handsome and strong, about 14 stone, and struggling like a children's cartoon character to stay perched on the front bonnet of the small four-seater powerboat as it is being rocked violently by scores of screeching children.

The Bay City Rollers are crammed into the back two seats and there is a panicked driver unsure as to whether to push away the children or try and rescue them – some appear to be drowning in the lake in which the boat is adrift. Paton has a cigarette wedged in his mouth as he grips the boat's small windscreen while trying to steady the band's 18-year-old guitarist Stuart Wood, who is stood up in the boat and trying to shift its gearstick to reverse away.

One of the children is about 14 or 15. Her tits are enormous and she is dressed like the band in an overall type costume with tartan trim and wearing a tartan scarf. Paton can't make her let go of the boat. The lake is about 400 metres long and 100 wide. If the girl, and they are all girls, go any deeper some will surely drown.

They have already risked their lives running across a live racetrack with souped up Ford Escorts hurtling past at 100mph. They have avoided the police, leapt over barriers, battered down stewards and waded through a putrid swamp of water just to get to the edge of the lake. Now they are hysterical. The swamp had much broken glass in it, their plimsoll-ed feet – in homage to the band's uniform battered Adidas high top trainers – are cut and there is blood in the water.

Paton has already been in the water once. There are frogmen, in black wetsuits, coming to try and rescue the girls. There are hundreds more screaming and sobbing girls wading and doggy paddling toward the boat. The band's 19-year-old singer Les McKeown, has already been dragged off the boat and into the lake. The girls, many of whom have his name inscribed on their backs or bottoms of their costumes, left deep scratch marks on his thin chest. His bollocks and cock are bruised from their clutches. Still Paton cannot prise this girl's hands free from powerboat. He grimaces, fag in gob, and pushes the heel of his shoe hard into her shoulder.

And this is normal for The Bay City Rollers. They are pop's hottest act. They have been at number one for the past six weeks now with their single 'Bye Bye Baby'. Their second album, released with indelicate haste following the success of their first, is also at number one. They are at the very pinnacle of their fame in the UK. They have their own weekly children's television show on ITV, their own magazine, a clothing range, and a vast slew of merchandising including board games and pillowcases.

Right now, in Mallory Park, Leicestershire, in the middle of England, 100 miles north of London and 300 miles south of the band's Edinburgh home, they are three weeks into a sold out six-week UK tour that has been so chaotic, hysterical and dangerous, that there has been talk in Parliament of banning the group from playing live. Already there has been a death linked to the group, a policeman supposedly killed by the fans as he tried to hold them back.

Every night on the tour, theatres are ripped up, hundreds of police are required to control the crowds, St John ambulance staff cannot cope with the thousands of girls fainting or in shock or sent into hysteria and there have been hundreds of hospitalisations for broken limbs in hair-raising crushes. Being a Bay City Roller means no respite from this. Their hotels are under attack, they require police escorts to travel between gigs and fans surround their homes 24-hours a day.

Today was supposed to be relatively undemanding public appearance for a BBC Radio 1 Fun Day. It was the third such annual event organised by the BBC and was being broadcast live to the nation, in an era when only few commercial stations had been granted licenses. As at the previous two BBC Radio 1 Fun Days, which took place at Brands Hatch racetrack, there was a special caravan close to the racetrack from which to broadcast. Here the DJs planned to interview visiting pop stars while commenting on the high-speed races; some involving celebrities among a programme of more serious car races. It was a nonsensical idea but the then controller of BBC Radio 1 was a motor racing fan and had pushed it through. The previous year motorbike stunt star Eddie Kidd had jumped 12 Radio 1 DJs.

This Sunday had already seen The Wombles, a novelty pop group dressed as characters from the popular kids TV, plus various Radio 1 DJs such as Tony Blackburn, driven around the track waving to the crowd. DJ Johnny Walker signed autographs. Showaddywaddy, the Fifties revivalists who were label-mates of the Rollers, had been water-skiing on the lake in their brightly coloured drape jackets. The Three Degrees and Slade were due at the event to be interviewed. Helicopter rides with DJ Noel Edmonds were on offer. There was also a giant hot air balloon on site offering rides. The event had been heavily trailered on Radio 1 for two weeks beforehand. It was "a day out for all the family".

It was a grey overcast day out, cold, without sunshine. The Rollers' appearance was supposed to be secret, but it was apparent as soon as the live broadcast began at 12 o'clock that the news had leaked. The event had never attracted this sort of crowd numbers; already there were 46,000 inside Mallory Park, breaking the attendance record for the racetrack. The security was woefully inadequate, primitive even.

Many in the crowd were dressed in the Rollers' trademark costumes waving tartan scarves and banners declaring their love for the band. To the tune of 'This Old Man', they had kept up this unrelenting chant:

B-A-Y, B-A-Y, B-A-Y C-I-T-Y, with an R-O, double-L-E-R-S, Bay City Rollers are the best! Eric, Derek, Woody too, Alan, Leslie, we love you!'

And as far as the eye could see there was a line of white and tartan-clad young females, thousands more of them, heading toward Mallory Park and Mecca, a sighting of the Rollers in the flesh. People were abandoning cars, bikes and scooters and walking the final mile or two.

BBC Radio 1 had begun broadcasting appeals for the public to stay away hours ago. Now there was a crush around the Radio 1 caravan. Curious fans suspected the band might already be inside. The barriers and police could not stop them. More girls joined the crush, thinking something was going on. DJ Paul Burnett, who was broadcasting live from inside the caravan, said "everyone was caught on the hop". Scores of girls were injured in the crush. "The nurses did a marvellous job," said Burnett. "It was like a battlefront."

For the next two hours St John Ambulance volunteers dealt with many more cases of fainting, hysteria and girls with bumps and bruises as Roller fans jostled for the best viewing position near the caravan. With racing due to begin, it was decided to decamp the broadcasting facilities to a hospitality marquee set up on an island in the lake that was in the centre of the racetrack. The island was close to one edge of the lake, about 15 metres in, nearest the part of the racetrack called the Strebbe Sraight. It was about 70 metres long and 30 metres wide and accessed by a wooden bridge. The BBC felt they could secure the bridge with the limited security that they had organised for the event.

The island also had a tower on it, usually used as a marshalling point and for observation during races. DJ David 'Diddy' Hamilton started broadcasting live from what he described as a 'hut' on the island at 3pm. He began by announcing the event was closed. "We've not got room for any more," he said. The crowd was now estimated at 70,000.

Fans of the Rollers were keenly aware they had a gig in Torquay that evening starting at 8pm so their appearance must be imminent. There had been helicopters in the air all day, and one landed on the island bringing in The Three Degrees. Roller fans, mostly aged 10-14, were already gathered in their thousands dangerously close to the racetrack, near the swamps and the lake. The 'tartan army' was making a headache-inducing noise that came down a notch when they realised the helicopter did not contain their quarry.

Hamilton explained to listeners how it had got a bit 'hectic' by the Radio 1 caravan so 'with everybody's safety in mind' they had come to the island in the middle of the track. His voice was transmitted via loudspeaker to the crowds. "Helicopters are flying in and out," he said. 'One of those should be bringing along The Bay City Rollers who are coming to pay us a visit.' The screams went up ten decibels.

The sound of revving engines – the helicopters, boats and cars being prepared for races – combined with the girls' screams to make a hellish cacophony. The start of the Radio 1 DJ and celebrity race was delayed due to Rollers fans on and near the circuit. "People are not where they're supposed to be," said Hamilton.

On the grid for the 'Radio 1 Pro saloon Championship' were BBC DJs Tony Blackburn, Dave Lee Travis, Emperor Rosko, John Peel, Noel Edmonds and Annie Nightingale. The celebrities were thin on the ground and including session drummer Cozy Powell. When the race did start – 10 laps of the 1.3 miles circuit – two cars span off precariously. The Rollers fans were not concerned with safety and had still not retreated.

The Rollers and Paton looked down on the event from the air. They'd played the previous night in Bournemouth and had flown up by light aircraft to a nearby airfield. Paton was loaded on Valium, the only way he'd been able to cope with the pressures of superstardom thrust upon them. Even with the Valium he was all nerves, smoking 60 cigarettes a day. He insisted on travelling everywhere with the band, even on holidays. He shared hotels rooms with them, was often featured in their media appearances, routinely photographed and commented upon by journalists who'd dubbed him the 'sixth Roller'.

He was now among the few managers in rock history to become a household name, seen as the seventies equivalent of Brian Epstein in the same way as the Rollers and Rollermania was compared to The Beatles and Beatlemania. He was described as "the man behind the Rollers, their manager, adviser and above all, their friend". Paton idolised Epstein and like him had been forced to keep his homosexuality a secret. But the similarities ended there. Paton was a different animal to the refined Epstein and the Rollers, essentially talentless, were no Beatles.

Paton was the Svengali who controlled every aspect of the band's career, had made them. They were his puppets. He spoke on their behalf and was famed for preventing them from meeting girls or drinking alcohol, pitching the group as wholesome kids' entertainment. He had just released a pulp autobiography, the blurb of which proclaimed him as the band's 'guiding light and father-figure'. The paperback had gone to number one in the book charts on publication, even outselling the hugely popular Frederick Forsyth thriller *The Day Of The Jackal*.

The band's 24-year-old drummer, Derek Longmuir, who was pretending to be 21 said, yes, the book revealed all the band's secrets. Then he and the rest of them snorted with laughter. Derek himself was hiding darker aspects of his personality; he would later be convicted for possessing child pornography. Paton's ultra clean-cut 'boys next door' image was clearly a joke. The band was soaked in drugs and other Rollers would subsequently claim they were raped by Paton or experimented with homosexual sex and serial groupie sex. At the time, within the industry, rumours swirled that Paton may have been abusing certain members of the band physically and sexually. They were not taken seriously as a band. Paton himself had recently announced that 'Bye Bye Baby' was the first single that the band had actually played on (and it was their eighth single release).

He had been struggling recently to sleep. The band's huge success to date had been confined to the UK with pockets of Europe slowly being charmed. Now there were complicated plans to take the band to America, Australia and Japan. There were also more TV dates, interviews, new recordings to organise and a bewildering array of business arrangements to manage. It was only recently he'd packed in his job as a potato deliveryman and lorry driver after almost a decade as manager of various incarnations of the group. Paton was ill-equipped to operate within the music industry at this level.

It was Paton, however, who had become adept at orchestrating situations like today where the band would be mobbed for the benefit of the media. He didn't see danger, only headlines.

The helicopter touched down on the island, dropped the band and Paton, and took off again. This manoeuvre was dangerous enough; already some girls had managed to sneak onto the island and the first glimpse of the band's arrival sparked much chaos. Thousands more girls pushed through flimsy security barriers, past the limited police presence, and hundreds started wading out into the lake.

Although it had been announced the band would be driven around the track to greet the crowd, a mass panic took hold. The girls wanted them now. More ran across the racetrack to get closer to the lake. The celebrity race had finished and now there was serious racing going on, a Formula Ford race. Marshalls and other racetrack officials had never encountered anything like it. "Hell broke out as hundreds of tartan clad crazy schoolgirls proceeded to run across the track, totally oblivious of the cars racing by," said one race mechanic. Some of the girls had lost control of their bladders.

DJ John Peel was having trouble taking it all in. The Rollers had climbed the observation platform and were waving to the fans. Tony Blackburn was conducting boat rides on the lake accompanied by a Womble. There were score of girls all dressed in Rollers chic, screaming, their faces vivid pink, plunging into the muddy water. "I was standing outside the hospitality tent talking to Johnny Walker," said Peel. "I said, 'Mark this well, because you'll never see the likes of this again in your life.' I just thought, 'If I live to be 200 years old, I am never going to experience anything like this again in my life. As a kind of cultural event, this is almost without parallel in our century.'"

With scores of girls now in the water, the powerboat on the lake accelerated back to the island with Tony Blackburn flung onto the floor and the Womble almost thrown overboard. "The only security – and it seems barely credible – was provided by the BBC Sub-Aqua Club," said Peel. "So you've got all these people in frogman outfits with flippers and goggles standing on the bank, catching these girls, carrying them back through the mud and depositing them on the other bank and they just turned round and came back again. Noddy Holder [of Slade] went over the bridge and walked through this crowd of people and they paid no attention to him at all. He must have thought in that moment, 'It's all over, it's the end for us.'"

In the pandemonium, plans for the Rollers' lap of the racetrack were abandoned. Hamilton dragged them into the hut for an interview. As soon as Hamilton mentioned the name McKeown, the screams grew louder than ever. Wood was asked how the tour was going. At the mention of his name the screams went up again. "Really really great tour," he said. "Nobody's been hurt or anything like that."

The band's other guitarist Eric Faulkner, who was 21 but pretending to be 19, declared that the band had the "best fans ever… the most beautiful girls in the world." More screams, even louder.

Hamilton wanted a word with "the old man" of the group, meaning founder member Alan Longmuir, Derek's brother. He would soon be 27 but Paton had begun knocking years off his age around 1971 to the extent it was difficult to know how old he was pretending to be; around 20. But a newspaper had this past week exposed his real age. Paton had resolved to get rid of him – too old, too hard to control; he was drinking and seeing girls. There was a rumour Alan had actually offered to quit in the light of the exposé. "I don't want to say nothing about it," he told Hamilton.

Faulkner said the band was trying very hard to persuade Alan to stay. He said, in Bournemouth the fans had handed in a petition with thousands of signatures pleading for Alan to stay and the fan club was getting thousands of letters asking the same. Faulkner added that the fans had got hold of Alan on stage last night, during a mini-riot.

"It was a bit frightening," Alan said. "I thought I was going to lose my trousers."

The screams went up again as he said it. There was a state of euphoria. Girls, some only nine or 10, continued to wade into the boggy water to be closer to the hallowed flesh. The thin line of stewards could do little to stop them. The frogmen did their best to drag them back. There was a huge crush building by the bridge. More fans were criss-crossing the racetrack.

Hamilton made an appeal for the Roller fans to keep away from the racetrack. He said, sounding worried, "They're all over the place now".

This prompted more screaming [all the screaming was clearly audible over the airwaves]. "In the interest of their own safety, if they can hear me over the address system, they must keep away from the race track otherwise racing won't be able to continue," Hamilton said. There was more wild screaming: he's talking about *us*.

Hamilton cut short his interview with the band. Thoughts turned swiftly to getting the band away from here – the island, the racetrack, Leicestershire. Hamilton was booked to compere a Rollers gig in Wolverhampton the following Sunday. "See you in Wolverhampton," he told them. Then he asked them to pick out a favourite record for him to play. They picked The Beatles' 'All You Need Is Love'.

Hundreds of fans had now made it onto the island. "The shed was only a tiny thing and it was surrounded," said Faulkner. "They all wanted to grab us. The Three Degrees [who were in the hut] were getting all emotional." There were reports that St John Ambulance was dealing with 160 casualties and that 23 children had been taken to hospital. The helicopter could not land again safely amid the confusion. There was no escape. Altogether now; all you need is love.

Paton suggested they should go on the lake in a powerboat and try and placate the crowds. Love love love. Security helped them past the girls clawing at them wildy, sobbing and screeching, and they clambered aboard the boat. "Eight hundred kids jumped into the water to swim across this lake," said Paton. "We decided to get into this boat and go around the island give everyone a chance to see the guys. The whole thing became more involved. The kids wanted to touch them."

Out in clear water they were safe from danger. But now hundreds of girls were swimming out to them. Tony Blackburn and the Womble were back zipping about the water. "There were that many boats in our wake, and there were all these girls swimming over to try to reach us, we were worried they would be run over or something," said Faulkner. "We were making it worse being on the water."

A nurse was pushed into the water while one police officer went into the water three times to help children who appeared to be in trouble. "I was worried someone would drown," he said. Around 40 girls who were near drowned were rescued from the lake and a fire extinguisher was turned on other fans to prevent them getting in the water. "They went mad," said a police spokesman. The security organised by the BBC was so inadequate race marshals were pulling girls who couldn't swim out of the lake. One marshal was trampled as he rescued a girl from the lake. He suffered broken ribs. At an emergency first-aid post, 30 girls were laid out on floor.

Hamilton announced to Radio 1 listeners that they had, "Got the Rollers away" and now they were "on a little boat in the middle of the lake... I don't know where they're going to go from there... they are marooned in the middle of a lake... waving."

"These rather short and stubby girls, sort of like tree trunks dressed up in tartan, are wading across this weed-filled water, which was disgusting," said Peel. "And the sub-aqua people were sort of standing there in their rubber outfits catching these strange children. And the helicopters are coming in overhead and there is lots of car noise and screaming."

The Rollers' boat went over to help some of the kids who seemed to be drowning. "Then there were enough girls on one side of us to grab on to the boat and it tipped over," said McKeown. "The Wombles had to come to our rescue. They dived in to help pick up all the stray Rollers fans from the water. We just thought, Jesus Christ, what's happening?"

"Half the group was pulled into the lake," said Paton. The Rollers clambered aboard a second boat where they did a quick lap of the lake and headed back to the shelter of the broadcasting hut to wait for their helicopter ride to be able to land. There were girls in their tartan kits laid out on the lake banks, wet and sobbing uncontrollably. Many of them were in need of urgent medical attention: 35 more whisked away to hospital. St John Ambulance staff treated many hundreds more on site for hysteria and cut feet.

DJ Emperor Rosko, who'd had the band on his Radio 1 show many times, said: "It was the most surreal thing I've ever seen in life, like something out of a monster movie." The band barricaded themselves in the hut as the scuba divers in wet suits and flippers struggled on, and all the police on site lined the banks trying to prevent the girls going back in the water. Hamilton kept up the commentary, live on air.

The band was "safe but drenched, all huddled in a tiny room". Noddy Holder was in there with The Three Degrees now. "I'm getting a little bit worried actually," he told Hamilton. There was much screaming audible in the background. Radio 1 decided to abandon the rest of the days planned events.

"We had taken adequate precautions with safety barriers but unfortunately it got out of hand and it was decided to close the show," a Radio 1 spokesman told *The Sun* who splashed the story on their front page the next day: "Fan-demonium – Bay City girls plunge into lake at pop riot: Fun day terror as Rollers arrive at festival."

After 20 minutes, the helicopter descended. The band was bundled in, scratched, soaked and terrified. As the chopper tried to take off girls hung on to the undercarriage, the skids. Paton used his heel again. They were away. "Insane," said Faulkner. "Great fun for the teenagers," said Paton. "It was better than them getting mortally drunk in some pub."

"These guys are going to be wrecks when all this is over," said John Peel watching the helicopter ascend.

In just 11 days' time McKeown would knock over and kill a woman in his high-powered Ford Mustang on a wet road in Edinburgh and be charged with causing death by dangerous driving, a charge subsequently reduced to driving recklessly. Four days later, at a gig, he would beat a photographer unconscious with his mike stand and before 1975 was over he would also be arrested on suspicion of shooting a teenage girl fan in the head, though later found not guilty, and drink and demons would quickly consume him.

Paton would soon unceremoniously sack Alan, replacing him with a younger, prettier, sexier model. Alan would try and kill himself. Although he would deny it was a suicide attempt, Faulkner was rushed to hospital after overdosing on prescription drugs. Wood collapsed and was hospitalised. They were wrecks all right. But it was never over, not for them. There was no stepping out of this pantomime unscathed, the tragedy would never end, not for the next 40 years. There were endless horrors to come for certain band members and Paton: accusations of involvement in murders, child rapes and arson attacks, bankruptcies, corruption, prison sentences, breakdowns, pub fights, drug dealing, addiction and arrests, alcoholism, organised child abuse circles, child pornography... and more.

But for now the tour had to go on, the band had to go on. Tam Paton insisted.

ACT I

Remember

CHAPTER 1

Obsession

"I was 12 when I discovered I was gay. I used to bash my head against the wall. I just couldn't figure out what was wrong with me because nobody ever spoke about someone being homosexual. When everybody else was looking at girls, I was looking at guys. It was hard being gay and living with an alcoholic father too. He was a big, butch man, and I was always frightened to tell him what I was. I was always embarrassed about what I was. I always hid."

— Tam Paton

There would have been no Bay City Rollers without their manager Tam Paton. He assembled the group, hiring and firing boys to suit his personal taste, grooming them and controlling every aspect of their lives, both professional and personal. He was far more than a 'sixth' member of the group. He was their leader in every way and as such becomes the principal character in their story, a Machiavellian schemer, both hero and villain, the key factor in their rise and fall and the main reason why the story of The Bay City Rollers is a tragedy of Shakespearian proportions and complexity.

As such, there is a case to be made that the seven boys who were members of The Bay City Rollers between 1974 and 1977 when their fame reached its highest point – singer Les McKeown, guitarists Eric Faulkner and Stuart Wood, bass player Alan Longmuir, his replacements Ian Mitchell and Pat McGlynn, and his brother Derek on drums – were simply fortunate to have been in the right place at the right time. The other dozen-or-so boys who came and went were simply unlucky. Then again, depending on your point of view, they could have been the lucky ones considering the legacy of The Bay City Rollers. And Paton was in the thick of it.

Born on August 5, 1938, Thomas Dougald Paton grew up on a council housing scheme in Prestonpans, a small, rugged coastal town eight miles east of Edinburgh. The town was once a famous Scottish seaport and trading centre, exporting salt, oysters, glass, soap and beer, but during Paton's childhood the area was chiefly known for its coal mining and brickworks. When he turned 13 in 1951, the population of Prestonpans was 7,000 and most of the men worked in one of the two prominent local coal pits.

Paton's father, also called Thomas, ran a thriving potato wholesale business, delivering to Edinburgh's fruit and veg merchants, restaurants and fish & chip shops. His youngest son went to work for the business when he left school at 15. Paton's brother David, eight years his senior, was already working for the firm.

For an intensely industrial area, dotted with pitheads and factory chimneys, there was a romance to Prestonpans. The sunsets on the Firth of Forth, the vast estuary that brokered the River Forth and the North Sea could be breathtaking. There were secret tunnels on the craggy coastline that smugglers had once used, and in 1745 the town was the site of a famous victory for Bonnie Prince Charlie over the English army. Beautiful beaches stretched along the coastline a few miles away from Edinburgh.

It was a hard place, a typical mining community, insular and intensely patriarchal, with pubs along the historic main road full of mining men. Paton's two elder sisters were keen to escape, one moving to America, the other ending up in London via Edinburgh. His mother Isabella, or Bella, was a homemaker. She kept the house spotless and never tired of fetching cups of tea or cooking. Although Scotland's ancient capital city Edinburgh could be seen from Prestonpans on a clear day, it was a parochial environment.

As a boy Paton spent hours alone, training the family dog, Tweed, to do tricks. On Sunday nights he could be found at a small-time card game in the back room of the family's potato garage along the coast in Port Seton. The main area held a small mountain of potatoes and three big lorries, one of which Paton drove. This garage, the 'tattie shed' as Alan Longmuir called it, would become the rehearsal space for the Rollers.

Paton's father was a gambling man. He used money made from the potato business to buy a building on Prestonpans' main street where he ran an illegal betting shop (off-course betting shops were legalised in 1960), eventually renting it out to betting firm Coral, one of the first to take advantage of legalisation of betting. He subsequently continued to run his own book-making business from the family home. Over time Paton's father would acquire more property in the area to rent out.

In large part Paton Snr left the running of the potato business to his sons who became partners in Thomas Paton Potato Merchants. He was a hard-drinking, no-nonsense man, robust, with an eye for the dramatic gesture. When one heavily backed horse race went against him, he'd left the betting shop and a crowd of customers claiming their winnings, and walked into the sea, fully clothed, threatening to drown himself. In public his drinking seemed under control and although most recall his liking for drink, he did not fit the pattern of an alcoholic.

At 17 Tam Paton was conscripted to serve two years' national service, among the last group of teenagers to be compulsory enlisted before conscription was phased out. He joined the King's Troop Royal Horse Artillery, a ceremonial unit based in London, most often seen providing gun salutes on state occasions. He enjoyed showing off the uniform when on leave, the big fur hat, fancy braided jacket and long riding boots, and the pomp and ceremony of the events in which the unit took part.

Years later Tam claimed to have been abused by select high-ranking army officers while in the King's Troop in London. Paton also maintained that Lord Boothby was involved in the sex sessions. The former Conservative politician, who died in 1986, was a well-known political figure, then in his mid-fifties. MP for Aberdeen in the north of Scotland since 1924, he was a closet bisexual who campaigned for homosexual law reform. In his lifetime Boothby was never exposed, presumably because of his contacts in the media and establishment, but it has since been alleged that gangster Ronnie Kray supplied him with young men procured from care homes for gay orgies. In the past few years his heavy links to the Krays, whom he claimed to have met only three times, have been detailed by MI5, among others.

Paton alleged he was among a group of young conscripts invited to private quarters for sex with officers and Boothby. "He didn't talk about it as if he was abused," said his future partner Ray Cotter, one of several people Paton confided in. "But he said they weren't allowed to talk about it, told not to mention anything. Tam would often say, Lord Boothby was a right raver."

Released from the army in 1957, Paton returned to Prestonpans and to driving the potato wagon for the family business. Drawn to music, he took accordion lessons and joined a local band that played at weddings and at dance halls. His best friend from Prestonpans, Ron Fraser, the same age as Paton and a regular at the tattie shed card games, played piano. The leader of the band was Fraser's uncle who played sax.

Paton suggested to Fraser, a dental student at Edinburgh University, that they form their own band, recruiting a Prestonpans guitarist, John Hunter, and a young drummer. They rehearsed in the wooden garage at the side of Paton's parents' home, a space just big enough for a car where in time the Rollers too would rehearse. "You could hear the music all over Prestonpans," said Fraser. This was the genesis of The Crusaders, the band Paton would make into one of Scotland's best-known acts.

Paton, Fraser and chums could churn out crowd-pleasing traditional stuff, material popularised by accordionist Jimmy Shand and Scottish BBC TV show *White Heather Club* compere Andy Stewart, unsophisticated dances and reels. Paton sang, badly, but, according to Fraser, "He was shit hot on the box. If you had a wedding and Tam was there with the accordion everybody was on the floor dancing."

Paton wanted more. About to turn 21, he was obsessed by the pop charts of the era. The UK music scene was in transition with R&B and rock'n'roll–influenced acts such as Elvis, Buddy Holly and the Everly Brothers now edging out the big bands led by Ted Heath or Tommy Dorsey and the solo crooners like Frank Sinatra, Dean Martin and Perry Como.

Edinburgh's music scene, its nightlife, was similarly in transition. It was still focused on a handful of famous dance halls, notably the Palais, where Ted Heath or Joe Loss brought their big bands or 'dance bands' made up of between 12 and 25 musicians with emphasis on brass, woodwind and percussion. Concentrating on swing, jive, Latin or trad jazz tunes for dancing, these bands, often featuring a crooner, now began to cover contemporary pop hits as well. Smaller, more modern, jazz bands, often quartets like Glasgow's Clyde Valley Stompers, often played the dance halls in support of the big bands and these more versatile quartets were playing rock'n'roll as well. Incrementally but tangibly, a new musical era was dawning.

Paton often went out dancing in Edinburgh. He had a girlfriend whom Fraser recalled as beautiful and whose photograph was found in his possessions when he died. "Tam was a very handsome guy," noted Fraser.

"I was lonely at the time," Paton said. "The reason I slept with women is because of all the things that had happened to me. You know, growing up in a very Victorian Britain. It was very difficult… to be gay and be happy – or it was in my time. I don't think you can be gay and have a regular partner. I know there are gays who will disagree, but it was true for my generation. My generation was destined to live on their own."

Delivering potatoes may not have been the most glamorous of jobs but it plugged Paton straight into Edinburgh's late fifties teenage rock'n'roll scene which had fish & chip shops and cafes at its core. The city's best teen rock groups, The Falcons and The Blackjacks, in thrall to the American pioneers such as Chuck Berry and Little Richard, and inspired by new UK performers like Tommy Steele and Lonnie Donegan, played regularly at the Hotplate, a tiny room downstairs from a chip shop Paton delivered to.

Paton would claim the early Crusaders sound was influenced by Scotland's most notable underground early rock luminaries, Ricky Barnes and Alex Harvey. They were both from Glasgow, where the scene was characterised as being far earthier than the lighter more pop orientated Edinburgh, and seen then and for the coming decade as being more original. Harvey, who would go on to have a long distinguished career as a cultish rocker, was two years older than Paton and had swapped traditional jazz for rock'n'roll, famously winning a competition in 1957 to find Scotland's Tommy Steele. Barnes' band played loud, half rock'n'roll and half traditional material. Neither he nor Harvey, made it in England at the time, but Barnes became a defining figure at Hamburg's influential Star Club where The Beatles cut their teeth.

Paton was ambitious for his band and single-minded. "He went to a dance hall in a town called Musselburgh, between Prestonpans and Edinburgh, and saw a rock'n'roll band,' said Fraser. "Tam had never heard a band play live with a bass guitar before. He was struck by the funny noise. So Tam, being Tam, went straight out and bought a bass guitar for rehearsals."

Fraser switched from piano to bass guitar and in 1959 Paton added a second guitarist, Paddy Dixon, from Musselbrough, at 17 four years younger than Paton. Dixon, who stayed with the band for the next five years until he got married, recalled his first gig with the band as being at a wedding in Portobello, Edinburgh's popular beach area, its promenade studded by amusement arcades and ice-cream emporiums.

Dixon was paid £8 for the gig which considering he was on £75 a week wages at the time was an attractive proposition. He quickly fell into line with Paton's dictate for the group. "Things had to be right with Tam, everything had to be right," said Dixon. "We used to tune in to Radio Luxembourg and listen to the top 20 and when a new record came out we'd cover it. To get gigs you had to be able to do the top 20."

Paton picked the songs the band would play and often bought the sheet music from a store next door to an Edinburgh chip shop on his delivery round. "His musical taste was what we followed," said

Fraser who could read music and often, in front of a perplexed Paton, transposed the key of the music to suit the band.

Paton was better at networking. He spent lots of time at the local music shops buying sheet music, seeing what was new in equipment and instruments, and listening to new records in the popular listening booths. He often met up with other local bands at the shops, paying attention to who was who, and getting all the latest news. One of his elder sisters had married a Frenchman and they ran a radio and TV shop in Edinburgh.

The Crusaders picked up gigs at Saturday night dances locally, playing Prestonpans Town Hall or at the ballroom located above the open-air swimming pool in the town, then moving on to a string of nearby towns, other mining or fishing communities, where there were similar dances in dance halls or village halls. With no DJs to play pop and rock'n'roll records from the charts, The Crusaders thrived, not least because big bands and trad jazzers avoided such venues, fearing drink-related trouble. A Teddy boy inspired riot at a Ricky Barnes/ Alex Harvey double-header in Glasgow fuelled the perception that rock'n'roll meant violence, leaving a gap for smaller, tough, proficient, bands who could play songs from the charts.

Paton added a singer, 17-year-old Rod Reynolds, a black guy who looked a little like Emile Ford, the West Indian immigrant who was at number one in the UK with 'What Do You Want To Make Those Eyes At Me For?' Reynolds was from Tranent, a small town close to Prestonpans and Paton could often be heard repeating that he was Emile Ford's cousin, Wally Ford – a joke inspired by the town Wallyford near Tranent. It was unusual to have a black singer with a broad Scottish accent and Reynolds handled the crowd well. He would joke about being the black sheep of the family, as his mother and siblings were white.

Paton also had the bright idea to add a female vocalist, Dot Walker, to the line-up. He wanted the band to be able to play top 20 hits by popular female vocalists such as Connie Francis, Brenda Lee and Helen Shapiro. Walker also provided backing vocals and duetted with Reynolds on Everly Brothers songs. Paton still sang one number in the set, the 1960

Neil Sedaka US hit, 'Run Samson Run'. "It was a fun song, and we'd all run up and down the stage playing it," said Dixon.

The Crusaders earned good pocket money. Paton kept them in shape, kitting them out in red tartan American baseball style jackets featuring the band members' initials, a look later echoed by the Rollers. As the group grew more accomplished and professional Paton made sure The Crusaders played every Scottish town and city over the next five years, driving them from behind the wheel of their old Bedford CA van. "We never knew where we were going until we got in the van," Fraser said. All the band members had day jobs and so the gigs were mainly at weekends. There was no bridge built yet across the Forth so if the band were playing in the north of Scotland, they'd have to take a ferry across the estuary. They were regulars in Inverness, 150 miles to the north of Edinburgh.

Fridays and Saturdays were also busy days for delivering potatoes on the wagon, so Paton often corralled a band member to ensure he finished early enough to get home, shave and dress, and drive the band to the gigs. The Crusaders were often late for gigs but could be relied on always to show. Dixon recalls helping Paton on the wagon. "Tam was a big strong lad," he said. "They were eight stone canvas sacks of potatoes we had to carry on our shoulder down spiral staircases into a restaurant. Tam was a grafter, worked hard." As his helpers struggled with one bag of potatoes, Paton carried two eight-stone bags, one on each shoulder.

Ever on the lookout for opportunities, Paton hooked up with well-known agent Duncan McKinnon at Border Dances who booked gigs in southern Scotland, near the border with England. "He had a dance nearly every Friday, Saturday, Sunday in nearly every venue imaginable through the [Scottish] Borders," said Dixon. 'We did all the town halls locally [to Prestonpans] but our bread and butter was travelling all over Scotland, down the Borders, up north, through the west."

The west meant Glasgow, often seen as an anathema to Edinburgh acts. Via a Glaswegian agent, Paton often had The Crusaders gig in the city, at venues such as the Maryland and the Elizabethan club. Paton also secured the band a regular Sunday night booking at the popular dance at Lennoxbank House Hotel by Loch Lomond, just north of Glasgow. He was a shrewd hustler, often stretching the truth as to the popularity of his band, claiming, for instance, they were booked up three months in advance. "I was a terrible musician, but I could really sell an act," he said.

The Crusaders were a relatively clean-living bunch. They all had girlfriends at home, and with the amount of travelling there was little time for groupies. "If any of the guys got out for a quick one they were lucky," said one band member. "There were no drugs and very little drinking – Paton was virtually teetotal – just the fug of cigarette smoke in the van. Paton smoked heavily."

Their Borders agent, McKinnon, worked with an agent in the north of England who offered The Crusaders gigs there as well. They began to travel to England for weekends, playing places such as Fleetwood in Lancashire, Rotherham in Yorkshire, Hull in Humberside, often stopping off on the way home for a Sunday night gig in Carlisle in Cumbria.

These were long trips of over 400 miles and illustrated the hardships geography posed for Scottish bands if they wanted to find an English audience. One night the Bedford van got stuck in snow between Carlisle and Edinburgh, in Leadhills, one of the highest villages in Scotland, and the band had to spend the night in the freezing van. Even reaching parts of Scotland could be a killer. If the gigs were way up north, a place such as Strathpeffer, the band would have to be booked for two nights and accommodation provided above the dance hall.

McKinnon booked many English acts to appear in the Borders region and The Crusaders acted as a support to an array of charts stars such as Billy Fury, Joe Brown, Eden Kane and The Springfields. Paton was getting closer to fame. He updated The Crusaders' image, fitting them out in red matching suits from Burtons. Singers Reynolds and Walker wore a purple suit and dress respectively. Paton also ditched the increasingly dated accordion and moved onto keyboards, starting off with a Clavioline, as used on the space age 1962 UK number one hit 'Telstar' by The Tornados, which The Crusaders covered. Next he bought an organ and then a Vox Continental, the same as The Animals used. "He wasn't a brilliant two-handed pianist," said Fraser. "I'd often say I could play the piano better with my feet than he could with his hands." He played, said Dixon, "what was essential".

The band's original guitarist, John Hunter, got married and left the group and was replaced by Frank Conner on rhythm guitar. Conner had grown up in central Edinburgh, in the historic old town, a mix of old multi-family tenement buildings and newer council stock. He was still a teenager having started out as 15-year-old guitarist in The Falcons, Edinburgh's leading rock'n'roll band. It was quite a coup to get him in the band. "Tam was knocking on my door for a week trying to persuade me to join his band for this particular weekend gig," he said. "By the Friday night, the fifth time he'd come up to my door, I said okay."

Paton had plenty of work lined up for the group and the money – Conner was an apprentice joiner – was good. He would stay on guitar for the next three years. "The Crusaders were what I called a chart band," said Conner. "Tam wasn't into the blues like I was; he liked pop stuff, chart stuff. Tam's mantra was keep up with the charts. The Crusaders were pop but we stuck a lot of hairy old rock'n'roll in as well. I was a big Chuck Berry fan. The idea was to have people get up and dance."

"Tam was the frontman, the band leader, in The Crusaders," added Conner. "He got all gigs, drove the bandwagon, and he dealt with everybody, all the agents. He did everything but he acted like he was just one of the guys. We never got paid on the night. Every month or so Tam would get a cheque from [agent] McKinnon and out of that he took the fuel and divided up what was left. You couldn't afford to try and live off it. You played for the enjoyment and love of it. We spent most of the week together as a band: rehearsal on Tuesday, and Friday, Saturday and Sunday playing, and then we got a regular gig on a Wednesday at the Gamp, that's when we started coming into Edinburgh."

The Gamp was a new central Edinburgh dance hall, opened in 1962 by Stuart Hepburn who would go on to own the famous Varsity Music shop in the city. Alongside The Crusaders, Hepburn regularly booked Phil & the Flintstones who wore tartan jackets and were fronted by

15-year-old singer Phil Clark. Hepburn gave Paton keyboard lessons "because he was crap".

Hepburn had regular jazz nights at the Gamp, and the club also hosted visiting UK acts such as Johnny Kidd & the Pirates plus upcoming local blues bands. It was seen as a purist's sort of place, for real musicians. The Gamp, and other newly opened small dance halls and clubs like it, were a sign Edinburgh was recovering, like most major cities in the UK, from the damage inflicted by World War II and beginning to prosper. For the young in the city, there were jobs at Leith Docks, skilled and unskilled work at a variety of booming factories and much new building work to be had as the overcrowded inner-city slum tenements were demolished and replaced by new housing estates, or schemes as they became known, on the outskirts of the city. There was spare cash and a sense of optimism among a new generation.

Frank Conner often worked for the Waldman brothers, two London entrepreneurs behind many of central Edinburgh's new nightlife venues such as Bungies and the Place. Conner had helped with the renovations there, which was close to the Gamp. "We put in new floors, doors, everything, at the Place," said Conner. The Crusaders played the venue the night after it opened and ended up with a regular fortnightly slot. They also had a regular slot at another new central Edinburgh club, the International. It was owned by Jimmy Roccio, from a well-known, property-owning, Italian family in the city, and run by an intimidating character called Peter Williamson and his notorious partner Paddy Reilly – the two also ran Edinburgh casinos together. In the seventies the International would transmogrify into Fire Island, the city's first gay club.

"Edinburgh was full of clubs and we were very, very popular," said Conner who described Williamson as 'colourful' and 'a less extreme version of Tony Soprano'. As Paton's contacts grew, he also got The Crusaders gigs at the famous Edinburgh Palais, which could hold 3,000 punters on its sprung dance floor and had a famous revolving stage. This was the Edinburgh venue with the most sepia-tinted glamour of all the old dance halls, where Sean Connery acted as a bouncer, and usherettes guided you to the powder room or Cupid's bar on the balcony.

The venue was trying to modernise itself. In the UK The Shadows had begun to popularise the notion of a streamlined modern pop group set-up of bass, two guitars and drums but it was the success of The Beatles in 1963 that saw the demand for beat and group music dramatically increase. Most of the major dance halls and ballrooms, however, were stuck with big bands and crooners. The Palais experimented with booking local pop act like The Crusaders alongside popular beat groups like The Dave Clark Five. They also organised buses to take punters back to the schemes at the end of the night. "We'd play the Palais several times a year but not as often as once a week," said Fraser.

The Crusaders, whose set already included a cover of The Shadows' 1963 instrumental 'Atlantis', adapted fast to the impact of The Beatles and were soon including several of their songs in their set. When The Rolling Stones became the next big thing, it was the same. "That's what we were good at," said Conner. "People would come in the hall and hear live music like listening to the records. We were all good musicians."

It was at the Palais that Alan Longmuir first saw The Crusaders. "There was always two or three young lads standing at the stage looking at you mouths open," said Conner. "I came off and I was with Tam and these lads said, 'We've got a band. Would you like to come and hear us?'"

In the post-Beatles boom, there were plenty of new teen bands in the city trying their luck. Most had cottoned on the fact that Paton and The Crusaders, the city's best known act, might be worth getting to know. "They'd all congregate around the front of the stage looking up at us, the so called number one band in Scotland, thinking I can do that," said Fraser. "Tam got interested in some of these newer bands. He would go out in the week to these church halls where they played. They never played in the clubs we played in."

In 1964 Paton's main focus, however, was on making a success of The Crusaders. He dreamed of the big time and saw it within his grasp. "I craved fame," he said. "I was stupid. Girls used to throw themselves at me, a lot of good that was."

Around him, Scottish contemporaries were getting record contracts. Among The Crusaders' rivals was Glaswegian band Dean Ford & the Gaylords, with whom they shared a booking agent and sometimes a stage, both having bridged the chasm between the dance band and beat eras. When EMI, The Beatles' record label, held auditions in Glasgow for new talent, The Gaylords were snapped up but no hits came from the liaison.

EMI also signed Edinburgh's The McKinley Sisters, a female pop duo who played the Palais and Kirknewton Royal Air Force base where The Crusaders also had a regular Saturday night engagement every three or four weeks. Kirknewton army base, outside Edinburgh, was home to 500 American soldiers trying to intercept Soviet radio signals. Many of them were regulars at the Palais, where they had their own corner, and other Edinburgh clubs. Dot Walker was not the only Edinburgh woman to be swept up off her feet by a dashing American from the Kirknewton base. She married hers and left The Crusaders.

Paton was quick to find her replacement. Pat Fernie, Paton said, "put Dusty Springfield to shame with her voice and make-up". Paddy Dixon also left the band to get married and was replaced by a new rhythm guitarist who doubled as a third singer. Paton also persuaded one of city's finest musicians and a well-known character, Toto McNaughton, to join the group as a new drummer. McNaughton was 26, two years older than Paton, and a veteran of many Edinburgh groups. "He was a charismatic guy," said Conner. "He would do a drum solo and he would get up off the drums and he'd be playing his sticks on the necks of the guitars, up and down the mike, onto a radiator, and onto a chair and all the way back round to his drums and then one, two and back in. Everybody in town knew him."

After she appeared on the debut edition of Scottish Television's pop music show *One Night Stand* in early 1964, Glaswegian singer Lulu was signed up by a London label Decca. STV was Scotland's commercial channel, a rival to the BBC. The show featured four Scottish groups per show with one guest English group. It was presented by Pete Murray who was a Radio Luxembourg and BBC DJ and a TV presenter on a variety of pop shows including *Top Of The Pops*.

Prompted by all this, Paton took The Crusaders into Edinburgh's top recording studio, Craighall, to make an album. 'We did an LP in three or four hours, all covers of what was in the charts," said Dixon.

"We never did any original music," said Fraser. "There was no one in the band had any sort of desire or knowledge to compose tunes. We did hire studios and do recordings but nothing ever came of it."

The recordings never seemed to be good enough, not even to send off as demos, but in new mohair suits The Crusaders got a spot on the fourth episode of *One Night Stand* televised in March 1964, playing alongside The Gaylords and Frank Conner's old band The Falcons. There was a momentum building. When The Crusaders supported The Animals in Newcastle, Paton played Alan Price's keyboards. They also entered and won the regional heat of the National Beat Group competition and were booked to appear at the final at the Prince of Wales Theatre in London on Sunday September 27. The judges included Beatles' manager Brian Epstein, Ringo Starr, Cilla Black and BBC DJ Alan Freeman.

"They flew us down to London, first time I'd ever been in a plane, put us up in some fancy hotel," said Conner. The event was sponsored by the charity Oxfam and The Crusaders were up against 11 other acts, none of whom achieved notability beyond this night. The second half of the show, from 9.45-10.35pm, was broadcast live on television by BBC2 under the title *It's Beat Time*. The Crusaders came tenth out of the 12 acts. Paton was cut up. "I thought we were the most musical group around and we got slaughtered by four youngsters," said Paton. "I really felt bad about it. These other guys sounded bad but the youngsters were wanting it and that's what it was all about."

The band enjoyed the event, recalling meeting Ringo Starr. Paton claimed he got to ask Brian Epstein why the vote had gone against The Crusaders who'd played their usual covers set. He would weave this into an apocryphal tale. "Epstein said, 'You were a good band but just didn't have any image,'" Paton later recalled.

"I didn't even know what the word image meant," Paton said. "I couldn't even figure out what he had meant by it – people wanted to hear us not see the group."

This was disingenuous. Alex Harvey's band, for instance, had gone all out to be noticed: in silver lamé jackets, red shirts with rock'n'roll spelt out on them and white stack-heeled boots as far back as 1958. Scotland's first international teen pop star Jackie Dennis, a 14-year-old

32

singer from Edinburgh, wore a kilt or tartan trousers and was pitched as 'the kilted Elvis'. Paton had already coordinated The Crusaders into coloured suits.

Paton repeated the story of his meeting with Epstein endlessly. His words, Paton said, had a profound impact on him and hence the future of The Bay City Rollers. "Brian agreed we were the best but we had no image and that was what the pop business is all about."

Their failure at the National Beat Group event virtually finished The Crusaders. Drummer McNaughton quit and joined the Boston Dexters, assembled by the Waldman brothers. They certainly had image. The Waldmans based the band's look on 1930s gangsters and dressed them in pinstriped suits and on stage they even carried replica machine guns. They signed to EMI in January 1965 and future Rollers songwriter Bill Martin wrote songs for them.

McNaughton's replacement in The Crusaders did not survive long. He worked in a local music shop and one night, in a bad mood, after a gig in Dundee he refused to dismantle his kit and load it into the band van. Paton showed a ruthless streak. "Tam told him, 'If you don't go get your drums I'm driving off,'" said Conner. "He then started the engine and drove back to Edinburgh, leaving the drums in the doorway." The next day he fired the drummer.

Paton was 27 and weighing up his options. The Crusaders were still working with many of Scotland's best agencies, including Universal, who also owned the country's popular *Beat News* magazine, but Paton sensed they would never make it in a pop world being taken over by beat groups such The Kinks, Small Faces and The Who. Their time had passed. The new craze for Mod and American R&B was, however, at least in Scotland, a city thing and out in the country's rural areas, The Crusaders could still earn money playing the circuit.

The Beachcombers now set the pace among teenagers in the city's clubs. They were the first young, teenage, Edinburgh group to establish a set based on contemporary black American dance and soul music, chiefly the output of record labels Motown, Stax and Atlantic. They were camp, good-looking and ambitious. Their set included 'Heat Wave' by Martha & the Vandellas and 'Baby I Need Your Loving' by

The Four Tops. They had a strong female following with screaming at gigs where some girls would try to pull them off stage. They were a huge hit at the Top Storey club, one of the few new Edinburgh clubs that The Crusaders had failed to play at regularly. The owners, brothers Jimmy and Russell Craig, always preferred to promote a rival act they managed, Butch & the Bandits.

The Beachcombers also had a residency at the International Club. Paton knew their guitarist, 15-year-old David Paton, whom he'd first seen in his schoolboy band, The Elements. He also knew their manager, Kenny McLean, the drummer's father. Paton saw him as a rival. "There was always this thing between the two of us," said Paton, who was impressed with the reaction McLean's band generated.

Paton took on another new teen group, The Hipple People, as manager. A schoolboy outfit packing in a couple of hundred kids, mostly females, at the small Abano Club opposite the Top Storey, they had two singers, "like The Walker Brothers" said 17-year old David Valentine, one of the singers. The band had started out heavily influenced by the Stones, playing blues tunes by Howlin' Wolf, Lead Belly and Chuck Berry, before updating their sound and covering Motown/Stax songs like The Beachcombers, songs by girls groups like 'Keep Your Hands Off My Baby' by Little Eva, 'Remember (Walkin' In The Sand)' by The Shangri-Las, 'Baby Love' by The Supremes, 'He's Rebel' by The Crystals and 'One Fine Day' by The Chiffons.

"There were three bands in Edinburgh at the time doing a similar thing and getting a similar reaction," said Valentine. "Us, The Beachcombers and The Moonrakers." The Moonrakers, whose van was often seen covered in girls' names written in lipstick, were soon out of the running. Their promising career was derailed when a band member was attacked after a gig by a jealous gang and sustained severe head injuries, which led to permanent brain damage.

The Hipple People actually buttonholed Paton to become their manager. Valentine knew him as an "influential character around town" and approached him at the Palais. "Tam seemed to be quite good at getting his own band plenty of gigs in and around Edinburgh and the Borders."

Paton tried to persuade the group to wear frilly-fronted shirts and suits, much like hip, Mod-ish, Glasgow bands The Poets, who had charted on The Rolling Stones-affiliated Immediate Records, or The Beatstalkers, who wore tartan trousers and caused teenage riots in their home city and were freshly signed to Decca who hired Bill Martin to write songs for them.

The Hipple People resisted Paton's attempts at grooming, preferring the scruffier Rolling Stones approach. "I thought I was Mick Jagger reincarnated with the collarless shirts and faded jeans," said Valentine. "Tam just wanted us to dress a bit more effeminate, in lace shirts. It was mooted a few times." Paton also reproached the band's drummer for growing a beard, calling it scruffy, "… yet again showing his early leanings toward image as being all important if you were to succeed," added Valentine.

Paton used his contacts to get The Hipple People better and more prominent club gigs in Edinburgh at the Place, the International and Bungies. The band found him to be "likeable and approachable". He was closest to Valentine who was always the last to be dropped off after gigs in Paton's car, a flash, white Zephyr with tinted windows and white-wall tyres. "I'd have to listen to his long chats that lasted around two hours outside my mum and dad's house," he said. "There was no suggestion of all that sexual stuff. He didn't touch my knee once."

In June 1965, The Hipple People won the *Edinburgh Evening News* Beat Competition held at Dunfermline's Kinema ballroom. Despite this minor triumph, the band members were still helping Paton out on the potato lorry on Saturdays. "He always had two or three young boys helping him with the deliveries," said Valentine. "He liked to be surrounded by young boys. We were like the Barbary Apes on his potato lorry. We never thought anything of it. He used to tell us about his sexual conquests with the females when he was delivering potatoes. He was a tall good-looking guy."

Paton now wore jeans, cowboy boots and a fringed jerkin jacket. He remained intensely competitive. The Beachcombers auditioned for CBS Records in London and were signed by the label. The American company, soon to take on the charismatic Clive Davis as President, was establishing its own operation in London after five years of being reliant on UK distribution from Philips and EMI. After signing to CBS The Beachcombers moved to London and were handed a residency at the famous Marquee Club in Soho.

Paton also arranged for The Hipple People to audition for CBS, driving them 400 miles down to London in an old Volkswagen van after an early start. "Once we got there, Tam slept in an anteroom right through the audition," said Valentine. "Then he drove us all the way home the same evening. Scary." Fresh in every Scottish band's memory was the 1965 death of two members of The Blues Council, a promising Glasgow group whose van crashed on the outskirts of Edinburgh. The Hipple People failed the audition though CBS expressed an interest in signing the band's two singers. "We, in loyalty to the band, refused," said Valentine.

Back in Edinburgh the club scene was virtually unrecognisable from just a few years before. Although many of the venues were the same, the audience dressed differently, had a more aggressive attitude, and danced to a mix of live music and DJs playing Motown and Stax. There were all-night sessions where drugs, chiefly pep pills, were popular. Paton's diligence ensured The Hipple People became one of the city's top attractions, playing regularly at trendy clubs such as McGoos where hip London acts often played. With The Beachcombers down in London, the Top Storey also became a regular for the group. The Bonnyrigg Regal, just south of Edinburgh, was another as were the Regal Ballroom in Kirkcaldy and Dunfermline's Kinema. In June 1966, for a second year running, The Hipple People won the *Edinburgh Evening News* Beat Competition held at the Kinema ballroom. They also played further south in the Border towns such as Eyemouth.

"Tam relished being in the band scene," said Valentine. "He was very driven." Valentine, however, was about to start a university degree. Since there were problems with the other singer in the band, by late summer of 1966 Valentine had decided to quit, hiding under his bed when Paton visited his parents to try and persuade him to stay.

Throughout 1965 Paton had continued to play intermittent gigs with The Crusaders. Guitarist Frank Conner had left and become the guitarist in the big band at the Palais. "The big bands were finding that to play the music coming out they needed to have a guitar player," he explained. Conner played at the Palais for six months until the big band was axed completely. To his surprise, they were replaced by The Crusaders.

The venue was in financial trouble, losing the young crowd during the week to the newer clubs. There was talk of the Palais being closed down or becoming a bingo hall. Already other huge popular dance halls in Edinburgh, such as the Plaza, had been forced to close. Paton, friendly with the manager at the Palais, had talked his way into the gig as the house band. It was a huge venue, full of faded glamour, and Paton reshaped the group for a slot at regular Friday and Saturday night dances that remained busy. He gave them a new name too: The Tommy Paton Showband. It was essentially The Crusaders with three saxophones and two trumpets. They played all the old popular dance styles along with the same current chart hits as The Crusaders did but in an ersatz big band style. Ron Fraser, who had married Paton's cousin in 1964 when Paton acted as best man at the wedding, was now the only original member alongside him. "We were the last resident band in the Palais," he said. The Tommy Paton Showband name went up behind the stage in large letters.

Ronnie Simpson, who ran the influential Music & Cabaret agency in Glasgow, would become Scotland's main rock music agent in the late sixties and into the seventies. "Tam was just a big lump of a lad, very pleasant and very nice," he said. "He kind of stood at the front waving his arms about and if he saw someone coming in he needed to speak to he just walked off the stage and went to speak to them. He picked the tunes and the musicians would toot out the hits of the day."

Paton was also placed in charge of booking the acts for the Thursday teenagers' night at the Palais when young groups played. "That was when a lot of these young groups got a shot," said Fraser. "That's how a lot of them got in with Tam." Many ambitious young Edinburgh groups vied for Paton's attention, hoping he'd manage them to Hipple People-style local prominence or give them a break at the Palais teen night, which paid about £70. One was The Beat Hysters, whom he managed briefly, advertising the fact and his telephone number 'for bookings' in Radio Scotland's new magazine, *242*. This was a new pirate station launched in December 1965 in the wake of Radio Caroline. Paton was friendly with one of its DJs, Stuart Henry, who went on to work on BBC Radio 1 in 1967 and prove to be a useful contact when he became a regular presenter on *Top Of The Pops*.

Another, in mid-1966, was The Circle, formed around well-known local character Rob Thallon, then 18, who would go on to make a name for himself in the seventies as the owner of Edinburgh's top designer jeans stores and also as a brothel and club owner. Valentine also recalled Paton trying out another young teen act who played a short 30-minute set as support to The Hipple People at the Top Storey. The singer, Nobby Clark, was dating his sister. "They were called The Motown Stompers," he said. "They were rotten. They got booed off stage."

This unpromising audition was actually the beginning of Paton's association with the schoolboy group that would become The Bay City Rollers. Paton didn't think they were anything special, but he did note that singer Nobby Clark wore a pair of pink jeans.

Nobby Clark has protested that the band he fronted was never called The Motown Stompers but he did recall they were often booed off stage in their early days. "We changed the name for a very short time to The Motown Goodies when we were trying to find a decent name for the band," he said. He had joined the group in the spring of 1965 as a 15-year-old schoolboy, when they were called The Saxons.

Clark had been invited to try out as singer by his classmate Derek Longmuir, also 15, who played drums in the group. Formed in 1964 by Derek's elder brother Alan, then 16, and their older cousin Neil Porteous, 18, they'd originally called themselves The Ambassadors but never gigged under that name.

Clark lived on one of the new housing schemes in the west of the city called Clermiston. One of five kids, he and his large family moved there from a cramped, dark and damp city-centre basement flat. He said the school he and Derek (and Alan previously) attended always smelled either of boiling hops from a nearby brewery or boiling horse bones from the local glue factory. It was a tough childhood and a rough school that tended to guide pupils toward a trade.

The band played a mix of old rock'n'roll such as Chuck Berry's 'Too Much Monkey Business' and 'Wake Up Little Susie' by The Everly Brothers plus up-to-date American material such as 'Jump Back' by Rufus Thomas and 'At The Club' by The Drifters. Their first gigs were at the local youth club in a church hall on the same road where Alan and Derek lived. The brothers were regulars at the youth club and at the Protestant Church's Sunday school.

They practised once a week in a back room at the Longmuir brothers' parents' home, a busy first floor flat in a tenement building close to Haymarket train station at the heart of Edinburgh in the working-class district of Gorgie-Dalry. The brothers had two younger sisters and the house was often noisy. Their mother, who played piano and encouraged music in the home, was from the Scottish Highlands and her family had made their own music on accordions, piano and bagpipes during her childhood. Their father had been a maintenance man of the railways but now worked as an undertaker for the Co-op, going to work in a top hat and long coat. There was often a hearse outside the home. "He used to come along the street with the hearse and people would wonder who had died, but it was just him coming home for his lunch," said Alan.

The brothers had secrets. Alan, handsome and outgoing, confided in Clark that not long before they'd met he'd stuck his head in the gas oven and turned it on. He said he had intended to kill himself but "the meter ran out before it was too late." Derek, the quiet, insular brother, did not share his brother's enthusiasm for chasing the girls.

Their earliest memory was of a black dog that scared them while they played as kids. Alan had been a poor student, a truant, and part of a tough gang more interested in Elvis Presley than maths. He worked at a local dairy, mucking out stables and delivering milk on a horse and cart, before leaving school in 1963 aged 15. He'd worked as an office clerk for a year before switching to train as a plumber.

Porteous, the brother's cousin, had attended a different school to the other three, and was the original spark behind the group. Inspired by The Beatles, he'd bought an electric guitar and wanted someone to mess around with. Alan bought a cheap electric bass guitar, identifying with fellow left-hander Paul McCartney. Derek, who played a marching drum in the Boys Brigade, was just there: tapping out a beat on old boxes and tins. As they developed, Derek progressed to a toy, plastic Ringo Starr snare drum on a stand. He'd seen the hysteria that surrounded The Beatles when they played at the ABC in Edinburgh in April 1964.

After Clark joined, Derek's father bought a cheap drum kit for the group on hire purchase. There was not a lot of spare cash around. Porteous didn't see much future in the group, missed rehearsals and in July 1965 told the others he was leaving.★ He was replaced on guitar by Edinburgh schoolboy Dave Pettigrew who'd answered an ad Alan had placed in the local paper. More advanced musically than Alan and Derek, Pettigrew embarrassed the less able brothers when they rehearsed the then UK number one, 'Help!' by The Beatles. They dubbed Pettigrew 'Dave the Rave'. "That was us taking the piss," said Clark. "He was the exact opposite. He wasn't a raver. He was a very straight-laced guy." Charlie Smith, a school pal of Pettigrew's, hustled for gigs around the Edinburgh clubs with some success.

The band played at the new central Edinburgh club, the Gonk, supporting a new hip teen group, The Reflections who had a freakishly big-voiced 13-year-old singer called Colin Chisholm. Paton was familiar with Chisholm who had been on the scene a couple of years already, fronting Tiny & the Titans, regulars at the Top Storey and McGoos. He had both of Chisholm's groups play the Palais.

For a while the nascent Bay City Rollers went under the name The Deadbeats, until they discovered there was a bigger band called Rock Bottom & the Deadbeats gigging around Edinburgh. Influenced by the new crop of Edinburgh groups such as The Hipple People, they played songs they'd heard these groups play: 'Please Mister Postman' by The Marvelettes and 'Heat Wave' by Martha & the Vandellas. Cheekily, they even played The Hipple People's big number, 'Keep Your Hands Off My Baby' by Little Eva. "[They were] the standard songs all the bands were playing around the clubs," said Clark.

★ In the late 1980s, Porteous committed suicide, making him the sixth individual who'd been in The Bay City Rollers who had reportedly tried to kill himself – a remarkable statistic.

During his plumbing apprenticeship, Alan went one day a week to Napier College's technical department. Here he met fellow plumbing apprentice Gregory Ellison who played electric guitar but had never been in a band. They were the same age, 17, and became good friends. Alan asked if he wanted to join his group. He did. "Dave [Pettigrew] went on keyboards," Ellison said. They were now playing several Motown songs in their short set. "That was Nobby's preference," Ellison added. "It was the same as a lot of bands in Edinburgh. [The Four Tops'] 'It's The Same Old Song', ironically, was one of the songs doing the rounds. We did one or two Kinks numbers. That was more what I was into."

Ellison's elder brother also joined the group, on vocals, so now they had two singers like The Hipple People. "Mike was four years older than me," said Ellison. "It just happened. It wasn't something that was consciously planned. Two singers worked for us okay. Mike had quite a good singing voice. He had no intention of trying to oust Nobby. Two singers suited the type of vocal harmony stuff we were doing, a lot of Four Tops and Martha & the Vandellas."

Alan and Ellison often went out dancing together, checking out bands and girls. "Doing what young guys did," Ellison said. "Having a good time. We'd go to McGoos, the Gonk, the Place, Bungies. I wouldn't say we were out and out Mods but everyone was going about in three piece suits and funny shoes. If you picture Steve Marriott in the Small Faces, that was us."

Ellison and Alan were on a night out in the week when they bumped into Paton at the Top Storey when they asked to see the manager. He was chatting to Paton at the top of the stairs. "Just outside the door so they could hear themselves talking because there was a band on," said Ellison. "We'd had a bit of Dutch courage so we were asking the guy to give us a try, to book us. Alan said, 'You've heard of us Tam', just in the banter. I didn't know who Tam Paton was. Alan had an inkling. Really that's how we got talking to Tam and that's how Tam ended up agreeing to come along and listen to us. He wasn't really coming along to listen to us at all… he was coming along to see what he could do with us as a band."

It took a little more persuading that that, although Ellison had made a good impression on Paton. "A fine looking guy," he said. Alan was determined and he and Ellison went to the Palais to chase up Paton. "Tam was big time," said Alan. "He knew everybody on the circuit. We used to call him the one-handed piano player because when people walked in [at the Palais] he'd wave with one hand and continue playing." Paton recalled it was Alan "and his mates" pestering him at the Palais that caused him to agree to check out the teen band in rehearsal. He said it was only to "get rid" of them – to get some peace.

"He was the most important manager in Edinburgh," said Derek. "Everybody who wanted to play in a group was trying to meet him." Clark recalls Paton as "an impressive figure", well-dressed, well-connected, full of confidence and driving a flash car.

Paton watched them rehearse in the Longmuirs' tiny back room. "We had amps going, mikes set up and a drum kit in the room," said Ellison. "I don't how their mum and dad put up with it and the neighbours were not happy." Paton thought it was bit ridiculous but "they looked like a neat collection of people" and, he recognised, they were obviously determined, keen.

He put the band on at the Palais on a Thursday night. They were confused by the revolving stage. "As we were playing we moved the mikes onto the other part of the stage which wasn't the revolving part," said Clark. "And when we finished they started to turn the stage back and the microphones were getting dragged along the floor."

Paton had also got them a gig supporting The Hipple People at the Top Storey where they had gone down badly. They were eager for him to manage them. Derek and Clark were now 16 and both training as joiners, Clark on £35 a week as an apprentice. Derek, like his brother, had left school with no qualifications and "was glad to get out". He'd also been a truant, often given the belt and threatened with expulsion. He recalled walking out of his final English exam leaving a blank piece of paper.

The group moved out of the Longmuirs' back room to rehearse in a church hall in the Edinburgh suburb of Hermiston and it was around this time they settled on a new name, The Bay City Rollers. It was a confluence of influences. They were now including 'CC Rider' in their set, a song they'd heard on a single by American rockers Mitch Ryder & the Detroit Wheels. "We started talking about wheels and came up with Rollers," said Derek. Bay City came because they wanted something 'big', American/Motown sounding, and had stuck a pin in an American map at the Longmuirs' home. To them Bay City "sounded like a football club" said Alan. They had tried Bay City Stompers or Bay City Strollers before settling on Rollers. "We dreamed of being successful, everybody does, but we never thought it would happen," said Alan.

In July 1966 Paton lost The Hipple People and started to pay more attention to The Bay City Rollers. Among his first pieces of serious managerial advice was to lose Mike Ellison. "Mike was ousted by Tam," said his brother Greg Ellison. "As far as he was concerned there was no room for two singers. I think Tam thought that he might not be able to control Mike the same as us younger guys."

Paton didn't like the new name either. When he asked if they'd taken it from The Atlantic Rollers, a Scottish band that had been around during The Crusaders' early days, they looked at him blankly. He explained it would not sit easily across a single column in newspaper advertisements that were priced by the word. He was in favour of short band names.

"He wanted to call us The Poppies," said Ellison. It was an indication of his vision for the group; pop, teenage music. "When Tam came in it was like, Yeah he wanted us to be better musically but it was really all about image," added Ellison.

"To me," Paton would famously declare, "they were a tin of Heinz beans."

Stepping up the pace, Paton booked them gigs at the venues where The Hipple People played in and around Edinburgh. There were Monday, Friday, Saturday and Sunday night gigs at the usual clubs: the Place, Top Storey, the International, McGoos and Bungies. He was a busy man, still managing The Circle and Beat Hysters as well as playing with his show band at the Palais.

The Bay City Rollers would often play an early show in one club before a late night gig at another. The money was good for a bunch of kids earning very little as apprentices, in excess of £100 for a night's work. "We were playing sometimes two or three gigs a night," said Ellison. "We might play the Top Storey and then the International and they go out to Bonnyrigg [Regal]." The band quickly started to pick up the same sort of teenage female audience as The Beachcombers and Hipple People had. "What I heard was ghastly, but they obviously had something because the audience was screaming and shouting," said Paton. "I realised the popularity was how they looked and how tight they wore their trousers, if that's not putting it too crudely. And that was basically the start of the band."

"They had absolutely no musical ability, but people went crazy for them," he added. "I took a drummer friend to see them one night [Neil Smith who drummed in the show band], and he came away and said, 'What the fuck was that? How did that lot get such a reaction?' I said to him, 'They are five pairs of tight jeans and big hairy bollocks hanging out at the front', and he said, 'Thank Christ for that, because you'd never give them a contract on musical ability.'

"I couldn't give two fucks for them the first time I saw them," Paton added. "They were a challenge and I was a frustrated pop star. I always wanted to be on the music scene. I didn't have anything. So I did it."

Small gangs of girls had started following them from club to club but when it came to music they were novices. Visiting heavy Glasgow bands such as The Pathfinders or The Stoics, both favorites of Ellison, crushed the Rollers. In Edinburgh, as elsewhere, there was a trend towards groups getting heavier in the style of acts like Cream or Hendrix. The Jury, formed around the impassioned voice of former Place club DJ Linnie Patterson, was the best. They belted out 'Hold On I'm Coming' by Sam & Dave and 'This Old Heart Of Mine' by The Isley Brothers – two songs the Rollers took to use in their own set. The young Rollers were impressed that Paton was friendly with The Jury, a group that was managed by the Waldman brothers. In fact singer Patterson helped Paton out on the potato wagon on Saturdays. When the Rollers supported The Jury the young group was put firmly in their place. "It was embarrassing," said Ellison. "They were a fantastic band."

"No guys wanted to see us," said Clark. "It was all girls. The guys would boo us off stage."

The band quickly became Paton's number one concern. He recruited roadies to carry their gear and drove the group members around in his Ford Zephyr. He found them incredibly pliable. Not only had they axed Mike Ellison on his say so, they were happy to get fitted out for matching suits. "He wanted us to look smart on stage," said Clark. "The suit scene didn't go down that well with us but that was an image Tam wanted to create. None of us were comfortable with it." The suits were coral, an orangey pink, and made by a neighbour of the Longmuirs. They wore them with white shirts and big black bow ties. "It was hideous," said Derek.

The Rollers regularly visited Paton at his parents' home in Prestonpans where he still lived and he encouraged them to rehearse in the garage. His mum fussed over them, cooked them egg and chips. "His mother was supportive, a lovely woman, just a normal down-to-earth person," said Clark. "His father was quite a nasty character, drunk most of the time." Paton asked Derek and Clark to help turn his bedroom into an office, so they put up a partition and built him a desk. Clark thought his taste in decoration a "bit suspect" with fake rifles and hand pistols on the wall, and crossed swords over the fireplace. Paton was "always well dressed," said Clark. "He wore quite expensive clothes." But, because he'd been delivering potatoes, he often had filth embedded under his fingernails. Prestonpans, Clark said, "had a very bad reputation for a lot of violent behaviour... a scary place back then: the streets, the pubs everything, a lot of violence."

Paton's image was changing: a smart but casual suit, white shirt hanging outside his trousers unbuttoned to reveal a hairy chest and gold chain with medallion. He wore Chelsea boots and his hair was long and fair. He smoked almost constantly. His bedroom/office became the hub of the band's activities with a big map of Scotland on the door on which he would stick pins in places where the band played – his ambition to put a pin in every city and town on the map. "When we were first getting off the ground it was a really exciting time and Tam was just like another member of the band," said Clark. "We went everywhere together. The whole thing was an adventure."

They began by playing locally, places close to Edinburgh where Paton had contacts such as Prestonpans, Tranent, Bonnyrigg, Lasswade, Dunfermline and Rosyth, all places where teenage girls were as keen on the group as their city counterparts. Paton instructed a band roadie, Tam Smith, to keep girls away from the group before, during and after the shows. "Tam was a bit frantic," said Clark. "There was a bit of kissing and touching going on."

Other early roadies were George Greenshields, 'Big' Davie Gold, in his mid-20s, and Davie Purdie, who often drove the van. Gold could carry a Hammond organ on his back. The roadies were also useful if any of these out of town gigs got violent. "There would often be ten or 20 rows of girls and behind them rows of guys hating us," said Clark. Tranent Town Hall was notoriously tasty and Paton often had to intervene as jealous local lads, usually drunk, tried to attack the band. He was often seen sporting a black eye.

Paton seemed to be everywhere on the Edinburgh scene, also appearing as a DJ around clubs like Walkers, that had links to the International's ownership/management, and Casablanca, a proto-disco that was run by the Waldman brothers. He played top 20 hits and tried to get bookings further afield under the name of 'Patonas Portable Discotheque', assuming that an Italian flourish might sway club owners. He used The Crusaders' Vox AC30 amplifiers to DJ at teenage nights he organised himself around Prestonpans.

This new career was inspired to some extent by the fact the Palais closed for refurbishment in early 1967. Fights and stabbings there led to a decision to turn into a bingo hall. This spelled the end of not just the Tommy Paton Showband but also The Crusaders, and there were disputes among the members about who owned their expensive equipment. "At that time he seemed to be quite down about everything," said Frank Conner. "He just started doing the DJ thing to keep himself involved as he wasn't a strong enough musician to go and do gigs with other bands really."

None of The Crusaders interviewed for this book said they knew or even suspected Paton was gay. They insisted they never saw any indication of Paton's future sexual attraction to young men. All spoke about his kindness of spirit, generosity, fun-loving nature and powerful sense of humour.

Paton admitted he wanted to be a big star, and when he realised it wasn't going to happen he had decided to settle for second best, managing a band to stardom. Others, however, had already begun to suspect his attraction to teen bands was sexually motivated. From here on Paton would be surrounded by attractive young male teenagers.

Stuart Hepburn, owner of the Gamp club, said: "All that happened was Tam read *A Cellarful Of Noise* [Brian Epstein's 1964 autobiography] and copied Epstein. It's just like you go to California and it's, 'Film stars wanted, no experience necessary', and that's for the porn. And with Tam, it's 'good-looking boys for band wanted, ability to play not necessary'. It was fucking terrible." And it was going to get worse.

CHAPTER 2

Innocence

"The smell of fresh wet cunt permeated everywhere. There wasn't a guy in the place. It was sensational. It was a bit like seeing the Stones when they broke. You could smell sex everywhere. Then this band come on and they are fucking awful but the crowd are going berserk. You couldn't hear a word for the screaming."

— Tony Calder.

Nobby Clark met Keith Norman in June 1967 at an Edinburgh coffee bar called the Coffin. They were listening to The Beatles' new album, *Sgt. Pepper's Lonely Hearts Club Band*. Norman played keyboards in a teenage band called The Images, another novice Edinburgh act churning out familiar Motown and soul covers on the club scene. The two young men clicked. Clark, 17, took the Rollers to see the Images and suggested they ask Norman to join their group. The Images had a strong female following and many of them gravitated toward Norman who was just 16. "He was a great-looking guy, dark shoulder length hair," said Clark.

Paton was already familiar with The Images. They often played the Casablanca club, where he sometimes acted as DJ, and the band had actually approached him to become their manager. He was happy to have Norman join and the Rollers added a second keyboard player to their line-up. "Tam had this idea of how to build it up was to have more individual guys in the band that girls could take to," said Clark. "All the guys in the band had their own fan following. They came to see Derek, or me, or Alan."

Or Norman. He was from a well-off family that lived in a big house in Murrayfield and had been to private school. There was "something lost about him," Paton said. "He was sad but with a sense of humour."

The new Rollers line-up with two Vox Continental organs either side of the stage was unusual for the period and distinguished them from other bands in the city. Unlike Dave the Rave, a guitarist shunted onto the keys when Ellison joined, Norman was a talented pianist. The group started to sound better. Always a fan of vocal harmony, Clark introduced new songs into the set like 'Rag Doll' and 'Bye Bye Baby' by The Four Seasons, a group he admired. "We started to change the type of music we were doing," he said. "I moulded it to be more something other bands weren't playing."

Alan also suggested songs for the band and they tried to keep their set up to date, building up a list of cover versions. Still heavily influenced by American soul and R&B, they played 'I'm Your Puppet' by James & Bobby Purify and 'Soul Man' by Sam & Dave. Their 'anthem', according to Clark, was 'Please Stay', The Drifters' 1961 hit. "It was a huge song for us," said Clark. "The girls insisted we play it every night. I must have sung that song thousands of times. These songs, to the fans, became Roller songs."

They also offered up dance orientated, funky material like Edwin Starr's 'SOS', The Temptations' 'Get Ready', and Sam & Dave's 'You Got Me Hummin'', and zoned in on girl group material: The Chiffons' 'Sweet Talkin' Guy' and The Ronettes' 'Be My Baby'. "We were changing the set all the time," said Clark. "We had a long, long list of songs. Picked up off other Edinburgh bands? Yes, absolutely. 'Be My Baby' was huge for us."

They had ditched the bow ties but were still sharply suited and booted, Paton having fitted them out with a set of baby blue suits from Edinburgh's top men's boutique Our Man. In matching shirts, ties, and black Chelsea boots, the look was strong. They often huddled in Paton's office-cum-bedroom discussing what it would take to make it big, how dedicated they would have to be. Paton laid down some fresh ground rules. "He strongly believed that having girlfriends would be a distraction and we agreed," said Clark.

"At that time I didn't know Tam was gay," he added. "I don't think any of the other guys in the band did either. It would never have occurred to us. There was nothing effeminate about him apart from his high-pitched voice. I thought he was dedicating himself to making the band successful and didn't want distractions the same as we were.

"That was naïve when I look back now. After I left the band I looked back over the whole situation and I think the whole band was almost a grooming situation. Helping us to build up the trust and once the trust is there… Tam met my parents. He sat and spoke with them on a number of occasions. He was very friendly to my parents, they trusted him – they didn't have any reason not to. I'm sure it was the same with the other parents. Tam was a charmer, a charming kind of guy. He never tried anything in those days. I felt perfectly safe with Tam on my own and I know the other guys did as well. I'd often be on my own with him and I never felt ill at ease at any time."

Girlfriends were not only time-consuming. Paton sold the idea to the band that they mustn't have girlfriends so their girl fans would believe they were available just for them. Soon he was demanding they couldn't have sex with girls at all. "One of his ploys was to tell us stories that would put us off girls," Clark said. One was about a local couple having sex got who got stuck together. Paton told the band that women had a bone in their vagina that could come down and trap a man's penis.

Nevertheless, girls were throwing themselves at the band and some members continued to have flings. It became a group law, however, that if a relationship developed they had to leave the group. For the next five years Clark became celibate. "It was a ruling," he said. "Paton was very strict about it. It was down to this, how keen you were to become successful and I know in my case and Alan's and Derek's, we were so dedicated to making this band successful even if we did have something going on the side it was never going to be that important."

"Tam wanted 100 per cent going into the band," said Ellison. "No time for wenching, courting, no time for women. So if you were, and everybody was, everybody had a girlfriend... it all had to be hidden. I don't think we were that naïve, but we never knew Tam was gay. He wouldn't brag about his sexual conquest with women with us but the indication was he was heterosexual for sure. Tam never tried anything on with any of us to my knowledge. It wouldn't have mattered a damn if he was gay. I knew back then some guys swung the other way and what did it matter? These things don't matter a damn."

Alcohol was also forbidden and to ensure his stipulations were met Paton made sure, while they all worked during the week, evenings were taken up with rehearsals or gigs or planning meetings in Paton's bedroom. On weekends, during the day, he had them on the potato wagon. "It was his way of keeping us under control," said Clark. "If we worked the potato lorry we weren't getting up to mischief. It started off as bit of laugh [riding around the city] but I could see what was behind it. We all took shots at doing it. I'd be doing it one weekend, Derek would do it another, Alan and me another. Sometime we were all on there. It was really a means to keep us busy, try and keep us under control."

Under Paton, The Bay City Rollers made steady progress. He made sure they didn't waste the money they were earning and that it was all channelled back into the band. "My old Hofner was traded for a Fender Stratocaster and we got a brand new Ford transit, double wheeled, long wheel base transit," said Ellison. "That was the thing for all the bands to have. You got one with the windows and the seats and you ripped out the seats at the back and stacked the gear up. Tam had it so well organised he made it look quite professional. He would have the roadies driving the van and setting the gear up and he would drive us in his car, the white Ford Zephyr, and we would go on round the back and do the gig and disappear. This was all Tam's dream."

"The drill was get out of the van, on stage, do the set, leave," said Clark. "No familiarity and we got better and better at it. Other bands hated us for it." It was the "inaccessibility", said Derek, "that made people want us even more." Alan added: "Tam promoted this untouchable idea and, gradually, we built up a big female following. We had to sneak off somewhere if we wanted to be with a girl because if the fans knew or saw, it would somehow damage our image."

The band, at this stage, "all got on really well", said Ellison. "We were just like any other bunch of young blokes, except Derek, who I liked but who kept himself to himself. Everybody took the mickey out of everybody else. Nobody ganged up. We were all equals in the band and everyone had a measure of respect for one another."

Paton used The Bay City Rollers as a template for other young bands that approached him. The Index was one such schoolboy band; bassist Billy McGhee was only 14. They were all from a housing estate in the south of Edinburgh called the Inch. "There were two main managers in Edinburgh at the time, Tam and Kenny McLean, The Beachcombers' manager," said McGhee. "We approached Tam he said Yeah, he could be interested but come and see one of the bands I've got."

The Index went to see the Rollers play a popular dance hall in the Greenhill area of Edinburgh. "They were his number one band," said McGhee. "We were really impressed by their level of professionalism for such young guys who obviously didn't have the same musical ability as the big Glasgow bands."

Paton agreed to manage The Index. "We were in awe of him," said McGhee. "He looked expensive when he turned up at your gigs. He looked like a proper manager, had great presence. He was tall, proud, well built. People looked up to him. He looked like he was in command, which he was when it came to his bands."

The Index was a fashionable looking five-piece dressed down in mix and match of jumpers, shirts and jackets. Paton put them in suits; light green, with shirts and big bow ties too. "Tam used to guide us towards what we should be playing, the kind of stuff that was popular," said McGhee. The Index started to include 'Please Stay' in their set. "We bolstered our set up with all the standards," said McGhee, "and a lot of stuff that was in the charts."

"Tam knew how to make a band popular even if you weren't any great shakes musically. He had this whole regime based on image. He was all about stage presence, the way you dressed – he had us in suits straight away, we had to get a good van so we'd be presentable, respectable, when we turned up. He made us get a car so that the band would be separated from the gear and roadies. Everything had to look professional. It all became about image."

As he did with the Rollers, Paton advised The Index to reinvest their gig money. "Tam said nobody should be taking a penny out, all the money you earn goes back in to pay for new equipment, a van, suits," said McGhee. "We followed his guidance." Paton would take only a nominal amount from the group for the gigs he arranged, less than 10 per cent. It did not seem to be about the money. "He wasn't interested in the money," said McGhee. "We looked after our own finances. He just wanted his bands to be famous. All he would take off us was £15 a gig."

Paton applied the same rules to The Index as he did the Rollers: no girlfriends and no booze. "It wasn't enforced quite as strongly for his other bands because the Rollers were always his number one band," said McGhee. "They got the big treatment, we got what was left but it was still great for us." The Index never helped out on the potato wagon. "That was exclusive to the Rollers," said McGhee. "They had that privilege."

"We were straight-laced young guys but we liked to go for a pint," McGhee added. "We had to do that very sneakily. Tam had such a hold over the Rollers. One gig we did with them in town, we snuck out to the pub and Alan came with us, the most normal guy in that band. Enjoying a quick pint was us being rebellious."

The Index visited Paton's Prestonpans office for weekly band meetings. "He kept close tabs on his bands," said McGhee. "There was a map of Great Britain on the back of the door [in his bedroom] and he had all these dots on it where his stable of bands had played. He said, one day that will be a map of the world."

"We didn't know Tam was gay," said McGhee. "None of our band was gay. You did hear stories about Tam, rumours used to kick about. I was still at school and they'd say, 'Oh you cannae have girlfriends, Tam must be a poof!' It was typical schoolboy stuff. But you never believed it. It never became an issue for our band; he never approached anyone in our band. We were too young and naïve to realise we might have been being groomed."

As he had with the Rollers, Paton began to tamper with the line-up of The Index. He felt their singer, Gillie, who was black, was not right for the group. "He kept putting it to us, saying Gillie's not cutting it," said McGhee. "It was very awkward; we respected Tam and thought we need to do what he's telling us to do. He put us in a hell of a spot. We eventually got another guy in to sing."

Paton soon added a significant third teen group to his stable, The Tandem. One of the band, 15-year-old Archie Marr, who played organ and guitar, worked in Our Man and was a future Bay City Roller. Paton was a regular at the Our Man shop, owned by two gay men, and Marr had actually sold the Rollers their baby blue suits. He'd been to an historic private all-boys George Heriot's School in Edinburgh, said to be a source of inspiration for J.K. Rowling's Hogwarts School from the Harry Potter books. "My parents thought I was destined for better things," he said. "But if you were going to be working in a boutique Our Man was the one to be in, where the top people would buy their clothes."

The Tandem played similar music to The Index and the Rollers and to a similar audience. "We were always second slot to the Rollers," said Marr. "They were Tam's baby – he always nurtured them. Tam made them successful in Edinburgh before any record came out. It was all Tam's doing. He wouldn't let girls near the band so they became desperate to go and talk to the guys. He made them look like stars even though they weren't and then people started believing it. He'd get all the lassies screaming. The Tandem and Index were put on the same gigs so we were capturing the same audience and following in a smaller way but it wasn't about music. It was about image.

"Tam's policy was always, no sex, no drugs, no rock'n'roll. He based his model on Brian Epstein. He wanted all the members in the group to be seen to be obtainable by the fans. There was method in his madness. We must have been quite naïve at the time. A 30-year-old man sharing a house in a mining village with his mum and dad, wearing cowboy boots, surrounded by young men… it's a no brainer. But our mind was full of girls and groups and getting on and getting some fame. We always kind of surmised Tam was gay but we never challenged him, it was irrelevant."

The Tandem and The Index, as well as the Rollers, played about four or five times a week each, often booked together. "He made us popular on the back of the Rollers," said McGhee. "We played with them as a support band then the girls would come see us next time we played. Tam controlled the whole thing. We were all the same in his stable."

As well as the Edinburgh clubs, Paton continued to supply his acts to the surrounding towns. Bonnyrigg Regal was a regular gig, at least every three weeks. It was a late night venue, open until 2am. The Index supported Dave Dee, Dozy, Beaky, Mick & Tich and Wayne Fontana here. Paton took over as promoter at the nearby Rosewell Institute near Lasswade for a period in 1967. He booked The Bee Gees for a gig here with his three bands acting as support. Paton even played the venue himself at a Christmas dance. "We managed to persuade Tam to come on stage with us dressed as Santa Claus," said McGhee. "He played Christmas songs along with us on his accordion."

There was also a concerted attempt to establish fan bases further afield in Scotland. "We travelled around every town hall in Scotland," said McGhee. "People were just dancing, there'd be no booze. People would go to the pub and then go to the dance after. These were busy places. We'd be playing clubs in Edinburgh during the week and then all local town halls, down the Borders, up north. Playing five nights a week was normal."

At Shotts Town Hall, half way between Edinburgh and Glasgow, a drunken gang attacked the Rollers. Paton's Zephyr had its tyres slashed and windows broken. Clark described another town hall gig where the girls were trying to grab his legs while he sang. Clark said he was teasing the girls when bottles were thrown at the stage and soon there was a full-scale riot. One of the band's Hammond organs and Derek's drum kit were thrown off stage. The police rescued the band. These were hard gigs even without the violence, at town halls in places like Motherwell and Airdrie – edging toward Glasgow, a city the band avoided. They'd head to places out in the sticks, unglamourous working men's clubs in remote villages like Gourock. There were gigs in church halls, in YMCAs, and in Butlins holiday camp in Ayr.

Bigger venues such as JM Ballroom in Dundee, the Trocadero in Hamilton and the Beach ballroom in Aberdeen also became regulars. One of Paton's early tricks for getting a positive reaction, ensuring a return booking, was to hire a coach to take girls who screamed at the band in the Edinburgh clubs out to venues elsewhere. He wouldn't charge them and they would create the right vibe. "All the locals used to think, 'Wow this is special,'" said McGhee. "And next time he didn't need to take busloads of girls from Edinburgh, he had created the same reaction in other cities. He spread that all around Scotland."

"At that time we were probably playing four or five gigs a week," said Clark. "Some of the gigs were mid-week and a lot of these places would be so full a lot of the fans couldn't get in. No matter what night it was they would travel all over the country to come and see us. It was quite a phenomenon. We had a staunch following of girls who would come to all the places. I think it took off because there was a jealously, a rivalry, when we played in other places. The girls that were from that area wanted to show how much they liked us and the girls who had followed us for longer were making their point by trying to pull us off stage and that kind of thing. It wasn't orchestrated. It came as a bit of a surprise to us all as it built up. It was all built on image."

Paton had a fixation for handing out publicity photographs of his groups. He would give away hundreds of 12×8-inch black and white pictures with his contact details on; early attempts to create publicity for his bands that were clumsy but effective.

In December 1967, he had the Rollers walk the nine miles from Edinburgh to Nazareth House children's home in Lasswade. They seemed to be dressed as cavaliers and had gifts for the children. "All marched up in fancy dress," said Clark. "It was billed as a charity walk and was covered by the *Edinburgh Evening News*." Ellison recalled Jimmy Savile being involved. "We did all the walks with Jimmy Savile," he said. "Walking up to the children's homes was done for a good cause but to be fair it was also done for publicity. We had swords and feathers in our hats. We made a donation to Nazareth in Lasswade. Savile came up. He was asked by Tam to lend his name to it, purely for publicity for the band."

In September 1968 there was another charity walk with Jimmy Savile, now working for BBC Radio 1. It was followed by a well-publicised football match: Savile and friends versus The Bay City Rollers and friends. The match featured on the front page of the *Edinburgh Evening News*. The money raised was donated toward buying a swimming pool for handicapped children at St Joseph's Hospital, Rosewell, just south of Lasswade, a Catholic church-run institution. "We did a couple of these sponsored charity walks with Jimmy Savile," said Billy McGhee. "Tam got us into that."

Paton orchestrated other stunts. He and the Rollers spray-painted the name of the band, often just their initials 'BCR' across all the new bridges of the M8, a motorway being built between Glasgow and Edinburgh, and on the walls of Princes Street, Edinburgh's main shopping street. The band were charged with defacing property and had to scrub it off. It created quite a stir and there were many photos of the graffiti and the band in the Scottish newspapers.

"That was all Tam's idea," said Clark. "We had to go to court and we got fined. But who cares? It was great publicity. Tam had all the papers he could get hold of taking photos of us scrubbing the graffiti off. With promotion and publicity he had the knack of doing the right things. Tam did a lot of things to draw attention to the band."

Even without a record, Paton was able to get photographs of the Rollers in Scottish music magazines such as *Beat Scene* and *Hitmaker*. He was also getting the band regularly in *Jackie* magazine, a weekly for girls, published by DC Thomson from Dundee. It sold 350,000 copies a week, the best-selling teen magazine in the UK. The *Edinburgh Evening News* was also supportive.

By 1968 Clark regularly had girls camped outside his family house. "Sometimes they were there during the night and my mother would make them tea," he said. Fans also gathered at the Longmuirs' tenement home, centrally located and known to be the band's meeting place. "They were round all our houses," said Clark. "That was quite amazing without a record, or any TV or radio."

The Motown/Stax dance boom had peaked in Edinburgh. The trend toward psychedelia and progressive blues-rock had impacted on the city's famous dance hall and club scene. The Gamp and Bungies were closing. The city centre was also being developed and the Top Storey and McGoos would soon be lost. The Place was sold.

The Rollers were earning good money on the road, up to £400 a week, but needed to find new places to play in the city where their fan base remained strongest. Stuart Hepburn, who had run the Gamp, opened a new club called Oasis that they would now regularly play, sometimes on Sundays for an under-16s crowd. Another new club that would become closely associated with the Rollers was the Caves, in the arches under the South Bridge in Edinburgh. They played the opening night in July 1968 when BBC Radio 1 DJ Stuart Henry acted as compere. Despite one of the band being punched in the face that night, the Caves club became a regular Saturday night gig for the band.

They also often used the Caves as a rehearsal space. Their set now included 'Hey Jude' by The Beatles and "a couple of Hollies songs", said Ellison. Billy McGhee recalled the Rollers playing material by The Idle Race, Jeff Lynne's critically acclaimed but commercially unsuccessful late sixties band. Clark enjoyed the vocal twists and the music, avant-garde rock, was a step forward for the band.

Paton persuaded a musical director from BBC Scotland to assist the band at the Caves club. "He could listen to a record and he would pick out all the chords for you," said Ellison. "The minor fifths the diminished and augmented chords we'd never heard of because we were pretty basic. He said to me, 'Never mind these bloody cowboy chords.' He did good things with the band, started us going better musically."

Paton worked his contacts at BBC Scotland. He was friendly with the influential Ben Lyons who produced broadcasts for Radio 1. The Index recorded for Lyons at the BBC sound studio in Edinburgh.

Paton was still working all day on the potato wagon, often driving all night with his bands in his Zephyr as well. In the summer of 1968, his behaviour began to cause some concern to the Rollers. He had persuaded them, bar Norman who worked in a chemist shop in the city centre, to accompany him on holiday to Spain. He was 30 now.

Derek and Clark and Dave 'the Rave' Pettigrew were still teenagers, and none had been outside Scotland before. Outside the Longmuirs', girls in the street waved them off. Clark recalled how on the trip Ellison got badly sunburned and, with his skin blistering, how Paton insisted he had the panacea but instead poured Old Spice aftershave on Ellison's back. It was, said Clark, the first sign of Paton's "sadistic tendencies". He continued to do his best to control the band, furious when they escaped him to go drinking. He was "going crazy" said Clark, pacing up and down, shouting and swearing.

Back in Edinburgh with handsome tans after a week on the beach – a key motive for the holiday – Ellison decided he'd had enough. "We were okay as a band and we were getting better," he said. "But I didn't like the way the band was going because it was getting too much image. I'd have liked to progress the musical side of the band rather than the image side. But that's not where Tam was taking it."

He had also met a girl, who would become his wife. "It was frowned upon," said Ellison. "Tam went about on your nights off chasing you. He would be spying, coming round to see where people were going. It was really that bad. Really controlling. It was too regimented for me. I enjoyed the band when it was fun. I enjoyed playing and when it was all loose, when it was a laugh."

Dave Pettigrew also left the Rollers. Originally the guitarist in the group, his role as second keyboardist was becoming superfluous and any hope he had of replacing Ellison on guitar was quickly dashed by Paton. He already had his eye on a new guitarist for the band. He'd long been an admirer of David Paton and the 19-year-old was back in Edinburgh after The Beachcombers' career had failed to ignite in London. Paton already had David, or Davie, as he was known, working on his potato lorry. He was perfect for the Rollers: great-looking, slim, with long straight hair and very popular with girls. David Paton appeared much younger than 19 and had the generic look familiar to all the male teenagers Paton wanted sex with – dark-haired, button-nosed, girlish.

Davie was also known to be among the most talented musicians on the Edinburgh scene. Although he admitted the Rollers had "a mystique about them that aroused my curiosity" he didn't really want to join the band, churning out cover versions to screaming teens. "I wanted to push myself musically, and I didn't think I'd be stretched with the Rollers," he said. Paton was very persuasive and persistent. "He offered me a new Gibson Les Paul, a Marshall amp, clothes, a good wage and gigs five nights a week," said Davie.

The new line-up had the band sounding at their best with Norman on keyboards and Davie on guitar, both skilled musicians. "Their enthusiasm was intense and their thoughts were always on the band and how to make it even more successful," said Davie. "The music was left in our hands, and Tam was out there working hard to make a dream come true. We were just an Edinburgh band but creating hysteria at every gig." Davie soon experienced being chased by fans around Edinburgh. "A Roller couldn't walk down the street without being recognised," he said.

They pursued heavier guitar music, tackling more expansive tracks by Cream and early Deep Purple such as their first single 'Hush'. "We were playing all the time and we were trying to improve and get better," said Clark. "The band, live, with certain line ups, musically was really hot. The early period with Keith Norman and the two keyboards was great and then when Davie Paton came into the band things took off again and we went through another great musical period. Davie was a real musician. He could play lead and sing great. We could do three part harmonies and we'd cover Beach Boys songs and Crosby, Stills & Nash." The Rollers also tackled a couple of mid-sixties Dylan numbers: 'Positively 4th Street' and 'The Times They Are A-Changin''. A new favourite was an album by Dylan's backing band, The Band, called *Music From Big Pink*. "We covered a lot of songs off that album," said Clark.

Live, they were still mobbed by girls. "We couldn't go anywhere or do anything without being mobbed by screaming girls," said Davie. They were also increasingly provocative in their stage wear, Paton having decided the matching suits were a little dated now. Clark proved to be a dab hand on his mother's sewing machine. He and Alan would go buy fabric to make trousers, shirts, and jackets for the band. "It was a great feeling to be making our own stuff," said Clark. Even in green velvet trousers and short pink satin jackets with a frill on the back, the screams kept coming. So did the aggression from jealous gangs of lads. Davie was impressed to see Paton step in and stop any trouble at gigs.

Paton took the band on another holiday in the summer of 1969. "The holidays were because we were knackered," said Clark. "We were working so hard, full-on all the time, and we needed a break." They slept on the beach in France and bummed around Paris after the van broke down en route to Spain. Paton was impressed with Parisian fashion, particularly men in black sheer lace see-through shirts and matching trousers. Back in Edinburgh Clark knocked up similar costumes for the band, in different colours. The girls could barely contain themselves.

Keith Norman was next to leave. He was rumoured to be seeing a girl, so Paton went on the warpath, sitting outside Norman's parents' house at 10.30pm. Norman was shocked to see him there. Paton confronted him. He confessed and left the band. Clark felt terrible. "He was a close friend," he said. "Tam was not physically violent with the band but he was verbally violent. Verbally he was very disruptive. He was a bully no doubt about it."

The incident served to make Paton even stricter on girlfriends. "I learned quite a lot from Keith," he said. "Girlfriend are bad news for lots of reasons. I literally had to tie up their nights off with Chinese dinner, whatever it takes to keep them focused. Without dedication to purpose, it's a disaster."

Now playing as many as six nights a week and rehearsing either in the garage at Paton's parents' house in Prestonpans, where he still lived, or at the potato garage in Port Seton, their manager had effectively tied up all the band members' spare time. They were driven everywhere in the van by a roadie or Paton would pick them all up in his car. "Tam was very strict with us," said Davie Paton. "If we had a night off Tam would take us to the pictures and drive us home at bedtime. He used to take me to my house and watch me going up the stairs. But I had a car and when he'd gone I'd drive to meet a chick. He'd be round two hours later. He'd see my car wasn't there and be chasing all over town looking for me!"

This was not normal behavior. Another incident also seemed out of character. At one rehearsal at the tattie-shed he handed the band a huge lump of cannabis. None of band even smoked cigarettes at the time.

"What do you do with it?" asked Alan.

Paton rolled a joint and gave it to them. Clark said he felt dizzy, sick, and horrible. "I always questioned what that was all about. I never really got to the bottom of that one but there was obviously something in Tam's mind. It was a strange thing to do. There was a dark side to Paton that I'd begun to find quite disturbing. What he showed, his public face, and what was going on inside his head were obviously two different things. Tam obviously knew what his game was, kept it to himself quite well but he obviously had other ideas in his head."

Paton was more determined than ever to have success. He had seen The Gaylords, his chief rivals in Scotland from the days of The Crusaders, change their name to Marmalade and reach number one in the charts with a cover of a Beatles song 'Ob-La-Di, Ob-La-Da'. The first Scottish band to achieve this, they celebrated by wearing kilts on *Top Of The Pops*, and continued to do well for the next couple of years.

Paton tried to get the Rollers a deal in London. "I spent 14 days going round the companies, coming back to a van each night which I slept in, wrapped up in newspapers. I had no tapes, just photographs, and was trying to sell the group on that."

Back in Edinburgh he replaced Keith Norman with an ambitious 15-year-old called Alan Dunn who was from Bonnyrigg and had been in Edinburgh bands since he was 10, most recently Penny Black who had been playing the Caves and the International. Dunn had approached Paton about the possibility of Penny Black supporting the Rollers. He was invited to Prestonpans and asked if he wanted to join the Rollers. Dunn was a bass player.

"I said, 'Is Alan Longmuir leaving?'"

"No, it's Keith."

"But Keith's a keyboard player. Why do you not take Kenny McFarlane out of my band because he plays the keyboards?"

"No, no, I want you."

"I can't play the keyboards."

"Don't worry, Alan, I'll teach you."

Paton approached Dunn's parents to get their permission for him to join the Rollers. Then he sent Dunn to the Edinburgh organ studio three nights a week to learn to read music and play the band's Hammond. Norman agreed to stay on in the band until Dunn was up to speed.

During this period Dunn was approached by a rival manager, Martin Frutin, who was also interested in building up a stable of teen bands. Amongst his roster was Size 5, a band Dunn had once played for. Frutin also managed The Hitchhikers, The Avenue and The Breadline. He was well connected and would soon become part of Paton's social circle. "They both must have been eyeing me up," Dunn said. "Frutin had a pink house down Portobello. I went there and he gave me Quaaludes and then he gave me a tight pair of hipsters to try on, really tight so all your private parts stuck out. He had this big fancy chair for me to sit on and he shut the curtains via remote control. He had this control that triggered all the lights in the room as well. Tam warned me. He said, 'Watch him, he will do bad things to you.' Tam knew what Frutin was all about. He said, 'Keep away from Martin Frutin.'"

Dunn was soon helping out with the others on Paton's potato wagon. The band called him Benjamin. "Alan Longmuir turned round and said, 'You'll get called Benjamin because every time someone said Alan we'd both turned round.' The first thing I learned when I joined the Rollers was how to light a fart. That was the initiation to get into the Rollers."

"The first rehearsal I had was in the garage at the side of Tam's father's house. It was 'She Came In Through The Bathroom Window' [from the Beatles' *Abbey Road* released in September 1969]. Davie Paton sat on the drums and showed Derek how it went. Then he went to Alan Longmuir and showed him what the bass line was. And then he sat down on the organ and showed me how to play it. The rest of the rehearsals we were in the tattie shed – what a mess it was in there, it was horrendous. We were all crammed in; I was sort of standing out in a staircase. All the tatties were in there, paper and books all over the place."

Dunn had already started attending Rollers gigs. "To begin with I'd stand on the side of the stage and watch Keith playing," he said. "That was for months. We used to travel around in Tam's Zephyr with its electric windows and I'd sit in the middle of the front seats one leg either side of the handbrake with Tam pulling on the handbrake, hurting me. For the gigs I used to strip off naked and put on these high-waisted trousers. I must have had my blinkers on. My mind was all about the music and the band. But not once did Tam try anything. There was many a night I got dropped off last because the guys stayed in Edinburgh and we'd go through to Bonnyrigg. We'd park up and Tam would talk away to me, about the band, what we should do here, for hours."

Dunn spent Saturdays "tattie humping" and on Sundays he'd go riding horses up the Pentlands with the band. They had progressed from riding Icelandic ponies to horses from a stable run by a family called Bygate at Penicuik on the east side of the panoramic 20-mile Pentland hills range. "It was big horses," said Clark. "It was great to get away from everything else going on. We all thought we were cowboys. We paid for that out of the band money. Any money went in the pot and things were just paid for, same as when we went out for a meal at night."

Dunn was soon forced out of the band. He was beaten up and pushed through a window by two lads jealous of him being a Roller. "I cut the tendons on my arm and I couldn't play the keyboards," he said. "That was it. I was out of the band." Dunn would resurface briefly in a new teen band called Keyhole, which also featured future Rollers Eric Faulkner and Eric Manclark. He then slipped from the scene.★

Billy Lyall replaced Dunn as keyboardist in the Rollers. He was 16, from Edinburgh, a classically trained pianist and flautist, hence his nickname Hot Lips. He was effeminate, good looking and the first Roller to openly have sex with men – although he said he 'did dabble in girls'. "Billy was gay," said Paton. Lyall said he had simply

---

★ In the mid-seventies he tried to commit suicide by taking an overdose. He'd been at a club when a Rollers song came on. "I'd been drinking," he said. "I'd been getting headaches and the doctor gave me 500 Paracetamol. I got really down thinking I should have been there, having the success. That was my ambition to be in a band. I threw the pills down my neck and lay down to die." Only having his stomach pumped saved his life.

answered an ad asking for an organist and "didn't know what group it was". His first gig with the Rollers was at Hamilton Trocadero. "I didn't realise how popular they were until the gig," he said. "I was shaking like a leaf when I saw the place was bursting at the seams with girl fans." Clark made him a pair of trouser from gold velvet curtain material. "When Billy joined, Davie and Billy together raised the bar musically," said Clark.

Clark, who stayed close to Lyall into the late seventies, said Paton and Lyall "may well have" started having sex. Lyall died of AIDS in 1989. Lyall was "very openly gay", said Clark. "I had no idea about anyone else. It was my naivety... at the time normal people in families never ever discussed anyone being gay or bisexual. It was quite a hidden thing, so when people say they didn't know Tam was gay, I believe it."

At the end of 1969, *Transplant* magazine, dubbed 'Scotland's Teenage magazine!', asked its readers to vote for the best group in Scotland. The Bay City Rollers were second behind The Poets. Remarkably Paton's other acts, The Index and The Tandem, were also in the top 10, The Tandem at number three. Paton said jealous rival bands would frequently pilfer the Rollers' equipment and tamper with their van by putting sugar in the fuel system and pouring brake fluid on the paintwork.

Paton was now pre-occupied with getting the band a record deal. The stories of screaming and mass hysteria the band generated were spreading. Even on a cold March evening in 1970, there were groups of girls outside a club in East Kilbride, near Glasgow, waiting to glimpse the group leaving as, guarded by Paton and five big roadies, they were hurried into a black transit van with tinted windows. Paton told *Transplant*: "We get hundreds of letters begging us not to go to London." The magazine stated that "no other Scottish group has collected such a following without a chart hit" and that an "amazing number of girls follow them gig to gig".

At the start of the new decade heavy rock was making in impact not just on clubs and venues around the UK but in the charts. Bands such as Free, Black Sabbath and Deep Purple were making news. In Edinburgh Ten Years After, The Nice and Led Zeppelin played the Usher Hall, Deep Purple played the Odeon, Pink Floyd played the Student Union.

Bands dressed down, guitars were turned up and there was a general mistrust of lightweight pop. "It was the period of what became known as 'heavy' music," said Paton. "Everyone was trying to see this as the new in thing and here were we playing what is known as a teenage music." Paton always maintained that "heavy" music did nothing for entertainment.

The Bay City Rollers just kept on doing, said Paton, "what we knew best". He threw another pretty face into the mix. Eric Manclark, who was 16, joined the group in March of 1970. He looked about 14 and was from the same Edinburgh Inch district as The Index and a school friend of Eric Faulkner. In fact the two attended the same school as Davie Paton and The Index's Billy McGhee. Faulkner at one time dated McGhee's now wife.

Clark told a story of how they'd all been on the potato wagon when Paton first spotted Manclark.

"Can you play the guitar?" Paton shouted at him.

"No."

"Well, would you like to be in a group anyway?"

The real story is a little more convoluted. Keyhole was a band playing regularly at Stuart Hepburn's Oasis club. A recuperated Alan Dunn was bassist in the band. "Hepburn was manager of Keyhole," he said. "He also had the Keyhole café just round the corner." Dunn said that when the band's guitarist left, he was tipped off about future Roller Eric Faulkner. "He was a wee fat guy but he could play," said Dunn. "But his mate Eric [Manclark] was there and he was good looking so I thought bring both into the band and Eric [Manclark] can just stand on the stage and pretend – just smiling at the girls, which he did. Eric and Eric were best pals."

Paton saw Keyhole playing at the Oasis club and decided Manclark had to be a Roller. "That's what Tam was all about, good-looking guys," said Dunn. For now Faulkner stayed in Keyhole. "We were at this party and I was telling Faulkner about the lighting farts thing," said Dunn. "You've got to learn to light a fart if you want to be a Roller. What the silly bugger did was take his pants down and let out a fart and he tried to light it and set fire to his bum hair. What a stink."

The Rollers were not happy about Paton forcing Manclark into the band. Clark, whose father had died from throat cancer in January 1970, said: "It was maddening for everyone who was serious about the music." But "he was great looking guy," said Clark. "He was very popular with the girls. He was a lovely guy but not a guitar player. Davie Paton had the job of teaching Eric to play guitar. At the start he was just on stage and not plugged in. Then after a while with the group he may have been plugged in but turned down so it wasn't heard. He did try and learn but he was never much of a player." He was dark-haired, button-nosed and girlish. A photograph of him in the band looks almost criminal. The Longmuirs and Clark look like older brothers to him and Davie Paton.

Ronnie Simpson and his business partner Alex Scott were now the main booking agents in Scotland, the biggest agents in Britain outside London. Their company MAC was based in Glasgow and supplied bands for almost every venue in Scotland. They had helped get the Rollers gigs at places such as the Two Red Shoes ballroom in Elgin and Green's Playhouse in Dundee and had helped build the band in the west of Scotland. The Rollers played "out west" often for Simpson, in Gourock, Wishaw, Motherwell and Bellshill. They still stayed clear of playing in the centre of Glasgow though.

"The Glasgow bands were always the bit more together musically and that's what over time audiences came to expect," said Simpson. "The Rollers had a reputation with the little girls, the screaming hordes. They were quite good-looking young guys. All you had to do was put them on stage. It wasn't just Edinburgh, they were getting the same reaction in provincial ballrooms. They were very popular at the Olympia Ballroom in East Kilbride, not far from Glasgow, the Trocadero in Hamilton, Kinema ballroom Dunfermline. I was booking them all over. Tam would get them gigs when it suited them in Edinburgh but I don't remember Edinburgh being his target area. It was more to get out and round the parts of Scotland. Tam had made friends with and spoken to the right people, like me. It's a handy chain. I'm looking for bands that keep my ballroom managers happy and Tam's looking for someone who can put him in the ballrooms.

"And the managers of these ballrooms they always love a thing like this," said Simpson. "What can you put on the third Monday of the month? Put on the Rollers, they'll pull four or five hundred little girls. That's a couple of grand you're earning and by the time you've thrown in the coca colas and the cloak room money it's bonus time." MAC took between five and 10 per cent of what they charged the venues to book the band, and they could charge up to £600. "They were always late for gigs," added Simpson. "Not because they were arrogant little twats, it was because Tam wouldn't leave the house until Tam looked the part. After he got in from the tattie round, he had to get himself done up and then go and collect the band. They were famed for not turning up on time and everyone eventually allowed for that."

Paton was never on time, admitted Clark. "We called him the late Tam Paton," he said. Simpson saw how the Rollers' teenage crowd could be manipulated. 'If you put a couple of stewards at the back and you've got the girls lined up at the front of the stage, six or eight deep, then, once the band starts, you have stewards pushing them in. If you push people in, they push back. By the time you're in the second number it's going like a fairground."

Simpson had wanted to take over as manager of the band but he couldn't speak to them directly. "No-one could get near them," he said. "You'd think, 'We'll catch them early before the gig and have a word with them about coming to us'. The first person you see is Tam and you go, 'I can't speak to them while he's there' but he was always there because he is the band. He delivers the tatties, comes home and gets a shower and shave, gets all dressed up and, when he's ready, the band move. They rehearse in his garden so he knows exactly what they're playing. I was interested because there was obviously money there and I'm dealing with people in London and Tam knows nobody."

"It was a closed shop," said Clark. "Tam used to think up ways and schemes to keep us busy and away from girls and business people."

"I lost my voice one night trying to talk him into adopting me as a co-manager," said Simpson. "The band just sat there gawping and I think Tam fell asleep. It came back to me that the band wasn't interested. But

I later heard it was Tam who wasn't interested. They were his baby. He wanted to be better than Brian Epstein and have a band that was better than The Beatles. Maybe there was a little bit in there where his mind had gone."

One of the London people Simpson was dealing with was Tony Calder, the former co-owner, with Rolling Stones manager Andrew Loog Oldham, of Immediate Records, famed for its success with Small Faces and its links to the Stones and Jimmy Page. In 1969 the label had number one hits with Amen Corner's '(If Paradise Is) Half As Nice' and Fleetwood Mac's 'Man Of the World' but had recently gone into liquidation. The tough and resourceful 27-year-old Calder had now hooked up with London agent David Apps to pursue a new venture. Apps worked at MAM, a record label, agency and management company founded by Gordon Mills, the manager of Tom Jones and Engelbert Humperdinck. Calder and Apps had linked up with the main agents in Scotland, the Midlands and the South of England to discover new acts.

"The idea was to find the acts through the agencies, get them record deals, build them up into being the new big band and then have the benefit of having them tied to your agency," said Simpson. "So you're getting your 10 per cent of £3,000."

Calder had already taken three Scottish bands off Simpson: Northwind, Hate and Tear Gas, all hairy rockers of the type currently in vogue. Calder and Apps had formed a label called Famous and cut a deal with EMI-owned Regal Zonophone to release their albums. "Tony's way of running things was he found the people with the money and took the money off them to supply all this stuff," said Simpson. Famous was, supposedly, being backed by an American oil company but there had been no breakthrough hits.

Simpson suggested Calder check out the Rollers in Edinburgh. "Having spoken for most of my life to ballroom managers and promoters the main thing was bums on seats," he said. "Let's not worry about the music. The Rollers were a band that could pull in hundreds, whereas you could have a band like Northwind that would be lucky to get 100 people."

Calder, Loog Oldham's partner during the Stones' rise in the early sixties, said Simpson had described "something weird happening" in the city, a "sensation". He was intrigued. Simpson took him to the Caves club. "I knew where the stage was and I knew what was going to happen," said Simpson. "So I said, 'Stand here you'll get a great view'. When the band came on the girls came screaming round every corner and he was caught right in the middle of it."

"Christ what is this?" Calder said.

"This is The Bay City Rollers," Simpson said.

"Oh, we must have them."

"The crowd were just unbelievable," said Calder. "The smell of fresh wet cunt permeated everywhere. There wasn't a guy in the place. It was sensational. It was a bit like seeing the Stones when they broke. You could smell sex everywhere. Then this band come on and they are fucking awful but the crowd are going berserk. You couldn't hear a word for the screaming."

Calder was introduced to Paton. They discussed Brain Epstein who Calder had worked for as a PR in the early days of The Beatles. Paton told him about Epstein turning down The Crusaders, purportedly claiming this had occurred even though he'd slept with Epstein. "He couldn't talk about anything in the rock'n'roll business except Brian Epstein had turned him down after he'd fucked him," said Calder. "Brian liked rough trade, the rougher the better."

Calder said during their initial conversation, Paton suddenly excused himself. "He said, 'Look, I'll be back in half an hour,'" said Calder. "'We're just going to deliver a couple of sacks of potatoes to the whatsitsname chip shop.' I thought good job I'm not on drugs, you'd have thought you were going bonkers. He wasn't that tall. He was smaller than me and I was 5ft 11 but he was broad. He was a humper and he'd drive the band to the gig all sitting among the bags of potatoes."

Calder recommended his partner David Apps see the band as soon as possible. He also saw them at the Caves. "The kids were being held at the top of the street by the police," said Calder.

"The club was packed, there were queues outside, and the band was going down a storm," said Paton. It was an impressive scene. Even more impressive to Apps was the take on the door. "You know, these kids have all paid," Apps said to Calder.

"So we sat down with the band and Tam and we said, 'Look we'd like to sign you and we'll get you a record deal,'" recalled Calder. "Tam pulled me to one side and said, 'You see the singer, he won't be in the band the next time you see them.' I said, 'Why not?' He said, 'Well he won't let me shag him so I'm going to fire him.' Well, then I knew I was in an LSD movie. This guy with rough hands and potatoes in sacks in an open top truck talking about shagging the singer and firing him because he can't get 'at least a blow-job out of him'. Tam said, 'But don't worry we'll replace him, it'll have the same effect, don't worry, the new guy's better looking.' Apps was convinced someone had spiked us and we were in a take-out movie, we thought we were going to get killed, it was like being in a snuff movie, your turn next, it was surreal, like an acid trip. I just said, 'Well can you get the new guy to sign the contract?'"

Davie Paton was leaving the group. His reasons, he explained, were personal and musical. "I couldn't stand the lifestyle," he said. "After not having a girlfriend for a year I was getting quite depressed." He said he had once taken a girl out in the group's van and been tailed by Paton for two miles. "I was tired of it," he said. "I'd been listening to bands like Free, Genesis and Led Zeppelin. I wanted to be doing something like that.

"I didn't leave the Rollers on the brink of success without thinking it through," he added. "I came to realise I didn't want to be a Roller no matter how successful they became. I saw the way it was going. I didn't want any part of it. Tam Paton had his dream and he was definitely pulling the strings. It wasn't my dream."

"Wonderful guy, couldn't spend enough time on the band either," said Paton of Davie's departure. He replaced him with Neil Henderson, a 17-year-old Glaswegian from Paisley, who moved to Edinburgh to join the band. He said he was "glad to get into a good professional band" having been in a semi-pro band. Henderson "wanted to go full-time" and by October 1970 he did.

The band, apart from Davie, were overjoyed and overawed by what Derek called "showbiz execs from London" signing them up. "These people assured us they were going to make us famous, the next Beatles, and get us a big sum advance." The band members all packed in their days jobs, having been told they were going to be needed in London a lot and that a fabulous career was opening up.

Without consulting a lawyer, Paton signed the Rollers to Calder and App's production company, Realization 7. He was sold on Calder's connections and had been desperate to strike a record deal for years. "Tam wanted me to go up front in business meetings," said Calder who organised for a promotional film to be shot to capture the hysteria around the band. He intended to shop that around labels in London. Paton hired six buses and filled them with Edinburgh girls for a gig at the JM Ballroom in Dundee that was captured by three cameramen.

On June 21, 1970, Paton planted an article in the *Sunday Mail*, the Sunday edition of the Scottish tabloid, *Daily Record*, that suggested the band would soon record a first single and album on a new label. Paton showed his early adeptness at stretching the truth for the press. "The boys have had so many recording offers recently that choosing the right one has been very difficult," he said. "It's almost certain the Rollers will have a single out by the end of the year."

He explained how recently the Rollers and two roadies had driven to London to record their first single, another exaggeration – the band were cutting demos for Calder and Apps. Paton told the *Sunday Mail* he had followed by plane. He said they'd had £175 between the nine of them. The pressure of work and a bad weekend financially had prevented him from being able to raise more cash. It meant the Rollers slept in the van for four nights in London as they recorded. He talked of a Billy Lyall penned song, 'Take One Or The Other', being a future A-side. Then things started to go askew. Calder got cold feet and was less enthusiastic. The deal looked as if it would fall apart. There was interest from Dick Leahy at Bell Records but he was more interested in the group's image than their songs.

Billy Lyall was disheartened. He left the group. It was suggested Paton forced him out because of he was too aggressive in pushing his own songs on the group and also that Lyall was, in his own words, getting "too close" to Derek. In April 1971, Paton replaced 17-year-old Lyall with 18-year-old Archie Marr from The Tandem. "I joined just in the nick of time," said Marr. "Paton said, 'Archie, I was going to ask you to join the Rollers a long time ago because Billy Lyall was really dissatisfied but I didn't want to break up The Tandem. But since The Tandem have broken up the job's yours.' I thought it was a chance I might regret if I didn't take it. Tam was a good guy. I liked him. Billy Lyall was quite a tortured soul. Nobby told me that Tam and Billy Lyall were having a thing but I don't think that's why he left."

The other groups in Paton's stable had suffered over the past year as Paton's focus narrowed on the Rollers. He had little time for them during his negotiations with Calder. "As soon as Tam got into that world, stepped up into a different league, we kind of got forgotten about," said Billy McGhee of The Index. "Our gigs started falling away. He had less time for us and we had depended on him so long, maybe for five years." The Index broke up.

The Tandem, according to Eric Faulkner who would soon be joining the Rollers, had 'a bit more cred with the guys' than either the Rollers or Index. Marr said that for the past three and half years they had been "doing quite well locally", often playing the Oasis club, and had played "up and down and all over Scotland". "We were not as popular as the Rollers," Marr said. "We always took second slot to them. Although we were under the umbrella of Tam's management, we were direct rivals."

Two members of The Tandem had actually left to form a short-lived band with Davie Paton called Fresh who signed to Decca. For a brief moment future actor Ken Stott, who lived three doors down from Marr in Liberton, just south of the Inch estate, was in the band. "When the band was on its last legs," said Marr, "just playing to pay off the money we owed on equipment. I was going to throw in the towel. I though this is not for me; my playing days are over. That's when Tam intervened."

I asked Marr if he felt he'd been asked to join the Rollers because of his musicianship or his looks? "The latter," he said. "I wasn't a great musician. I was passable. Tam thought I looked good and would blend in."

Calder said Dick Leahy at Bell Records became interested in the band after he'd played Leahy the promo film shot in Dundee. Leahy recalled it slightly differently. He could not remember ever seeing a promo film of the band. He claimed he'd first been tipped off about the band by Chas Peate who ran a small independent publishing company called Belsize Music and was keen to sign the band.

Leahy was 33, and had been a well-known A&R manager at Philips Records. His first job was at Ford in Dagenham, but he wrote to Philips Records' boss Jack Baverstock saying he could pick hit records. He got an interview and was soon working as Baverstock's PA, the hip young man at the company who purportedly knew what his generation wanted. His rise had been prodigious and Philips had hits with acts such as Dusty Springfield and the Walker Brothers. In May 1970 he was appointed Managing Director of Bell Records and was keen to stamp his identity on the label. "Chas pushed me a couple of times, 'C'mon Dick, if you come up to Edinburgh with me, it'd add weight to it' [Peate's proposal to sign the band]."

Bell Records was an American label that had established a London office in 1967. Active since the fifties and throughout the sixties, it had collected a diverse roster of American acts, mostly exquisite R&B, such as The Delfonics, The O'Jays, Solomon Burke and Lee Dorsey. Alongside the soul music, the label had an eye on the pop charts with acts such as The 5th Dimension, The Box Tops and Tony Orlando & Dawn. The white side of the label tended toward soft rock or bubblegum, releasing novelties by studio acts such as Crazy Elephant.

The label's American owner Larry Uttal, 48, had throughout the sixties made Bell one of the top three labels in America in terms of singles sales. The father of two grown children, he was nevertheless gay and would die from AIDS in 1993. He was a colourful character who had made shrewd production deals with several pre-eminent, mainly southern, soul music producers who brought him material and acts, and he had recently signed his first 'heavy rock act' Mountain.

In 1969, Uttal had sold Bell to Columbia Pictures Industries, staying on as President and running the company autonomously. Bell was now poised to release records by The Partridge Family, the group in a new American sitcom produced by Columbia Pictures TV arm, Screen Gems, about a widowed mum and her five kids embarking on a musical career. Bell would thus become unfairly identified with 'bubblegum' material, aimed squarely at eight to 14 year olds, not least because the sitcom would make a major star of 20-year-old David Cassidy, a future Bell solo act. The Rollers, moreover, identified Bell with its great soul catalogue, having covered one of the label's mid-sixties hits, 'I'm Your Puppet' by James and Bobby Purify.

Despite its rich history in America, much of Bell's releases had not translated to Europe, nor had the label attracted major talent in the UK. "It was a tiny label in the UK," admitted Leahy. Bell had, however, one serious English talent: songwriter Tony Macaulay. In January 1970 Bell scored a number one in the UK (and top five in America) with his song 'Love Grows (Where My Rosemary Goes)' by Edison Lighthouse, essentially a studio project with a revolving cast of musicians. Macaulay had previously written hits for Marmalade and penned the immaculate 'Build Me Up Buttercup' for The Foundations. For Bell he scored another huge hit in 1970 with 'Blame It On The Pony Express' by one of the label's American stars, Johnny Johnson & the Bandwagon. In 1970 he would be voted Songwriter of the year by BASCA, the British Academy of Songwriters, Composers and Authors.

Leahy had been tasked with finding more English talent for the label in the UK, material that would translate across Europe. "It was run totally as a subsidiary of Bell New York and therefore anybody I wanted to sign I had to get approval," he said. "Larry [Uttal] was a great believer in signing producers and they'll find acts." Leahy was set to transform the label in the UK, so much so that over the next four years its European success would eclipse the American output. "I was reviewing all the Bell acts and getting rid of all of them except for one or two," said Leahy. "For me it wasn't working. It was during that period the Rollers came into it. I'm cleaning out, sweeping out [the company], not knowing what the hell I'm doing by the way. The arrogance of youth, this is not working, this is not working…"

Leahy went to Edinburgh with Chas Peate to see the Rollers play. "There were 700–1,000 people and I heard not a word or note of what was played," he said. "It was total mania going on. It seemed to be back to pop music, back to the ballrooms, having fun. What influenced me most [in my decision to try and sign the band] was in my last year at Philips Records I went to Henry's Blues House in Birmingham to see [Black] Sabbath when everybody had turned them down. I just watched the audience [and sanctioned the signing of the group to Philips subsidiary Vertigo]. It just kicked in when I went to Edinburgh, sign the audience. That was it, sign the audience. It was the audience that made the impression."

After the show Leahy met Paton. "Tam was a very unusual character," he said. "He was a potato farmer and a control freak. Of course he didn't fully understand the industry and that was totally apparent to me. But it was his band. He was an early person to do what [Simon] Cowell has done with One Direction. He just put local musicians together and formed a band out of them and told them what to do."

Paton told Leahy he'd made a deal with Tony Calder to represent the band. "That's when Calder came into the picture," said Leahy. He and Calder negotiated a deal for the Rollers that earned Calder's production company a £75,000 advance. Leahy also had Calder sign an inducement letter. "If you sign an act through a third party and you're investing the money, if they remove themselves then the band is automatically signed to the company," said Leahy.

"Dick said, 'We're going to make a lot of money,'" said Calder. "I said, 'You are, I'm not, I'm selling you the contracts. I cannot handle it.' David [Apps] and I tried to work out various scenarios and in the end he said if you don't want to do it, doesn't matter how much money you could make, you can't do something you don't enjoy and that was the clincher."

Calder had grown suspicious of Paton's motives. "Everybody was saying, 'You know he's fucking some of the band up the bum,'" he said. "Everybody! He was shagging them in the back of the potato wagon. I didn't know whether they were in the group or not. I presumed they were in the band. He'd be in the group one minute and the next minute he's not there. He's been fired and someone else has taken over. It was horrific. You didn't know how old the band members were. Tam would lie. I couldn't do a meeting with Tam. It made me feel ill. You wanted to scrub your hands after you shook hands with him. It really was that sick. He had the dirtiest fingernails. I never knew if it was from sticking his fingers up some kid's arse or from the potatoes. If you get blood on your fingernails at night the next morning it's black... looks like dirt. Do you really want to be having breakfast with Tam Paton looking at his dirty fingernails where he's stuffed his finger up some kid's arse whose sitting at the table crying because his arse is bleeding?... no thanks."

With the deal done Calder wanted no more to do with Paton or the Rollers. "I said to David [Apps], 'I'll take the cheque round to the bank and special it.' My opinion of Dick went down at that time. He was desperate for success and he needed a hit to keep his job. I understood that. I'd have loved to have a hit too... the amount the people who would have bought the record in Edinburgh would have put them in the Top 20. I just didn't want it on my conscience.

"Dick Leahy was an opportunist," Calder added. "He was very cool, calm, collected but terrible dress sense and he needed a good hairdresser. But he was a good record man. We got on real well over music. So when we were talking about songs we were on the same wavelength. He was a pleasant guy to deal with."

"Tony was good enough to phone me to say it was happening and to apply your inducement letter which I did on behalf of Bell Records," said Leahy. "So now they're signed to Bell Records directly instead of through Calder. I don't know if Tony disappeared or what he did with the money. It's not my job." The Bay City Rollers were Leahy's first major signing to Bell in the UK.

Calder's production company went into liquidation. A second recording session booked for Olympic was cancelled. It was claimed that the money Calder had taken from Bell did not reach the band. The Rollers felt badly let down. "The months that followed were very confusing," said Nobby Clark.

"Calder had run cold on the boys," said Paton. "He was just too busy and lost interest as fast as he got that cheque. I was as green as grass. The straw was coming out of my ears. I knew how to get work. I knew how to get photographs and I knew if a gig was £600 there'd be £60 for petrol and £200 for HP [to pay off the amount the band owed on equipment and the van]. But I didn't know anything about getting advances. It was a completely new ball game to me."

"What made it especially tough was jobs in our part of the world weren't easy to find," said Alan who had packed in a job earning £300 a week. "Derek and Nobby started knocking on doors looking for work," Paton said. "Alan and couple of the others were mixing cement for a building firm. There was work on the potato wagon and some washed windows and cars."

"Tony had no intention of doing anything with the band," said Clark. "He was obviously just a businessman who saw an opportunity to make some money."

Nevertheless, the Rollers still had a recording contract with Bell, albeit not a very good one. "An inducement letter means you take over the contract with the same terms and conditions," said Leahy. "Maybe I changed them, I can't remember." Bell had just signed former Monkees singer Davy Jones to a solo contract that stipulated he was not allowed to choose his songs or producers. The Rollers contract was similarly tough.

Clark, now almost 20, said the royalty rate Bell was offering the band was 4 per cent. This was the percentage the band would earn from the price of any record sold; low but not that unusual for a new band in the era. However, they would only start to earn that tiny percentage once they had paid back the costs of recording and promotion *and* the advance, namely the £75,000 that was missing. "It was a shit deal," said Clark.

"Tam went down to London with straw coming out his ears," said Archie Marr. "We were young, not interested in the money. We just wanted to get on *Top Of The Pops*. We'd sign anything, Tam would sign anything."

Already feeling that the band had been ripped off by Calder – "His intention was always to sell the contract to someone else to make money" – Clark wanted to consult a lawyer regarding the new deal with Bell. "The biggest rip-off was it gave the record company carte blanche to spend as much as they wanted off our earned royalties on promotion without us having any control," said Clark. "They could spend all our money to make themselves a fortune."

Paton went ballistic.

"You're going to fuck it up for everybody," he screamed. "After all the years of hard work."

Alan, 21, backed Clark. Paton grew angrier.

"What the fuck do we need a lawyer for? You can see what's in the contract!"

"His eyes were bulging, his voice getting higher and squeakier, his arm flying everywhere," said Clark. "The rest of guys were too frightened to say anything."

Under duress, the new contract with Bell was signed. There was the promise of an increase to 5 per cent in royalty payments during the second and third years of the deal. Paton didn't let the details concern him. He had finally got what he wanted: a record deal and a shot at the charts. Fame, he told the Rollers, would be theirs.

"It was a disaster waiting to happen," said Clark.

CHAPTER 3

Frustration

"The idea was – as with The Monkees and others – break a teen band with a real hit and then capitalise with the girls continuing to buy future product through the teen press/photos and fan base... The point – as a producer and writer – was that you didn't have to produce a real hit every time because image would carry groups through several OK tracks until the next real hit."

– Jonathan King.

Chris Denning was Dick Leahy's Promotions and Marketing Manager at Bell Records, working out of the company's small Mayfair office. "He was a great friend of Jonathan King," said Leahy. "Jonathan was always interested in producing stuff, making money. He came swinging by the office to see Chris and played me 'Johnny Reggae' and I made a deal for it. That's how I knew Jonathan. He was looking to do something and I gave him a shot with the Rollers." Paton, nor the Rollers, had any say in it. King was producing the Rollers debut single for Bell.

Conceived, created, produced and directed by Jonathan King, the song 'Johnny Reggae' was attributed to the Piglets. It was a novelty song and went to UK number three on Bell in 1971.

"Dick Leahy approached me, telling me they were huge in Scotland," said King. "Normally I paid the studio costs and thus own the rights in perpetuity but I allowed Bell to pay studio, arranger and musicians costs and I simply chose the songs, routined the band, did the sessions and collected a fee and ongoing royalty (which I never got)."

King was sure of himself, claiming to be among the biggest record producers in the UK at the time. He was certainly prolific. Alongside 'Johnny Reggae', he scored hits in 1971 with 'The Same Old Song' by Weathermen [UK number 19], 'Sugar Sugar' by Sakkarin [12], 'Leap Up And Down (Wave Your Knickers In The Air)' by St Cecilia [12] plus two others, 'Lazy Bones' and 'Hooked On A Feeling' – its B-side called 'I Don't Want To Be Gay' – under his own name [both 23]. None of these were on Bell, and were released by a variety of labels.

A 27-year-old Cambridge graduate, King had risen to prominence in the music industry with his 1965 hit 'Everyone's Gone To The Moon'. That single began a long relationship with Decca Records that was ongoing. He had also established himself as a personality on TV and radio and wrote pop music columns for a variety of periodicals.

The Rollers met him at his plush Kensington apartment. He had a white Rolls-Royce with tinted windows. Paton was flapping about how much the journey down had cost the group. King played them a selection of songs he was considering for their debut single, including two of his own. The young, penniless, band was intimidated. Nobby Clark was keen to take up the mantle of Billy Lyall by writing songs for the group but Paton was angry with him when he suggested it.

The band returned to London for a recording session at Olympic. They need not have bothered. It was a testing journey down, the better part of six hours, and their van broke down leaving them to travel the last 80 miles in a breakdown van. Paton had booked a cheap hotel room, which he and the band shared. For four days they lived on ham sandwiches. He told the group not to let on to Leahy or to King how shabbily they were living in London.

The struggle to get their gear down proved pointless. "They never played on the songs," said King. "Only Nobby sang, all the rest was me [and arranger/pianist Johnny Arthey]. I simply didn't make those sorts of tracks [where the band play] unless they were signed because of their musical ability. This band simply needed a hit and I didn't make hits that way."

Paton recalled that King told him, "I'm not farting about with a stupid fucking band. Just give me the singer."

"That quote sounds very unlike me," said King. "I would never be so rude or hurtful. As I remember, the band all attended the sessions (to sing backups) and were fine but I decided my own vocal backups were better."

King recalled he only ever did the one session with the Rollers, cutting four songs:

'Keep On Dancing' by The Gentrys (a top five hit in America in 1965), 'We Can Make Music' by Tommy Roe (a recent US single release that failed to make the Top 40 in America or the UK) and two of King's own songs, 'Jenny' and 'Alright', both of which Clark disliked intensely. 'Keep On Dancing' was notable for the fact that it was actually one short recording repeated to stretch the record out to the length of the typical pop single of its day. The second half of the song, after the false fade, is the same recording as the first. The Rollers' version was an almost exact copy of the original – if anything, more simplified and the hook even more exaggerated.

"Nobby was fine… no problem at all with him," said King. "The idea was – as with The Monkees and others – break a teen band with a real hit and then capitalise with the girls continuing to buy future product through the teen press/photos and fan base. I never thought the guys were cute enough to get a real fan following. I was clearly wrong, but right at the time. The point – as a producer and writer – was that you didn't have to produce a *real* hit every time [viz Spice Girls and others later] because IMAGE would carry groups, bands etc through several OK tracks until the next real hit."

The recording highlighted how little control the band had over their own future, in fact how little anyone thought of them as a group. Similarly, Leahy did not take Paton seriously. He felt he was "someone who'd tagged on with them" rather than a serious manager. The group might have wanted to be a band but the reality was that they were fronting another Jonathan King novelty record.

'Keep On Dancing' was chosen by Leahy as the band's first single on Bell. It was the obvious choice from the King session, the catchiest track with the most energy. Released in June 1971, it picked up good reviews in the music press. *Melody Maker* called it, "one hell of a good pop single" while *Record Mirror* reviewed it as "very commercial… sounds like a giant".

King told the press the band was "going strictly for a type of number that is mainly rhythmic". He described the single to *NME* as: "A happy sort of sound that the kids can sing with a smile on their face."

The Rollers gave their first interviews under the direction of Bell's promotions manager Chris Denning. Paton sat in and contributed. He dubbed the band's music "anti-heavy" in *Disc & Music Echo* in which he was labelled a "tattie-humper" and part-time potato lorry driver. "If anything we're more commercial on stage than 'Keep On Dancing'," said Clark. "That's what people want in Scotland. Progressive groups are guaranteed to empty the halls. We do some chart stuff on stage, quite a lot of harmony and things like 'One Fine Day' by The Chiffons." Derek added: "It's mainly pop stuff, the sort of stuff we like, Tamla [Motown] and that sort of thing. We all write in the group and hope to write some of our future records. Depends if they are good enough or not."

There was talk of the band staying loyal to Scotland, boasts that they hadn't "uprooted and come to London in search of fans and a record contract". "We'd never move to London," said Derek. "So many groups move and then split up." Scottish agents, the band said, were reluctant to book over the border "but hopefully with the record out now" there might be some English gigs in future.

NME was told the group's average age was 18 and in Scotland they were "recreating the hysteria that happened in the early sixties". The band were said to split time "between making their own stage clothes and rehearsing". Alan was pretending to be 20 and Derek 18 – two years younger than they actually were.

Denning, then 30, was proving an excellent appointment by Leahy as Bell's Promotions Manager. He joined the company in October 1970 and was well connected to music journalists, TV and radio people. He had worked as a DJ on Radio Luxembourg and (short-lived pirate station) Radio London before becoming one of the first DJs on BBC Radio 1 in 1967. He left the BBC in 1969, supposedly over a conflict of interest resulting from a promotional position he held at Decca Records.★

Denning was indiscreet about his gay sex life. He and Kenny Everett, who worked together at the BBC, were often seen out chasing young men together. Tony Calder told this author that Denning had offered to suck his penis during one late night in the office. "I was saved by Kenny Everett," he said. "Kenny said to Denning, 'C'mon queer we're going out looking for kids.' Denning was like a dog following Kenny Everett around."

BBC Radio 1 DJs Johnny Walker and Dave Eager played 'Keep On Dancing' and it made the Radio 1 playlist, picking up widespread plays. It was voted Hit Pick by Radio Luxembourg DJs, meaning the station played the song every hour, and described as "bubbling under" in the charts. The BBC had a monopoly on radio broadcasting in the UK (until 1973) and Radio Luxembourg, based in Luxembourg, was its only serious commercial rival station once the Government outlawed pirate stations like Caroline and London. Many BBC Radio 1 DJs, including Denning and Walker, began their careers with Luxembourg.

Paton called Denning "a marvellous guy" who "really fought for the record and wouldn't take no for an answer". "We're going to make you a hit," he told Paton.

"Denning helped me create Bell [in the UK]," said Leahy. "It was a small circle [of key figures in the music industry] in those days." Leahy was part of that circle. "If I thought I had something really worthwhile I could talk to certain key DJs who had their own playlists. I'd only ever do it if I thought I had a great one. Radio was king."

★ Denning would later claim to have been a rent boy from the ages of 13–18. His many lengthy jail sentences (almost 14 years in total) for sex offences relating to young boys began in 1974. In 2014 he would be jailed for a further 13 years for a string of sexual offences against boys, some as young as nine.

At the time of the Rollers first single, the dark arts of radio promotion were under close scrutiny. Corruption appeared to be rife. In February 1971, an undercover exposé by the *News Of The World* alleged that promotion men at record companies were offering sexual favours, cash and free holidays to BBC executives and disc jockeys in return for airtime. Ultimately Janie Jones, a singer who ran sex parties at her home in Kensington, was jailed for three years on 26 charges, which included controlling prostitutes and offering them as bribes "to BBC men as inducement to play records".

The men in the case were often referred to as Mr Z or Mr Y, or "unnamed broadcasters". It was suggested that Jones organised orgies involving BBC staff, call girls and others at her home, while executives and celebrities looked on from behind a two-way mirror. The court heard how Mr Y, "a television producer", might have made a 14-year-old girl pregnant and could therefore be blackmailed. Mr X answered questions about a cheque for £1,400 he gave to one of the girls but said he didn't know she was a prostitute. "I thought she was much too young to be involved in anything like that," he said in court. A shop assistant, aged 18, told how Jones took her to filmings of *Top Of The Pops* at the BBC in Shepherd's Bush and promised her work in modelling and television commercials if she "played her cards right" – which meant going to bed with producers and show business people.

The BBC launched an independent inquiry led by a QC. Jimmy Savile was questioned by a legal team over the allegations but refused to co-operate. *Top Of The Pops*, which he hosted, was the subject of a separate but related police inquiry in 1971, led by the same detectives, into claims that a 15-year-old dancer on the programme had been "used" by disc jockeys and other celebrities. The girl, Clair McAlpine, subsequently committed suicide. She had named Savile in her diary.

The corruption in the industry did not seem to be as organised as that which would soon engulf the American industry, where the Mafia was suspected of playing a heavy role and huge cash sums changed hands between promotions men and DJs. In the UK it seemed to be seedier, the climate deeply unwholesome.

Assisting Denning and Leahy to promote 'Keep On Dancing' was Jonathan King. "I never came across any payola trips," he told me. "I certainly never paid anybody to play my hits. I was always a very good plugger. Like with my other hits at the time I tended to plug my own productions. Chris was an excellent promotion man too and broke many Bell hits."

'Keep On Dancing' entered the charts at 37 in early August, jumped to 26 and then rose to 20 the following week. Denning called Paton to say they'd got *Top Of The Pops*.

The Bay City Rollers were on the first step of the ladder.

"I was living with mum and dad up in Liberton," said Archie Marr. "The telephone rang. It was Tam. He said, 'Archie we're flying down to London tomorrow morning, we've got *Top Of The Pops*.' It was my first time flying. We stayed at the Royal Norfolk Hotel in Paddington. It sounds grand but it was a budget hotel. We went to the BBC [in Shepherd's Bush], had a dress rehearsal and pre-recorded it on Wednesday night."

The date was September 1, 1971. Denning was there. The band wore matching brown suits and patterned shirts open at the neck. Alan was pushed to the front alongside singer Clark who was allowed a red suit. "We try and look smart on stage," said Derek. "We hate to see a group going on stage dressed in jeans."

"They looked like a cabaret band," said Paton. Certainly in comparison to the more colourful and loose Rod Stewart and the Faces who were on the same show performing 'Maggie May', the UK's second best-selling single of 1971.

The Rollers watched their TV debut at a Cheshire hotel the following day. They were due to play their first gig outside Scotland at the New Century Hall in Manchester, a gig organised by Dave Eager, a DJ at the venue. Eager, who lived in Manchester, was close friend of Jimmy Savile and had acted as his assistant for many years before landing his own shows on BBC Radio 1. The 23-year-old would prove to be a useful ally for the Rollers. "They went down a storm, and I got them three more bookings at the venue," said Eager who made the chorus from the Rollers debut single a jingle for a club tour throughout the UK that he presented live on BBC Radio 1.

"We spent the night in Dave Eager's flat," said Marr. "I don't know why we never stayed in a hotel. He was a stand-in DJ for Radio 1, didn't have a regular slot. I think he was gay but he never came on to us."

The exposure on *Top Of The Pops* pushed 'Keep On Dancing' to number nine in the charts, its peak position. There were more photo sessions and more interviews. Derek, alone, handled one with *NME* that referred to the bands "13-year-old teenybop" fan base. "Our audiences are young and we like it like that," said Derek. "Young audiences give us the best reception. Yes we do get grabbed and pulled off stage… we love all that. The screaming bit is definitely on the way back. Everywhere we go people keep telling us the underground scene is fading… on the circuits we've been playing pop music is coming back." Derek explained that he didn't smoke or drink and hated "music snobs" that he encountered "a lot on the underground scene".

The group played a clutch of dates around Scotland in September including the Glasgow Flamingo Ballroom. Paton could now charge around £800 a night for the group but they were still heavily in debt, paying off approximately £20,000 in installments for the van they'd bought and equipment. Paton had also spent £6,000 on photographs that he sent to every DJ at the BBC – "I was sending them each one photo a week" – and music journalists at *NME* that he thought "was the big paper at the time". He also started a fan club from his office in his parents' home, recruiting teenage fans from Edinburgh to assist him. Everyone who joined got a photograph. The fan club address was his parents' house and the girl in charge was called Wilma. "She existed," said Clark. "A girl called Pauline started to run the fan club in the early days and Wilma took it over and started to run it very well. They were fans, young women who wanted to be involved."

Paton kept the perilous state of band finances from the band members, placing each one on a wage of £80 a week, and borrowing money off his parents to keep the ship afloat. "He sank money into the Rollers when he didn't have to," said Marr.

The success of 'Keep On Dancing' attracted hungry London agents and managers to the Rollers. Barry Perkins of Starlite Artistes, whose main acts were the Troggs, Marmalade and the Tremeloes, was one of the first on the phone to Paton. Starlite also had links to producer Mickie Most's acts such as Hot Chocolate. It was a small world and Perkins, 39, who would go on to become the Rollers' co-manager, had, during the sixties, enjoyed a successful career as an agent at Kennedy Street Enterprises, Manchester's number one music agency/management firm. There he had handled Kennedy Street's main act Herman's Hermits who Mickie Most had produced to worldwide prominence. Dave Eager was also linked to Kennedy Street and the DJ was pals with Marmalade too.

Starlite was actually owned by Peter Walsh who had been around the music business as a promoter/agent/manager since the fifties. A cigar-smoking wheeler-dealer, with slicked back dark hair and a moustache, dressed in a conservative suit, he looked as if he was still in that decade. Under his guidance a number of late-sixties acts, among them the Move and Love Affair, had prospered but his real success had been with the Tremeloes whose early to mid-sixties hits had sent them stratospheric. Walsh also personally handled Marmalade, once The Gaylords, who now had scored seven top ten hits. Paton instinctively disliked him, even more so when Walsh suggested that he take over as the Rollers' manager.

Paton described marching the band into the Starlite office on Gloucester Place in Marylebone. "Peter was probably what they imagined as a manager," Paton admitted to Johnny Rogan in his book *Starmakers & Svengalis*. "Big moustache and big names in his past. Luckily that didn't wash with the group … They really believed everything I was doing for them was right. It was beautiful."

Perkins was still eager to become the Rollers' agent in England and talked of the gigs he could get the band now they had charted. Short, stout with thick-rimmed glasses, he was ambitious to carve out his own slice of the business. The catch was Starlite charged a whopping 25 per cent commission. Clark recalled Perkins schmoozing the band by taking them out to a London club where Paton was anxious about the amount of booze and girls around. "He behaved like a teacher on a school trip. I didn't take to [Perkins]," said Clark. "He was not likeable."

However, when Perkins called Paton soon after to say he could get the group a gig in Bournemouth for £1,750, he grew a lot more likeable. "Oh God this is it!" Paton shouted at the group excitedly. Unfortunately the gig was for over-21s and the band did not go down well. In fact many of Perkins early English booking for the Rollers were ill thought-out and they often found themselves in cabaret venues the now past-it Tremeloes might play. Out of their comfort zone without an audience of screaming teens, the hastily assembled line-up was not gelling. Marr and Neil Henderson had a ferocious punch-up at one gig.

The band mixed these shows with familiar venues around Scotland booked months in advance and where the hit single intensified the level of teen adulation. Paton had borrowed money to buy a new car, a large Vauxhall Viscount, and drove the band around in that. Two roadies, Davie Gold and Davie Purdie, followed in the van with all the gear. Only Paton, Marr and Henderson could drive and took turns behind the wheel of the Viscount for long trips down from Scotland for the English shows, often one-nighters. "There was lots of driving and not much glamour," said Marr. It was hard coming from hysteria in Scotland to obscurity in England. Harder still were the many nights they slept in the van or the Viscount. "When the record did well we thought this is the big break," said Alan. "But it wasn't. We started gigging more and it got harder on road."

"We travelled the length and breadth of the UK in that car," said Marr. "We would say, 'Oh look at this girl, look at that girl' but I never once heard Derek say anything about girls. His brother was girl daft. Alan would always say, 'Imagine getting her.' Derek would always say, 'Shut up, shut up'. But I never suspected he was gay. We never knew Tam was gay. We always inwardly thought he was but we had no proof and it didn't really matter."

Working about five nights a week, the tensions between Marr and Henderson, both 18 and the only band members who drank alcohol at this stage, intensified. Clark and Paton were often seen arguing too. "Nobby and I had an argument with Tam which he hated," said Marr.

"He turned round and said, 'Ah you always side with fucking Nobby'. I said, 'Don't be daft Tam', but you couldn't speak back to him too much. He would lay into you; he had a right tongue on him. He was obstinate, very opinionated but without Tam there would be no Bay City Rollers. Tam kept us on the straight and narrow but he was too strict. Girls were taboo: out of the equations, no girls involved at all."

"I didn't get on with Henderson," said Marr. "We had an argument in the backstage band room after a gig, an argument about harmonizing. He was slightly out of key. I ended up throwing a snare drum stand at him. We fell out. All the rest of the band was kind of trendy and Neil was a weegie, meaning a Glaswegian. Tam got him in the band but he wasn't a great guitarist. I think Tam fancied him but if there was anybody straight it would have been him."

Although some shows earned good money, they also took work in youth clubs in England for £500. Set against, the amount the group owed plus the travelling expenses, the six-piece band weren't making a lot. This was compounded by the fact the band would not make money from Bell for some time.

Leahy took the Rollers, King, Denning and Paton out for a slap-up meal at a top London restaurant to celebrate the single's success and talk about a follow-up. The Rollers were overawed. "We'd never been to a place like it," said Marr.

"Have what you want. It's on Bell," said Leahy.

They ordered champagne, lobsters and steaks. "It was charged to the band account and set against [record] royalties," said Clark.

Bell had released 'Keep On Dancing' in Germany, France, the Netherlands and Norway but European success, despite muted promo TV appearance in Germany, was some way off for the Rollers. This was partially due to the set up Leahy had inherited at Bell in which European releases were licensed to EMI. Bell's records tended to get lost in the vastness of EMI's operations, especially in Europe where there were individual sub-licensees in each territory. "I'd gone around Europe and it was obvious we had to take more control," said Leahy.

In late 1971 he announced he was making Bell an independent label in the UK while still utilizing EMI's pressing plants and distribution network in the UK. In Europe Polydor would distribute their records. "I took it to independence," said Leahy. "We were getting stronger then."

Bell was doing well under Leahy. They'd had the UK's best-selling single of 1971 with 'Knock Three Times' by Tony Orlando & Dawn who also scored huge hits with 'What Are You Doing Sunday' and 'Candida'. The Piglets, Johnny Johnson & the Bandwagon and 'Keep On Dancing' had all been among the top 100 best-selling singles of the year. The Rollers were at 99.

Leahy had signed a host of new acts to Bell: solo singer Miki Antony, model Twiggy and teen appeal glam rock hopefuls Hello. "It was just before the glam period, just as it was kicking off," said Leahy. "I was fascinated by what a few people were doing, particularly Tony Visconti." Having produced David Bowie' *The Man Who Sold The World*, Visconti had produced the year's hot new act, T. Rex, whose singer Marc Bolan wore glitter make-up on *Top Of The Pops*. His singles, 'Hot Love' and 'Get It On' had both gone to number one. Bolan's chief glam rival was Slade who also scored their first number one in 1971.

In December 1971 Bell moved to what would become a permanent home in Charles Street, off Berkeley Square, Mayfair. "By total coincidence within two days Mickie Most moved in next door," said Leahy. Most, famed producer of Herman's Hermits and Donovan, would see his new company RAK Records, home to Hot Chocolate and Suzi Quatro, rival Bell in the coming years.

Before the end of the year the Rollers played at a youth club in Walton-on-Thames called Scene 71. As the club was close to his home in Weybridge, Chris Denning invited the band and Paton to stay at his home for two nights. They were hoping that Jonathan King would come up with another hit for them but there was no news on any future recordings. Paton had called Leahy about it but there was no firm news. On their first night at Denning's, Paton suggested to the band, in front of Denning, that one of them should have sex with their promotions manager.

"Chris would probably do more for us if one of us slept with him," Paton told them.

Clark freaked.

"It definitely won't be me."

"I don't know what else happened that night, we didn't ask, but Alan and I slept on the floor with one eye open," said Clark. "I was beginning to see Tam in a completely different light. I felt we were becoming pawns in his game. Around that period I had my doubts about whether I wanted to continue with it. Nothing terrible happened at that point. That was the early stages of Tam and I going in different directions. I didn't like the way he was beginning to turn things around on us."

"In his kitchen Denning had a big family size tub of KY Jelly," said Marr. "I said to Nobby, 'What the fuck has he got that in the kitchen for?' I dare say conversations between Tam and Denning would be Chris saying to Tam, 'Have you nobbled any of them yet?' But Denning never made a pass at me."

On the second night Denning took the band and Paton to the Walton Hop youth disco. Clark felt uncomfortable around Denning and at the Walton Hop that night. He described it as being like a school disco. Now the focus of allegations of child abuse, the Walton Hop club was often frequented by Denning and King, who was found guilty in 2001 of sexual offences, including buggery, against boys aged 14 and 15. One of the club's DJs was Rob Randall, in his early thirties and a journalist on *NME*. Randall interviewed the band during their stay with Denning, a piece headlined: "There is room for teen idols".★

Eric Manclark, now 17, left The Bay City Rollers in November 1971. "He needed getting sacked, he couldn't play," said Marr. "He had a Marshall stack with his amp on standby. It wasn't switched on. He had fingers like shovels. He was tone deaf. Tam had him in the band because he looked good and Tam fancied him."

As he did not contribute significantly on stage, Manclark did not need replacing and the band was once again a five-piece. With King stalling, Leahy hooked the Rollers up with Tony Macaulay who had continued

---

★ In 2002 Randall was fined and put on the sex offenders register for an indecent assault on a teenage boy.

to write for Bell acts such as The Fantastics, Johnny Johnson & The Bandwagon and The Drifters. In 1972 he scored the label another huge hit with '(Last Night) I Didn't Get To Sleep At All' for The 5th Dimension. Marr and Clark recalled visiting Macaulay's sumptuous penthouse in Kensington where he played them a song he suggested they record. Clark recalled recording a vocal on the track that had been recorded by session musicians. Macaulay, however, shelved the project. "Tony thought it sounded too much like another of his hits," said Marr. "I thought it was great, that it should have been put out."

It was now apparent why King was reluctant to commit to recording a follow up to 'Keep On Dancing'. He was starting his own record label, UK Records, to be distributed by Decca. "I decided they were *not* going to be the next big teen thing and suggested Dick [Leahy] and Tam find another producer," said King. "After I dropped the band and formed UK Records Tam kept asking me to take them over but, as I felt they were has-beens and also would never have 'stolen' them from Bell (against my morality), I turned him down numerous times. And lived to regret it!"

King was evidently unaware that Paton was gay. "I never really knew Tam personally," he said. "I knew nothing about his private life and he certainly knew nothing about mine. I remember he had dreadful teeth and got them fixed after the first Rollers hit. I called him (to his face) 'the Potato Farmer'. He always was a perfect gentleman with me and I suspect with everyone else. The Rollers *only* succeeded because of Tam. Anyone else would have given up after 'We Can Make Music' flopped. I would say Tam was 95 per cent the ingredient for their success."

With 'We Can Make Music' chosen as the Rollers second single, Leahy hoped that the fact it was produced by King, widely considered a hot hit-maker by industry tastemakers, would make up for its flaws which were manifest. Clark sounded uninterested. The track's hooks had none of the commitment or attack of the Tommy Roe original. King had sped up Roe's version and it sounded thin and weedy.

Even Denning struggled to get people interested in the single. The band did mime to the song on long-running ITV pop show *Lift Off*

With Ayshea, aired at the beginning of May 1972. Made by Granada and filmed in Manchester, it was ITV's main music show to rival the commanding BBC *Top Of The Pops* and, shown at 4.25, aimed at kids. This was the Rollers' first contact with Muriel Young who would go on to produce the Rollers own TV show, *Shang-A-Lang*, and a slew of other pop shows for Granada, which held the ITV franchise for the north west of England. The Rollers' appearance on *Lift Off* failed to trigger any significant airplay.

'We Can Make Music' did not chart. Paton said it "died the most horrible death". Dick Leahy seemed unconcerned. He and the staff at Bell, where David Bridger replaced Denning who left to help King run UK Records, had a new superstar on their hands, David Cassidy, whose first major hit single and album came earlier in the year and whose new single, 'How Can I Be Sure', was on its way to number one. *The Partridge Family* was airing on British TV and their records were also shifting in huge numbers too. In America, Cassidymania, as it was dubbed, was already in overdrive, with mass hysteria at huge concerts. In Texas he played to over 110,000 people over a weekend. All this was coming to the UK and over the next two years the 22-year-old teen idol was set to make Bell a fortune with a string of hit singles and albums.

"I was very busy with Cassidy," said Leahy. "He became more or less an English project. The Rollers almost slipped through the slipstream of what was going on because suddenly the label was happening and the Rollers weren't."

Bell was also starting to do well with new signing Gary Glitter. His debut album had gone Top 10 in the UK and he scored two top 10 hits in the UK in 1972. He was set to become a major star for Bell over the next couple of years.

Like Jonathan King, Leahy said he was unaware that Paton had a sexual interest in the Rollers. "I suppose with the benefit of hindsight and I have thought about this... if you look at the history of Jonathan [King] and Chris [Denning] and Tam, it seems to tie together. In hindsight I'd say there seemed to be a lot of shit going on [in the industry] we didn't know about and probably didn't suspect, apart from Savile. I think everyone suspected that.

"At the time it never occurred to me. Frankly it was the furthest thing from my mind because all I was trying to do was make a hit record. It never crossed my mind. It certainly didn't bother you if they were gay, not important to me at all, never has been, unless it gets predatory and, in hindsight, maybe it was. Who knows? But maybe there was a little cabal. The early history [of the Rollers] might suggest there was."

The band was certainly surrounded by gay men. Alan Blaikley, 32, was the latest. He lived with Ken Howard, 33. Tasked with resurrecting the Rollers on record, the pair were Hampstead schoolfriends who after university began their careers at the BBC in the late sixties, scoring early success as songwriters by writing the 1964 number one 'Have I The Right' for The Honeycombs. As managers of Dave Dee, Dozy, Beaky, Mick & Tich, they wrote eight UK top 10 singles for them between 1966 and 1969. Many viewed the band and Blaikley and Howard's songwriting as puerile, pastiches of whatever more credible sixties groups were producing. The songwriters were also involved with other sixties teen bands, including The Herd featuring Peter Frampton, had written a Eurovision song for Lulu and singles for acts as disparate as Rolf Harris, Frankie Howerd, Marmalade and Elvis. The pair had struggled to get a fresh group off the ground in the new decade and the Rollers were about to find out why. Leahy, of course, had been A&R chief at Philips, the home to Dave Dee, Dozy, Beaky, Mick & Tich, and felt he owed them a shot.

"Howard and Blaikley seemed like two obvious gay guys," said Marr. "They lived together in a beautiful place [Ken Howard had a home in Swiss Cottage]. They picked us up at the Royal Norfolk Hotel in a Rolls-Royce silver shadow, metallic ice blue, cream leather upholstery."

The songwriters played the group a potential single, 'Wouldn't You Like It?' Ken Howard sang the song to the group while playing an old Farfisa organ. The Rollers thought it was a joke. "All I heard was 'Wouldn't you like it, baby, baby, wouldn't you like it?'" said Clark. "I thought Oh my God, what have we got now?"

Howard later claimed he was astonished by the behaviour of the group who never swore or drank in his presence. Even more astonishing was how a scenario unfolded where the group and Howard ended up frolicking in a swimming pool. Howard recalled Paton appearing and ordering the group to bed instantly. "They immediately stopped and went off to bed meek as lambs," he told *Svengalis & Starmakers'* author Rogan during the early eighties. "I have seen many groups over the years but never anything like that."

'Wouldn't You Like It?' was poorly constructed and not to be confused with the song of the same title that the Rollers recorded in 1975. It featured strum-a-long sixties verses that were abruptly interrupted by repeated chants of the title that was supposed to be backed by a stomping Glitter beat. The beat sounded so weak and naff it was comic, like fingers drumming on a desk. Howard and Blaikley had also thrown in a saxophone solo. Clark was the only Rollers required to perform during the recording and he did it well. Leahy, however, suggested Howard and Blaikley could do better.

The band went back on the road, mixing Scottish gigs with gigs in the north of England, sometimes in working men's clubs and cabaret venues to people in their thirties and above. Sometimes the money was good, up to £1,000 a gig, but the reaction was generally not. "Whenever we appeared in Scotland, there'd be fantastic scenes," said Paton. "Then we'd drive over the border and nobody was interested."

Peter Walsh at Starlite was behind these gigs and he was struggling. It was now almost a year since the band had charted with 'Keep On Dancing'. At venues in places such as Birmingham the band could still expect a £1,000 fee but for a Scottish band, the economics of travelling meant very little profit. A string of awful English gigs in the north east sapped the band's morale. At the Top Hat in Spennymoor, near Durham, they shared the bill, memorably, with a comedian and a dog act. In Sunderland, Paton recalled the gig being interrupted by the announcement that pie and peas were on sale at the back of the hall. During a week at the Fiesta club in Stockton on Tees, another tough venue in the north east, tempers frayed and Paton ripped the band to shreds with personal insults, one by one. When he got to Clark, the singer screamed: "Don't you fucking dare start on me." Paton was shocked to be talked back to and stormed home to Edinburgh.

"He was like a spoiled kid sometimes when he couldn't get his own way," said Clark who was now keen to exert some control over the band. Much to Paton's anger, Clark had started smoking. The singer also wanted to record his own songs. Paton organised and paid for several sessions for Clark and the band at Craighall studios in Edinburgh where they cut an album's worth of original material.

Nevertheless there were more arguments between Clark and Paton. "I was beginning to dread being in his company," Clark said. "I felt empty and shallow." The commercial pop industry was interested only in the band's image. "We were just a vehicle to drive Paton's ego," Clark said.

They still slept in the back of the van or at budget hotels. "We shared rooms but Tam would always have a room by himself," said Marr. "But we'd pair off in three rooms, two in each, but Tam would never let the same two share consecutive nights. Nothing to do with sex, he didn't want two of us getting pally to gang up on the other members or gain strength to voice their opinions because Tam wanted to be the boss and he was the boss."

One night in a hotel in Birmingham, Paton made a pass at Marr. "He started kind of rubbing me up and he said, 'You're fucking getting a hard on'. I said, 'Stop that or I probably will, now get out of the room, bugger off' and he did. It was just playing around, he knew it wasn't on and that was it. Nothing went any further because he knew it wasn't to be. I was straight."

Marr didn't tell the rest of the band. "I would if I'd thought he was really aggressive but he wasn't. I didn't think it was important. His attitude toward me didn't change afterwards. He didn't ask me not to tell the others. He knew I wouldn't bring it up and he wouldn't, and as nothing transpired, nothing was said. It didn't sway me toward leaving the Rollers. I was just fed up."

"I knew about his approach on Archie, but it was treated as a laugh," said Clark. "The same thing happened to one or two others [in the group] but it was always treated as a laugh and a joke. Tam never isolated anybody, got them in a position where they were isolated with him in a situation they couldn't get out of. At that time we all realised what Tam was. But it wasn't that threatening."

"Tam used to say there's no such thing as a straight man," added Clark. "He thought that every male had a tendency toward homosexual behaviour... he believed that because it made his situation more acceptable to him."

Marr told the others he was leaving on a ferry from Liverpool to the Isle of Man for a gig at the Royal Lido in Douglas. "I said to Tam in the hotel, 'Tam, it's not for me mate.' I thought there'd be glamour. The only glamour was *Top Of The Pops*. It took four hours on the ferry. I thought to myself, 'Where's the glamour?' I was quite glad to leave."

Marr went back to working at Our Man and Paton had no shortage of young men lined up to take his place. He had kept a beady eye on the developments in teen groups in Edinburgh since The Index and The Tandem had split. "Tam was always looking for guys in case someone else left the band so he'd have someone lined up," said Clark. "He was also trying to find another Rollers, another band with as strong an image. But all these bands were all secondary to the Rollers."

It was a small scene and the principals all knew one another. Keyhole, the teen group he'd plucked Manclark from were still around. Marr's brother played with them as well as former Roller Alan Dunn plus 17-year-old Ken Stott who'd been in Tandem. Eric Faulkner had also passed through the group with his best pal Manclark. Members came and went and the group's name had now changed to The Witness. Like the Rollers, they played the usual pop and Motown cover versions, lots of Four Tops. They had supported the Rollers at Scottish gigs and were keen to be managed by Paton.

Also on the teenage scream scene in Edinburgh was The Phoenix who were playing six nights a week in the city at clubs like the International. They were the Rollers' main rivals – although the Rollers played Edinburgh infrequently now as Paton feared over exposure – and there was antagonism between the two bands and their female fans. They had a black singer and played covers of Eddy Grant's R&B band The Equals. Paton had already approached the band's guitarist, Brian Spence, to join the Rollers after Davie Paton left. Spence had briefly played in The Index before they split. "I was 16 when I got asked to join the Rollers," said Spence. "I travelled around with Tam to a couple of gigs. He was quite famous for wrestling with the kids in the back of the potato lorry. Tam was so positive the Rollers were going to be massive, from day one whenever he spoke about them, they were going to be the biggest thing in Britain. I had a rehearsal. Tam said he was going to kick Davie Paton out.

"He was very clever in his assessment of people and how to manipulate people, especially young guys," Spence said. "What he said to me at the time was, 'Davie's stopped washing his hair that means he's not interested anymore'. If they stopped washing their hair then it was time for them to go! What it really was about was if he started to lose control of somebody he'd want someone else in. I felt bad about it and phoned up Tam and said 'I'm not doing it.' That was when Henderson got the gig."

Now Paton approached Spence again. "I was up for it this time," Spence said. He was now 18. "I went to see about it with this guy John Devine and Eric Faulkner. They were in a band called Kip. I didn't do a proper audition then, it was irrelevant as far as Tam was concerned. What your playing was like had nothing to do with it."

Spence was ultimately passed over for the Rollers. But Paton did take on a new group Spence was putting together with Colin Chisholm, former Tiny & the Titans and The Reflections singer, now 19. He found them a drummer, Gordon Liddle, 22, who became the flatmate of Rollers new roadie, Jake Duncan. In January 1973 Paton organised for the new group to record a two-track demo at Craighall in Edinburgh produced by former Roller Billy Lyall who was now working at the studio. "Tam named the band Bilbo Baggins," said Spence. "We'd never heard of it, we couldn't even say it first, what the hell does that mean?" It was the name of a character in J.R.R. Tolkien's 1937 novel *The Hobbit*.

To replace Marr in the Rollers, Paton was more interested in picking out someone from Kip. 'I sort of psychoanalysed them every time I interviewed them for the job," Paton said. He would eventually end up choosing four teenagers from various Kip line-ups to join the Rollers. "They soon got the name for being the reserve team for the Rollers," he said. "They were perfect for this role because they were very young and this is what the Rollers are all about."

Paton had in the past used Kip, formerly Sugar, to support the Rollers, The Index and The Tandem in and around Edinburgh. They'd got to know Paton at the late-night Continental Café in Edinburgh, a regular after gig stop-off. Kip had gigged heavily in late 1971 and early 1972, earning close to £300 a gig. They had even supported their heroes Slade. The band's guitarist, 18-year-old Eric Faulkner, described their set up as "a three piece glam stomp, no frills".

Faulkner was from Moredun, an area that joined onto the Inch estate and he knew The Index and Davie Paton. He'd been in Keyhole when Eric Manclark had been ghosted away to join the Rollers, and he now auditioned for them by playing a version of The Velvet Underground's 'Sweet Jane'.

In the event, Paton chose John Devine, Kip's bass player to replace Marr. He was younger than Faulkner, more handsome, taller, slimmer, with higher cheekbones and cute dimples that drove the girls wild. "I tended to pick Rollers on personality rather than musical skill," Paton admitted. "I always thought that you could take someone who had a fantastic image and train them to play whereas you can have the most fantastic musician but then you'd probably have to spend a fortune on plastic surgery or something like that to get him right as far as image is concerned."

Faulkner was in luck, however. Neil Henderson, now almost 19, was out of the group too. He later said he quit as he "wanted to make it as a musician rather than play in a band that was being manufactured". He would surface a year later as guitarist and songwriter in hit Glasgow pop band Middle Of The Road, fronted by Sally Carr, and famed for their 1971 number one 'Chirpy Chirpy Cheep Cheep', a novelty record. The follow up 'Tweedle Dee Tweedle Dum' made number two. The hits had run out by the time Henderson joined but there was work across Europe.

Paton drafted in Faulkner. Clark said the band was "falling apart", blaming Paton's rules. "He was absolutely obsessive and jealous of us even talking to girls," he said. Having seen so many changes in personnel, Clark and the Longmuirs doubted the band could continue. "I never got on well with Eric [Faulkner]," Clark said. "I didn't take to him very well. As a band you just have to work with these things. I certainly was never very close to him."

Alan Longmuir was now 24. To him, Faulkner and Devine were almost from a different generation. They were brash, trashy and loud. They idolised Slade and T. Rex. Alan had been the most outgoing member of the band, keeping spirits up during long nights in the back of cold vans. Now he was depressed and sleeping in the back of the van no longer appealed. A handful of gigs, at a working men's club in Darlington, where the band were required to play two sets either side of the bingo, at Fraserburgh Town Hall in Scotland where the van's windows were smashed, and at Peterborough where the van broke down, suggested a band going backwards.

Faulkner and Devine saw things differently. The band's PA system was better than anything Faulkner had played through before. They were both eager and were soon helping Paton on the potato wagon, bringing some much needed fresh energy to rehearsals in the garage in Port Seton.

Faulkner's parents had just vacated the family's fourth floor Edinburgh flat in a high rise in Moredun and were leaving the city. He was staying with his aunt in the Inch. His father, a welder and shop steward at the Bottle Works in Portobello, a member of the British Communist Party and ultimately a Scottish Trades Union Congress delegate for the Boilermakers' Union, had got a new job. His son was a smart lad, a keen fisherman and rugby player who'd left school at 16 with eight O-Levels. He had briefly worked as a roof surveyor but his head was full of dreams of pop stardom. He was sacked from his job when he refused to cut his long hair and instead picked up odd bits of manual work through pals.

Faulkner's elder brother had played him Clapton and Fleetwood Mac but his tastes were more pop and he'd been in and around the Edinburgh band scene since he was 14. He was used to rough gigs and in Dumfries he was amused to see Paton fly off the stage to attack a gang of lads that were hassling the band and females in the crowd. Paton, he recalled, landed several punches and knocked down four men.

Unlike Clark and the Longmuirs, Faulkner was also expecting great things from working with Howard & Blaikley, and was a fan of their work with The Herd. The new-look Rollers were invited to Chappell Recording Studio on London's New Bond Street but not required to play on a newly written song called 'Manana' that Howard & Blaikley intended for the band.

"Manana, Manana, nana nana, repeat twice and then repeat again," said Faulkner. The word Manana, meaning tomorrow or later in Spanish, was repeated over 70 times in three minutes. In the studio the predominant strings were supplied by a full-blown orchestra and augmented by whip cracks and plenty of Spanish sounding percussion. It was catchy and cohesive and totally banal. In the final hours of the recording session, a Clark-penned demo, 'Because I Love You', from Craighall was cleaned up for inclusion as the single's B-side.

Leahy agreed to release it. Cassidymania was engulfing him. There were 10,000 fans at Heathrow to greet the Partridge Family's favourite son to England and 15,000 outside the Dorchester Hotel. The Bell Records office was also overrun by his fans and the British media couldn't get enough of Cassidy. His second album of 1972 was at number two, equalling the chart position of the first.

Clark, with a song about to be released as a B-side, and an album of demos recorded, was advised by Leahy to secure a publishing deal and guided next door to Mickie Most who alongside his record label also owned RAK Music Publishing. Most routinely tried to sign up the copyrights on any original songs RAK released as singles. Paton went ballistic when he found out Clark had met Most to discuss business.

Paton was intimidated by Most's experience and his own ignorance at what a publishing deal entailed. He eventually decided that everyone in the band should share the publishing, even though Clark had written the song, and this would apply to any future songs written by any of the band members. Leaning heavily on Barry Perkins for advice, Paton set up an entity called Bay City Music to collect any publishing income derived from the band's self-penned songs. Clark was allowed to assign the copyright of 'Because I Love You' to RAK Music but the company would pay any money earned into Bay City Music.

The five band members and Paton were all equal shareholders of Bay City Music, but Clark objected to Paton collecting his 15 per cent management fee and having a share in the publishing company. Paton got aggressive. "He was abusive," said Clark. "He called me every name under the sun. We were bullied and blackmailed into signing the agreement." Again, Clark thought about leaving the band. He spoke to the Longmuirs.

"We can't give up now, we've come so far," said Alan.

Clark felt horrible. "This was all I knew. I loved these guys, so I decided to give it another six months."

Leahy was hopeful for 'Manana'. The band went shopping for new clothes, favouring a much more relaxed look – tight trousers with bell-bottoms, fancy shirts and tops and platforms boots – that suited the long hair everyone was now sporting. Paton even took them on a short band holiday to Hammamet, Tunisia, so they could all get tans. He was growing more obsessive and tried not to let the band out of his sight, "in case we got up to something he did not approve of" said Clark who, along with Alan, was growing increasingly frustrated with the band rules.

'Manana' was released in September 1972. Howard & Blaikley entered the song into the Radio-Tele Luxembourg (RTL) Grand Prix International, a competition to find the best produced song in Europe, and it was selected as one of the 12 songs to be performed live at the modernist, 1,000-seat Nouveau Theatre in Luxembourg.

It sounded naff, like a second-rate Eurovision Song Contest, but promised the band much exposure on Radio Luxembourg and across its affiliated radio stations in Europe under the RTL banner, particularly in Germany, France, Belgium and the Netherlands. The band was told the show was also being televised to 12 European countries and they could be playing to an audience of 40 million.

Faulkner and Devine rushed to get their first passports. Paton drove them down to London Airport in his Viscount in late October. On the M1 a wheel came loose and the car crashed into the banking. Amazingly no one was injured. On the flight over, Howard & Blaikley talked to the band about their performance, suggesting they paint themselves in gold and silver body paint for the show.

It was an industry bash that attracted executives from most UK record labels and industry figures such as songwriter Bill Martin who was soon to take over as songwriter for the Rollers. Along with the band and Paton were Barry Perkins, Dick Leahy and Bell Promotions head David Bridger. All the bands – from Germany, France, Belgium and Holland – and assorted guests were put up in the Holiday Inn hotel just a few hundred yards from the HQ of Radio Luxembourg. In addition to the 12 contenders, Slade were performing at the event as they were picking up an 'Act Of The Year' award.

The Rollers sprayed their torsos gold and silver. There was plenty of bare flesh: Clark and Alan went topless, while Devine wore just dungarees and Faulkner wore a short unzipped jacket. "Tam wasn't that enamoured by it but I insisted we do it and it was a good image at the time because it got a lot of attention," said Clark. "It was just try and be different really."

A 12-man jury made up of European music and television journalists voted 'Manana' the contest's winner. The show was in its fourth year and no previous British song entry had ever been a hit in its own country although some songs had done well on the continent. The instant pop of 'Manana', however, many felt was going to be a best seller in the UK and Europe.

The after party at the Holiday Inn was a schmooze fest where David Bridger worked the room expertly. Paton was on sparkling form too, although he chastised Alan for drinking champagne. Faulkner said the band made a key contact that night in Ken Evans, programme director for Luxembourg's British Service. Paton also met Wayne Bickerton at Polydor who would soon sign Bilbo Baggins. Dick Leahy, in a dark green velvet, high-collared suit and ostentatious frill fronted shirt, with silver buckles on his shoes and long wavy hair combed into a fringe, looked like a pop star himself.

"David Bridger was a very good promotion man, excellent radio man, excellent contact point," said Leahy. "He was bit lairy [rowdy] but who wasn't? He was my David Most [Mickie Most's brother], a charmer, Jack the lad… he was damned good. He was seriously great for Bell… he knew everyone and he got records played."

The events of the contest were reported in *NME* and *Music Week* in the UK, in *Billboard* in America and across Europe. Unlike 'We Can Make

Music' that Bell had only released in Belgium and Germany, 'Manana' was released in France, Portugal, Spain and Germany and Belgium – all countries where RTL affiliated radio stations were plugging the record. There was even a promo of the single circulating in the US. It was an indication of the extent of Paton's continuous changing of band personnel and of Bell's still not fully coordinated European operations that some countries' single sleeves featured pictures of the band with Archie Marr and Neil Henderson in the line-up.

"'Manana' broke us abroad," said Alan. "It was in the charts in Finland, Belgium, France and Germany as well as Israel and we even got a chance to appear in Belgium and Germany." The record made number nine in the German charts. Perkins managed to get them a two-week tour with Middle Of The Road in Belgium in "big venues", according to Faulkner. Paton crowed the single had gone to number one in Israel, "the first number one for my boys".

In the UK the band promoted the single on *Lift Off With Ayshea*, shown on November 8. Bell's Bridger plus Howard & Blaikley organised for the band to be dressed up in "summer holiday gear", recalled Faulkner. He said he ended up in "Robinson Crusoe ripped trousers and straw hat" and quipped that at the time he wondered which member of the group was going to be 'Girl Friday'.

Bridger struggled to get the song on BBC Radio 1's playlist, however, which determined how many times a week a song was played. Faulkner recalled they re-recorded the single for Tony Blackburn's Radio 1 Breakfast show in the BBC's Maida Vale studio and there was talk of a potential *Top Of The Pops* slot on the new release spot. In fact Clark recalled having his body painted gold for a filmed performance of 'Manana' that was supposed to be used by the show if the song broke into the Top 50.

The band returned to Chappell and cut two more Blaikley & Howard songs, 'In Love's Dominion' and 'I'd Do It Again'. The tracks were stuck in the early to mid-sixties, clearly the work of songwriters whose best days were long gone. There is version of 'In Love's Dominion' on the pair's website credited to Dave Dee but the vocals sound like Clark. Everything about the song, from the overblown strings to the timpani drums, was clichéd. 'I'd Do It Again' sounded like a third-rate Herman's Hermits and was again massively over orchestrated.

By early 1973 it was clear, despite everyone's efforts, 'Manana' was not going to make the UK charts. Anyone who heard the new Rollers recordings knew these wouldn't be either. "It wasn't right, it just wasn't right," said Leahy. Disappointed not to make the UK charts, the band's mood was bolstered somewhat by the success of 'Manana' on the continent where Clark insisted it sold over one million copies. In January, Bell flew the band to the Midem festival in Cannes, an annual music industry business event, where David Bridger was trying to promote the group to various European contacts. Any positivity generated by the Grand Prix win, however, would soon be gone.

Ahead of them were cold hard English winter months in the back of a van as the band gigged to stay alive.

CHAPTER 4

Confusion

"Tam Paton ran a bit of musical chair situation. If there were five Rollers on stage, he always had another couple in reserve in case anyone stepped out of line. Tam ran a very tight ship."

– Phil Coulter.

Paton bought a huge new car, an American Dodge station wagon. With the back seat folded down there was enough room to sleep in it. He often drove the Rollers down from Edinburgh to London, but could not always attend their gigs as he needed to work on the potato wagon. The band members were still on £80 a week wage and still helped Paton on the wagon or scratched around for odd jobs. Faulkner moved out of his aunt's and was living in squalor in a bedsit. He often ate at Paton's parents in Prestonpans after band rehearsals or at the Longmuirs' home. Paton, Alan and Derek all still lived at home.

Clark also lived at home and Faulkner was a frequent visitor. He was keen to help Clark work on writing songs. The live set now featured several of Clark's own alongside Motown favourites such as Marvin Gaye's 'I Heard It Through The Grapevine' and long-standing rock cover versions such as Bob Dylan's 'The Times They Are A-Changin''. It was impossible to play the orchestrated 'Manana' live.

Faulkner and Devine were keen to harden the band's sound to make it more contemporary or add pop quirks that would make the band stand out. A mandolin was sometimes used on stage and Faulkner played a viola as the band took on Beethoven's Ninth as heard in the controversial 1971 film *A Clockwork Orange*.

The film fed into the mix and the Rollers tried to update their image, a process largely led by Faulkner. He saw a parallel between the gangs in Edinburgh's housings schemes and the one at the centre of *A Clockwork Orange*, as unemployment hit levels not seen since the forties. Edinburgh had some terrifying gangs such as Young Niddrie and Young Gillie and Faulkner's older brother had briefly run with one. These gangs not only liked fighting, they liked fashion, often setting the trends in the city.

Faulkner was keenly aware of the strong images projected by Slade and other popular English bands. As a newcomer he had little influence over Clark and the Longmuirs but he was determined to be an individual and create a new band look. Paton too was encouraging the Rollers to wear clothes the fans could identify with. He was dismissive of Clark's fondness for flared trousers.

The Jook were a key influence for Paton at the time. Formed by Edinburgh songwriter Ian Kimmett, who'd been working in London, they featured local lad Ian Hampton on bass. Hampton knew Paton and the Rollers from the Edinburgh club circuit in the sixties. Paton was unmoved by the Who-influenced sound of the four-piece but liked their image, an update of Slade's old, skinhead-influenced, Levi's, boots and braces look via the Edinburgh schemes. Their trousers were cut loose and wide with exaggerated turn-ups, in bright colours including white, and they coupled the trousers with tight striped jumpers, bovver boots, scarves and bog brush haircuts – spikey but shoulder length.

Paton saw The Jook play in Edinburgh and complimented Hampton on the 'bonny' image. The band was signed to RCA, label mates of The Sweet, who were at number one with 'Blockbuster' in early 1973. The Sweet, who would score two more huge hits in 1973, had gone for a totally overblown comic glam look in huge platform boots and multi-coloured shiny one-piece costumes. They were vocal supporters of The

Jook and Mickie Most had signed them to a publishing deal without hearing a note. The Jook, however, never scored a chart hit.

Slade, although they too had gone for a comic glam look, were a major influence still on Faulkner. He started to wear garishly-coloured hooped socks and Dr Martens boots. The socks had been popularised by Slade singer Noddy Holder and were commonly referred to as 'Slade Socks'.

Faulkner, like Paton, was aware that the band's young audience in Edinburgh needed fresh stimuli. Alan would soon be 25, Derek and Clark were both 22; they were losing their teen scream appeal. Their fan base in Scotland remained strong in certain areas, notably Hamilton and Aberdeen, but was wavering in Shotts, Motherwell, East Kilbride and Glasgow. Their giant roadie Davie Gold often had to fight back gangs infiltrating the gigs. When the stage was invaded Faulkner used his guitar to beat them back. The band's other roadie, Davie Purdie, was hospitalised with a head wound. Paton was also in the thick of the fighting. Equipment was routinely trashed. A guitar, Derek's drum kit and the primitive lighting the band carried alongside their own PA in the back of the Mercedes van were all damaged.

There was still a hardcore of screaming fans, the coachloads of Edinburgh girls, who could make venues close to the city but much of the thrill was gone. Paton tried to remain upbeat. The fan club had swelled to 2,000 members but it was clear he was struggling to sustain the group. "Tam didn't know what to do, quite frankly, at that time," said Bell boss Dick Leahy. Paton continued with his expensive policy of handing out photographs of the group, "going through thousands of them", said Faulkner. The band was virtually his whole life. "I was lonely," he said. "I was in love with The Bay City Rollers."

He was also around £30,000 in debt. "Even I was beginning to think they were one-hit wonders," he said. "But I wouldn't give up on them. I had slogged for the Rollers to the point I almost thought I was a member." Overwhelmed by fears and doubts, he understood the process of record company accounting even less than he did the mechanics of publishing. 'Manana' had sold all over Europe. 'Keep On Dancing' had sold over 100,000 copies. He knew they should be making money but the complexities of overseas licensing, for instance, befuddled him.

He often discussed the business with Barry Perkins who seemed happy to explain but it didn't sink in. Sub-publishing deals in foreign territories and the various (reduced) percentages of those deals was a complicated area even for experienced operators. Paton had still not even consulted a lawyer over the basics of the contract the band had with Bell. Perkins guided him to the offices of accountants Goldberg Ravden who Starlite Artistes used and who at one time had offices in same building as Starlite. Stephen Goldberg and David Ravden were ambitious young men and moving into business management, looking after Twiggy and Hot Chocolate among others. Paton was cautious about letting outsiders look into the band's messy finances, afraid to expose his own naivety. Goldberg was known to be a clever man, a brilliant negotiator.

"It was a very naive business," said Leahy. "Running a label you didn't give a shit about who was looking after the artists. You thought, 'I'll do it through the records; that's my job. I'll make the records and make it work. The rest is up to them.' We were not taking a piece from anything, not performance, publishing or merchandise… just making records. That was our job."

Paton fell back on what he knew best and that was gigging. Perkins continued to book them and the band spent the next six months slogging round the UK, often six nights a week. Alan recalled the routine of setting off from Edinburgh at 6am on Thursday to reach gigs in Torquay or Bristol and returning to Scotland on Sunday after more nights sleeping in the back of the van. The Rollers didn't have a life beyond this and Alan was growing more depressed. "It was like being in the army," he said Alan. "If Tam said jump, you jumped."

Perkins and Peter Walsh had used the Rollers and Paton to get their Starlite clients, the Troggs, a deal at Bell. The band's singer Reg Presley returned the favour and helped the Rollers get gigs in the south west of England where he was based. They also returned to Bournemouth to play the Chelsea Village, where Jimmy Savile had connections. There was a big showbiz set and regular parties in Southampton where the Rollers also played. The city was home to the regional Southern TV company, where Mike Mansfield worked. Mansfield, in his early thirties, would soon move to London Weekend Television and become the pre-eminent director and producer of pop music shows of the era. He had long dyed blond hair, was well-connected with many in the industry including the Bee Gees' flamboyant manager Robert Stigwood, and would prove to be a key ally of the Rollers.

Life on the road was hellish, the travelling particularly, and the gigs were often thankless experiences. Outside Scotland they struggled to make an impact anywhere: Manchester, Southend, Swansea Top Rank, Cardiff, Doncaster, Poole, Cleethorpes, Sheffield… the gigs kept coming and so too the muted reactions.

It was a measure of their lowly status that Perkins did not think the Rollers could play in London where the crowds would inevitably expect something more up-to-date. By the time the band was back in Scotland, they were often out of pocket and utterly deflated. Faulkner recalled the band's Mercedes van packed up in Newcastle. Paton had to rely, again, on the largesse of his mother to be able to afford a replacement.

Bell ignored the Rollers. Paton struggled to get Dick Leahy on the phone. He was at the helm of one of the UK's most happening record labels, enjoying its best year yet. As well as Bell's success with David Cassidy, Tony Orlando & Dawn scored 1973's highest selling single with 'Tie A Yellow Ribbon Round The Ole Oak Tree'. Gary Glitter, who took the absurd glam rock look to new extremes, had two chart toppers in 1973, including 'I'm The Leader Of The Gang'. He also chalked up two number twos during the year and his second album also went to number two in the UK.

Leahy was also having success with a solo singer who went by the stage name Barry Blue. He wore blue and pedalled lightweight teen-pleasing glam pop, scoring a number two with 'Dancing On A Saturday Night'. He also had a hit with a song about "breaking the rules and loving a schoolgirl", a common theme among glam pop that promoted a culture in which the moral boundary surrounding under-age sex became blurred. At Bell, The Drifters were even back in the UK top 10 with 'Like Sister And Brother'.

"In those days the Rollers were almost the last thing on my agenda," said Leahy. "I'd made Bell a very successful label." He enjoyed playful competition with his neighbour Mickie Most at RAK. "It was, 'Let's see who can have the most hits this year,'" said Leahy. "I was operating at the limit of my ability in those days. The philosophy was: make a hit record, get on *Top Of The Pops* and conquer the world. Mickie Most and I dominated *Top Of The Pops*. We used to walk into one another's offices, and say, 'what you think of this song?'"

Just when they needed it most, the Rollers had a little bit of luck. Songwriter Bill Martin visited Leahy at his Mayfair office. A Glaswegian, he was 35 with a determined streak and impressive pedigree. He and his songwriting partner Phil Coulter had written Sandie Shaw's 1967 Eurovision Song Contest winner 'Puppet On A String' and followed it with 'Congratulations' for Cliff Richard, which came second in the 1968 Eurovision. They had also written for Cilla Black and penned 'Back Home', the 1970 England football team World Cup song. Martin had left school at 15 and worked in Glasgow's shipyards. He was a tough man who had fought his way to the top, a salesman and a hustler. "There wasn't a door he wouldn't have gone through," said Coulter. "He made stuff happen."

Martin suggested to Leahy that he and Coulter could replicate the success Nicky Chinn and Mike Chapman were having next door at RAK. The songwriting and production team of Chinn/Chapman were behind the huge success of The Sweet and were now writing hits for RAK acts Suzi Quatro and Mud, both enjoying significant chart success. "Bill said, 'We can do that,'" said Leahy. "I said, 'Okay Bill, you're a Scot. I've got this little band I signed a few years ago. All I know is when they get in front of people they excite them. Do you want to work with them, do you want to give it a go?' That's how it started, almost as a last resort."

"I always wanted a [hit] Scottish band," said Martin. He'd known of Tam Paton, "a potato salesman", back in the mid-sixties. "He kept trying to get a band with me but I thought he was a bit of a poof and I didn't want to become involved."

Martin negotiated a great deal for himself and Coulter with Leahy, guaranteeing them, as producers, a high 4 per cent [equal to the band who had to share that between the five of them and their management], and, as songwriters, total control of the material. It also tied the band to them as long as they kept producing top 20 hits. "Yes it was a tough deal," said Leahy. "Frankly no one else wanted them and business is business. If it doesn't work you pay nothing anyway."

Coulter, 31, from Derry in Northern Ireland, recalled auditioning the Rollers at a rehearsal studio in the West End of London. "They were young kids, wet behind the ears, very green, and trust me not great players, not great musicians," he said. "It soon became obvious that was not their forte. I concluded these guys were still coming to terms with their instruments. I couldn't afford the time, and I didn't have the interest or the energy to spend days and days or weeks and weeks in the studio trying to get them up to speed. My brief from Dick Leahy was, Go away and make hits. Simple as that: I didn't have the luxury of rehearsing these guys for days on end to get them up to speed. The only viable way of working with them was to lay down the tracks with session players."

He chose to lay down those tracks at Mayfair Recording studios, situated above a chemist in South Molton Street in Mayfair. "One sign said 'Mayfair Studios' and just underneath was a sign from the chemist, 'Ear Piercing by Experts'," said Coulter. Producer and songwriter Mike Leander, who was behind Gary Glitter, used the studio for all the acts he had signed to Bell: Glitter, the Glitter Band and Hello. Peter Shelley also used the studio to create the hits of Alvin Stardust, memorably 'My Coo Ca Choo'. It was glam hit factory.

The Rollers argued with Paton because Martin and Coulter were writing the A and B-sides of their new single. It was in their contract. Everyone, by now, knew the financial worth of a B-side on a hit single [in that era, in terms of record and publishing royalties, the same as the A-side]. "I had a lot of aggro with Nobby," said Paton. There was also general unhappiness over the fact that, yet again, they were not be playing on their own record. Paton got, in his own words, "very angry". He spoke to the group "one by one", explaining the importance of the recording session. "I honestly believed if it didn't happen we'd be finished."

Mayfair Studio was owned by John Hudson who acted as engineer for all the sessions that took place there. "He was a very important part of the whole soundscape of the Rollers," said Coulter. For the Rollers' records Coulter called on his first choice session players: Clem Cattini on drums, Joe Moretti or Chris Ray on guitars and on bass either Les Hurdle or Frank McDonald. The keyboard player was Cliff Hall. "That would have been the team," said Coulter. They made the Rollers' records for the next 18 months.

"Nobody could beat the shit out of a drum kit like Clem Cattini," said Coulter. "The directions I gave Clem when we got to one particular chorus was, 'Hooligan!' Clem knew exactly what to do. As often as not when it got into the part after the drum break and into the last couple of choruses where it goes through the roof there would be two of us at the piano, Cliff would be at the bottom end and I would be up doing the jangle top end with two hands… doing that rumble.

"There was a lot of tricks. My hands were so sore from doing claps that I came up with this idea of two planks of wood with like drawer handles screwed on. As an overdub I would go into the drum booth and put the two planks between my knees to anchor them down and you just hammer them together for the claps for the off beats."

"The Bay City Rollers didn't have a sound," added Coulter, "so it was up to me to come up with a sound that would be identifiably theirs. I was going for something that would be hooky, accessible. It was a kind of bopping at the high school hop thing I was trying to recreate, a bit of that vintage fifties, that feel-good happy feeling."

Coulter's template was 'Da Doo Ron Ron' by The Crystals. 'That's two minutes 40 seconds of pop heaven," he said. "The soundscape is overpowering. Phil Spector at his best. The real turn on apart from that great lyric is it's not only three chords it's three notes… that's some achievement. I was doing my own 'Da Roo Ron Ron'."

He was not keen to have the band or Paton in the studio. "Making records for me is a serious business, I don't encourage entourages in studios," he said. "I think it is a distraction from the main business and it's not a social event so I would bar people. Subsequently I got accused of being a control freak."

114

Clark was required to provide the vocals. The first song he sang on was 'Saturday Night'. "The songs were stronger with these guys, came across fresh," he said. A version of 'Saturday Night' would be the band's first American number one – but not for another 18 months. It was built around a huge chant where Saturday was spelt out letter by letter, an idea of Martin's. "I said to Phil let's write a cheerleader song, like the American football games. O.H.I.O. Ohio," he said. "One of my favourite sixties songs was The Who's 'My Generation' where there was a line, 'Why don't you all just f-f-fade away'. It's almost like he's going to say fuck off. We came up with S-S-Saturday night. That was the key of the hook and the best part."

This version of the song speeds up noticeably toward the end. "I was getting excited," said Martin. "I'm shouting at them to keep going and it gets faster and faster." It also lacked the fatness and percussive depth that would mark out future Coulter/Martin productions for the Rollers.

The band went back on the road. 'Saturday Night' sounded like a hit but the Rollers standing in the UK was not good. Bell promotion man David Bridger worked it hard. Radio Luxembourg was supportive but it was over 18 months since the band had last had a hit in the UK, a lifetime in pop.

Martin pushed Leahy to support the record. There was a series of high-profile support slots with popular bands like Sweet and Mud. "It was good for us because we were unknown in England," said Clark. "We played to some big crowds too. I'm not so sure the crowd who came was really the crowd we were looking for. Our following was mainly female. We did okay from it. We did gather quite a few followers from that because they all joined the fan club. It was a slow process. Mud had a big following of guys but Sweet was more female fan orientated. We did get quite a lot of publicity because we were on the tour with them, a lot of magazine and music papers followed the tours, we got publicity out of it, raised the profile."

Clark also recalled the pre-publicity for 'Saturday Night' as being positive. "I didn't read one bad review," he said. *Record Mirror* called it a "chart cert". Faulkner recalled Paton informing the band the record was going in the top 50 and they should prepare to travel to London to film *Top Of The Pops*. The record charted at 51, "one tantalizing place from definite inclusion on the show", said Faulkner. He was gutted. Bridger was unable to get the record on BBC Radio 1's playlist and it quickly disappeared. "It sold about 118 records and my mother must have bought every one of them," said Martin.

The record was also released in Belgium, France and Germany. Following the success of 'Manana' in these countries, particularly Germany, there was suggestion of TV work on the continent and an imminent European tour – neither materialised.

Faulkner saw the near miss as a sign of encouragement, a reason to dig a little deeper. Clark and the Longmuirs did not. They were tired. "We were all pretty depressed about not being able to get back into our own charts," said Alan. Clark said he had become "completely detached". He was in some sort of inner turmoil. Looking at his pictures from the era, the once handsome Clark almost seemed to have shriveled up.

Paton did his best to keep up morale. He bought a new van, a plush Ford Econoline, and accepted Perkins' offer of a short tour of Ireland, included gigs in the north where the conflict between unionists and nationalists had created an atmosphere of disorder. With British troops patrolling the street and the Northern Ireland parliament suspended, there was a virtual state of war in the country where bombings, violent clashes, and murders were increasingly frequent. Paton said the band was frightened to be going there but the dates would generate a much needed £11,000.

Driving them was new roadie Jake Duncan, who replaced Davie Gold and Davie Purdie and would become a long-standing member of the road crew. A former drummer with a band called Krutch, he didn't have a driving license but had fixed up the band's lighting rig. "You'd find bands out there [in Northern Ireland] like The Equals or Herman's Hermits who'd had their day," said Duncan. "You wouldn't go there unless you needed the money." They played in Belfast, where the atmosphere was "tense", according to Clark. Although intimidated by having to cross army checkpoints and deal with armed policemen on the streets, the gig, in a hotel, went well. "We were the only live band who would agree to perform there," said Clark. "The place was packed and it was a fantastic night."

Duncan recalled how while clearing the stage he was approached by a young girl: "My sister wants to bang you," she said. "Eventually the girls went out of control – nothing had prepared me for the way these girls behaved. When we ran into some trouble at some of these gigs, Tam could handle himself. Some guy gets hacked off because Eric is attracting his girl's attention and wants to come up on stage to have a go at Eric... Tam would sort it out. He wasn't violent but he could handle himself."

It was the beginning of Ireland's love affair with the Rollers. "We didn't realise every other group refused to play in Northern Ireland," said Paton. In Enniskillen someone in the crowd was shot and the band's van became a makeshift ambulance. But it was a rare sign of violence as the band got wild receptions in Dublin's Revolution Club, Galway, Bangor and Cork where they were supporting Dublin band Thin Lizzy who'd scored a recent hit with 'Whiskey In The Jar'. The Rollers returned to Ireland and played Northern Ireland several times over the coming months. The gigs "helped keep the band alive through the lean times", said Faulkner. Each visit drew stronger reactions. "It was out of control in Ireland before England. They had a strong following there like they did in Scotland," said Paton.

There were also gigs in Jersey and Guernsey. It was here, in the Channel Islands, that Faulkner finally cut his long hair, asking Clark to give him a 'bog brush'. Faulkner was increasingly influencing the other band members to dress up. There is a picture of Clark in platform shoes, striped socks, trousers cut just below the knee and tight jumper. He was not convinced. "Just things to try out," he said. His hair stayed long. "I didn't like the long hair," said Paton. "It took us a long time to try and make Eric cut his hair. But in spite of all that, it was Eric who created his own 'tufty' style. That had nothing to do with me. He created that style himself. He was creative himself on that type of thing."

Faulkner was running with the "boot boy" look. He bought a pair of wide, white, Skinner jeans from an Army & Navy store and turned them up to just below the knee to show off his striped socks. He wore braces festooned with badges and sometimes a wide white tie. The final touches to the new image "were staring me in the face", he said. "I'd watched the *White Heather Club* with my mum often enough to know what a band from Scotland would have in its image." He bought a white shirt with tartan shoulder inserts and a tartan scarf to hang from his guitar.

The Rollers were exhausted by the touring, sometimes still sleeping in the van, and still uncertain of their future. Paton himself was disillusioned with Bell, claiming they refused to listen to him. "They all had their own ideas and nobody wanted to listen to mine," he said. The group, particularly Clark, was giving him tremendous trouble. "He was becoming neurotic about his songwriting," Paton said. After 'Saturday Night' had flopped Paton thought that "the show was over". "That's the finish," he said to himself. They were now £75,000 in debt. "I thought we had really had it. And I was scared. We were deep in debt and I couldn't think what other company would be interested."

Derek told Paton he was thinking of quitting. He'd found work as a joiner. "I kept saying we could still make it," said Paton. Derek, he said, burst into tears and was persuaded to give it another six months. His mother was seriously ill with chronic bronchitis and heart problems. Clark had already told Paton he was quitting. He said he would stay until they found new singer. Alan took the news badly but Paton, although he'd be glad to see the back of Clark, felt it was just another tantrum.

The sense of doom within the band was not helped by the fact Paton had finally managed to score Bilbo Baggins a deal with Polydor, signed in October 1973. With the assistance of Barry Perkins and Peter Walsh, Paton had persuaded Wayne Bickerton, the head of A&R at the label, to see the band in Edinburgh. "At a tiny gig," said the band's guitarist Brian Spence. "There wasn't many people there. Bickerton liked the band and offered us a deal... it all happened really quickly. I've no recollection of ever seeing any contracts."

Bickerton and his songwriting partner Tony Waddington had just cut 'Sugar Baby Love', a number one in the UK for Polydor act The

Rubettes, their own glam pop construct who would go to have a string of hits. Bickerton was looking for more bands to hang songs on.

At the time, the Bilbo Baggins' drummer Gordon Liddle was sharing a flat with Faulkner who was kept abreast of all the developments. Paton was spending an increasing amount of time with Bilbo Baggins. "We'd rehearse until 11 at night. We'd go back to his and sit listen to him talk for three hours up in his bedroom," said Spence. "Tam would intrigue you with the whole gay scene. We're taking over the world, so-and-so's gay and this politician is gay and he's gay… we got in situations where we were surrounded, found ourselves in places where everyone was gay and we were the unusual ones. He'd say let's go out and we'd end up in someone's flat somewhere and it was like a den of inequity. It wasn't that big of a deal. Bowie came out and there were straight guys having sex with other guys just to try it out. I know someone who got involved in it and they just brushed it off, didn't see himself as gay because they'd tried it. Tam loved a young boy, he always loved young guys… if he thought there was any chance he'd have tried it. He had guys a lot younger than 16."

Paton was also keen on styling Bilbo Baggins. "What he suggested to us was, 'You've got to dress like the kids,'" said Spence. "We started wearing the Sta-Press trousers rolled up. Our drummer's mother made us tartan [bomber] jackets. I had these big baggy jeans, rolled up and I dyed mine and used tartan stuff to patch them up. We were wearing this and the Rollers were still wearing the satin trousers and satin jackets. The first time we did it at a gig, the response was unbelievable, clocked on to it right away."

During the band's first recording session in London they complained to Polydor that their van had broken down and they didn't have the money to get it fixed. "They said. 'Why didn't you use the money from your advance?'" said Spence. It was approximately £10,000. "We said, 'What money, we didn't get any money.'" The recording did not go well. The band changed some of Bickerton's lyrics and when he asked why, they told him they thought they were 'shit'. "We just didn't do ourselves any favours at all," said Spence. The band would have to wait until summer 1974 to release their first single and their first national TV exposure would only come in July that year.

Faulkner took close note of the Bilbo Baggins image: the tartan bomber jackets, striped socks, hugely wide trousers with exaggerated turn-ups, baseball shoes, tight V-neck T-shirts and jumpers, some with the band's names on them. "Bilbo Baggins were better than the Rollers," said Paton. "They were a very strong, musical band."

"Shimmy shammy shong – we used to make up songs, remember."
"Hidey hidey ho, we used to kiss hello, remember."
"We would hum-a-lum to the beating of a drum, remember."
"I wasn't overly excited by the lyrics," said Clark. "But when Phil [Coulter] sang it over the backing track I loved it and through we could be onto something here."
Faulkner was less impressed.
"Sha La La La La La La LA Shooby do eh!"
"You want us to sing that?" he said.
"Yep then: Remember all the little things we used to say."
"Sha La La La La La La LA Shooby do aye."
"Wonder why we ever had to say goodbye?"
"I knew those lyrics were never going to get a Pulitzer Prize nomination, that wasn't the point," said Coulter. "We were not looking for Grammys. We were looking to sell records."
"I'd written, We used to sing along... da da da da da... remember," said Martin. "Tra la la la, we used to sing to you... remember. I used to hum it and then Phil said, 'Why don't I add in this one, Sha la la la' ... so it was really two songs we stuck together. Phil was a great finisher. He was very good with words, I'm not the lyric writer, I was the ideas man, came up with tunes and lyrics but Phil had the patience to finish things."
"A common misconception is that with Bill and I it was a music and lyrics partnership," said Coulter. "He was good ideas man, I would have a song half-finished and he'd say, 'No it's too complicated.' He had great street ears, a very commercial nose. But he wouldn't be involved in the nuts and bolts of the music end of stuff."
The recording at Mayfair studios was brief for the band. As on the 'Saturday Night' session, the backing tracks were already recorded by Coulter and his session men. Coulter had even sung a guide track

for Clark to copy. Again, the B-side was another Coulter/Martin composition. Faulkner was disgruntled. "Who's going to play all those saxophone and brass lines at the gigs?" he complained to Paton.

There was no great enthusiasm from Bell either. Paton had been to see Leahy and begged for this one last chance. "I think he felt sorry for me," Paton said. "I was begging. I begged Dick Leahy. I begged him to give us another kick at the ball."

Leahy had planned to drop the band. This last single, 'Remember', was to be given a perfunctory release in the UK and that would be it. He was in the process of signing a new band Showaddywaddy. A new Bell act signed in America, Terry Jacks, had delivered 'Seasons In the Sun', a soon to be a number one smash in both UK and America. David Cassidy was at number one in the album charts with *Dreams Are Nuthin' More Than Wishes* and on the singles chart with 'Daydreamer', his UK success at its peak. Gary Glitter was so popular that even his backing band, the Glitter Band, was about to start having hits. 'Tie A Yellow Ribbon Round The Ole Oak Tree' had sold one million copies in the UK.

Faulkner recalled driving back to Edinburgh from the recording in Paton's Dodge "pissed off with it all". He felt the band had been belittled. The mood was sombre. Even Paton was silent. "I thought about leaving," Faulkner said.

Another Irish trip was lined up. Faulkner was amazed at the crowds. A string of gigs in England were cancelled. Clark wanted out. He was deeply into the Californian sound of singer-songwriters such as Jackson Browne and Joni Mitchell and bands such as The Eagles and Crosby, Stills, Nash & Young. "It was not where rest of band, especially Eric was at," he said. "The Rollers sound was just not appealing to me. I was unhappy with being controlled."

John Devine was also planning on leaving. "To get married," said Paton who had known about his desire to leave for some time but kept it from the band for fear of sinking morale even further. "We decided if this one flops we pack it in," said Derek. Paton was desperate. If 'Remember' flopped that was the end of his Rollers dream. He could not sleep. His mind raced, endless scenarios of what could be done to save the situation. He did what he was best at. He rolled up his sleeves and grafted. Paton was manic.

He borrowed almost £1,000 (over £10,000 today) off his parents for printing and postage and paid for 10,000 postcard-sized flyers featuring the group's image with the words: 'New Single – Remember – Out Soon!' He, his mother and his mother's friends went to work. Paton had a couple of thousand fan club members and managed to get hold of the names and addresses of the David Cassidy fan club members. He also bragged of buying up issues of teenage pop magazines such as *Popswop*, aimed at nine-13 year-olds, and girls magazines such as *Jackie*, and lifting from them the names and addresses of the kids writing in for pen friends or to swap pictures of Donny Osmond or David Cassidy. Postage alone was close to £300 (£3,000 today). "I sent these cards everywhere," he said. "I sent them to DJs, to television producers, to everybody. That picture went out everywhere." Paton did the dirty work: wrote out the addresses, licked the stamps and posted them. "I used to sit and pray every night," he said.

"The response," Paton said, "was phenomenal." He credits this promotion with helping break the single when it was released in November 1973. Bill Martin certainly had something to do with it too. "He was the best promotion man I ever encountered," said Coulter. "He got the Radio 1 Play of the Week, the Luxembourg Power Play." The single was being played every hour, every night on Luxembourg. BBC Radio 1 was behind it. "I'm a street fighter," said Martin. "I get in there and do it."

In early 1974 the Rollers mimed the single for an episode of *Lift Off With Ayshea* that would be aired on January 9. Faulkner, 20, wore his turned-up white trousers and tartan-trimmed white shirt. His hair was beautifully cut. Alan had got with the decade and had a brutal bog brush haircut. He wore a tight V-neck jumper and short flared trousers trimmed at the hem with tartan – the earliest hint of the Rollers signature look. Derek had a similar get-up in white, his hair still long. Devine, behind the keyboard, had the same jumper as Alan but in a different colour. His denim jeans were exaggerated wide with three-inch turn-ups and he wore basic plimsoles. The others were still in platform shoes.

Only Clark had not converted to the Bilbo Baggins/Jook style look and wore his long dark flares. Worse for Paton was the fact he was getting serious about a woman. "He had fallen in love," he said disparagingly. Clark said "it had no bearing on my decision". He simply didn't want anything to do with the band. "I was fighting with Tam daily," he said. "I was sick and tired of it and just wanted out."

Faulkner tried to convince Clark to stay. "I said he was mad, that it was the biggest mistake he'd ever make."

There were more cancelled gigs. Paton continued his endless postcard mail-outs to boost sales of 'Remember'. He wondered about promoting from within. "At first they wanted me to be the front man but I said it wasn't for me," said Alan, who was now 25.

'Remember' was selling, 200 a day, 300, and then 1,400 a day. The band, although outside the top 40, were the week's 'star breaker', the best-selling single outside the charts. The band was asked to appear on *Top Of The Pops*. Paton kept Leahy and Coulter/Martin in the dark about Clark leaving. He begged Clark to appear on *Top Of The Pops*. Surely now the record was a hit Clark might change his mind about leaving? Clark agreed to do the show. It was the start of what Paton hoped would be a turnaround. There was also a gig he'd lined up in Perth. Clark refused to do it.

Paton snapped. With Faulkner he'd recently seen play live a local five-piece band called Threshold formed by Alan Wright, 18, a former member of Faulkner's old band Sugar before they became Kip. Threshold had been knocking around for a year, gigging around Scotland with a residency at Edinburgh's new Americana club. Wright was a local personality, a fashionable hairdresser at the top salon in town. Paton wanted to manage the band but they were undecided about going down the pop route: some members wanted to be rock musicians and didn't fancy cutting their long hair. Apart from Wright they dressed down in scruffy denim, playing songs by Free, Deep Purple, Stealer's Wheel and popular chart material such as David Bowie's 'Ziggy Stardust'. But their audience was predominantly female.

Their singer was a handsome, skinny local guy with a crooked smile called Les McKeown, only just turned 18. Alongside Wright he was the band's sex symbol. He was a Bowie freak and during his time with the band he'd started to dress more elaborately than the others, in women's platform shoes and tight yellow flares. His hair reached half way down his back although it was cropped at the fringe.

It was Paton who had actually recommended McKeown to Threshold. McKeown had got to know one of the girls, Pauline, who helped run the Rollers fan club, and had invited himself out to Prestonpans with an eye on hustling Paton. "He kept coming down to see me," said Paton who eventually pointed him in the direction of Wright.

Wright was the best looking and best dressed member of Threshold and Paton had tried to persuade him to join Bilbo Baggins. During the uncertainty about Clark, Paton had also asked McKeown if he'd ever consider joining the Rollers. He felt he wouldn't take much persuading. "We were in a bit of state," admitted Paton. "The hard times we had had were beginning to show. I was starting to feel I had had enough." Clark's refusal to play gigs when the band needed the money infuriated him. The refusal to play Perth was the last straw. He made his mind up to get McKeown into the group. "I literally turned the car around and grabbed him for the gig that night."

"The next thing I knew I was in Eric's flat trying to learn all these songs I'd never heard," said McKeown. On stage he got by "reading lyrics off the back of a loudspeaker".

"Les was thrown in at the deep end," said Alan. "The first time on stage he was so nervous he was shaking – he was just this wee guy from Broomhouse [housing scheme]."

McKeown was "raring to go", said Paton. His spirit and ambition gave the group strength, gave Paton strength "like when Eric joined the group," he said.

Paton told Leahy he had replaced Clark, a remarkable turn of events as the band was due to appear on *Top Of The Pops*. "I seem to recall Nobby was tempted by RCA to go solo," Leahy said. "I talked to him. If that's what you want to do because he saw no future in the Rollers, he'd been with Tam for years, probably earning nothing."

Bill Martin had devised a look for the group for *Top Of The Pops*. Five matching long sleeve red T-shirts on which his and Coulter's secretary

Sheila Lazarus had stitched two stripes on the arms and numbers on the front, like an American football team. She made up five sets of trousers too, four white, one black. "And the trousers were short," said Martin. "She didn't buy enough material and anybody can say what they like but that is a fact."

McKeown had his long hair cut into an approximation of a bog brush and headed down to London in the Dodge with Paton and the band. The country was in the grips of an economic crisis. The troubles in Northern Ireland – there were deadly bombings in England now – seemed part of a more general darkening in the country. The UK was in recession. The Conservative Government had declared a state of emergency and introduced a three-day working week in an attempt to conserve electricity. Almost 1.5 million temporarily unemployed people registered for unemployment benefit. After a lengthy dispute, the coal miners went on strike seeking a pay rise to keep their wages in line with inflation that was running out of control at 20 per cent. Growth was down and a war in the Middle East had caused an oil crisis that saw oil prices quadruple globally. The oil crisis caused the price of vinyl to increase – for singles from today's equivalent of about £3 to £5 and rising. Albums cost between £15 and £20 in today's money.

Only services that seemed essential – hospitals, supermarkets and newspaper printers – avoided the three-day week, and during those days longer hours were also prohibited. TV companies were required to cease broadcasting at 10.30pm to conserve energy. The BBC was in turmoil; there were threats of strike among the technical workers, stoppages and shortages.

A promotional appearance by the Rollers on BBC's popular children's show *Crackerjack*, filmed live at BBC Television Theatre in Shepherd's Bush, was cancelled. *Top Of The Pops*, unusually, was filmed on Tuesday rather than Wednesday night at the BBC in Shepherd's Bush. McKeown had to pre-record a new lead vocal for 'Remember' and the group all tried on their new outfits that they all coupled with platform boots or shoes. Faulkner wore his hooped socks. Devine was the odd one out in black trousers. The group performed enthusiastically, all raising their arms above their heads to encourage clapping along. McKeown shone, totally in the moment, bursting with an infectious happiness.

As arranged, Clark flew down to London on Wednesday to film *Top Of The Pops*, only to be told "they had made a special arrangement and already recorded the show." It seemed a cruel trick to play on the man who'd been in the band for over eight years. "He had got a bit old-fashioned," Paton said.

"All the time Nobby had put in to that band and Tam just brushed him aside," said Jake Duncan. Paton promised to pay Clark the royalties he was owed and his share of the band's assets. "[It] never materialised," he said. He did sign a solo deal, with CBS, but his subsequent career never took off. Paton, he said, tried hard to make sure it didn't. As the Rollers' star rose he was accused of using his influence to block Clark's progress. Clark also had trouble escaping the former singer of the Rollers tag. "It was terrible," he said. "I was trying to carve out a solo career and all people wanted to ask me about was The Bay City Rollers." His descent into madness, suicide attempts and alcoholism began.

The Rollers' *Top Of The Pops* appearance was aired on Thursday, February 7, 1974. The band stacked up alongside Suzi Quatro, The Sweet, Alice Cooper and T. Rex. Paton wouldn't allow them to socialise after the recording. "I always thought this takes away some of the 'star' quality from the act," he said.

Their *Top Of The Pops* performance was repeated on the show on February 21. They were in the Top 40 with 'Remember' selling 5,000 records a day now. After they recorded a new performance on March 7 with the same line-up and in the same uniforms, the record peaked at number six in the UK, with total sales of over 250,000 copies. Bell rushed it out in Germany, where it made the top 40, France and Australia.

On March 16 they were on the cover of *Record Mirror*. John Devine in his baseball boots, Les in his women's platforms, and Eric with even more tartan on his white shirt, on the pocket and down the fly front to match his shoulder inserts. He and Les seemed most committed in the wide white trousers that stopped mid-calf. The others had lengthened theirs. Compared to the glam rockers that dominated the scene, in their sweet – home-knitted, declared McKeown – little jumpers, all smiling, the Rollers looked young and fresh.

McKeown was put on the same wage as the others, £100-a-week, and recalled the band being featured in *Jackie* magazine and finally appearing on *Crackerjack* and also the BBC kids' TV show, *The Basil Brush Show*, hosted by a puppet fox.

"From then on you knew they were going to be big," said Leahy. "You didn't know how big but you certainly knew they were going to be successful and that it wouldn't be just one hit. Les brought the energy Ron Wood brought to the Stones when he joined, shook them up... he had tremendous energy."

Paton had been warned against taking McKeown into the group. He had a swagger about him, even at 16 when he'd first come onto Paton's radar, that suggested trouble. By then he'd already been convicted of grievous bodily harm and malicious damage. "I can handle him, he's all right," Paton said. He had grown up in a tenement block on Edinburgh's Broomhouse council housing estate built in the late forties, the youngest of four boys in a poor family. One brother was put away for a while in a "special school" for troubled kids. Another was put in a young offenders' home where, it was later revealed, he was abused.

His father was a tailor and profoundly deaf and dumb. The family had created their own sign language. "He couldn't quite understand everything that was going around any particular subject," said McKeown. He often communicated via violence. McKeown watched him beat his older brothers "many a time".

He was softer on the younger McKeown. "He would sit me down and he'd get his big bunch of keys and he would straighten my legs and smack them over my knees," he said. "So he never punched me in the face or tried to break my arms. It was a set punishment." He made McKeown's stage clothes.

His mother had tuberculosis and he worried for her health. He was trouble at school, cheeky and unruly, quick to lose his temper, highly-strung and tense. He left with no qualifications after being expelled when he was barely 15. He did not respond well to authority and had gone through a succession of menial jobs before joining Threshold, his first band, in early 1973.

Roni, his elder brother by five years, was a DJ in the Edinburgh clubs and a popular figure with his mates and the girls. McKeown wanted to be just like him. He had grown up listening to his records, blues, Motown, Roxy, Bowie, Led Zeppelin. "I loved all kinds of music," McKeown said. He was desperate to escape from the scheme, its crime, drugs, prostitution, depravation and gangs. He was determined on a career in music. He was already helping out as an unpaid teaboy at a recording studio, Radio Edinburgh. McKeown said he was even having guitar lessons off Faulkner before joining the Rollers.

Threshold and Roni sold themselves as a package, a DJ and a band for an all-encompassing evening. They'd had plenty of bookings, travelling around Scotland playing small clubs and dance halls every other weekend, for £100 a gig, picking up a strong local female fan base. Alan Wright was in charge and prohibited girlfriends from the gigs. There were plenty of girls on the road. Wright and McKeown grew close; play wrestling in the back of the van. He introduced McKeown to marijuana. McKeown also enjoyed homosexual experiences. "Experimentation was rife," he said "We tried everything because we could."

"I realised I was bisexual before I was 18," said McKeown. "It was what young people do when they are fooling around, I was quite the lad at school and we occasionally had two or three people involved in fooling around... let's say it started with a couple of guys with a girl and then it got bigger and then it got into party mode and that's when that happened. It was not something I thought was disgusting or unusual in any way... it was not until you start to see other people's reaction to gay people and bisexuality, that's when you start to have the problem with it, you think, wait a minute everyone thinks it's a bit weird."

The band's drummer Jon Gillam, then 17, said that although Broomhouse "was a rough working-class area", with Edinburgh's main prison on its border, McKeown was not a hooligan. "He didn't go out looking for or creating fights, or trouble, or stealing, that wasn't Les at all," he said.

McKeown idolised the androgynous Bowie, whom he'd seen play live and met in Edinburgh. "Most times we'd be round his house, that's all we would bloody listen to," said Gillam. He said McKeown was "perhaps more effeminate than the rest of us but not overly so. He'd be dressing up a bit more, being more flamboyant on stage whereas we'd be playing in jeans."

McKeown claimed it was his tight stretch nylon trousers that his father had made for him that attracted Paton. He said he was wearing no underwear when Paton saw him perform in them. McKeown initially found Paton "strong and scary... nobody in their right mind would mess with him", but also "a good-looking geezer who looked after his hair".

McKeown had heard from guys on the circuit that the Rollers were "a bunch of poofs". When he joined the band, Faulkner, two years older, but from a similar underprivileged estate, told him that one of the group rules was no girlfriends. McKeown responded that no one told him what to do and Paton, cautious about losing another singer, told McKeown that if he did have a girlfriend – Lynn, apparently, was her name – he must never mention it in the press and she should never be seen with him. He must seem accessible to the fans. He agreed. Following the success of 'Remember' there were already girls starting to hang around his parents' home in Broomhouse where he still lived.

The band continued to gig in Scotland and around Edinburgh but McKeown was not instantly popular among the hardcore fan base that demanded the return of Clark. They made "rude noises", he said, and even spat on him at gigs. Now they were a chart act Paton and Barry Perkins at Starlite could charge £2,000 and sometimes £3,000 for gigs and according to Paton this "lifted the morale". "Derek had started smiling again," he said. In England the band found themselves accepted in the same ballrooms where audience before had been lukewarm. "There was even the odd scream," said Paton.

Paton now replaced John Devine. He had promised the gig to a pretty dark-haired teenager called Stuart Wood who had just turned 16 and was in the latest version of Kip. He was concerned that the success of 'Remember' might mean Devine no longer wanted to quit but Devine knew Paton had sounded out Wood and was "quite happy to go". Paton told the rest of the band of his decision. Faulkner was shocked. Paton maintained Devine had met a girl and wanted to settle down. Faulkner said he was leaving for "family reasons". Like all the various ins and outs of group members, the suspicion was always that there was a sexual undertow to the decision. In the case of Wood it seemed clear cut.

"It was a good gig to get in the Rollers," said Pat McGlynn, a future Roller himself, 15 at the time and a then member of Kip. "Woody was good looking and Tam fancied riding him, basically, to cut the story short."

McGlynn was from a rough area of Edinburgh and in the Young Niddrie Terror. He ended up in Kip after being caught stealing a guitar from an Edinburgh music shop run by the band's then manager Tam Scott. McGlynn was on probation and pleaded with Scott. "He told me I was a good looking wee boy and he said if I came for an audition for the band he wouldn't call the police." Wood was in the band when he auditioned and despite the fact he couldn't play an instrument, McGlynn was asked to join. "We were all learners," said McGlynn. "We used to back up The Bay City Rollers. Tam Scott knew Tam Paton."

He'd been in Kip for about a year when Paton offered Wood the Rollers job. "While he was in Kip, most of the band would go home with Tam Scott but before Wood was about to join the Rollers we knew something was going to happen because Tam [Paton] started coming to the gigs and taking him home."

Wood, or Woody as he became known, was the second born of three brothers, a healthy lad who didn't drink and loved swimming. His father was a Royal Mail chief inspector and also a Royal Navy reserve. His mum was a school cook. The family lived in Marchmont, an affluent residential area of Edinburgh, just south of the Old Town, in the city centre. He was well-behaved at school – generally kept in line by his father. Paton described him as "the boy next door type" and chose him because he was "young", he said.

The £100 a week wage Paton was offering doubled what Wood was earning as an apprentice electrician. He'd left school with few academic qualifications. He already knew Faulkner and though he was no great guitar player – "I knew five or six chords" – he was enthusiastic. Before the joined he had the "tufty" haircut, as it became known, and copied the Rollers' clothes. His first gig was at Birmingham Town Hall where he mucked up the keyboard introduction to 'Remember'.

Even though the band were starting to earn good money on the road, when they came to record the follow up to 'Remember', they stayed in the same Royal Norfolk Hotel they always did. They also still shared rooms. Three double rooms, two in each [Paton and the five band members] on a rotating system although the Longmuir brothers never shared with one another. "In the case of Woody it is a necessity because he is still very frightened of the dark," said Paton.

"Tam Paton ran a bit of musical chair situation," said Phil Coulter. "If there were five Rollers on stage, he always had another couple in reserve in case anyone stepped out of line. Tam ran a very tight ship. Woody was a late draftee into the band. I thought he was a very average talent. He made up the numbers in the band and looked the part."

Coulter nevertheless appreciated what McKeown brought to the band. "I was delighted when Les was drafted in," he said. "He had a pleasing quality in his voice which you can't be taught or learn. He was an engaging young fellow, good personality, a natural performer. He fitted naturally into that whole thing of being a pop idol, he loved it – he was just to the manor born. Les was the star of the band, the guy who had the charisma and the smarts. He was the brightest most talented of the whole bunch. Les doing lead vocals was the biggest contributor to the hits."

The new single was already recorded by Coulter and the session players by the time the band got to London. Coulter had recorded a vocal for McKeown to sing over. "That's the way it was done," he said. "We had to drag a few of the others in to do sha-la-las and shoobie-doobies but they weren't really great at that. So I would have been on with Les doing the backing vocals after we'd laid the lead voice. A signature touch was on the fade out of the choruses there is a high falsetto singing a counter melody, that's me… my Alfred Hitchcock moment."

The song Martin and Coulter had come up with was 'Shang-A-Lang'. Martin had two versions of what inspired the lyric. 'Da Do

Ron Ron' was a core influence, the onomatopoeia in the song he said. 'Shang-a Lang', he said, was inspired by the noise he'd heard coming from the shipyards as a youth in Govan, Glasgow. "For a shipyard noise, I couldn't write clang clang, because Judy Garland had had a hit with 'Trolley Song': 'Clang clang clang went the trolley,'" Martin said. "So eventually I came up with, 'We sang shang-a-lang as we ran with the gang, doin' doo wop be dooby do ay'. The rest of the lyrics are about nostalgia for early pop. 'With the jukebox playing and everybody saying, music like ours couldn't die.'"

Martin also said: "If I swore my mother would hit me. We weren't allowed to swear. I would go, 'Aw shang-a-lang'. My mother would say, 'What's that?' I said, 'It's just something I say to stop me swearing.' Phil said, 'We should use that, that's good.'"

It was also suggested the song was inspired by the street gangs prevalent in Scotland. "There were lots of gangs in Govan at the time [of his growing up], lots of razor gangs and what have you," Martin said. "Blue suede shoes is in there, it was all mixed in like a pot pourri. It was phenomenal, it took off like a rocket."

'Shang-A-Lang' was the best Rollers single to date, the strongest lyric and the most complete backing track: the closest Coulter/Martin ever got to Spector. Coulter had hit on a pulse and rhythm that had a unique identity, a more liquid, funky version of the Glitter stomp. "Normally when a drummer is starting to play his rhythm he's playing his eighths on a high hat," said Coulter. "I did away with that and that dotted rhythm I put on the floor tom. Clem [Cattini] was doubling up with the stopped guitar, the playing of the two low strings on the guitar. The accumulations of that gave you this kind of throbbing. On 'Shang-A-Lang', the dig-a-ding [hook], that explosive thing, was not only guitar smashes and floor tom it was my percussion player Roy Jones who doubled that up on timpani."

The Rollers debuted the single on the first ever edition of a new Granada TV show called *45* at the start of April. It was produced by Muriel Young, who also produced *Lift Off With Ayshea*, and presented by two Radio 1 DJs: Emperor Rosko and Kid Jensen. It was filmed in Manchester which Paton and the band preferred to London as the journey time from and back to Edinburgh was almost halved. They had dropped the football shirts and tartan, opting instead for white trousers, short and wide, and a mix of skinny-rib jumpers, shirts and white braces and little jackets. The platform boots stayed with Faulkner and Wood showing off their hooped socks.

David Bridger at Bell pushed the record hard. He was getting a little out of control, said Leahy, but he was effective. In the UK, the record was playlisted by Radio 1. Radio Luxembourg was also behind it. Paton's BBC DJ pal from Edinburgh, Stuart Henry, had recently joined the station. Bell Records was now one of the most influential labels in the UK, certainly in terms of singles. Showaddywaddy's debut single was on its way to UK number two. The Drifters scored another huge UK hit with 'Kissin' In The Back Row' and 1974 would be another huge year for Gary Glitter with three big hits singles, including another number one, while the Glitter Band scored three top 10s. Now the label also had the Rollers breaking out, and it was finally prepared to give them full backing in terms of advertising and promotion.

"Bell was a force to be reckoned with," said Leahy. "I'm not sure it would have happened without Bell because we'd built something by that time. The monopoly that supplied Woolworth's and all the big chains said to me, 'Why won't you give us a discount?' I said, 'Because frankly you buy all our records.' We'd got that powerful by then. It was a combination of the promotion efforts of David Bridger and Bill Martin and Bell becoming a very hot label that broke the Rollers."

A certainty to make the charts, it was just a case of how big a hit 'Shang-A-Lang' was going to be. The band was booked to record *Top Of The Pops* to be shown on April 18. A day before the recording, the Longmuirs' mother died of a heart attack. The brothers were in shock, Derek in tears. They flew to London and recorded the show. It was impossible to tell how upset they were. They both sported smiles as they mimed 'Shang-A-Lang'. Alan was about to turn 26, Derek was 23. They were both playing at being 21. Faulkner, 20, was being 18 while Wood, 17, and McKeown, 18, did not need to lie. It was this aura of youth and innocence that marked the group out from their contemporaries: Mud, Gary Glitter, The Rubettes, Slade and Sweet.

These acts looked like men, not boys, and wore exaggerated costumes and outrageous make-up. Wood looked like he could have a young teenage girlfriend.

The appeal of the band, Derek said, was this youth. "The people who follow us are like the group, the same age, there's more communication between us and them than, for example Gary Glitter. Now Gary is a great guy and we've met him several times but he's about 35 and young kids of 14 and 15 cannot really communicate. Then there's the fact that he wears glittery suits which cost thousands of pounds. Kids cannot go out and buy things like that. But they can communicate with us because they can also go out and buy what we wear, and they'll cost just what they cost us. Things like tartan scarves and short trousers."

"All that Woodstock bit is over," said Faulkner. "Audiences are younger now, and that's where we come in. We are about the same age as the kids who come to see us. We know how to entertain them. And that's what they want – entertainment. Many people writing about us in the music papers are nearly 30. They've grown away from the kids. The girls who come to see us think of us as boyfriends. And in a way we think of them as girlfriends."

The Rollers were fresh-faced and came across as unaffected kids, bragging of their mum's knitting their jumpers and the cheapness of making their own trousers. The platform boots and shoes were the only real concession to glam pop. The group they most resembled was The Wombles, the novelty pop group dressed as characters from the hit TV show that was 1974's most popular act, selling an incredible amount of albums and singles. The music had the same happy glow. Phil Coulter recognised this: "Record company executives had believed comfortably beforehand that kids buying records were 16, 17, 18 and 19 [the average of Marc Bolan's fans was 15]. Then it finally dawned on them, finally, that the kids buying records were seven, eight, nine and 10. That was the gap in the market."

The promotion for 'Shang-A-Lang' ran into mid-May, including three further appearances on *Top Of The Pops*, and two more on *45*. The song peaked at number two in the UK, selling over 250,000 copies, and made the Australian top 40 and the German top 50.

For Paton it meant the money coming in from gigs could be hiked further and bookings became easier. He had kept them on the road through most of April and May and now there was a huge tour booked for June. For Dick Leahy, it was a final hit at Bell Records. His four-year tenure as Managing Director of the label's European operations expired on June 7 and he had decided not to renew his contract.

Over in America, Clive Davis was now a 'consultant' to Columbia Pictures Industries, Bell's American owners. The foremost executive the American record industry had ever seen, in 1973 Davis was famously sacked as President of CBS Records, the biggest and most powerful record label in America, under a cloud of a scandal that involved payola, the Mafia and fraud against CBS to the tune of over $500,000. He was said to have billed CBS $100,000 to pay for the bar mitzvah reception of his eldest son (written off as a party for Liza Minnelli). He was also alleged to have used CBS money to rent a summer home in Beverly Hills, pay for his wife's jewellery and for the $250,000 renovation on his New York home.

Davis had been dragged through the mud during a high-profile Government-led investigation into corruption within the American record industry, chiefly the use of drugs, money and gifts to persuade DJs and record stations to play records. He was facing charges relating to filing false income tax returns that could result in five years behind bars. Ultimately, Davis pleaded guilty to one count of this indictment, not paying taxes on almost $10,000 of vacation expenses that had been charged to CBS. The government dropped five other charges against Davis and he would escape with a $50,000 fine. He would quietly settle the civil case brought against him by CBS where he was accused of perpetrating fraud to the amount of approximately half a million dollars. The scandal threatened to overshadow his success at CBS where, with acts like Janis Joplin, Bob Dylan and Simon & Garfunkel, he had overseen a 600 per cent rise in profits and watched the CBS stock price double during his six-year tenure as President.

The skilled Harvard-educated lawyer, who oozed personal charm, was essentially being tasked by Columbia Pictures with phasing out the Bell Records imprint and starting a new record label. Columbia was contributing $10 million to the new partnership with Davis plus any artist Davis wanted to sign from the Bell roster. He also got a 20 per cent equity stake. The company was pragmatic about the charges hanging over Davis's head. A senior figure at the company quipped that if necessary Davis could run the label from jail. "I came in to look for a six-month period on a consultant basis at the artist roster and the executives at Bell," Davis said. "I had an opportunity to go over the roster of some 30 artists and keep all of them, some or none. At the time Bell Records domestically [in America] was losing a considerable amount of money [no big albums]." Davis would ultimately wind up dropping all but three Bell artists: Barry Manilow, Melissa Manchester and The Bay City Rollers. By November 1974 Bell Records would be defunct and reorganised into Arista Records (although the name Bell Records would be used for the next two years on UK releases).

"Columbia Pictures more or less fired Larry Uttal – the President and former owner of Bell Records – and brought in Clive and started Arista," said Leahy. "This coincided with Bell UK having masses of hits on the charts and me thinking about what to do with my life. Larry gave me a proposal to start a new label and Clive invited me to have a chat. I went to NY to meet Clive and he really wanted me to stay at Bell but at that time people were offering me deals to go on my own and I just thought if I don't do it now, I'll never do it. Clive was very gracious." Leahy formed GTO Records and went on to have hits with Donna Summer, The Walker Brothers and Billy Ocean.

Paton was confused as to what these high level management and ownership changes would mean for him and the Rollers. "I don't have a very high opinion of the London music business," Paton said. "They seemed to think because we were based in Edinburgh we knew nothing about our business. Well, they were wrong."

In fact, they were right. His calculations were crude: he said the band had made about £50,000 from 'Remember' and the same again from 'Shang-A-Lang'. His negotiating skills and understanding of international music business affairs were equally basic. The Rollers' four-year contract with Bell would be up in 1975. The idea of him negotiating with the experienced and ultra-savvy Davis and whoever was going to be the new head of Arista in the UK was almost laughable. Paton certainly had no appetite for it.

He divested much of the responsibility now to Barry Perkins who left Starlite to become the Rollers' business manager and he also agreed to Perkins' suggestion to take on Goldberg Ravden as the band's accountants, thus freeing him to focus on his "personal management" of the band. "There's absolutely no way Tam would have been able to make a deal with someone at a higher intellectual level and not lose control of the band," said Leahy. "Maybe that's why he worked with a Barry Perkins."

CHAPTER 5

Explosion

"They fell into that trap of believing that this success was because of some inherent magic within their bodies, some talent exuding out of all of their presence, disregarding the fact that this was all very carefully put together, and these records were carefully crafted. They got the notion that they wanted to be more involved; they wanted to write the songs."

– Phil Coulter

In Glasgow there were 3,000, all "hysterical kids", said Paton. Two and a half thousand turned up to the Tottenham Royal in north London. "We had a 2,000 watt PA and it was completely drowned out by the screams of the girls," said Faulkner. "On stage we got showered with rings, bangles, all kinds of jewellery." There were 4,000 in East Kilbride: the atmosphere electric and fans going wild. After the show, the bouncers formed a human chain to get the band out of the venue. It failed. "Alan was nearly crushed," said Faulkner.

There were similar scenes at ballrooms around the UK, queues down the street and pandemonium inside. The band was returning to some of the venues for a third or fourth time and the managers were invariably ill-prepared for the upsurge in the Rollers' following. The fan club had swollen from 4,000 to 25,000. "Only £2.50 to join," said Derek.

Alongside the mostly pre-teen and young teenage girls, Derek noted the Rollers also had following of boys, "a new generation between the ages of 13-16", he said. Paton said one third of the fan club members were "guys".

"You'll need barriers," Paton often told venue managers. "There'll be a riot," he predicted. Nonsense, they'd tell him, we've had them all here: Slade, Led Zeppelin, Rod Stewart, T. Rex. Even before the band took the stage, their panic would start to rise. The rising crowd squall came with tears, high-pitched, deafening screams, and girls fainting as a crush built by the stage front. After the band took the stage the venue managers saw that the crowd was out of control: there was pushing, screaming, girls rushing on stage to grab the band, hysterics. They often begged Paton to get the band off. The shows might last for a mere 30 minutes. There was talk of band members being covered in bruises from the attention.

"The great thing was that it didn't matter that they weren't great players or great at tuning their guitars," said Coulter. "You couldn't hear because the kids screamed from the start to the end... it didn't seem to matter. This was hysteria, proper hysteria."

Sometime it grew ugly. In Margate, Paton recalled the venue manager hired help from the local fairground to control the crowd. Thugs he called them. He said he saw them kicking and punching the fans to try and control them: "It was disgusting."

In early June 1974, pop music weekly *Record Mirror*, a colour tabloid and an early enthusiastic supporter of the Rollers, reported that Derek had been rushed to hospital after collapsing before going onstage at a gig in Glasgow, suffering from nervous exhaustion. Doctors advised him he would need at least a week convalescing. Derek would later claim the incident took place at home and was an asthma attack – although he never suffered another such attack. Paton said he had got really ill following the death of his mother. He was hospitalised for a week and away from the group for almost three weeks.

The shows went on, Derek's place on the drums taken by roadie Jake Duncan. "We thought about cancelling the rest of the tour but it would be such a disappointment to fans we have decided to carry on," Paton told *Record Mirror*. "I think we have far too many bookings in a short period of time and the pressures have been ridiculous. I'm taking the group off the road for a month, a fortnight of which I hope we'll spend at a health farm so the lads can completely get away from it all."

"Tam went after another drummer in one of his bands in Edinburgh," said Duncan. "But the guy wasn't available. I said, 'I think I can do this.' The only thing I couldn't get together was the drum roll on 'Keep On Dancing'. I got £300 that week [the same as the band members]. I was on £150 by that point [as a roadie]. I thought I'd won the lottery. On stage, once the girls start screaming you couldn't hear a damn thing, not a damn thing. Our PA system could just not cope."

Record Mirror listed the remaining 16 UK tour dates for June. It was a mixed bag of clubs and small town venues, including Caeser's Palace at Dudley, Samantha's Disco in Sheffield, Theatre Royal in Norwich, Tiffany's in Hull and Blackpool, South Pier Pavillion at Lowestoft and Bath Rugby FC. From Wales to Wakefield, Bognor to Chesterfield, the reaction from the fans was similarly over the top. "We get a lot of wrecked seats," said Faulkner. McKeown had grown into his role. He was enjoying himself on stage. They were only 13-year-old girls and if they did get on stage and try and manhandle him they were easy to push off. The adulation was incredible. His hair got more coiffured and he grew more cocksure. He was "the cherry on top of the cream cake", said Paton.

The mechanics of the band's touring operation was still rudimentary. "Once the band started to happen, it was me and another guy, Ted, as the crew," said Duncan. "We were just going gig to gig. The band left straight after the show. It was the only way they could get out of the building. We didn't see them until the next day. The van was obliterated. I tried to clean it but gave up. It was covered in lipstick, spray paint, scratched with names… someone had tried to get in the back door using a pair of nail scissor and the scissors snapped in the lock so we couldn't get the back doors open."

The band travelled with Paton. He had started to "tighten the reins", he said, explaining how he did not want band members "falling in love" and leaving as others had, he claimed, in the past. The group was forbidden from having girls on the road and anyway, he said, "They just do not seem to be interested." They still shared hotel rooms with each other and Paton. "For the first couple of years after I joined they were all celibate as far as I could see," said McKeown. "I'm pretty sure Faulkner and Woody were virgins."

"We hate groupies," Derek said. "They don't appeal in the slightest. We like plain, Bay City Rollers fans, they're our type of people." Occasionally Paton would take the band to a gathering. "The first time we went to a party, I thought it funny that there seemed to be lots of young lads but not many lassies around," McKeown said. "It didn't take too long to find out why." He assumed that "that sort of thing" was normal in the music business.

The band scored their second front cover in June. *Popswop* magazine was the leading pure pop music paper of the era, a colour magazine that sold in excess of 750,000 copies. The band drew praise for their "Youthful, happy-go-lucky style of music and stage presentation ideal for ballrooms and clubs". McKeown wore a home-knitted child's jumper on the cover, far too small and decorated with flowers. The band listed their favourite acts: McKeown named Lulu, Glitter and Mick Ronson; Faulkner, often in these early press mentions referred to by his real surname of Falconer, named The Bee Gees and Deep Purple; Alan picked The Beatles, Gilbert O'Sullivan and Led Zeppelin while Derek chose Elton John and Santana. To the chagrin of Wood, John Devine was featured as one of the band members.

The mistake was down to the fact that the Rollers did not have their own press officer and the in-house PR at Bell Records was already dealing with several huge hits acts. Glitter and Cassidy had their own outside PR representatives. Paton stumbled into an ad hoc solution. London-based music photographer David Golumb, in his late-twenties, supplied pictures to music magazines, including the popular music weekly *Disc*. He also had contacts with a host of girl and teen magazines such as *Jackie*, *Mirabelle* and *Valentine*, all boasting huge readerships. Golumb had photographed Sweet, Marc Bolan, David Cassidy and Rod Stewart. He was interested now in the Rollers. "They had something and I thought they were going to be big," he said. "They had their own little thing, their own identity. I'd been doing pictures of pop acts for long enough to see what was going to be commercial. That's what got me onto it; it was something I could see. It was good for photos. I told Tam I could probably get them some publicity. It went from there."

Paton invited Golumb to Edinburgh. He took up close and personal shots of the band at their parents' homes and at Paton's office in Prestonpans. There was a *Clockwork Orange* vibe to the look of the band, in their short white wide trousers and hooped socks, patterned platform shoes – made in Carnaby Street now – and tight jumpers: a look that was a derivative of Scottish street gangs. Golumb captured the band better than anyone in this phase. There was only the briefest of hints of tartan in their image, a scarf or the patches on Eric's shirt or Woody's jumper. The look was in embryonic form: Faulkner had scribbled 'Eric', and the initial 'E', in biro on the pockets of a white denim jacket.

Golumb's photographs also show the closeness Paton and the band enjoyed. One shot in Paton's Prestonpans bedroom/office saw the group huddled close around him as he rested a hand on McKeown's thigh. "If you'd suggested to me anything was going on I would have said you're nuts," said Golumb. "Tam hid the fact he was gay. I didn't know. He was quite a masculine sort of guy. The Rollers had a clean image. I never ever saw anything sexually going on in any way… and I never saw drugs. Tam was very dictatorial but they were quite happy to do what he said."

Golumb was as good as his word; his exclusive photographs of the group were widely used. *Disc* became hugely supportive of the band. The Rollers also appeared on the cover of *Music Star*, aimed at the glam rock teen scene and often featuring Slade or Gary Glitter on the cover. "There were so many pop magazines," said Golumb. "It was a big time for teenybop magazines and kids magazines." Most wanted colour photographs for 'pin-ups' such as *Popster*, a music monthly that folded out into a huge poster. Golumb's photographs were also perfect for teen girl magazines.

The situation suited Paton. He could control the band's image – he wanted them smiling – via Golumb whom he appointed the band's official photographer. Golumb was also free. He just earned whatever he could from the magazines that used his photos. Over the next 10 months the situation was worked to saturation point. Golumb dropped his other work to focus exclusively on the band. There were endless sessions at his studio in north-west London, the media never left wanting for a new Rollers photograph. In fact by the end of 1974, the Rollers would launch their own photograph-led monthly magazine. "They were great to work with," Golumb said. "They made good pictures. Any gimmick they'd go for. We dressed them as schoolboys. When Christmas time came along it was choirboys and Santa costumes. I did so many sessions with them... hundreds of them."

The themes of most teen/pop magazine articles about the band were established early and would be repeated ad infinitum: the girls that turn them on, their hopes and dreams, their private fears, their intimate secrets and favourite bands. Wood had a chance to mention Paul McCartney and 10cc plus his love of V-neck jumpers, cartoons and milk. His ambition was to "make people happy". *Music Star* described him as "the one everyone would like to hug and mother because he is so cute and cuddly".

Disc called Paton the Rollers "manager, guiding light and father figure". "We're clean cut and poppy and our image is just like being one of the kids next door," said Derek. McKeown added that the image was not a construct: "We're just the same off the stage as we are on the stage. We don't dress up in glitter and put make-up on and things like that. They can identify with us. We're just like the boy next door."

One odd story did emerge from these early innocuous press encounters where image topped content. Faulkner – favourite colour: black – was described as going through a "lonely phase" and had gone on a blind double date with Alan and his girlfriend Sue. His date was Sue's sister who had been described to him as "a bit tall and not exactly beautiful". The pay-off of the anecdote was that the blind date was Derek dressed up in drag and Faulkner had only cottoned on when he tried to kiss him.

Bill Martin and Phil Coulter came up with a quick follow-up single to 'Shang-A-Lang', a summer anthem about schoolgirl holiday romance called 'Summerlove Sensation'. It had the same throbbing rhythm as

'Shang-A-Lang' but with bells as well. The lyrics were also beautiful. Coulter was in the zone, producing work that eclipsed Chinn/Chapman and Mickie Most, full of charm and heart. " 'Summerlove Sensation' is melodic and has that descending thing where we used the tubular bells to spell out the melody," Coulter said. "It had nice bright summery feel to the song. The bells was another little touch, a little ingredient other guys [producers of the era] weren't using that puts a little sheen on the whole operation."

Again, only McKeown participated in the recording. Faulkner, in particular, was beginning to tire of this arrangement. "What bugged the Rollers most was Phil would not let them play on their records and used session musicians," said Martin. "We made all the records in Mayfair Sound and we were very quick. Phil used session musicians because they were very quick. The Rollers weren't that great [as musicians]."

Faulkner also continued to pester Paton about the band recording their own songs for the new single's B-side. He was writing plenty. "It got so bad that at one stage I pleaded, 'Next time we make a record can I be there?'" he said. "I was told to shut up and go away."

"I wouldn't give them a B-side," said Martin. "That was the biggest mistake I made. I should have given them the B-side. But they couldn't write a song. It was a joke. They had to realise the driving force was me and Phil. We maybe should have given them a B-side but we didn't. That was a mistake but the biggest thing of all was they thought they could play on their records. We didn't have time to do three months in the studio to do one record… we would do three records in one day. We were proper producers/writers. They were just a vehicle."

Martin had been aggressive with the band at the taping of a TV show. "You've got to pretend you're putting a production thing together but really you've got a tape," said Martin. Coulter wasn't there. "This was when the Rollers were getting on the edge and wanted out. McKeown said, 'Oh this will be great, let's see how we'll do the drum sound.' I said, 'I'll drum sound you right through the fucking drums you little prick.' There were no fists. I would blow him away if I hit him. They're wee skinny boys. I don't go about punching people. I'm very aggressive mouth wise."

Before he left Bell, Leahy had put in motion the band's debut album, scheduled for release in September. He saw how things were developing with Coulter/Martin. "It had started to go wrong," he said. "I'd talked to Bill about you've got to change the deal... you've got to give the band the right to write at least their B-side and, of course, he was hard ball. Then I left so I never got to see the solution to that. I do recall having a conversation with Bill where I said, 'You should recognise you've got a hit act on your hands and you should relax a bit' [but] he just wouldn't do it."

On the insistence of Martin, McKeown re-recorded the vocals on 'Remember' and 'Saturday Night' for inclusion on the debut album. Both tracks were also strengthened by Coulter with overdubs. "Our relationship with the group did start to sour," said Coulter. "They fell into that trap of believing that this success was because of some inherent magic within their bodies, some talent exuding out of all of their presence, disregarding the fact that this was all very carefully put together, and these records were carefully crafted. They got the notion that they wanted to be more involved; they wanted to write the songs. There was even a suggestion they wanted to sit in on the recordings, sit in on the mixing. When I heard all of that, that's an anathema to me. Committees never made a hit record."

The fact that the band did not play on their own records was a fairly closely guarded secret. Even so, the Rollers felt like they should. They also wanted some of their own songs on the album, at least. There were arguments with Coulter/Martin who had a contract stating they had the final say. The band was also unhappy that their producers were earning more record royalties than they were off the records. Ultimately four of the band's own songs would appear on their debut album, chiefly Faulkner/Wood compositions. Faulkner described the sound of them as "happy rock".

"It was a gesture," said Coulter. "I'd like you to do some songs on the album and come along and play them, so they could feel a bit of ownership and participation. They would have played and then we would have dickied them up a bit afterwards. It was just so they could feel a bit better about it and become a little bit involved."

The songs were rushed and the idea that Wood and Faulkner might record vocals for some of the tracks complicated the recordings. It was a time-consuming process that frustrated Coulter and Martin. For the album, they also recorded two long-standing cover versions in the Rollers' set, songs they had first started playing in the mid-sixties, 'Please Stay' and 'Be My Baby'. "The covers thing kicked in after the fracture of our relationship," said Coulter. "It was their desire to have more of their songs recorded and have more of a say on how and where they were recorded that stuck in my throat." Faulkner was the most vociferous Roller in this regard. "Yes, Eric," said Coulter. "Up until then Tam was only too delighted that as an answer to his prayers he'd teamed up with a writing production duo who were giving him hit after hit after hit with no flops. He wasn't about to rock the boat."

While recording, the group was still touring despite Paton's pledge of time off. In July there were major gigs at Preston Guildhall, Liverpool Stadium, New Century Hall in Manchester and in the Isle of Man. Golumb was now doing primitive merchandise for the group. "Getting posters put together and badges, pictures, stickers," he said. "I started all that, standing outside selling them." It was clear, almost immediately, that he couldn't cope. "I said to Tam, 'If you want to make money you need people standing outside the theatre and at the theatre. Tam wasn't bothered about it, not at the beginning."

The band was also making tentative steps into Europe. In early July they appeared on Holland's TV pop show, *Top Pops*, plugging 'Shang-A-Lang' and later the same month played a free concert in a park in Harlow in Essex. The Labour-dominated town council had been using the local park for a series of free concerts featuring bands such as Mungo Jerry and Fairport Convention. In incredible scenes between 18 and 20,000 turned out to see the Rollers, all aged 12-16. The size of the crowd overwhelmed the band and the organisers. The local newspaper, the *Harlow Gazette*, said that it was amazing there were no fatalities.

The Rollers showed up half an hour late. The teenagers were hysterical, pushing at the crash barrier that soon broke. Teens were pushed into the artificial pond at the front of stage. Others were crushed. A fleet of ambulances rushed 11 to hospital including a seven year old. Thirty more teenagers were treated on site. A St John Ambulance Brigade staff officer declared it a 'near major scale emergency'. The teenagers suffered severe bruising to chests and abdomens, fractured ribs, hysteria and shock. Fresh in the memory was the May 1974 death of a 14 year old in a crush at the front of the stage at a David Cassidy gig in London's White City stadium. An incredible 650 people had been left injured at the show.

The police advised the council to prevent the group from playing in Harlow. The council decided to go ahead with the concert, fearing a riot if the Rollers didn't play. Faulkner, on stage, said that from the first number the 'kids were pressing forwards'. The band dropped songs "trying to get it over with as quickly as possible before someone got hurt in the crush", according to Faulkner. "It got worse and worse. It was terrifying."

'Summerlove Sensation' was debuted by the band on *Lift Off With Ayshea* on an episode aired on July 29. They also mimed to 'Shang-A-Lang' on the show. On the same episode was Paton's second band Bilbo Baggins who finally had their debut single out, 'Saturday Night', written by Bickerton/Waddington. Their image for the show, dictated by Paton, saw them in short-legged tartan-trimmed trousers, baseball boots and tartan jackets.

The record was a star breaker and the band was due to record *Top Of The Pops*. However, a dispute with the Musicians Union over their involvement in the recording of backing tracks forced the show off the air for several weeks. The single failed to make the top 40. The band did a round of promotion. "Tam would insist that any time we did an interview we had to mention his name," said Brian Spence. "He would get upset if you didn't mention his name in an interview."

By the time of their follow-up, 'The Sha-Na-Na-Na Song', another Bickerton/Waddington effort, Paton had switched the image of Bilbo Baggins to white bomber jackets and then school blazers, both sporting a 'BB' insignia cloth badge. "He had a copy of the *Lift Off* show and he destroyed it once he had the Rollers wearing our stuff," said Spence.

The Rollers always insisted their dramatic change in image to their famous tartan-trimmed uniforms was inspired by a drawing sent into the fan club of a boy dressed in 'Roller gear' walking hand in hand with a girl on the beach, art inspired by 'Summerlove Sensation'. The truth was Bilbo Baggins had already adopted a rough approximation of the tartan look and Paton decided to use it for the Rollers. With a few tweaks, and some professional design work, it was going to send the Rollers into the orbit. At the time, Paton was just trying anything that he thought might work.

His relationship with Bilbo Baggins did not seem healthy. "I went with this girl after a gig and the band told Tam," said Spence. "So Tam gets on the phone a few weeks later. He said, 'I don't know what you've been doing but I've had this girl on the phone and she says she's pregnant.' He let this drag on. I was thinking I'm going to have to leave the band and eventually I found out it he was making it up. I was really stressed out about it. We decided to give it him back. The band told him Brian's left home and gone missing. Tam flipped when he found out it was a joke on him. Went nuts."

"Tam was a constant liar," added Spence. "He'd play military albums and you'd hear marching and he'd say, 'Can you hear that, can you hear the spurs? That's me.'"

"Have you ever killed a man?" Paton would ask Spence. "I have. I've got a shirt with a hole in it."

"We were just young and gullible but you couldn't trust anything he said," said Spence. The band actually sacked Paton as manager briefly. They went to Peter Walsh at Starlite Artistes. "He encouraged us to leave Tam and was going to manage us." The management agreement with Walsh lasted until the band found out it was him who had pocketed their £10,000 advance from Polydor. "So we left him and went back to Tam but Tam was never the same after that. If anybody left him, or even if he kicked them out, he wouldn't want them to be successful afterwards."

Paton wasn't predatory towards Bilbo Baggins. "We managed to stay clear of it but maybe that's because we didn't look like young boys," said Spence. 'Our bass player looked like a real caveman.'

With the Musicians Union strike causing the suspension of *Top Of The Pops*, Paton decided the Rollers should go on holiday. Faulkner was sent to a health farm to lose weight. McKeown went to the South of France, purportedly with his mother and father. Paton, Derek, and Wood flew out to Jamaica and were there for Paton's 36th birthday on August 5. This was the holiday the just-turned 17 Wood said he wished he'd not gone on, alone with two older men, both sexually interested in adolescent males, holidaying near Noël Coward's home in Montego Bay. It was a destination recommended by the highly suspect Martin Frutin. "Tam, Woody and Derek blew a good few hundred in Jamaica," said McKeown, less than cryptically. After nine days, rhapsodised as idyllic by Paton, the holiday was cut short when the strike that had affected *Top Of The Pops* ended. The band was needed to perform. "They were fresh and full of vitality," said Paton. "They looked really good with their dark brown skins contrasting with their white trousers and T-shirts."

'Summerlove Sensation' was used as the playout disc on *Top Of The Pops* on August 8. The record shot into the charts at number four and the band reconvened in London to mime to the single for a 'live' episode shown on August 15. The tartan uniforms were not yet in operation although Faulkner wore a tartan scarf around his neck. The show was hosted by The Osmonds who were recording all week at the BBC's Shepherd's Bush Theatre for their own daily 25-minute show on BBC1.

The clean-cut family group was a huge and established act in America, where they had scored their first number one in 1971 and had their own Saturday morning cartoon series. Osmondmania was used to describe the fever they generated in teen fans but their American success was dipping as they tried to spread the gospel of their Mormon religion. The slack was made up by their 1973 breakthrough in the UK following the success of the 'Crazy Horses' single. Their current single 'Love Me For A Reason' was at number one in the UK. Several band members, notably Donny and Marie (who was only 14), were also having solo hits. *Melody Maker* called her the 'nicest slice of jailbait seen in years'. The Osmonds continued to trade on their clean-cut image, famous for not drinking and not having sex (until they got married).

Thousands of girls gathered outside this recording of *Top Of The Pops*, all there for The Osmonds. Here was one group with whom Paton was happy for the Rollers to socialise. In fact, as opportunistic as ever, he decided he would borrow an aspect of their clean-cut image and throw it into the Rollers' mix, insisting the Rollers never drank alcohol. Soon there would a Faulkner/Wood song about not having sex before marriage, 'When Will You Be Mine?'

The Rollers did not need to heavily promote 'Summerlove Sensation' in the UK. There was one further *Top Of The Pops* shown on the August 22 but no other UK TV shows. The single peaked at number three. Paton was now planning ahead. "People are just beginning to realise how big this group is going to be," he said. "Our fan club is probably the largest in the country right now. It stands at 30,000 and we get 2,000 letters a day. Our first album is out soon, it won't be the greatest album in the world and we'll probably laugh at it ourselves in five years' time. But it's a start from which we can build. By the beginning of next year I would say people are going to sit up and take notice of us. They're going to have to."

Arista Records had a new Managing Director in the UK. Appointed by Clive Davis in August 1974, Englishman Tony Roberts, 31, was a former managing director of Warner Brothers Music UK publishing company where he'd signed the group America and Rod Stewart & The Faces as well as handling David Geffen's publishing: Crosby, Stills, Nash & Young, The Eagles and Jackson Browne. "I was very much into that kind of artist," said Roberts. It was the sort of music Davis foresaw at the new Arista. "Clive wanted to do at Arista what he'd done at CBS," Roberts told me. "He wanted to sign people like Bob Dylan, Barbra Streisand, Simon & Garfunkel, Blood Sweat & Tears, he looked down his nose at these poppy acts a bit."

As Davis made the transition of Bell into Arista, he outlined to Roberts that any pop acts would remain under the Bell imprint while more serious artists would be on Arista. "He wanted me to be signing acts like Dire Straits and Elton John and Queen," said Roberts, who would have a tough task turning Bell, celebrated for its hit singles and pop roster, into an album-orientated rock label. "Even though we had nine records in the Top 20 when I took over [in the UK]. Because they were all pretty lightweight stuff, Clive didn't really want to know. He wanted to build Arista with quality acts."

Roberts took over Leahy's office in the old Bell offices on Charles Street and was shocked at how small it was. "I could touch all four walls standing on the desk," he said. "I had Gary Glitter and David Cassidy as well as the Rollers. We had fans on the steps all the time. We had to climb over them all the time... all the time."

Davis was keen for Roberts to develop the company's A&R department. Previously, Leahy had not just run the company but signed all the acts. As head of A&R, Roberts would hire Andrew Bailey, formerly the London editor of *Rolling Stone* magazine. David Bridger, who had been running Bell as interim boss, was promoted to Director of Promotions. There were seven other staff, all females, when Roberts took over.

Roberts met The Bay City Rollers' managers, Perkins and Paton, on his first day in the office. "Tam said we've got a problem," said Roberts. "The boys have fallen out with Bill Martin and Phil Coulter and they're never going to go in a studio with them again. I said, 'Don't be ridiculous we're just happening, we're just beginning to be successful'... he said, 'Well I'm sorry but they're absolutely un-persuadable... we're never going to go in a studio with Bill and Phil ever again.'"

Roberts dug out the Coulter/Martin contract that stated they were locked in until such time as they stopped making Top 20 records. "I got Bill in, I'd known him for years, since 'Puppet On A String', and said, 'Look I'm sorry. You can lead a horse to water but it's not going to work. I've done my best but it's not going to work.' He said, 'Well I couldn't care less. I've got a contract and I want it honoured.' I said, 'But Bill they're not going to go in the studio with you, I don't care what the contract says. So let's be friends, let's be gentlemen, let's see if we can work something out'... which we did."

Roberts bought out Coulter/Martin's production rights (but not their publishing copyright on the songs); their 4 per cent, meaning the pair would not get paid record royalties on any future use of the tracks they had produced for the Rollers, including the, as yet unreleased, new songs for the album. It cost a fortune. "It was a six figure sum," said Martin. He recalled negotiating with Clive Davis directly. "I personally thought they would never go on if they didn't have our writing and producing," said Martin. "Clive didn't want to get rid of us but he said, 'I won't have a band.'" Martin was not happy.

"I said to Clive Davis, 'It's hard enough to make hit records when everyone is pulling in the same direction,'" said Coulter. "But there's friction here because now they're dragging their feet… and they think they can do it better than I can, this has become a situation which is pretty untenable.' We could have played really awkward and said, 'Okay let's drag them into the fucking studio and make records.' The friction was less coming from Les than other quarters but it's not my nature to go in the studio and know as I'm walking through the door there's going to be confrontation… edginess. The buy-out was the only sensible way to resolve that situation."

The search for Coulter/Martin's successors was not urgent as the band's debut album was already finished and there was enough material for one more single. Barry Perkins, described as "a tosser" by Bill Martin, however, needed to move fast. With four of the Rollers' own songs on the upcoming album and now, without Coulter/Martin at the helm, potential for the band's songs to feature on future singles, he needed to strike a publishing deal for Bay City Music, the company formed to hold the rights to all self-penned Rollers songs.

Freddie Bienstock was interested in acquiring Bay City Music. 'Viennese Freddie', as he was sometimes called, owned Carlin Music. Born in Switzerland, he came to London in the early sixties after working for music publisher Hill & Range in the penthouse of the famous Brill Building in New York. At Hill & Range he had supplied songs to Elvis Presley. Songwriters were so keen to have their material recorded by Presley, Bienstock had been able to get them to turn over a substantial portion of their publishing royalties in what became known as an 'Elvis tax'. In London Carlin looked after Phil Spector's publishing. They owned the copyright on 'Be My Baby', one of the songs on the Rollers' album.

It was one of the major publishing houses in the UK, winners of 10 consecutive annual Top Publisher awards in the UK trade periodical, *Music Week*. Bienstock was among publishing's shrewdest and most well-connected figures, one of the music industry's most powerful moguls.

He had also established the Hudson Bay Music publishing company with songwriters Leiber & Stoller, who wrote 'Jailhouse Rock' for Elvis among many others. Hudson Bay would publish some of the Rollers' hits in America.

Carlin owned the copyright on over 100,000 songs including such staples as 'Fever', 'The Twist' and 'What A Wonderful World' and musicals such as *Cabaret* and *Fiddler On The Roof*. Bienstock would eventually take over Chappell Music, the world's largest music publisher (with a catalogue of 400,000 songs) in a deal worth £100 million.

It is unclear how much Carlin paid for Bay City Music, or the terms of the deal. Perkins, then almost 44, had a major gambling habit to feed and may not have been as on the ball during negotiations as a man without such burdens. It is also likely that Paton did not fully understand the complexities of publishing agreements. At the time, Faulkner was delighted to be able to tell the press that one of the songs he wrote for the album may be covered by what he called a "quite well known artist". It never happened.

Paton described Faulkner as "moody" and although he appeared confident suffered from a "nervous stammer". "We're very close although he can be a bit of rebel," said Paton. "Sometimes he doesn't accept what I say but we always end up doing what I say in the end."

Paton hoped the band would develop as songwriters and expressed an interest in signing other songwriters to Bay City Music. He still held an interest in the company, as did Perkins. "Les wanted to write the songs and Eric wanted to write the songs 'cause that's where the money is and that's when the trouble comes in," said Paton. "With the publishing company I put it down that everybody would share five ways. That was to stop the bickering, like, 'Oh he wrote the last one, so I'm gonna write this one...' So, I thought if they all had a share in each song... and they could only have it for five years, that would be it, basically. And then after the five years the person who actually wrote the song could get all the royalties back. The songs were usually credited to Faulkner/Wood and that's where the jealousy came in from Les' end. And that's also where I got the blame and Les' hatred for me comes from. I was supposedly defending Eric and Woods."

True or not, Paton said he had been offered over half a million pounds for his 15 per cent management contract with the Rollers and a wage to stay on with the group. He never revealed who offered this – "A consortium," he said – but stated the band insisted he turn it down.

What was clear, however, was the Rollers were about to start generating huge amounts of money. Their debut album *Rollin'* featured a front cover portrait of the all-smiling band that placed Derek in the very centre wearing a top bearing the image of Charlie Chaplin that had previously been worn by John Devine – the band often shared clothes. David Golumb had taken the shot and there was not a flash of tartan in sight. Released in late September, the album was at number one by early October and would stay on the charts for an incredible 62 weeks, selling over 300,000 in the UK alone by Christmas. The Rollers would have earned approximately 50p per album sold from record royalties. It positioned itself ahead of Paul McCartney's *Band On The Run* and *Tubular Bells* by Mike Oldfield. It also made the top 10 in Australia and the top 40 in Japan. Paton could barely contain himself. His first number one.

Faulkner complained in the press that they'd only had four days to record it. He said he was "very disappointed" with the album and described the production as "diabolical". "They don't really mean what they say," said Paton. As far as he was concerned the only downside was the Coulter/Martin album track 'Jenny Gotta Dance' that sparked a rumour Faulkner had a girlfriend called Jenny. At the fan club girls were writing in threatening to commit suicide if this was true.

"The first album is essential Rollers," said Coulter. "That was the sound of the Rollers, that's what broke them and gained them all the fans." It featured just one more new Coulter/Martin original, 'Give It To Me Now', and contained all the A-sides they had written for the group to date. The Rollers' own songs had a kiddy-like charm, particularly 'Ain't It Strange', but the lyrics seemed deliberately faux-naif.

The album was followed by a new Coulter/Martin-penned single, 'All Of Me Loves All Of You' that Roberts kept off the album for this purpose. It was backed by 'The Bump', another Coulter/Martin song, that many felt was the stronger track. The A-side was pure puff, all chugging rhythm and nonsensical lyrics similar to 'Remember' with a massively syrupy sing-a-long chorus. Paton, remarkably, told the press he disliked it, calling it "sloppy sentimental stuff".

"What about the guys in the audience? They won't like it will they?" he said. "I don't think it'll get to number one. In fact, I've got a bet on that it won't. You can't get to number one without strong material no matter how popular you are, and we need better material. I think the boys themselves can write better than that."

The split with Coulter/Martin had not been publicised yet. Paton thought he was being cunning. By suggesting the pair had lost their touch he hoped to lessen the impact when it was announced the band had lost their hit songwriters.

The band debuted 'All Of Me Loves All Of You' on a new Tyne Tees pop show, *Geordie Scene*, which was hosted by Paton's pal, BBC Radio 1 DJ Dave Eager. Tyne Tees held the ITV franchise for the north east of England. The band followed this with an appearance on *Top Of The Pops* on October 11, repeated on October 24, and then on *Lift Off With Ayshea* on October 15. The Rollers appeared on the cover of *Disc*, dressed in what appeared to be undertakers outfits – black top hats and smart suits and ties. It was another Golumb effort, accompanying an article promoting an upcoming 24-date British tour headlined 'Ready For The Road'.

The venues were similar to recent tours undertaken by Sweet, Mud and Gary Glitter, taking in major cities and lots of smaller towns. Tellingly, the Scottish shows had already sold out, as had the gig in Newcastle, but the English shows in towns such as Ipswich, Bournemouth and Hull had not. Paton was worried. He called the Rollers a 'working man's band', meaning he felt they played best to audiences in working-class cities such as Liverpool, Manchester, Newcastle, Glasgow and Edinburgh. He worried about dates in places such as Chatham, Oxford and Hanley, which he identified as "Conservative" and "reserved".

'All Of Me Loves All Of You' peaked at number four and did not chart anywhere else in the world. It seemed Paton had doomed it with faint praise. Coulter/Martin took the single's B-side, 'The Bump', and gave it to a group called Kenny, a manufactured boy band, who wore matching wide red trousers and featured the letter K on their matching T-shirts and jackets. The record came out on Mickie Most's RAK and the band was managed by Peter Walsh at Starlite Artistes. 'The Bump' rose to number three in the UK charts in November and Coulter/Martin had fun with Kenny throughout 1975, scoring three more top 20 hits, including the memorable number three 'Fancy Pants'.

To maximise the exposure the Rollers tour would bring, Barry Perkins hired Alan Walsh, a former music journalist, as PR for the Rollers. It was now too dangerous for the band to play clubs, ballrooms and Mecca dance halls. Paton said the Rollers were ready for the 'big venues'. This tour saw the group booked into major concert halls, including a London gig at the Rainbow Theatre, where The Who had famously played for three nights in November 1971. Pink Floyd had recently played the 3,000 capacity venue, also for three nights, and Queen were about to use it to cut a live album.

"It was a bit of instant money," said Walsh, who was doing PR as a sideline to his music journalism. Perkins paid him approximately £450 a week. "I didn't particularly like Barry," he said. "He wasn't the sort of bloke you'd want to go for a pint with. Barry was the guy who wielded the stick. If there was anything strong to be said it used to come from him. Tam was okay as long as you did what he wanted you to do."

Walsh travelled to Edinburgh to meet Paton at his parents' house in Prestonpans to discuss the tour. Also travelling to Prestonpans was the tour's promoter Jef Hanlon, a streetwise 31-year-old Mancunian. "Tam lived in a semi-detached house and he had the box room and he ran the fan club from there," he said. "He was sat there with cardboard boxes full of fan letters… used to try and answer them all himself. It was all a bit strange in his mum and dad's house. Tam was a bit weird."

Hanlon had a longstanding business partner who was gay and cottoned on to this fact about Paton straight away. "Of course nobody ever came out in those days," he said. "I never confronted Tam with it. There was nothing to confront. What he got up to behind closed doors was none of my business. In the sixties people were getting arrested in toilets for homosexual acts and it hadn't moved on a lot since then."

Hanlon had started out at Kennedy Street Enterprises in Manchester, where he had first met Perkins, and where he had been tour manager for Wayne Fontana and Herman's Hermits. He had worked closely with Perkins during that time but it was not through him that Hanlon got involved with the Rollers. In fact, Hanlon – who would go on to become one of the most respected music promoters in the music business over the next 40 years – did not like Perkins. "He was a Southerner but he was living and working in Manchester," Hanlon told me. "Something happened at Kennedy Street and he left. Then he came back and his title was business adviser and he was based back in London. He went totally big time. He wouldn't talk to anybody unless he needed to. You can never afford to go big time because when you're up there it's very easy to be nasty and unpleasant to everybody. You think you've got power but eventually the tide turns and you have a quiet year. Barry became unpleasant. It was a massive disappointment."

Hanlon was now working as part of RAM (Rock Artist Management), a company co-formed by Mike Leander, Gary Glitter's manager and producer. RAM had had a strong relationship with Bell and Dick Leahy and Hanlon had booked tours for Bell acts: Gary Glitter, the Glitter Band, Hello (who broke into the top 10 in late 1974) and Barry Blue. He was the go-to guy for teen glam pop concert tours of the era.

Paton took Hanlon to see the group rehearsing in the tattie shed in Port Seton. "They had to finish the rehearsal before the potato wagons came back from the deliveries," Hanlon said. "I was there to give them a bit of guidance, whether they realised this or were told this is unlikely. They just thought the big promoter from London was getting on a plane and flying to Edinburgh and going to see them for a day or two and watch them rehearse. They'd never done any concert halls before and there is a slightly different technique to it than playing in clubs. The bigger the hall is the more you have to take your time talking and let your voice go to the back of the hall and come back again. We talked about movement on stage and lighting."

The tour was still basic. There were no stage props. The band had a new PA, 6,000 watts, that they hoped would lift the music above the screaming. It was still just Jake Duncan driving the truck with the band's gear in it with one or two more roadies. Hanlon organised for two small lighting towers. The no-frills operation was due to Paton's parsimoniousness, said Hanlon. "A genie tower, one each side of the stage, telescopic tower, 10 or 12 Par Cans each, and then the follow spots up in the gods," Hanlon said. "An amplifier each, set of drums and three microphones along the front. That was it. They had no aspirations to do a Pink Floyd. It wasn't appropriate for what was going on."

In the tattie shed Paton had Faulkner and McKeown show Hanlon a routine where they'd both get down on their knees facing one another and gyrate and touch one another. Wood and Alan would do the same during the stage act. "Tam was into all that," said Hanlon. "He just wanted a bit of guidance and reassurance. I didn't stay there more than two days. We worked on the length of the set. The idea was to start off strong, cool it down and then build it up towards the end."

The preparation for the tour also included a young, unnamed female designer and a tailor who were creating new uniforms for the band, or "stage overalls" as Paton called them. Tartan was used in a major way. It would make Eric's tartan scarf and his white shirt with tartan trim – on the fly front, shoulders, two breast pockets and small arm pocket – look subtle. The band's trademark short wide white trousers were given thick tartan stripes down the seams and on the hems. There were short jackets with tartan collars and tartan cuffs. These also had their names or initials – 'E' for Eric Faulkner or 'W' for Wood – on them. There were more scarves, sometimes wrapped around wrists as well as necks – another gang influence. Poor Alan wore an outfit made entirely of tartan with white trim. He hated it. "The minute I got a chance, I'd rip off all that garb and put on a pair of jeans," he said.

The band still wore striped socks and platform shoes. Wood's had a 'W' on the side and cost over £30 (£300 today). The tartan suits cost close to £70 (£700) each. "A fan sent us this fantastic drawing of us with tartan stripes down our sleeves and trousers and we adopted that," said Faulkner. "It became the Rollers look." There was a clear lineage to the development of these costumes but it was chiefly the enthusiasm of Faulkner and the skill of the designer that brought them to fruition.

The first show of the tour was at Birmingham Town Hall on October 18. "We stopped the traffic in the centre of Birmingham," said Hanlon. "The town hall was in the middle of a massive one-way system and they did an 'Osmonds' on it." 'They' were London-based security firm Artists Services, who provided protection for David Cassidy (they had been at the White City disaster), Gary Glitter and The Osmonds, as well as high end rock acts like Led Zeppelin and Deep Purple. Hanlon had worked with them on his Glitter tours. "Patsy, Billy, Paddy the Plank, Fat Fred, Billy Francis and Danny Boy," he said. "Big tough boys." Paton hired them to look after the Rollers during the tour. "Doing an Osmonds" was all about creating hysteria.

"This big furniture van broke down in the middle of this one-way system," said Hanlon. "Very inconvenient... it was when all the fans were mobbing up about an hour or so before the show. The traffic stopped and the papers picked it up and ran with it, 'Traffic stopped by Bay City Rollers fans'. No one ever noticed this big removal van that had allegedly broken down. I wonder who organised that? And it went on from there and it seemed to become a competition between the fans from each town to go crazier at each gig, to top what they'd read about in the papers that morning about the gig the night before. And the media whipped it up and whipped it up and exaggerated it. It got into this competition, Newcastle can outdo Glasgow, and it went all round the country like that, getting crazier and crazier and crazier. The stuff with Sweet or Glitter Band wasn't as intense. The Rollers audience was nearly 100 per cent young girls between the ages of 10 and 15 and they just went potty."

Alan Walsh had used his contacts to talk *Melody Maker* into reviewing the Birmingham gig, positively. Although a 'serious' weekly music paper like its main rival *NME*, *Melody Maker* had covered teen acts such as Jackson 5, The Osmonds and David Cassidy. Although *MM* leaned more towards serious rock its editor, Ray Coleman, believed in covering the whole range of popular music so was not averse to sending its writers to report on Rollers' concerts and the chaos they inspired.

The Rainbow show fell early in the tour, the third date, on a Sunday night. Outside the venue was a crowd of girls in Rollers merchandise:

tartan scarves, rosettes and caps. There were also groups of lads in short baggy trousers. A man called John Collins, who had been doing the same for Gary Glitter, handled the merchandise for this tour. There were also records, posters and programmes on sale. It was estimated that 20,000 programmes retailing at £2 a piece were sold and 15,000 tartan rosettes at £3 each.

The gig and the tour in general attracted touts selling bootleg merchandise and forged tickets. Artists Services would have serious conversations with the touts about what might happen to them on the way home if they didn't get lost. It could get wild on the road; touts, bootleggers, even local gangs who didn't like the idea of 1,500 girls screaming at the Rollers and wanted to attack the band.

Hanlon managed DJ Dave Eager and got him the job at *Geordie Scene*. Now he employed him as compere for the tour. "That was new," said Hanlon. "Others weren't doing that. If we lost the crowd and we could see we were losing it, we had signals and I'd go to the side of the stage and get the boys off. They didn't like it obviously but I made them come off stage and quieten down and send the DJ on to say 'Listen go back to your seats otherwise the show's over, you're going to hurt yourself'. A lot of the Rollers' concerts collapsed into chaos after about 30 minutes."

At the Rainbow, fans in the stalls rushed to the front of stage out of control. Hanlon became embroiled in a major row with a police inspector who wanted to stop the show. "I was telling her how stupid that would be because she'd have more grief if she stopped the show than if she let it go on," he said.

It was hard to tell what the band was playing through the wall of screams. 'Shang-A-Lang', 'Keep On Dancing', 'All Of Me Loves All Of You', some old favourites from their sixties sets, 'CC Rider', 'Great Balls Of Fire' (sung by Alan), 'Shout', 'Be My Baby' and Wanda Jackson's rockabilly classic 'Let's Have A Party'. It didn't seem to matter. When Faulkner and McKeown faced each other on their knees the roof came off. "Have you ever loved a boy?" teased McKeown. "The little girls wee'd themselves and there were panties here and there and goodness knows what," said Hanlon. Many of the fans were sobbing uncontrollably.

Golumb was on the tour as the band's photographer. "It made for good pictures as well," he said. "I mean I felt sorry for the kids, right at the front of the stage they had these bouncers pulling them out, they were fainting, pulled out up on to the stage. It was frenetic. St John Ambulance was there every gig, out in the corridors they were so busy. The kids just got so overwhelmed by the whole thing. The fan mail used to come in by the sackfuls. When I went to the theatre sometimes the girls would hand me teddy bears to give to the boys and cards… each theatre there'd be bag loads of stuff."

At the Rainbow show, McKeown led a sing-a-long of 'Happy Birthday' as it was Faulkner's 'nineteenth birthday' the next day. He would actually be 21. Up in Prestonpans the fan club received 25,000 letters and 5,000 parcels addressed to Faulkner for the birthday. It took two GP vans to deliver them. Some birthday cards were over six feet tall. He was sent gold rings, silver bracelets and toys. "His looks have generated the biggest fan mail, and one look at the audience tells you Eric is the favourite," *Melody Maker* had noted. Valentine's Day was always another bumper post. On stage, at the Rainbow there were 11 large teddy bears, Roller scarves, rosettes, knickers inscribed with sexual suggestions, small teddies dressed in scarves. At other shows the band were hit in the face by jewellery. The band's 60-minute set also saw Alan play an accordion on Dylan's 'The Times They Are A-Changin''. Faulkner seemed to think album tracks such as the unbelievably soppy 'Just A Little Love' and 'Angel Angel' "go better than the singles". Although "'The Bump' gets them going as well," he said.

The reviews were histrionic. 'Rampant Rollers in London' reckoned *Record Mirror* who had "never seen anything like it", writing of a mania "beyond the Osmonds or Glitter". To the delight of Walsh, the *Daily Mirror* devoted an entire page to the gig, flagging it on their front page. Walsh was friendly with the paper's showbiz editor Pat Doncaster and "the chief photographer Kent Gavin was hot for exclusive Rollers photos which I arranged", said Walsh. "The photographer David Golumb had an arrangement with Tam at that time and he did all the photography and he farmed out his pictures. The only time they did decent photography other than with this guy was when I set it up with the *Daily Mirror*. To make page one of the paper was a real coup at the time. Once the national papers switched on to it, it was a matter of servicing them rather than going to them to try and get publicity for the band. The *Daily Mirror* switched onto The Bay City Rollers very early on and in a big way. I did quite a lot of things with the *Mirror* and the band."

"It was sheer excitement being at the centre of such hysteria," said Wood. "You just had to lift your hand on stage and instantly 2,000 girls would go berserk. That felt amazing. But it used to get real crazy when we'd be trying to escape from a venue."

"The Rollers travelled around in a big American station wagon with Tam driving," said Hanlon. "Artists Services had a VW van with mesh over the windows and a sliding side door and a big foam mattress on the floor. The emergency exits at the venues are always set back three or four feet so nobody can stop the fire exits opening by parking a car or putting something solid outside. Artists Services would park the van right up to the exit doors, so nobody could get between the wall and the van, slide the door and the lads used to get hold of the band, sometimes by the scruff of the neck or the seat of the pants and sling them onto the foam and they're away. It was always chaotic."

Faulkner recalled an event that left him terrified when the wheel of the van came off while leaving the venue. The van was quickly surrounded by screaming fans. They had to jump out and get a taxi with girls chasing them. "They are so excited they don't know their own strength and it's dangerous," he said. "I had the shirt, trousers, shoes and socks literally ripped off me by crowds of girls," said Alan. "It could be bloody frightening. People would go mad. We'd have to stop concerts mid-flow because things got too dangerous. We were frightened that someone would be killed." All the band members kept a look out from the stage for girls who were being crushed or had fallen or fainted.

They sometimes played two shows a day. At the Edinburgh Odeon, for instance, there was an early evening show and one slightly later. Both had to be stopped by Hanlon until calm was restored. The stewards were often inadequate. "You couldn't call them bouncers," he said. "Some of them were OAPs." He was forced to hire outside help to help corral the stewards and patrol the crowd. He preferred firemen. "They are fit and trained in first aid," Hanlon said. "And most firemen are good human beings, used to life and death situations and caring for people under extreme distress." In Edinburgh 35 of them earned £50 each a show. They couldn't stop the front rows of seats being destroyed by the fans. "Our damages bill was extraordinary on that tour," said Hanlon. "They all moved forward and flattened the seats... and the seats were all 30 or 40 years old. The concert halls were all oldish places, so most of them got a new set of front stalls out of me." Twelve girls fainted in Edinburgh and more pretended they had. They would leap up and try and touch the band once they had been dragged out of the crowd and onto the stage.

"At the concerts I was more concerned that nobody got crushed and killed," said Hanlon. "I had a major job every day dealing with the police who were concerned about the hysteria and then the press got on it, following us everywhere, counting how many girls were taken to hospital or how many girls had fainted. We used to get an injury report after every gig... and I'd write it down every night.

"I had to try and guide the Rollers to not create any trouble or get into situations we couldn't handle with the security we had," Hanlon said. "I was very careful because ultimately I'd signed the contract with the theatre and I was responsible for everything. If someone breaks a washbasin in the ladies toilet I get the bill for it. If somebody gets hurt then my insurance and the theatre's insurance argue who will pay for it – the boring part of putting on concerts. I signed the contracts and I was liable for everybody, I had duty of care to the public and the public on those shows did not want to be cared for. It was scary, it was terrifying. It was just me... there were no mobile phones. I used to have a bag of coins to pump into a call box to phone the office in London."

Hanlon was forced to hire his own security to travel with him, three club bouncers from Glasgow. "It was a life-threatening situation... very stressful. The lead guy was Bobby Preston, Black Bob as he was known, a champion weightlifter. They didn't drink, my Scottish guys. They were fit as fiddles. If we had firemen or stewards Bob would organise them and he would stand at the front centre stage and when the crush came down he was like a radar dish and if he saw a head disappear he was strong enough to push his way through and grab the little girl who'd gone down or fainted and drag them out. He'd get hold of her round her waist and carry her out, arms above his head, and put her on the side of the stage where the St John would pick them up. It was scary and you were playing with very young kids, who'd probably never been to a concert before and never been let out on their own before in a lot of instances."

Two anxious fathers and one mother arrived in Edinburgh, up from London, searching for their daughters who had run away to see The Bay City Rollers.

The fans found ways to try and meet the group. One guy was found in a cupboard in Aberdeen dressed in a lookalike uniform. Two girls were found hiding under a stage. When these fans came face to face with the band, they would often break down in hysterics. Paton orchestrated such meetings, usually in front of the press, and other minor publicity stunts to keep the band in the news. No photographs were permitted unless they were wearing stage gear. They grabbed headlines visiting a fan in hospital who had been knocked down and was unable to attend any dates on the tour. McKeown said Paton usually brought young boys backstage to meet the group. "He'd say, 'Be nice to them' or 'You might need these one day,'" McKeown said.

After the shows, Hanlon stayed behind to count the broken seats "because a lot of theatre managers would exaggerate the numbers," he said. Hanlon would not see the band until the next show. "They were scooped away and locked up in their rooms every night," he said. "They had security in their hotels making sure they didn't come out of their rooms."

"After the gigs they vanished to a hotel," said PR Walsh. "And they'd have two to a room, twin rooms. For some reason they seemed to favour the Holiday Inns."

"Tam was like a mother hen, he used to hide them all away," said Hanlon. "I didn't know if Woody could talk, he was very shy. It wasn't like most tours where you finished and went back to the hotel and go down the bar and everybody's there having a few drinks before they go to bed. You never saw the Rollers. Most of the time they weren't even in the same town as the rest of the tour personnel because they had this thing of staying in hotels 10 or 20 miles away so nobody would know they were there.

"Tam was always a bit iffy. He had five young boys and he kept them tightly on a leash. They never walked out on their own. He'd say, 'Right boys we'll get in the car now' and they'd all get in the car. They weren't allowed to drink beer, they weren't allowed to do anything. Even if we were in the same hotel, which happened sometimes, you never saw them. They went to their room, they were locked in their room and they came out the next day when you had to get in the car and drive in the next town."

"There were subplots," added Hanlon. "Apparently some of the band were Tam's boys sort of things. There was a gay subplot going on pop music, TV and radio, a fair proportion working in those industries were homosexual. There was a whiff of it round the Rollers but you'd have to be relatively sophisticated to smell it."

The band still shared rooms and the members never had the same roommate two nights running. "The unlucky fifth one had to share with Tam," said McKeown, who maintains that despite being cooped up together the band were not close. He said the only band member he had a "real conversation" with was Alan. Wood and Faulkner, he said, were "joined at the hip" and "mutually and exclusively best buddies". McKeown sensed "something odd" was going on, that there was a "secret everyone knew about but me. It was like they'd all had their initiation."

McKeown found the group's obedience toward Paton's wishes astonishing. "His size and strength played a big part," he said. Paton had been known to kick down doors when he lost his temper. The Rollers also heard the stories about him killing a man, or men in this instance, while in the army in Cyprus. He patrolled their hotel rooms at night and would routinely check their rooms when they were out.

"Paton was constantly, constantly, constantly ramming the concept that women were dirty fish, dirty, smelly fish, you don't want any of them, you want to be one of the boys," said McKeown. "He'd say,

'Look at all these people who are successful and gay', and he'd say, that's how you do it in this business blah blah blah, that's how you get good proper friends... In one way what he said was kind of true; if you toe the line you reap the benefits."

They were now reputedly paid £20,000 a night for shows. Hanlon took a percentage of their net after paying for advertising, hall rental and other expenses. "It was 90/10 or 85/15 in their favour," he said. "The venue rental was roughly 30 per cent of the box office take and then you had extras, not too many with the Rollers, broken seats, extra security, advertising. You didn't need a lot of advertising but we used to do big ads at the beginning of the tour for people's egos and so the business knew what was going on. You could say 40 per cent of the box office went on all that. Then the group would have the cost of driving round, hotels. When you're getting down to a net it's something around 50 per cent of the take to split between the promoter and the group.

The Rollers played Manchester the same night as David Essex, who had the best-selling single of 1974 with 'Gonna Make You A Star' but he was forced to cancel one of his two proposed shows. The hot ticket was for the King's Hall, inside Belle Vue amusement park. Prices were £15, £10 and £5. It was the largest capacity venue on the Rollers tour, about 3,900, also used as a boxing arena, shaped like a big bowl. It was the biggest gross on the tour as well at just over £40,000. Net would have been £20,000. The whole tour, not including merchandising, would have netted about £400,000. Paton also had the band advertising Gale's honey, peanut butter and lemon curd. Gale was the UK's biggest manufacturer of honey, and the band held out Gale pots gormlessly in the ads.

The tour also boosted sales of the *Rollin'* album, now selling 75,000 copies per week, while the fan club was now routinely getting 5,000 pieces of mail a day. "Half of them are marriage proposals," said Faulkner. "The other day Woody got a letter from a seven year old enquiring if he was married." Paton would use the fan club to control the band members, often intimating someone might need replacing as they weren't getting much mail that week. "He might say, 'Derek you're not very popular right now, you'll need to be extra-friendly to me – sorry! – the fans,'" said McKeown. "The implication was clear – toe the line or there's plenty more where you came from."

It also generated more press coverage. At the start of November they were on the cover of *Record Mirror*, the first stage shot of the band in their new 'stage overalls'. Over time the costumes would become less primitive, more stylish, but the effect was instant. It was an unbelievably strong look even though only Alan's outfit was white. Derek wore black, Faulkner and McKeown blue denim while Wood was in red. Faulkner accessorised his uniform with a number of badges, a recurring motif for the future, most significantly a large smiley face one. They were still wearing platforms.

Girls had started turning up at the gigs in imitations of the uniform. It was easy to copy with just a ribbon of tartan sewn onto a pair of jeans or jacket. If they wanted to go one step further, there was soon to be the Rollers 'own boutique' where fans could buy T-shirts and 'Rollers socks' and approximations of all the Rollers clothing. The real name for the trousers was apparently 'Short Bags'. It was a postal boutique and it was unclear who was running the mail order business and where the money was going. It seemed likely Paton and Perkins had taken a back-hander to allow an enterprising soul to crack on. It was all good promotion.

Walsh had *Sounds* review a date on the tour at Lewisham in south-east London. The rock weekly devoted a page to the Rollers and said the gig really started as soon as the fans arrived. It was a spectacle. The band was again forced off by Hanlon to calm the crowd. Eager was wheeled on to ask everyone to stay calm. Back on stage Faulkner and McKeown knelt and faced each other, bumping into one another gently. There were more damaged seats. McKeown told the crowd: "I think all you girls are beautiful."

"Les is a fantastic frontman," said Hanlon. "I compare him to Rod Stewart: the consummate rock star [Hanlon spent nine years as Stewart's European agent] who knows exactly what he's doing in each microsecond of his performance – he knows how to get a crowd going, where to stand, when to go hard or when to go soft. And Les had the same instinctive ability, he wasn't as refined or sophisticated as Rod but he was a great frontman, it was natural to him. Eric was an okay guitarist and the rest of them were just very average."

Walsh took *NME* to meet the band at the Holiday Inn in Slough, a hotel 20 miles from the centre of London and close to the M25 and Heathrow that had become a Southern base for them. "They didn't live in any kind of luxury," said Tony Roberts, the head of Arista UK who was forced to visit Slough for a meeting. He drove there in his Rolls-Royce. "Most of the bands I met had floors of suites in hotels and were guzzling Dom Perignon but these guys were all huddled up in these pissy little rooms in the Holiday Inn. And sharing rooms. Bizarre. I was used to staying in the [five-star] Four Seasons [and the] George V in Paris."

"Tam found it a lot cheaper than staying in central London," said Walsh. "Mentally they were never stars, they were always just the little kids that were being looked after by Tam and completely controlled by Tam."

Paton sat in on all band interviews. The *NME* one did not go well. Faulkner had been handling much of the press on the tour but this time it was 18-year-old McKeown. *NME* described how Paton controlled the group and mocked the singer who wasn't "allowed a girlfriend because it would spoil the image of the band". They said Paton was denying McKeown the right to say what he really thought. McKeown was peddling Paton's lines about the band being anti-heavy music and anti the "intellectual thing", and how he just wanted to "entertain" the fans – although he preferred to think of them as "friends".

"How this guy is reciting all this crap about entertainment… he must be daft if he buys all this shit," said *NME*.

Paton tried to suggest that his favourite music was psychedelic rock by claiming to have managed Writing On The Wall who had formed out of Edinburgh act, The Jury, and he bristled at *NME*'s suggestion that the Rollers were superficial. "But isn't that pop, how a person looks?" he said. "When there's so much trouble, terrorists blowing up things, kids want to be entertained, to be happy. They want to go to a concert where they can scream, wet their knickers and have a great time. Isn't that what music's really about?"

"Surely there's nothing wrong with being in love and these kids are in love with the Rollers," he added.

Afterward he was not happy. "The *NME* make me so angry," he said. "They reckon they're so bloody intellectual but underneath it all they don't know a blessed thing about music." There were no more *NME* interviews and Paton banned the group from reading it.

The pop press was easier to deal with. For *Jackie*, the magazine that outsold all the music weeklies added together, Golumb photographed them on roller skates. *Record Mirror* did not call Faulkner out when he declared: "We just like to think of ourselves as entertainers – that's the name of the game." The magazine put the band on their cover again at the end of November. There was mention that Paton "forbids" them to mix with girls, however. "We try not to think about them as long as we're busy it takes our mind off other things," said Faulkner. The question about girls would come at them again and again during interviews Walsh organised. Faulkner became adept. His textbook response was: "No, unfortunately... we just haven't got time, we're always working and touring so it wouldn't be fair to ask a girl to put up with that kind of thing. Of course we all want to settle down eventually."

An idea was put to Paton that would help the band circumvent any misinterpretation of their agenda by the media. They should have their own magazine. "If you can sell 100,000 or 200,000 once a month there's good money to be made," said PR Walsh. "It was also a time when artists did not want, or did not ask for, a percentage of the cover price."

Walsh was not involved in the creation or the publication of *The Official Bay City Rollers* magazine. Issue number one would debut in December 1974 and the glossy colour magazine would run until 1978, in total publishing 43 copies. The cover price started at £2, high compared to the pop press at the time that generally sold for between 50 and 80p an issue. The editor was named as Andy Macdonald but Walsh suggested this was a pseudonym. The magazine was anodyne stuff, packed initially with Golumb photographs. With Christmas coming the band were done up as choirboys. If it was not a group shot, the band took it in turns as the individual cover star.

The text inside peddled endless propaganda and lies, rewriting the band's history. "Crammed full of bullshit," said McKeown. It virtually deified Paton, "the sixth Roller" who featured regularly in the magazine and was often cited as the reason for the band's success. He was more than a manager, he was "their friend" who had "nursed and groomed them with care" and "slept in the back of the van with them". Much was made of how "canny with money" he was. There was a constant running of lists of 'likes': The Osmonds, Bowie, Cassidy, Stevie Wonder, Roxy Music… Faulkner wanted to write a number one, McKeown was crazy for fast cars, Derek loved animals, Woody wanted to make people happy and Alan, the countryside one, liked fishing, walking and horses.

There were also "facts" about the band such as detail about their haircuts, called 'Tufties'. Faulkner had a "100 per cent tufty". McKeown had "Tufty brushed back". The Longmuir brothers had "50 per cent tufties". Wood had "almost but not quite the same" as Faulkner.

The main attraction of the magazine to fans was new and exclusive photographs. The production office was in London and the monthly, with low production costs and high sales, would soon be earning a small fortune. It seems unclear if the band profited although almost certainly Paton and Perkins, who made the deal, did.

Inside the Rollers, or someone pretending to be them, wrote regular messages to fans while they "lay in bed with a glass of milk". The magazine also printed lyrics, fan letters and soft focus, fairy tale stories about the band members. McKeown, a talented sculptor apparently, might pursue a career in films. Wood cried for hours when he found out Santa didn't exist. Girls, aged 13, wrote poems declaring their love. "I would do anything for them," one wrote. "Kiss them, hug them and wouldn't you like to know what I'd do!" There were even sexual overtones from letters printed in the magazine from 11-year-old fans.

The band stayed in the womb of their Slough Holiday Inn refuge, with Paton their umbilical cord to the real world. Golumb hired a film projector and films to help them to relax. During a day off on the tour Paton had walked with them from the Mayfair offices of Arista to the Odeon cinema in Leicester Square to see a film. Dressed in their costumes, they soon attracted a swarm of girls. "They called me a poof because I wouldn't let them near the boys," said Paton. He wanted more of this. David Cassidy and The Osmonds were surrounded by fans wherever they went.

"Teenagers were rebellious," said Hanlon. "Respect for anyone elder didn't count for anything. Young kids were throwing themselves at pop artists. They were climbing up drainpipes to get into their rooms. Inhibitions were put to one side, kids had a more aggressive attitude. The girls were throwing themselves at anyone in a group... it happened... and a lot of times if you were a famous pop star it was a job to keep them off."

In mid-tour the Rollers made their first appearance on London Weekend Television's Saturday morning kids TV show, *London Bridge*. They appeared on a segment of the show called Saturday Scene, which featured pop star interviews and various promo performances. Head of Promotion at Arista UK, David Bridger, was regular face on Saturday Scene interviewing bands. At LWT, Paton made contact with Mike Mansfield, who was involved in the show and about to start his own stand-alone pop programme for LWT.

A crowd of fans at the front gate forced the band to climb in over the walls of the studio on London's South Bank by the Thames. Derek was interviewed alone by Saturday Scene's young female host Sally James. Paton did not like the band being interviewed by females and generally prohibited it. Afterwards, they had to leave the studio with a police escort in a van with bars on the windows.

Back in Edinburgh, Faulkner found his flat besieged. He decided to start looking for a "cottage on the outskirts of the city". He said he was also looking for a place "down south" so he didn't have to use hotels. "It is impossible to go out," said Wood. "If we want something from the shops we have to send someone out to get it." The normal scenario, he explained, would start with four or five girls following him and build to about 100.

None of the band had invested any money in new homes. They were now on a wage of approximately £300 a week. "Money doesn't seem to worry them which is quite strange," said Paton. They appeared happy enough with their newly bought stereos. Only McKeown had a car. He had splashed out, investing in a second-hand electric blue Ford Mustang with wide wheels which cost £25,000 and, he bragged, could travel at 160 miles an hour. "I feel like I'm flying, it goes so fast," he told girls magazine *Pink* just after he bought it. "I love speed, the thrill of going 100 mph… anything with a bit of rush to it." Paton spent £50,000 on a new "large American car" to ferry the band about in.

Alan and Derek were looking for new homes on the outskirts of Edinburgh. Up to 200 girls regularly gathered outside their father's tenement in the city centre, unscrewing the door handle, nameplate and letterbox. The police often had to move them on. "We've always had a fan following but never anything as bad as it is now," said Alan. "You couldn't walk the street. They were constantly outside the house screaming and shouting. You never had your own time. We were prisoners of our own success. It was insane. It got scary. I became so fed up and frustrated. I was the oldest in the band by three years and felt I had a life to lead. I had great respect for the fans as they made the band what it was but I yearned for a bit of privacy. I no longer had any control over my life. I got depressed and felt desperate.

"Most of the time all I ever saw was inside a hotel room,' he added. "I used to try to get out by myself to go for a pint – sometimes they didn't recognise you if you were wearing ordinary clothes. They didn't seem to realise that we didn't walk around all the time in baggy tartan trousers and platform shoes." Paton sometimes followed Alan to the pub to spy on him. Alan also went fishing to find some peace. "Sometimes," he said, "I wish it would just all stop."

There was no chance of that. Even before the current UK tour ended Paton was already lining up another one starting in April 1975. He and Perkins were also eyeing up dates in America, Japan and Australia.

Immediately after the exhausting, emotionally draining month long UK tour ended in Plymouth on November 16, there were more dates for the group in Europe. They flew to Belgrade in Yugoslavia to perform on a TV show and at a pop festival. Paton crowed this prompted 7,000 Yugoslavians teens to write letters to the fan club. He was now predicting the Rollers' fan club would be the first in the UK to have 100,000 members. By January 1975, Paton was pleading, to no avail, for fans not to send any more gifts. There was not enough room to store them. Still run by Paton's mother from their Prestonpans home, the club's subscription fee was raised from £2.50 to £3.50. For a time there was a pen pal service in operation, exchanging names and addresses of teen fans.

Germany was believed to be the most serious long-term European territory for the Rollers in terms of record sales and concert dates. They spent a week there in late November with Paton hoping to cram in as many shows, appearances and interviews as possible. As Clive Davis restructured Bell into Arista, the Rollers and all Arista product continued to be distributed by Polydor in Europe.

At the historic Hamburg Musikhalle, capacity 2,000, the gig's 3pm start reflected Polydor's feelings about the age of the Rollers' audience. Sandwiched between gigs there was a visit to a children's theatre where the group and Paton spent time with 40 young stage hopefuls on a double-decker bus. They also visited the Munich office of influential German teen pop magazine *Bravo*, a million-selling but rather strange weekly magazine that ran a popular sex advice column for teenagers and sometimes featured full frontal nudity of teen models while also playing an influential role in promoting pop acts in Germany.

In the UK, the *Rollin'* album was platinum, the seventh best-selling of the year, and all four of the band's 1974 singles were in the year end's top 100 sellers. 'Shang-A-Lang' was the top seller at number 50 and in total the band had sold well over one million singles. They returned to Manchester to film a Christmas edition of *45* for Granada TV. Muriel Young, the show's producer had seen the band develop over the past six months and now witnessed the effect the Rollers had on their fans first-hand. She was 51, with a long career behind her. She had been an actress, children's TV presenter and Radio Luxembourg DJ before moving into production work as head of Granada's children's department. She was married to a TV director but the couple had no children. Paton, who suspected she was gay, became a pal.

The band recorded three songs for the show, 'Angel, Angel', 'Shang-A-Lang' and' Be My Baby'. For one segment of the show they dressed in Catholic choirboy costumes of white smocks, ruffle collars and cassocks.

The special was filmed at the Hardrock concert hall and outside it was overrun with fans. Inside those selected to be in the audience rushed the stage. In total the band had made 22 TV appearances in the UK in 1974 but this was the most significant.

It was their final appearance in ungainly, ugly platform boots and shoes. On December 29, on the front cover of *Record Mirror*, they finally appeared in the Adidas high-top sneakers that completed their iconoclastic look. Wood described them as 'sort of sports shoes', costing £120 a pair. The show also convinced Muriel Young to pursue an idea she had of offering the Rollers their own Granada TV pop show.

Paton was overjoyed. He had been anxious about the recent success of a band called Pilot, formed by former Rollers Billy Lyall and Davie Paton, who had scored a hit in November 1974 with their second single 'Magic', written by Paton and Lyall. They were signed to EMI and 'Magic' sold in excess of one million copies, reaching the top 5 in America and Canada. They followed this with 'January', a song written by David Paton that went to number one in the UK in January 1975 and was also a chart topper in Germany and Australia.

Tam Paton, although enjoying his own success, could not find it in himself to congratulate his former charges. "Good songwriting, no image," he said. "That was the sad thing about it."

It irked him that Pilot had got a number one single before the Rollers. It also cast doubt about his own decision-making, as he'd let David Paton go from the Rollers. After Pilot split in 1977, David Paton would go on to play with the Alan Parsons Project, Camel, Pink Floyd, Kate Bush, Elton John and many others. At the time he said: "I don't know how they'll get on now they've split with the writers [Coulter/Martin]." He suggested they take one of his songs called 'Boys Will Be Boys'.

With their own TV show all but guaranteed, Tam Paton felt certain it was only a matter of time before the Rollers would crush Pilot and the rest of the competition with their own number one single.

CHAPTER 6

Mania

*"Then some MP started to ask questions in the Houses of Parliament...
should The Bay City Rollers be banned from playing live because it's
dangerous to children? I was getting calls from the police. Two days before
the concert the Assistant Chief Constable of that city or town would phone
me up and say, 'What are your plans for getting in and out of our city?'
They'd say, 'Well we'll give you a police escort.' They used to change
traffic lights, clear roads... they'd meet us and insist on giving us the police
escort which was crap because everybody knew who was coming with the
blue lights and two police cars and the VW van in the middle of it."*

– Jef Hanlon

Clive Davis was still in the process of sifting through the Bell acts
to see if he wanted to keep any on Arista. Jef Hanlon, partner
with Gary Glitter's manager/producer/songwriter Mike Leander at
RAM, said Davis ruined Glitter's career. "He insisted on taking him
to New York and making records there and the records never became
hits – Glitter never made it in America." In 1975, after two more
top 10 entries in the UK, Glitter's career went into free-fall. "Clive
is so dominant," said Hanlon. "A heavy duty egotistical maniac sort
of guy."

175

David Cassidy's hits were drying up since he stopped touring and he struggled to make the top 10 in the UK during 1975. Hello scored another big hit single in the UK and Europe with 'New York Groove' but the group had no chance in America, especially under Davis. The one act Davis did seem certain on was Barry Manilow, a gay American singer who had thus far failed to trouble the charts in the UK. That changed with his single 'Mandy' that climbed to number one in America and became his first British hit. Crucially for Davis, Manilow was an act capable of shifting serious quantities of albums in America. His first album for Bell had gone platinum [one million sales] in the country and his just released second album had gone double platinum.

The Rollers were Arista's best-selling UK act. "Gary [Glitter] was also huge but the Rollers were bigger," said Tony Roberts. "What frustrated them all was that nobody could crack it in America." Roberts felt good about the deal that he'd made with Coulter/Martin. Although it had been an expensive goodbye, the 4 per cent record royalties the company now didn't have to pay the pair was stacking up into nice money. He didn't expect the songs they cut for the Rollers to still be selling but he realised that there would be a Greatest Hits album in the not too distant future and there was the possibility of the Rollers' hits starting to sell significantly around the world, maybe even in America. The band's 1974 sales had been almost exclusively in the UK.

Also selling well at Arista UK was Showaddywaddy, the Teddy boy revivalists who covered mostly fifties or early sixties hits. They were on a run that would see them score six top 20 hits before the end of 1975. Roberts was friendly with the band's producer Mike Hurst who had produced Cat Stevens early run of hits in the sixties. Roberts considered asking Hurst to step into Coulter/Martin's shoes and produce the Rollers.

Also in the frame for that job was Phil Wainman who had, in partnership with Chinn and Chapman, produced an incredible seven top five records for Sweet dating back to 1971. The group had, however, recently opted to write their own material and was consequently on the slide.

Roberts was close to David Walker who managed Wainman but was worried about choosing either Hurst or Wainman lest it be interpreted as "giving a job to my mates; the old boys' act". In the end he chose Wainman. "My choice, my decision… it was a good decision," he said. Roberts also brought in Colin Frechter as musical director on the project. Frechter, in his early thirties, had been musical director on the Troggs' run of sixties hits.

Roberts had a reputation for being ultra-straight in business – *too* straight I was told by one industry insider. "There was nothing sneaky or underhand about the books in England," he said. "I was as honest as the day is long. Lot of people said to me what a bloody idiot I was." He had a low opinion of Perkins and Paton. "Dreadful, awful men. Tam was always very nice to me, polite and courteous. But I knew what they were. Why Tam needed Barry I have no idea. I never trusted either of them… at all."

Roberts was in no doubt about Paton's sexual relationship with certain band members. "I thought some of them were gay," he said. "I heard so many rumours about them… but that was an era of a lot of fairly repulsive people. Everybody knew about Savile, everybody knew about Jonathan King and everybody knew about Tam Paton. People put two and two together … without really having any evidence or proof. The whole thing was pretty sleazy, in fact a lot of the acts were pretty sleazy.

"The girls themselves weren't entirely innocent,' Roberts added. "They used to throw themselves at the bands. I was offered all kinds of sexual favours by very young girls when I was running around with the Rollers and David Cassidy and Gary Glitter."

The Sweet had played at Phil Wainman's wedding in 1969 when David Walker was his best man. Walker had recently helped Wainman disentangle his relationship with the band and Chinn and Chapman and was looking for a new project for the producer. There was strong interest from Mud, Chinn and Chapman's other main act. The band was planning to leave the songwriters/producers and their record label, RAK, after seven top 10 singles including three number ones since 1973.

Wainman had put together Sweet's early singles with session musicians, among them himself. "I played with a few of my mates and we put the tracks down and the boys came in and sang," he said. He was 28, and had a fine pedigree as a drummer in a number of sixties bands, including The Paramounts who became Procol Harum. He had also drummed for Jimmy Cliff. Although Chinn/Chapman songs dominated Sweet's oeuvre, Wainman co-wrote songs as well as produced, notably 'Little Games' for The Yardbirds.

After Roberts approached Walker, Wainman met Perkins. "A funny fella," he said. "Used to do all Tam's running around." He then flew up to Edinburgh to meet the band and Paton. He bought a tartan bow tie to break the ice. "They had a huge following so I thought I just have to make good commercial records and we're away," he said. "The work had been done – not by me. I was following a number one [album]."

Watching the Rollers play a couple of songs in an Edinburgh studio/rehearsal space, Wainman started to realise the difficulties he might face by taking the job on. It had been stipulated to him that the band must play on any forthcoming records. There was fear that if it leaked how their previous hits had been made, and there were already strong rumours swirling around the industry, it could potentially derail the band. There was a suggestion that radio might abandon them.

"They couldn't play," said Wainman. "Getting them in tune and to play together, to look at one another while they played, to play as a band was going to be tough. Their strengths were not in singing and not in playing but they looked great."

Wainman took the job in return for a 2 per cent royalty. "Initially they were very tough to work with," he said. "Very tough. I had to rehearse them and rehearse them and rehearse them before we went into the studio." The rehearsals took place at Slough Holiday Inn. "One of their favourite haunts," said Wainman.

In the ever-helpful *Record Mirror*, the issue dated January 18, 1975, Paton announced that the band was going to do their own TV series with few further details. He also broke the news that they had split with Coulter/Martin. "There's no animosity," said Paton. "It's all been very nice but it's like everything else one must move on. That is all it is. A lot of people thought there was a lot of aggravation but there was absolutely nothing. It was a friendly parting."

"We're grateful for everything they have done for us, we learnt such a lot from them," added Faulkner. "We're still good friends."

"Everyone in the music industry went into a bit of a shock when they heard the Rollers split with Coulter/Martin," admitted Paton. He was waiting for the collaboration with Wainman to produce some results before publicly announcing that the Rollers had not played on their past hits.

Wainman took the band to record at the residential Chipping Norton studios in Oxfordshire, a converted old manor house. Booked in initially for four weeks, they would stay for six, recording enough material for almost two albums. "The boys stayed at the studio and I booked myself into a little local hotel. I didn't want to get involved in any of the shenanigans, the dilly-dallying. The first thing they did when they got to the studio was to try and take my trousers down. I had the record company on the phone saying, 'Has anyone made a pass at you yet?' I said, 'Well they've tried to take my trousers down if that's what you mean' and they were falling about laughing. They didn't hide the fact that stuff was going on. Tam even flattered me. I told him I was very happily married and maybe he should look elsewhere… he was outside my hotel door for half an hour talking deep and meaningful to me."

Wainman also said Paton beat the band up while he recorded them. Faulkner, Wood and McKeown were both just over five foot seven and lightweight, the Longmuirs not much bigger. "Unfortunately the boys used to come in bruised when Tam was around," Wainman told me. "He did bash them about. I didn't get involved in any of that… it was just very sad, very sad. I was upset when I'd see a couple of the boys come in black and blue but it was only when Tam was around. I'd say, 'How did that happen?' and they didn't want to tell me and I didn't really want to hear it but I had to show concern because it was quite obvious. If someone comes in with a black eye or a scratched face, you know what's going on but they didn't want to discuss it and I'm glad they didn't because I didn't want to get involved in the politics and open up a whole new can of worms."

Wainman had enough to occupy himself getting the band to play on their own records, especially on the songs they had written themselves. "I taught them how to play drums," he said. "I taught them how to play guitar and we just worked stuff out. It was a crash course. They were so willing to learn. They wanted it. They were desperate to be good. The deal was that they played on the songs. My brief was: they had to play. And the records took three or four times as long as they should have done, to actually make that real."

He worked the band hard, starting at midday and routinely working through until 4am. "I'd yell at everyone… no-one sleeps while I'm awake," he said. In the studio, Colin Frechter helped the band develop their own songs, played keyboards on them and assisted with all the harmonies. "But the boys did sing and play on everything," said Wainman.

"I was there as a musician," said Frechter whose relationship with the band would continue through their next three albums. "I helped them play the tunes. Phil was the production side and I was the musical direction side. Phil asked me if I'd go in and do a similar job with the Rollers as I had with The Troggs. I'd go down in the studio and coach or drag them through the musical side of it… just generally advise them musically on how to do things. Someone had to put the vocal arrangements together and tell them what to sing… and that was me. The backing vocals ended up being Eric, Woody and me… and occasionally Alan."

Frechter disliked Paton. "He played one guy off against another in the band," he said. "One day he's best friends with one of them and the next day he's best friends with another." Sometimes it seemed sexual to Frechter, who claimed he reacted strongly to the approach. "Nobody approached me again and I became a mate. I was married, had kids. I was aware some of them played silly buggers. I know they were locked up in hotels and virtually never saw the light of day.

"Paton was a very strange guy,' Frechter added. "I knew what the situation was but I wasn't prepared to get involved in it. Tam was a Svengali. They were his boys. Derek was a very gentle guy, I presumed he was gay, a nice fella. With Woody, Eric and Les… a lot of young people do that – they play around before deciding which way they're going to jump. That was my impression."

Frechter played keyboards in a band called Big John's Rock'n'Roll Circus with singer John Goodison, a project Wainman and Goodison had developed for the songs they wrote together. Wainman used some of these songs on the Rollers' album including a couple of tracks, 'When Will You Be Mine?' and 'Rock And Roll Honeymoon' that Big John's Rock'n'Roll Circus had already cut. "The tracks were already down and it saved us a load of time," said Wainman. "I brought the multi-tracks down to Chipping Norton and they put the voices on. There was a Bay City Roller vocal sound so we weren't going to mess with that but the rhythm section... yeah, it was easier [if the tracks were already made]."

Alan was supposedly the singer on 'Rock And Roll Honeymoon' but it didn't sound much like him. "No, don't think it was," said Frechter. "I sang on virtually everything, simply because we'd have still been there doing it if I hadn't. Woody was quite good, the best technical musician of the lot, the best musical person. Eric was the one with the most ideas but he wasn't as good a player. Les was good... he was very young and I don't think he realised how good he was. He sang the songs for Phil and Bill but I don't think they got anything special out of him... with us Phil was quite careful how the voice went on."

McKeown said he hated recording with Wainman for that reason. "He'd run the track, first couple of words would come up, he'd stop the track, and make me do it again," said McKeown. And again. And again. "The control room was about 19 feet up and you're down here [in the live room], feeling very small. It was fucking so annoying, I blew my top loads of times."

Some of the songs Faulkner and Wood had written for the album were unoriginal but at least they more sophisticated than those they'd contributed to the debut album. What would become the title track, 'Once Upon A Star', had lyrics contemplating stardom and 'Hey! Beautiful Dreamer' sounded very trippy in a Beatle-esque way. "At that time The Beatles was one of the main influence we had," said Frechter.

"The band was writing songs that leaned that way a little bit and that's kind of what we were after."

With Coulter/Martin out of the way Paton also wanted to contribute. He had the band record 'Keep On Dancing', their 1971 breakthrough hit, for the album. He also suggested they cut 'Bye Bye Baby', a song that had been in the Rollers' set for almost a decade. Paton did not play Wainman the original version of the song, recorded by The Four Seasons in 1965, as a guide but a cover version by British group The Symbols made in 1967 that had not made the top 40. "It was actually a better version than The Four Seasons in a way," said Wainman. "The harmonies on it and the whole thing were terrific. Tam played me that and said, 'I think this is a hit, Phil.' And I said, 'I think it's a number one. But we're going to have a hell of a job making it with the boys.'"

"When we came to doing the choruses and the counter melodies and the counter-counter melodies of 'Bye Bye Baby' we only did one chorus," said Wainman. "And we then used a very primitive way of spinning in the choruses [repeating the one recorded chorus throughout the song] otherwise I'd have still been making that record to this very day. It was like a cheat, a way of getting there quicker."

Another major song cut during this stay at Chipping Norton was 'Give A Little Love', also a future single. "Something I wrote with John Goodison," said Wainman. "We wrote it for the girls. Mud heard it and wanted it. I said, 'You can't because we've already recorded it with the Rollers. We'll write something especially for you, a more adult version', and we did 'Show Me You're A Woman'." Wainman produced an album with Mud after the session with the Rollers. 'Show Me You're A Woman' was a top 10 hit for the band in late 1975.

"I recorded and mixed 'Bye Bye Baby' and 'Give A Little Love' together," said Wainman. "The record company was delighted when I gave them those tracks. I said, 'I think I've got single number one and single number two and to me they both sound like numbers ones.' If you go with 'Bye Bye Baby' first you have to follow it with a record that crosses over, one that becomes a mums and dads type record. Mums and dads would buy it for the little girls and it was something you could wave a scarf to."

Roberts was astounded by these two tracks and would base the next stage of the Rollers career around them. "I think we worked wonders with a band who could barely play," said Wainman. "Tony couldn't believe it was possible."

Word had leaked that the Rollers were in Chipping Norton, apparently via a lady in the fish shop up the road. "There was a garden full of kids camping outside," said Frechter. "They camped there for the best part of six weeks. We asked, 'Do your parents know where you are?' They said, 'Oh no, they're all right.' A couple of kids came up from Southampton. They wanted anything the Rollers had got. Some of the band smoked and they wanted a fag end. We went in the studio one day to find a couple of kids had got into the toilet."

"Word got out and there were busloads… there were girls absolutely everywhere," said Wainman. "I used to take them out bottles of milk."

The band took time out from recording to attend the Carl Alan Awards at the Lyceum Ballroom on the Strand in London. They spent time getting measured up for new uniforms and relaxing, swimming and in the sauna, at the Slough Holiday Inn. Paton, 36, was sharing a room with Wood.

The annual Carl Alan Awards were not band orientated and honoured acts that had made a significant contribution to the dance and theatre industry, like dancers and choreographers. Mecca, which once owned the most extensive network of dance halls and entertainment venues in Britain, presented the awards that were named after the company's joint Chairmen, Carl Heimann and Alan Fairley. Royalty general handed out the gongs, and The Beatles had picked up awards in 1964 and 1965.

On January 29, 1975 the Rollers collected their golden statuette for an 'outstanding contribution' to the Ballroom Dancing Industry, presumably for the gigs they'd played at various Meccas in 1974. The awards were handed out by Princess Anne. "It was the biggest thrill of my life," said Derek. She enquired about the Rollers' short trousers. Faulkner said they'd bought them on the 'never never' and that was why they were so short. When the band had paid all the instalments they hoped their trousers would be full length.

'Bye Bye Baby', with a Faulkner/Wood song on the B-side, was scheduled for release on February 28 and filming of the band's own Granada TV show was due to begin at the start of March. As the extended recording session with Wainman wound down, with enough basic material recorded to fill two albums, the group and Paton found time to go shopping for houses. McKeown bought a £375,000 modernist pile in Edinburgh where he lived upstairs and his family downstairs; "A big house so we can all live together," he said. Alan bought what he called "a little cottage" just outside Edinburgh. It was later revealed to be on 15 acres of ground with its own section of river and a stable full of horses. Faulkner bought a remote Scottish cottage at a "secret location", miles from the nearest shops, costing around £43,000 (£400,000 today) and was said to include 50 acres of land, and he was also said to have bought his parents a new home. Paton found Little Kellerstain, a secluded ranch-style compound in rural Gogar, five miles west of Edinburgh city centre on Scotland's east coast, newly built and costing £29,000 (£275,000 today). Derek bought an "amazing ultra-modern bungalow" that cost, like McKeown's pile, today's equivalent of £375,000. "It's somewhere in Fife," he said. "But I have not had time to sleep in it yet. Maybe I'll get a couple, of days off sometime and be able to go there and take a really good look around it."

Derek said the band had got "a great deal with an insurance company" that guaranteed them close to £1 million when they reached the age of 40. "We've got an accountant who does the lot for us and we've got different investments and things," he said, referring to Stephen Goldberg. Derek was in charge of the band's cash float of around £2,000, which they all dipped into for day to day expenses. He said the band were still on a wage of around £300 a week. "Well if we got anymore we'd probably just go berserk so we need protecting from ourselves," said Derek, posing now as 19.

"Every penny of the band's mammoth earnings is carefully tucked away by band manager, canny Scot, Paton," wrote the *Edinburgh Evening News*. "He raps their knuckles if he catches them frittering it away on booze and cigs and keeps them too busy to spend it on long-legged blondes."

The Crusaders, 'Scotland's number one band', circa 1959. Tam Paton far right. Note matching tartan jackets with band members' initial on breast. COURTESY OF FRANK CONNER

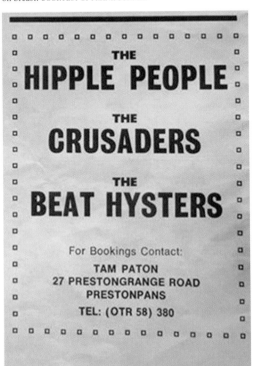

THE
HIPPLE PEOPLE
THE
CRUSADERS
THE
BEAT HYSTERS

For Bookings Contact:
TAM PATON
27 PRESTONGRANGE ROAD
PRESTONPANS
TEL: (OTR 58) 380

Paton advertising his management roster, 1966.
COURTESY OF DAVE VALENTINE

The Hipple People, 1966, resisting Paton's attempts to groom them. COURTESY OF DAVE VALENTINE

INDEX

PERSONAL MANAGEMENT:
TAM PATON
TELEPHONE PRESTONPANS 380

The Index, who alongside the Rollers and The Tandem were one of Paton's three main late sixties acts. The top picture is how they came to him and the bottom picture is after Paton has groomed them. COURTESY OF BILLY McGHEE

Pre-Paton Bay City Rollers, 1965, as The Saxons. Nobby Clark on vocals, Derek on drums, Alan far left. COURTESY OF NOBBY CLARK

The Bay City Rollers, 1969, groomed by Paton. From left, Derek Longmuir, Billy Lyall, Alan Longmuir, Davie Paton and Nobby Clark. Davie Paton and Lyall would soon leave and form hit act Pilot.
COURTESY OF NOBBY CLARK

Transplant magazine, a popular Scottish teenage magazine, features three of Paton's groups in a vote to find the best group in Scotland in 1969. COURTESY OF BILLY McGHEE

WHO ARE THE BEST GROUP IN SCOTLAND?
That was the question we asked last month.
And the answer—as far as September was concerned— is THE POETS. And not far behind them were the Bay City Rollers and Tandem. The full list of the Top Ten is . . .

1—POETS	6—BEGGAR'S OPERA
2—BAY CITY ROLLERS	7—PLATFORM
3—TANDEM	8—DREAM POLICE
4—TEAR GAS	9—KAYWANA STOCK
5—CHRIS McCLURE	10—INDEX

May 1972, appearing on ITV pop show, *Lift Off With Ayshea*, promoting second single 'We Can Make Music'. New additions Neil Henderson (on guitar) and Archie Marr (on keyboard). REX/SHUTTERSTOCK

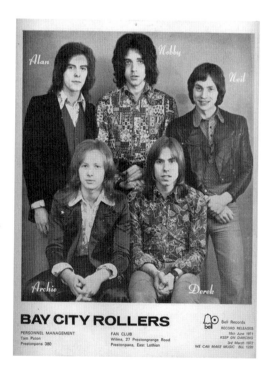

Bell Records publicity shot, 1972. COURTESY OF NOBBY CLARK

March 1974, *Record Mirror*, the band's first front cover. New members John Devine Eric Faulkner and Les McKeown had replaced Henderson and Marr and original singer Nobby Clark.

Promoting third single 'Manana', topless, at the Radio-Tele Luxembourg Grand Prix International in September 1972. An early taste of life in the band for new boys Faulkner (left) and Devine (right).

A short-lived new band image from 1974, orchestrated by producer Bill Martin. New boy Stuart Wood has replaced Devine. From left: Alan, Derek, McKeown, Wood and Faulkner: the famous five.

Threshold, 1973, the Edinburgh band Les McKeown (far left) sang in pre-Rollers. COURTESY OF JON GILLAM

Bilbo Baggins, June 1974. Paton's new Edinburgh act. He would soon have the Rollers adopt the look and Baggins would fade into obscurity.

Advertising Gale's honey, 1974. Paton cashing in on the early hits. DAVID GOLUMB ARCHIVES

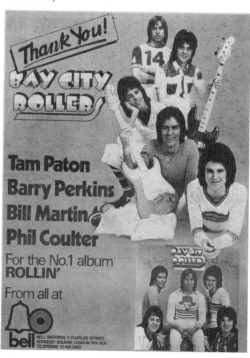

Bell Records advert thanking the band and their managers and producers for their success of the Rollers' debut album, 1974. DAVID GOLUMB ARCHIVES

Among the sacks of potatoes in Tam Paton's infamous potato wagon, 1974. Paton liked to pretend wrestle among the potatoes.
DAVID GOLUMB

The band and Paton in Paton's bedroom/office at his parents home in Prestonpans. Note his hand on McKeown's knee.
DAVID GOLUMB

The pre-tartan Longmuir brothers in Edinburgh. The sartorial influence is Clockwork Orange and Scottish gang culture.
DAVID GOLUMB

McKeown with his mother who he often bragged had knitted his jumpers. DAVID GOLUMB

Paton cancelled a visit to Spain for TV and concerts and a tour of Scandinavia so that Faulkner and Derek, about to turn 24, could spend time at the exclusive Champneys Forest Mere health spa in Hertfordshire. He wanted them to look their best for the TV show and invited the press to meet the pair in these luxury surroundings as promotion for 'Bye Bye Baby' began. Derek also talked up the upcoming spring tour of the UK. He said the two shows booked at Hammersmith Odeon were going to be recorded for "a feature film for the cinema". He said there was "no story line, nobody gets kidnapped, it's just us at the Hammersmith Odeon."

Jimmy Tarbuck was at the health spa alongside Cilla Black's husband, Bobby Willis, and Lady Kilmarnock, former wife of Kingsley Amis. Tony Curtis had once driven a Lamborghini into the lake of the rambling manor estate. Derek and Faulkner stayed for two weeks at a cost of £200 per week (£1,500 today) each. David Golumb took lots of photographs of them enjoying saunas, Faulkner draping his legs over Derek, getting massaged in just small towels, relaxing in bath robes, out horse-riding or boating on the lake.

They got large features out of it in *Record Mirror* – 'Rolling in Health Wealth and Happiness' – and *Melody Maker* plus in girls' magazine *Pink* and in *Music Star*, a colour pop weekly full of pin-ups. Paton, who virtually conducted the interviews himself, told all the journalists how the pressure of "five weeks of recording" had nearly given the band a nervous breakdown. "They were in a virtual state of collapse, a doctor told them you are not physically ill but you have nervous exhaustion and will have to rest," he said.

Paton would soon be writing a pop column for *Disc* in which he declared he "kept the boys away from the girls to preserve their image". "I was trying to guide them one way and maybe I was overpowering," he said. "I never meant to be overpowering, it was all done in the interest of their careers." At Champneys he outlined their daily routines, mentioning a diet of salad and fruit. "The boys are not slimming or anything," he insisted. Faulkner and Derek reiterated how they had finished the new album and had been working "solid" in the studio, recording up until the early hours every day. "The last one got to number one and this one had has just got to be better," said Faulkner.

The pose also gave Paton a chance to show off how clean-cut the band was. He pressed home the line about their abstemiousness. "We pushed the celibacy and non-drinking a lot in the early days," he said. "I made a big point out of it. I tried to turn them out as a nice group, different from the others around at the time."

Wood travelled down for a few days. Paton talked enthusiastically about the lads showering, taking baths where "massaging hydro jets spurt out onto their bodies" and "rub downs". He said he was having hypnosis to help him relax and stop smoking.

McKeown, who did not attend Champneys, outlined what he felt was the real reason for the health spa visit. He said that Derek and Faulkner had "both got overweight – particularly Eric who tends to get fat very easily". He said Faulkner's nickname was the Incredible Bulk. Alan was also absent, apart from one brief photoshoot, at the spa get together. Paton was growing tired of having him in the band. His attitude was wrong and he'd soon be 27. Although he was pretending to be three years younger he looked like a man, especially alongside the others. Alan also liked to drink and hang out with girls. Paton was in Faulkner's ear about replacing Alan.

The Rollers debuted 'Bye Bye Baby' on March 1 on the first pilot episode of Mike Mansfield's new LWT pop show, *Supersonic*, alongside performances by Rod Stewart, Gary Glitter and Alvin Stardust. "When I was with the band the only other person of any great consequence was Mike Mansfield," said Wainman. "I made the aural and he made the visual and together it was special… it was a nice period of pop. Mansfield was very influential. He knew what he was doing in his studio… same as I knew what I was doing in mine."

"Tam didn't make any decisions," added Wainman. "I would work out a timetable with Mansfield. He was instrumental in making the band as successful as they were. Mike and myself used to decide on what the band were doing and then tell Tam. The boys need to do this TV thing there, there and there and I said, 'I've got an album to make and I need this, this and this'. Mike and I would sit down and work it out between us. Mike's contribution was on a par with what I did. Everything they did [on TV] was a spectacle.... Mike stage managed that."

Supersonic would begin airing regularly in September and the Rollers would often feature. Unlike *Top Of The Pops*, which was chart-based, this 30-minute pop show simply offered the best teen acts of the era miming live in front of a young audience. Mansfield presented the acts on screen as well as acting as the show's director and producer.

He would soon be directing *Shang-A-Lang*, the name of The Bay City Rollers' own pop show on Granada, and later in the year would direct the show that introduced the Rollers to America and remains the best example of their working relationship. "There was only BBC and ITV," said Mansfield, explaining the impact these shows would have on the British public. "There was no Channel 4 even. On the radio there was only Radio 1 and Capital Radio (the first London commercial radio station awarded a license), the commercial stations were just starting out. I was director for six shows of *Shang-A-Lang* as a favour to Muriel Young, the wonderful Muriel. They had a lot to thank her for."

Mansfield travelled to Prestonpans to meet Paton and the band. Segments of *Shang-A-Lang* were shot on location, such as on a farm riding on tractors. "I went to the potato factory," said Mansfield. He would soon be employing as his 'second in command' a young Bay City Rollers roadie called Hilary Tipping. Mansfield was pragmatic about Paton. "From the son of potato merchant to being one of the great impresarios in the world is quite an amazing feat," he said.

Mansfield was becoming a flamboyant showbusiness figure. His luxury mansion in Wimbledon was noted for its large sauna in the basement and an enormous living room with white walls, ceiling, curtains and carpet and even a white grand piano in one corner. To top it off he had a white Rolls-Royce. McKeown recalled Mansfield introduced the "bum shot" to *Shang-A-Lang*. "I was never quite sure if that was for his benefit of the audience's," he said.

The band recorded the first batch of *Shang-A-Lang* shows in two busy days in Manchester on March 4 and 5. "They all look very healthy and are beaming with vitality and vibrancy," said Paton. The show ran for

25 minutes with an ad break and the band would shoot, in total, 20 episodes in just two further two-day stints, on April 9 and 10 and May 13 and 14.

The shows were all filmed in a Granada TV studio in front of around 100 screaming teens, all dressed up like the Rollers and clutching tartan scarves and waving banners. The band in a mixture of tartan-trimmed uniforms – Faulkner, McKeown and Wood showing plenty of hairless bare-chest – mimed to three of their songs per episode. The show also featured a special guest act per episode plus more lightweight scenes featuring the band where they got to talk and act up. The Rollers performing was the main draw, always backed by screams from the audience. A wave of the arm from McKeown set off waves of squeals. Although they held onto instruments, it was clear they were nothing but dolls, with no attempt made to conceal they were playing to backing tracks. Nonetheless, the effect was electric and live. They often chugged along with three guitars up front while occasionally a keyboard was wheeled on for Faulkner to bash away on. They were all smiles, projecting a convincing youthful optimism.

Paton said he hoped the show would appeal to boys as well as girls but a planned segment where McKeown would talk cars was dropped. Wood famously played the simpleton, with a huge 'W' on the front of his tiny jumper. Faulkner added multiple badges on his scarves, braces and memorably down the front of his trouser fly. The set was brightly coloured, cheap, with the distinctive cartoon lettering used for the band's promotional items spelling out the title. They, ultimately, came across as genuine, awkward when asked to speak in front of camera. Alongside the now trademark white and tartan get-ups, they were turned out in an array of lurid outfits. There was a lot of a tartan-trimmed banana yellow and putrid pink. They looked outrageous, in their Adidas high tops, scarves, and tartan costumes. The spectacle, including the manic crowd, was a high-water mark for seventies pop.

The first episode was scheduled for Tuesday April 1 at 4.20pm, a timeslot designed to coincide with kids getting home from school. The show would run every week at the same time for 20 weeks with some repeats on various ITV networks. There was a petition raised in

Edinburgh requesting the show be put back to a later slot, for over 16s who might be working, but Granada said the "programme will be of appeal to younger viewers up to the age of 16".

By the first episode, 'Bye Bye Baby' was at number one in the UK charts. BBC Radio 1 was behind it – the band were guests of the Friday evening *Roundtable* show. There was a remarkable run of *Top Of The Pops* performances beginning on March 6 and continuing, weekly, until April 24. The commercial channels also wanted the band: they were interviewed and mobbed at Capital radio and promoted the single on LWT's Mansfield-connected *London Bridge* Saturday morning kids' show for a couple of weeks; one week taking over the entire Saturday Scene segment.

They were an unstoppable force. The *Sunday Times* financial section reported on a shortage of cheap tartan fabric in several cities. Inescapable. Ruffling feathers. Elton John said he was "sick of them being thrust down my throat". 'Bye Bye Baby' stayed at number one for six weeks, selling nearly a million copies in the UK alone – the biggest selling single of 1975. The single went top 10 in Italy, Norway and Germany and top 20 in Holland, Austria and Belgium.

Paton took the opportunity to announce in March that the Rollers hadn't played on any of their previous records. "I wish I could say more," he said. "The whole British recording industry is full of con tricks like this." A spokesman for Arista UK (still routinely referred to as Bell in the UK) said: "It's true. We weren't happy about it but now the boys have proved with 'Bye Bye Baby' that they can do it alone." Paton felt that he'd handled the transition away from Coulter/Martin well.

The band was featured on the cover of popular children's magazine *Look-In* that centred on ITV programmes, as *Shang-A-Lang* started its weekly run. The band would feature on an extended run of these *Look-In* covers, one band member per week, all painted in acrylic by Italian Arnalso Putzo who also painted iconic posters for films such as *Get Carter*.

On the second edition of *Shang-A-Lang* the band previewed three tracks from their upcoming album, now titled *Once Upon A Star*. The packaging was an elaborate fold-out affair but deeply unattractive at first glance. The full-length Golumb shot of the band used on the back cover was strong – they were tightly packed and touching gently crotch to bottom – although only McKeown wore high-top Adidas trainers with the Longmuirs and Wood, a tartan scarf tied round his wrist, in dated platforms. Faulkner wore the popular Grafters Monkey boots of the era. The front cover did not feature the popular cartoon lettering used on the TV show and had a cartoon graphic of the back of a biker – Rollers writ on the back of his jacket – riding into the sun with a seriously inappropriate image of a blonde with huge breasts hanging over the word 'Bay'. Folding back the images of tiny individual headshots poking out on the top of the sleeve revealed five more pages of elaborate design, each featuring a large headshot of a band member.

The only single on the album was 'Bye Bye Baby', the rest was essentially filler, seven of the songs credited to Faulkner/Wood. It didn't matter. Everything was selling.

The band's own magazine was doing tens of thousands of copies per month and heavily promoting every product the band had for sale. *Pink* magazine ran "exclusive pictures" from Paton's "own scrapbook". There were features in a slew of other girls' magazines such as *Mates*, *Tammy*, and *Bunty* and in the new Mansfield-affiliated *Supersonic* magazine, launched before the TV show began regularly. It was all barely believable stuff: cute tales of first dates, stories about Faulkner wolfing an entire chocolate cake sent by fans, or how Alan never does the washing-up or how McKeown once nipped off for a Chinese 20 minutes before a gig.

Tony Roberts at Arista UK was also backing the album with extensive adverts in the music press. *Mirabelle* readers got a special promo disc included in the magazine featuring excerpts from the album and short messages from the Rollers. The band heavily promoted the album on *Shang-A-Lang* and Mike Mansfield ran what was billed as a *Once Upon A Star* half-hour special on a Saturday morning on LWT.

The album was number one by early May and stayed on the charts for 37 weeks, selling over 300,000 copies in the UK alone. It went top five in Australia and top 30 in Japan. Asked about working with Wainman, compared to Coulter/Martin, Faulkner said: "The main difference is that there is a swopping of ideas."

190

Tickets for the UK tour sold out fast. Scenes of hysteria were reported in Scotland around their purchasing. Hundreds of fans brought sleeping bags and queued all day to get tickets for the Glasgow Apollo show that opened the six-week tour on April 27. The band was booked to do two shows, one at 5pm and one at 8pm, meaning 6,200 tickets were available. The police had to be called in to control the queue. Some girls were photographed sobbing as they neared the front. The manager of the venue said the demand meant they could have sold out "for a week" but "we could only get the Rollers for one evening". A second Glasgow date was eventually squeezed into the tour itinerary, as was a second Edinburgh show.

During another couple of days filming *Shang-A-Lang* in Manchester in April, with Cliff Richard as a studio guest, disaster struck. A policeman died soon after controlling Rollers fans. "Trampled policeman dies in pop frenzy" was the *Daily Express* headline over a story about how at a crowd crush in Manchester, a 45-year-old police sergeant died of a heart attack as he tried to hold back hysterical fans.

A 15-year-old Edinburgh teen, Angela Stevenson, helping out at the fan club still based out of Paton's parents' house in Prestonpans, explained how she had travelled down from Edinburgh to Manchester in a bus with associates of the band for the TV show recording. After the show, there were loads of fans outside, screaming for the Rollers she said. "When they spotted Tam's mum in the bus, they were convinced that the Rollers would be there too. We tried to tell them they weren't, but they lunged towards the bus, banging on the windows, one of which shattered. It was really frightening."

It was unclear how the policeman actually died, later reports suggested he'd had a heart attack the day after the incident. Paton offered his widow a ticket to the Glasgow concert that she accepted.

Straight from school until about nine in the evening, and most weekends, Stevenson helped out at the fan club. "Every day for about three years," she said. She would send envelopes stuffed with signed pictures and newsletters. The secretary was still named as Wilma but the membership price was creeping up towards the 50p mark (£5 today). The membership kits included two large posters, six individual postcard-size pictures, an introductory letter, a life-line number and a leaflet enabling fans to obtain Roller souvenirs plus the promise of three newsletters per year and a Christmas card. In charge was Paton's mother Isabella, 70, and her pal, Mary Snedden, 73. The HQ: the shed in Paton's family home's back garden.

The tour schedule swelled to over 36 dates, stopping in 36 towns. Irish dates added prior to Glasgow were treated as a warm-up. Every ticket sold out. Paton said this was last chance to see band "for perhaps a year".

Much to the chagrin of their tour manager Jake Duncan, the Rollers were still rehearsing in the potato shed in Port Seton. Just as the last tour, there was going to be little in the way of stage production. He was tired of Paton's "way of doing things", he said. Duncan quit the set-up. "Tam was too preoccupied with everything that was going on and the success of the band. He was too busy running about all over the place, didn't pay any attention [to the touring mechanics]. I felt I'd been there for a few years and it was time to be paid a little more money. I couldn't get to even talk to him half the time. I got frustrated. The pressure these boys were under, just day to day, was relentless. Just getting from place to place was chaos. Everybody wanted a piece of them. Tam, even with Barry Perkins' help, was finding it difficult to do it all. It was manic, moving at 110mph all the time."

Paton was frantic. He was concerned about the merchandise on this tour after so much "unauthorised" material on the last tour. There was also much Rollers merchandise flooding UK shops. He promised official watches, scarves, caps, socks, T-shirts and posters would soon be available. Add to that: key rings, underwear, pillow cases and curtains, rosettes, mirrors, pendants, handkerchiefs, money boxes and stationary kits.

Artists Services were again being employed to provide protection for the group on the tour and the owner of the company, Don Murfet, had hooked Paton up with Paul Pike, a 27-year-old who now began to handle the band's official merchandise. Pike was also doing The Osmonds' merchandising in conjunction with Murfet. "We had a meeting at Barry Perkins' house in Kent," said Pike. "And we took it over. Tam decided he needed to make some money out of it."

"There was a hell of a lot of touting," said Pike. "My biggest problem was to try and clean up the unofficial merchandising because it was rife and the band weren't earning any money out of that. One major company called Coffer Sports, based in Manchester, had a whole range of stuff they sold outside gigs but their main business was in retail. I went to see them, two lovely blokes, Ronnie and his brother, and said look rather than me start fighting you and getting legal restrictions on you, why don't you just go legal? They credited me with turning their company into a legal organisation. They actually sought licenses. It was the obvious thing to do, they had distribution and were already selling the stuff."

Woolworth's would soon carry a huge stock of Rollers stuff and Pike made a deal with C&A for them to design their own range, including tartan-trimmed trousers called 'Roller Strollers'. Soon there would be jigsaw puzzles, tea towels and even a Rollers board game. "There were a lot of licences out there but there was a sense of product control in the production," said Pike. "Tam had the final say over licensing. We had to run everything past him. I don't think we gave Tam much that he turned down. We used to meet quite often in the Slough Holiday Inn with Tam and Goldberg Ravden. Stephen [Goldberg] was the main guy we dealt with on a licensing basis. We just gave him the royalty figures every quarter. It was up to the licensees to supply us with their royalty statements and pay us and we'd pass it on.

"Normally, under licensing, it's about 12.5 to 15 per cent of the wholesale that went to the band," added Pike. "And we would have taken a percentage of that. We would have probably taken 20 to 25 per cent of the royalties coming to the band."

Adverts appeared in pop magazines like *Record Mirror* for entire Roller outfits, jackets, shirts and trousers, for £100, with various tartan options – Royal Stewart, Dress Stewart, Dress Gordon, Macbeth tartan, Mcleod tartan. There were also adverts advising girls to call a special number for a "personal" message from the band.

Pike set up a mail order company running out of Don Murfet's huge HQ near Pentonville prison in north London. From here Murfet ran myriad operations alongside his security company, including rehearsal space and band travel. It was Murfet who supplied the band with films and full projection equipment to keep them entertained in various Holiday Inns around the country.

The mail order business, FanFare Rollers Ltd, was run in conjunction with the fan club. As soon as it was set up it began receiving 5,000 orders a week on an average spend of £12 each. "We sold what we were selling on tour and some of the licensed stuff," said Pike. "We'd be supplied by the licensees for mail order as well. We would have produced the merchandising for the fan club, any offers Tam put out."

Interviewed by the *Daily Mirror* for an item headlined 'The Price of Teeny Lust', Pike predicted that by the end of 1975, Rollers' merchandise would have generated £9 million in sales. He said FanFare was getting "about seven or eight sackfuls of mail a day". He said the band was on 5 per cent royalty for every article sold. He highlighted the £5.50 jigsaws and said they would sell £750,000 worth of them. Pike told the *Mirror* that the majority of fans were 11–14 but "it doesn't stop there because you find kids of four are being bought things which apply to the Rollers".

"The £9 million I quoted for 1975 was a bit ambitious," Pike told me. "I don't think we did anywhere near that. I was probably bigging it up for the journalist. We only did the UK and a few territories in Europe. I went across to Denmark for a few shows over there and Sweden."

In the UK Pike planned to tow a caravan full of merchandise that he would park outside each venue. "Tam was an interesting character," he said. "He had the band under total control. They didn't do anything without him knowing about it. He was a complete control freak. He was paranoid about any of the guys being seen with girls."

Meanwhile, Barry Perkins was trying to convince Clive Davis that the band had a future in America. Davis was unimpressed by 'Bye Bye Baby' despite its success. He considered The Four Seasons' original a classic and didn't want Arista associated with what he felt was a weak cover version. Davis had been calling contacts in the UK to ask about the band, including Jonathan King. "He asked, 'Could the Rollers happen in the USA?'" said King. "I replied, 'My head says no but my heart says yes'. He said he'd go with my heart. And he has told me many times since it was totally my response that made him work the band."

Davis was finally free from the nightmare that had derailed his life for the past two years. In May 1975 a federal grand jury in Newark had indicted him on the six counts of filing false income tax returns pertaining to his improper CBS expense reimbursements. A jurisdictional call transferred the case to Manhattan, where Davis arranged to plead guilty to a single felony – failing to pay taxes on CBS-financed vacations in 1972. In handing down a fine and a suspended jail term, Federal District Court judge Thomas Griesa excoriated the press for subjecting Davis to "unprecedented... appalling innuendo" and went out of his way to note that the crime was in no way connected to the activities of CBS promotion man David Wynshaw and Patsy Falcone. Wynshaw, described by Paul Simon as "Davis's CBS procurer", pleaded guilty of conspiring with Falcone, an associate of the Genovese family crime syndicate (and manager of Sly Stone and other CBC acts), to defraud CBS up to a reported $2 million by billing for fictitious services performed by equally fictitious companies and was sentenced to a year in jail. Falcone was given a two-year term on the same charges to run concurrently with a ten-year term he'd recently received for heroin smuggling. It would take a further 18 months for Davis to put the last of his troubles behind him by finally settling CBS's civil suit.

Initially, Perkins did not get to see Davis in New York. Carol Klenfner was despatched to meet him. Carol had just started her own PR Agency, CJ Strauss (her maiden name) after years working for one of New York's major rock PR agencies, Gibson and Stromgberg, where she'd handled Elton John, Cat Stevens, The Eagles and The Doors among many others. Already CJ Straus was hooked up with The Who and Davis had used Carol to work on Gary Glitter. Her link to Davis was through her husband, Michael Klenfner, who'd worked for Davis at Columbia Records as director of national promotions. "When Clive was dismissed, Michael was his first hire at Bell Records/Arista (as Head of Promotions)," she said. "As he was setting things up and reorganising the label I was brought on as the firm's PR consultant department in the early months of Arista."

Davis wanted Carol to meet with Perkins to "see if I thought there was anything there to work with", she said. "A lot of Bell acts needed to be sorted through. He looked at their roster and tried to gauge who was worth promoting and who should be left, what was marketable and what wasn't." Perkins was staying at the Plaza Hotel in New York, in "one the smallest rooms, one of the notorious broom closet rooms", said Carol. He had insisted Carol go to his room because he wanted to show her the scrapbooks of newspaper clippings he had brought with him. "The little bed in his little room was covered in these scrapbooks," she said. "There was riots, pandemonium, screaming girls... it was all Rollermania and it was endless and it was very impressive. The band looked anything but generic, they had a unique look and the hysteria was powerful, it said a lot... so I recommended to Clive that we do something with them."

She arranged to take two American journalists, Danny Fields, the editor of the country's best-selling teen magazine *16,* and Lisa Robinson, the editor of *Rock Scene*, a colour monthly that often featured glam English acts such as Bowie, Roxy Music or Slade, to Glasgow to witness the opening show of the Rollers' UK tour. "It was very clear to me that the Rollers were not music for me, my age group," Carol said. "I knew that immediately. I also felt kids 10 or 15 years younger than myself deserved to have the same crazy love experience with a rock'n'roll band as I had had and not everyone was into the Osmond brothers and that kind of bland, homogenised music and look."

The Rollers' warm-up gigs in Ireland were covered in both *Record Mirror* and *Sounds*. The latter put the story on their cover. They played two shows in Dublin on the same evening. Fans unable to get tickets started throwing bottles at the police cordon which led to a baton charge to break-up the crowd. Inside there were 20 broken seats but no injuries, reported *Record Mirror*. The troubles in Northern Ireland continued and the Rollers remained one of the few bands to play Belfast; the gig patrolled by the police and the army.

Supporting the Rollers in Belfast was a local young teen band Young City Stars. They featured on guitar a 16-year-old called Ian Mitchell. They had been going a couple of years and had already supported visiting

UK acts such as Marmalade, Kenny and Smokie. The band had released a single in 1974, a cover version of a David Cassidy song. Their singer, Damian McKee, also 16, one of three brothers [Terry was 14, Colin was 13] in the band, told me: "We were basically a cover band playing the chart hits, Gary Glitter, Mud, Sweet, Suzi Quatro but mostly we were playing Rollers stuff."

"We went on and started to play and girls were going ballistic," McKee said. "We were wearing Rollers gear, we were a tribute band nearly as such, we just played nearly their whole set... and we didn't even think we were doing anything wrong. Tam nearly had a heart attack when he came in and heard us playing 'Shang-A-Lang'. He shouted 'Get the fuck off the stage, who the fuck do they think they are?'... he wasn't too pleased."

The Young City Stars were managed by a former bodybuilder and one-time Mr Northern Ireland who was now a major agent in the country. He had already sent the group to London to record. After the show, Paton spoke to him and arranged for the group to visit him at his home in Prestonpans. He was very interested in them.

In Glasgow the pressure was intense. The Scottish media were out in force. *Melody Maker* and *Disc* were in attendance for cover stories. Carol Klenfner was flying in with her important American journalists. There was also talk of the show and events surrounding the show being filmed for a huge American kids TV show *Wonderama*, seen by 20 million kids, aged seven to 14, every week. American agent Sid Bernstein, who had promoted The Beatles' concerts at Shea Stadium, was also in attendance. "He was a heavy duty New York gentleman in business," said Jef Hanlon who was again promoting this UK tour.

Paton was hugely impressed with Bernstein's Beatles connection. Bernstein, who had an array of Epstein stories, had recently been negotiating with Abba to take them to America. He'd seen the press clipping on the Rollers. "I saw that magic word 'hysteria'," he said. "I wanted to check them out."

Bernstein had also spoken to Clive Davis but he said Davis had told him: "Don't do it. They don't play their own instruments. If you bring these kids to New York you'll lose your credibility. Leave it alone."

197

Bernstein was not deterred and arrived in Glasgow to see the city centre overrun by Rollers fans. Police from three other divisions had to be drafted in to help the city boys. There were thousands of girls outside the Apollo, mostly dressed like the band, many without tickets, plenty of them already in hysterics, sobbing and wailing. Bernstein had travelled over with Barry Reiss, Arista's business affairs manager, who was as circumspect about the band as Davis until, Bernstein said, he saw a "huge trailer" flogging "caps, vests, scarves… everything in tartan". "There was no longer a question that bringing the Rollers to America would make good business sense," said Bernstein.

"I never saw anything like it before," said Carol Klenfner. "The entire city was at a standstill. There were police barriers and screaming mobs of 12 year olds. These kids were young. The fresh faces of these kids in their home-made costumes was so powerful and so sweet. As Americans we were struck by how poor Scotland was as a country."

This tour would test Jef Hanlon's resolve. Although the same security was in place, Artists Services and his own Glasgow club bouncers, the intensity was ratcheted up a notch from the late 1974 tour. Hanlon pleaded with fans to be careful, to not get hurt in the "excitement to get close" to their "idols". He warned that when fans crush against one another the weight at the front was "like being pushed against a wall by a double decker bus".

It was not just difficult for the band to escape after the show but also to get into the venues. "It was total mania," he said. "We would arrange to meet somewhere three or four miles out of the town, a filling station, or a lay-by, some local park or whatever. Then they'd swap out of Tam's big American station wagon (still being driven by Paton and containing the band and a young teenager, Martin Donald, who purportedly looked after the band's clothes) and get in the van and go in. Then after the show the van would go back to where they'd met up and they got back in the station wagon and off they went.

"Then some MP started to ask questions in the Houses of Parliament… should The Bay City Rollers be banned from playing live because it's dangerous to children? I was getting calls from the police, not hassle.

Two days before the concert the Assistant Chief Constable of that city or town would phone me up and say, 'What are your plans for getting in and out of our city?' They'd say, 'Well we'll give you a police escort.' They used to change traffic lights, clear roads… they'd meet us and insist on giving us the police escort which was crap because everybody knew who was coming with the blue lights and two police cars and the VW van in the middle of it."

In the foyer Paul Pike was experiencing his first Rollers gig. "We put all these tables out with the merchandising on it," he said. "They got flattened straight away. We had to call security to come and rescue us. They were all over us… we learned very quickly. We had the van outside venues but most venues wouldn't let us use it because there wasn't any room for it. We used the van to haul all the stuff around and then set up inside. Eventually we got security on there. It was only Glasgow that took us by surprise. It was the first time we'd ever done it, we just thought everyone would queue up and they were enthusiastically pushing and all the tables collapsed.

"Me and Gerry [Slater, co-owner of Artists Services] used to stand on stage at night, looking for girls who fainted to pull them out," Pike added. "It was all hands on deck. Lots of girls fainted and we'd take them backstage to St John Ambulance. They immediately recovered and then you had to get them back out again. There was no health and safety regulations."

The band turned up just before show time with no time for a sound check. This would become routine. It did not seem to matter. The screaming was absolutely piercing and invariably drowned out the music. A bagpiper took to the stage and then the band appeared. The scenes of carnage eclipsed the previous tour as kids surged out of their seats and forward to the stage. Some beat the stewards and security and clambered on stage to launch themselves at Wood or McKeown. The first Glasgow show was stopped twice.

DJ Dave Eager was again acting as gig compere and urged the crowd to calm down. On other dates on the tour Hanlon would use bigger name DJs, such as the BBC's David Hamilton and Emperor Rosko or Peter Powell from Radio Luxembourg, to do the same job. While the band was off stage the bouncers moved the many splintered seats. Two girls were taken to hospital, one with a suspected broken leg and the other with concussion. The half dozen nurses on duty were kept busy with girls constantly being carried out of the main auditorium gasping for breath.

In between the two shows, Paton, as always was surrounded by an eager crowd of adults and children, all hoping he could fix it for them to meet the Rollers. Paton took a girl with a kidney complaint backstage but she collapsed at first sight of the band. "All the boys gathered around her, trying to bring her round," said Paton. "They gave her autographs and pictures and things but she didn't know a thing about it."

Bernstein also went backstage after the first show. "Paton and I made a deal right then and there," he said. "We signed a one-year contract granting me the right to represent The Bay City Rollers in America."

The second show of the evening was even wilder. "The balcony was going up and down like a yo-yo," said Hanlon, "but they're designed to have play in them." One girl pulled out lifeless from the throng down the foot of the stage sprang back to life and tried to grab McKeown. It took three men to carry her out kicking and screaming. Another girl of about 10 simply looked at the stage and burst into tears. A steward led her out. McKeown seemed in his element. He had the kids singing along to 'Remember' and every time he waved there was renewed frenzy in the audience. When he blew a kiss out it was bedlam. The old trick of Faulkner and McKeown facing one another on their knees caused another crescendo. McKeown stopped this second show himself and verbally blasted security. He asked, "Who's the guy pulling wee girls by the hair and punching them? Get this creep out of here." The show ended with 'Bye Bye Baby'.

Afterwards the band was whisked away to a hotel out of town. Paton had organised an aftershow reception for his VIP guests at the Albany Hotel in the city. The band was not required. The hotel was mobbed. Limos pulled up and girls screamed for the arrival of Tony Roberts, Sid Bernstein and the producer of *Wonderama*. These executives had a taste of Rollermania as the fans banged on their cars and clutched at them as they got out. The police were eventually forced to move in.

"The hotel was mobbed," said Carol Klenfner. "The fans stayed outside the hotel and screamed all night basically... it was pretty crazy. Danny [Fields] and Lisa [Robinson] were very impressed by it. It wasn't about the music to them but the phenomenon factor of it... you couldn't argue with that; that wasn't manufactured." Inside Paton and Perkins worked the room, handing out press kits, Paton with a glass of milk in his hand. "Tam was the charmer," said Carol. "There was a lot of fun around Tam. Barry was the man who looked like an accountant. He seemed like he was doing the back office work. Tam had a way with words. He walked into a room and things started happening."

Sid Bernstein told *Melody Maker*, for a cover story that would be printed on May 3, that: "My impression of this band is they are phenomenal. For three or four years now the kids in America have been starved of this type of band." The *MM* cover shot was of Faulkner and McKeown on their knees facing one another on stage, headlined "Rockin' Rollers". PR Alan Walsh was still working his contacts.

For the cover story in *Disc* that appeared the same day ("Rollermania"), Bernstein supplied more quotes. "The man who brought The Beatles to America is about to do the same thing with The Bay City Rollers," wrote their reporter. Bernstein told *Disc:* "I strongly believe the people of America are ready for the Rollers. Right now they are looking for new heroes and the boys could be just what they want." Bernstein outlined plans to present the Rollers at New York's Madison Square Garden in November, followed by other major venues. McKeown was quoted as saying that if things went well they'd stay in America for "three or four months". Paton said: "To be honest, we'd like to try and escape this country for a little while otherwise we may be in danger of overexposing ourselves here."

Danny Fields was 34 and gay and *16* magazine was the most influential teen publication in America: two million teens saw it every month. "We had heard, Lisa Robinson and I, before we went there, that some of them might be gay," he said. "Our plan was to go to Glasgow and stay with them in this big stately home turned into a hotel between Glasgow and Edinburgh and we were expecting to come back to New York with the truth about these big teen idols. We were supposed to go look around to see how many beds had been slept in, that was our plan. There were only 20 or 30 rooms in the whole place. We looked in but we saw no examples of any mischief. They were on their best behaviour. Only between myself and Tam was there this understanding that we were both totally gay and out… and we had out friends in the UK music industry, Elton John and his manager John Reid and the gay mafia. It knows itself, knows who it is. That's who we were."

Fields, who had worked as publicist for The Stooges and MC5 and had recently become co-manager of The Ramones, would be a key ally for the Rollers in America even though he had not got his scoop in Glasgow.

The wild scenes in Glasgow, and there were many boys involved as well as girls, were repeated on the short Scottish leg of the tour. In Dundee one girl collapsed outside a hotel that fans thought the band were staying at. She turned blue and was whisked off to hospital. "To get out of the theatre in Aberdeen we had to get out over the roofs and take fire escapes," said Faulkner. In Leeds on May 4, the *Guardian* reported that some fans had "faint scars on their forearms" where they had drawn blood while scratching 'Eric' or 'Les' with a pin. "Mine turned septic," said one girl. The *Guardian* wrote about a "monstrous regiment of girls". Another newspaper headline described "Teeny terror – Rollers fans crash 20ft from balcony".

The merchandise was flying out. "The biggest sellers were always badges and posters and that sort of stuff," said Pike. Some 35,000 programmes were sold. As on the past UK tour, there were problems with touts. "We advised fans to look for the official table, usually in the foyer, and just buy stuff from inside the theatre," said Pike. "In Liverpool, the kids were giving touts a hard time and in Southampton three touts were chased up the road and had a bucket of water poured on their stall. You can never entirely stop it but we did our best to keep it to a minimum. One guy following the tour we called King Tout. He'd get a local shopkeeper to give him the shop for a day and sell stuff in there… wasn't a thing we could do."

Two days after Leeds there was pandemonium at Newcastle City Hall. It took more than 70 police, 40 special stewards and the entire staff of the concert hall to control the screaming crowd of more than 2,400 inside. There were also 1,000-plus outside that did not have tickets. The screaming and chanting began when the doors opened just after seven and, before the concert started, young girls – aged 11 or 12 – were in floods of tears, some having wet themselves. When the show started it was soon stopped. One girl, wearing a tartan rosette and with her jacket covered in Bay City Rollers badges, flung herself at the stage. Hundreds followed her. Police reinforcements were called. It was impossible to hear which number they were performing. Above everything else came the sounds of splintering seats as the front three rows gave way under the pressure of the hysterical fans. Girls were trampled in the crush as another row of seats buckled. The Rollers played their last number – and ran. Outside an out-of-control mob of girls tried to overturn a van they thought contained the band, while hundreds more refused to disperse and chanted and screamed for an hour before finally wandering off into the night.

There was a three-day break in mid-May so the band could film more episodes of *Shang-A-Lang*. The studio again filled with screaming teens. All through the tour their TV show went out every Tuesday. The band mimed to tracks from *Once Upon A Star*, still number one in the LP charts, and past hits. Alan was now often kitted out in an all tartan costume. Derek was chosen to interview guests such as Bruce Welch from The Shadows and chat show host Russell Harty.

There followed the debacle at Mallory Park, detailed in this book's prologue, and then another huge incident in Cardiff where the band were again forced off stage. "Twice in three days riots have hit concerts," wrote the *Daily Mirror* under the headline: "Young girls run wild at pop shows." In Cardiff there were 90 police, 70 first aid volunteers, 70 security guards and 3,500 fans. Much of the blame was laid on the "suggestive gyrations" of McKeown who was said to be "teasing and tempting" fans. Alan was pulled into the crowd and row upon row of seats were destroyed. The police formed a chain at the front. There was a fleet of ambulances outside. One fan, her arms and legs flailing had to be held down by six first aiders. St John Ambulance staff treated 246 young girls and 25 were hospitalised with suspected fractures from crush.

Paton suggested cutting some dates to alleviate the pressure. Wherever the band went in the UK, city centres were over-run with fans. "It was mass hysteria," said McKeown. "We really feared for the safety of the fans. It got so ridiculous that MPs wanted to ban us. We got mentioned at the dispatch box."

"In some ways," said Faulkner, "1975 was the beginning of the end for the Rollers. We got banned because of all the headlines. We couldn't get a license to play anywhere. So we went to America where we could work."

The rest of the tour went ahead. Seventy were hurt in Swansea where hundreds of fans laid siege to the Dragon Hotel where the band stayed. *Disc* put the band on the cover again, except this time just a photo of a fan being wrestled off stage. "Security men: Gorillas, goons or just men doing a job?" was the strapline. In Manchester the Rollers left the stage twice before Paton pulled them off early. In Preston, Alan said he would be leaving the band after his real age had been revealed as 26 and not the 21 that had been claimed in publicity material. Then Alan decided to stay, yielding to public outcry. "I'll stay, Roller Alan tells fans," the headline. "It was all a bit daft," he said. "Reporters were even trying to track down my birth certificate." In Southport he and Faulkner were pulled from the stage and mobbed.

Then there *was* a tragedy but not at a gig. After a show in Great Yarmouth the band had a day off. McKeown flew back to Edinburgh and spent it at home. The following day, May 29, he prepared to travel to the airport for a show in Bristol. It was raining heavily. McKeown was behind the wheel of his Ford Mustang, a car he had often rhapsodised for its speed and power in print. All the band members had their shtick and McKeown's was cars and speed. In his case it was genuine affection. "Wow, it is so fast," he said of the Mustang. "I have been streaking around Scotland." He had only passed his test in 1974. The Mustang was a hell of car to handle.

He was driving along Corstophine Road when he hit her. It was said to have happened close to a well-known tricky bend. The woman walked out in front of him but it was claimed he was going too fast. "Roller Pop Star hits widow at 60mph," the court was later told, as reported in *The Sun*. "I was driving at about 40mph and this woman was standing at the side of the road obviously undecided about whether or not to cross," he said later. "I blipped my horn and it seemed that she had seen me and was going to wait. Then she suddenly stepped out into the road. I swerved to avoid her but I had no chance. I was sideways on when I hit her and then crashed through a brick wall."

McKeown and the other occupants of the car – a woman said to be his girlfriend and one of his brothers – were unharmed but the pedestrian, 76-year-old Euphemia Clunie, had been killed. McKeown said he was pulled out of the wreckage by a passing nurse and that the owner of the house whose brick wall he'd demolished invited him in for a whisky stiffener.

Some witnesses claimed McKeown had been going as fast 70mph. Corstophine Road is part of a long stretch of road that goes from the city centre out west to the airport. The speed limit varies on this stretch between 30, 40 and 50 mph.

The Rollers cancelled that night's gig in Bristol just minutes before the start. Fans heard the news from BBC Radio Bristol and struggled to take it in. "When Les killed that old woman on the way to Edinburgh Airport I had to go out on the steps of Bristol Colston Hall where the screaming hordes were to confirm there was no show tonight," said Jef Hanlon. "That was a character building experience."

The next day the crash was on the front page of both the *Daily Mirror* – 'Bay City Rollers Death Crash' and *The Sun* – 'Bay City Roller In Death Crash'. The latter published pictures of McKeown and Paton on its front page with the strapline, 'Concert off after widow is killed'.

McKeown was charged with causing death by dangerous driving and a court date was set for November. He was almost certainly facing a two-year stretch.

Remarkably McKeown was back on stage the next day, in Southampton. The following day he played the first of the tour's two consecutive major London show at Hammersmith Odeon. He was resentful toward the rest of the band and Paton. "They didn't see it from a helpful, human way," said McKeown. "It wasn't like, 'We're going to get through this together', it was more like, 'We need you on stage tomorrow, you wee cunt, so you better stop fucking crying'. I was 19 years old, I'd just killed someone, and it seemed like everyone around me was pretending it hadn't happened or it didn't matter."

The two London dates, at the 3,000 capacity venue, had been a long time in the planning. The band had been offered the much bigger 17,000-capacity Earls Court but that venue was considered unsafe for the Rollers; that there was no way of controlling such a large number of fans in one place. "Kids would definitely get injured," said McKeown. "We couldn't take the risk so we turned down the offer."

During the first night at the Hammersmith Odeon, 250 girls became so worked up that they had to be treated for shock. *Melody Maker*, reviewing the show, called it "pure bedlam". *Disc* called the fans a "seething horde". The atmosphere was electric. One fan spent £200 on merchandise. There were police on horseback, hundreds trampled, as the "tartan hurricane" passed through town. It got them another cover of *Record Mirror* with more than 500 fans injured at the second Hammersmith Odeon show.

There were only two dates left now but finally McKeown cracked. On June 2, in Oxford, as teenagers stormed the stage, ambulance office Bill Cooper accused McKeown of leaping off stage and causing a riot. Steve Hartley, a photographer, said he was knocked out by McKeown following "several blows from McKeown's mike stand".

"There was no reason for his action," said Hartley. "He went berserk."

"I just lost the plot," said McKeown. "I burst into tears, couldn't handle it anymore. There were all these fans and when I started crying they came forward wanting to mother me. And then my attention suddenly focused on the orchestra pit. There were girls coming over and getting hurt and all these photographers were taking pictures of them, and for some reason in my twisted little mind I thought that was out of order so I jumped into the orchestra pit and started beating up a photographer."

McKeown was arrested on assault charges and required to appear in court in November, a date set for just before his court case for causing death by dangerous driving. A St John Ambulance nurse had also been struck in the melee. Hanlon was glad to see the end of the tour after a final date in Newcastle, a second visit to the city. "I was really pleased we got through the tour without anyone getting killed at the gigs," he said. "To my knowledge no-one got seriously injured at the shows. I put it down to the fact I brought the Scottish guys down and they were in the middle, organising the local fellas."

"It was after that that I slowly started getting into all different kinds of drugs," said McKeown. He claimed Paton already allowed him to smoke marijuana, just not around the others. Now he "dabbled in smack" and drank Jack Daniels. "I really went off the edge into my own private hell," he said. "Seeing someone lying dead in the street is something you never get over."

But America could not wait. Paton drove them forward.

CHAPTER 7

Disconnection

"There were certainly a lot of quickies [with Rollers fans]. You would do it in hotel service elevators, linen cupboards, all the best romantic places. If you ever did get in a room every time there was a knock on the door, I'd hide her in the loo, wardrobe or under the bed, and tidy our clothes before opening the door. I was nervous because of the constant intimidation, continual threats of being sacked, which we had all been conditioned to think was the end of the world."

— Les McKeown

There was no relief from the pressure for McKeown or for any of them. Paton told the press that the band might have to leave Scotland and possibly the UK. "We'll quit, warn Rollers," was the *Record Mirror* headline. The new addresses of all the band members and of Little Kellerstain, Paton's Prestonpans mansion, were common knowledge among hard-core fans. McKeown's mother was said to be unwell because the fans kept a constant vigil outside the new home they shared with McKeown and there was always screaming and photographs being taken. McKeown bought a flat in London to escape. "In a part of London where the neighbours won't know me and where nobody is going to find me," he said.

Wood's parents had to change their phone number 20 times. The fans stole bricks from their wall around the home and would graffiti their love for Wood on the house, upsetting the neighbours. His mum was unhappy and unwell. His younger brother was harassed at school. He'd even been mobbed in Portugal during a short break. "We got hassle from fans from all over the world," said Wood's father, John. "They would hang around outside the house and take anything they could find. The neighbours' wall would be covered in graffiti and I had to buy gallons of paint and cover over it. Then I bought some hardboard and asked fans to use that. It filled up in two days. We had been there for 23 years but it became so crazy we decided to move." Not before the house was broken in to. "I found three boys in the house and they were after Stuart's gold discs," his mum said.

Two Edinburgh families named Faulkner and McKeown – no connection to the band members – were victims of fan harassment. Faulkner's father was unwell and suffered an alarming episode where he briefly disappeared, said to be related to memory loss. Faulkner and Wood were supposed to be moving in together to the remote farmhouse with 50 acres of land that Faulkner had bought but two squatters had already settled in and needed evicting first. Fans had already started to gather outside, even though it involved two buses, one train and a taxi from Glasgow to the farm in remote West Calder – and was five miles from the nearest shops. The pair would eventually move in and the fan attention continued. Paton, who installed high levels of security at Little Kellerstain, said the band was "getting depressed". "If the Scottish fans don't leave the Rollers alone in the privacy of their own homes, there will be no alternative except for them to leave Scotland altogether," he said. "The boys must have time on their own and they're not getting it."

"It was so totally different from normal life that we could have been in space," said Alan. There were still rumours he might quit the band. "Too old at 27," one article suggested, accompanied by a picture of a grinning Alan in a schoolboy uniform.

"I feel like I'm past my peak at 19," said Faulkner, who was actually closer to 22. "I wish I felt creative instead of tired all the time." Every

Saturday hundreds of girls from around the country rolled into Edinburgh hoping to catch a glimpse of the band. They would invariably end up en masse heading out to Prestonpans and Paton's new home to join up with girls from England already camped out. "You were their whole life for a year or two, more important than their father or their religion," said McKeown. "You were their little God, probably more powerful than God."

Throughout June, *Shang-A-Lang* kept the band on TV in the UK every week. Slade, Gary Glitter and Showaddywaddy were all guests on the show. Paton also organised for his second act Bilbo Baggins to appear with their third single, 'Hold Me'. Peter Powell chose this as his Hit Pick on Radio Luxembourg but Radio 1 ignored the track and it flopped. Perkins and Paton tried to sell the band to Tony Roberts at Arista UK but he was not interested. On July 13 the Rollers played the rescheduled show in Bristol. The venue spent £15,000 hiring extra police. It would be the band's last show in the UK for over a year. "We'd love to do more gigs but it's difficult now," said Faulkner.

In July the Young City Stars visited Paton in Edinburgh. The band's Rollers gimmick had made them popular in Northern Ireland and they were earning good money gigging locally. "Tam had spied Ian [Mitchell]," said singer Damian McKee. "There must have been something going on with Alan [Longmuir] and he decided to make a move. The only way he could do it without it becoming blatantly obvious was to bring us all over to Scotland, under the pretence he was going to manage us or do something with us."

"He picked us up in a station wagon, and we stayed out in an amazing hotel in a stately home just outside Edinburgh," McKee added. "He took us round to show us his new house he'd just bought. He had no keys so he got one of us to climb in through the window and we opened the door up. Tam had no intention of becoming our manager. He was after Ian.

"We were just so happy to be going over we did not think Tam had an ulterior motive that might have been sexual," McKee said. "Any innuendos or cracks would have been, 'Oh your man is a bit of a woofta'. We wouldn't have realised what that entailed. When today you hear all the horror stories, the grooming, what went in some of these children's homes, looking back now, actually that was probably the same situation only we didn't realise it. We were naïve and had stars in our eyes."

In America, Carol Klenfner was raving about the Rollers to her husband, Michael, Head of Promotions at Arista. "He got excited," said Carol. "One of things Clive [Davis] liked about Michael was his enthusiasm and his ability to promote that which he was enthusiastic about." Arista's Head of business affairs, Barry Reiss, who'd seen the band in Glasgow, was also positive and Sid Bernstein was bursting with hutzpah. He was negotiating with sportscaster Howard Cosell, who was set to host a new high-profile Saturday night variety show on American TV in September. Bernstein called the show an "almost carbon copy of The Ed Sullivan show" that had launched The Beatles in America. Bernstein planned to launch the Rollers on the new Cosell show and began a series of meetings with his producers at the ABC network to thrash out a deal.

Paton visited New York but achieved little. He went cruising the gay bars with *16* magazine's Danny Fields. Here he saw fist-fucking displays. "It'd be the stage show," said Fields. "Someone coming out with someone on his fist and we'd laugh and say, 'What's the next bar'… it was the cruising bars era."

Clive Davis remained unmoved by the Rollers. Gary Glitter hadn't made it in America. None of the British glam acts, not T. Rex [who Carol Klenfner had actually worked PR on], David Essex or Slade, had made it in America. At the time Davis was preparing Arista for the release of Patti Smith's debut album, *Horses*, and had recently signed Gil Scott-Heron, another radical performer, to the label. Pressured by Bernstein, Klenfner and Weiss, he spent an afternoon listening to the Rollers output thus far in his office on 1776 Broadway. These were the old Bell Records offices and were not grand. Davis was planning to move the label to a new flashier home in New York just off Fifth Avenue, on West 57th Street, known as music row. CJ Strauss was based there, as were multiple music publishing companies, managers, agents and the influential trade music weeklies, *Record World* and *Cash Box*.

Davis liked the band's planned new UK single, 'Give A Little Love', even less than 'Bye Bye Baby', which had been released in America but with almost zero backing from the company. He listened to their *Once Upon A Star* album and was astonished at how poor it was. Then he put on *Rollin'*, the first album, and he found a track he liked, 'Saturday Night'. Told that it hadn't been a hit in the UK when it was released as a single in 1973, Davis said it didn't matter. It was full of hooks. "Anthemic and melodic," he called it. This was the single to launch the band in America. "I thought it was awful," said Paton of the song. Davis also planned an album, exclusively for North America, to ride on the back of the imagined hit, basically a greatest hits package, all the singles to date, plus a few album cuts from *Once Upon A Star*, notably just two Faulkner/Wood originals. One of them, 'Marlina', would be the B-side of 'Saturday Night'.

In the UK, the band was promoting new single, 'Give A Little Love', a slow ballad, the band's most cloying moment yet. Faulkner/Wood were again credited with writing the B-side. The TV debut of the song came on *Shang-A-Lang* on July 8. Two days later they were on *Top Of The Pops*. The single shot to number one in the charts. The Rollers appeared on three further episodes of *Top Of The Pops*. One of the appearance was a Mike Mansfield-directed promo of the band miming the songs while sat on the bonnets of four gleaming Rolls-Royces. Derek was said to have just got himself one, although he was more often seen in a Citreon CX 2200. The band was seen miming the track four more times on *Shang-A-Lang*, including on what would be the final episode of the show on August 26.

Paton, whose recent best-selling autobiography was promoted as "The story of a man and five boys", said the band were now going into hibernation and would keep a "low profile over the next few months" in the UK. There would be no more *Shang-A-Lang*. "We were offered another 20 weeks but we have turned it down because we wanted to cool it in Britain between now and the end of the year," he said. "*Shang-A-Lang* starts to go out in Australia in the next few weeks... the series has taught the Rollers a lot about television and it hasn't done them any harm. Although I am aware the show had plenty of critics I just feel they should have shown more patience." There was a rumour that Muriel Young offered the series to Bilbo Baggins to host but Paton had not pursued it.

Life for the Rollers grew more frenetic as they hurried to complete a new album and to promote themselves across Europe. Germany was proving to be fertile ground. 'Bye Bye Baby' had gone top 10 there and 'Give A Little Love' was also in the top 20. They were featured on the cover of *Bravo,* German's most popular teen pop magazine which was now enthusiastically backing the group. They also visited Helsinki in Finland and Stockholm in Sweden. "Forty girls gave chase through the hotel in Helsinki," said McKeown. "In the sauna, the swimming pool... it was mayhem. If you stopped and thought about it too much it would probably screw up your head. You just go along with it."

McKeown was having sex with fans. He couldn't resist. He found the thrill of getting caught added an extra "sparkle". "There were certainly a lot of quickies," he said. "You would do it in hotel service elevators, linen cupboards, all the best romantic places. If you ever did get in a room every time there was a knock on the door, I'd hide her in the loo, wardrobe or under the bed, and tidy our clothes before opening the door. I was nervous because of the constant intimidation, continual threats of being sacked, which we had all been conditioned to think was the end of the world."

There was also a first visit to Australia to squeeze in but not for McKeown or Derek who were left behind. "They were getting pretty tired because it was push push push," said the band's official photographer David Golumb, himself exhausted and soon to back off from his role. "The managers and record companies wanted to squeeze as much out them as possible because they didn't know how long they were going to last. If there was a demand, they just had to go and do it."

The Australian *Women's Weekly* had already covered the band's concert at Hammersmith Odeon, reporting back on the "hysteria over five clean-living lads from Edinburgh... a pop group who profess to drink milk, deplore drugs, and indulge in none of the wild gallivanting often associated with pop stars." The band's first two albums had both been top 10 in Australia. 'Bye Bye Baby' had been a number one single there and 'Give A Little Love' was at number two in the country.

The *Sydney Morning Herald* predicted a wild airport welcome for Wood, Alan, Faulkner and Paton – "the wildest seen in Australia since The Beatles". In the end only 300 teenage girls turned up at Sydney Airport, although they caused a commotion, screaming and chanting as the band touched down on August 26. Paton said the band were here to "talk to their fans" for two days. After Sydney they would be visiting Melbourne, and possibly Adelaide and Brisbane. He was still working on getting *Shang-A-Lang* shown on Australian TV.

In Sydney the band did interviews with radio station 2SM amid hectic fan scenes and their hotel was also mobbed. Paton made sure they were mobbed in Melbourne, guiding them toward a gimmicky drive down the middle of Bourke Street, one of the city's busiest, in an open-topped car. Their appearance on Melbourne radio station 3XY was also crowded with fans. Paton said Rollermania was just starting in Australia where the group was getting 34,000 fan letters a week. He claimed they received 20,000 letters a day in the UK. They would be back in Australia later in the year for a tour, the demand for tickets successfully invigorated.

There were more European dates to play as summer faded, including an eventful trip to Copenhagen to play at the 1,800-capacity Concert Hall. Two Yorkshire girls of 17 and 18 brushed aside the bouncers and climbed on the stage to kiss each band member in turn. Afterwards one held McKeown's hand and kissed him outside the theatre. Faulkner declined so the other girl simply yanked out a tuft of hair from his head.

After the show McKeown discovered a fan working as a chambermaid at their hotel so she could meet them. McKeown welcomed her into his room but when he heard footsteps outside he insisted she hide on a balcony, dressed only in her underwear. She had turned blue by the time Paton had left his room. Paton routinely inspected the band's hotel rooms to check they hadn't smuggled girls in. "I often got caught trying to hide a girl under my bed and he found them hiding a couple of times," said McKeown. "As far as Tam was concerned going with a girl was the worst sin you could commit as a band member. Paton would physically drag the girls out of the room."

The fans were persistent and before leaving Denmark McKeown recalled coming "face to face" with about 10 teenagers in his hotel corridor. "They immediately charged me," he said. "Before I could unlock the door they had torn all my clothes off."

While they were in Copenhagen Paton and Perkins were interviewed together for the esteemed American rock magazine *Creem*. They spoke to a young Cameron Crowe who would go on to write for *Rolling Stone* before becoming a Hollywood film writer and director. Crowe noted that the band's hotel was surrounded by a crowd of pre-pubescent girls – "most had kept a nightlong vigil" and "some had travelled all the way from Britain".

What Crowe really wanted to know from the pair was whether the band would succeed in America. "I really think the Rollers will happen in the States," Paton told him. "There's a lot of people still sitting back, I know, saying that it can't happen. I remember when they said that in Scandinavia. I remember when they said that in Australia. Now, in those places, it's just as bad as it is in the UK. It's *neurotic* in Australia… New Zealand… Africa… we're number one in Germany now, too. Japan is next."

Crowe also asked about the injuries at concerts in the UK and about McKeown's recent fatal road crash. "The papers insist that death follows us around," said Perkins. "The most horrific instance was when we did a TV show in Lancashire. The day before, a policeman had a coronary thrombosis. The next day he showed up for work at the station and died. The day afterwards the headlines said 'Rollers riot kills policeman'. It's just incredible."

"Nobody has ever died at our concerts," added Paton, going on to optimistically predict that in 10 years' time "people will talk about the Rollers the same way they talk about The Beatles". "We learned from the mistakes The Beatles made over the years," he said. "Look at the hassles they got into. Money hassles, publishing hassles. Then they all got on their Hare Krishna kick. I don't know if that will happen to us. I don't think so. We're all very sensible."

Finally, it was in Copenhagen that Paton signed up the 15-year-old Gert Magnus, lead singer of a manufactured pop rock band called Mabel that had supported the Rollers in Denmark. They had a record out in their own country on Polydor, who distributed the Rollers' records in Europe. "He could see at that time all the girls went really crazy for us," said Magnus who was cute and dark haired with the ragamuffin look Paton liked. Paton told Magnus' mother and father that he was going to make their son a star and moved him to Scotland to live with him at Little Kellerstain where he stayed for the next two years. Magnus said he was being paid an outlandish £25,000 (the equivalent of almost £250,000 today) a year by Paton. "I think Tam thought I could become a Bay City Roller," he said. "At the start he wanted me to be a new Bay City Roller but after a while he was thinking for me to go solo."

Paton sent him for guitar lessons in Edinburgh. "Tam was like a father for me… he really watched everybody and said, 'No you can't do that with my son'. Tam always took care of me when we went somewhere and they wanted sex for doing something like TV shows or something. I was not like that so I told Tam that and he took care of me like his own son.

"No members of The Bay City Rollers ever pressured me for sex," he added. "They were my friends. But at the time I was thinking maybe they had been through the same as what was happening to me with the guys in the music industry."

Pat McGlynn, then 17, was also staying at Little Kellerstain at the time, recalled Magnus. "It was a hard time living in LK," said Magnus. "We couldn't go outside because there were always lots of girls outside. There was a camera [on the gates] and you could stand and look at the girls, and there was a fence all the way round the house. He had four dogs. And Tam didn't want us to go out. He was very much taking care of me. There were lots of older gay guys coming to the house… I was not very old, so he really took good care of me."

Paton recorded three songs with Magnus, two of which 'Rain And Tears' and 'Wham Bam Shang-A-Lang' sounded excellent on paper. He started to shop him around in an attempt to secure a record deal under the nom de plume Baron Gert Von Magnus and got him features in American and Japanese magazines and UK newspapers such as *News Of The World* and the *Daily Record*. The rumour mill, predictably, went into overdrive. Paton's interest in Magnus seemed highly suspicious, acutely sexual. One suggestion had it that Paton had kidnapped Magnus who was Danish royalty. "He was no Baron; we only pretended he was to give it a publicity angle," said Paton. It would be a while before Magnus's UK pop dream died and Paton made a sexual move on him. In the meantime he stayed. Paton bought him pinball machines and a trampoline for the garden at LK so he didn't get bored. "When he went to United States he always bought presents back for me and the other guys, such as watches." The trampoline became a popular part of the entertainment at Little Kellerstain. The Rollers were photographed on it with Paton and all the old queens who visited the house would happily bounce up and down talking about their various conquests.

The Rollers were back in the studio with Wainman and Frechter to complete a new album in time for the Christmas market. The bulk of the tracks had been recorded in Chipping Norton studios earlier in the year. There was nothing of substance there to follow up 'Give A Little Love', which would be included on the album as its main draw.

"You wouldn't put all your eggs in one basket so what you'd do is hold something back for the next album and then you'd have singles and add those to the next album and give people a reason to buy that album too," said Wainman

The main task at hand was to come up with a new single. Uncle Phil, as the band called Wainman, had several suggestions but Faulkner was convinced he'd come up with a number one of his own, called 'Money Honey'. The title was as unoriginal as the simplistic main riff of the track – a song with the same title written in the fifties by Jesse Stone had been recorded by Elvis, The Drifters, Little Richard, Jackson 5 and Gary Glitter among many others. The Rollers track was improved by the sound of police sirens running through it. Wainman also put Derek through a significant ordeal making him double track his drums.

"Every single band gets ahead of themselves, they want to become Lennon & McCartney and Eric and Woody wanted to write all the own songs, and they didn't write a good one in my time," said Wainman. "'Money Honey' is not bad but you're following two number ones. You don't want to follow it with a top 20 or top 10, it's not good enough. But the boys were stamping their feet and saying we're putting it out."

Wainman was not happy. "They wanted to write but Phil wanted to either pick earth-shattering great songs or put his own songs on, he didn't want to fill in albums with their songs," said Tony Roberts at Arista UK. "Phil either wanted great songs like 'Bye Bye Baby' or his own songs basically. He didn't want their songs. Once again I had a problem not similar to the one I'd had with Coulter/Martin. Les was quite difficult in those days... he was probably one of the ones that caused the rift with Bill and Phil [Coulter] and I'm not sure he got on that well with Wainman producing them either."

Roberts's chief reason to accuse McKeown of causing unrest was the fight he witnessed at the Arista office in London. "My promotion manager, David Bridger, was fighting with Les on the stairs," he said. "I had to sort that out. It was a nightmare. Bridger was a key part of the team; he liked to think he was the team. It was a dreadful day; they were having a fist fight on the stairs in the office."

"With the Rollers, I tried to do my best to let them have what they wanted but at the same time it had to marry with having hits,' Roberts added. "I'd say to them, 'you've got to record the right songs for you, there's no point just writing songs.' I think they felt they were better than they were, that was the trouble."

Melody Maker interviewed Faulkner in Chipping Norton studios in early September. He was written up as "highly strung, vulnerable, a dreamer quivering with nervous sensibility". There was said to be "romanticism in his cornflower-blue eyes" and that in person his "classically pretty baby-face is magnified beyond a fan's wildest dreams".

He and Wood, now living together at the remote farmhouse, had written more new songs. They were talking about building a recording studio in their home. "We've been recording for eight days and six of the songs we've done are ours," Faulkner said. "We know that we appeal to a certain market more than others and you've got to accept that. I feel we're holding back some of things we'd like to write. We've got to write commercially at the moment."

Faulkner was still claiming to be 19, although the journalist knew his real age. She wrote that his "fib" was "rather tragic", an "indication of the immense pressure he is under to achieve the impossible, to halt the march of time and stay caught in a time-warp, a Peter Pan, forever the teenager's teenage idol."

Faulkner also said, tellingly, in this interview: "I know about things that you shouldn't know at our age. About being ripped off and conned and what have you."

He was grilled on the band's acquiescence to Paton's rule of no girls. "Well, we've never been a band who dragged girls into the back of the van," he said. "We always thought bands who did that were unprofessional. We've always basically been what we're said to be now. None of us are raving alcoholics or anything. That's not just publicity. I know you think that we get orders and that we say 'yes, sir' and do everything we're told. But if we didn't want to do something we wouldn't do it. It's funny but it depends on what you want. If you feel you've got to do something bad enough you just give up certain things. I think you'll find that whoever is best in their field is really dedicated."

Is he resigned to his apparently celibate way of life?

"I was resigned to it four years ago," he replied.

Sid Bernstein firmed up the band's appearance on the Howard Cosell show for the end of September, having sold the producers on the idea by promising that if they had the group on they would need to have "police barricades around the theatre" and that "kids will be lined up for days waiting for ticket". The show would get "tremendous press coverage", he said.

He outlined his vision: first the band would appear live on the show, via satellite, from a special concert in London intended, Bernstein said, "to show the hysteria around the group – the kids wearing tartan, the whole scene". The following week he intended the group to be in New York to appear live at the Ed Sullivan Theatre where the show was filmed. "The Rollers will put Howard's Cosell's show on the map," he predicted. The two appearances on the hour-long national primetime show, *Saturday Night Live With Howard Cosell*, aired at 8pm, would reach approximately 80 million Americans.

Already, in August, there had been a clip of the band used on *Wonderama*. Bernstein had begun winding up the American media for the Rollers. He had begun to talk about the band playing the 70,000-capacity Superdome in New Orleans and making $1.5 million. He had even bigger plans for New York. "I've got hold of Shea Stadium – that's 55,000 – and I'm trying to get Yankee Stadium for the next day. That's 75,000," he said. "I bet I can fill both ball parks back to back." He called the Rollers the "most important young group since The Beatles".

Carol Klenfner was also working the American media. Arista had scheduled the American release of 'Saturday Night' and the eponymously titled American compilation album to coincide with the Cosell show. "Sid Bernstein got involved as the American manager and that was significant because he was the American manager/promoter of The Beatles," said Carol. "On one hand Sid brought a lot to it but on the other hand he made a terrible misstep of comparing them to The Beatles... which they never were or could be. It was a quote we had to always disown... it was a PR misstep. The Shea Stadium thing also haunted us. Sid was the nicest guy, a real sweetheart of a person, a colourful New York character, and who doesn't like that? But it was difficult sometimes... Sid was trying to pump some air into it."

Carol said she had a "pretty clear picture" of what her company CJ Strauss was trying to achieve. "If I try to hype this band they're going to get sunk, it's not going happen," she said. "I'm going out to journalists who are into much more complicated, esoteric music. But I have these incredible scrapbooks filled with news clippings so I put together a series of mailings. I did nine or 10 and I called them 'Bay City Rollers Bulletin' number 1, 2 and 3 etc. I put five clippings in each bulletin and let the clippings speak for themselves. Every week I sent it to about 1,000 people, people in radio, tastemakers, journalists, other record company people. It was a teaser campaign and it worked beautifully. By the third or fourth one everyone was buzzing about what's going on here? Look at the funny tartan clothes, the fans dress up, the band is weird looking with the short pants and the fans are even more funny-looking... it's unique, it's different, it's fun."

"There was an awareness immediately amongst most of us who were working on it, certainly at Arista, that they skewed young," Carol added. "That's where we were aiming. Clive was more inclined to be involved in more artistic things that were to his liking but he wasn't averse to making money. And people were ready for the band, it was a novelty, it was something different, it was not for you but for your younger sister. The whole thing was, let's see how far we can take this kind of enterprise."

Her husband, Michael Klenfner, 29, Head of Promotions at Arista, was now busy working his contacts at radio stations. "Michael really worked hard with them," Carol said. He was a big Brooklyn-born personality, a fixer, who had worked with major acts such as The Beach Boys, Bruce Springsteen and Led Zeppelin. He had actually started out as bouncer at the Fillmore East rock venue and moved on to be a promoter before joining CBS Records. He was well known and well liked in the business, a brilliant salesman. His contacts in radio were numerous but the Rollers were a difficult sell. The band's sound was not suitable for FM radio stations that were overtaking the AM pop stations in popularity in America. "They weren't going to be played by the album orientated rock stations," said Carol. "The first thing was to forget about the FM progressive market." There was a tight playlist on AM stations, particularly in New York where only 13 songs were rotated between beer and chewing gum ads.

On September 1 there was a major article about the band in the respected weekly paper, the *Village Voice*. It highlighted the problems the band might face in America, namechecking Slade, T. Rex and Gary Glitter as British acts who had already "got lost" in the country. It explained how in America FM radio stations thought T. Rex and Slade "sounded too bubblegum" while AM radio stations thought they sounded "too underground". The *Village Voice* recapped the Rollers' appeal: "cheerful unpretentious songs, blatant sartorial gimmicks... creating hysteria in an audience, the gigs are scenes of mass fainting, trampling, panic and hundreds of young girls requiring hospitalisation."

There was also mention that "most British hotels have banned the group" due to fans camping outside, that they travelled incognito and stayed out of restaurants for fear of being mobbed. Sid Bernstein told the *Voice* they didn't smoke, didn't do drugs, didn't swear or drink alcohol, preferring milk. That image he said was "rare", appealing to parents. "With that kind of image parents aren't so restrictive as far as giving money to spend on concerts and records," he said. *Village Voice* concluded the band might fill the vacuum left by The Osmonds [now playing Las Vegas] and David Cassidy [trying to become a righteous solo artist] and called them a "merchandiser's dream" that would soon be appearing on "pre-teen lunchboxes".

An interview Paton gave to the Associated Press news service reached hundreds of regional American newspapers, providing headlines such as 'Bay City Rollers to invade US rock scene' and 'Brace Yourself America, here come The Bay City Rollers'. There was much emphasis on the "nice boy" image that was compared to The Beatles of 1964. "The Rollers will grow musically just as The Beatles did," Paton said. "I'm not saying the Rollers are the new Beatles but some of the comparisons are inescapable." The *Chicago Tribune* said that with Cassidy, "now a barely trustworthy 25 and trying for a more mature new image", and the Jackson 5, "growing up" there was a gap in the "teenybopper market" and the band were aiming for 10-15 year old girls. In the UK, the *Tribune* reported, the band was "the biggest thing since The Beatles".

The recent bad publicity surrounding McKeown was airbrushed out of the American publicity push. There was no mention of his facing charges for assault and death by dangerous driving – not exactly clean-cut, nice boy stuff. "They weren't real stars in the way that things like that would cross the pond," said PR Carol.

Paul Gambaccini, an American in London, offered a counterweight to the froth in the respected rock monthly, *Rolling Stone*, in an article headlined, 'Bay City Rollers Skate on thin Hype'. He called the Rollers the "most vigorously promoted pop act of year", their success based on "excessive marketing" and "media saturation". He named their children's TV show and pointed out that their tartan costumes were easy and cheap to copy. Gambaccini also took umbrage with Bernstein calling them "the most important young group since The Beatles", suggesting they might be the new Archies, the late-sixties merchandising creation of Don Kirshner, a manufactured group whose records, most notably 'Sugar Sugar', were made by session players. He noted that 'Saturday Night' was made by session musicians and concluded that the band was propelled by "publicity, accidents and other people's wishes".

Mike Mansfield was directing the appearance that would, in part, be shown live on the debut Howard Cosell show on September 20. In the morning he'd had the band performing on his recently launched Saturday kids' LWT show, *Supersonic*, playing a rare version of 'Shout', which would also be aired at the filmed 'concert' that evening.

Due to the five-hour time difference between London and New York, the evening show began at 1am in the morning. It was perhaps the Rollers' greatest ever performance: played out in front of close to 1,000 girls at a London Weekend TV studio on the South Bank. Mansfield had set the group up in a square in the middle of the studio and they were surrounded on four sides by banks of hysterical fans, all in Roller gear and wearing or waving tartan scarves. There were small walkways off the square so band members could get closer to the crowd.

As various members wandered from side to side of the square, or walked toward the fans and reached out their hands, there could be little doubt they were miming but it didn't matter. At one point Faulkner was pulled into the crowd and his guitar ripped off but the music continued to run smooth. Wood swapped from electric guitar to acoustic mid-song when a strap broke and his part continued without pause. McKeown was yanked into the audience, his hair pulled violently, and, though he was mobbed for almost 10 seconds, his vocal continued uninterrupted. The band looked spectacular, full of energy. McKeown was bare-chested, and the girls were wild throughout the 45-minute performance. McKeown and Faulkner did their on their knees bump and grind together; a clear simulation of sex. The whole thing climaxed with a run through of 'Saturday Night' that was broadcast live in America on the Cosell show. By then the band had been showered in feathers, giant balloons and bubbles and the stage was covered in various items thrown by fans. Mansfield used quick cuts between cameras to keep the energy at its maximum.

It was an increasingly hysterical show with the fans screams a constant backdrop and, despite the presence of burly Artists Services security, Faulkner was dragged off stage and into the crowd by fans during the song. Paul Pike, who was acting as security, said Paton had "got some of the real hard-core fans to rush the stage which none of us knew about".

"I put my back out that night trying to hold them back. When the show finished Tam had everyone bandaged up… it was all in the papers the next day."

"The crowd rampaged onto the stage," Mansfield told me. "They knocked Woody out. Tam had arranged with the security guys to let the crowd storm the stage. Having the band bandaged afterwards was a great story."

Paton insisted two band members had been knocked out by over-zealous fans. Associated Press picked up the story and it made headlines in American newspapers where it was reported that girls, "mainly 12 to 15, had broken through security" and knocked McKeown and Wood unconscious for several minutes. "The group has seen worse," commented Paton. "We get knocked over a great deal," said Faulkner. "It's an occupational hazard."

The band did not appear live in New York the following week on the Cosell show. The sports presenter was proving to be a disastrous variety show host, not suited to comedy. The reviews were awful for his debut performance watched by an incredible 25 million people. The show was routinely chronically hectic and unprepared and it would be cancelled after just 18 weeks. On the September 27 episode the Rollers were on the show but it was another clip from the London concert. The full concert would be shown in America under the title, *And Now… The Bay City Rollers*, on up to 30 regional, city TV stations in the coming months. NBC would pick up the recording for a national broadcast (on November 29) in a deal apparently brokered by Bernstein.

The Rollers finally arrived in New York on September 29 planning for a few days' promotion ahead of their live turn on the Cosell show on October 4. The time of arrival – TWA Flight #703 at JFK at 2:35 pm – had been leaked and any American fans they had picked up from the Cosell exposure were urged to buy the album, call radio stations and meet them at the airport. "We leaked a lot of information about where they were going to be, as any smart press agent would," said Carol Klenfner. "The idea was to create little scenes, get it going." Fans were "half encouraged" to come up to the CJ Strauss office.

In the event there was around 200 fans at the airport. Bernstein said there would have been more but kids were still at school. "We understood that the majority of fans would be under driving age so we made some bussing arrangements," he said. "There were loads of kids in the suburbs with no transport so we arranged for a few buses to bring them in." It didn't matter; all three six o'clock news programmes carried news of their band's arrival. "There were more fans there than I expected, we got pulled and scraped – the usual," said Faulkner.

The location of the band's New York hotel was also leaked and McKeown found two girls hidden in the wardrobe in his room at Hotel Westbury on Madison Avenue. "They were mobbed at the hotel," said Carol. "Screaming throughout the night." There was a press conference at the hotel in which the band was seen sat behind jugs of milk. "It was all a bit surreal really," said Faulkner. "We were thinking, 'Are people actually going to buy this? Are they going to believe that we drink milk?' But it seems that the media wanted that."

Then they went to dinner. "We took them to a restaurant called Maxwell's Plum in Manhattan," said Carol. "It was a fabulous legendary restaurant. They were young and sweet. Les was certainly the most sophisticated with the best sense of humour. The Longmuir brothers were very dependable, nice guys. Woody was adorable, Eric was the good-looking one – you could sell him as almost the Paul McCartney one. Tam was fun to be with. At dinner, he said to me 'Carol, I don't know if I've given the boys a blessing or a curse.' He only let them drink milk. He would dip his fingertips in a glass of water and flick it on one of the band's necks and say kerchew!

"Tam never came out and told me that certain members of the band were gay or bisexual," she added. "But there were rumours… and I did think it was odd they were sharing hotel rooms. It seemed like there might be some kind of hanky panky going on between some of the band and Tam."

Arista worked the band hard. The next day began at 7am, and crammed in 10 visits to radio stations and the rest of the week was filled with more interviews with radio, magazines and newspapers. The band planned to fly to Bermuda after filming the Cosell show for a short break. There was a strong sense Bernstein may have over-hyped them. Only half a dozen fans camped out in the band's New York hotel lobby. The band was also free to walk the streets. This was not Beatlemania.

"We've done more work on the road than most groups have," Faulkner told the American press. "A lot of people feel we're like The Monkees – we've just been put together and somebody else is cutting the records in our name. Not at all. I'm annoyed when people say 'You're a big hype.'"

"We ain't no hype," said Paton. "We've been together eight years since they were 13 or 14 [Paton had continued to lie about all the band members' ages]. We are controversial. They say we start riots. I never saw any riot. They do put out their hands and touch the audience but Sinatra does that so did The Beatles."

The teen press in America all interviewed the band but the amount of coverage the band could expect to receive depended on the success of 'Saturday Night'. Danny Fields, simultaneously managing The Ramones and writing for *16*, took McKeown to dinner with The Ramones. "All the Ramones loved The Bay City Rollers," said Fields. "Both acts were fascinated with each other. There was not that big a divide between their hearts. Patti Smith was as much a marketing plan/scheme as the Rollers were." The Ramones admitted that 'Blitzkrieg Bop', their debut single released in February 1976, was a "direct homage" to the Rollers' 'Saturday Night'.

Fields saw the role of Michael Klenfner behind the scenes as crucial in breaking the band in America. "He was a real promotion's man promotion man," he said. "The millions to be made were in albums, and hit singles generate hit albums – that's where the record company makes their money. Radio is the lowest form of life, where the disgusting people are, and they can make a song a hit. You have to go in and make these people think you're one of them… to debase yourself." Record promotion, even following the payola scandal Davis was caught up in, was a dirty business: the industry was peopled by characters that would sacrifice any ethical standard in order to sell records. The Rollers were lucky to have Michael Klenfner on their side.

Arista extended their hospitality to the band; dinners, lunches and shopping trips. While Davis had been President at CBS, the label was infamous for inviting working girls and boys to entertain guests at record conventions. McKeown later claimed Paton raped him in an American hotel room when he was 18 or 19 after being given Quaaludes, a sedative and hypnotic drug often prescribed for insomnia but infamous for enhancing sexual feelings when mixed with alcohol. He would be 20 in November. This was his first trip to America. In his autobiography he claimed that by the time the band got to America they were taking "various medication" to help them sleep "at the right times, be awake at the right time and do everything else at the right times". He said that, in fact, for a "fair wee while" there'd been "a stash of stuff to help us out as and when we'd needed it".

Paton had already admitted he was gobbling Valium. Speed pills were also on the menu. So too were Quaaludes. "Everybody took Quaaludes," said Danny Fields. "It was fun to take them. You don't just take them for sex although it enhances sex. It is not a date rape drug. You can't slip it on someone and it makes them feel good and it makes them feel like they want to get laid."

In his autobiography McKeown did not mention the rape but said he had "the weirdest and most horrible" dream while in America. In his book the notion he is dreaming often acts as a prelude to revelations about inter-band sex such as band members openly masturbating in front of others. This "dream" involved Faulkner, Wood, Paton and himself in a hotel room high on speed and Quaaludes. He said while the three of them indulged in sex he took photographs. He said later he found the roll of film removed from his camera.

The band had a stroke of luck when Bernstein found out via a contact that The Temptations had pulled out of filming for an NBC Ann-Margret TV special, a popular variety show that dated back to 1968, built around the acting and singing talents of the popular Swedish American host. The star of hit films such as *The Cincinnati Kid*, *Carnal Knowledge* and *Tommy*, Ann-Margret had also performed on screen with Elvis. At one time she was promoted as a female Elvis but her musical career never really took off. She was more of an all-round entertainer and had even been a character in an episode of *The Flintstones* cartoon. She was a hugely loved American star.

Bernstein quickly organised for the band to replace The Temptations. They played 'La Belle Jeane' from *Once Upon A Star* with Faulkner on mandolin and then 'Saturday Night' with Ann-Margret, dressed up as a Roller, singing with them. This was played out, for some reason, in front of a crowd of OAPs, some pictured knitting. The show would be broadcast on November 20.

Jackie magazine in conjunction with Capital Radio had sent over two 15-year-old competition winners to enjoy four days in New York with the Rollers. They wrote – for a later edition of *Jackie* – of visiting the Statue of Liberty, United Nations building, Manhattan, Greenwich Village, the top of the Empire State building with the band. The Rollers also wanted to see Harlem.

The competition winners also went to the live recording of the *Saturday Night Live With Howard Cosell* TV show. The band was given a police escort to the Ed Sullivan Theatre on Broadway and 53rd Street, and there were a mob of fans outside. John Wayne was appearing as a guest alongside a tiger-taming act. Phil Wainman had flown in to co-ordinate the Rollers' sound. "That was supposed to be live but it wasn't," he said. "They did appear live and they did sing live but did we feed their live performance through to the TV audience? The answer is, no. I had a tape with me. We set the whole thing up at the auditorium; we put microphones on the girls screaming and we played the track to the auditorium. The producer wasn't up for it initially until I explained to him the boys had come a long way and it'd be a shame if I had to stick them on a plane back because they will not play live."

The conceit that the band appeared from inside a giant tartan box wrapped with big bow, and stamped 'With care. Made in Scotland', was novel. But following a small explosion and puff of smoke, and the unfolding of the box, the performance fell strangely flat, nothing like the hysteria generated at the recent London show directed by Mike Mansfield. Bernstein said that initially he'd managed to persuade the producers of the show to allow him a third of the 600 tickets to give away to Rollers fans. "But at the last minute they switched their position in case the Rollers fans interrupted the rest of the show," he said. "Instead of getting 200 tickets, I got 60." Clive Davis got four and Bernstein got four. "That meant only 52 young people got seats and they were all put up in the balcony so it was subdued, controlled and there was something wrong with the sound. It turned out that a transmitter in New Jersey was malfunctioning so they couldn't be heard properly. That was an unlucky break."

Bernstein continued to defend the group. "There were hundreds of kids outside the Ed Sullivan Theatre," he said. "I don't like to make comparisons to The Beatles but I've never seen anything like it since then." It fell on deaf ears. The truth was the rest of the country had grown ambivalent to the revolving cast of New York's latest media darlings. In the Midwest, West, South and Northeast, there was almost hostility toward what New York tried to sell as the next big thing. The harmless, cute, vapid Rollers were a classic case in point.

Bernstein lowered his expectations. "My hopes now are to bring them in, in early spring, into venues that they will be totally comfortable with and that will give them very strong contact with the audiences. That'll be halls ranging from 3 to 5,000 seats. I was carried away by the wild imagination I have... I want to do what I think is best for them and their audience. There is always time later on to go back to thinking about my wilder schemes."

He remained upbeat however. He said he had as many as 30 to 40 calls a week to his office inquiring about merchandising after the Cosell show. "Three or four manufacturers a day wanted to make Bay City Rollers T-shirts," he said. "I have never had such an experience." Bernstein wanted to handle licensing of the Rollers' merchandise but it was taken over by 'Honest' Ed Justin who operated out of the Columbia Pictures building in New York. Columbia Pictures owned Arista. Justin had been in charge of merchandising for Screen Gems, the television production subsidiary of Columbia Pictures, for three decades. His office door had the 'Honest' crossed out. He had marketed everything from *The Flintstones* and Yogi Bear to David Cassidy. "We get five per cent royalty on each item," he said. "We don't do any work but grant licenses; no designing or manufacturing — we just collect money." The

Partridge Family he said had earned almost $1 million in royalties in two years. The big money was in commercials.

Justin was confident the Rollers logo would "adorn millions of artifacts in the next 12 months and the band will receive vast sums". There was talk of one company planning to include a record by the Rollers on the back of specially marked cereal boxes in America. Justin said he had made no deals yet. It would be "unfair to license them before they have made it". "I can get a better deal when they are a hit and it would be premature right now," he said. "I am waiting for their record to get to number one."

Straight after appearing on the Cosell show, later the same evening, the band and Paton left New York and flew to Bermuda for a few days' rest. Of course there was a photographer at hand to take pictures of the band "relaxing", all perched on little 50cc bikes with baskets. The real reason they were in Bermuda, it seemed, was to open offshore bank accounts, presumably to filter any future US earnings.

There was a flurry of activity behind the scenes regarding the band's business affairs that went unreported and was difficult to unravel. None of the main players will talk openly about it; some are dead. It happened as 'Saturday Night' slowly began to take off in America. On October 18 the single was at number 64 on the *Billboard* singles chart. The band's American compilation album was at number 89. The single was certain to rise higher as the unstoppable Michael Klenfner had secured the song on the playlist of WABC, the major New York AM station. Other important radio markets such as San Francisco, Chicago, Atlanta, Philadelphia and Boston, were reporting that the song was also getting favourable responses.

Primarily, and most significantly, the band was required to agree a new deal with Arista Records to supersede their old contract with Bell. The appointment of 'Honest' Ed Justin to handle the band's merchandise was likely part of the deal.

Barry Perkins seemed in the thick of the deal making. Certainly, the two heavyweight New York lawyers appointed to make the deal were well known to Arista boss, Clive Davis, well known to anyone in the music industry. One was dandyish Marty Machat, who represented The Four Seasons, James Brown, Phil Spector and Leonard Cohen and negotiated contracts for the Stones, The Kinks and The Who. The Brooklyn-born Machat did a lot of work with Allen Klein, the infamously tough New York accountant who'd managed The Beatles, Stones and Mickie Most's stable of acts. Phil Spector would accuse Machat of stealing from him, and there remain many questions over financial aspects of Leonard Cohen's career. Twenty-three years after Machat's death in 1988, a New York federal judge awarded the American government $3.2 million in unpaid taxes on his estate.

The other lawyer involved was Eric Kronfeld who had started out working for Machat. He had negotiated the contract between Philadelphia International Records and CBS when Clive Davis was President and it was malpractice by Philadelphia in terms of radio promotion that sparked the payola investigation that rocked the American industry. Davis, however, was impressed with Kronfeld and retained him for personal legal services. He would go on to be chief operating officer of PolyGram for a decade until he was demoted in 1997 for making racist remarks. He was known to be a Pit Bull Terrier type of lawyer, a colourful character who talked movie gangster tough and was involved in the careers of The Eagles, Eric Clapton, The Who and Lou Reed, whom he managed for 12 years. He was close to a significant portion of America's major music industry power brokers and had been involved at Arista in arranging the contracts for new signings, The Outlaws. Kronfeld also represented Paul Rothchild who'd produced The Doors and Janis Joplin.

Until his death in 2013 Kronfeld spent three decades successfully breeding racehorses, and was said to have bought his first two horses in England in 1975. That same year Barry Perkins had persuaded Arista's UK boss, Tony Roberts, to buy a horse called *Supersonic*, the name of Mike Mansfield's TV show. Roberts said he bought it in conjunction with Phil Wainman's manager, David Walker, and Perkins. "We kept getting bills for feed and vets and I'm not convinced it ever existed," said Roberts. "I think Barry was copping the money."

Tony Roberts was being sidelined by Davis and was not involved in any of the negotiations for the Rollers' new contract. His two-year contract with Arista was winding down and he was made aware it would not be renewed. "The reason was Clive felt I was too much Gary Glitter and Bay City Rollers and not enough Dire Straits and Queen," Roberts said. "Clive said he wanted to get somebody who would be signing more of those kind of acts."

Roberts' final signing at Arista UK was Slik, a Scottish act, featuring Midge Ure as singer, who were produced by Coulter/Martin. The pair wrote 'Forever And Ever' for the group in late 1975, a number one hit. Davis did not think Slik had a chance in America and didn't give them one.

"It was difficult," said Roberts. "Clive signed a number of acts I had a lot of trouble with [in the UK]. He was signing acts that weren't particularly commercial for the UK like Gil Scott-Heron. Machat and Kronfeld were very famous showbiz lawyers," added Roberts. "Machat was famous for being a really sharp guy, a little bit like Allen Klein. They both had reputations. Bills like $150,000 were quite normal to them. The American lawyers were very tough guys to deal with." Roberts was replaced by Bob Buziak, Arista's West Coast boss who moved to London at the request of Davis. Buziak was close to Davis whose reputation for knowing every last detail of company business, often clocking up 18-hour work days, was legend.

Stephen Tenenbaum was appointed to act as the Rollers' American accountant. Tenenbaum was only two years older than Paton, at 39, but a world apart. His accountancy firm, Eichler, Tenenbaum & Co, acted for major stars and specialised in scrutinising the music industry, conducting audits of record labels for publishers and artists. In 1972 he told *Billboard* magazine he had never been involved in audit of a record company that didn't involve recovery (of money) for an act. The more records an act sells the greater the chance of error, he said, adding that record labels offered only 'reluctant' amounts of cooperation. He had long called for accounting systems within the industry to be modernised.

McKeown said he had seen Perkins, the group's business manager, getting visibly excited by the money the band was generating: "It's a big pie, a big pie!" was a Perkins catchphrase. Perkins told the *Birmingham Post* that the Rollers might leave the country because of "crippling taxes". It was, he said, the "the only sensible course from a business point of view". Derek said 83p out of every pound went to the taxman.

Mike Mansfield called Perkins "a very nefarious character" who he suspected of taking back-handers. Stephen Goldberg he called "a rather strange and not a very pleasant character". "A lot of the money went missing I can assure you," Mansfield said.

It has been suggested that Perkins was keen to feather his own nest rather than attend to the band's best interests. Paton was not capable of dealing with men like Machat, Davis, Kronfeld and Tenenbaum. He still relied on his mum to help run the band's fan club. Perkins did the business.

The schizophrenic nature of what was now Paton's life was ably demonstrated as the teen press in America began to seriously cover the band. By November, 'Saturday Night' was in the top 20 and the band had their first *Tiger Beat* front cover: 'Make way for The Bay City Rollers'. The magazine was a West Coast rival of *16* and packaged teen idols for adolescent girls. Its content was largely made up of the sort of fluff associated with the Rollers' official magazine and in the coming months, as the Rollers featured endlessly, often lifted direct from there: all about the band, on stage pictures, in the studio, how they stay in shape, meet Tam (a recurring theme was each band members saying they owed everything to Paton), Rollers fashion and crucially the *Tiger Beat* girls they want to date! "We don't have anything to do with groupies," said Derek. "It can give you a bad reputation."

The band would start an unprecedented run of consecutive covers on *16* in January but the magazine was already cashing in on the group with a special one-off devoted to the Rollers. Although it covered much the same material as *Tiger Beat*, in the coming months *16* had the edge thanks to the access allowed to Danny Fields. The magazine was also located conveniently close to Arista and the offices of CJ Strauss. *16* urged readers to send in "$1 for a surprise package" that was "more pix and more private secrets". *16* also attempted to make the teen idols appear approachable and "attainable" for their young readers – "surrogate boyfriends". In *16* it was revealed that McKeown smoked but more crucially how he "loves reading fan mail".

Davis asked Bernstein to bring the band over for a five–city tour in December to stimulate added interest. He wanted them to play smaller Midwestern cities before the big tour scheduled for spring. Bernstein rejected the idea. He wanted to see the reaction to the Ann-Margret special and the NBC concert special. He estimated the band would potentially earn between $16 and $40 million dollars in America in 1976. "My theory is to give them heavier TV exposure than their predecessors to make them more recognizable," he said.

In the UK the band was back on the treadmill promoting their new single 'Money Honey' – according to McKeown the lyric was a dig about the greed Faulkner saw in the record business – and upcoming album, *Wouldn't You Like It?* There was special disc free with *Supersonic* magazine, featuring the single and an exclusive interview with Mike Mansfield. They were featured on the front cover of *Melody Maker.* 'Can the Rollers crack America?' They wrote that 'Saturday Night' was expected to shortly make the top 10. It was said to be galling for an experienced and skilled live group like Slade, who toured the US constantly for three years but had yet to chalk up any meaningful sales, whereas the Rollers' only public appearance so far was on a TV show. An Arista spokesman told the paper: "The excitement level at the company is very high but the growth potential does depend on what happens next. I hear they have been recording new material in England a lot depends on that."

The Rollers' impact was now being felt around the world: not just Japan, Europe and Australia but in countries like Iraq. They were huge in Baghdad. In an October issue of the Communist Russian magazine *Sovietskaya Kulturam* the Rollers, together with "sadistic films and pornographic literature" were said to be part of a big-business plot to stupefy the masses. 'Money Honey' was in danger of getting lost in the American rise of 'Saturday Night' and the controversy that now surrounded McKeown with both his court cases due to be heard. On November 12 he was fined £10,000 for what was called a "violent and unprovoked attack" on the photographer at the gig in Oxford. He was also handed a three–month suspended prison sentence.

On November 16, two days before McKeown was due at Edinburgh Sheriff Court to face a charge of causing death by reckless driving, the

Rollers appeared at the Saturday Scene British Pop Awards at Wembley Pool. Some 8,000 Rollers fans watched them play a short set alongside Alvin Stardust, The Wombles and Gary Glitter. They mimed to 'Money Honey', 'Shout' and 'Bye Bye Baby'. *NME* said that during the latter number, as the fans went crazy, 'they were the best band in the country'. When host Sally James announced the Rollers had left building, the fans went into hysterical abandon, hurling themselves at the stage.

More hordes of hysterical girls attended McKeown's trial. Rumours circulated that Paton had lined up a substitute singer in case McKeown, who was said to be facing up to 10 years, ended up in prison. The teen tipped for the role was 16-year-old apprentice joiner Martin Donald, a 'wardrobe assistant' during the spring tour of the UK. It was also suggested the good-looking Donald had been in line to replace Alan when he said he might quit after the scandal broke about his real age. Donald couldn't even play an instrument and in all likelihood Paton promised him a role in the Rollers so as to be able to take advantage of him.

McKeown's trail attracted a slew of misinformation. One witness definitely said McKeown was speeding. It was claimed he was going as fast as 100mph. There was a suggestion he was drunk and probably high. A crucial part of his defence appeared to be the OAP he'd killed wasn't wearing the spectacles she'd normally wear to see and was walking erratically. Then "at the eleventh hour", said McKeown, the nurse whom he claimed had helped him from the wreckage "appeared from nowhere" and convinced the court there was nothing McKeown could have done to avoid the accident.

The fans screamed with delight when McKeown was cleared of causing Euphemia Clunie's death. It was noted he'd been driving at 40mph in a 30mph zone and he was found guilty of the lesser charge of driving recklessly, fined £1,500 and banned from driving for a year.

McKeown was said to have displayed little concern at the time for the woman or her family and instead rebuked his QC for being "fucking useless". Paton said he had employed the top barrister in Scotland for McKeown, a senior legal figure, "to go into a small court to defend him". He added: "He gets off with killing somebody, but still people look at me like I'm the bad man."

The following week in *Record Mirror* Paton denied that he had a replacement lined up for McKeown and said he had never seriously considered McKeown would be jailed. If he had been "we would have waited on Les because The Bay City Rollers are a five-man unit and each one is equally important." Paton added that Martin Donald was one of three young men who had formed Kip, with whom he was also involved.

The same day McKeown left court a free man, the Rollers mimed 'Money Honey' for an appearance on *Top Of The Pops* shown on November 20 and repeated on December 10. Compared to the previous two UK singles of 1975, there was only a short promotional burst for 'Money Honey' as the band had a commitment to tour Australia. On November 22 they mimed the single on LWT's *Saturday Scene* and the following week did the same on Mansfield's *Supersonic* show.

The single peaked at number three in the UK. Out of the top-selling UK singles of the year it ranked at number 65, compared to 'Give A Little Love' at number 11. 'Bye Bye Baby', of course, was the best-selling UK single of the year. It was no disaster, especially considering the circumstances of its release and as it was the first single written by Faulkner/Wood a cause for some celebration. The band members were all rightly pleased. According to McKeown, however, Paton was not. He sought to crush Faulkner's self-esteem and make him feel inadequate – a tactic he used on every band member. He screamed at Faulkner, "Look what you've done, we only got to number three because of you – the Rollers are finished!"

The new album *Wouldn't You Like It?* was a platinum record before it was released with huge advance orders of close to 400,000. As the band picked up platinum discs for their first two UK albums from boxer John Conteh – cue Rollers in boxing gloves poses – Paton told the press: "These lads won't finish with nothing in their pockets like so many other groups. We're too canny for that." The fan club now had over 100,000 members.

The *Melody Maker* review of the new album was scathing. It was called "musically incompetent from a musically incompetent band". The paper said there was no "secret talent" lurking in the "creative sources within the band" meaning Faulkner/Wood who were credited with writing 11 of its 12 songs. These songs were "so weak as to be instantly forgettable" with "not the slightest trace of musical potential". The lyrics were "pathetic". It was difficult to disagree. It was also difficult to know why Faulkner had given the album's title track the same name as an abandoned Rollers song recorded while Nobby Clark was the group's singer. Why, also he had made the song overtly sexual?

The rest of the Faulkner/Wood songs on the album were either lachrymose teeny ballads such as the Faulkner-voiced 'Shanghai'd In Love', corny and derivative inoffensive upbeat rockers such as 'I Only Wanna Dance With You' or middle of the road attempts at Beatles-esque adult pop such as 'Here Comes That Feeling Again'. Much of the material had been recorded earlier in the year with Wainman at Chipping Norton studios with overdubs done at Eden studios in Chiswick, west London, a facility run by Colin Frechter's brother-in-law. One track *Melody Maker* singled out as rising above the mediocre was 'Eagles Fly', an American-sounding acoustic track with sophisticated harmonies that the band had recorded afresh with Colin Frechter at Eden. The final song on the album was an instrumental, 'Derek's End Piece', seemingly named after Derek's cock.

It was barely an album, just a random collection of songs, reflective perhaps of the problems the band was now experiencing with producer Phil Wainman. Faulkner questioned why 'Money Honey' was not on the album, although 'Give A Little Love' was. There were other tracks he felt should have been included too. Nonetheless it did the job, filled the gap, and as The Bay City Rollers album that came the closest to being entirely self-penned is something of a rare gem. Arista UK advertised the fact the album sleeve folded out to make a colour picture of the band. Wood was pushed to the front now, showing his bare chest and utilising the Paton-directed trick of leaving the top button of his trousers undone. It was supposed to be sexy. The band was beginning to look a little worn out, prostituted.

The album peaked at UK number three. It also went to number three in Australia, where 'Money Honey' also made number three in the singles chart. The band arrived on December 2 for a short 10-day sold out tour of the country and New Zealand. It was estimated they'd sold 60,000 tickets for the gigs. Their arrival was big news. Daily Melbourne newspaper *The Age* reported on fans camping out to buy tickets. The Australian *Women's Weekly*, a monthly magazine, gave them a huge spread that ignored McKeown's recent court appearance amid much fluff about their "boys next door" appeal and "unspoiled, unaffected, amiable" personalities. "And they're single."

McKeown claimed that his mother gave him a couple of Mandrax tablets – the UK name for Quaaludes – to take on the flight and an Australian doctor wrote him a prescription for 100 more when he arrived. Paton was now using them frequently to relax [the drug was also a muscle relaxant] his young sexual partners for what could be painful penetration. McKeown made up a story about using the pills to drug the band and Paton to sleep so he could sneak out and meet girls for sex. He later admitted that was a lie. The band asked McKeown to share the drugs. The murk behind the scenes thickened. Faulkner privately felt that Wood had been "brainwashed" by Paton and was "pathetic" in allowing himself to be so manipulated by their manager. In public, the front remained. Faulkner told the Australian press, the band was clean cut. "That's just the way we are," he said, calling drugs "old-fashioned".

McKeown said the promoter of the tour had organised a group of prostitutes for the band at the hotel, presuming they'd be like every other visiting UK band. Paton raged. There were thousands of fans outside the hotel in Melbourne, all dressed in Roller gear. The band was hugely supported by 3XY radio station, offering reports on their arrival, interviews with the band and their music on rotation. Some teen fans had booked into the hotel hoping to meet them. A mix-up between security and promoters left the band stranded outside the hotel and their car was rocked and pounded by the fans. "Rollers set the city rocking," was *The Age* headline.

At the 5,000-capacity Festival Hall the chaos continued. The band was playing two shows, one at 6pm and another at 8pm. When McKeown reached out his hand to the crowd there was pandemonium. Ambulance officers treated score of girls for hysteria. The over-enthusiasm of fans did not concern Paton. "We haven't had any deaths," he repeated. In the street afterwards there was hundreds of fans flat out, distraught, sobbing. Twenty minutes into the second set at Festival Hall, Wood collapsed on stage. The group carried on without him.

The band flew to Canberra. Wood collapsed again on the plane. An ambulance met them at the airport and he was taken straight to hospital. Two 14-year-old girls kissed McKeown enthusiastically and wept when the band left the airport. The local newspaper, *The Canberra Times*, put Wood's illness on their front page on December 4. Without Wood, the two shows in the city, again at 6 and 8pm were both cut short. At the 6pm show, 20 girls were pulled out of the 1,800 crowd with heat exhaustion.

It was reported that due to Wood's illness – described as nervous exhaustion and a few days later as heat exhaustion aggravated by a throat infection – the New Zealand leg of the tour was cancelled. Derek said the tour was well organised but tiring and they were all suffering from "exhaustion". Wood was expected to be out of hospital in time for the show in Brisbane, four days away. While he was unconscious in hospital, a teddy bear was placed on his pillow and photographs taken for the press. Cute. Manipulated.

McKeown reported of multiple female fans at his hotel all ready and willing, sexually aroused and gagging for it. *The Canberra Times* reported an awkward meeting with six young competition winners, girls aged 8-14. There was prolonged silence – no one knew what to say.

Two hundred teen and pre-teen fans were at Sydney Airport to shriek for the band. Wood remained in hospital in Canberra. "Tam did say if things had got worse he'd have put me on a plane [home]," said Wood. "It was a virus and dehydration." Girls scrambled on top of a police car to get a better view of the group. The police spent their time confronting sobbing girls who appeared to be suffering from hysteria. "We didn't have a chance to see anything in Australia," said McKeown. "It was like being part of an army the rules were so strict."

The tour stopped at Newcastle Civic Theatre and Adelaide where 500 fans stormed the stage and the show had to be stopped for 15 minutes. Sydney was another two-gig day. Again around 200 fans met the band at the airport. About 100 had to be carried out of the first show at the 5,000-capacity Hordern Pavilion after fainting or collapsing. It was described as the wildest concert ever seen in Sydney with police starting to carry girls out to waiting ambulances during the first number. The show was cut to 40 minutes because it was feared someone would be killed. The second concert was stopped after just five minutes as a crush got dangerous. Paton warned the crowd the band would not come back unless things calmed down. Twenty girls fainted and had to be taken out. The concert lasted just 25 minutes.

The gig put the band on the front cover of the *Sydney Morning Herald*: "Hysteria as pop group hits Sydney". Four teens were taken to hospital, aged 14 and 15, and described as suffering from "bruising, hysteria and a sprained ankle". Over 30 others were treated at the scene. The newspaper described the pavement outside as resembling the "casualty clearing station".

Just days after returning to Edinburgh, with news that 'Saturday Night' was almost certain now to reach number one in America, on Thursday December 18, a fan was shot in the head outside McKeown's home in Torpichen, near Bathgate, West Lothian. McKeown had long expressed his annoyance at the constant vigil fans held outside his home. That night, as usual, there were about a hundred or so. McKeown said it made it "impossible to relax and unwind". Nonetheless he said he was having a party with a house full of hangers-on and people he said were vaguely connected with the music business. He printed this in his autobiography even though his alibi differed in court. There was a suggestion that some fans would make it past the front gates of the house and try and crawl up the driveway. The game was to shine a spotlight on them from the upstairs lounge window and aim.

Newspapers reported that Margaret Ness, aged 15, required stitches after being shot in the forehead with an air rifle. The police visited McKeown and found his air rifle and he was charged with recklessly discharging a loaded firearm. Ness said she had been trying to deliver a Christmas card. She said she was sat on a low wall outside the house when she was shot. Ness had made dozens of trips to the house.

McKeown was going to jail. He was still on his three-month suspended prison sentence for assault. The band's UK PR Alan Walsh said: "My role moved from promotion to protection. It became more that I was there to stop the bad publicity and encourage the good publicity. With the shooting an airgun out the window and hitting a fan... my job there was to dampen it down. I just stone-walled. We just said it was an accident and he apologised and damped it down really. Didn't let it develop into a bigger story. The fact I was a trained journalist and had worked that side of the road enabled me to appeal to other journalists, don't build this up into something it wasn't. It was an accident and it's all over. They were prepared to accept that because they could see the band was likely to get bigger and bigger and they didn't want to kill it off and make enemies of me and the management by tearing them apart over that incident."

"We were in the process of negotiating with British Caledonian Airways [at the time the UK's foremost independent, international scheduled airline]," said BCR merchandise chief Paul Pike. "We'd developed a seven colour tartan. We were going to turn that into the official tartan because you can't copy it. We were going to launch it for the American tour. Three things happened to put British Caledonian off: first he knocked over the old lady, then he clocked a photographer over the head at Oxford, and then the third one was the shooting of the fan ... that was the final straw for Caledonian. They were going to give the Rollers a plane and deck out the air hostesses in the seven colour tartan for America."

The Ness case would not reach court until September 1976. Until then, McKeown would operate under the threat of a prison sentence. There was fogginess to everything now: a sense of unreality. The schedule was unrelenting. The band played two shows in Belfast, the most violent city in the UK, at the ABC Theatre on December 22. It got them another *Melody Maker* cover: "Rollers Storm Belfast". All proceeds from the gigs were going to charity. In Belfast they rode in a bulletproof, armour-plated Land Rover and the teen fans still tried to get at them, rocking the vehicle from side to side.

During a radio interview neither Faulkner nor McKeown knew what charity the gigs were in aid of. Paton interrupted and said it was for a non-sectarian organisation that sent kids of all religions on holidays away from the six counties. He was not sure what it was called. He asked the interviewer to start the interview again. "They're not strong on Irish politics," he said. Wood told *Melody Maker.* "There's the troubles but then everyone's got troubles." He said the troubles were "a bit silly. Why not forgive and forget?"

The Belfast gigs were manic, with 100 bouncers and 100 police holding back 4,000 screaming girls. Once again, the support act was the Young City Stars. They visited Little Kellerstain over Christmas and shortly afterwards guitarist Ian Mitchell "started to get a bit funny", said singer Damian McKee. "Then Ian disappeared off for two or three days so he'd obviously gone back over on his own." Mitchell left the Young City Stars. "I had a fair suspicion he was away over to Edinburgh," said McKee. "I didn't know for sure he was going in the Rollers but the talk at the time was Alan wasn't happy. You put two and two together."

Paton was keen for the Rollers to be seen doing charity work to enhance their image, damaged by McKeown's recent recklessness. He had already overseen the group being filmed visiting children in hospital for a Christmas episode of *Top Of The Pops,* that ran of December 23, to the tune of 'Give A Little Love'. Paton was also active away from the cameras, bagging up the endless stream of cuddly toys sent to the fan club and taking them to a children's home, Nazareth House, in Lasswade, run by nuns and riddled with abuse. Paton had been visiting there since 1967. In the mid-seventies he went regularly with bags of these cuddly toys and the staff there knew him well.★

The Rollers were back on *Top Of The Pops* on Christmas Day, performing 'Bye Bye Baby'. There was little escape from them that day, the star on top of the pop Christmas tree. Many fans would have received as a Christmas present the band's first annual, a thick colour

---

★ In 2000 a nun named Sister Alphonso was convicted on four counts of cruelty to children in her care at Nazareth House. It was reported she had abused and humiliated children there between 1965 and 1980. In the same case, Peter Blaney, 54, a former helper and resident at the home was jailed for six years for regularly sexually abusing two brothers, one who was nine at the time, at the home between 1969 and 1972.

hardback detailing their year in soft-focus hues but with great pictures. After *Top Of The Pops*, at 5pm, there was *The Bay City Rollers Show* on Granada. This was originally supposed to be their own hour-long TV special but was now advertised as "with Gilbert O'Sullivan" who performed the bulk of the material on the show, alongside guests such as Elton John and Showaddywaddy. In fact there was only one Rollers song during the entire hour-long programme. Then at 6pm they were stars of *Mike Mansfield's Supersonic Christmas Special* alongside Gary Glitter, Marc Bolan, Slade, Mud and The Sweet.

There was no doubt 1975 had been the Rollers' year. They had even inspired songwriter/producer Nick Lowe, who had recently left Brinsley Schwarz, to write a tribute song, 'Bay City Rollers We Love You', attributed to The Tartan Horde (it was a hit in Japan). They had also hooked up with Cadbury to promote a chewy caramel ladder chocolate bar called Curly Wurly that saw them featured on the wrapper. Paton had pushed them to the very limit of their credibility and capabilities. They needed some time off. It was never going to happen. In early January 'Saturday Night' reached number one on the America charts. It was at number one in Canada too, top 10 in Germany, where they were on the cover of the January issue of *Bravo*, and at number two in Holland. The song's co-writer Bill Martin said the single sold in excess of 20 million copies worldwide. The compilation album Davis had thrown together for the American market rose to US number 20, selling 500,000 copies, and went to number one in Canada, selling a further 100,000.

The band knew what it meant. "We had started to move away from tartan, that was getting a bit jaded now, we'd done it for two years," said Faulkner. "We got to America and we were right back to square one again."

It meant more pills, more flights, more hotel rooms, more miming, more abuse and more screaming.

CHAPTER 8

Compulsion

"Tam started me on drugs. When we got a wee bit tired, he'd give us amphetamines. He'd keep us awake with speed, black bombers, and then it becomes a little culture, doesn't it? I've got this great stuff from a chauffeur, Mandrax, whatever, so you end up almost showing off to each other what stupid drugs you've taken."

– Eric Faulkner

In New York Arista boss Clive Davis was guest speaker at a meeting of the Entertainment Analysts Group, comprised of 35 Wall Street analysts specialising in the leisure-time industries including broadcasting, movies, theatre and the record business. He told the assembled men that Arista was "very substantially profitable both domestically and internationally". The licensing fees from EMI, which distributed Arista internationally [Polydor still handled Europe outside the UK], was "well into seven figures", ie tens of millions.

Davis attributed this to the signing and development of new talent and the successes of three carry over artists from the Bell days – Barry Manilow, Melissa Manchester and the Rollers.

He also pointed to Arista's successes in America with new artists like southern rock band The Outlaws, former Raspberries singer Eric

Carmen and Monty Python among others. Davis explained that Arista's success has stemmed from "the signing, nurturing and development of new artists". He did not mention Patti Smith, a critical success but not commercially strong – without a hit single *Horses* did not make the American Top 40. Arista's heavy backing of Gil Scott-Heron garnered similar results, although a 1975 album of his did make the top 40. Davis was also about to sign Lou Reed, managed by his lawyer Kronfeld, to give Arista even more cutting edge kudos. He also signed critically acclaimed folk singer Loudon Wainwright III.

All this enabled Davis to boast that "no company that's come into the record business since A&M" had had the initial success that Arista enjoyed. Profits, he declared, were up 700 per cent by the end of 1975 and "1975 was the largest year in the record industry's history". His former label, CBS, paid the company close to a $5 million advance to sell music by Arista acts in the Columbia Record Club, a mail order business.

Davis' reputation was significantly recovered following the expenses and payola scandal. He was on a seemingly unstoppable up curve. As such, he had found the song he wanted the Rollers to record to follow up 'Saturday Night', a Tim Moore song called 'Rock And Roll Love Letter'. He was unequivocal about this and also planned to have another Rollers album out by the time Bernstein had promised to tour the group. Bernstein had told Davis his plan to bring the group to America for "an adrenalin shot" – more promotion – in January and then his "gut" was telling him March for the tour.

Davis cobbled together a package of songs (all by Faulkner/Wood) from the band's UK albums two and three, *Once Upon A Star* and *Wouldn't You Like It?* but intended to hang the American album on 'Rock And Roll Love Letter' which he felt would be a huge hit single.

The Rollers were not keen on the song Davis wanted them to record. The success of 'Money Honey' had buoyed their sense of self-sufficiency in the songwriting department. They had assumed that it would be their next American single and that they would have a significant say in the future of their career but Davis was adamant. "I'm pretty relentless," he said.

Phil Wainman, already teetering on the edge after seeing only one of his songs included on *Wouldn't You Like It?*, would be the first casualty of this stand-off. He had spent a week rehearsing a new set of Faulkner/Wood songs with the group that he felt "weren't really worth cutting it". Then Davis ordered him to record 'Rock And Roll Love Letter'.

"Clive Davis didn't even want to put their music out initially," he said. "It was Sid Bernstein who arranged everything. Clive was a musical snob and didn't see the potential in the band until they had 'Saturday Night' at number one. Then when he did get involved the American market was something he wanted to concentrate on and he sort of forgot about the UK. When it went to America Clive wanted to put his own stamp on it. 'Rock And Roll Love Letter' was his contribution to The Bay City Rollers. It had to be recorded. The boys said, 'Well you go and tell Clive where to stick his 'Rock And Roll Love Letter'."

Davis visited London to make it happen, staying at the luxury 5 star Dorchester Hotel in central London not the Holiday Inn in Slough. He wanted Wainman to stay on as band producer. "I was summoned for an audience," said Wainman. "He was saying to me, 'Let this thing run, don't rock the boat, just work with the boys.' I said, 'Clive you don't understand. The boys don't want to record that song, they've told me they don't want to record it because they've got a load of material of their own they want to record.'"

"It started to get a bit bitchy," he said. "Clive got bitchy with them and they got bitchy with him. I was piggy in the middle and that's when I said to Clive, 'You know what, I've had enough. I've got a career of my own. I don't really need to be dealing with this kind of crap' and that was it. I went. The band was dumbfounded that I could up and walk out. They thought I was desperate to stay with them." Wainman would go on to work with punk act Generation X and post-punk group The Boomtown Rats, including producing their hit 'I Don't Like Mondays'.

It is interesting to note, in light of the band's subsequent troubles with Arista over royalty payments, that after a lengthy legal dispute of his own regarding his royalty payments Wainman settled out of court with Arista in 2005 for an undisclosed fee.

Colin Frechter stepped up from musical director to produce 'Rock And Roll Love Letter' in Nova Sound studios in central London, previously used by The Who. "They were already trying to put it together when I got to the studio," he said. "I helped them get it down on tape." Davis did not see Frechter as a long-term replacement for Wainman and began looking for a new producer for the group but he was happy with the track. "He wanted the voice lifting in the middle and I remixed it as he requested and sent it off," said Frechter. "He phoned back and said, 'I love it, it's going to be the next single.'" Frechter stayed with the band, acting as musical director for their next studio album, in the interim writing the live arrangements for Brotherhood Of Man's April 1976 Eurovision Song Contest winner 'Save Your Kisses For Me', 1976's best-selling single in the UK.

The Rollers flew to America on January 15 and met with Davis. He had acquiesced to their demands to release 'Money Honey' as the Rollers' next American single, only it seems because of the elongated, problematic recording of 'Rock And Roll Love Letter'. "A mistake," said Carol Klenfner. "They wanted to grow, develop, they had aspirations of being more... but I'm not sure their audience wanted that for them."

Bernstein got them on the Cosell show again, miming to 'Money Honey' and 'Saturday Night'. The level of fan hysteria had moved up a gear following their number one success in the country. The frothy coverage in *16* continued. They would appear on the cover of the February issue as they had the January issue: 'Roller Riot! Join the Gang on the Bay City Bandwagon! How to meet them! Only *16* tells you how! Personal fax and new pix!' The band was photographed clutching cuddly toys. There was also a Rollerline for fans to call for up-to-date info.

Danny Fields, of *16*, was with the group again for much of this visit. He not only wrote them up but photographed them exclusively. "In the exhilaration of their conquest of America," he said. "Tam was good fun, good to go out with, hang out and laugh at people. He got a kick out of everything, got kick out of New York. And he was really good on the road, I learned a lot from him. I learned attitudes from him... and ways of changing mood when you are on the road with musicians, or a band, or five young guys. There were people wanting to get to them and I saw how he manoeuvered that and how he dealt with security, unwanted arrivals and expected arrivals… he was very cool and very good at that, he was a pro. I learned from him."

Of the band Fields was closest to McKeown. They hung out together alone. Fields recalled a night in a hotel in Biscayne Bay, Miami, when they took a boombox and sat at the edge of the pier, listening to Pink Floyd and smoked a joint. "He was a good-looking kid and in America the pictures being used were my pictures 80 per cent of the time," said Fields. One of America's most revered music archivists, Fields recalled that, "not one of the band said the gayest thing or made the gayest gesture when I was in with them". Nor did he see them with female groupies. "It was as if they were little priests or acolytes and we all assumed they were continually, always and eternally virgins. That's the way they were being marketed and that's the way I was tacitly enlisted to perpetrate this. There were some things Tam said about them where I wanted to ask him what did you mean by that but I didn't want to tip into that subject where the boys were concerned. He may have wanted to for a second; he had to tell someone, he could tell me anything but not about the band because I was professionally committed to perpetrating the virgin legend, myth, the virgin birth, and I was happy to do it."

In New York, Paton continued the UK shtick of having the band visit children in hospital and they were photographed with kids at the Queens Psychiatric Hospital. Arista Promotions boss, Michael Klenfner, was on hand again to guide the band and 'Money Honey' through the American radio process. With a number one single, this was proving easier. Already New York's FM station, WXLO, an adult Top 40 station, was playing 'Money Honey'. Klenfner had the band interviewed on the station and also flew them to key stations in Atlanta, Philadelphia (where they were greeted by the mayor), Boston and Detroit. They also made appearances on local TV stations, for one memorable mime to 'Saturday Night' Derek was absent and McKeown was positioned on drums. The band was still in full tartan wear, wearing scarves and bare-chested.

The dates Bernstein had planned for March did not materialise. 'Money Honey' quickly climbed the *Billboards* singles chart, peaking at an impressive number nine. 'Money Honey' was also a second number one single in Canada and another top 20 in Germany. "They were fun, it was a fun ride," said Carol Klenfner. "Maybe we got them farther than they imagined, cooking this up. It was legitimate in the UK, pandemonium, and our attitude was, 'Let's see what we can do in the US' and it was pretty successful in the *16* audience. The Rollers appealed to girls who weren't into David Cassidy, who weren't into that mainstream look. They appealed to individuals. They were for girls who wanted something a little different. But it's hard to fill a stadium with that. They were a little off-centre, that was their appeal."

The album Davis had hastily assembled for America, titled *Rock 'n' Roll Love Letter*, was in stores by March. Production standards were low. It featured the same cover photo of the band as seen on *Wouldn't You Like It?* and the title of the album did not quite match the name of the Frechter produced 'Rock And Roll Love Letter' which was featured on the album alongside 'Money Honey'. It didn't matter. Although the album peaked at 31 on the *Billboard* charts it sold over 500,000 copies, significantly more than UK number one albums were selling. It also went to the top in Canada, selling over 100,000 and replacing the band's previous American album at number one. This was some feat for band that had not yet played in America or Canada.

Davis set in motion 'Rock And Roll Love Letter' as the band's next single. The Rollers did not agree and determined to prove him wrong. Amid a flurry of European promotional engagements they spent a weekend recording new original material with English producer Muff Winwood. A former member of the Spencer Davis Group, alongside his talented brother Steve, Winwood now worked as an A&R man for Island Records. He had produced The Sutherland Brothers, Spooky Tooth and Sparks for the label, gaining much acclaim and chart success.

"I was running Island's studio complex in Basing Street," he said. "I was called by the band's manager, Tam Paton, and asked to do it. I think they had liked what I'd done with Sparks. He said that they were desperate to record their songs. Their producers had said they hadn't got any songs any good and the band was saying we want to record them. I think it was Tam's idea that they find somebody and just ask that somebody if they would like to cut a couple of tracks with them."

It was arranged that the Rollers would arrive at the studio on Saturday morning and Paton needed two songs finished and mixed by Sunday night. "I said, 'Well what do the two songs sound like?' and he said, 'That's irrelevant, you've just got to record them,'" said Winwood. "I turned up at the studio at 9am and at 10 a van pulls up and I think 'Oh here they are'. Out of the van comes two delivery guys and they had 10 or 12 giant cardboard boxes of basketball boots, all dumped in the studio. I said 'What they hell are these for?' They said, 'Oh the guys have a deal with this company.' About half an hour later the band turned up, two or three and then a couple separately. The first thing we all did was not talk about music at all. We all sat down in the reception area and opened all these boxes and were passing round these boots and I got myself two free pairs of boots.

"Finally the roadies turn up and the equipment gets pushed in and we start to record. They'd only got two songs. I didn't have any choice. My main job was to make sure the songs were constructed right and arranged right, and I just had to do everything in my power to make sure the songs came across as commercial as I could make them. I was a producer that 99 per cent of the time worked with artists who wrote their own material. Wainman and Coulter were the kind of producers who like Simon Cowell found songs for artists – come into the studio and this is the song you're going to record. I never made a recording like that. I was very good at taking a song in its raw state and helping the band shape it into the best possible thing it could be. Sometimes they had too many verses before they got to the chorus or there was no middle bit or the middle bit was too long or they played a guitar solo in it that was too long or it didn't end properly or it didn't have a decent introduction. I'd say you'd be able to make this song better by doing this or that and then they would do it. I wouldn't do it for them, they would. I'd just give them the ideas on how to do it… that's why they chose me."

Winwood was impressed by Faulkner's ability. "A very good little musician," he said. "At the time they were derided in the music industry, everybody who had anything to say hated them and thought they were bunch of nobodies. But Eric was very helpful in the studio putting the stuff together. I knew Phil Wainman, I phoned him up when they asked me. He said, 'Oh bloody hell, rather you than me.' He gave me the impression it was going to be hard work but it was okay and that one song was very good ['Love Me Like I Love You']. It was obvious which was the A-side and the B. I was expecting it to be really tough and dragging these guys through the process. In fact they were well together, the bass player was very good too. We managed to cut the tracks reasonably quickly. Their music wasn't my kind of music but I was very surprised with their musicianship and they coped very well. And on top of that they were extremely hard working. They worked hard in the studio. Not one outside musician on the session."

News leaked that the band was in the Island studio complex. "At the time it was in a very rough part of Notting Hill," said Winwood. "You looked left and right if you left at midnight. But for the entire 48 hours the street outside was full of girls. You couldn't go out, we had to send outside for food. We managed to get both songs recorded and mixed by Sunday night and I never saw them again."

Winwood was paid close to £75,000 for his time. He bought a cottage in Cornwall with the money. He still has it. He went on to become a long-standing executive at Sony. He claimed that it was only in 2005, after Sony took a stake in Arista, that he began receiving his 2 per cent royalty on the record.

'Love Me Like I Love You', credited to Faulkner/Wood, was the band's finest moment as a self-contained unit. It had great harmonies, cool hooks, and a classic chorus. Paton determined to get it out as the next UK single as soon as possible. It put him at loggerheads with Davis who had scheduled the release of 'Rock And Roll Love Letter' as a single for April.

The demand for the band was overwhelming. Faulkner described himself as a "walking zombie". He said he had been prescribed amphetamines to suppress his appetite. Paton was constantly chiding him to watch his weight. "That made him hate me," Paton said. "He felt it didn't matter if he was 20 stone that people would still pile in to see him. But it doesn't work like that. I don't care who it is, even Led Zeppelin. There's an image there." Faulkner found he enjoyed amphetamines and had becoming addicted. He was taking downers like Secanol and Valium to help him sleep. He also admitted to experimenting with LSD.

"Tam started me on drugs,' Faulkner said. 'When we got a wee bit tired, he'd give us amphetamines. He'd keep us awake with speed, black bombers, and then it becomes a little culture, doesn't it? I've got this great stuff from a chauffeur, Mandrax, whatever, so you end up almost showing off to each other what stupid drugs you've taken."

There was plenty of Quaaludes [as Mandrax was more commonly known outside the UK] and a plethora of other tablets in different colours, greys and reds, which were amphetamines.

There was promotion in Italy at the end of January, a German TV show (the popular *Disco*) on February 14, charity appearances in London for the sick and needy and at an award ceremony hosted by Trade publication *Music Week*, where the band dressed in kilts to collect an award for the best-selling UK album of 1975. Derek collapsed on stage in February.

Crucially for McKeown, on February 16, Hilary Tipping, a 21-year-old Rollers roadie, provided him with an alibi for the shooting of the fan outside his house. Interviewed by police on January 4, Tipping had not mentioned that he was the one who pulled the trigger. Why? "I was never asked," he said. Now he made a voluntary statement to McKeown's lawyers, the day before McKeown was due to appear at Linlithgow court where he entered a not guilty plea. Although the case was not heard until September, it lessened the chances of McKeown being sent to prison.

Paton described Tipping as a friend of his. "There was always a story attached to that that I had paid him to take the blame," said Paton. "I think that may be a ghost that may eventually come back to haunt mister McKeown." Tipping was described as a normal bloke, with long hair, who suddenly left the Rollers organisation and was next seen on the *Supersonic* TV show sitting beside Mike Mansfield wearing eye make-up. "My producer Hilary worked with them," said Mansfield. "He was their road manager for nearly two years. Les was already under probation for assaulting a photographer, he would have gone to prison."

"Sure a lot of people assumed I had arranged a phony alibi," said McKeown. "It was some time before this guy who had been staying with me came forward and admitted it was him. Afterwards I felt sorry for him and gave him a minor job in the Rollers organisation. It backfired as plenty of people wrongly assumed the job was his reward for providing a false confession."

Since McKeown joined The Bay City Rollers they had never really been a "band", in the traditional sense. They were a purely manufactured phenomenon, and Paton had tried to keep the members separate from one another and had always treated McKeown differently from the other Rollers, allowing him more freedom. Faulkner and Wood were the only two who had been significantly close. Alan was disenfranchised and Derek plodded along, serious and business-like. They came together as the Rollers for whatever was required but that was it. McKeown said he felt like an outsider in his own band. Paton urged him to get his crooked teeth fixed having himself spent thousands on his own rotting set: he was left with three teeth and a mouthful of bridgework that would cause him a lifetime of problems. McKeown refused to have his teeth done but there was always the sense Paton could replace him any moment. There were a lot of willing teenagers at Little Kellerstain.

He was lost with no sense what was going on in wider terms. In his autobiography McKeown described a significant change in the band's business structure in early 1976 thus: "Eric employed someone called Colin to look at the band's complex web of finances". As McKeown understood it, the copyright of the songs which "had passed to Carlin reverted to Bay City Music and Eric says that Colin then began selling the songs worldwide, but to whom it's not clear."

Colin Slater was a PR representing Gary Glitter, David Cassidy and the James Bond films with his business partner Fred Hift, an experienced *New York Times* and *Variety* journalist who was director of advertising and publicity for Europe and the Middle East for 20th Century-Fox.

Slater had spent the previous five years, since 1971, working for Harry Saltzman, the producer of the Bond films. He was American but based in London. He was sharp.

"We did 70 per cent film and the rest music, rock'n'roll, because I liked it but Fred didn't,' said Slater. They also represented acts for GTO Records, Dick Leahy's new label. "Dick Leahy was a very close friend, part of a small group of my very best friends. He alerted me to some problems with the band involving Tam – his behaviour and his competence – and recommended me to the boys. I took over Bay City Music instead of doing a run on the management contract which would have landed everybody in court forever."

Slater was appointed Managing Director of Bay City Music, the band's publishing company and initially worked out of an office in their accountant Stephen Goldberg's building on 42 Duke Street in Mayfair. After two months he moved to a new band office on Heddon Street just off Regent Street, close to Piccadilly Circus. It would become the band's new HQ for the coming years and as soon as they moved in the place was swamped with female fans. There was recording/rehearsal studio attached to the office that the band sometimes used. David Bowie had posed in front of the building for the *Ziggy Stardust And The Spiders From Mars* album cover.

The opening of the new London office also coincided with Faulkner buying an apartment in London, in Chelsea, just off the King's Road. Slater helped him furnish it. It offered brief respite from the fans until the address got out and Faulkner's new home was also surrounded. Paton also started looking for a London apartment, choosing one in a residential block out in West Finchley.

Slater was not on a percentage like Perkins and Paton. He was on a salary and worked for "the company" as he called it. "I didn't sign anything and I never touched the money," he said. Slater claimed that right away he found "in-depth problems with the music publishing" arm of the Rollers' operations. Perkins had acted out of self-interest, he claimed. Carlin ended their connection with Bay City Music.

According to Slater, he spent "most of 1976 and 1977" renegotiating the band's publishing contracts in territories around the world, including the UK, Germany, Europe, Australia, America and Japan. "By the time I got to Australia, this guy picks me up in a Holden limo and as we're riding into town I said, 'And who are you?' He said, 'I'm your publisher here in Australia.' I said, 'Right, we need to be looking at your contract to see if it's any different to the copy I didn't have.' They rescinded the contract, told me how much we earned and I rolled it into the new advance and had it paid as a single cheque. I tried to do a deal with a company in Russia but they accused me of subversion."

Perkins and Paton were cut out of the new publishing deals Slater made, collecting only the percentage of income they could claim under their management contract. Their ownership of a percentage of the copyright of the Rollers songs ended. In America Slater said he declined a significant offer of an advance to sign over the songs in favour of setting up the band's own independent publishing companies to collect income. This was TGK Music and PD Music and both companies were registered in New York at 1776 Broadway, the address of the band's accountant, Stephen Tenenbaum.

"Tenenbaum set up the companies and all of the songs [and their revenue streams] went into those two companies for the United States and the Far East," said Slater. "And all the songs went into Bay City Music for the UK, Europe and Australia." He said he had no idea what TGK stood for and suggested PD "was a joke that worked". "The cash flow from the US all went through Stephen Tenenbaum's office," Slater said.

While all this was unfolding Perkins hung on grimly. But Slater claimed he uncovered more deceit. "Perkins was doing it with everything," he said. "He was doing it with the merchandising. The merchandising had remarkable problems that could only be caused by either gross incompetence or enemy action. I met Sid Bernstein in New York and he told me what the previous merchandising deal was and I smiled and said nothing to do with me, but just roll with a new deal on this and this is what I want. The merchandising was a total mess... terrible deals had been done. I had a meeting with the British equivalent of the postal inspectors where apparently 14 per cent of our shipments [the band's own mail order business not the company run by Paul Pike that had been sidelined by Paton/Perkins] never arrived at their destination and people were demanding their money back. I hired three people to write cheques… to return the money. I hired someone else who took over the merchandising out of London… and we saw revenues triple in four or five weeks."

During his tenure with the band – from January 1976 until the end of 1978 – Slater said he only met Paton four times. "As soon as he realised things were happening and I was travelling round the world doing business on their behalf he left me to it," Slater said. "Tam went to Heddon Street long enough to build a 12-inch dias on which to put his desk so that everybody sitting in front of the desk had to look up at him then he never came in. I had the biggest office suite in the building and if he wanted to talk to me he came over to me. The only conversation that lasted longer than two minutes involved his dislike of TR7s [a sports car he had bought]."

Slater's impression of the band was that they were "still teenagers, in mind if not body" and that "they regarded themselves as hugely wealthy". McKeown, he recalled, demanded a Range Rover. Paton already had one up in Edinburgh. "I bought Les a Range Rover," said Slater. "But then you get four other phone calls, where's my Range Rover? Why do you want a Range Rover, you live in London. Okay, I'll take a Nikon camera. Okay I'll send you a Nikon camera."

Slater lived in Barnes, and travelled to work in a limousine. His next door neighbour owned a limo hire business with an office on Regent Street, so they rode into town together. Faulkner noticed this. "Eric rented another limo from the same company and kept it for a month," said Slater. "The guy who owned the company said to me, 'You guys owe me, $200,000.' Everybody else in the band was ordering their own limousines." Slater ended up buying the company for the band. "It was cheaper to buy him out," he said. "He had the only white Rolls-Royce Silver Wraith available for hire in town on permanent rent to RCA for Perry Como. So for a while Perry Como's car was owned by Bay City Music."

The new contract with Arista had still not been signed. "Clive sent Elliot Goldman [Arista's Executive Vice President and General Manager with direct responsibility for all areas of its business operations] over to talk to me," Slater said. Slater then flew to New York to meet Davis.

"I started off by saying I need $10 million to pay for this forthcoming [world] tour as tour support. He said, 'Is there anything else you want?' I said, 'Yes, 20 per cent worldwide [record royalty] and you pay the producers on top of it.' Basically he was fuming but I had him because 'Money Honey' was in the charts and he didn't have a contract.'

Slater did not get 20 per cent out of Davis. But the new royalty agreed with Arista [approximately 12 per cent but with many caveats] did significantly improve what the band were getting under their old contract – that had stood at approximately 8 per cent in the UK and 4 per cent for the rest of the world.

"I forwarded my weekly reports to Stephen Goldberg and they went to his contractual lawyer, David Landsman [who went on to work with U2]," Slater said. "Basically I was involved in stitching the band's business together in a sensible manner and, also, as much as possible trying to keep their earnings offshore. We were looking at 60 per cent corporation tax, 98 per cent personal income tax." Slater claimed the band had a significant offshore account in Gibraltar, a tax safe haven. "British tax laws were very strange in those days,' he said. "You stayed in England, you paid 98 per cent, but if you took your business offshore, there were no taxes. You didn't have to hide anymore, you just had to put it somewhere that was not in England. The other insane thing was if you kept your money offshore for seven years it became tax-free anyway, you could take it back to England tax-free."

Paton was complaining of suffering from heart palpitations. He could not converse sensibly with Slater. Going up against Davis terrified him. He knew that his long-time business associate Perkins had been rumbled. The only aspect of the band he still controlled was their minds. In late February he took the radical decision to fire Alan, who would be 28 in June. He summonsed the band's founding and longest serving member to Little Kellerstain. McKeown said he was instructed to go to a pub in Edinburgh to collect him. "Alan went into Tam's office and came out crying," he said. "Tam had told him that he wanted him to leave the group – he thought that was best for Alan and the Rollers."

There were myriad reasons suggested for his firing of Alan. He was too old. He was drinking too much and had fallen in love – spending too much time with the woman and not the band. Paton put some of the blame on Faulkner. "Eric was the one behind the sacking of Alan," he said. "Alan was coming and going to the studios and they were flying him up and down to and from Scotland. Eric was the one saying, 'He is not even interested and we'll have to do something about this.' And I went along with Eric. I'm not washing my hands of it, I was a part of it too. I think it suited Alan. Alan just thought, 'I've got my farm, I've got my horses, my beautiful girlfriend and I got a few million in the bank.'"

"I had a fallout with Tam because I wanted to get a life," said Alan. At Little Kellerstain there were several cute teenagers eager to take Alan's place in the Rollers: Martin Donald and the Kip boys; Gert Magnus, still without a record deal, and Pat McGlynn. Paton had been on the look-out for Alan's replacement since the scandal over his real age had blown up the previous year. He plumped for Ian Mitchell, the five foot six inch Irish teen, now 17, who had been living with him at Little Kellerstain since leaving Young City Stars.

Mitchell said that he was told he would be joining the Rollers by Radio Luxembourg DJ Peter Powell on April 1, 1976. It was unclear as to why Powell happened to be hanging out at Little Kellerstain at the time. Paton made Mitchell get a "tufty" haircut and gave him some fan club merchandise to wear. "The next day the press arrived," said Mitchell. "Not just a couple of reporters but van loads of press." He posed for pictures with his new band mates, who he didn't know and had barely met before. They turned up dressed normally and donned their Roller gear – at one time Paton had made them wear the clobber at *all* times – posed with Mitchell and left.

The news put Mitchell on the cover of the April 10 issue of *Record Mirror*. The photographs of Alan and Mitchell were almost grotesque. Alan, having been asked by Paton to hang around to smooth the transition, wore a pin stripe suit to indicate his return to civilian life as he handed over his role in the band – and tartan clobber – to Mitchell, a 'Bay City lookalike' as *Record Mirror* called him.

He looked younger than his age, around 14, and posed with his hairless chest on show. He made the others: Derek, 25, Faulkner 22, Wood,

19, and McKeown, 20, look old in comparison. The appointment sent alarm bells ringing among the band. If Paton could sack Alan, then who might be next? They felt old looking at this new chicken in their midst. "A little stranger in the band," said McKeown, who resented Mitchell taking centre stage in the band photographs. "Paranoia crept in," he said. "It was the beginning of end," said Derek.

Paton declared to the press that it was not true that he just looked for "a pretty face" when choosing new band members. He said they must have "special qualities" to be a Roller. "They have to be interesting and they must have the ability to play," he said.

Alan handled the media the best he could. The line was he had decided to walk. "I don't think the magic's there anymore," he said. "I lost a lot of interest in the group and I think that was keeping the other guys back. I've got this house in the country and I love my horses. I want to spend more time there. It's not a question of age, lot of stars are much older; it's just a question of personality. I feel I've disappointed a lot of fans who followed me personally but Ian is younger and will probably work a lot harder." He said he was "well-off" but not a millionaire.

In a special message for *Tiger Beat* in America Alan [really Paton] said he wanted to "give someone else the chance to experience the wonderful life of a Bay City Roller". He wanted to relax and "have a peaceful life for a while". In actuality, Alan was depressed and hitting the bottle, whisky and beer. He had lacked confidence in the studio and felt ridiculous dressed in Roller gear.

Mitchell told the press he was the "happiest guy in the world". He had seemed to cope well with living at Little Kellerstain, although the drinking and drugging he enjoyed would become, for him, a life-long and life-threatening problem. "Everybody was frightened of Tam," he said. "If he said jump you jumped."

"It was interesting for everyone," said Danny Fields as *16* covered the change-over in band personnel for another cover story in the magazine with Mitchell as cover star and a strapline that read: "An intimate look at the new member". "For the magazine, it was, Meet the new Roller. For the band, he said, it was a "challenge"

Paton invited Fields to Edinburgh to stay at Little Kellerstain. "He opened up to me," said Fields. "Here are my boys, aren't they lovely, I'm proud of them. I'd go into his room to say hello or goodnight and he'd be in bed with one boy each side. They were not children, they were street boys who looked pretty happy to be there... better there than on the street or being beaten up by their father. It had a certain domestic and nice feel... the boys were better off than they would have been in the gutters of Edinburgh.

"He wanted to be a good son and to me what it looked like with those boys he wanted to be a good parent as well," added Fields. "Tam I always thought was a benevolent John, he was fond of the boys, they were like adored pets, he petted them like he would his pets."

Paton also took Fields out in the city. "He got on so well with the lower classes because he was of them," he said. "He went to meetings of senior citizens of limited means and he'd be the band leader and dance with the women and play the accordion. He'd sing old songs. He was wonderful for those people."

Mitchell was unprepared for life as a Roller. He said the schedule was "crazy". The band flew to London to shoot a promo film for new single 'Love Me Like I Love You'. Mike Mansfield was directing. It did nothing for the song, featuring the band spinning on a table that with clever camera angles made it appear as if the band were on top of a silver globe. The band formed a circle holding hands with Alan in the middle before he disappeared and Mitchell was magically revealed. There were glitter globes and a waterfall effect in the background. The band then took to swings. There was a long lingering crotch shot. Mitchell was still in a pair of fan club trousers and a tight T-shirt with a tartan scarf round his neck. It was grim stuff.

The promo was shown on *Top Of The Pops* on April 8 and repeated on April 22. Paton had fought to have the song released as a single in the UK, claiming that the record shops had already imported the band's new American single 'Rock And Roll Love Letter' and fans were buying it. He argued that the sale of imports would have an impact on sales of an official UK release of the song. 'Love Me

Like I Love You' was granted a limited release in the UK, Europe and Australia. Alan, illustrative of the haste of his departure, featured on the promo adverts for the single.

Mike Mansfield was directing the popular primetime LWT *Russell Harty Show* and got the band the show's coveted music slot, shown on April 16. The band also flew to Ireland to pick up an award from *Starlight* magazine, 'Ireland's No 1 Young Entertainment Weekly'. It required a 6am flight from Glasgow to Dublin, a meeting with kids with serious illnesses, interviews at the hotel – surrounded by 200 teens – with the national newspapers; the *Evening Press* and *Sunday World,* and with RTE, Ireland's national broadcaster. In the evening they were due at the Country Club to collect the award. About 300 fans waited outside and a limo was sent as a decoy – the band was bundled in the back of a van. The following morning they flew back to Glasgow on the 10am flight.

"When they made schedules for us, two things were always missing: time to eat and time to go to the toilet," said McKeown. "There was no human touch. We were in a constant mouse-on-a-wheel scenario."

'Love Me Like I Love You' rose to UK number four [seven in Australia]. 'Rock And Roll Love Letter' [its B-side, Faulkner/Wood's 'Shanghai'd In Love'] was also now available in Europe, although not the UK. It was an odd and confusing situation, frankly a mess. In Germany it was the latter single that entered the charts, peaking at 13. *Bravo,* like the American teen press, put Mitchell's arrival in the band on their cover. So did UK magazine *Look-In.* Overnight Mitchell was a star.

The band was being trailed for children's news programme, *John Craven's Newsround*, shown daily at 5pm on the BBC1. Craven and the crew travelled on a flight from London to Edinburgh with the band to film at Little Kellerstain. Craven, on camera, wondered if they were concerned that some journalists in the UK were claiming they were finished? The episode was shown on April 30.

Faulkner felt the criticisms keenly: he had been badly stung by the press reaction to the *Wouldn't You Like It?* album. He did not feel the two recent hit singles he had written were treated seriously. Paton was, sensibly, pushing the band to become middle-of-the-road entertainers.

Faulkner did not share that vision. He "wanted to go into a Meat Loaf or Zeppelin scene", Paton said. "He couldn't get the we're going heavy phrase out of his head." He and Faulkner were now often at each other's throats. Paton had no confidence in Faulkner's songs.

Faulkner wanted Frechter to produce the band's next album but Clive Davis was now auditioning American producers. In three days the band was due to fly to America to begin promoting 'Rock And Roll Love Letter', a song Faulkner had never wanted to record. He denied what happened next was a suicide bid.

At Little Kellerstain, where he was spending the night, Faulkner swallowed too much Seconal and Valium. "I was getting screwed up," said Faulkner. "I took too many downers." The pressure had caught up with him.

Mitchell found him on the floor in one of the bedrooms. He kicked him gently to wake him up. "All this greenish yellow stuff started coming out his mouth," said Mitchell. He was "in a coma, near death", said Paton. An ambulance was called and Faulkner was rushed to hospital. Paton jumped on it as a "nice little publicity move". He called the band's new PR, Bess Coleman, 33, who worked for Tony Barrow International, the illustrious Mayfair publicity firm. Coleman was a tough lady who handled PR on The Beatles' early sixties American tours. She was also a trained journalist who had edited American teen magazine *Teen Life* before moving back to England and into PR.

Paton made anonymous calls to newspapers alerting them of Faulkner's plight. "There were photos of him coming out of hospital four days later and going into hiding," he bragged. "It may sound cruel but bands are built on publicity. I always sought publicity in a big style, in a big way. Whenever I could get them on the front page of the national papers I went for it. Because that was about all they had going for them. In my own mind I had nothing but image to sell. It was just another front page as far as I was concerned."

Later Paton asked Faulkner why he'd done it "I was tired, tired," Faulkner replied. "He was sadly depressed," said Paton. "We'd been in Dublin and London and done three TV shows in two days. I think this was a thing that had been coming on for a long long time. Eric had no interest in life except for being a Bay City Roller." An official press release said he'd had a nervous breakdown.

The band flew to America without Faulkner on April 18 for a week of promotion beginning in Los Angeles. 'Rock And Roll Love Letter' was in the *Billboard* Top 40 (and would peak at 28). It also charted at six in Canada (and nine in Australia). Its producer Colin Frechter claimed he never got a penny in royalties from the single. They were welcomed at LAX by around 300 fans. Michael Klenfner was at hand to guide them through the promotion, beginning with a visit to Disneyland where they were interviewed for *Rolling Stone* magazine. The journalist noted Paton's 60-a-day cigarette habit and the fact he and group "still maintain the frantic, punishing pace of newcomers".

Paton laid the blame for Faulkner's OD on the English music press's vicious attacks on the group. "I think they're all very unhappy," he said of the band. "They're happy being Rollers but I think they're disillusioned with the constant attacks on them, that people say they're rubbish. It can't help but affect you." The journalist mentioned that in their press bios four of the five Rollers had stated Paton as the biggest influence on their lives. Paton responded that he just wanted to be their manager.

"Pop stars last five years if they're lucky," Paton told *Rolling Stone*. "It's like being thrown into a massive big pit that has gold and everything in it, and you say to these five guys, Okay lads, let's get as much of this gold in your pockets as we can because we have to get out of this hole in five minutes."

Wood finally got a chance to speak. Although proud of the songs he and Faulkner wrote he admitted to inexperience. "In the really good bands the guys are 35, 36," he said. "When the screaming dies down we should be musically ready." In answer to the band's critics he said: "If it's such a load of shit why are 500,000 buying the record? The criticism really got Eric down. I suppose the pressure got too much for him. We share a farm and we go there to relax but they're always fans showing up. We don't have any kind of private life. Eric just couldn't take it anymore."

The band's schedule was frantic. Los Angeles was the home to *Tiger Beat* magazine and the band visited their offices. The magazine milked it. They called Mitchell "the boy too beautiful to live". He said he loved milk, hot baths, honesty and sincerity, and, of course, reading fan mail. There were new shots of him posing bare-chested with his trouser top button undone. In fact the band shots were getting increasingly risqué: standing nude in showers, their modesty protected by a shower curtain or naked in a bath full of bubbles, laid out on beds with legs akimbo and buttons undone and one infamous photograph of Wood totally nude with just a long scarf dangling from his neck. In the Californian heat, there were opportunities for shots of the band in swimming trunks by the pool and McKeown started to wear little cut-off denim shorts.

Tiger Beat was getting sacks full of mail for the band. There were ample new shots of McKeown, often posing bare-chested. The magazine, like *16*, began to advertise a Roller's Hotline telephone number for up to the minute news. There were adverts asking fans to send in $1 for a variety of cheap products such as stickers. *Tiger Beat* ran cover after cover on the band in the coming months, detailing the same sort of stuff as *16*. *Rolling Stone* wrote that: "They chronicle the most vacuous minutia in a giggly style patterned on cloakroom exchanges of 12-year-old girls."

It was all bubbly stuff with headlines such as: 'Talk Like Them! Dress Like Them!' and 'How to Catch a Roller!' Derek was described as shy but he liked hugging. Wood loved nice letters. Faulkner was said to favour a white sandy beach or a mountain trail on horseback. Readers were invited to 'Write today and it could be the beginning of a great relationship!'

At *16*, they were advertising Rollers "kissing kits – super size kiss pin-ups of each member", a guide on How To Dress In Roller Gear, Revealing Tell-Tale BCR Secrets! Tour news! Rollers Love-O-Scopes, and the evergreen, What They Look For In A Girl plus, tantalisingly, What It Would Be Like Kiss Woody? Wood was popular in America and featured solo on a *16* cover. The emphasis of the *16* coverage was on new pictures – Scrumptious Colour! – of the group often packaged as things such as "our secret scrapbook". They too, like *Tiger Beat*, were getting sacks full of mail for the group

Others were cashing in too. The Topps Company, which made baseball cards with a stick of chewing gum in each packet, made Rollers cards to collect and trade. "At one point you could buy Bay City Rollers panties with our picture on front," McKeown said.

The singer said life now was like being in "a permanent trance". "You start withdrawing," he said. "That's what happens when people resort to drugs or booze," McKeown admitted. In America in 1976 there was a new drug on the menu: cocaine. "One sniff leads to another, leads to buying it," he said. "I was greedy with that stuff." This was on top of the constant pill-popping. "Eric's scare did nothing to abate the flow of pills," McKeown said.

Michael Klenfner had them visiting LA radio stations and appearing at record stores for signings – 1,200 fans showed up at one signing. Klenfner enjoyed having the group drive around in an open-topped car so they could be seen – and mobbed. They travelled to San Francisco for more of the same, radio and in-stores, and then on for more in Denver, Dallas, Miami and St Louis, where over 5,000 fans showed up for an in-store appearance.

Without Faulkner, the band taped two national TV shows, miming 'Rock And Roll Love Letter' on *Midnight Special*, a Friday night music show that ran after the popular *Tonight Show* featuring Johnny Carson from 12.30am until 2am, and *The Merv Griffin Show*, a massively popular talk show that ran, depending on what part of America you were in, during the day or in the prime-time evening slot.

Asked about Alan, Derek said: "He's relieved all the hassles are over." The official press release stated that Faulkner "got into somebody else's prescribed medication when he was in a period of depression". Asked if McKeown had killed a woman, a band spokesperson said they had "never heard of any such incident". McKeown said Paton still had keys to all their hotel rooms, and would regularly go through their stuff. "He was strong, intimidating and a bully, totally dominant, a control freak who indulged in head-trips," said McKeown. It was "abusive", he said. Mitchell said he was earning $8,000 a week. "He's only been in two weeks and already I see the stress and strain on him," said Paton. "I sometimes wonder will it be a Marilyn Monroe situation. The only thing I can give them is the money. I don't know if making him a Roller I've given him a blessing or curse."

There was no let up. They flew back to England on April 26 and the following day there was another morning flight to perform at an award show in Germany, organised by *Bravo*. The band, with Faulkner back, collected an award for most popular group of the year.

Davis selected Jimmy Ienner to produce the band's next album. The 30-year-old American had produced Eric Carmen's recent solo album that included the power ballad hit 'All By Myself'. He had also produced four albums with Carmen's previous band, the clean teen power pop Raspberries, as well as albums by Grand Funk Railroad and Blood, Sweat & Tears. He was loud and tough. "Clive was asking me to get involved in many projects, as all the companies were," he said. "This one tickled me." The decision could be seen as Davis' revenge for the band's recalcitrance over 'Rock And Roll Love Letter'. The new contract Arista had with the Rollers gave the label unbridled artistic control. It was obvious what Davis thought of the band's songwriting, not much. "Arista retained 50 per cent artistic control, and that damn clause came to haunt us," said Faulkner.

Ienner met the group in London to discuss material and rehearse songs. Most of the new album would be cover versions, including two songs, 'Let's Pretend' (already cut by The Raspberries and written by Eric Carmen) and 'My Lisa' on which Ienner owned the publishing. He and his brother Don owned CAM, a publishing, management and production company. Don ended up as Arista's promotions chief in the eighties. They were also going to record 'I Only Want To Be With You', the 1963 Dusty Springfield track. This was a song Davis had chosen and envisaged as the group's next single.

Ienner also presented the band with a track about the fleeting nature of pop stardom, 'Yesterday's Hero', a 1975 hit in Australia for John Paul Young. The Rollers were apparently in on this joke. "I'd say in two years' time you're going to be shaving twice a day and then what's going to happen?" Ienner said. There were three other cover versions including The Beach Boys' 'Don't Worry Baby' and 'Dedication', a track written by prolific English songwriters Guy Fletcher and Doug Flett whose songs had been covered by Elvis, Ray Charles and Cliff Richard.

Faulkner was not happy. "We wanted to write more of our own material, but they wanted more cover versions," he said. He was disillusioned. "It didn't mean anything," he said. "The band was just sailing on what we'd been doing. We weren't even interested anymore." He had little fight left in him. He put forward two old songs, 'You're A Woman' and 'Rock'n'Roller' and there was one other band song on the album, purportedly written by Mitchell, McKeown and Wood, called 'Write A Letter'.

The rehearsals were painful. "It was difficult because we were learning new material that I'd brought to them or that they had and we were reworking," said Ienner. "It was a lot of work... it wasn't fun, you moved incrementally. And they had to go on their own for a while and learn them more." Paton had no input into the selection of the material for this album nor the choice of recording location: Soundstage studio in Toronto, Canada. The band would be there for five weeks from the beginning of June. The studio was new and co-owned by Canadian producer, Bob Ezrin who had produced Alice Cooper's run of hit albums and was now working with Kiss.

Before recording began the band spent two weeks touring Europe starting May 15, with seven dates in Germany including the famous Circus Krone building in Munich, one of the largest circuses in Europe that doubled as a 3,000 capacity venue. The other venues ranged from 2,000 capacity (Hamburg) to 8,000 (Essen). There were 5,000 capacity venues (Frankfurt and Oldenburg) and one 7,000 (Dusseldorf). This, the band's first proper German tour, was both lucrative and covered enthusiastically by *Bravo* magazine. The Rollers had scored five top 20 hits in Germany, three already in 1976 but not yet gone higher than number 10. The touring set-up was still basic, no frills. Wood had switched to bass to accommodate Mitchell on second guitar. The band eyed their new member cagily. He was high on adrenalin. He wanted to party after the shows.

Ienner saw the band in Helsinki on May 18. The mania at the hotel took him aback. "I couldn't believe I was watching girls climb up flagpoles screaming Les's name, Eric's name, Woody's name… it was cold and wet and they were climbing up this flagpole outside the hotel. This I've never seen. At the gigs the girls were all fainting."

The Rollers touched down in Canada on June 1 with 5,000 greeting them at the airport, their best reception at any airport yet. If the band thought they would enjoy a quiet few weeks recording they were in for a rude awakening. This was a country where they had scored two number one singles and two number one albums. To avoid fans it was necessary to book two hotels, the Harbour Castle Hotel and the Four Seasons, and attempt to use one as a decoy. Decoy limos were also employed. It meant the group were trapped again, locked in hotel rooms and rushed about in the back of a van.

"It was ridiculous," said Ienner. "I was the old man of the bunch and girls were knocking on my windows. I had to have security on my door." McKeown talked about "mass orgies and mass drinking binges". He said it was normal to open his hotel door to be confronted by naked girls, or girls in just overcoats. He said the groupies hung out in lifts waiting until a Roller got in. "And then the girl takes her clothes off," he said. "Not scrubbers but beautiful chicks from respectable and wealthy families."

Ienner knew Toronto well. He had a long history of working with Canadian bands and artists such as singer songwriter Bruce Cockburn, David Clayton-Thomas, lead singer of Blood, Sweat & Tears, and rock band Chilliwack.

Ienner used "some of his guys" in Canada during recording of the new Rollers album, guys from Blood, Sweat & Tears and from the group Lighthouse. "It was about the time element," he said. "We were on a very tight schedule. That's what the Rollers recordings were always like… they were always ready to go on the road again. So we had to expedite things we were doing to meet the time frame. We didn't have time for the guys to do everything. My guys augmented things, they didn't replace or take over, they augmented."

The Rollers got some of their own way through musical director Colin Frechter. "They wouldn't do it unless I was there," he said. "Jimmy

[Ienner] was a larger than life character and not the easiest person to work with. I was musical directing, largely arranging the vocals, doing bits and pieces of guitar and keyboard. We were locked in the studio, you couldn't get out with all the fans outside, same with the hotel."

Mitchell sang lead vocal on what would ultimately be the album's title track, 'Dedication'. "He was better than Alan," said Frechter. "He was a very cocky young lad. The Rollers were massive as a band. We used to say he's only been in the band five minutes and he's more famous than they are. Les had an issue with him, as if to say it's our band not yours."

Paton flew into Toronto as did Michael Klenfner of Arista. There was promotion to be done. Elton John was in town and dropped by the studio. So did journalist /photographer Kaz Utsunomiya from leading Japanese music magazine, *Music Life*. Arista was now distributed worldwide by EMI and in Japan Toshiba EMI were busy priming the market for an imminent tour, due at the end of the year. All the UK and American albums were available in the country already, all making the top 40. There was even a Japanese only album, *Souvenirs Of Youth*, which featured all the band's Nobby Clark era material. The breakthrough in Japan though had been a recent singles compilation album called *Rock And Roll Love Letter* that had gone to number one, remarkably without the band having set foot in the country. Utsunomiya spent an afternoon doing interviews in the studio while Elton John was there. He was amazed by the Roller fans' behaviour, watching as they almost turned over a car outside the studio. "A seriously fat car," said Ienner.

Also visiting the group in the studio was 25-year-old Australian Jack Strom. He'd met the group briefly when they appeared on a pop show on Channel 9 during the Australian tour at the end of 1975. Strom had been a floor manager at Channel 9, the Melbourne station that had the highest ratings in Australia. He was now managing Australian TV personality Ernie Sigley and producing his variety show for Channel 0/10, the third biggest station in Australia. Sigley wanted to make other programmes for the channel. Strom had heard that the Rollers would be returning to tour Australia later in the year and had contacted Paton about the possibility of making a documentary on the visit.

"Tam was very friendly and said it sounds like a great idea," said Strom. "But he said the problem is if you do the promotion when we're there it may be a year until we come back again. What we really need is promotion before we get there to promote the tour. I would prefer you to cover the Canadian tour [due to start in August] and use that as promotion when they come to Australia. He said, 'You need to talk to my lawyers in New York.' "

Strom spoke to Marty Machat who told him that the BBC was also interested in doing a documentary and "you will have to convince us you should do it". Strom flew to New York. "I said, 'I want to shoot this documentary and use it in Australia and you can use it in other places but we want it in Australia as a special for 0/10,'" he said. Machat asked about budget, indicating the BBC had a "reasonable budget". "I said I don't have a budget really," Strom said. "I can't offer you anything, just the use of the documentary when it's finished: our budget is so small it's just going to cover the shoot. The budget was about £50,000. He said, 'It's ultimately not up to me, it's up to the boys, you need to go and live with them for two weeks in Toronto while they're recording the *Dedication* album, get to know them and they can decide if they want you or the BBC to do it, they will need to feel they can trust you.'"

In Toronto, Strom hung out with the band by the hotel pool, which was closed off for the band's exclusive use, and went to the studio to watch them record. He got on well with Ian Mitchell. After two weeks he flew back to New York. Machat told him, "Okay the guys are very happy for you to do the documentary. They like you. They can relate to you. We were similar ages." Machat told Strom to head home and "by the time you get there, there will be a contract for you".

"This huge thick contract had a couple of problems," said Strom. "It said as soon as I shoot the footage it belongs to them, which means they can take it away from me even before I'd edited it into a programme if they wanted to. Secondly I had no rights to record any of the sound and thirdly I couldn't go on stage with my crew. How do you make a documentary about a band and their tour when you can't record any of their music or go on stage? This was a problem. Also they wanted the right to approve the documentary before it went to air in Australia.

So numerous calls to Marty [Machat] later he finally said, 'I've spoken to the record company, spoken to the guys, they really want you to do it, you write the contract and we'll sign it.' It was agreed that after two screenings in Australia they owned the rights to it."

Strom organised with Paton to visit Edinburgh in July to begin shooting once the band had wrapped up the album and then he would travel with them across Canada. "Tam was very open and he described them as an image-band," Strom said. "I don't think he tried to convince anyone, let alone the boys, that they were in the band for just their musical ability. Everyone knew they were there for what they brought to the group in terms of character and personality and quirkiness and looks. Ian for instance was not there because he was the best guitarist, he was someone all the girls would love."

"I didn't know if any of the band members were gay at the time because it wasn't a question I ever asked," Strom added. "I knew Tam was. I had suspicions about some of the boys."

As the band concluded recording in Toronto there were rumours that McKeown was thinking of leaving. He was tired of Paton controlling his life. The June issue of Mike Mansfield's *Supersonic* magazine ran an article headlined: 'Les – Is this Goodbye?' "Les was the one who had a little more of a problem in how it was going," said Ienner. "I don't think it was unhappiness as much as it was frustration over certain things."

Ienner said it was "an open secret" that Paton abused some of the band members. "I heard rumblings from Arista but I heard it more from other people in the business. Any time anything came up about Tam, I would look in their eyes and I could see fear. I don't mean because of Tam. I mean because of... 'Please don't ask me about this, please don't look at me too hard'... there was that in some of the guys. It was a horrible thing to see and that's why I'd never go near it unless it needed to be gone near. It seemed to have affected everyone somewhat differently. When I looked into their eyes I knew they'd suffered."

Sid Bernstein had finally got the band a gig in America. It took place on June 26 at Atlantic City's Steel Pier Music Hall in New Jersey. Atlantic City was a then crumbling beach resort and Steel Pier was one of several piers in the small town. The Stones had played the venue in 1966. Atlantic City was about to legalise gambling, revitalising itself, and the Music Hall had new owners. It was over 100 miles south of Manhattan but many fans had made the trip there from New York.

The place was packed with 2,200 adolescent girls, a sell-out. Hundreds of fans, all dressed up in Roller gear, waving scarves and banners, rushed the stage even before the band appeared. There was a Japanese film crew and 20 photographers waiting for the band outside. They arrived in a limo that was immediately over-run with girls who climbed on the roof, on the bonnet, mass of hysteria that sprawled across the road.

There was a strong police presence inside the venue and almost as soon as the band took the stage another stage invasion. Paton took the band off and urged calm. They reappeared and played for 45 minutes as multiple girls fainted. One 12 year old was weeping. "My friend just passed out," she sobbed. "My other friend is passed out, and my other friend is missing and I don't know where I am."

"I didn't figure it would be as wild as this," the *New York Times* quoted the group's "beaming business manager" Barry Perkins as saying as "the audience screamed, yelled, clapped, stomped and ground their sneakers into the plush velour of the seats."

The *New York Times* reasoned that the music was "bright and jubilant" and the band "appeared young, clean-cut and cute – a great deal like the early Beatles." *Rolling Stone* magazine took a different view. They called the band "insipid and uninspired". Bernstein had them booked to return to America for a short 15-date North American tour in mid-August. Many of the dates were in similar size venues.

The band was looking forward to returning to London and Edinburgh for a break. Before they did, they flew back to Toronto for what Perkins described as a "reception" for Toronto-based radio station, CHUM, Canada's most influential and listened to top 40 pop station, as part of the station's Summer Music festival held in the city's famous plaza, Nathan Phillips Square. The plaza covered 12 acres and featured a large reflecting pool/ice rink, peace garden, elevated concrete walkways, a permanent stage and many sculptures, a Henry Moore among them. It was supposed to be an undemanding appearance for the band to collect platinum disc awards for the two recent Canadian number one albums. 'Saturday Night' and 'Money Honey' were also both among the top 10 best-selling singles in Canada in 1976.

CHUM had heavily advertised the band's early afternoon appearance. Some DJs were even calling it 'Bay City Roller day'. The event was free. Organisers had planned for 15,000 to attend. On June 27 the square was actually overrun with 60,000 and many were hurt in what quickly turned into a crush. There were chants of 'We want the Rollers' with girls fainting and screaming. It was a hot day, 30 degrees. Some fans had been there since five in the morning. It was frantic, panicky. One girl had her leg broken. There were repeated warnings for people pushing forward and a police barricade formed. The band appeared and there was a surge forward.

"They were kicking the police," said Mitchell. The organisers took the band off the stage after a few seconds. A policeman took over the microphone and started to angrily admonish the crowd. "We've got some people injured down here," he said and then threatened to call off the event. "Please don't move," he implored.

The band came back on for the presentation. The crowd went wild. There were girls passed out held up only by the crush of bodies around them. The police officer took the microphone again and warned the crowd; people were getting crushed at the front. The presentation was called off. "It was like a weird Twilight Zone episode," said Wood.

The band's getaway limo was mobbed. There were thousands swarming around the vehicle, many on the roof, banging, screaming. The roof started to cave in. It was scary. "But brilliant at the same time," said Wood. "We believed the hype," McKeown said. They were superstars. Gods for that brief moment.

CHAPTER 9

Darkness

"I was green until I got friendly with Les and he opened my eyes to girls. With Paton it was all to do with boys and gay sex. Me and Les had lots of girls but the trouble was if you got caught with a girl Woody would go back to Paton and tell him everything. I never saw any of the other band members sleeping with girls apart from Les."

– Pat McGlynn

Jack Strom arrived in Edinburgh with two cameramen to begin filming what would be the defining documentary on the band. Strom was treated as a friend and hung out with the band members when the cameras were off.

He filmed their lives in Edinburgh, even interviewing their parents. "We got a really good insight into the families, the friends of the boys and the way they lived," he said. "We filmed Tam's mother helping with the fan club, opening the envelopes. Woody's parents were such lovely people. We walked up to their place and there was a girl stood there with some flowers for Woody's mum. When she saw Woody she passed out on the spot."

The band and their families were not living lavishly. "Woody's parents, John and Joan, lived very frugally," said Strom. "John still worked at the

Post Office. Eric's parents were not wealthy at all. Ian's parents were not wealthy." Joan Wood was a school dinner lady. She was interviewed by *Record Mirror* and mentioned three girls from Denmark and three from America camped on her doorstep. She said she received a "lot of letters" from fans. "The only time I get the police is when they make an awful noise," she said. "There's not a day goes by without someone coming."

Strom would use Wood's car, a Range Rover four-wheel drive, to get about the city. "It was a big monster of a car and the fans would recognise it," he said. "Every time I stopped at the lights or the end of the lane leading up to Tam's place the fans would come out and rip bits off the car. When we went to their studio, which was in a big Victorian building outside of Edinburgh [Castlesound Studios], the fans were hiding in the bushes. The fans were everywhere."

Wood admitted on camera that he purposefully kept his shirt open and his trouser buttons undone as a turn-on. "That's what it was about," Strom said. "It was an image band designed to excite the fans."

Strom met Alan at a pub in Dollar, a small historic town about 40 miles from Edinburgh, close to his farm. "We went back to his home, filmed him with his horses and he spoke about how he wanted to focus on the farm and lead a quiet life." Alan said he was learning about sheep farming and planned to get some sheep of his own. His girlfriend, who was 17 when they met, lived close by. He spent a great deal of time at the local pub, downing endless pints, often riding there on a horse. He was also downing bottles of whisky.

Record Mirror revealed that Alan had attempted suicide. "I did try to do myself in, it didn't work and I'm very glad it didn't now," he said. "The basic problem was pressure. It never stopped ... we had to go there, do this, then go somewhere else. Always on time, always another plane or car to get into. In the end we were just like zombies... that's what I felt like anyway. I bought a house and couldn't get any time to spend in it or get it together. It was stupid. I was really disillusioned with the whole pop business."

Strom asked Faulkner about his overdose, if it had been a suicide attempt. "It wasn't a hard-hitting documemtary to find out about the dirty life of the Rollers," said Strom. "It was designed for their fans and a particular timeslot but I did ask the question of Eric. He said, 'Well I couldn't sleep and I took some sleeping tablets and they had to take me to the hospital because I took too many. I took an overdose but it was an accident.' I accepted what he told me was true."

"What I captured was some sadness with the boys," Strom added. "We interviewed Les and you could see there was sadness in him. He was telling me how his father was deaf and never got hear him play music."

At Little Kellerstain, Paton flaunted his young male companions. There was Vince, the singer in Kip, and Graeme, who liked to dress up as a Roller, and another young lad called Plum. Pat McGlynn was floating about and Gert Magnus was still in situ. Paton had not got the Danish teen a record deal but had taken him to Japan, Germany and America and was still lavish with his spending on the youngster. When Magnus wanted to visit his home in Copenhagen, Paton gave him his credit card and he would stay in the best hotels in the city with a chauffeur-driven car to get around in. "He paid it all," Magnus said.

Strom would hook up with the band again on their North American tour. Ian Mitchell was a guest on *Top Of The Pops* on July 8, just there for a chat. Mike Mansfield directed an hour-long LWT special on the band called *Roller Coaster* that was shown on July 31 with Twiggy as special guest (Rod Stewart pulled out). Mansfield had filmed the Rollers playing 'live' in Eden Studios and in the LWT studio, without an audience in both locations. Ienner was supposed to have sent rough mixes of the new album but they never arrived. Colin Frechter was put in charge of the music for the show. "It took a week to put together and we made it up as we went along," he said. "We recorded the tracks, we voiced them, we mixed them all in a week. The last session I kept the sound engineer up all night."

The band, with Wood, Faulkner and McKeown toning down the Roller gear and even appearing in non-Roller costumes, gave a convincing impression that they were playing live in Eden, with amps, wires and headphones all displayed. They played album tracks from *Wouldn't You Like It?* alongside a smattering of new tracks from the forthcoming *Dedication* album. 'It wouldn't have been playing live but we recorded the tracks again," said Frechter. "It's like an alternative version of that album. When I compared our mixes to the ones Jimmy had done it was like a different band."

Faulkner was in full-on "heavy" mode for 'Rock'n'Roller', one of the few tracks he had written for *Dedication*, a Slade-like stomp on which he, Wood and McKeown all shared vocals. Mitchell got the full close-up star treatment on the track 'Dedication', on which he handled lead vocal, with his stars and stripes shirt [Wood had a matching one] open to the navel and his top trouser button undone.

Roller Coaster went out on a Saturday night at 6.30 pm. It was supposed to suggest the band had matured. But without the screaming girls in the audience it was a flat, strange viewing experience. Some of the new album tracks such as 'Let's Pretend' (with Wood and Faulkner both on piano) and 'Don't Worry Baby' were almost cabaret. It was easy to forget McKeown was not yet 21, just a few months older than John Lydon whose Sex Pistols were about to release their debut single. McKeown and the Rollers seemed to belong to another era, alongside the ersatz pop rock of Leo Sayer and Showaddywaddy. The show made the band appear so middle-of-the-road that they made Abba – the best-selling singles band of the year – look almost edgy. They had become hopelessly showbiz. There was certainly a career in it but it was not one that Faulkner wanted. He did not want to become the light entertainment fodder Paton now foresaw them as. Ironically John Lydon had admired the rough and ready 1974/5 version of the Rollers and the band's manager Malcolm McLaren had greatly admired the commotions they caused in the media. He said the Pistols were just The Bay City Rollers in negative. Faulkner still felt the Rollers could become a serious rock force, given a chance.

Now living in London, away from the rest of the band, he was also starting to take more of an interest in the band's business affairs. As the chief songwriter in the Rollers, Faulkner was keenly interested in Bay City Music, the band's publishing company, and eager to discuss with Colin Slater, at the band's new Heddon Street HQ, the deals he had been negotiating for the band's song catalogue in territories around the world. It was complicated: each territory had different laws regarding music publishing royalties and in each territory there was often more than one organisation collecting the royalties – there were 12 in France – and you needed to be affiliated with each. This was why the band had needed two publishing companies in America: one for ASCAP and one for BMI.

Faulkner pored over the detail. He should have been earning significant amounts from publishing, even if he had to split the song revenue evenly with the rest of the band. The monies, all being channelled through the band's accountant, Stephen Goldberg, were not filtering through to him, or not, as he saw it, in sufficient amounts.

Slater highlighted to Faulkner how he felt the band's business manager Perkins had been taking back-handers. Faulkner had never trusted, or liked, Perkins. He determined to oust him. "I didn't get rid of anybody – maybe Freddie Bienstock," Slater said. Faulkner was also eyeing Paton with some suspicion but other band members, namely Wood and Derek, tended to think Paton was a good manager. Wood said so repeatedly in interviews and continued to do so until 2015 when he decided otherwise.

Perkins' involvement with the Rollers' finances was highly questionable and the deals he'd struck on their behalf also seemed nefarious. Paton had frequently mentioned sacking him. Now he was. After the band unburdened themselves of him, Perkins had no further significant involvement in the industry. When he died in 2014 he was penniless and living alone in a council house. His marriage had collapsed and he spent his final 15 years working for a taxi firm in Bournemouth, first as a driver and then as PR manager. He had worked as a taxi driver in London prior to that. In his final years, he lived beyond his means and admitted he'd gambled away hundreds of thousands. He was struggling to make even £10 bets by the end. It seems likely that, if not greed, his gambling habit was behind his ripping off – and it seems clear that's what it was – of the Rollers. Who potentially exploited Perkins' weaknesses remains unclear.

The band's Heddon Street HQ was constantly besieged by scores of fans. If any member of the band was seen inside, hundreds would quickly gather outside. Slater continued to run the business without interference from Paton. He felt everything, once Perkins was gone and Paton sidelined, in terms of business, was healthy. He liked the band's accountant Stephen Goldberg. He told Faulkner he felt Goldberg was "a gentleman and wonderful guy". Slater did not believe Goldberg was stealing from the band. "He was far too smart to do that," he said. Paton was concerned about the ramifications of the sacking of Perkins. "I did hear of a conversation he had with Stephen Goldberg along the lines of I want to be assured my 15 per cent is intact," Slater said. "I don't know what happened with that. I thought Stephen was a straight guy."

There was a now an idea floating around that as well as keeping their income offshore, the band might benefit from a tax loophole that meant they would be allowed to pay no tax on earnings should they leave the UK for 12 months. It was an option they were considering for the tax year beginning April 1977. The decision was said to depend on foreign earnings over the next few months. Slater told me he had never heard of the band's business vehicle ALK Enterprises, the company created in America to allegedly control, at least, the entire financial operation of the band's American and Far East income, so as to minimise tax payments. Paperwork would later be made public showing that ALK Enterprises Ltd was in operation by October 1976. It was featured on a document, with that date, that showed the company then owed the Rollers a figure of close to $5 million. If, as he claims, Slater was unaware of the existence of ALK, what chance had the band members to untangle the labyrinth that was their finances? Slater was, after all, their man in London handling the band's business.

Mitchell was finding life stranger than he imagined it would be inside the band. The strain was showing. They had done a photo session for the new album cover with *Vogue* and *Sunday Times* photographer Allan Ballard who was making a name for himself as an esteemed rock photographer. Mitchell said that as they were looking over the results at Paton's home, Wood expressed his dislike of a photo where he felt his hair did not look right. "I said it looked fine," said Mitchell. Wood, he said, ran out of Little Kellerstain crying. "Eric got right in my face and shouted, 'Don't you ever talk to my friend that way!'" Mitchell said. "They both figured I was taking Tam's side." Paton would chide

Mitchell if he showed any concern for the others. "So you're becoming buddies now," he would say.

On the band's debut tour of America in August, Paton continued to insist the band members share rooms and he continued to rotate who went with whom. Arista had lined up 'I Only Wanna Be With You' to be the lead single from *Dedication*. It was the obvious choice. 'Yesterday's Hero' was the only other meaty, uptempo track on the album.

Derek said the group had "set success in North America as its goal". Eight of the upcoming 15 tour dates were in Canada, where 'I Only Wanna Be With You' peaked at number three and the *Dedication* album went to number five. In Toronto at Maple Leaf Gardens the band played to a healthy 9,000 fans with the police again struggling to handle the Rollers' young crowd in the city. Mitchell was agog. A fan handcuffed herself to the back bumper of their transport. "We didn't know she was back there and we were doing about 30 miles per hour," he said. Another fan climbed through the bathroom vent of their touring bus. "She was crying because she got stuck halfway through," said Mitchell.

In Regina the band had a police escort from the airport to their hotel but there were only 35 hardcore fans waiting. In Edmonton Northlands Coliseum, in front of another crowd of 9,000, there was a reported 27 girls who fainted as the crowd rushed the stage. One was taken to hospital. The Rollers played for about 40 minutes, leaving the stage twice when the crush of fans became too dangerous. The third time they reappeared, the venue manager stopped the show. Paton was furious. "There is no way we are ever coming into this stadium again," he said. "The manager was more excited than the teenagers."

Jack Strom and his two-man crew were capturing it all. "We travelled right across Canada doing some huge concerts in huge arenas," he said. "There's footage of me rescuing girls who had passed out, dragging girls out of the audience. Tam was stopping concerts, telling everyone move back, go back, the girls down the front are getting crushed. There's footage of Tam telling the boys what's happening backstage. There were screaming fans bashing the cars, thousands of fans, hysteria everywhere."

"We filmed on planes, at concerts – eventually they let us on stage, at radio interviews, in hotels," he said. "There were women with babies in their arms crawling up the fire escapes, people coming up the goods lifts, up the back stairs, trying to sneak through to meet the Rollers. We filmed in airports when there were kids running across the tarmac. The band was pretty much kept to their rooms with security guards. I saw people trying to get into their rooms. The band weren't very happy. Sometimes they wanted to go out and they were told, 'No you can't leave it's too dangerous'. If they were on the streets it would be risky from a safety point of view. Les was crying one night because he wanted to leave the hotel and go buy some records at the local record shop and Tam said 'No you can't go out on the street.'"

"Tam wanted to keep them inaccessible because he thought that would make girls want to try harder," Strom added. "It created this pandemonium. If a girl won a competition to meet the Rollers, she'd come backstage with a camera. If she took a picture of the Rollers with other girls, Tam would rip the film out and throw the film away and give the camera back to her. He didn't want the fans to think they had girlfriends or that some girls could access them."

Strom found the business organisation to be strangely loose. "There were guys coming up to Tam in Canada saying, 'I want to sell posters at the gig,'" he said. "Tam would say, 'Okay you go sell the posters for $10 and give me $5.' It was a bit rock'n'roll sometimes. I was surprised people would just turn up off the street with posters."

In America, the teen press continued to heavily feature the band. The Rollers had been on every cover of *16* since January. The magazine was getting 15,000 letters a month from girls aged 9–14 and their circulation was on the rise. Mitchell was often the star attraction – "I'm the luckiest boy in the world" was one headline. And there was the usual band features, wearing thin now: Roller diaries, pin-ups, excusive pictures, tour news and even Derek talking about his pet dog and pet goldfish. As Mitchell's star rose there were questions being asked about the paunchy-looking 22-year-old Faulkner. 'Is He Too Far Out For You?' was a *Tiger Beat* headline as rumours surfaced that the guitarist was into the occult.

Clive Davis saw the band perform on the tour, at a show in Philadelphia. He said he was shocked at the volume of the female fans' screams. "I had never heard anything like that before in my life," he said. In a room at the back of the venue, 40 girls were laid on the floor having passed out.

There were no major shows in New York or Los Angeles. "The record sales and fan club inquiries point to the fact that those aren't our areas," Paton said. The band punctuated the live dates with visits to radio stations and 'autograph parties', where they sat signing posters of themselves for fans.

In Buffalo, the venue organised for police to announce, before the band went on, that if any fans left their seats, they'd be thrown out. The venue was heavy with security. During the first song McKeown leaned over from the front of the stage and held his hand out to a girl. She reached up and took his hand and he kissed it. The room exploded. The fans over-ran the security.

Melody Maker's New York-based US Editor Chris Charlesworth joined the tour at one point. "Paton ordered me not to bring any girls back to the hotel," he said. "Usually when I'd been on the road with groups there were loads of girls to shag. Especially with Slade, bloody hell, the more the merrier, certainly with The Faces it was ridiculous. Tam just didn't seem to like women at all. It was a men-only situation. I thought it was very weird."

Charlesworth was with the band as they were mobbed by 1,000 fans at Logan Airport in Boston, Massachusetts. He described the rush to the waiting limo from the plane as terrifying, surrounded by shrieking fans – that all looked like Rollers – with the police wading in. Mitchell was even tossed to the floor by one police officer who mistook him for a female fan. Safely on the road, Paton, chain-smoking, described the event as everyday while "checking his supply of Valium".

"I was surprised it had transferred from the UK to America," Charlesworth said. "Slade never made it and they were a thousand times better live. It seemed ridiculous. At the gigs you couldn't hear much because everyone was screaming but it was obvious to me they weren't very skilled. They sounded thin and weedy; weak."

Paton, Charlesworth said, didn't have a lot of self-confidence. "It seemed as if he'd lucked into this thing and didn't quite know how to handle it and was asking anyone he could for advice, even me," he said. "He seemed a bit out of his depth."

Although they were playing relatively small halls, not all the concerts in America had sold out. Reviews were mixed. The *Chicago Tribune* said a gig at the city's 4,000-capacity Uptown Theatre was scarcely 'half-filled' and the band was 'awful'. Their short, 45-minute set had barely developed and still included 'Let's Have A Party' and 'Shout' alongside new single 'I Only Wanna Be With You' and fan favourites 'Saturday Night' and 'Money Honey'. "It's true careers have been built briefly on less but not much less," the *Chicago Tribune* concluded. A show in Detroit was cancelled although Paton denied it was because of poor ticket sales.

A young David Copperfield acted as an opening act on some dates. The crowd never stopped screaming so hiring magicians like Copperfield or a children's party act was the only entertainment that seemed viable. The fans paid no attention. It was all about the Rollers. Some had been waiting outside the venues from 3pm and the ritual of meeting with other like-minded kids to trade gossip or pictures from their scrapbooks was as much a part of their day as the show. The gigs were routinely wrapped up by 9pm. It left the band with long evenings free. Paton tried to organise a hook up with Elvis when he discovered the band and the American icon were staying in the same hotel. Elvis' long-time manager Colonel Tom Parker politely declined.

Paton caught Mitchell with several women in America. He was not happy. Paton accused Mitchell of destroying the band's image. Fame had gone to Mitchell's head. Charlesworth wrote in *Melody Maker* how the new member "contributed little" on stage. He was also often drunk and rebellious off stage. There was an alleged encounter of some sort with a female employee at a hotel. She rushed from the room. Paton managed to hush the incident but Mitchell's days as a Roller were numbered.

Paton was increasingly struggling to keep the clean-cut image alive as the band members disintegrated. Most of the band now chain-smoked, drank excessively and were addicted to drugs. They were having sex too. More than 12,000 fans were said to have resigned from the fan club when a rumour got round that McKeown had spent time in a hotel room with a groupie. Magazines and the fan club in Scotland got hate letters, often accompanied by torn-up photographs of the singer. McKeown denied the incident and was said to be close to suffering a nervous breakdown. "There's not a Roller that's not suffering from nerves," said Paton. He said that all the band members were on Valium.

"They're exhausted now," Paton told Charlesworth for *Melody Maker.* "The whole thing is terribly tiring and the pressure in enormous. It was no wonder that Brian Epstein ended it all for himself."

"We came here expecting a mild reception but it's been anything but," Faulkner added. "The airports, hotels… they're everywhere. Obviously the majority are 14, 15, 16-year-old girls but at the back, in the balconies, there's a lot of people who come to actually hear us and check us out as musicians."

The band did make it to Los Angles during the tour but only to shoot TV promos for 'I Only Wanna Be With You' including on the debut episode of the short-lived (and unsuccessful) ABC, Bill Cosby-fronted, variety show, *Cos.* They had a showbiz, top hat and tails, dance routine to perform that took them days to master. They were also guests on the syndicated daytime variety talk show *Dinah!* hosted by singer and actress Dinah Shore. Mitchell stole the show by making a sandwich with chips and ketchup. They band were back on *Midnight Special,* showcasing the new single plus 'Saturday Night' and album track 'Rock'n'Roller'.

In LA, word got round that the band were staying at the Century Plaza Hotel in Hollywood. Some of their wealthier and older fans booked into the same hotel. "We were followed round the world by two chicks from Ohio," McKeown said. "They were always booked in the hotel. A hardcore of maybe eight to 12 girls kept re-appearing."

"They couldn't escape the fans looking at them," said Jack Strom. "They'd be trying to relax around the pool but they couldn't." While in Los Angeles, Paton took them to Bill Gaff's birthday party and the band mixed with his guests including Rod Stewart who Gaff managed. Mitchell also celebrated his birthday in America. He was 18. "I bought him a suitcase and a hairdryer," said Strom. "His suitcase was torn and he didn't have a hairdryer. Everything happened so quickly for him. He'd been dragged from obscurity and thrown in at the deep end."

Dedication peaked at 26 on the *Billboard* album charts, selling in excess of 500,000 copies. They were now writing their own reviews in large adverts: "The Bay City Rollers now reaching the peak of their power, are about to explode with their finest album! It's a beautifully curated album, which includes their hit single 'I Only Wanna Be With You'. People are already astounded and are asking 'can this really be the Rollers?' It damn well is, is the reply! Both the single and the album will definitely be hailed as brilliant milestones in the unfolding Bay City Rollers story. From mellow gems to rousing rockers, The Bay City Rollers are moving on, and everyone, everywhere will soon move with them."

'I Only Wanna Be With You' rose to number 12 on the *Billboard* singles chart, convincing the band, and Paton, that America was their biggest potential market for the future. There was talk of Paton negotiating for a weekly TV series in America. One British paper reported that the group had actually signed a $20 million deal with the ABC network. A second larger American tour was being planned for the following year. Sid Bernstein would not be involved, however. Paton unceremoniously ditched him and sought representation with International Creative Management [ICM], a new talent agency formed in 1975 through the merger of Creative Management Associates and International Famous Agency. The merger made ICM one of the largest talent agencies in the world with offices in New York, Los Angeles, Washington and London. "He never seemed to have the boys' best interests as his top priority," said Bernstein who did not go quietly, threatening to sue Paton for commission earned during his time as American manager of the band.

Returning to Edinburgh, the Rollers had only four days respite before a short UK tour started. There was no time off however: they rehearsed for two days, made a promo film for 'I Only Wanna Be With You' (with Mike Mansfield) and mimed to the single on *Top Of The Pops*, shown on September 9 and repeated on the 23rd. Mansfield also booked them on LTW's kids' show *Saturday Scene* and his own LWT

Supersonic programme. 'I Only Wanna Be With You' peaked at UK number four.

Dedication also went to number four on the UK album charts but sold less than 100,000 copies. The UK edition of the album did not feature the current hit single but included 'Money Honey', a track released almost a year ago in late 1975. It gave the impression that Arista UK, now run by Davis' close associate Bob Buziak, was becoming negligent toward the Rollers' UK career – and that Paton had abandoned many of his duties as manager.

In America, Paton had told *Melody Maker*'s Chris Charlesworth: "The current British tour may be the last. Not because the Rollers don't want to play in England any longer, but because halls, promoters and agents don't want to know. The risk of damage is too great. I'm not saying this is a farewell tour to drum up publicity. Unless things calm down and the fans behave themselves, we may have to abandon touring at home. We don't have any choice. I wanted to play Hammersmith Odeon but they wouldn't have us and it took me a long time to agree with the New Victoria people. It will come to the point where there is nowhere for us to play in England."

Faulkner said he hoped to present the band in a more sophisticated light and wished the screaming would die down. The tour lasted 11 days and took in 11 towns: Dundee, Edinburgh, Glasgow, Manchester, Birmingham, Sheffield, Newcastle, Liverpool, Cardiff and Southampton. With the exception of London the venues were all the same as on the previous spring 1975 tour.

Radio Luxembourg DJ Peter Powell acted as compere on some of the shows and supporting the Rollers on all the dates were Bilbo Baggins, who had a new look based on a street gang from Leith – long, faded denim coats worn over high-waist baggy white trousers – but had still not made the charts. A third single, the AC/DC-esque 'Back Home', had flopped earlier in the year. Paton had recently forced out the band's bass player, evidently because he did not look the part, but had failed to persuade Alan Longmuir to take his place.

"No-one from the Rollers came to speak to us in our dressing room apart from Les McKeown who'd come to have a chat," said the band's guitarist Brian Spence. "He'd almost disassociated himself from the band. Tam couldn't control Les like he could the others. Les was like a street kid from quite a hard family... a Ned [non-educated delinquent]. He was the genuine thing. He just did what he wanted."

Bilbo Baggins had recently recorded a version of 'Let's Spend The Night Together' in the hope of a chart breakthrough but it was not released and when their Polydor contract expired they split from Paton. The band's drummer Gordon Liddle, then 25, who had being staying at Little Kellerstain, would go on to study law and become a Sheriff.

In Scotland, where the tour began, it was pandemonium as usual. Glasgow fans broke glass doors at the band's hotel, and a huge police security operation was needed for the show at the Apollo with nearby streets blocked off.

Paton had already put the Rollers on the front page of the Glasgow *Evening Times* by talking about them becoming tax exiles and living abroad. "We are paying a fortune in taxes," he said. "The boys all have very large investments, mainly in banks and building societies: the interest alone would keep them going for the rest of their lives, but they lose a fortune in income tax. We are looking at plans to live abroad. The only problem is it would mean we could get back into Britain for only a few months a year." He mentioned moving to Ireland.

Paton also broke the news that he was getting married later in the year. He would not name the bride to the *Evening Times* but talked wistfully of regret that he had not settled down at 21 with a wife, a council house and six kids.

The lucky lady was soon unveiled: Czech-born, 28-year-old London art student Marcella Knaiflova. She and Paton, 38 (or 36 as he told the press), posed for photographs. The Rollers stood behind toasting the couple. The engagement photo was taken in Manchester before the band's gig at Belle Vue King's Hall and widely circulated.

"That was advised," said Paton. "I had the *News Of The World* floating around at the time. If the press thought that the band had a homosexual manager, you know, they could all be rolling about in bed with me. So, I got wangled into this stupid engagement thing. It was the one decision I didn't take for myself, it was taken for me by a female publicist."

Andrew Drummond, the head of the Scottish office of the *News Of The World*, to whom Paton had regularly supplied stories, was just one Scottish journalist to have seen the numerous boys at Little Kellerstain first hand and heard all the rumours about Paton. "I could call Tam up anytime," said Drummond. "As a journalist I was more into getting stuff in the paper than being able to tackle what was actually going on. I couldn't have tackled that at that stage. You see how many newspapers tried to do Savile at the time... the atmosphere just didn't allow it. So much went in on those days that the media turned a blind eye to. Gary Glitter had dinner parties with journalists where young girls attended."

It seemed in Edinburgh that Paton' sex life was an open secret. His Rolls-Royce was often scratched and, according to him, "filthy things were written on it". "You definitely knew something was wrong at Little Kellerstain, he was having his way with young boys but there was no way to prove it," said Drummond. "The necessity was getting stories about The Bay City Rollers which is what the punters want to read about. I probably did give Paton a little heat but I don't think that would have prompted him to get engaged."

Nonetheless, what was going on inside the increasingly fortified Little Kellerstain – security was paramount to keep out fans – was attracting widespread suspicion. The high brick walls topped with barbed wire and the endless parties and flow of young men, not least the troubled, apparently suicidal, band. On stage McKeown routinely changed the words to 'Shang-A-Lang' to 'Shag-A-Lad'. One British newspaper, under the headline 'Locked behind the Gates of Colditz', suggested Paton controlled the group, preventing them from having girlfriends. "They said I locked them in behind barbed wire," said Paton. He was also compared to the original Svengali created by George Du Maurier in his novel *Trilby* and immortalised in the 1931 movie *Svengali*, a ruthlessly maleficent hypnotist whose subject obeyed his every command.

It was Bess Coleman, at Tony Barrow International, who organised the engagement stunt. A story about Paton's actual sex life would have been devastating to the band's career. If their manager had been unveiled as gay at the time – particularly in America where religion encouraged strong anti-gay feelings – the Rollers would have been put in an awkward position. This was an unenlightened, bigoted, era. Freddie Mercury of Queen – then breaking into the mainstream with their huge hit 'Bohemian Rhapsody' – hid his sexuality for years until *The Sun* forced him to 'confess' to having sex with men in 1986. Elton John, another gay performer, married a women in 1984. Barry Manilow also hid his sexuality. Even as late as 1999 in the UK, there was shock when a member of boy band Boyzone declared himself gay.

There was a suggestion that Kniaflova was actually Bess Coleman's partner, adding another level of irony to the whole charade. The picture of Paton and his fiancée was used widely in the press and Kniaflova actually moved into Little Kellerstain. "She lived in the house for some time," said Gert Magnus who lived there at the time. "The *News Of The World* were trying to find out about lots of things. So he did that to get peace. There were a lot of rumours... but they didn't find out because there was this lady living with Tam but in another room."

Magnus, now 16, did not stay around for much longer despite the money Paton was paying him. Paton kept promising his record would come out soon but it never came to anything. He moved Magnus down to the apartment he owned in West Finchley in London. "It was a place to get away from the press and everything," Magnus said. "We stayed there for some time... there was not a lot of people around like at LK, it was very quiet." It was here, Magnus said, that Paton made his move.

"He was starting to try something. I got really scared. I was thinking I didn't want that shit. I was there for the music. I just said no. He was not physical but tried to talk me into it."

Magnus' close friend and mentor, influential Danish pop journalist Per Lyhne, came to visit and helped Magnus escape. He was soon back in Denmark where he formed his own band who had some success with an album in 1979. "He decided he wanted to go back because he was going into banking or something instead," said Paton. "And he was missing home and he went back to Denmark."

The Rollers tour continued out of control. Fans went berserk at Edinburgh Odeon with thousands locked outside and hundreds treated for shock. The show was stopped and the band led off stage halfway through. Mitchell claimed some of the English shows outside London were not sold out. In London at the New Victoria Theatre, the Rollers played one of the final shows at the historic 2,500-seater venue before it closed for five years. It was business as usual. At least 210 hysterical fans were treated for minor cuts and bruises after flattening the first three rows of seats. It made the front page of the *London Evening News*: 'Rollers Face Ban in London'. The Greater London Council had voiced concerns about the band. There were pictures of young fans in distress outside the venue. It was to be the band's last UK concert of the decade.

Outside Little Kellerstain 12-year-old Christine Moore was thrown into the air in a collision with a passing van as she jostled with other young fans for a glimpse of her heroes. She was irreparably brain damaged. The crowd had thought the band were in the van. Moore suffered a fractured skull and two blood clots on the right side of her brain requiring immediate surgery. She was in a deep coma for five weeks then in hospital for six more months after she woke up.

Paton could no longer cope. He was admitted to hospital with shooting pains in his neck, complaining the top of his head was completely numb. He was having a nervous breakdown brought on by tension and drugs use. "I was definitely on the verge of suicide," he told *Starmakers & Svengalis'* author Johnny Rogan. "There's no doubt about it. I was frightened to death. It sounds crazy. I was going off my head." He also admitted to Rogan that he took *LSD* after leaving the hospital.

On September 25, there were more sensational headlines, 'Roller cleared of gun charge', as McKeown was found not guilty of firing the air rifle at the 15-year-old fan in December 1975. Over 100 fans cheered the verdict at Linlithgow Sheriff Court. McKeown had denied recklessly discharging the loaded air rifle. The court was told 22-year-old Hilary Tipping had used the weapon while McKeown was in the bath. McKeown said he was home with his girlfriend and had just cleaned his air rifle when he heard a noise on the path outside. He shone a portable lamp out of the window and there were some girls in his driveway. Asked if he had discharged the air rifle out of the window, McKeown replied, "No".

There was a possibility of proceedings against Tipping. Mike Mansfield said: "Nobody did take the rap. Hilary pleaded guilty to discharging a fire arm but was never accused of shooting anyone… it was all very strange."

McKeown put his house up for sale, guide price £37,000 (equivalent of £350,000 today). He said he was buying an old mansion in a remote part of Scotland. "My family can't stand the nuisance of fans hanging around the house anymore," he said. "The fans are upset when they are told I won't come out to see them. They don't realise that I need to have peace and quiet." He, like Faulkner, also had his own flat in London. He had also invested in a new Jaguar car. He was constantly harassed in London too. "There were about 30 fans that simply wouldn't go away," he said. "They'd be outside your house all day and night. I'd say, 'I can't devote my life to you. We can't fall in love and live happily ever after.' And they'd just smile and say, 'But you don't mean that, Les.'"

The Rollers work schedule was unrelenting and they embarked, unenthusiastically, on another stint of European promo. 'I Only Wanna Be With You' was top 20 in Austria and Belgium and top 10 in Holland, Germany and Italy. Mitchell said there were a number of fist-fights between band members as they flew in and out of countries to mime on TV shows, propped up by pills and threats from Paton. Both he and Wood were pictured in hospital in October 1976. Faulkner had been in hospital in the previous month, reportedly having his sinuses drained. Wood was said to be having a splintered bone removed from his nose. Mitchell, it was reported, had a growth, a node, removed from the back of his throat. It was unclear if the incidents, and explanations, were a PR stunt, a cover or genuine.

The Rollers played overwrought gigs in Belfast and Dublin before Paton had them parade through an excruciating promotional stunt in Glasgow. As he no longer had direct access to the band's finances he took to cashing in as best he could. This was a new low. Paton had the band, in costume, traipse around several local businesses including: Lefferty's the builders, Sloan's restaurant, Maryhill carpets, Marshall & Beaumont's leather and sheepskin manufacturing, MFP protective clothing and safety equipment, Rich Rags boutique and Garvie's lemonade factory. All these companies used photos of the band posing in their premises in future adverts. McKeown and Mitchell were photographed bare-chested. "All of us love all of City Cash Tailors," was one such embarrassing ad strapline. There was another, for Wellhall garage, with the band leaning on a Lada four-door saloon. As the day had unfolded, hundreds of girls had begun trailing them and a police escort was required. The girls threw themselves against the police and attacked the band's transport. The whole debacle made an eight-page special in the *Edinburgh Evening News*.

Paton, purportedly a multi-millionaire himself, declared that all the band members were now millionaires – apart from Mitchell who was seen around the city on a Honda 50cc motorbike (although he soon acquired a Mini). His sacking now a forgone conclusion, Paton had already lined up his replacement in the band: Pat McGlynn, 18 (17 for the press), dark-haired, slight and child-like, the same look as Mitchell. Paton had known McGlynn since he was 15 and a novice guitarist with Kip. He'd been a wild kid, a gang member, brought up around his father's scrapyard. In Kip he'd played alongside Stuart Wood before Wood was ghosted away to join the Rollers in 1974. More recently McGlynn had been singing in his elder brother's band, Wot's Up, who were gigging around the UK and attracting record company interest.

McGlynn knew the Little Kellerstain scene well, describing the recently departed Gert Magnus as "a good looking wee guy". "They were all after him," he said. "I told him to watch himself. Tam wasn't protecting him. He was keeping him for himself and then when he'd finished he'd pass him on." McGlynn was also friendly with Ian Mitchell who had been living at LK for most of 1976. He said Mitchell, like Magnus, was also lusted after. Mitchell would not comment although he said that he had been "chased" around LK by "a top showbusiness manager" who "demanded sex".

Paton had signed McGlynn up while he was under age. "I had a memo from Tam saying sign this boy immediately," said Colin Slater. "I interviewed him and he said, 'Do you want to hear me play guitar?' I said, 'No that's not necessary, I want to see your birth certificate.'

He was under 18, so I flew his parents down and had them sign the contract."

McGlynn was a virgin. "I'd never had sex with a girl," he said. "I was more into fighting. My first experience of sex was with that bastard Paton when he abused me on his couch."

Paton had already offered him Mitchell's role in the Rollers but the transition was messy. McGlynn appeared on the front cover of an issue of The Bay City Rollers official magazine, which had risen in price to £3, before Mitchell's exit was announced. McGlynn was said to like "horse-riding, swimming and trampolining plus Stevie Wonder, The Bee Gees and The Eagles". His most thrilling experience was, predictably, "meeting Tam Paton". He was photographed taking a bath and giving the obligatory thumbs up.

McGlynn had never left Scotland before and didn't have a passport. There was a suggestion that Mitchell might stay for the upcoming tours of Australia and Japan before McGlynn joined the band. Mitchell travelled to Los Angeles for promotional appearances on TV shows as Arista released 'Yesterday's Hero' as the second single from *Dedication*. The Rollers were featured on the cover of *16* for a tenth consecutive month. "They're coming back – and *16* tells you how you can get to them!" Mitchell was, again, featured heavily in the magazine. There were shots of the band on the trampoline at Little Kellerstain; all, apart from Derek, in tiny denim shorts – McKeown, Mitchell and Wood had nothing else on. Mitchell would actually feature on the cover of the December issue of *Tiger Beat* (the top button on his pants undone) even though he'd been ousted by then: 'Rollers – Are they telling the truth about themselves?' was the headline.

The Rollers recorded promo slots for the new single on the *Tony Orlando and Dawn* show, *The Merv Griffin Show* and mimed to 'Saturday Night' for an edition of *Midnight Special* devoted to the year's "million sellers". 'Yesterday's Hero' peaked at 54 on the *Billboard* charts and at 22 in Canada.

From America, Mitchell and Derek reportedly went on holiday together in Barbados. Wood travelled to Jamaica while McKeown spent time with Peter Powell in Luxembourg. Faulkner went back to

London. Mitchell by his own admission was flying off the rails, drinking heavily. He returned to Little Kellerstain and, he said, took a bottle of mild tranquillisers: an apparent third Rollers suicide attempt. "There was always the worry he might go off and do something dramatic," said Paton. "When you've already had two overdoses in the group that thought is always in the back of your mind."

The ever-obliging *Record Mirror* announced Mitchell's exit on November 13. The official line was that he had quit. "Joining the Rollers was my dream but it slowly turned into a nightmare," he said. He spoke of life as a "virtual prisoner" and a "gruelling timetable". McGlynn was in.

On November 27, McGlynn was introduced to the world via *Record Mirror*. Hurriedly poured into McKeown's old costume, the photographs showed him in a tartan-trim outfit that clearly didn't fit properly. "I don't have any of my own yet," he said. He was due to fly out to New Zealand in three days to start a tour that would also take in Australia and Japan. His passport had been rushed through. McGlynn said he'd been lined up as a prospective Roller for the past six months. "Tam said he was making the Rollers up to six," McGlynn revealed. "To tell you the truth it was when Eric took an overdose," Paton said. "I thought then he was reaching the danger point and that he might leave. That's when I thought of Pat."

McGlynn admitted he did not know the band material, having had only one rehearsal with them. He said Wot's Up had covered 'Summerlove Sensation' but he would have a chance to learn the other songs during two days' rehearsal in New Zealand. The act still included material the band had played in the mid-sixties such as 'CC Rider' and 'Shout'.

In the same *Record Mirror* article Paton said he was fed up with the way he was being portrayed in the media. "People seem to think I'm some kind of monster," he said. "They seem to think I go around hotel corridors brandishing keys and locking the boys up for the night. It's not true. I don't run their lives. I'm not a monster."

The seven Australian dates were as crazed as they had been on the previous visit to the country, almost a year ago now. On stage the band were frightened by the scenes. McGlynn was overawed. The *Dedication* album had reached number three in Australia and 'I Only Wanna Be With You' was at number eight. In Melbourne 200 fans had to be treated outside the concert by ambulance officers. Inside, the arena was full of sobbing and screaming fans with bouncers shifting unconscious girls on to the stage to be carried through the back doors where four ambulances were waiting.

The show was stopped twice. One mother who was there with her daughter told *The Age* newspaper: "I am scared stiff someone is going to get killed." A St John Ambulance man said: "We think there is going to be a catastrophe before the night's out. We can handle the fainting but someone will be crushed for sure." The police called in back up to prevent 500 fans locked outside the hall rioting. 'When the Rollers play, sanity goes pop,' was *The Age* headline.

There was a series of riots, injuries and criticisms from the Australian press as the dates progressed into early December. The Minister of Health for the state of New South Wales threatened to ban the group from the country unless they toned down their stage act. "We came to Australia to entertain teenagers not the Australian press," said Paton. The Australian *Women's Weekly* ran a competition to meet the band that attracted 20,000 entrants.

There was a close call in an underground car park in Sydney when the gates didn't close behind the group's limo and 4,000 fans poured down a ramp to surround the band. It was dark, hot and noisy. The fans swarmed all over the car and its roof buckled. There were only 12 police. The limo was trashed but the band escaped unharmed. "That was the worst occasion," McKeown said. "There was a feeling we were about to die."

Interviewed at Sydney's Boulevard Hotel, McKeown said: "I love being a Roller. It's like a dream come true... all I care about is to perform in front of an audience." During the visit, one newspaper said McGlynn answered questions "like a programmed computer" but McKeown was clearly going through the motions too.

In Melbourne the band appeared on the popular ABC TV music show *Countdown*. The studio was packed with screaming girls, hundreds locked outside. McGlynn smiled but looked lost. Wood and Faulkner seemed on autopilot and refused to look at the new recruit. The Jack Strom documentary, titled *Don't Stop The Music*, was aired for a first time. It was 70 minutes long and Paton loved it. It was also shown in New Zealand, the UK (by the BBC) and in Canada. "I won an award for direction," said Strom. "I was very proud of it." Incredibly, the documentary, whose ownership reverted to the band, was subsequently "lost". It has never been shown on TV since.

Strom also organised for the Rollers to appear on the variety show he was producing, the *Ernie Sigley Show*. The band was interviewed in the Hilton Hotel with thousands of kids outside. "I put my arm out the window and they all screamed," said Strom. "During the day they did a motorcade through Melbourne in an open-top car, through the main shopping area. The city came to a standstill. You could not move, thousands and thousands of kids everywhere, just extraordinary."

McGlynn was already struggling. "I expected Woody to be like he was when we were in the band before, a nice guy," he said. "But he was a totally different person now to the Woody I knew."

One night in Australia a fire alarm meant all the guests had to evacuate their hotel. "Les told me if it hadn't been for the fire Tam would have sexually abused me because he'd spiked my drink and I was unconscious on the bed," said McGlynn. "I was taken to hospital unconscious. Tam was drugging everyone he wanted to get his way with – drug them and abuse them. He was just an animal. Les pulled Tam off me a couple of times when he tried to rape me or he spiked my drink."

Paton told Colin Slater that McGlynn had started the fire and was a pyromaniac. McGlynn's days in the band were numbered. "Paton was a bastard," said McGlynn. "Paton had people sorting out sex. It was all laid on a plate. I must have seen hundreds of teenagers go through his hands."

Encouraged by McKeown, McGlynn admitted to taking advantage of the willingness of the band's female fans to have sex with a Bay City Roller. "I was green until I got friendly with Les and he opened my eyes to girls. With Paton it was all to do with boys and gay sex. Les and I had lots of girls but the trouble was if you got caught with a girl Woody would go back to Paton and tell him everything. I never saw any of the other band members sleeping with girls, apart from Les. I did see young guys going into Derek's room," he said. McGlynn said he presumed they were sexual partners. "Derek creeped me out."

McGlynn said Paton would call him to his hotel room to be "interrogated". "It would be once a week if you were lucky," he said. "Otherwise it was twice a week. Woody would be going back to Tam grassing everyone up, especially me and Les – if we had girls or were smoking pot or anything, and we'd get called to the room to be interrogated for hours." McGlynn said these interrogations, routinely had sexual overtures. "You never got peace in that band," he said. "Basically Paton was trying to abuse you and turn you gay. Paton was trying to fill me with drugs all the time… that's how I ended up taking drugs because most of them came from Paton. I didn't know what drugs were before I joined the band." Paton, as he had done with Faulkner, told McGlynn he needed to lose weight and had him on amphetamines as well as Quaaludes.

After the final Australian show, in Perth on December 8, the Rollers and Paton moved on to Japan. *Dedication* had become the band's second Japanese number one album and they were welcomed at Tokyo's Narita Airport by an incredible 30,000 fans. Paton and the Rollers were astonished. "What The Beatles did in the UK it's almost like The Bay City Rollers are remembered like that in Japan, even today," said McKeown.

Their hotel, the Tokyo Hilton, was besieged by over 3,000 fans. The ensuing mayhem led the hotel to ban rock bands. The fear of serious injury in the crush when they left and returned to the hotel was ratcheted up when one girl caught her hand in the hotel's revolving door and started screaming. She was okay but everyone knew that something could go badly wrong at any moment.

"There was always people screaming," said Bob Gruen, one of New York's hippest and best photographers. He was on the tour with the Rollers working for *Music Life* magazine. Famed for his pictures of The New York Dolls, John Lennon and Blondie (Debbie Harry was said to be a fan of the Rollers and was pictured posing with the *Rock 'n' Roll Love Letter* album), Gruen had struck up a good relationship with the

Rollers since photographing them during their first visit to New York in late 1975 and again on subsequent visits to America, including their most recent short tour there. "I made more money photographing them than any of the bands I was working with at the time," he said. "We had built up this relationship where I was with them any time they were in the States."

It was the first time he'd met McGlynn. "All of a sudden there was a new guy because the manager needed a new guy," he said. "It seemed rather manufactured; that said he hired pretty well. They were more like a theatre troupe than a band, with union rules: you want to be in the band you don't go out to a club on your own, you don't have an outside girlfriend."

Gruen had worked for *Music Life* in Japan in 1974 with Yoko Ono and in 1975 with the Dolls. "They asked me if I could get the same kind of access with the Rollers in Japan and if I could they would pay for my trip." Carol Klenfner called Paton to okay it. "He said he'd be happy to have me in Japan," Gruen said. The esteemed photographer travelled across the country with the band for gigs in Kyoto, Kyushu and Osaka. "I was in the limo, the dressing room, the helicopter," he said.

"Tam was very professional, friendly," said Gruen. "We didn't socialise. They didn't go out to nightclubs or anything like that. I didn't often go back to the hotel with them. They'd go back and I would go develop my film. When I was in a hotel, they would get a big take-out order of hamburgers and milkshakes and things kids eat, French fries, and they'd get stoked on that and maybe have a pillow fight and at 8.30pm I was done. Me and the security guard went out in Japan late at night. At 8.30pm, after the pillow fight, the door would close and I don't know what went on. What I did know was there were no groupies involved. The fans were so young; you're not going to let 12-14 year-olds in your room. That was an absolute rule, no girls allowed."

The fans still tried to get in. McKeown found two had somehow managed to get onto his balcony in Osaka. The endless promotion and interviews in Japan would see the band saturate the country's music media. They featured on two *Music Life* covers, and in the coming months would feature on the cover of *Young Rock* magazine and five covers of *Rock*

Show magazine. "It was a working group," said Gruen. "They got up in the morning and we went to one event after another. It was a non-stop schedule and 8.30pm at night, back in the hotel and done."

Gruen had some videotapes with him featuring upcoming New York acts like Blondie and Patti Smith that he played the band. He also showed them a documentary he'd made on The New York Dolls as they travelled between cities on the tour bus. "It was an odd moment," he said. "Several of them were just passing time, something on the screen not particularly interested, but Les was fascinated. Les was a great lead singer, very cute, very savvy, he had a charisma... a really talented charismatic guy. He was studying the video and Tam was putting him down. Tam said, 'Oh they wear make-up, oh they're just pretending, our band is really good, their band isn't. They broke up, we're a success.' Tam seemed a little threatened by the video."

The band returned to the UK from Japan on December 21. There was the brief lull before, on January 7, the Rollers played at the Santa Monica Civic Auditorium in Los Angeles. The band's new American agency, ICM, eschewed the hype of the Sid Bernstein era and focused on establishing the Rollers as a working band in America. This meant, initially, showcase gigs in Los Angeles and New York.

The 3,000-capacity venue in the beachfront area of Los Angeles was a credible venue for the band and they were received enthusiastically. A catastrophe had been narrowly avoided prior to the show when a young diabetic fan had to be rushed to intensive care after doctors struggled to get through the crowd of screaming girls to treat her. The fans refused to clear a path and the young girl was left on the verge of death. She survived.

The show in New York the next day at the 3,000-seater Palladium (also known as the Academy of Music) on East 14th Street was also marked by near tragedy. A 12-year-old fan was rushed to hospital after being accidentally pushed in front of a car by girls running across a busy street to catch a glimpse of the Rollers. There was an electric atmosphere inside the old theatre and many girls in tears as the crush at the foot of the stage intensified. One review noted the fans, "girls aged 12-18", were all wearing tartan, even tartan underwear. ICM began to plan a large American tour for the group in 4,000 to 5,000-seater venues for early summer.

Arista released the title track from *Dedication* as a new single. McKeown had redone the lead vocals, replacing Mitchell. ICM had contacts in all areas of the entertainment industry and had the band feature on popular kids' TV show *Wonderama* and on one of America's most popular day-time TV programmes, *The Mike Douglas Show* (shown on February 1). 'Dedication' peaked at 60 in in the *Billboard* singles chart and at 70 in Canada.

The band spent almost a week in New York promoting it. McGlynn was on the cover of the February issue of *16*. The magazine promised his "most daring pic" and delivered him nude apart from a strategically placed scarf. The magazine continued to churn out fluff: "Derek's love secrets", "Eric's moods", "Les reveals how to thrill me", "Woody – what it takes to be his love!" and "Rollermania! - Have you got it? What to do about it!"

Tiger Beat also continued to feature the group on the cover but the magazine was taking a slightly different position on the band. They featured pictures of new boy McGlynn heavily but inside there were articles about the pressure the band felt. 'Your Love is Hurting the Rollers' was one headline, the fan attention said to be "causing them heartache and pain". Paton, again, talked about his Valium use "to keep me going" and he said Mitchell was the happiest Roller because "he just left". Faulkner said: "Most people want to know us only because of who we are now. You really can't trust anyone." The volume of fans outside their New York hotel forced them to switch bases. There was also news that a 16-year-old girl in Chicago had accidentally shot and wounded her 15-year-old pal during an argument over the Rollers.

McGlynn said that, during this short stay in America, Paton was feeding him a constant supply of amphetamine and cocaine. He was so worried about Paton making sexual advances towards him that he was sleeping with clothes on. "The guy was pestering me every day while I was in New York," McGlynn said. "He was trying to ride me and would stand there on his bed at the hotel with his cock out wanking off in front of me and trying and to get me to suck it."

McGlynn said there were other men involved in Paton's games in New York. "There would be parties in the room... all these guys in bed together, trying to take pictures of you in the nude or trying to get you to join in." McGlynn said one night in New York he stabbed Paton with a knife to fend him off during an assault. McKeown said McGlynn had been the unlucky band member that night, designated to sharing a room with Paton. He recalled how McGlynn rushed into his room "hyperventilating" with Paton charging after him. Having slammed and locked the door, McKeown said the pair stood terrified as Paton tried to kick it in. Finally hotel security dragged Paton away. "The next day at the airport Tam was literally chasing Pat around, trying to get hold of him," McKeown said. "He was so out of control by then, he didn't seem to care what the press saw or said."

The Rollers met with Clive Davis at the Arista offices in New York. He had chosen a new producer for the band to work with and a batch of new songs he wanted recording. Harry Maslin, 28, had been an engineer at the Hit Factory studio in New York working with acts such as Carly Simon and Dionne Warwick before moving to the equally well-known New York studio, Record Plant, where he worked with David Bowie in 1975 after Bowie fell out with producer Tony Visconti. Maslin had produced Bowie's hit single 'Fame' and then gone back to the Hit Factory to produce Bowie's highly regarded 1976 album *Station To Station*. He'd recently produced a solo album with Bowie's then guitarist Earl Slick. As well as the Rollers, Davis hired Maslin to work on a new act he'd signed to Arista called The Hollywood Stars, touted as a West Coast New York Dolls.

Maslin was soft-spoken and easy-going and he and Davis would go on to work together on various hit future projects, notably Air Supply. "He has a gift for picking songs," Maslin said of Davis. "He's got a percentage of being right that's higher than anybody I've met in the business."

Davis had chosen four songs he wanted the Rollers to cut: 'It's A Game', 'You Made Me Believe In Magic', 'The Way I Feel Tonight' and 'Love Power'. The band also had demos of new songs they wanted to record, chiefly by Faulkner/Wood although McGlynn was keen to get involved.

"It seemed to me that the band's relationship with Clive was fine at the time," said Maslin. "They made mention that they did not always agree with his choice of material for them, but nevertheless they understood the dynamic... he was the Supreme Leader. It is not unusual in the relationship between the artist/act and the head of the record company for there to be a little stress. Clive may not have seen them on the level of the super creative groups of the day, but he knew what he had and they were making the company a fortune. Their vision, as I perceived it, aside from making hit records, was to legitimise themselves to their peers of the day and to incorporate more of their own material on their albums."

The band would meet with Maslin to begin recording in Gothenburg, Sweden, at the end of February. The studio chosen, Tal and Ton, was owned by Bob Lander who had found fame as a member of The Spotnicks, Sweden's first international breakout band. Maslin did not know who had chosen the location. "They could escape some British tax law if they did the actual recording outside of the country," he said. Paton was not involved in any of the discussions regarding the new album. "Not in the picture," Maslin said. The producer did not intend to rehearse the group. "I enjoy the spontaneity of working out a song. To me, capturing that spontaneity is part of the process."

After short holidays – Wood and Derek went to the Caribbean together – the Rollers were back in Scotland on February 8, 1977. Paton and Derek hooked up with Jimmy Savile for a fundraising event relating to the horrific November 1976 murders of a nurse, a patient and police officer by two inmates of the State Hospital in Carstairs who had broken free. Savile met local primary school pupils before, at Motherwell Town Hall, he compered a benefit gig for the families of those killed. The Rollers were there as special guests.

At home in Edinburgh, McGlynn broke down and told his father what Paton had been doing. "I didn't want to," he said. "But I couldn't stand it anymore. My father went crazy and went away to the police and reported him." McKeown claimed that McGlynn's father "beat the shite" out of Paton.

"I was going to expose him," said McGlynn. "I was threatening Tam and talking about exposing what really went on in the band. I ended up going to the police. But Tam knew someone in the police... it was like a gay Mafia. Stephen Goldberg was gay... most people around the band and in Tam's circle were gay. A lot of them liked them young, 15 or 16. They looked after one another. I told Alan [Longmuir] about how Tam abused me and he knew what Tam was like."

McKeown excused himself. "We didn't all know everything about what was going on with the other ones," he said. "Stuff happened that wasn't talked about, obviously."

McGlynn was still with the group when they flew to Miami to record a TV special for *The Mike Douglas Show*, miming songs from the *Dedication* album and all their recent singles in front of a live audience on a makeshift stage on the beach. They were also filmed fooling around on Miami beach for 'fun' segments on the show. The band members were shown trampolining, driving around in a beach buggy and ganging up on McGlynn to aggressively drag him toward the sea for a dunking. There was enough recorded material for multiple shows that went out over three days, February 21 to 23.

On February 25 they were back in Europe, in Germany, miming 'I Only Wanna Be With You' on the *Scene 77* TV show. McGlynn had featured on the cover of the January issue of *Bravo*. 'Yesterday's Hero', the band's current German single, peaked at 13.

They travelled to Gothenburg on the west coast of Sweden at the end of February and spent March with Maslin recording their fifth album. It was cold and they stayed in two rented houses close to the studio, driving around in a Volvo estate incognito. The studio was in a building that had originally been a prison. "A couple of the solitary confinement cells were now echo chambers," said Maslin. "It was pretty cool and an interesting experience."

Maslin would become well known for bringing an MOR sensibility to the acts he worked with, especially on single releases. His work with the Rollers was an early indication of where his career was heading as he tried to move the group into a more adult direction.

The most pressing concern as far as Arista were concerned was to cut new singles. Davis has made it clear the songs he had chosen were key to the project's success. 'It's A Game' was written by Chris Adams from the Scottish folk rock band String Driven Thing. Maslin loaded the chorus with strings. "That is something I pride myself in doing," he said. "Quite often I would sing the orchestral part for the arrangers, sing the melody for a string or horn part and have them orchestrate it further. When it came time to record, I would alter or adjust parts [of songs] in the studio when I found it necessary, the better to fit what I heard for the song."

Maslin said that all the music on the new album was played by the group "except for any obvious orchestral or keyboard parts". The Rollers were respectful of Maslin. "I'm not sure if it was because of my previous work or just that I treated them as a band and had due respect for them as well," he said. "I was given the feeling that they were not often taken seriously as musicians previously and I sensed they appreciated my demeanour toward them. I found them to be very nice guys and eager to please. They were more than capable of playing on their tracks. They were not of the calibre of the great studio musicians, but that was fine. If it took a bit longer to get results, no problem. In the end I think they started sounding more like a band and were looking toward the future, and that was good."

McGlynn had developed into a decent, funky guitarist and was keen to be involved further in the songwriting on the album, making valuable contributions to the band's own material, notably on the song 'Sweet Virginia'. Faulkner/Wood had brought their best work to Sweden, specifically 'Don't Let The Music Die' and 'Inside A Broken Dream', both intensely sad songs. Maslin gave them astonishing orchestral treatments. It became easily the band's best work as a group, full of genuine pain and lament. Faulkner would later claim he had written almost all the Faulkner/Wood songs himself. 'Inside A Broken Dream', he said, was "about the music business" but with "undertones or hidden meanings about somebody being ill and lying in a hospital bed with nurses around them finding it hard to distinguish dreams form reality." McKeown gave his best vocal performances to date on the material.

"Les took direction well and I had no real problem with him while recording vocals," said Maslin. "He was a good singer and had very eclectic tastes. He did appreciate David [Bowie] and many others. I recall the two of us listening to Jackson Browne's *The Pretender* album more than once with great appreciation."

As well as Browne, McKeown was listening to more un–Roller-like material by Waylon Jennings and Pink Floyd. Outside the studio, McKeown said the band experimented with acid in Gothenberg and that McGlynn got himself strung out on the drug. "Pat was a decent player but was indeed a bit on the wilder side," said Maslin. "I do not recall hearing of him setting fire to a hotel room but I wouldn't put it past him." There was a suggestion that McGlynn had made a move on Maslin's wife and that he was caught having sex with the wife of an Arista executive. When these rumours landed back at Little Kellerstain, as all Roller news inevitable would, Paton flew into a rage. There were endless calls back and forth between Edinburgh and Gothenburg. Although not involved in the decision to appoint Maslin, Paton saw it as a coup for the Rollers to be working with Bowie's producer and feared McGlynn's behaviour might have derailed the project.

McKeown suggested there was further upset when some of Faulkner's guitar parts were re-recorded by a session player and Faulkner found out. "Les is making up stories," said Maslin. "If we used a session player it could have been because Eric was ill on the day and I had to get the work done, it certainly would not have been for the lack of confidence in Eric's ability." Ruben de Fuentes from The Hollywood Stars claimed Maslin hired him to play guitar on "a couple of tracks" on the album.

Paton did briefly visit Sweden, Maslin said. "He was always pleasant to me and I put away any rumors that were floating about," he said. After recording basic tracks in Sweden, overdubs on the album were completed in various studios around the world. Maslin recalled using Konk and EMI studios in London, plus Mountain in Switzerland and another studio in Vancouver.

Paton needed the band back in Scotland for the start of April to appear at a press conference to announce their involvement in an anti-smoking campaign launched by the Scottish Health Education unit. No fee was involved, Paton was keen to point out. McKeown and Faulkner confessed to smoking, listing boredom during concert tour hotel stays and one-time ambitions to become 'hard men' as the cause of their addiction. So Derek, Wood and McGlynn found themselves featuring on TV ads and with their faces plastered on giant anti-smoking posters. It was said that 50 per cent of young Scots aged between 16 and 19 smoked.

During April the band also appeared in front of 8,000 in Berlin at the Bravo Super disco, picking up an award for most popular band in Germany. McGlynn was cold shouldered during the event by the other band members. After a detour to pick up an award in Luxembourg from Radio Luxembourg, they travelled to Munich to mime 'It's A Game' and 'Rock And Roll Love Letter' for TV show *Disco 77*. McGlynn seemed to have lost interest in the charade now. While the others, maybe by force of habit, committed to the mime, he could see how foolish they looked and made fun of it, smirking and strumming half-heartedly. The band was back on the cover of the *Bravo* magazine for their May issue. New single, 'It's A Game', peaked at number four in Germany, their biggest hit in the country.

The single was also issued in Australia (where it reached nine) and the UK. It was their first single in their home territory for almost six months. There was a promo video for the song that saw the band superimposed on a chessboard – McGlynn was a pawn. None of the band was wearing Roller gear and all their trousers, although flared, were back to full length. The tartan-free image spoke of adulthood although 23-year-old Faulkner could not resist embellishing his white jacket with a small letter 'E'.

On May 3, as McGlynn was readying himself to travel to London to record *Top Of The Pops* to promote the new single, Faulkner and Wood called him at his parents' home. He was out. They didn't want to play with him anymore. They sang 'Bye Bye Baby' down the phone, he said. The Rollers recorded the show as a foursome. It was shown on May 5 and repeated on May 19. They then flew out to America for a much-anticipated 21-date North America tour, leaving McGlynn back in Edinburgh. On May 6, his sacking made the news: 'Bye-Bye Pat as Rollers sack new boy' and 'Rollers sack their new recruit' just two of the headlines.

Paton pleaded ignorance and told the press: "I still don't know why the scene has gone sour but I'm hoping to speak to the Rollers later today and I'll be flying out to join them for part of the [American] tour later next week. I'm extending my operations and have been involved for quite a few weeks now with other groups under my control. I haven't been really close to the Rollers over the last couple of months. I can honestly say I am shocked by what has happened but the four have made their decision. It's their right to do so but I still want to find out what went so badly wrong."

The band issued a statement: "We all honestly believed that he [McGlynn] would be a valuable asset to the group and fit in well musically and personality-wise. Unfortunately things haven't worked out the way we hope and after long discussions we have decided in the best long-term interests of The Bay City Rollers it would be better that he no longer remained a member. Needless to say we wish him well in whatever career he pursues."

There had been a rumour that Wood had also wanted to leave the group. Perhaps because of his dislike of McGlynn. Wood said: "The other two guys [Mitchell and McGlynn] got toppled into it and it went to their heads. We might take an older guy sometime, someone who'd played in a successful band but otherwise there's no way we'd take someone in off the streets again."

"We paid off Pat to leave the band," said Colin Slater. "I had to get his father to come down to sign for it. We gave him money and his father signed a receipt for it."

McGlynn rejoined his brother's band Wot's Up and, remarkably, there was some talk in the media of Paton managing them. In the press the story that would stick about why McGlynn had been forced out of the band was that he had been complaining about being paid only £200 a week. Derek explained that was because he was only in the band on "a trial basis". In fact, McGlynn was well-remunerated, paid in excess of £30,000 for the tour of Australia and Japan.

There was no way McGlynn wanted Paton as his manager. He needed to escape completely from the abuse. "Part of the reason I got away from him was because he wanted me to drop the proceedings against him with the police," he said. "I didn't know what to do but in the end I didn't bother making a statement and that's how I got out of the management contract."

'It's A Game' peaked at number 16 in the UK singles charts. It was the band's final top 20 single in their home country. On the label of the seven-inch single someone had inscribed a special message for Paton: "Special thanks to Tam Paton – P.S. It's a game."

CHAPTER 10

It's A Game

*"I like punk rock. I think it's genuine. I'm a strong supporter of that.
Punk rock's only a variation. It's like guys in the street saying the same
thing as Jackson Browne is saying on a more understandable level. I like
it because it's music that makes people think. I'm friends with that guy
in the Sex Pistols, Johnny Rotten, met him in a club one day, and he's
a nice guy."*

– Les McKeown

The Young City Stars had replaced Ian Mitchell with 16-year-old
Andy LeGear and, while Mitchell had been in the Rollers, had
continued to ply their covers set successfully in Ireland to appreciative
young female fans. Now, in a surprise about-turn, it was announced
Mitchell had returned to the band and Paton was managing them. Lead
singer Damian McKee was now 18. His brothers Terry and Colin were
16 and 15, respectively.

Mitchell had actually contacted McKee about rejoining before being
sacked from the Rollers. "I found out he wasn't too happy with what
was going on," McKee said. "He told me he wasn't getting on with
Les. He asked me, 'If I get out of this, can we get the whole thing back
together?' I looked at it like I know he's a wee bit of a bollocks but

at least we can notch the whole thing up a bit. We might as well get something out of it."

McKee visited Mitchell in London. "He showed me a bit of the world he was involved with," he said. "He had a few quid and we went off to Luxembourg and met Peter Powell. I don't know what he was thinking but I said, 'We need to get all the boys over.' No way was I leaving them." The band stayed at a hotel in London at Mitchell's expense.

"We were in a hotel for months," McKee said. "And then Tam came back on the scene and we all got talking again. I basically asked him if he would manage us. Tam was non-committal at first but then he brought us all up to Scotland and we stayed in Eric's place, a farmhouse up in the mountains. We weren't on a wage. We didn't get anything. We were kept boys."

Mitchell said that he was "contractually obliged" to Paton or "there is no fucking way in hell I would have had him as a manager". Paton fancied LeGear and had an eye on the younger McKee brothers. Faulkner had long moved out of his Scottish house – it kept being broken into by fans – and Paton had The Young City Stars ensconced there for the early months of 1977. "It was a really old farmhouse," said McKee. "But it had been beautifully renovated, no expense spared. There was big extension of a kitchen put on to it."

One night there was a chip pan fire that threatened to bring down the entire building. "Luckily the stone walls stopped it getting into the main body of the building," said McKee. "It burned the new extension down. We were not popular boys."

Paton wanted the band to change their name. They wrote a few suggestions down, among them Rosetta Stone, copied from an old Barry Blue B-side. "We had no name for about a month," said McKee. "We were pressurising Tam because we knew when he got the name he had to do something. He was doing a radio interview one night and he was asked, have you got a new band and he said 'Aye, the wee band's called Rosetta Stone.' So we went 'Oh right he's picked the name.'"

For a time the band were moved into Little Kellerstain. Was Paton grooming them? "Probably yes, when you look back," said McKee.

"But he had charm and a way about him." Paton appeared to be no longer interested in Mitchell, even though, as a former Roller, he would be the main draw of the new band. "Tam didn't want Ian back again, he didn't want Ian on the scene at all," said McKee. "Tam and Ian fought it out. Ian was a rebel generally. We'd be gigging and the next minute he was gone. That was always the case with Ian. But I was able to handle him; get him on stage if he was drunk. I think alcohol got him in the end. As far as Tam was concerned he wanted professionalism… getting on stage not pissed and on time."

Paton managed to sign Rosetta Stone to a record deal with Private Stock, a label owned by Larry Uttal, the one-time owner of Bell Records. Private Stock had just released Blondie's debut album and the label was also home to Frankie Valli of The Four Seasons and David Soul of *Starsky & Hutch*. "I don't know if it was a good deal or not," said McKee. "We were totally naïve, we hadn't a notion about the finances. If you asked about it you were made to feel as if you were questioning Tam's honesty. If you mentioned, how much was this, how much was that, he'd say, 'Do you think I'm ripping you off?' So you stayed away from it. We didn't really have money or see any."

As he had with the Rollers, Jonathan King produced Rosetta Stone's debut single, a cover version of Cream's 'Sunshine Of Your Love'. Scheduled for release in August 1977, King speeded up the original and tried to turn it disco. The band was booked on a tour with Gary Glitter to help raise their profile. Paton told the band not to worry about their arses. "He's into little girls not boys."

Contrary to his recent press assertions, Paton had no other groups under his control but the fledgling Rosetta Stone, no empire to oversee that might detract him from Rollers business. Gert Magnus and Bilbo Baggins had both left him. Kip was a pipedream for boys more likely to end up in Paton's bed than the recording studio. The simple truth was Paton had lost interest in the Rollers; they no longer excited him. He had, in private, embarked on a period of wild sexual abandon that would culminate in a prison sentence. All he needed to keep him happy he could find at Little Kellerstain. When there were no parties, he would hunker down and watch endless movies. His favourite was

311

the epic biographical film, *Patton*, about American General George S. Patton during World War II. He was addicted to Valium and took other drugs. Paton saw himself as untouchable, his mind as muddled, muddied and messed up as the Rollers. He asked Colin Slater if there was any need for him to accompany the Rollers on their upcoming American tour. He was told no.

Arista had decided against putting out 'It's A Game' as a single in America and instead were releasing 'You Made Me Believe In Magic' as the lead single from the new Harry Maslin-produced album. It was a sophisticated disco-tinged ballad written by Len Boone, a Philadelphia based songwriter who scored a solo recording deal off the back of this song, one of his first efforts. Maslin had given the band a contemporary gloss far removed from their rumbustious breakthrough American sound.

The tour had been due to start in Canada but the dates were postponed and the band travelled straight to Tennessee to rehearse. For the first time the band had a travelling stage show. Chessboard squares would cover the stage and four huge chess pieces positioned for the band to hide behind at the start of the show. These were sometimes mistaken for giant tombstones. The band even had special guitars made to resemble chess pieces.

It also had a name. The *It's A Game* tour opened on May 9 at Westchester Premiere theatre, 30 miles north of Manhattan. The venue was close to 4,000-capacity and the start time was 9pm, late for the Rollers, a sure sign of intention – they had grown up. The stripped down four piece also wore more normal clothes, with only discreet hints of tartan. The sets were longer too than ever before, 90-minutes, and the first half an hour given over to ambitious material from the new, as yet unreleased, album.

There were some huge venues to fill on the tour, such as the 5,200-capacity Toledo Sports Arena, but the ticket sales were healthy. The band had made some devoted fans. Since April, 40 girls in Toledo had been in the local papers kicking up a fuss in malls to publicise the Sports Arena gig "to make sure advance sale of tickets will be big enough so that they don't cancel out".

Very early look at the tartan stage overalls, or costumes, the band adopted in late 1974. The platform boots would soon be replaced by Adidas high-tops. PICTORIAL PRESS

Paton in America, 1975, sporting a look more often associated with Flavor Flav of Public Enemy. Paton enjoyed cruising New York's happening gay bars. BOB GRUEN/WWW.BOBGRUEN.COM

Wood being 'bathed' in shaving foam by Alan, an attempt to present the band so as to appeal to teenage girls but in retrospect looks awkward. DAVID GOLUMB

Faulkner and McKeown sporting exquisitely tailored outfits and battered trainers as the look is perfected.

The debut issue of the band's own monthly magazine launched in December 1974 that sold hundreds of thousands of copies until it folded in June 1978. DAVID GOLUMB ARCHIVES

Wood, Longmuir and Faulkner in Australia with Jack Strom who would shoot the defining period documentary on the band, *Don't Stop The Music*. COURTESY OF JACK STROM

The band posing with Clive Davis, the boss of their American record label Arista. Davis took much of the credit for the Rollers' success in America. BOB GRUEN/WWW.BOBGRUEN.COM

"Everybody was frightened of Tam," said Alan Longmuir. "If he said jump you jumped."
GEORGE WILKES/HULTON ARCHIVE/GETTY IMAGES

Paton instructed the band to flash their chests and either unzip their flies or unbutton their trousers for photo shoots.
JORGEN ANGEL/REDFERNS

American fans laid out after fainting or suffering from hysteria at the Rollers' US debut show in New Jersey.
BOB GRUEN/WWW.BOBGRUEN.COM

Fans reach out to touch Faulkner, as the band grow expert in teasing a reaction at their concerts. JORGEN ANGEL/REDFERNS

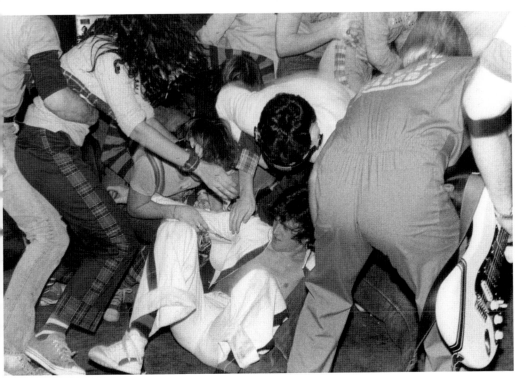

American fans mob McKeown on stage. BOB GRUEN/WWW.BOBGRUEN.COM

Paton announces his engagement to Czech-born, 28-year-old London art student Marcella Knaiflova, a stunt intended to curtail growing rumours about his private life. Pictured is new boy Ian Mitchell (centre), a replacement for Alan.
PA IMAGE/ALAMY STOCK PHOTO

A BBC Radio 1 Fun day at Mallory Park in Leicestershire turns into chaos. COURTESY OF LEICESTERSHIRE CHRONICLE

Paton and security attempt to protect McKeown from fans at Mallory Park. COURTESY OF LEICESTERSHIRE CHRONICLE

Although the audience was still mainly young kids and there was the occasional matinee show to perform, without Paton on the road the band felt free, adult, and almost real. The 23-year-old Faulkner, in particular, was letting loose. The band certainly no longer needed to hide their alcohol in milk. Wood was 20, McKeown 21 while Faulkner and Derek, who was now 26, were pretending to both be 21. As a four piece they were a tighter musical unit than they had ever been but it was still ragged around the edges and their ambition to be taken seriously did not match their aptitude and was plainly at odds with their audience.

The screaming continued: fans were trampled in Philadelphia and the crush in Dayton, Ohio, began before the doors opened. "One day they're not going to be screaming at concerts, they're going to sit there and listen," predicted McKeown, towing the line about the Rollers' new mature musical direction.

Jeff Grinstein followed the tour across the country. He was an 18-year-old New Yorker who had been around the band since late 1975, helping Sid Bernstein organise their American fan club as well as hosting popular Rollers parties in New York. "There were no adults at the gigs on the tour," he said. "It was all girls and a few parents stood at the back."

Grinstein had actually just returned from Edinburgh where Bernstein had sent him in the hope of signing Pat McGlynn to a management contract. McGlynn was back living with his parents in Niddrie. "I stayed at Pat's for four nights trying to get him to sign a management agreement," said Grinstein. "Sid and I really wanted to manage him." Grinstein said he was shocked by the behaviour of McGlynn's family. "We were chasing a squirrel in the back yard all day and that ended up being dinner that night," he said. "It was like the Beverly Hillbillies."

The Rollers were still being propelled in America by coverage in the teen magazines. McKeown, fast emerging as the band's main star, featured on the cover of *16* and *Tiger Beat*. Among the usual features – "ten pages of intimate behind the scenes pix!" – *Tiger Beat* asked: "Are they leaving younger fans behind?" The Rollers, the magazine wrote, were dating on the road, smoking, and "even drinking".

Yet, they were still trapped. Even without Paton patrolling the corridors, the band were often stuck inside their rooms as hundreds, sometimes thousands, of fans gathered outside their hotels. In one town in the south of America the local Sheriff had to be called because two girls, both aged around 13, had driven a Cadillac down from Los Angeles to follow the band. The car was borrowed from the father of one of the girls and full of McDonald's fast food wrappers. The band often registered at hotels under the names of different trees; Faulkner was an oak. Derek was said to be fascinated by flamboyant American businessman Jack Stephan who ran a successful, heavily advertised plumbing franchise business. Derek spoke of an ambition to have 200 vans with his name on the side running around Scotland fixing plumbing problems.

Not all the concerts on the tour were sell-outs and some were flops. ICM's booking of 4,000 to 5,000-seater venues was not appropriate for certain areas. Gigs in Buffalo, Dallas, San Diego had to be postponed. Another, in Salt Lake City, was cancelled at short notice due to "equipment problems". The band was, however, due to return to America in early August for more dates and would reschedule some of the shows. But between these disappointments there was enough of the old Rollermania to keep the show on the road. In Minneapolis a wooden balustrade in front of the stage collapsed and a swarm of fans fell into the orchestra pit, crushing a security man whose leg was broken. At a radio event in Chicago they judged a dance contest at the city's baseball park.

The band visited over 20 cities and towns on the tour, taking part in endless radio promotion and publicity interviews. The hard work paid off as 'You Made Me Believe In Magic' was selling well and would rise to number 10 on the *Billboard* chart, a great result following a couple of flops from the *Dedication* album. It also climbed to five in Canada (25 in Germany and 36 in Australia, their final top 40 in both countries). The tour, which closed on June 4, also grossed over $2 million including merchandising.

Back in the UK, the scenes at Little Kellerstain were growing more frivolous and outlandish. The addition of Rosetta Stone, with three members 16 or under, to a swinging scene that already included many teens mixing with older men, did not seem to register with Paton, who was almost 29, as being particularly dangerous. His intention was to stir up controversy with his thrusting new young act and let people think what they wanted. To the outside world, particularly in the UK, the new act, the rotating Rollers, the LK compound, guarded by aggressive dogs and with walls topped by barbed wire, all added up to a total that seemed increasingly sinister. What had Paton got to hide?

He continued to treat the Rollers' musical ambitions dismissively. Faulkner was not amused by Paton's attitude nor the debauchery at LK and threatened to leave the group. There was talk of a solo career and of him managing and producing other groups. Paton revived some interest and attempted to reassert his iron grip on the band. Wood and Derek remained loyal to him. McKeown admitted he was fearful of Paton, still easily persuaded to obey his command. One of his brothers had got a record deal with Polydor and Paton browbeat McKeown into thinking his own family was now taking advantage of his and the Rollers' success. McKeown said he felt isolated from the band and did not know whom he should trust: again he thought about a solo career. There was a rumour that he'd got an American girl pregnant and abandoned her and the child.

The band's old road manager, Jake Duncan, now 24, had rejoined the Rollers' crew for the recent tour of America. He continued to look after the band and their equipment in Edinburgh. "Tam was up to all sorts of high jinks up at Little Kellerstain," he said. "There were lads wandering all over his house. When the band had spare time they weren't interested in going to LK and Tam wasn't interested in having them there. The band was concerned that what he was doing was throwing a bit of a shadow on their professional operation."

'You Made Me Believe In Magic' was released as a single in the UK in July and the band undertook a hurried bout of promotion. Faulkner was photographed dressed as a Geisha girl. McKeown said the guitarist looked like 'Paton's bitch'. When they appeared on Granada's new kids' pop show, *Marc*, hosted by Marc Bolan (produced by Muriel Young and aired in the same time slot as *Shang-A-Lang*), Faulkner wore eye-wateringly tiny denim shorts. Only Wood wore anything that resembled Roller gear during the appearance. The Rollers made just one appearance on *Top Of The Pops* to promote the single, shown on July 21, and it peaked at a disappointing 34. It was the band's final top 40 single in the UK. Throughout July and August, Granada were repeating old episodes of *Shang-A-Lang*. Where had that band gone? The new *It's A Game*, released in July in the UK, peaked at 18 on the album charts.

Rosetta's Stone also appeared on the *Marc* show but their debut single failed to chart in the UK. The band picked up TV exposure in Germany, and toured there extensively. They also toured Japan. McKee recalled the accountant they shared with the Rollers, Stephen Goldberg, charged them £70,000 for bookkeeping for the Japanese tour. Goldberg was said to visit Little Kellerstain to have Paton sign various documents. "I think Goldberg had him tied up completely," Damian McKee said. "The only way Tam could get his money was if he screwed everybody else. I couldn't prove it but that was my impression of the situation. He had to let everything else go if he wanted his own money."

The band was keen to move out of Little Kellerstain. The five members were told they could buy themselves a house each. "Then it was, 'You can't all afford a house each, you'll have to double up somewhere,'" said McKee. "So it was four houses and then three and then a couple and then one and the one was nearly none." McKee said he "pushed and pushed and pushed" to finally get the house where the band ended up living together: a cottage in the Scottish countryside in West Linton. They did not even own their own tour vehicle; it was leased.

A second Rosetta Stone single, a cover of Amen Corner's 'If Paradise Is (Half As Nice)' soon flopped in the UK, despite an appearance on BBC TV's *Jim'll Fix It*, as did their debut album. They continued to gig in the UK in small venues, often playing to the same crowd of hardcore young female fans, many of them Rollers devotees. Mitchell was the first to quit. The band's popularity in Germany and Japan meant Paton could keep them working throughout most of 1978. They never made any money. Andy Le Gear grew ill. "He was growing hair all over his body, he'd got himself so thin it was unbelievable," McKee said. Their relationship with Paton was, by all accounts, deeply unhealthy.

Alan Longmuir was clearly missing the game. He came back with a solo single 'I'm Confessing'. The front cover featured an old shot of him in Roller gear and large lettering declaring, "Ex Bay City Roller". It was released by Arista and co-produced by the Rollers' old music director/producer Colin Frechter. "Hard, hard work," said Frechter. "Alan was feeling a bit left out. The idea was to give him a record to do to make him feel better." It was not released in America and did not sell well in the UK or any other territory. The others laughed as Alan gave interviews to promote it, declaring how he had "more sex than hot dinners" while in the band. "Someone must need publicity," said Faulkner. Paton, however, considered putting Alan back in the group.

The band returned to America for 19 more dates in early August 1977 to coincide with the American release of the *It's A Game* album. Arista lined up 'The Way I Feel Tonight', another slow, heavily orchestrated ballad, written by jobbing UK songwriter Harvey Shield (and already released by him under the name Shields), as a second American single from the album. To promote the album the band hosted an entire edition of *Midnight Special* with acts such as Roger Daltrey and Electric Light Orchestra appearing as guests. For the first time on American TV the Rollers played live.

They looked, on first sight, bewildering. Faulkner wore blue eyeshadow, a black leather jacket, tiny denim cut-off shorts with the words 'Spank Me' writ across the bottom, plus leg warmers. "He looked a right twat," said McKeown who was high on cocaine. Wood, proving to be an accomplished bass player, had huge white harem trousers and, crucially, just a hint of tartan on his sleeveless top. They played a selection of songs from the new album including 'It's A Game' and 'You Made Me Believe In Magic'.

There was audible screaming from the audience. A small string section and saxophonist added to the sound. Faulkner was loud and Derek was brutally basic, almost amateur. For a rip through 'Yesterday's Hero' the band were stripped back to basics, just the four of them bashing away. It was an impressive spectacle. However, there was no cohesion between this raw sound and image, particularly Faulkner's new look, and the new, sophisticated, album they were supposed to be selling.

Many of the band's American live shows were at state fairs with the Rollers part of a huge bill of entertainment. In Ohio, the fair lasted for 13 days and attracted over two million visitors. Also on the 'fair circuit' were acts such as Dolly Paton and Bob Hope plus the Barnum & Bailey Thrill Circus. "Kiss and Elton John do them and they earn you $100,000 a time," Faulkner told a visiting *Record Mirror* who covered part of the tour. 'It's mania time again' was the headline. The magazine wrote that the Rollers "may have lost some of their following in this country, but in America it's starting all over again."

"Things are going really well in the States now," said Faulkner. "We've had seven hit singles so far. The new single is in at 30 with a bullet." 'The Way I Feel Tonight' peaked at a respectable 24 in the *Billboard* charts and at 23 in Canada. The band stayed in Los Angeles whenever the dates allowed and made promotional appearances in the city on *American Bandstand* and *The Merv Griffin Show*. Three weeks after its release *It's Game* was at 23 on the American album charts and had sold over 500,000 copies. The new material was suitable for MOR rock stations with its echoes of The Carpenters, The Moody Blues and Wings. The album went to 14 in Canada and 10 in Australia.

There were dispiriting moments on the tour, partly through bad planning. There was no chance the band could hope to fill the 10,000-capacity Salt Palace in Salt Lake City, Utah. At the Milwaukee State Fair Park they were required to play a matinee show for kids. They were an hour late for the second set, appearing at 9.30pm. The heavy security presence insisted the fans remain seated. Twelve girls still fainted. In Detroit at the Michigan State fairground the band had to go on stage at 5pm. It was difficult to keep motivated. The band often sounded ropey, with terrible harmonies, bludgeoning through the upbeat numbers.

At venues more suited to the band's American stature, there were reminders of the heat they could still generate. In Seattle they played the 3,000-capacity Paramount and filled it with screaming girls, all standing on the theatres seats going crazy. Some had queued through the night to get tickets that would put them within 10 feet of the band.

There was plentiful groupie sex on offer for the band with fans prepared to climb fire escapes and crawl through windows to avoid security. *Tiger Beat* put the band on their cover again, reporting on how McKeown had been seen "out on the town" with different girls in cities the Rollers visited. The headline was: 'They're ready for romance!' The magazine also asked the crucial question: "Are they ticklish?"

The Rollers had been on every cover of *16* since January 1976, a remarkable run that would continue throughout 1977 uninterrupted. Often McKeown was alone on the cover although Derek did feature on one late 1977 *16* cover for an "at home with" feature. While the band toured America, among the usual exclusive photos and posters, the odd quote of depth featured in *16*. "Me being a Roller is a sideshow," McKeown told the magazine. "It's me playing a part."

Derek talked about getting interested in "contracts and clauses and things... So many people are ready to rip you off. We've made some bad business deals, but you learn as you go along." He added that he had just bought a new sauna for his home. "Eric's new look" was also much discussed in *16*. He continued to wear his Spank Me shorts and leg warmers, enjoying himself on stage singing Bowie's 'Rebel Rebel', the final track on *It's A Game*.

It was easy to laugh at them but they had reached a status in America few British bands ever would. In Canada they were mammoth. There was a hugely triumphant show in Toronto, the band playing to 18,000 at the National Exhibition Stadium. Paton missed the date. News filtered through to the band in Los Angeles that he had "confessed" to being homosexual in *The Sun*. Asked about this, Wood said: "He probably just refused to deny it and they made up a story out of that. I refuse to comment on Tam's sexual abilities but he probably just told the truth – that it was none of their business."

In America, the Rollers were also asked their opinion on punk, a movement now gripping the UK media. Their answers revealed the schism between the band members, a reminder that Paton had thrown them together somewhat randomly, and their attitudes. "I like punk rock," said McKeown. "I think it's genuine. I'm a strong supporter of that. Punk rock's only a variation. It's like guys in the street saying the same thing as Jackson Browne is saying on a more understandable level. I like it because it's music that makes people think. I'm friends with that guy in the Sex Pistols, Johnny Rotten, met him in a club one day, and he's a nice guy."

It was put to Wood that The Bay City Rollers were sometimes mentioned in the UK press as being Britain's first true punks. In fact in America, the Rollers were surprisingly featured in John Holmstrom's influential *Punk* magazine. "Les is a punk," said Wood. "He's been a punk for the past 15 years."

"I think we should be aware of trends," said Faulkner. "But all the greatest groups, the Stones, the Who, have managed to stay themselves and have remained above current fads. That's how we'd like to be – aware of what's going on underneath but ourselves above all that." He added that he never listened to what he called the Rollers old "dated" material. "I couldn't bear to listen to *Rollin'*," he said. "Look out for the next album, that's going to be a real shocker."

The band made a famous visit to their "namesake city", Bay City in Michigan, on August 24, toward the end of the American tour. It was where the pin had apparently landed all those years ago. Like many things in the Rollers' story, it was a lie. Nonetheless the Mayor of the 48,000 population town named August 24 'Bay City Roller day' and he, alongside the entire City Council, Chamber of Commerce and staff of local radio station WHNN, waited to welcome the band on the City Hall steps.

There were also 5,000 Rollers fans, mostly decked out in tartan, waiting for the group. Some had been there since 6am. The band arrived at 3pm with a police escort motorcade, put their handprints and signatures in trays of cement and held an autograph session.

After three more dates, the tour concluded with a desultory gig in the middle of a kid's playground in an amusement park. "We were so glad it was the last show," said McKeown. There was a short break in the schedule. "It was fantastic to be away from one another," he added.

"The band were sick of one another," said Paton.

But the punishing schedule would soon restart. It had to. The band had been advised, or told, that due to their colossal earnings from overseas they needed to spend a year out of the country, from April 1977, to avoid tax. "The in-fighting started after they became tax exiles from Britain," Paton added. "That had to neglect this country. It is very sad but tax drove them to do it."

A lucrative 18-date tour of major sports halls and arenas in Japan began on September 15, running until October 10. *It's A Game* had gone to number one in the Japanese album charts and the band were featured in a TV advert for Kit-Kat chocolate bars on Japanese TV. The adulation of the Rollers in Japan – 120,000 fans gathered at Narita International Airport to see them arrive – was frightening. There were terrifying crowd crushes at almost all their public appearances and in one instance the roof of the band's limo buckled under the weight of fans. One Japanese teenager committed suicide after having her concert ticket taken off her. Her school apparently had forbidden her to attend the Rollers' show. She had jumped to her death from a high building.

Seven shows were scheduled over four days at the 12,000-capacity Budokan Hall in Tokyo. "Tickets were $100 each," said Colin Slater who was on the tour as the band's management representative. "People were coming from China, Thailand Australia." Asked if a tour advance of $2.5 million paid to the band sounded about right, he replied: "Sounds light."

Slater had almost completely usurped Paton now in controlling the band's business affairs. "The Rollers gave me a bonus, bought me a BMW CSL," he said. "They said, 'Well with Tam he introduces us to thousands of people but he never tells us what they do. We noticeably are aware of the fact, you bring in an Italian guy, or a Japanese guy and we know what he does within minutes, what he does for us and what he's going to do.' That seemed to me to be very strange, that Tam had introduced them to so many hundreds of people but had never explained what any of them did."

One of the new publishing deals Slater had recently made for Bay City Music was for Japan with Watanabe Music. "They had an office in London run by Akira Nakamura," said Slater. "We had dinner several times and then I invited him to meet the band. He said, 'Really, I've been calling Tam for five years and he never wanted to meet with me and he didn't want me to meet the band.'"

Nakamura's boss, Misa Watanaba, who owned the huge and influential Japanese company, also wanted to meet the band. Slater arranged for her to meet them in Paris. "I didn't want the band to set foot in England [for tax reasons]," he said. "It was Woody, Eric and Misa, maybe Leslie, in a Japanese hotel in Paris and we were all getting along well, drinking champagne and this lady, who speaks very little English, turned to me and said, 'How much?' I said, 'Have your lawyers call our lawyers and let's start at $8 million for Japan.' She said, 'And for how long?' I said, 'Until you get your money back.'"

Slater said the music publishing revenue, in terms of advances, that he had secured for the group while he'd been managing director of Bay City Music was in the area of $25million. "Bear in mind we took nothing in the US. We were offered $15 million from Salvatore Chianti, the President of Universal MCA Music. I asked him, 'What would you do?' He said, 'I'd open my own business in New York,' so that's what we'd done."

As an indication of how much money the Rollers' songs were earning, Slater said 'Don't Let The Music Die', released exclusively as a single in Japan to coincide with the tour, was covered a total of 365 times by various artists. "Also with the songs they recorded that they didn't write," said Slater, "I went to all those song publishers in London and LA and said we're going to record this song, we need to get 15 per cent share of the publishing… and that was successful on every occasion."

Slater also estimated that the merchandising revenue the band had now generated was close to $16 million. There was serious money flying around. Paton, far from being pleased, thought Slater was getting too clever by half but there was nothing he could do. He did not understand the basics of many of the deals Slater had struck never mind the intricacies. On his passport, as his profession, it still said "potato merchant".

The band members were simply prisoners in Japan, locked in their hotel rooms when not wheeled out to perform. It was impossible for them to go out on the street. The shows at the Budokan were recorded for a live album that was planned for future release. "One of the most beautiful things I've ever heard," Slater said. "Essentially we had 12,000 kids who couldn't speak English but they had learned the words singing along. It was amazing." This album never surfaced at the time but would finally be released as *Rollerworld* in the year 2000.

As a document of the era it would prove to be an everlasting swansong.

ACT II

Curse of The Bay City Rollers

CHAPTER 11

Decline

"I had a terrible row with Tam and left. I warned him. I said if you don't watch you'll end up with nothing... and that's just what happened. By Christmas of 1979 he didn't have £300, everything had gone, all taken away from him."

– John Gorman

Brothers Sid and Marty Krofft started out as puppeteers in the fifties, touring Europe and America as part of the famous Ringling Bros and Barnum & Bailey Circus, and had subsequently enjoyed a celebrated career on stage and latterly on TV in their chosen profession, beginning with *The Banana Splits*. They were rarely without a hit kids' puppet-driven show on Saturday morning American TV from 1971 to 1978 and were close to the pre-eminent American boy band of the era, The Osmonds. In late 1975 they had created the career-defining *Donny And Marie* TV show for the family, a soft-focus variety show that had proved so popular that it split the family and virtually ended the group's serious musical aspirations.

Sid Krofft was almost 50 and his brother Marty in his early forties when they met Tam Paton. It was heavily hinted at that at least one of the brothers was gay. The Kroffts' various TV shows had been loaded with gay-friendly characters, a considerable feat for the era: Freddie The Magic Flute from their hit *H.R. Pufnstuf* show is often considered to be the first gay character on American TV.

Neither brother ever came out but in 2006, questioned about his sexuality, Sid explained he lived alone because, "I'm married to my art". In the late seventies entertainment business, those enjoying a gay lifestyle, like Paton, tended to protect themselves from media exposure and identify with others in the same position. In America it had only been a few years since the country's eminent Psychiatric Association had declassified homosexuality as a mental disorder.

When it was suggested to him, Paton was enthusiastic about the possibility of The Bay City Rollers and the Kroffts working together on a Saturday morning kids' TV show. The band had some form in the area although over two years had now passed since they had starred in their own knockabout kids TV series, *Shang-A-Lang*, in the UK. His chutzpah required some fine balancing and outright lying: the Rollers were falling apart at the seams. This was almost entirely a situation of his own making but he didn't see that; the man who had sacked three band members in quick succession and belittled their creative impulses. He had worked and pushed them to breaking point and they were in a state of anarchy. Paton had virtually given up trying to sort it out. But the opportunity presented by the Kroffts was too good to let slip by.

The band was currently in Switzerland recording their sixth album in the exclusive Mountain Studios in Montreux. Harry Maslin was again producing. After the end of 1977 Japanese tour, operations had slowed over the past few months as the band stewed in a mix of discontent and sickliness. The pressure remained intense and the cracks were clearly showing. A recent, January 1978, performance on the hip late night American TV music show, *Midnight Special*, had seem the band tear through old tracks such as 'Money Honey' and 'Wouldn't You Like It?' with an aggressive sound and dressed-down look. Performing live, the four-piece had played with a blunt New York Dolls-style slash and burn. Wood, about to turn 21, on bass, with a punky earring dangling from one ear, looked a lot like a young Keith Richards. McKeown was in a black outfit featuring zips and rips. Alongside the punk energy, the band channelled more mature material from their most recent album *It's A Game*, including the beseechingly maudlin epic, 'Don't Let The Music Die'.

It seemed futile but Faulkner was serious about gaining the band credibility. Even Houdini would have struggled to escape from the band's teen pop image. But Faulkner put everything he had into it. McKeown, however, was not committed to this grittier version of the group and was eyeing a solo career. He appeared to be carrying an almost unbearable weight.

McKeown viewed Faulkner not as musically brave but as self-absorbed and rather pathetic. "Eric really did think he was John Lennon born again, and you know, he has never written anything you can spit on," he said. "But his attitude, his pomposity is unreal." The pair had huge arguments about the songs on the new album that they were recording in Switzerland.

McKeown talked openly about it being his last album with the group. There was a rumour he had been offered a minor part in film called *Think For The Sun* and was going to sing the movie theme as his first solo offering. He would later brag of spending his time in Montreux having regular secretive sex sessions with the girlfriend of another band member. The band member, he laughed, had even written a song about his love for the girl for the album.

Mountain Studios was a new, state of the art facility, located inside Montreux Casino on the shoreline of Lake Geneva at the foot of the Alps. It was owned by rock band Queen who would record many albums there. The studio had been booked for the Rollers for three months at a price of over £300 an hour. That meant studio time alone on the new album was costing them over £300,000. Maslin was another major expense.

Paton said he'd had "terrible dramas" just to try and get the group together to record. Then, in Switzerland, Paton said that McKeown complained that the air in Montreux "wasn't good for his throat", affecting his ability to record vocals. "And the hatred between Les and Eric at the time was horrendous," Paton added. "There was horrendous jealousy between the two. Les had terrible problems with himself. He wanted to be the centre of attention all the time. We also had Eric and Woody who felt they were Lennon and McCartney. I thought I was going crazy, I thought this is mental – this is the end."

Although he had rarely contributed in the area before, McKeown was demanding some of his own newly penned songs be included on the album and disparaged those written by Faulkner and Wood. Arguments between the band members was now commonplace. McKeown had recently been writing with an outside collaborator, 21-year-old Glaswegian Scobie Ryder, who was writing the soundtrack for the McKeown-linked feature film, actually called *Touch Of The Sun*, shot in Zambia, and starring Oliver Reed.

The fact McKeown and Faulkner seemed to dislike one another suited Paton. The pair had much in common and would have proved a formidable front had they come together to confront their shared concerns. They were both, for instance, growing angry about the lack of clarity over the band's financial position. Instead of tackling the issue with Paton directly, they argued among themselves about certain business aspects of their career such as the revenues from copyright on the songs. McKeown was now thinking about a future when there'd be no Rollers but their songs would still have the potential to earn future revenue. Though many of the band's song publishing deals had recently been rewritten, with advances running into the multi-millions, the exact amounts and fine detail were unclear to the group. The publishing money, and other band income streams, had not filtered through to the individual members yet.

Both Faulkner and McKeown were keen to get to the bottom of the internal band memo over the split of the song copyrights. It was understood the copyrights, initially split six ways between Faulkner, McKeown, Wood, the two Longmuir brothers, and Paton, and latterly said to exclude Paton, would revert to the original songwriters after a set period of time – five years according to Paton. Almost exclusively the catalogue of 40 or so of the band's original songs were penned by Faulkner/Wood. McKeown was now waking up to what that might mean for him in future. Up to this point he'd been happy that his voice was on the records, when often the rest of the band weren't.

He knew well how sensitive Faulkner was about writing songs for the band. How the guitarist had long fought to record his own material against the will of their record labels, Bell and Arista, who insisted on the heavy use of material from outside songwriters, particularly for singles. McKeown enjoyed now winding the portentous Faulkner up about the songwriting. The pair had never got on with one another. He recalled they'd had had a vicious fistfight soon after he joined the band when Faulkner demanded he dump his then girlfriend. In fact, McKeown was at loggerheads with every member.

"Right from the beginning it was always me against the rest of the band," McKeown said. "We argued about everything; who got the most fan mail, who got the most close-ups on TV, which songs to record, which venues to play, who had the best spot on stage, who was the most talented. Eric used to get upset and threatened to walk out on tour unless I stopped upstaging him."

While the inter-band arguments, about songs and the creative direction the new album might take, raged, they could block out any deeper psychological issues troubling them. The band was largely deeply unhappy, depressed and confused. They did not discuss their feelings, particularly in relation to their manager's extraordinary sex life and its effect on certain band members. Some of the Rollers had been keeping Paton's secrets for years. It was now becoming increasingly difficult to keep a lid on what was going on with Paton and they were worried about the implications.

Two recent major pieces had appeared in the media that suggested that some members of the band were Paton's sexual playthings, a rumour that had long circulated within the music industry. Paton was being increasingly less than discreet about his lifestyle and was continually surrounded with attractive young men, mostly teenagers, both professionally and socially. His long-standing contact at the Scottish office of the *News Of The World*, Andrew Drummond, had recently interviewed him at Little Kellerstain and wrote about what he saw, and had heard, for the best-selling Sunday tabloid, albeit obliquely.

"There were all sorts of boys hanging around," said Drummond. "Paton was in a dressing gown. They were all in dressing gowns." And they all looked under 18 to Drummond. "He didn't seem to care too much about laws. He even sent a boy to pick me up and take me to the house for the interview. The boy had a driving license but he didn't look old enough."

Drummond said he got the impression that "one or two" of the Rollers had a sexual relationship with Paton. "Paton had created this group and felt it was his right to leap into bed with some of the guys," he said. The headline on his article dubbed Paton a Svengali and hinted at his undue influence over the Rollers and his teenage entourage.

Drummond admitted he had nothing "watertight" to back up his impressions of sexual impropriety and it was not the focus of the article that fell far short of a shocking exposé of life inside the Rollers camp. It did not even out Paton as gay. At the time, Drummond said, it was not a great idea to come out as gay in the UK, not, he quipped, a great "career move". "*The Sun* was still going on about poofs 10 years later," Drummond said. What he had seen first hand and what he heard from several sources, including Ian Mitchell, convinced Drummond that there was some sort of abuse at the heart of Rollermania and he would continue to pursue Paton into the eighties.

Another controversial article also surfaced in early 1978, and this one was far more explicit about the band's supposed homosexual liaisons. In it, the writer alleged that some of The Bay City Rollers preferred sleeping with each other to girls. Published in Denmark in – according to McKeown – "a Danish gay magazine called *Coq*", it was almost certainly written, he said, by Per Lyhne, who had been close to Gert Magnus. Due to tight libel laws, and perhaps the niche readership of the COQ publications [the company notoriously and openly published paedophile magazines for those sexual attracted to underage teenage males], the controversial Danish article had gone almost entirely un-noticed in the UK. Not by McKeown. He over-reacted and sought to establish his own red-blooded credentials. He gave an interview to the *News Of The World* in which he claimed to have slept with a million women and when it came to sex had "tried just about everything".

Not only was Paton enraged that McKeown had gone to the media without his consent, for a group that had long been built on a clean-cut image and whose fan-base remained almost exclusively girls under 16, McKeown's comments, like Faulkner's efforts to remould the group, came across as desperate and deeply misguided. Deluded even.

"It didn't feel like we were really a band at the time," said Wood. He recalled the atmosphere in Switzerland while recording the new album as "depressing", "negative" and "terrible".

Into this situation Paton introduced the expectant Krofft brothers in April 1978. The sunny picture Paton had painted for the pair of a thriving and harmonious band relied heavily on stressing the recent success of the band's *It's A Game* album which had done well internationally and the popularity of a new compilation album, *Greatest Hits*, released in late 1977, that had gone gold in America. In the UK, although the hits were drying up, they had featured in a Granada TV special over Christmas 1977, taking over an episode of kids' TV show *Get It Together*. Paton pointed to this and explained how they had been advised to become tax exiles and hence could not work their home territory as they once had – hence the declining chart success in the UK. This was partly true. Elsewhere in Europe, however, he said he was optimistic of the band growing in popularity.

Although they had ditched their tartan uniforms, the band, crucially for the Kroffts, continued to have strong brand recognition among American teens as regular cover stars of the influential *16* and *Tiger Beat* magazines. In December 1977 the Rollers had actually played a one-off concert to 20,000 people in Boston alongside other teen stars Andy Gibb and Shaun Cassidy and they could still command regular guest slots on popular America variety TV shows. Paton continued to play the media. Despite the fact that as a four-piece they had never sounded better, he had gone ahead with reinstating the band founder Alan Longmuir to add a further twist to the continuing soap opera that was the band's career. That move had created a stir, particularly in America. It had made a cover story for the January 1978 issue of *16*, their 24th consecutive cover – 'Alan's Back! Will Alan Put the Rollers Back on Top'.

It was not just a PR stunt. Paton had hoped that Alan would be a steadying influence and might curtail some of the internal band bickering. Dubbed the "reluctant Roller", he'd always been considered the most down-to-earth Roller, the normal one, 'Big Al' who enjoyed the simple pleasures – a pint, a woman and a laugh. In a 2008 interview he would cite as a highlight of the band's career the moment he'd sat next to Olivia Newton-John in the make-up room at *Top Of The Pops* and seen "one of Pan's People without a stitch on". He was also a handsome man, a genuine hunk among a group of waifs and strays, someone the Kroffts could picture playing well on TV.

Although he had ordered the Rollers to be at their most accommodating, the meeting between the Kroffts and the band in Montreux went better than Paton could have hoped. It rekindled some of his smouldering love for them. They were real professionals, practiced at burying their turmoil and conditioned to charm. Protestations, chiefly from McKeown, that starring in a Saturday morning kids' puppet show might not complement the band's new adult image and musical direction were bluntly rebuffed by Paton who argued in favour of the priceless publicity they would get from starring in their own coast-to-coast weekly show in America. "This will be great for you," Paton assured the band.

Paton no longer really cared what was best for the band. They had already lived long past what he felt was their built-in expiry date. What he cared about now was milking it. The fee the band's new American agents at ICM were negotiating with the Kroffts would help push up the band's earning in the past year to close to £30 million. There were plans for the show to be screened in the UK and in other territories around the world. Paton thought it would keep the business in rude health for at least another year and wouldn't require much of his own input. He had long been suggesting they forget their musical aspirations and focus on becoming all-round light entertainment fodder. It was a win-win situation for him.

While negotiations continued he attempted to manipulate the situation. He planted stories in the press about how other American TV networks beside NBC [the network who planned to air the new Krofft show] were interested in the band doing an American TV show and revealed how he'd recently turned down a big money approach to do an American Christmas TV special.

In principle the deal with the Kroffts and NBC was quickly agreed. But, on reflection, McKeown now said he didn't want to do it. That he wouldn't do it. He screamed long and hard against the idea of starring in a kids' TV show "for five-year-olds… alongside a bunch of puppets". But no one could scream longer or harder than Paton.

Filming on the Krofft show began in Los Angeles in June 1978. McKeown continued to show contempt for the decision to do it but he was there. His suggestion that the band members all simultaneously quit in a show of solidarity, dissolving any contractual obligations they had, caused some bewilderment. Effectively, he was proposing ending the group. His attitude further alienated him from the rest of the group who had begun, with Paton's nudging, to accept the new project as an opportunity to advance their American career.

Marty Krofft said McKeown was "nothing but trouble" and that signing the Rollers was "the biggest mistake" he ever made. As soon as they touched down at LAX, the arguments started, "about cars and private swimming pools", said Paton.

The Kroffts were using the trusted Bob Levinson to act as PR for the new show. His firm, Levinson Associates, had offices in LA (where Levinson lived and worked) and in New York, and represented teen stars such as David Cassidy and The Osmonds as well more credible acts such as Stevie Wonder, Elton John and Fleetwood Mac.

Levinson recalled meeting the Rollers and Paton at Marty's sumptuous Sunshine Terrace mansion in Laurel Canyon where the band was due to stay while filming the show. A beautiful location, the area was rich in counter cultural history and home to many of LA's top rock musicians.

"Les and a couple of the other guys went out on Sunset Strip to a [hip] club called Carlos 'n Charlie's," said Levinson. "They were still palling around. But Les was very unhappy and not quiet about it. I told Les one evening that I felt he was making a mistake I'd seen so many other band members over the years make. They assume the success is entirely due to them and not to the group, so they are ready to go off and be bigger stars than they were before. It rarely works out that way.

The other band member's egos were in control. It was Les who sparked whatever problems there were, whatever differences of opinion."

Levinson met Paton just this once, and only briefly, at Marty's mansion. They exchanged pleasantries. "He wished me good luck with the boys and then flew back to Scotland," said Levinson. "That was his last contact with our office. At no time did we deal with management. Our focus was on the show. The Rollers had a built-in following and we just had to use the show to build the audience based on that."

The filming took place at KTLA on Sunset Boulevard, a historic studio once home to Warner Bros Pictures. *The Jazz Singer* had been filmed here and the studio had recently been designated as a Historic Cultural Landmark. It was a popular location for modern studio-based TV shows to be filmed. The *Gong Show* was filmed at KTLA and the Kroffts had previously used it for the *Donny & Marie* show.

The Rollers had built their career on miming their songs on TV, and this would be a key component of the new show, but none of them had ever trained as actors. The skits they had performed in the past for *Shang-A-Lang* had only a charming amateurish quality. The idea of them starring in their own feature-length film had long been talked about but never materialised. They weren't felt to be competent or charismatic enough. "They were barely qualified to host a supermarket opening much less a 60-minute weekly series," wrote Hal Erickson of the band in his respected book length critique of the Kroffts' TV career.

During initial rehearsals for the comedy sketches the band tended to be insular, unsure of their abilities. A thumbs-up gesture had been enough to get them out of many tight spots during their countless past public appearances. This was now real showbusiness with lines to deliver, scenes to act out and dance routines to execute. The band's keenness to work at their craft had marked them out from their peers during their rise and there remained some of that old zest left in some of them. They began regular rehearsals with a dialogue coach and choreographer. The schedule was again punishing; the Rollers had to record enough material to fill 13 one-hour shows.

Initially they were persuaded back into matching band costumes, a version of their old iconic 1975/6 look. The half-mast, flared 'stroller' trousers were out but the band looked strong again in the famous all-white uniforms, satin now, with flourishes of tartan. They were required too to focus on their past glories musically: miming on the giant sound stage to their biggest American hits such as 'Saturday Night', 'I Only Wanna Be With You' and 'Rock And Roll Love Letter'. This was all played out before a live audience of screaming young girls.

In the final edit, the Kroffts tended to pull away from these "concert" segments mid-song and cut to band comedy skits before returning to the performances. The skits were hit and miss. Faulkner, his accent, despite the elocution lessons, deeply Scottish, seemed to be set-up as the band lothario and there were a surprising amount of inferences to sex and dating thrown in for a kids' show. Derek, the band's perma-smiling, 27-year-old drummer, delivered his lines in a steady, frill-free, no-nonsense approach, much like he played drums.

He was the only blond in the band and popular with fans not just for his looks but because he seemed so overwhelmingly nice and kind. He loved animals and was never crude about women. Everything he said, in fact, about the band and life, was balanced to the point of blandness. Although he was the quiet one, Paton had long trusted him to run their day-to-day cash affairs, and had recently given him permission to sign cheques and make withdrawals from the band's bank accounts.

Wood elaborated on the Stan Laurel-like simpleton shtick he'd mined during the *Shang-A-Lang* TV series. Alan was handsome and McKeown was stick-thin. Neither seemed to have much of a personality when not performing with the group. Over the course of filming, the group performed in kilts, cowboy outfits, matching Californian beach wear and memorably in white union suits (one-piece long underwear) with tartan-trim for "at home" sequences when they were seen to all sleep in the same bed.

The skits worked best when the theme was on the band's perceived rabid female fan base with guest stars from other NBC shows, such as Erik Estrada from *CHiPs*, the new hit motorcycle cop drama series, playing along. Some were funny: the over-zealous gossip columnist interacting with the band and interpreting everything they said as a "scoop". Other comedy sections were plain daft with the band often rescued by Mr Munchy, a giant fat puppet able to swallow humans.

The band also made a series of farcical silent sketches – at funs fairs, moving house etc. – that ran speeded up to the familiar soundtrack of the pop jazz instrumental 'Yakety Yak'. The tune had been popularised as the Benny Hill TV show theme music and the skits were basically their homage to Hill who was a hit in America at the time and a band favourite. "Our hero is Benny Hill," McKeown had said in late 1974.

One stage routine involved the band dancing and miming to a medley of fifties rock'n'roll hits. Faulkner and Wood performed some convincing moves; knee slides, twists and steps. However, dressed as fifties rockers with greased back hair, in denim and leather and then, later in the sequence, in golden Teddy boy suits, the band looked ridiculous. They also popped up incongruously in the surreal puppet/ live action segment of the show called Horror Hotel that featured many Krofft puppet characters from their past children's hits including Witchiepoo who ran the hotel of the title. McKeown excused himself from one appearance at the hotel where the band went through several lame scenarios before playing for hotel regulars, Horatio J. HooDoo from *Lidsville* and *H.R. Pufnstuf* characters Seymour the Spider, Orson the Vulture and Stupid Bat.

With the exception of McKeown, the Rollers tried wholeheartedly to play silly and zany and linked the show's various segments with earnest professionalism. As the hits ran out, the band mimed to a variety of songs for the concert segments from across their catalogue, including obscure tracks plucked from their first two American albums such as 'Too Young To Rock And Roll' and 'Let's Go', and material from their not yet completed new album such as 'Love Brought Me Such A Magical Feeling', written by jobbing British songwriters Charlie Spencer and Barry Kirsch. They performed the latter song without McKeown. Wood took lead vocal with Faulkner and Alan backing him. It was a doe-eyed, sugary, sing-along that threatened to explode into epic soft rock but never did. It had promise.

The girls in the audience kept up the screams but the vast stage and glitzy effects plus the hotchpotch of outfits chosen for them did not portray the band in their best light, and these performances had none of the excitement of their defining mid-seventies UK TV appearances directed by Mike Mansfield.

The hip and raunchy *Midnight Special* punk look and attitude was buried beneath showbiz schmaltz, the band going through the motions in get-ups such as beige safari suit style outfits with tartan-trim, tartan waistcoats, or in shiny silver and gold, and even in a smart casual wear – sensible slacks and checked shirts. McKeown was developing a mullet and pranced, grinded and posed up front inappropriately. There was no quality control and no one for the band to turn to for help. Paton, who had controlled their image so tightly in the past, was back in Edinburgh trying to make it with Rosetta Stone.

While filming the show, the band and producer Harry Maslin were also putting the final touches to the album they had started in Switzerland. Maslin, an LA resident, had hired Allen Zentz Recording in Hollywood, recently used by Michael Jackson to record his *Off The Wall* album, to add orchestral arrangements courtesy of the LA Philharmonic and keyboards from Nicky Hopkins, England's best-known session player, famed for his work with the Stones, Who and Kinks.

The idea was for the album and the new TV show to be launched simultaneously, each benefitting the other. It was the sort of cross-media marketing that had seen The Bee Gees become huge American stars on the back of the recent *Saturday Night Fever* film soundtrack album. McKeown said he alone raised serious concern about the material on the new album not being cohesive with the Saturday morning kids' TV puppet show they were in the middle of filming.

He was thinking of the despondent sentiment on slow, moody Faulkner/Wood songs such as 'Strangers In The Wind' or 'Another Rainy Day In New York City'. It was not exactly the sort of music you would associate with the crazy band goofing around on kids' TV. He also thought the two grown-up love songs on the album, both written by Iain Sutherland of Scottish folk duo the Sutherland Brothers, would be wasted on kids. Sutherland had written and recorded the original version of 'Sailing' made famous by Rod Stewart. McKeown was a fan and thought the Rollers version of Sutherland's 'When I Say I Love You (The Pie)' was amongst their most adult, and best, work.

"All his stories are bullshit about the show," PR Levinson said. "Les was preparing to leave the band. It was a business decision. The band's credibility was not going to be damaged in America by doing the show. It was fine for the coverage in the teen magazines. In America the notion was that they were strictly a band designed for the teen market. They were never going to be Fleetwood Mac."

The Rollers had never stayed in Los Angeles for an extended period. Although they had been round the world several times, visits to most cities tended to follow the same routine: media, gig and locked hotel room. McKeown now could finally cut loose and enjoy himself. The others said he had "gone Hollywood".

McKeown moved out of Marty's mansion and into a suite at the famous Chateau Marmont on Sunset Boulevard where Jim Morrison had lived at one time. He avoided the parties at the Krofft mansion, preferring celeb discos and edgier parties where he could rub shoulders with A-listers such as Jack Nicholson, Alice Cooper, Ringo Starr and the Stones. "Everything was freely available," he said. "There was always someone on hand with a little vial [of cocaine or heroin]. There were fans knocking on my door saying, 'Please sleep with me' and girls flying all the way from Japan begging me to take their virginity."

He went to the premiere of *Grease* with Hollywood teen actress Jodie Foster, famed as the underage prostitute in *Taxi Driver*. The press also reported on a liaison he was supposedly having with Swedish film star Britt Ekland, 13 years his senior at 35. The sex symbol was one of the most photographed and talked about celebrities in the world. She was famed as a Bond girl, the one-time wife of Peter Sellers and as the recently cheated-on girlfriend of Rod Stewart.

Ekland was managed by Paul Cohen, a Brit who had settled in LA after writing about pop stars for UK teen publications such as *Jackie* magazine. Ekland's break-up with Rod Stewart had created headlines and Cohen was known to be a sharp operator. If he could link Ekland with somebody to make a positive news item he would. McKeown, young and virile, fitted the bill.

Alan Longmuir also found the Los Angeles party scene irresistible. He recalled rubbing shoulders at star-studded parties with The Who's Keith Moon, Led Zeppelin's John Bonham and Deep Purple's Ritchie Blackmore. "Drugs were everywhere," he said. "I never had to pay for them. I experimented with everything back then. At producers' houses there were big bowls of coke and guys would walk round, their noses pure white." He recalled tripping on LSD in the recording studio.

There were also, Alan said, women everywhere. "I once opened my wardrobe and there were two of them inside," he said. Girls chased the band, many lied about their age, altering their ID cards. One 14 year old bragged of sleeping with Faulkner. "We'd go to their rooms, usually just two or three of us girls," she said. A scene developed with some band members and these underage girls (who freely admitted lying about their ages to appear older) at the Le Parc hotel in West Hollywood, centred on marijuana, wine and sex.

The band also kept a couple of rooms at the iconic, famous and luxurious Beverly Hills Hotel where major movie and music stars had stayed throughout the decades. The hotel had 23 bungalows or cabanas that provided privacy for many in Hollywood and the music business. Clive Davis, the boss of the Rollers' record label Arista Records, often used one when he was in Los Angeles. A lot of business was done in the cabanas and around the swimming pool at the hotel. Alan recalled being at the bar of the Beverly Hills Hotel with Robert Redford and Barbra Streisand. Always a drinker, he was now boozing to excess, downing bottles of brandy or whisky. He continued to function as a Roller however.

McKeown began to miss rehearsals and turn up late for filming. On one occasion he was said to have kept a special guest star, the acclaimed actress and singer Doris Day, then in her late fifties, and the whole crew waiting on set for hours. When he finally showed up, Day told McKeown how unprofessional she thought he was. She said she was prepared to go through with filming but would never work with the band again. McKeown appeared unconcerned.

Paton, who adored Doris Day, was apoplectic when he found out. McKeown he said was "going off his head". Even when the singer was on time he increasingly made things awkward on set, demanding his own dressing room and changes to the scripts, complaining about the embarrassing nature of many of the skits he was expected to perform. Sometimes he simply, unexpectedly, disappeared, keeping scores of people waiting for his return.

"People were telling him he was a superstar and he felt he should have his own dressing room and limo," said Derek. "He wouldn't show for rehearsals and script meetings. It was a bit embarrassing for the band."

"Les got into friends who were filling his head with nonsense," said Faulkner. "They were telling him he should get a butler, a maid, a Rolls-Royce, and someone to drive for him. Listen, we're just a band, and you have to keep your feet on the ground in this business."

The others continued to record segments of the show without him, sometimes making fun of his absence. "Les was mixing with the wrong people," said Paton. "I felt sorry for him. The TV people were used to dealing with temperament but Les still upset them with his antics. It was an impossible situation. NBC were ready to throw it in."

McKeown missed business meetings and was openly hostile to the other band members, claiming at one point he would refuse to even pose with the band for photos. He wound up Marty Krofft to such a point the producer finally snapped. McKeown claimed Marty pinned him against a wall, pulled a gun and threatened to kill him.

On set, a cream pie was pushed in McKeown's face. Faulkner said that the TV crew hired a "pie man" to get McKeown and the band didn't know anything about it. Other reports suggest the band, the Kroffts and the crew all agreed McKeown should receive the pie in the face for being so difficult to work with. McKeown reportedly stormed off set and headed back to London, claiming he'd been booted out of the band. 'Les Gets A Pie and the Axe', sang the *Tiger Beat* headline. He was "too unruly and disruptive" to be a Roller the magazine stated. McKeown told the press he was hurt and didn't think the others wanted him back. 'Did Les leave or was he pushed?' asked *Tiger Beat*.

On July 7, 1978, less than four weeks after they'd started filming the show, the *Edinburgh Evening Times*, ran a front-page story claiming that

The Bay City Rollers were breaking up. Paton, the source of the story, was said to have just returned to Edinburgh from LA. He quipped that there were "17 lawyers in LA" trying to work out "who gets what" from the band's multi-million pound career. "I think it would be disgusting for them at this time to split," he said. "I have been out to America three times talking and discussing with these lads about their decision. I have told them they must get their differences together. But there is nothing more I can do or say to them."

Paton had committed the band to major tours of Japan and Germany. They also had a new album, which had cost close to half a million pounds, due out and a coast-to-coast American TV show on NBC, one of the so called Big Three networks in the country, to promote. The *Edinburgh Evening Times* reported that McKeown's "walk out" could cost him £5 million.

The Krofft brothers were astonished at the news. Had they built their entire show around a band that was now going to split up? Bob Levinson had quite a task to PR this disaster. By August, however, most American teen magazines were running with his version of the story that suggested everything was okay. McKeown was not sacked and had not left the band permanently. He had merely been told to go home and get his head together or, as *TeenView* magazine put it, "get Hollywood out of his system". The line was that, when his attitude had improved he would be back in the band.

Paton took a more direct approach at a press conference held at KTLA studios in August to launch the TV show. He said: "We set off on a tour of Japan next month and if Les doesn't join us he will be sued for the money we would make from the tour." He estimated proceeds from the Japanese tour at close to $14 million.

McKeown had not been sacked, Paton repeated. The rest of the group wanted him back but only if he got rid of the "glitter-glamour nonsense". He would have to prove he still wanted to be a Roller, Paton said. He flew back to London for an emergency meeting with the singer.

On Friday September 8, at 8pm, NBC screened an hour-long preview special of the Kroffts' new show under the banner: *The Bay*

City Rollers Meet The Saturday Superstars. The *Krofft Superstar Hour*, as the new show was billed, would start the next morning. During the preview the band were seen miming their big hits on garish stage set-ups, gamely plugging cartoons, The Fantastic Four and The Godzilla Power Hour, and introducing the puppet/live action segments, Horror Hotel and the Lost Island. They also sparred with special guests such as Scott Baio, best known as Chachi in *Happy Days*, and famous New York Jets quarterback turned actor Joe Namath. The reviews were unkind. "The lowest of lows ever achieved in the name of entertainment," said the influential *Los Angeles Times*. McKeown called the show "sickening".

The band was not available to help promote the Krofft show at this crucial time. They had already arrived in Japan and would be there until late September. After several arguments Paton had succeeded in persuading McKeown to join the group on the 10-date tour. Here the fervour for the band, stoked by two previous hysterical tours and three number one albums, remained strong, "intense and fraught" said McKeown. The demand for band-related material had seen a plethora of Roller releases rushed out. Earlier in the year the self-explanatory compilation album, *Early Collection*, had sold remarkably well peaking at three in their LP charts, while the late 1977 *Greatest Hits* package had gone top 10.

McKeown had not rehearsed with the group prior to the tour. Paton, anxious to avoid a whole lot of bother ahead, decided to give it all a miss, deputising John Gorman to accompany the band to Japan in his place. An amiable 42-year-old Welshman, Gorman worked for Paton out of the band's Heddon Street office in London, chiefly for Rosetta Stone. He'd been a pop music promoter in South Wales during the late sixties and early seventies, a one-time close friend of Billy Fury. He'd had "a bit of breakdown" that stopped him working in music before Paton had offered him the job with Rosetta Stone.

At the start of the year, in January, Gorman had accompanied the then four-piece Rollers on a short sold out seven-date tour of Germany partially sponsored by *Bravo*. They played to around 50,000 fans but the tour, extended to Switzerland, Holland and Belgium, was characterised by frequent arguments between McKeown and the others.

Gorman was readied for more of the same in Japan. They were playing in 10,000-12,000-seater venues in Tokyo, Osaka, Shizouka and Nagoya. "Les was leaving and there were arguments," said Gorman who recalled the tour advance paid by promoter, Siejiro Udo, being close to £1.5 million. Udo was also supplying five-star hotel accommodation and first class travel.

While the band had rehearsed in Los Angeles without him, McKeown had been on holiday in Hawaii. He'd asked his close pal *Bravo* photographer Wolfgang 'Bubie' Heilemann to fly over to Waikiki and the two had then flown together to Tokyo. The band was already in the country having arrived direct from Los Angeles. The first date was at the huge Budokan Hall. Wood stayed on bass and Alan, the band's bassist from 1965 to 1976, was on second guitar.

After the concert McKeown went into the packed hotel bar and ordered drinks for everybody. Gorman asked, "Who is going to pay for this?" McKeown answered, "That's your problem." Gorman called an unhappy Paton who paid via his America Express card.

Gorman's focus was to make sure everything ran smoothly for the band but he had been told to look after McKeown specifically. "I kept him away from the others," he said. "And I had to make sure he didn't sneak out of the hotel." Getting into the hotels was also a problem with "fans everywhere", said Gorman. The band often entered through the hotel kitchens.

They travelled to Osaka by plane and were welcomed by 40,000 fans at the airport. Their limo was surrounded but they survived another terrifying crush. The animosity between McKeown and the band simply simmered. They tended to avoid one another whenever possible, eating at separate restaurants, sometimes staying at different hotels. He wound them up when he could, referred to them as his backing group and left the stage during the gigs so the audience would cheer when he came back on. In retaliation McKeown said he felt the band ordered the lighting crew to turn off his spotlight on stage during certain songs. He also claimed the band were deliberately changing key just as he was about to start singing so that he would sound out of tune.

It was petty stuff but the show went on. Then Paton turned up. "I was surprised," said Gorman. "He wasn't coming when we left."

Paton aggravated the situation. "There were scuffles behind the stage," said Gorman. "We sorted it out. I stopped it. It was only throwing cans of Coke at one another." Things got worse. There was pushing and shoving on stage. The real fighting took place "out the back" said Gorman. "We couldn't keep Les and Eric apart," said Paton. "Every place we went, they were fighting with each other. I couldn't blame one without blaming the other."

"There was a huge clash of egos between Les and Eric," said Alan. "They just couldn't sort things out. There were a lot of arguments. There were a lot of drugs going about too and we were working under intense pressure."

McKeown asked for his own security man to protect him from the others. "It was like being in a bad marriage and I wanted out," he said. "The others didn't want me to go and we had the most awful fights – real kicking and punching and swearing fights."

Paton claimed they gave Gorman a nervous breakdown. "He was virtually crying," he said, adding that Gorman later tried to sue him "for thousands because he said he would never be the same again, that he had never experienced anything like this."

Things reached a nadir when McKeown felt the need to bug Faulkner's hotel room to see what was being said about him. He soon wished he hadn't. Listening back was not pleasant. Despite his desire to leave the group, he was scared by the thought of quitting, crying with worry. "We were a sick band at the end," said McKeown. "Eric and I couldn't stand being in the same country as each other, never mind the same room. Tam thought he was God, Eric thought he was God, and there were five gods in the group."

The denouement to this unhealthy squabble was played out on stage in Shizouka. During the songs Faulkner or Wood sang the lead vocals on, McKeown, in black leather trousers, purposefully tried to attract the crowd's attention. Finally Wood snapped and kicked out at McKeown, sending him off the stage. Four security guards were called to prevent McKeown retaliating. The city's police were also involved. "Horrendous," said Paton. Promoter Udo was deeply concerned over the remaining dates.

Gorman said that Paton abandoned ship and flew back to Scotland. He had been on the tour a week. Once he was gone the hostility became manageable, Gorman said. He insisted they all go out to dinner together. "I had them all talking," he said. "I calmed everyone down, got them round the dining table, which was a first." The final week of the tour passed without further incident.

"We all travelled back together," said Gorman. "There was no fuss on the plane. When we got back to Heathrow we all went one way and Les went the other. We went into London and Les went up to Scotland."

The *Krofft Superstar Hour* ran for eight weeks on Saturday mornings in the 11am time slot on NBC and trailed in the ratings behind the carton shows *Tarzan And The Super Seven* and *Scooby's All-Stars* on rival networks. Then, on November 4, the show was slashed to 30 minutes, renamed *The Bay City Rollers Show*, and moved to a new time slot of 12.30pm.

The Rollers' new album, titled *Strangers In The Wind*, had been released in America to coincide with the launch of their coast-to-coast TV show. On their return from Japan, McKeown was uninterested in promoting it and the release was, like the TV show, struggling to find an audience. The rest of the band did what they could to promote the work. There was interest among America teen magazines but the Rollers now had to compete with fresher, younger or more novel teen stars impacting on the American market: Shaun Cassidy, Leif Garrett, Andy Gibb, John Travolta and a new cartoon costumed rock group, Kiss. The Krofft show was even a little gauche for the *16* or *Tiger Beat* audience.

To their intense frustration the Rollers found themselves trapped in the American public's perception as a band for children. The TV show gained coverage only in the kids or teen sections of regional American newspapers, next to the puzzles and cartoon strips. The band had hoped the new album might help win over an older and more mainstream demographic. They fancied the album had sentimental, melodic, easy listening/soft rock appeal. Members of the band had always had a soft spot for The Carpenters and hoped to gain some traction among the

American adult contemporary audience. But they had been firmly pigeonholed and critics viewed their TV show as a wheezing last gasp of the band's cheap teen pop appeal. No one wanted to listen. Conversely, *Strangers In The Wind* had nothing for kids on it, no simple catchy pop tunes. This, in comparison to their early records, was a bloated, self-indulgent and druggy album. Paton actually liked it.

"The album wasn't designed for the audience that the show intended to draw," said PR Bob Levinson. "The band was being pulled in two directions. I could publicise the album in the teen magazines and the music trades but it was a going to be a difficult sell if the band was not on the road in America." Levinson would soon be voted Publicist of the Year by *Billboard* magazine, largely due to his ability to work regional newspapers ahead of tour dates, enhancing the possibility of local music retailers stocking the band's product. "We were kings of the road," Levinson said. The Rollers were in no fit shape for another American tour.

Rumours that the band had split up spread and without the availability of McKeown it was impossible to even book promotional TV appearances in America to mime to the album's lead single, 'Where Will I Be Now'. There was no cohesive marketing campaign behind the project. Without a hit single, without a tour, and pitched around an embarrassing flop TV show, the album struggled. The Krofft show was certainly no great advert for their musical talents. Essentially it had turned them into the sort of anachronism in America, an inconsequential variety turn similar to how they were perceived now in the UK.

The mainstream American press was savage. The show was pilloried and best-selling American weekly magazine, *People*, read by several million Americans, called *Strangers In The Wind* the worst album of the year "bar none… absolute MOR dreck".

Arista Records President Clive Davis was not happy. He had chosen almost all the group's singles since late 1975, usually finding the song and insisting the group record it. The band had not always agreed with his choice but had understood Davis was in control of the machine that was going to market the project. His focus had always been on the right sound and song for the American market and that was another reason for the group's rapid decline in the UK.

'Where Will I Be Now' had not been one of Davis' best choices and seemed to reflect the 46-year-old's loss of interest in the group as a commercial proposition. It was a slushy torch song written by Chris East, who had written the recent country-tinged hit 'My Kinda Life' for Cliff Richard. McKeown did not have the big voice required to carry the song. Maslin's sophisticated production; the sweeping string orchestration and Hopkins' keyboard interventions, also swamped the band's quirky identity. It was ultimately bland.

The Rollers had given the newly minted Arista its first number one hit in America when Davis was desperate for one and helped establish the new label. The group had gone on to sell millions of albums for the label, earned Arista a small fortune. But Davis was a pragmatist. He always saw them as a gimmicky pop band, and now the teen craze for them was spent. The group keenly felt Arista's current indifference toward their career. The label had recently taken out an incredible 50-page plus self-aggrandising advertising feature in *Billboard* magazine to celebrate their third year anniversary. It featured a loving profile of Davis, and every aspect of the company but the Rollers were barely mentioned. They knew what they'd done for Davis and the label, as much as anyone. The band felt Davis owed them. Beneath his debonair existence, however, Davis had a reputation for being stingy with sharing the credit for his successes. He seemed able to compartmentalise his life with ease. There were rumours, later confirmed in his autobiography, that he enjoyed secret homosexual trysts with young men away from the bosom of his family.

Success meant everything to him. He measured it by the profit Arista made and he now saw the Rollers as a drain on those profits. He had fully exploited them commercially. The band was imploding, the lead singer self-destructing, the TV show was a flop and so was the new single. The new album, *Strangers In The Wind*, had cost the label close to half a million dollars and pre-orders were poor. Davis was known to be ruthless in business. He had other acts he would rather work on.

The band, crucially, had little support elsewhere in the company. Their standing at Arista had been significantly diminished by the recent departure of promotions manager Michael Klenfner. A loud and enthusiastic ally of theirs, he had played a significant hands-on role in breaking the band on American radio and always had the trust and ear of Davis. Now Klenfner was working in a senior role at Atlantic Records and the band had no one to fight their corner within Arista. They also missed the influence Klenfner had wielded on their behalf over American radio. Few, if any, stations were picking up on the new Rollers material.

There was no firm announcement about McKeown's departure from the band. The question mark about his future hung over this entire period. In November McKeown had shared the cover of *16* magazine with Kiss. The headline was: 'Les in Trouble!' Alongside behind the scenes pictures from the making of the Krofft TV show, the magazine suggested that McKeown's absence from the group could be permanent. Wood was featured as a cover star on the next issue of *16* magazine with the headline, 'Rollers are breaking' and a special Roller Hotline number to call for distressed fans. The magazine asked "Where are they now? When will they be back?"

The band's single, 'Where Will I Be Now', did not even make the top 100 on the *Billboard* charts nor did the album, *Strangers In the Wind*, which peaked at 129. It was a significant failure, one from which their American career would not recover. A second single from the album, the achingly slushy acoustic Faulkner/Wood penned 'All Of The World Is Falling In Love', was dead on arrival. A planned third single, another Faulkner/Wood composition, the mournful 'Another Rainy Day In New York City', was aborted.

It was not just a disaster in America. In most territories, the reaction to the new album and the singles taken from it was equally devastating. The material failed to register in the UK charts or in the band strongholds of Canada and Australia. The only exception to the poor reception, was Japan, where the album climbed into the top five.

Had Arista decided the band was worth fighting for then perhaps an answer could have been found to this career slump. Davis himself had resuscitated several other acts via shrewd choice of material. The band felt that there was no appetite at the label to even discuss a future for them. They floundered, looking for someone to blame.

Like McKeown, who was consulting independent lawyers about his position in relation to leaving the band, the other Rollers began to wonder about what they could rescue from the situation. They felt persecuted by their record label and unloved by Paton who was often unapproachable, evasive or plain uninterested. The flop album had, however, focused their attention onto the business of their finances. They were concerned about the lack of money filtering through to their individual accounts when they'd turned over vast amounts in the past few years. They felt there was a huge hole in their finances.

With Paton increasingly out of his depth business-wise, Colin Slater, Managing Director of the Bay City Music publishing company, had acted as ersatz manager of the band. Slater had restructured and managed Bay City Music and overseen other aspects of their business. He estimated that the band had, while he'd been with them, generated close to $100 million in various advances, monies that were kept offshore to avoid tax in the UK. He said, as an example if the revenue the band might have been earning from sales and from publishing, the *It's A Game* album, the band's album prior to *Strangers In The Wind*, had generated four million presales worldwide and the band had sold close to 150 million records in total since 1975.

It was unclear what figures the Rollers songs were generating in America (where they had not accepted an advance in favour of starting their own independent company) – but it was likely in the high millions. Slater, however, could not significantly help the band. He did not control the cash. He said he simply channelled all his business reports through the band's longstanding UK accountant, Stephen Goldberg, and the various contractual lawyers Goldberg recommended.

Goldberg was the man several of the band members thought held the answers then to what they saw as a shortfall between band income and their own earnings. They were eager now to access key documents and contracts held at Goldberg's Mayfair office. Already having problems with Paton, who was asking questions about the safekeeping of his percentage of the band's revenue, Goldberg, the band said, made it clear he did not welcome their interfering in his business. His attitude, they found, was always defensive. The band had never entirely trusted him, felt he was a slimy character, and resented the huge fee he charged them and his largesse; his flash Rolls-Royce and big house.

Independently of Paton, on the advice of an English lawyer they consulted, the band hired Martin Goldberg, an experienced, measured, chartered accountant from the major Manhattan accountancy firm Prager & Fenton to audit Goldberg Ravden on their behalf. The band referred to Stephen Goldberg the 'bad Goldberg', and Martin Goldberg, who worked from Prager and Fenton's London office, the 'good Goldberg'. The two were not related.

Prager & Fenton was a firm historically active in the entertainment industry and where Allen Klein, who at one time managed Phil Spector, The Beatles and the Stones started his career. Martin Goldberg had worked for the company since the sixties and enjoyed pursuing rip-off guys, prolific in those days, in the record and music publishing industries. He relished the chance to investigate the Rollers' affairs.

He first met Paton and immediately afterwards warned the band that their manager was completely mad, not to be trusted and had probably feathered his own nest at their expense. Experience told him the band was likely being taken advantage of from almost every angle – management, accountants, lawyers, their record label...

The good Goldberg also been asked to investigate, with a view to auditing, their American accountant, Stephen Tenenbaum, the other figure, beside Stephen Goldberg, who appeared to have a significant measure of control on the band's finances and business structure. Tenenbaum had actually, at one time, worked for Prager & Fenton. The Rollers had always felt intimidated by Tenenbaum's swish New York office, his famous clients and powerful friends. Like Paton, they had never fully understood the complex structures put in place to manage their money.

Clive Davis was said to be tight with Tenenbaum. Before Davis moved Arista to a new upmarket address in 1976, the label and Tenenbaum's offices were both located at the same New York address, 1776 Broadway. Tenenbaum had been involved in the band's financial set-up in America since January 1975. He was instrumental in setting up ALK Enterprises, the company that controlled the Rollers' business in America. ALK, it transpired, had even signed the deal with Arista on behalf of the Rollers (delivering, by letter of assignment, the services of each member of the band). The individual Rollers were not personally signed or directly connected to the label at all. ALK, in simple terms, owned them and all their rights. ALK oversaw the publishing companies that controlled the Rollers songs in America, touring revenues, merchandising deals and recording royalties. It bounced the money around various companies under its control to best utilise the most efficient tax route necessary in relation to corporation and personal tax. Between ALK and the band members' individual limited companies there were said to be up to 30 other companies. For instance, three companies had been involved in signing the band to Arista.

The deal with ALK had been sold to the Rollers in a hurry after a show in Canada. Pushed into it by an insistent Paton, they signed several documents in the dressing room there and then. They had thought no more of it until now. Many English rock stars in the seventies had moved away from England to avoid high levels of tax or set up complex, legal, corporate structures to minimise their tax position.

For the band members, the structure of ALK made their position and their finances mysteriously opaque, almost unfathomable. They were reluctant to ask Tenenbaum for explanations for fear of looking foolish. McKeown said Martin Goldberg found ALK had made one payment of close to $150,000 to a recipient whom the band was unaware of. Within the various ALK companies there were tens of millions of dollars being administered. It baffled the band. All they knew was their personal bank accounts did not reflect what they felt they had earned and that ALK was very expensive to run in terms of accountant and lawyer fees. In fact, the band reckoned the fees charged by Stephen Goldberg, Stephen Tenenbaum and the various lawyers who acted on their behalf ran into the multi-millions. It was estimated they had paid Goldberg Ravden alone close to £800,000 in fees. In New York, one bill from Marty Machat was reputedly close to $500,000.

The band felt they had made a good move hiring Martin Goldberg to investigate their financial affairs, a positive step toward taking control of their own future. They hoped they could now get on with the business of trying to rescue their musical career.

Paton was rarely seen at the band's head office on Heddon Street. It was becoming a ghost office, an expensive one in a central London location with fancy furniture in the plush lounge, three separate rooms and a recording studio downstairs where the band could rehearse or record.

Colin Slater had recently left the company and returned to LA. He said he had left the company in "good shape". Just before he left, Slater recalled Faulkner, McKeown and Wood voicing concerns about the fees Stephen Goldberg and Stephen Tenenbaum were charging them. "I tried to point out to them that they were the only wall they had between them and the IRS (Internal Revenue Service, American tax collection) and the Inland Revenue and if they didn't like what they were doing, did they really want to do it themselves?"

Another man leaving Heddon Street was John Fogarty, an assistant to Stephen Goldberg. The band's decision to appoint Martin Goldberg to audit his boss put him in an awkward position. Fogarty had worked for Rod Stewart's manager Billy Gaff before joining Goldberg Ravden and since 1977 had been in charge of the day-to-day Rollers' finances, "paying bills and getting the band to sign off cheques" he said. Everything, he said, had to be authorised by Goldberg Ravden, even Paton's expenses.

Fogarty also looked after Rosetta Stone and Hot Chocolate for Goldberg Ravden and had often worked out of one of the smaller offices at the Rollers' Heddon Street HQ. He felt the band was always well advised but that it was up the band to act on that advice. The Rollers, Fogarty said, "were young boys and not from a sophisticated business background". He left Heddon Street and Goldberg Ravden to set up his own publishing company.

John Gorman, who had never seen the point of Fogarty, was also on his way out. He had a furious row with Paton about the band's business set-up, particularly the fees being paid to Goldberg Ravden: "£16,000 a week for him, £16,000 for him… What are they doing?" he demanded of Paton. "We do all the things in this office. I walk across and they put it in a book."

"That's when I finished,' Gorman said. 'I had a terrible row with Tam and left. I warned him. I said if you don't watch you'll end up with nothing… and that's just what happened. By Christmas of 1979 he didn't have £300, everything had gone, all taken away from him."

That left Anne Baxter, Paton's long-time secretary, and Barry Evangeli who took over Gorman's duties, and an eerie sense of quiet foreboding, at Heddon Street.

Faulkner was back recording in November, in Dublin Sound Studios in Ireland, and denying any rift with McKeown. While concerned about the band's finances, he was not short of money. In London he had a flash apartment in Chelsea just off King's Road, behind the famous Peter Jones department store, worth half a million pounds. He'd splashed out £25,000 on a bed for the place from Harrods and had the best home stereo in the world, a $50,000 Bang & Olufsen quadrophonic system. The company had provided it free in exchange for Faulkner posing for an ad that ran in *Gramophone* magazine: "Eric Faulkner of The Bay City Rollers listens to his own music on Bang & Olufsen". The apartment had shag-pile white carpeting, 30 gold discs on the walls, and there always seemed to be voluptuous women staying there.

Despite the recent disappointments in America, Faulkner had no intention of giving up on living the rock star life. He had funded the hiring of the studio in Dublin, plus the hiring of a producer, engineer and top class session musicians, to assist him make a solo album and perhaps put down some ideas for a new Rollers record.

The rest of the band, on holiday, had no immediate financial concerns either. Wood had invested in two pubs in Gibraltar and property in Scotland. He drove a gold BMW. Alan and Derek Longmuir also had several properties in Scotland, including a farmhouse and hotel.

McKeown also owned property and drove an expensive Range Rover. He too was self-funding the recording of solo material. He'd hired the expensive Konk Studios in London, established and managed by The Kinks. It now seemed certain he wouldn't be coming back to the fold, had finally left The Bay City Rollers. It was something of a relief for the band. "Great he's gone," surmised Wood. "At that point everybody hated everybody."

The Rollers felt they might carry on with Faulkner as singer. They had not entirely given up on McKeown returning and this seemed like the best interim, compromise, solution. Alan, Derek and Wood were finding it difficult to see how the group could survive without their lead singer; history was not littered with bands that had.

Although perhaps there were tax breaks to be had from recording in Ireland, little else made sense of Faulkner's efforts in Dublin. If *Strangers In The Wind* was too adult-themed for the Rollers' young audience, the solo album he planned to record was sheer lunacy. It was an ambitious musical adaptation of 18th Century visionary poet William Blake's epic *The Four Zoas*, a prophetic and uncompleted book supposed to act as a summation of Blake's mythic universe. There was a lot of free sexuality in the work and exploration of divided identity. Blake had been cited as an influence by beat poet Allen Ginsberg and songwriters Bob Dylan, Van Morrison, and Jim Morrison. The main instrument on this solo album was to be an instrument Faulkner had invented called a Viotar, a guitar/violin hybrid.

On the other side of the Atlantic, Faulkner was still being chased around on TV by Mr. Munchy. The Krofft show continued through to January 27, 1979 with increasingly poor ratings before being axed. It was a disaster for the Krofft brothers. They would not make another kids' TV show until 1983.

At Dublin Sound Studios, Faulkner also developed songs that would form the basis of a new Rollers album. Some of these songs had been around for a while, such as the bleak 'Stoned Houses,' and had been castigated by McKeown who had disliked the material intensely. Faulkner had hired Peter Ker as a producer for the work in Dublin. Ker, a former guitarist with a number of British sixties acts, had co-written the massive Arthur Brown hit 'Fire'. He owned his own studio called Pathway in London where new wave acts such as Elvis Costello and The Police had recorded. As a producer he was working with contemporary British new wave acts such as The Motors who had scored a recent top five UK hit with their 'Airport' single. He had also recently produced hotly tipped Edinburgh power pop band The Headboys.

Ker was a laidback guy with long grey hair and grey beard, the type of producer who was happy to let things develop and only intervene when necessary. He and Faulkner got on well. At Faulkner's request, the owner of Dublin Sound Studio, Phil Green, had organised an engineer for the pair, Rod Thear. He was a veteran engineer with many years' experience working with groups such as The Rolling Stones and Led Zeppelin at London's famous Olympic Studios, before moving to Ireland. He'd recently been working with The Animals' singer Eric Burdon. The closest he'd come to pop, he said, was engineering 'three or four' Slade albums at Olympic. Faulkner had been a huge Slade fan.

Thear recognised Ker straight away. "I said to Pete, 'What you doing here?' He said, 'I could ask you the same question.'" Also in the studio with Faulkner were two of the UK's top session men: drummer Clem Cattini, a feature on at least 44 UK number one singles who had played on the early Coulter/Martin-produced Rollers material, and bassist Mo Foster who had played on a huge list of recordings with musicians including Jeff Beck, Ringo Starr and Scott Walker. Also in the studio was 15-year-old Mariella Frostrup, now a well-known journalist and TV presenter. "I said we need a tape op and Phil [Green] said, 'Right I'll find someone,'" said Thear. "She was good fun. She wasn't a trained tape op. We had to show her how to do things but she was enthusiastic."

Slowly, the other Rollers drifted to Dublin: the two Longmuirs and Wood. They and Faulkner stayed at the historic, upmarket Gresham Hotel in the city centre. Here, together, they made the decision to look for a new singer.

"It was something we had to do," said Derek, now almost 28. "You see Les began to feel he was bigger than the group, that he was irreplaceable and that the group couldn't survive without him. It got so that we all began to believe that the group couldn't survive as a group with him. It was wrenching but it was something that had to happen in order for the Rollers to survive."

CHAPTER 12

Failure

"They knew no better, they were very simple Scottish boys, very basic, not well educated. Some of them could hardly read. And Tam came in and promised them the world. Woody would tell me Tam was a good manager. I would say, 'Yes he did make you famous, but that's only one aspect. He took your innocence and your future. You made a deal with the devil. Was it worth it?'"

– Stephan Galfas

Duncan Faure was 21, based in Los Angles, and managed by Freddie DeMann who also managed Michael Jackson. DeMann was in his mid-thirties and one of the most powerful managers in the American music business. Faure had only recently left his native South Africa where his former band, Rabbitt, had been the country's undisputed number one rock/pop act and he, with his long strawberry blond hair and a button-nosed androgyny, had been a huge teen heartthrob.

Rabbitt's hit records had barely registered outside of South Africa. It was, said Faure, the band's press cuttings that initially wowed DeMann. "We were front page every day in South Africa," he said. "Freddie saw that. He also had the videos."

Faure, who played keyboards, guitar and sang, shared the lead role in Rabbitt with guitarist and singer Trevor Rabin. Although they generated the same teen hysteria as the Rollers, with girls fainting at their gigs and bras and knickers thrown on stage, and often wore outrageous costumes, they were considered to be serious musicians. "We were a phenomenal band musically," Faure said. "Rabin was already the original 'world's greatest guitarist' and I was there beside him – the two of us were pretty monster guitar players together." Faure had been a qualified guitar teacher since he was 15.

For three years, from 1975, Rabbitt ruled South Africa. With their mix of glam and prog rock recalling Queen, Elton John, The Beatles and Pink Floyd, they recorded three gold albums (25,000 units was gold in South Africa) and packed out 3,000-seater capacity venues. "Sometimes three shows a day," said Faure, who wrote many of the band's hits.

There was interest in the group from around the world and talk of touring America and Europe. Capricorn Records, a label linked to Atlantic Records, released their music in America. ELO manager Don Arden came close to signing them.

The talk and interest ultimately came to nothing. South Africa was a pariah state. The Afrikaner-dominated National Party had governed the country since 1948. Non-white political participation was outlawed, black citizenship revoked, and the entire public sphere, including education, residential areas, medical care and common areas such as public transportation, beaches and amenities, segregated.

The anti-apartheid movement had grown in intensity throughout the seventies and most mainstream artists boycotted South Africa. The Soweto uprising in 1976 has seen further sanctions introduced from abroad and brought fresh focus to the injustice in the country. Up to 700 black students had been killed by police when 20,000 marched to protest against Afrikaans being introduced as the medium of instruction in local schools. There was almost universal disapproval of apartheid policies.

Rabbitt, a white South African rock band, was a difficult sell to the world. In 1977 there were 4.3 million whites in South Africa, constituting 16.4 per cent of the population. Co-star Trevor Rabin left the group and moved to London. He too would wind up in Los Angeles, joining rock band Yes who would score a massive American number one in 1983 with the Rabin-penned 'Owner Of A Lonely Heart'. Rabin went on to play guitar with Seal, Tina Turner and Michael Jackson as well as writing scores for films such as *Enemy Of The State*, *Armageddon* and *Gone In 60 Seconds*.

After a tour of Rhodesia in early 1978, Rabbit broke up and Faure left the country too. "I wanted to go overseas because the political situation was completely incorrect," he said. He did not want to talk about the two years' mandatory military service white South Africans served after leaving school but, yes, he'd done it. "It's an embarrassing situation, black South Africa. When I came to America it was hard for me to look people in the eye. When people asked, 'Where are you from?' I'd change the subject."

DeMann was eyeing a solo career for Faure. A profile of him had recently featured in the September 1978 issue of *Tiger Beat* magazine. He was being treated well. DeMann had taken him, along with the Jackson brothers, to see a recent Rolling Stones gig in New York. Faure was a hustler, determined and bright. He widely distributed his showcase video.

A copy found its way into the hands of Eric Faulkner in Dublin. He played it to the band. "They watched it and thought, 'Well, here's the guy,'" said Faure. It was November 1978. "I got sent a first class air ticket to Dublin. It was really exciting. I called Freddie in New York and said, 'I'd had an offer to join the Rollers, do you mind?' He said, 'No you have my blessing.' At that time the Rollers were a household name."

He met the band at the Gresham and went to Dublin Sound Studios for a jam. "I was showing off on the piano," he said. "The next thing Woody was sitting next to me: they could see I could play. I was almost instantly in the band. It was, 'Wow.' It felt like home. Derek, Alan, Woody and Eric were such good people. We went to the clubs [in Dublin] and the girls were swarming, there was one on the first night wanting to drag me home. I went back with the band because I didn't know how serious they were [about the band's famous no girlfriend rule]. I thought I might be fired."

"The next day Tam flew in and he came to the hotel," Faure said. "Half an hour later we all got a plane and flew to Edinburgh. We get to the house [Little Kellerstain] and it was swarming with kids. There was Rosetta Stone, five of them, the five of us, Ray [Cotter, Paton's new boyfriend] of course and Tam's entourage. Tam was good to me."

"When I joined his power had been eroded really," Faure added. "He was never problematic to me. What went on from 1974 to 1978 I don't know. The other band members never opened up to me about Tam."

Unlike the band, Paton immediately realised that a major drawback with Faure was his South African nationality. A 13-date German tour booked for 1979 would be problematic. "No way were they going to let a guy with a South African passport into Germany," he said. Maybe, he suggested to Faulkner, he could talk McKeown into coming back for the tour.

The band was headstrong. Faure was in and, they insisted, as a full-time and equal member. They bought him £40,000 worth of equipment including an electric piano and handed him £10,000 to buy clothes. They also eased him into their social lives: taking him to see Elton John play in Edinburgh and London. John's manager John Reid had long been pally with Paton. Faure and John now became friendly. He had the new Roller stay at his home and would go on to help Faure get his Green Card.

The Rollers rented Faure his own apartment in London, in Pimlico. "Lovely apartment," he said. "I was well looked after." He said the fans kept an almost constant vigil outside the band members' houses. "Even though I was new in the band there was three or four cars every night outside my flat."

Paton inquired about getting Faure an Irish passport but was told it would take at least a year. The band's new singer was unveiled at a press conference that took place in Los Angeles. The teen magazines were keen to find out what the story was.

"Those magazines weren't looking to print anything negative," said the band's American PR Bob Levinson. "It was Les is going off to great glory, welcome Duncan, who is Duncan, what does he have for breakfast?" Faure was described in *16* as "someone unlike Les; quiet, cooperative and businesslike" who does "not party a lot". *Tiger Beat* asked, "Will you ever be able to love them again?" The magazine then gave several reasons why fans should be able to. "We feel we'll come out of this stronger than ever," said Derek.

The band then travelled to New York where Faure struck up a relationship with Beth Wernick who worked as a PR in Levinson's East Coast office. She was in her mid-twenties and recalled visits in limos to hip club Studio 54 for photo ops and shopping expeditions to buy leather trousers and jackets. The Rollers returned to Los Angeles for Christmas 1978.

Levinson suggested they visit a children's hospital. The band had Christmas lunch at Levinson's home in Los Feliz, near Griffith Park, and then visited the wards of an LA children's hospital. "Absolutely no publicity," said Levinson. "They didn't breeze through the wards for publicity pictures. There were no photographers. Even the hospital was told no publicity. They spent time with the kids. They drew pictures with the kids. They went to the cancer ward. It was heartbreaking. They were the sweetest people in the world to these kids. We finished and went back to my house. We had groupies, teen fans, on our lawn. They had followed the group… these fans spent Christmas on the lawn outside my house."

Back in London, media interest was becoming increasingly difficult to stimulate. It was almost two years since the Rollers had scored a top 40 hit in the UK, and they had not played live in the country since September 1976. Now seen as hopelessly dated, it did not help that they were represented by Tony Barrow, best known as The Beatles' press officer throughout the sixties. Barrow was an old-school operator who disliked modern music, particularly punk. He was months away from retiring from the PR world, leaving the Rollers without any UK PR representation.

The band hurtled into recording a new album in Ireland at Dublin Sound Studios with Ker and Thear producing and engineering. Faulkner had the bones of some songs recorded and Faure was bursting with fresh ideas. Faulkner also picked over songs from Faure's Rabbit past looking for material that might suit the contemporary art pop/new wave rock direction he wanted the band to take. There was a new enthusiasm to reach out to a fresh market, a sense of optimism.

Clive Davis was sure the band had reached the end of their run and that the band's effort was futile. There was nothing to suggest they had a future in America. *Strangers In The Wind* had cost a fortune to record and sold poorly. He did not want a repeat of that disaster to eat into Arista's end of year profits.

He was currently engaged in selling Arista Records. The label's parent company, Columbia Pictures Industries, had been through a prolonged period of disarray at boardroom level following a high profile scandal involving the movie division's studio chief David Begelman who had been caught embezzling over $200,000 from the company in 1977. The studio had scored recent hits with films such as *Shampoo* and *Close Encounters Of The Third Kind* but Begelman's misconduct threatened to derail the public company.

After much politicking, the Columbia board voted to remove President and Chief Executive Alan Hirschfield, a close ally of Davis, and was open to offloading Arista. Davis was keen to find a suitable buyer. German company Bertelsmann Music Group (BMG) had offered a phenomenal $50 million for Arista. Davis stood to make $10 million on his 20 per cent equity in the company if the deal went through and also retain his position as President of the company.

Davis pitched the prospects of Arista skilfully but the German company was essentially buying only one guaranteed superstar, multiple million-selling Barry Manilow, whose best days actually seemed to be behind him ; his latest album had flopped. Davis accentuated the positives: the career resuscitations of The Grateful Dead and Dionne Warwick at Arista, the nearly $100 million in predicted sales for 1981, the 40 gold [five of them albums by the Rollers who had also scored six top 40 American hit singles] and 11 platinum records racked up during his Arista reign. "Talent comes to me because they believe I've established a creative haven in which they can flourish," he boasted to *Newsweek*. "And talent attracts talent."

The Rollers had two albums left to deliver on their current contract with Arista. It was a difficult situation. The label had clearly lost faith in the group and had no real desire to promote them. Faulkner said the label would not pay the recording costs for the Rollers' new album. He said they stated that they had not been consulted on the choice of producer or the choice of material as the reason for doing so.

Faulkner decided the band would pay for the recording costs themselves rather than compromise over those key decisions. It was a foolhardy stance. The Rollers, however, were enthused by the new and original material they were recording in Dublin, a sharp collection of power pop with slashing buzz guitars and adult lyrics about cocaine, sex, regrets and ruminations on pop stardom. Mannequins and erections were mentioned on the Faulkner/Faure/Wood penned 'Elevator' and on Faulkner's 'Stoned Houses' there was a real sense of desolation. Gone was the soppiness that underscored much of the past Faulkner/ Wood songwriting.

The band was also radically rethinking their image. They paid for publicity shots that saw all five band members in brightly coloured suit jackets, smart shirts and ties, matched with leather trousers. The 'tufty' haircuts were toned down to neat, tight modern shoulder length cuts. Faulkner added a moustache. They looked very much as if they belonged to the current melodic new wave scene, very much like The Cars, who were breaking in America, The Police, Talking Heads or The Knack who were climbing to number one in America with 'My Sharona'.

Faulkner wanted to make clear this was a new band and planned to launch the new look and sound under the banner of 'The Rollers', dropping the Bay City. The uptempo, chorus-driven 'Turn On The Radio', written by the band bar Derek, was seen as a good choice as a lead single for the new album. They hired old pal Mike Mansfield to shoot a video for the track, a straight-ahead, as if live, performance. With Faure and Faulkner on guitar, Wood on bass, Alan was consigned to stand behind a bank of keyboards.

The song was released as a single in the UK and Europe in April 1979. Paton used what little influence he had at Arista to push the release through. Terrified of engaging with Davis, he rarely stood up for the band against Arista. He'd had no real say at the label's London office since Bob Buziak, one of Davis' trusted lieutenants, had been appointed Managing Director of Arista for the UK and Europe. Buziak had, however, recently left Arista and Paton had used the opportunity to find a sympathetic ear in the label's London office to help get the new single a release.

Things began promisingly. Music weekly *Sounds* made 'Turn On The Radio' its single of the week. Paton organised a series of interviews with British newspapers in which the group hoped to underscore their newfound grown-up image. "Tam was trying to get us away from the teenybopper image," said Faure. "And we were on the front page of *The Sun* or *Sunday People*, a sex and drugs story – Derek had more sex than hot dinners sort of thing. It snowballed."

In the interviews they talked about how the past pressures of pop stardom had led them to drink and drugs: pills, marijuana and acid. Despite the band claiming they had put this behind them, the papers jumped on the confessions, running with the line that the band's clean-cut image, famously preferring milk to alcohol, had been a lie. The band found themselves back on the front pages with tabloid headlines such as 'Living A Lie for Five Years' in the *Sunday People* and 'Drugs, Drink, Birds – The wild, wild world of The Bay City Rollers' in the *Daily Record*. In one of the articles Paton confessed to being the "worst of the lot" for drugs and said he'd been seeing a Harley Street shrink to get off them.

There was also upbeat talk of forthcoming live dates for the band in the UK but these would never materialise. The new single failed to get radio support from BBC Radio 1 and stalled, selling poorly. The band, evidently, was dead in the UK. The new album would not be released in the country.

Paton did not accompany them on their tour of Germany, even though this was a market where the Rollers might still prosper. In his place he sent Barry Evangeli, the former Anchor Records A&R man whom Paton had known since he worked in promotions at EMI. Still in his early twenties, Evangeli had been offered work by Paton when Anchor was closed down in 1978. He did odd jobs with the Rollers, and with Paton's other bands, Bilbo Baggins and Rosetta Stone. Alan

Longmuir was not happy, describing Evangeli as inexperienced. "He didn't have a clue," Alan said. "But Tam was coming on to him and Tam was more interested in that."

"Tam wanted to keep a grip on the Rollers but he'd kind of lost interest in them at that time," said Evangeli. "They were his money making-machine but Tam's mind wasn't really on the Rollers, it was more on Rosetta Stone. The Rollers insisted that Tam be on the tour because he wasn't devoting as much time to them but Tam decided not to go. It was bad vibes as soon as we landed at the airport [in Berlin]. Eric was kicking off at the representative at EMI [who now distributed Arista in Europe]. He was very peeved off they weren't getting the attention [from the record label] they were getting at the height of their success."

Faure recalled his first gig with the Rollers as being a *Bravo* magazine event in Berlin in front of about 20,000 people. "They threw me in the deep end," he said. At the same event was McKeown whom the band had not seen in the past six months, since the end of the Japanese tour. He was with his new writing partner, Glaswegian Scobie Ryder. The pair were putting together material for McKeown's solo career and actively looking for deals.

Ryder recalled McKeown at the *Bravo* event for a personal appearance. "The crowd were shouting, 'Leslie, Leslie', when the Rollers were on stage," he said. "The band were spitting blood because no one wanted to know about them." Faulkner recalled McKeown climbed on stage at the end of the Rollers' performance. "People were trying to unplug the PA, knock over amps," said Ryder. "It was madness."

Afterwards, the band and McKeown collided in a Berlin hotel, the Schweizerhof, where they were all staying. "We had our security, they had theirs," recalled Ryder. "Then it all kicked off in the bar." Alan claimed to have punched McKeown hard in the face "three times" while holding him by the scruff of the neck. McKeown was laid out. He was not a fighter.

"I went round the room swinging punches," said Ryder. "And they were swinging punches at me. I ran out into the street and Woody was chasing me down the road with Eric. I slid on the gravel and scraped all my arm and leg." Ryder smeared blood from the scrapes onto his face and posed for photographers, claiming the Rollers were bullies. "Les and I had a real laugh out of that," said Ryder.

"They were kind of shoving each other outside of a hotel," recalled new boy Faure. "They'd told me things about Les and when I met Les I could understand what they were talking about."

The Rollers' German tour dates that followed did not go well. "The first date wasn't even half full and it was pretty much like that for most of the tour," said Evangeli. "The venues were barely 25, 30 per cent full. Tam had booked auditoriums, big halls. Eric was the one who seemed to take it most to heart. He was miffed the tour wasn't a success because he wanted to prove to Leslie that it wasn't all about Les McKeown. Eric was the most serious, the spokesman out of the band."

The band was in Munich when they sacked Paton. "Woody came up to me and said you'll never guess what we've just done," said Evangeli. "I thought he'd kicked the door in. I got the impression that the Rollers didn't want to be associated with Tam anymore because although a lot of the publicity was about the Rollers it was also about Tam as well. Tam wasn't making any great secret of his sexual preferences by now. He'd got engaged [in 1977] but that was to get the wolves off his back for the sake of the Rollers more than anything else. I don't think the Rollers were too happy about some of the stories they were hearing about Tam. I think it was the band not wanting to be tarred with the same brush."

The following day, as the band prepared to leave Munich for a show in Stuttgart, Paton called Evangeli and ordered him to return to London. "I left them half way through the tour," he said. Evangeli met Paton at Heddon Street and they went together to the offices of Goldberg Ravden. Paton wanted to guarantee his management commissions.

"There was an almighty row, lot of threats made by Tam to Stephen Goldberg," said Evangeli. "Tam was wearing slippers for some reason, he didn't really have airs and graces he was a jeans and shirt person. He accused Stephen Goldberg of misappropriation. Stephen Goldberg was shouting down the stairs at him, 'If you feel like that then sue me.' He was quite calm about it really but there was a lot of effing and blinding from Tam."

"Tam wasn't a business guy," added Evangeli. "He left it to other people and trusted other people. I was fairly young but there were things said where I'd think this is not right. Tam would say he didn't have money to pay the mortgage on his flat in Finchley. Hang on a minute, you sold all these records and merchandise and you can't afford to pay the mortgage? It dawned on Tam a little too late what was going on. Meanwhile Stephen Goldberg was driving a beautiful black Rolls-Royce."

"The accountants totally misled me," said Paton. "We were taken in by conmen... it's as simple as that."

On behalf of the band, Martin Goldberg had completed his audit of Goldberg Ravden in London and had advised the band to hire lawyers to begin legal proceedings against the company. It was felt that Stephen Goldberg was not being completely forthcoming regarding access to all the band's documents and contracts. Martin Goldberg had also organised a meeting with the band's American accountant Stephen Tenenbaum to discuss the band's American operations.

Having walked out of a deal with Freddie DeMann, Faure felt the sacking of Paton was a mistake. "Alan and Woody had too much to drink and called him up and said he was out." It began to cross his mind that he might have made the biggest mistake of his career in joining the band.

They wrapped up the final German dates, cancelling several shows. Duncan said the German tour was "not a nice place to be". The Rollers had made a promo appearance on German TV, miming to 'Turn On The Radio' on the popular *Der Musikladen* music show, but the single did not sell in Germany and did not chart. The new album, now titled *Elevator*, was released in the country but it did not chart either.

Just as Paton had predicted, there were multiple problems arising from Faure's nationality. He was unable to get a work visa for a visit to Japan, the country where the Rollers could still guarantee huge sales. The *Elevator* album and two singles from it, 'Turn On The Radio' and the title track, were released as singles in the country. "It was my passport," said Faure. "I couldn't work there. It is a pity we never went. That was the best territory." Australia, another stronghold, had to be abandoned for the same reason. 'Turn On The Radio' was released there but with no band promotional visit, it sank. The album was never released in Australia.

After returning from Germany, the Rollers briefly entered Matrix Studios in London to record new material. Opened in 1977 it was being used by Adam & the Ants and Gary Numan. Again the band was paying for its own studio time. They then headed for New York and a meeting with Clive Davis. There were no singles planned for release in America from the *Elevator* album that was only being given a perfunctory release in the country.

The meeting did not go well. Faure said that Wood told Davis to fuck off. "That is pretty heavy," said Faure. "They assumed they could pick up the mantle and write and that was never their forte," said Davis. "The key is material, acts forget who wrote it and they decide they want to be the next Bob Dylan."

They got a warmer welcome in Los Angeles where they hooked up with PR Bob Levinson. The teen press were still keen and Levinson was able to make something from the band's recent controversial UK interviews. *Tiger Beat*'s June 1979 issue promised "the real story of the Rollers' recent interview on drugs". They weren't doing them anymore!

"Instead of helping us through the day drugs were slowly destroying us," said Wood. "Avoid drugs," said Faulkner. "I just went through life in a mechanical way. It was terribly confusing and wicked." Alan added: "I hope I never have to go through that hell again because it's not worth it. Not for all the money in the world!"

Levinson also managed to organise several TV appearances for the band, all filmed in LA. "TV was something we could set easily," he said. "A reputation doesn't disappear overnight." The band was paying him but Levinson had a genuine affection for them. "Just some of the nicest people we ever dealt with," he said. "They're one of the few acts I ever invited to the house."

They mimed the album title track, 'Elevator', plus 'Turn On The Radio', enthusiastically on *The Merv Griffin Show*. A heavy-looking Faulkner was noticeably out of breath when Griffin gently interviewed them afterwards. "They let us write the album this time," he said, adding that the band had changed their name to avoid the taxman.

The Rollers also appeared on the syndicated panel game show, *Hollywood Squares*, as one of the nine celebrity guests inside the 3×3 vertical stack of open-faced cubes. All five of them were crammed into one cube. It was not pretty.

Levinson also booked them on the syndicated *Mike Douglas Show*. Here they played 'Back On The Street', a song from *Strangers In The Wind,* on which Faulkner sang lead, and 'Elevator', on which Faure acknowledged the past with a tartan scarf. Many young fans of the band were in the audience.

The exposure had no persuasive effect on the position of Arista. There was no heavy promotion put behind the band. The band clearly needed a new manager to represent them. Jake Duncan, who was staying with the band in Los Angeles, suggested Brit Andy Truman who was resident in LA. They'd met while touring with idiosyncratic prog rockers Jethro Tull. "He was the best tour manager I ever had," said Duncan. "I said, 'I'll introduce you and then step away.' They needed somebody to get a hold of the situation."

Truman had only recently moved to LA and had formed the De Novo Music group in the city. He was not a known band manager but the Rollers were short of options. Faure had asked DeMann about managing the group. He didn't want them. They had met Kiss manager Bill Aucoin who showed some interest but chiefly in Faure as solo artist. Truman has since died and it is difficult to know what attracted the band to him other than desperation.

At the time he was acting as tour manager to heavy metal act Black Sabbath and his strength and interest seemed to be in the heavy metal/ glam metal scene. In 1983 he would become manager of American HM band Alcatrazz, featuring ex-Rainbow frontman Graham Bonnet, and several renowned metal guitarists including Steve Vai and Yngwie Malmsteen.

With Truman as newly appointed manager, the Rollers set off for a long tour of America through July and August 1979. The shows were not glamorous and included many bookings at fairs and amusement parks in backwater towns. They even played a safari park. The tour mainly bypassed major cities. The band travelled by tour bus.

"They said, 'We don't want a bus, we want a jet, we're the Rollers,'" said Faure. 'We did the bus but we had money for hotel rooms as well. We'd go back to the hotel until 3am and then Jake [Duncan] would pound on the door and pile us into the bus. We had a disco at the front and the back in the bus. The alcoholics would sit in the front and the pot smokers in the back. Ten or 20 cars followed the band wherever we went, full of fans."

The shows were hit and miss. "Arista had given up on the band and offered no assistance at all," said Truman. They didn't take stage sets or backdrops. If they were playing an amusement park such as Carowinds in Charlotte, North Carolina, they were essentially a side-show. At Carowinds, for instance, the entrance fee to the park was $24 and it was $6 extra to see the band in the 13,000-capacity Palladium Amphitheatre. At country fairs, a ticket to the fair would also include entrance to the band show. Some of the fairs had 50,000-seat venues and the Rollers' shows were badly attended. Despite a smattering of young girls in tartan, often with their mums and dads in tow, there were many testing gigs. The band's new look and sound was not a success.

"We didn't do 'Bye Bye Baby' for a while because it felt too poppy," said Faure. "That was kind of silly. We did eventually. Some of those [poppy] tracks; 'Rock And Roll Love Letter', 'I Only Wanna Be With You' and 'Saturday Night' are great live. I should have done more singing without an instrument but in those days I was glued to my guitar or piano."

Dotted throughout the tour were gigs in small venues in out of the way places like the Saratoga Performing Arts Centre. The 1,800 capacity venue was in a small town over 100 miles to the north of New York, and the fans, all girls aged 8-16, many dressed in the famous Roller gear, were rowdy. The show was sold out and they played a well-received 90-minute set. Such nights echoed former glories and were rare successes on what was fast becoming a spirit-draining experience.

"One gig haunted me," said Faure. "It was raining and there was no canopy and there were metal pipes. The money up front was $15,000 and Andy [Truman] rushed us into the bus and we had to get across the state line. I couldn't believe that. He didn't want the band getting electrocuted but people had been cheated... we cancelled and ran away."

A show in Philadelphia was called off on the day of the concert and on August 19 a gig at the 2,500-capacity Milwaukee Auditorium was cancelled. A spokesman for the local promoter said the Rollers had cancelled their entire American concert tour. Truman blamed "poor ticket sales". Refunds were being offered.

The Rollers played a last date in America, in support of pop art rocker Todd Rundgren, at the annual and hugely popular *Jerry Lewis MDA Labor Day Telethon* at the Sahara Hotel in Las Vegas. Then Faure cut out, returning to South Africa. He was looking at releasing a solo single with his old record label, Jo'Burg Records, utilising tracks he'd cut at Matrix earlier in the year.

Faure remained a major draw in his home country and, in the press, talked about bringing the Rollers to South Africa for gigs. There were offers on the table, he told the band. This was during the well-publicised apartheid era, so it was impossible that the rest of the band would not know what this meant. The British Musicians Union had adopted a policy in 1961 that its members should not perform in the country as long as apartheid existed.

In the early eighties, Frank Sinatra, Rod Stewart, Elton John and Queen would be pilloried for accepting multi-million dollar offers to play the infamous Sun City casino, opened in 1981, northwest of Johannesburg.

This was 1979. The Rollers would be among the first major acts to ignore the cultural boycott if they chose to go to South Africa. They would be forever tainted by what would be an apparent backing of apartheid. But the Rollers had nowhere left to run.

Scobie Ryder was a pal of McKeown's older brother Roni, who was a DJ at the trendy Maestro's club in Glasgow. Scobie was a 21-year-old Glasgow native and a well-known local character. He sang in bands and had regular after-club parties at his West End flat.

Roni brought McKeown to one of Ryder's house parties in 1978. McKeown was still a Bay City Roller at the time. Among the 40 or so other fashionable wannabes, McKeown struck Ryder as "introspective" and "worn down by everything", "miserable and almost shy".

"He took out a big handful of pills and he had them in the palm of his hand," said Ryder. "He said, 'Do you want one?' I said, 'What are they?' He said, 'I don't know.' So I knocked his hand up in the air, knocked out the pills, and said, 'Don't be an asshole. If you don't know what you're doing, don't do it.'"

A few months later, in late 1978, Ryder was down in London, squatting in a building on King's Road in Chelsea. He had a tape of his songs and was negotiating with record companies. He would soon sign a solo record deal with EMI and make a deal with Phil Coulter and Bill Martin as a songwriter. By chance he bumped into McKeown in a late-night shop near the World's End pub on the King's Road. "Les was getting ice cream," said Ryder. McKeown invited him to his home "just around the corner".

"It was this rather lovely mews house that he was renting and his mum and dad were there," said Ryder. "We had a few spliffs, a chitchat, and he went on to tell me how unhappy he was in the band. He said, everyone was fighting, everybody was arguing."

"Well, if you're unhappy, why are you doing it?"

"I don't know what else to do."

"If I was you, I'd get happy, leave the band. Fuck them. Go out on your own."

"Oh I couldn't do that."

Ryder said McKeown, who was a year older than him, was "in a terrible state. He was like a zombie. I had no idea about his real problems. I knew he was a bit emotionally fucked up but not about his bisexuality. He had that demeanour."

A few days later Ryder went round to see McKeown at the mews house with his acoustic guitar. "He wanted to have credibility, that was the whole point," said Ryder. "I said it's all about songs and if you had the right songs you could have a hit on your own, nobody cares who's in the band, you're the lead singer. You need to write your own songs."

"I can't do that."

"That's not a problem. I can fix that."

"I was quite happy to take half of something and do the work," said Ryder. "We made a deal. He would leave the Rollers and go solo and I would find a new band to back him and help him get identity and image. We agreed we'd say that he co-wrote the material. I'd give him half the credit and half the money from the songs. He could hardly write his name. He had no idea about songwriting and subsequently hasn't written a song to save his life. I made a commitment to stick with it, promised to stay with him for three albums. In return he would look after the rent. It was a mutual abuse situation. I was squatting. I wasn't really in great financial shape."

McKeown rented a house for Ryder near Harrods in Fulham. He moved there too. "Lots of girls, lots of crazy shit," said Ryder. They started to work on songs. Then they moved to an apartment near Regent's Park. It cost approximately £1,000 (£10,000 today) a month to rent. "He'd be away on tour and I'd be killing time waiting for him to get back," said Ryder.

Ryder used the Rollers rehearsal/recording studio at the band's Heddon Street HQ to record demos. "Tam was saying, 'Great, come in and try and write stuff' but I knew he was just playing games, trying to get me onside," said Ryder. "I told him to stay away. I made it very clear. We became enemies; I didn't like Tam one bit, horrible character. Les always said he locked himself in the hotel rooms and managed to keep Tam out but I got the impression him and perhaps some of the other band members had paid the price; that's part of the terror of the industry. It's a cesspit of abuse and people either play the game or they don't get anywhere."

McKeown discussed with Ryder concerns about the band's financial situation. "He was telling me he didn't know how much money he had," said Ryder. "It was preposterous."

"You're the artist but you don't know who's in control of your bank account?"

Ryder encouraged McKeown to ask awkward questions. Together they had a few adventures trying to find out what was going on with the band's business arrangements. Ryder even broke into Heddon Street one night, forced open the desk where the books were kept and took a set of accounts.

"I'm the reason The Bay City Rollers broke up," said Ryder. "I gave Les the confidence to step out of his misery." By the time McKeown decided to finally leave the band, he and Ryder had enough material for McKeown's first solo album "and a bit more". Ryder put together a band of elite session players including guitarist Alan Darby who worked with Eric Clapton and sax player Gary Barnacle who played with Paul McCartney. They went into Konk studios and recorded this material in early 1979 with McKeown funded the recording. It cost approximately £150,000.

"I said it's really simple, if you want something to happen, you better make it happen," said Ryder. They had a meeting with Clive Davis at the Dorchester Hotel in London. He found the idea of a McKeown solo career as laughable as the band's attempts to present themselves as a new wave outfit.

"Clive said we'd never make it," said Ryder. Not only that but Davis informed the pair that McKeown was still under contract to Arista. "As far as he was concerned Les was signed to him and Arista owned everything," said Ryder. "I stood up and said, 'Clive you've had great success but your trousers are bri-nylon, your tie's a kipper and if you want to stop me you're going to have to fucking kill me.' He went, 'My gosh, aren't you aggressive.' I said, 'We're going to do this. We will get the album out. Fuck you.' And we left."

Ryder suggested they put out the record independently. He went to a friend at MSD [Multiple Sound Distributors], a thriving UK specialist company who released compilation album packages such as *Twenty Country Classics* and *Golden Greats* by fondly recalled middle-of-the-road acts such as Johnnie Ray and the Bachelors. These budget albums, backed by TV ads, on labels such as Windmill and their own Warwick imprint, were highly lucrative and the company had just invested in its own multi-million pound pressing plant where they made records for rival TV merchandisers such as K-Tel and Pickwick plus records for companies such as Reader's Digest.

MSD, on the fringes of the business, agreed to manufacture and distribute McKeown's solo album and paid a small advance. McKeown and Ryder spent it on a launch party on the roof of hip Soho club Madame Jojo's. Ryder put together the packaging for the record. He did not expect to have success in England. "The knives were already out to kill Les," he said. "But if we could get it out in one place, we could get it out somewhere else. That was the thinking. Somebody had gone against Clive."

The album, *All Washed Up*, was released in England via McKeown and Ryder's own independent label, Egotrip Records, an in-joke about McKeown having left the Rollers on a reported ego trip. McKeown was eager to promote the project, proudly declaring he'd co-written all the songs and co-produced the album.

For promotional shots he donned a one-piece skin-tight spandex bodysuit slashed across one shoulder so it and one arm were left bare. This outfit, combined with cowboy boots or legwarmers, or one long spandex glove, and decorated by various bondage straps came in black, bright pink and banana yellow. With his mullet, McKeown looked preposterous, like he was auditioning for pantomime season. Live, he wore lightning symbols to cover his ears. The album cover showed him all done up in such an outfit and emerging from the sea onto a desert island having escaped from a plane crash that supposedly symbolised The Bay City Rollers.

"The styling was space age glam," said Ryder. "The idea was to be rock'n'roll. It was a touch of Kiss… fantasy. Some of the stage outfits were amazing. The band all had outfits too. I got his hair done, the mullet with the multi-colours. He went from being a teenybopper to a bit of a naughty rock'n'roller."

On October 22, 1979, the *Edinburgh Evening News* ran the first of a three-day exclusive with McKeown, "the rebel Roller". The headline was 'Tam's Puppets On A String'. McKeown, who would soon be 24, said he had earned and spent more than £2.5 million during his time as a Roller. Then he ripped into his former band mates. "A soon as I left the Rollers last year they started slipping badly," he said. "Now they are has-beens. Now the pop world is crying out for a James Dean of the 1980s – and that could be me. People will say I'm on an ego trip but I don't care. I've called my backing group Les McKeown's Ego Trip."

He said that the American girl who had recently claimed he was the father of her child was "a set up". "Someone is trying to embarrass me just as I'm about to launch as a solo star," he said, indicating he had a pretty good idea who that was. He said he had learned a lot about the floating of phony stories during his time in the Rollers

Paton, he said, was the master of the publicity stunt. "Half the stories about the Rollers were planted," he said. "It was nearly all made up. No news was bad news so he would invent juicy little tidbits to make sure the Rollers were on front pages. It didn't bother him if it cast the band in a bad light."

"It was not the pressure of superstardom that got the Rollers down it was Tam Paton's bullying," he said. "The band was terrified of him. We were told all the time what to do, where to go, how to dress, what to say and even what to think. We had no freedom. Being in the group was like being in prison. When I left I was almost incapable of making a decision for myself – even over simple things like what to wear or what restaurant to go to. It was like people who become institutionalised. I had lost the ability to look after myself."

The *All Washed Up* album and its lead single, 'Shall I Do It', failed to sell in the UK, as Ryder predicted. McKeown had dreamed of superstardom, TV adverts, radio play and mass media interest, but in reality he was only a curiosity, already a relic of a bygone era. He suffered, like the Rollers had, from the fact his last top 10 hit in the UK had been over three years ago. His debut album, like *Elevator*, was also no masterpiece. Ryder was inexperienced as a producer, and many of the songs seemed slapdash, but the material had some character and lots of hooks. It was well played, if generic, pop with splashes of reggae and punk. Elsewhere there were touches of the Rollers at their most cloying. It was difficult though to see why the singer had kicked up such a fuss to leave the Rollers if this was his musical vision.

McKeown worked his contacts in Germany and he and Ryder persuaded Metronome Records, owned by Polygram, to release 'Shall I Do It' as a single in the country. Here he first experienced some of his past success, performing on the popular TV show *Szene* to a familiar level of hysteria. The single picked up radio play and climbed into the top 10. The *All Washed Up* album, however, was not released in Germany. The situation with Arista was made clear to Metronome and they feared legal action.

Next, Ryder and McKeown took the material to Japan. It was only a year since McKeown had sold out a massive Japanese tour as lead singer of the Rollers. Ryder, acting as McKeown's manager, was able to strike a five-album deal with Toshiba EMI, the advance an incredible $100,000 per album. Toshiba EMI had licensed the Rollers' material from Arista up until 1978. Arista had now switched their Japanese licensing to Nippon Phonogram who had already started repackaging the band's hits on compilation albums as well as releasing the new work by the Rollers. Toshiba EMI obviously felt they could make money out of McKeown.

"Arista didn't have the clout in Japan that they had in other parts of the world," said Ryder. "We just did a great pitch and they went for it. We got a massive advance and 12 points [per cent of record royalties] per album." On the back of the deal McKeown was also able to secure an advance from leading Japanese publishing company Watanabe Music. They had recently paid a multi-million dollar figure to sign publishing rights to Bay City Music.

All Washed Up was released in Japan to coincide with a major tour. McKeown and the band Ryder had put together for him were treated as superstars. While the Rollers were unable to visit Japan due to Faure's passport, McKeown capitalised. The tour featured a date at the massive Budokan Hall. A second single from the album, 'Long Distance Love', was also discussed as a major TV commercial for Mountain Bell in Japan. There were several performances on popular TV shows between tour dates and McKeown's face was back on the cover of major Japanese music magazines such as *Rock Show* and *Music Life*. *All Washed Up* went Gold in Japan with sales of over 100,000.

Before 1979 was out, McKeown and Ryder delivered a second album, *Face Of Love*, exclusively for the Japanese market. The single, 'Sayonara', was easily their best joint effort yet, with shades of Rod Stewart's 'Sailing'. There were more major Japanese live dates in 1980. In London McKeown and Ryder shared a beautiful apartment in an expensive part of town. They zipped about town in McKeown's Range

Rover. "It was an amazing time," said Ryder. "We had loads of laughs. We were partying hard but Les wasn't off his face."

It was a shame they could not get the *Face Of Love* material to a wider audience but while The Bay City Rollers were tied up with Arista, so was McKeown. Only Japan would touch the material. "He was a phenomenal frontman, he had that special quality," said Ryder. "I really thought he had a chance to be a major superstar. He had all that potential."

McKeown still wasn't happy. "The more we went on the more Les resented the fact he was living a lie and he wasn't actually doing the writing or production," said Ryder. "He was playing Space Invaders, not doing anything. He started to object." The material began to be advertised as produced by Les McKeown, co-produced by Scobie Ryder. "How did that happen?" wondered Ryder. "Then the songs were self-penned by McKeown," Ryder said. "Hang on a minute. We got a deal here. It was basically his ego."

Free of Paton, McKeown was also indulging in drugs and drink. He made sure, however, that he, or his lawyers, kept a keen eye on the progress Martin Goldberg was making in investigating the Rollers' finances and the lawsuits that might ensue. He was highly suspicious that the band was trying to somehow rip him off. He talked about being owed close to £1.75 million (£8 m today) from his time in the Rollers.

He complained about being stuck with an American Express bill for close to $30,000 from his time in the band. He expected it to be taken care of but he said it hadn't been. Colin Slater's warning that without the protection of the Rollers' UK accountant Stephen Goldberg, the band members would have to deal with their own tax affairs and interest from the Inland Revenue, now seemed ominously prescient. McKeown was presented with a huge tax bill, estimated at a total of over £300,000 (close to £1.5 m today).

McKeown and Ryder had funnelled all their earnings through exclusive upmarket private bank Coutts. Ryder said he would regularly phone to check how much was in their account. At one stage it was over £50,000 and the pair headed to Los Angeles on a mission to score an American deal, staying in a villa in Echo Park. It was an ill-advised trip, as no American label would defy Davis, and there was, predictably, no major label interest in McKeown. The pair, nonetheless, had fun. "Until I phoned up the bank to ask, 'How much is in there?'" said Ryder.

"Why nothing, Les emptied it last week."

"I was beyond words," said Ryder. "I'd worked my ass off for 18 months. I took out a big kitchen knife and stuck it under Les's chin. He was laying on a sun lounger. I said, 'I could fucking kill you right now but I'm not going to do that because a wanker like you doesn't deserve a quick way out. What I am going to do is, I'm going to leave and when you see me again you better run like the motherfucker you are.'" Ryder returned to London. "I felt so betrayed," he said. "Les was like an abused dog. Eventually he's going to bite you."

McKeown argued how he'd paid for all the early recordings and never got the money back. "The deal was he'd look after those expenses in return for my commitment to getting him out the band and looking after him," said Ryder. "That deal changed after we started to make money."

Ego Trip disbanded. The two further albums McKeown released in Japan, in 1980, a live album and then a compilation, featured no new material. "Unfortunately for Les he still had two albums left to deliver [on his Toshiba EMI deal] after that," said Ryder. "He called me, 'Would you come in to do one more album?' Sure, put the money with my lawyer and I'll do it."

He and Ryder recorded the album *Sweet Pain*, again exclusively for the Japanese market. Released in 1981, it sold poorly. Promotion was difficult. McKeown had dropped the spandex for mature Bowie-esqe pale suits. He had no band.

His final Japanese album consisted entirely of cover versions, including a track called 'Roller Days' – a medley of Rollers hits. "He couldn't write any songs on his own," said Ryder. "He couldn't survive on his own, so he went back to where he was before. I felt sorry for him. Les was a fool to himself. I've often considered suing him. When I think of him I'm always disappointed. I gave more than I should have, gave him support when he really needed it and he let me down so badly."

McKeown ended up singing 'My Way' and The Village People's 'In The Navy' on Japanese TV. Like the band, he had nowhere left to run. His finances were shot. He had hundreds of thousands to pay on the outstanding tax bill. He'd fallen behind on the mortgage on his nine-acre spread in Torpichen, where his mum and dad lived. It was repossessed. His bank account was closed. He moved into a £100-a-week rented bedsit in Notting Hill Gate with a cooker in the corner and a shared bathroom. "It was horrible," he said. "I was fucked, basically."

He blamed everyone but himself.

Andy Truman and the Rollers ignored the cultural boycott and went to South Africa in late 1979. The apartheid regime was being attacked as abhorrent throughout the world; the UN had recently condemned the country at the World Conference Against Racism.

Duncan Faure's solo single, 'Honey Don't Leave LA', was doing well in his home country and Arista were persuaded to release a third Rollers single, 'Hello And Welcome Home', from the disastrous *Elevator* album exclusively to South Africa. It was a former Rabbitt song that Faulkner had revamped. It sounded very much like later-period Beatles.

Truman organised a series of concerts in 3,000 to 5,000 capacity venues, many of the same places Rabbitt had once filled. On the first night of the tour, in Welkom, 5,000 people paid to see the band. "The places were packed," said Faure. Truman had used his experience of touring to organise pyrotechnics that he was said were "better than what Kiss were using".

The band members stayed in downtown Johannesburg and had a good time, the darlings of a small scene of hipsters. Wood started dating Danielle Saint Clair whose father, Barrie, was a big shot film producer in South Africa, having recently executive produced *Zulu Dawn* starring Bob Hoskins, Burt Lancaster and Peter O'Toole. It was a prequel to the hit movie *Zulu*.

Via his daughter, Barrie Saint Clair saw the clamour around the Rollers and decided he wanted to involve them in his latest project, a film starring young German actress Olivia Pascal, famed for a string of German soft porn movie roles. The movie, *Burning Rubber*, based around drag racing, was due to start filming early 1980. Saint Clair offered Alan Longmuir the role of the male lead. He would play a downtrodden backwater car-mad motor mechanic who eventually makes good as a driver in the big race, beating Flash Jackson and getting the girl, Pascal. The band was given the task of writing the soundtrack and there were roles for Wood, Faure, Derek and Eric, as Alan's motor mechanic sidekicks (who also happen to play in a band – there was a club scene written in during which they could play a song). It was, finally, the Rollers' own feature film!

Faure was feted in Johannesburg and enjoying himself, maybe too much. "He was a bit of a loose cannon," said Jake Duncan who was with the band as tour manager. "He was a household name in the country. But it all went wrong over the space of a couple of months."

It started when one newspaper, the prominent *Sunday Times*, picked up on the band's recent drug confessions in the English press. They splashed on it. It snowballed. "Suddenly we were on the wrong side of the press," said Duncan. "Andy [Truman] may have rubbed the press up the wrong way as well. They started coming along to soundchecks, taking a couple of photos from the stage when there was no one in the venue and then printing that as if it was a show night. Then Duncan [Faure] swore on stage, 'Let's fucking rock', and his reputation started to fall apart."

"South Africa at the time was a very conservative country," said Faure. "I foolishly said [on stage], 'Sex and drugs and rock'n'roll', basically singing the Ian Drury song. It was blown out of all proportion."

Attendances at the shows dropped. Truman said in Durban and Johannesburg the band weren't allowed to use their pyrotechnics and, as a result, "we were forced to cancel other shows". He said he made a "business decision to cancel the rest of the tour after I'd spent $100,000 of my own money" propping up the tour.

Truman left South Africa over Christmas 1979, "first class to Paris on Concorde", said Faure. The band knuckled down to recording 10 new songs for the soundtrack to *Burning Rubber*. When Truman returned to South Africa in January the band sacked him. Faure called his claims to have spent $100,000 on the band "bullshit".

"He was very naughty," said Faure. "He saw five guys that were easy to get on with, easy to work and easy to take advantage of. A lot of the

South African concert money disappeared. He took the money. We don't know how much."

Filming on *Burning Rubber* began in February 1980 in Magaliesburg, north of Johannesburg. It was directed by Irishman Norman Cohen, best known for directing the feature length film versions of UK TV sitcoms, *Till Death Us Do Part* and *Dad's Army*, and three sequels to popular UK soft porn sex comedy film, *Confessions Of A Window Cleaner*. *Burning Rubber* was his final film. He died of a heart attack three years later aged just 47.

Alan over-acted as if he was still in a daft Krofft skit or even one from *Shang-A-Lang*. He was also playing a much younger character, in his early twenties, which didn't quite work. But he looked okay, a little like the star of the *Confessions* films, Robin Askwith, and the film had a strong, if basic, storyline. The locations and secondary characters were convincing and Olivia Pascal was alluring. The drag racing sequences picked up the slack in the script. There were some daft zany sequences but generally it was played straight. If they'd filmed it at the height of their fame, it would undoubtedly have been a hit and led to other film opportunities. *Burning Rubber* was released in May 1981 in Germany where Pascal was a star. It did little business elsewhere.

Faulkner was not involved in the filming, having flown back to London to produce a single for post-punk, new wave three-piece, Dolly Mixture. Faulkner cut a cover version of the Shirelles' hit 'Baby, It's You' with the group. Released in September 1980 by Chrysalis, it was disowned by the band who opposed the label's attempt to sell them as a teen girl group. Without Faulkner, they went on to work with Paul Weller's new record label Respond.

Jake Duncan had stayed with the band during the making of the film. At an industrial tribunal in August 1980, he described how Alan had called him one night "in a great panic" saying two sheriffs had approached him with a writ involving the group's alleged debts accrued from the cancelled tour. The figure was said to be in excess of $30,000.

The story was reported in a South African newspaper and others came forward to claim they were owed money by the band and were trying to trace them. After a tip-off they would be pursued there by more sheriffs, the group decided to move from the Marathon Hotel in Johannesburg. "As this was a civil matter I was told that I personally could not be apprehended by the police," said Duncan. He stayed at the hotel while the group made plans to stay with various friends north of Johannesburg.

On March 13, 1980 Duncan checked into the Marathon and took a call from Derek and two other members of the group. "Mr Longmuir told me that some dope had been left in the hotel room on top of a cupboard near the toilet," Duncan told the tribunal. "I verified it was there and it was cannabis. My first thought was one of panic. I didn't know what to do. I did not fancy going out of the hotel with it in my pocket."

The following day he put the dope in his briefcase with the intention of removing it. When he went downstairs the lobby was swarming with the police and press. Duncan was cautioned for withholding information about the Rollers. The drugs were found and he was charged with possession. The group was arrested that weekend for non-payment of debts. It was all over the papers. Duncan, in prison, found out the group had fired him via a story in a Johannesburg paper. He had not been told and denied he had resigned.

The band organised bail and took the next flight out of South Africa, avoiding any involvement in the pot bust. Duncan had to stay, and was tried in a South African court, receiving a suspended sentence. Back in Scotland he took the band to court for unfair dismissal and won. He had been on a wage of £500 per week. He was awarded just over £8,000. He told the industrial tribunal in Edinburgh that he now had to live "under the stigma of having worked with a group that most people consider just a joke".

In London, while the rest of the band was in South Africa, Faulkner had, at the band's expense, compiled material for a new Rollers album. It was the final one – the eighth – due to Arista on their current contract. Its completion meant they would be free of contractual obligations with Arista and be able to find a new, more welcoming, record label to work with.

The album was put together from odds and ends and included Faure's recent solo single. There were also offcuts from the *Elevator* sessions and a reworking of an old Rabbitt song. For Roller aficionados there were two tracks cut in early 1978 at Konk in London, prior to the *Strangers In The Wind* sessions – both songs were re-voiced by Faure. "There's some nice stuff on there," said Faure, "if you look for it."

Faulkner said he took the album master tape and 'just chucked it' at Arista's A&R department in London and got them to sign for it. Outside the offices that day he found piles of press cuttings and promotional material from the band's heyday thrown in a skip. Faulkner was self-medicating, struggling emotionally with failure.

The new album, titled *Voxx*, was not released in the UK or America. In June 1980 it was given a limited German and Japanese release. 'God Save Rock And Roll', a new Faulkner/Faure song from the 1979 Matrix sessions was released as a single from the album but in Japan only. The band, however, was still unable to visit the one last territory that wanted them due to Faure's South African passport and the issues surrounding apartheid.

The preparation of a court case against the band's former English accountant Stephen Goldberg would be a slow and expensive process, costing the band money that was fast diminishing. They had been forced to hire, alongside Martin Goldberg, a small army of solicitors, lawyers and barristers.

"There were board meetings with 40 people," said Faulkner. "The five of us were sat there thinking who they hell is paying for this?"

"It cost an absolute fortune," said Wood.

Having completed the audit on Stephen Goldberg, Martin Goldberg was now keen to audit Arista Records. The company Goldberg worked for, Prager and Fenton, completed two audits of Arista on behalf of the band, in America and in Europe. It was estimated that between July 1975, when The Bay City Rollers signed to Arista, and the end of 1978, the band was owed approximately $4.8million in outstanding royalties from Arista on record sales. Goldberg had met with the band's American accountant Stephen Tenenbaum and the pair did not exactly see eye to eye. The band had now hired a separate high profile (and expensive) law firm to represent them in America, Arrow Edelstein & Laird.

Faulkner, Wood and the Longmuirs were getting into deeper and deeper financial trouble. But what could they do? They were aware now that, like McKeown, they were facing huge tax bills of approximately £1.5 million each. Martin Goldberg had told them a story about how he was booed when he visited the HMRC head office hoping to broker a deal on their behalf. The staff had mistaken him for Stephen Goldberg.

The Rollers needed to get their hands on cash. They had been looking for a new manager since sacking Andy Truman. Freddie DeMann and Bill Aucoin were still not interested. Journey's manager Walter Herbert passed. So did Foreigner's manager Bud Prager. The funds were no longer there to record their own material. In fact, they would soon run out of money to pay for Martin Goldberg's services. They had already fallen behind on their payments to American PR, Bob Levinson. The bills from the various lawyers and barristers were overwhelming.

Al Dellentash was on a high. He was a smooth, 32-year-old mustachioed Italian-American New Yorker who was co-manager of Meat Loaf alongside well-known music attorney David Sonenberg. They had struck gold with Meat Loaf's 1977 *Bat Out Of Hell* album that would eventually tot up in excess of 34 million sales. Dellentash had Meat Loaf working on his follow-up album, *Dead Ringer*, and was hungry to expand his roster.

During his twenties, Dellentash had built up a fleet of aircraft and a multi-million dollar private jet leasing company with clients including The Rolling Stones, The Grateful Dead and Kiss. His planes had king-size beds, gold fixtures, fully-stocked bars and thick carpeting. Dellentash was a qualified pilot and had often flown the planes himself. The Rollers heard stories about him flying to Libya with a load of automatic weapons but did not believe them. They met him in his lavish office in New York, all gold and mahogany, apart from the pink room that had a pink grand piano at the centre.

"I had a private chef, and a full-time guy just to keep the fireplaces roaring at all times and a theatre room with a 20-foot screen," Dellentash bragged. "We'd host sex parties with all the best girls." He had a bodyguard called the Brick.

Dellentash told the Rollers he could get them a deal with Epic, Meat Loaf's label, also home to The Clash and Abba and owned by CBS Records. He put them up at the Olcott Hotel in New York and organised time in a studio, House of Music, out in West Orange, New Jersey, that he had an interest in. Meat Loaf had recorded parts of *Bat Out Of Hell* there and was recording *Dead Ringer* at the studio with producer Stephan Galfas, who owned House of Music. Dellentash wanted the Rollers to work with Galfas too.

Galfas, in his late twenties, had practiced law in New York and worked as a producer for Warner Brothers before starting the studio. "Al and David managed me at the time," he said. "Loosely," he added. "They were friends, they brought me work."

House of Music was just 10 miles from Manhattan and had been used by new wave luminaries Patti Smith, Talking Heads and Television. Galfas described the studio as "super high class, state of the art, on eight acres of land with a swimming pool and gym." It was totally private. "You could do what you wanted." There were limos to ferry musicians back and forth from the centre of New York. American disco funk group Kool & the Gang were making the studio a home and had recently recorded their platinum-selling *Celebrate!* album at House of Music.

In October 1980 the Rollers moved from the Olcott into a rented house in Maplewood, New Jersey, near the studio. They were given a station wagon to drive around in. "The band were having tremendous issues," said Galfas. It was mainly alcohol. "First time I met them they were drunk and a mess," he said. "Eric was depressed," said Faure. "He was drinking heavily." There was also a lot of cocaine around in the studio and some heroin. Faure said the band never did coke, maybe a little on Saturday night. "We smoked pot," he said. "Half the band smoked pot and the other half drank."

Galfas was not optimistic about working with the band. "They hated each other," he said. "They were passive aggressive until they got drinking and then all hell would break loose. They were lost about what to do. They were these lost souls." He did not tell them but Clive Davis had actually approached him to produce the band in 1977 and he'd met

Paton back then too. "He was very flirtatious and complimentary and he'd done his research into the work I'd done," Galfas said. Ultimately, though, that approach had come to nothing.

Dellentash, as he had promised, made a deal with Epic Records for the Rollers. It was a simple arrangement. He claimed to have taken a staggering half a million dollars advance for one album. The band would spend almost six months at the house in Maplewood, a pedestrian existence in the small sedate suburban town. They cooked at home, watched TV and listened to music. Faulkner drank booze to excess and ate lots of hamburgers and cake.

"It was a very large house," said Beth Wernick, the Bob Levinson employee, who often stayed there as Faure's girlfriend. "Eric was in the maid's quarters downstairs, the rest were upstairs." One morning she came downstairs and found two "punk, Goth looking girls" there. "Eric had paid for them to get a taxi to come and party with him," she said. "I called Del [Derek] and said we need to get these girls home."

Faulkner emerged in his underpants looking "disorientated", she said. He claimed the girls had put acid in his drink. "I wasn't sure that was true but we couldn't get him to put clothes on," said Wernick. "Blue underpants with red dice on them. We had to take him to studio in his underpants and then I took car and had to go shopping for clothes."

As word got around, fans of the band and curious local teenage kids visited the house. "Sometime there'd be 40 kids there," said Wernick. She soon had enough of that. The band "seemed like it had run its course," she said but "there was always the element of hope there, that they were still famous enough to turn it round".

"Woody and I still wanted to play," said Faure. "We'd be down in the basement in New Jersey playing and it was hard to get the others interested. They were kind of like, well we're done with this, we've toured the world." Alan was drinking heavily like Faulkner.

Sometimes they would waste the studio and Galfas' time, not turning up for sessions until they were hours' overdue. Galfas threatened to burn the studio tapes. "Turn up on time or fuck off back to Scotland," he said. They got more disciplined. "Slowly their confidence grew," said Galfas. "They stopped drinking all the time and started getting serious about the music. They started hanging out at the swimming pool, which meant waking up during the day."

One afternoon, rehearsing songs in the living room at their New Jersey house, Galfas asked if they could play him 'Saturday Night', their 1976 number one hit in America. He suggested Faure stand aside and let Wood sing. "It was like that moment in the movies when the heavens open up and the light shines down," he said. "They had that magic pop energy that only a handful of people on this planet ever had. Yes, they were sloppy as shit. They didn't have the chops of serious musicians, but neither did Television or Talking Heads or the Sex Pistols. They wanted credibility badly and they didn't understand they already had it. They didn't have enough confidence in themselves, didn't get how good they were."

For Galfas recording them, getting a great new album together, became a labour of love. He said he had not seen any money yet and the studio costs were $2,500 a day. "The money [from Epic] didn't go to my studio," Galfas said. "I gave them free time to make the record. I gave them the time and space to be able to find themselves again. I was a serious producer. I did it as a favour. There was no advantage for my career. I cared about those guys and they knew it."

Galfas grew closest to Faulkner. "Eric was really lost," he said. "He was having panic attacks every day, was nervous and insecure. He was like a little puppy at my side all the time because I would listen to him." Faulkner had started piling on weight and was noticeably bulky. It was hard for him to deal with the issue. "He tried to stay cute with his eyeliner but he was heavy," said Galfas.

He actually put Faulkner in touch with a psychiatrist in New Jersey. "I knew he needed it. The shit that had been going on was horrifying. The severity of what happened behind the scenes has never been exposed."

Faulkner saw the psychiatrist "a couple of times", said Galfas. "Tam would tell them that girls were nasty, they have diseases and they have babies and the band were too innocent to get that they were being played. Tam would fuck certain band members and say, 'You can't tell anybody because this is really wrong but let me fuck you in the arse again.' I spoke to Derek about vagina and he said, 'Oh no it smells, it's got disease, it gets pregnant and your whole life is over.' He couldn't even say the word vagina. He called it 'ja-gina'. Derek's issue was acceptance and wanting to be loved. That's what they all wanted. They were troubled, lost and searching, and trying to hold it together.

"They knew no better, they were very simple Scottish boys, very basic, not well educated. Some of them could hardly read. And Tam came in and promised them the world. Woody would tell me Tam was a good manager. I would say, 'Yes he did make you famous, but that's only one aspect. He took your innocence and he took your future. You made a deal with the devil. Was it worth it?"

"The alcohol and drugs were part of the escape from that," said Galfas. Faulkner was often drunk when dark secrets came tumbling out. Galfas would try to help as best he could.

"Well, did you ever think you were gay?" he'd ask.

"No."

Pause.

"But I don't know what I am. I have no idea."

The band reworked a couple of the rockier songs from the *Burning Rubber* soundtrack but the collaborative spirit between Faure, Wood and Faulkner had dissipated. The new tracks were now all either exclusively written by Faulkner or by Faure. The close relationship between Faulkner and Wood also appeared to be dead. They were often in conflict, arguing loudly and openly. "Woody was a mess too," said Galfas.

He was, however, still passionate and committed to the band. Unlike Alan, who was barely involved in making the new album and spent much time in the local bars. He also seemed to have trouble relating to his brother. "He was very uptight, judgemental, very conservative," said Galfas. Woody tended to play his bass parts on the record.

Faure said he did not enjoy the recording. His material tended to be overblown, with intricate keyboard and guitar work, ultimately sounding remarkably like Elton John. Galfas saw him as the weak link. "He didn't have the same musical roots," he said. Faulkner kept things simple, channelled contemporary UK new wave with some whimsical charm on his songs, 'That's Where The Boys Are' and 'Roxy Lady'. He took lead vocals on both.

The album sounded convincing but there was no obvious hit. Dellentash invited senior promotions and marketing managers from Epic to hear a playback. Faulkner turned up too – in drag. "Full make up, the full deal," said Galfas. "Mini skirt, stocking, heels… Seems to be an English tradition, straight men dressing up in woman's gear."

Epic, encouraged by Dellentash, put some thought into promoting the record. The initial copies of the album were released in a plain sleeve with no signifiers as to the identity of the band. The sleeve was just stamped with the words 'Collector's Edition' and 'Contains One Outstanding Rock Album'. Recipients were encouraged to guess the band's identity. A promo four-track EP, using the same concept, was sent to the radio and press. It picked up radio play in Canada.

Epic and Dellentash picked three potential singles from the album and the label put up the money for the band to shoot videos for each. The format was becoming increasingly popular with TV music shows, particularly in America. MTV, dedicated solely to music videos, was due to launch in August 1981. Dellentash had the new channel on a promise to showcase the Rollers' videos.

One of the videos was shot at an aircraft hangar Dellentash used for his planes. It featured one of his aircraft and the band partying with women in lingerie. The song, the Faure-penned 'Ride', was not subtle either. Another video for Faure's excellent mock pomp rocker, 'Doors, Bars, Metal', was a riff on the band's arrest in South Africa (as was the song) and was shot in an abandoned jail. Derek was dressed up in a Judge's wig. They were "well done", Faure said of the videos.

The album, titled *Ricochet* after an instrumental on the album, was scheduled for release in the UK and Europe ahead of America and Canada. The lead single, Faulkner's 'Life On The Radio' had whistling and bagpipes, a new wave throb and a gentle melody. It sounded contemporary and came with a simple, performance-based subtle, classy, black and white video.

The band played a few low-key club dates around New York in June. They sapped what little optimism the band might have had for the project. They were poorly attended desultory affairs. One club in Queen's featured mud wrestling on Mondays. They could not fill the popular 2,000-capacity Malibu club on Long Island. A handful of gigs on the West Coast were a little better. At LA's famous Whisky A Go-Go the capacity crowd of 250 welcomed the band's new approach. They also played the Roxy in LA and a casino resort in Nevada. It was a strange clutch of gigs. The money was poor but at least they were getting it in their hands.

Then things stated to go wrong. 'Life On The Radio' was only issued as a single in Australia and the Netherlands, going nowhere in either territory. Inexplicably, Epic chose Faulkner's soft metal rocker 'No Doubt About It' to be the lead single in the UK. There was no video for the track, which flopped in the UK, as did the album. The only other territory where the album was officially released was Canada and it bombed there too. Once the name of the band was revealed, almost all media interest had dissipated. Epic started to withdraw support.

One of the main problems was that there was no Dellentash to drive the project forward. He had, said Faulkner, "disappeared off the face of the earth".

On May 6, 1981, multi-millionaire Salvatore Ruggiero, aka Sal the Sphinx, Sal Quack Quack or Sally, was travelling in Dellentash's Lear Jet when it mysteriously crashed in the Atlantic Ocean, killing all on board. Ruggiero was a mob associate of New York's Gambino family and linked to the Sicilian Mafia in Canada. He had been on the run for six years.

The music business, it transpired, was just a sideline for Dellentash. It was revealed he was working with Ruggiero and was in fact one of America's premier drug smugglers. Since 1979 he'd been importing millions of dollars of Pablo Escobar's cannabis and cocaine from Colombia's famous Medellin cartel directly into New York. He was also involved in major heroin smuggling.

In the aftermath of Ruggiero's death there were serious questions asked of Dellentash about the whereabouts of a large shipment of heroin and quantities of cash. The crash also attracted the attention of the FBI who suspected Dellentash was involved high up in the chain of the mob or he was a Mafioso. He was, he later admitted, holding Ruggiero's heroin. He tried to move it and was busted. He said he was relieved when he realised it was the police who burst through the motel door. He thought it was a hit.

Dellentash would receive a 25-year sentence, 15 years for conspiracy to distribute heroin and 10 years for possession of felony weapons. In 1986 he testified in the high profile trial of Gambino crime family leader John Gotti and would be released from prison after serving just five years. "He was one of the biggest drug dealers in America," said Galfas, "I had no idea. I never saw him drink or do a drug. One day he called and he said, 'I'm not going to see you for a while, I'm in prison.'" Dellentash's major music industry client Meat Loaf would file for bankruptcy in 1983 and accuse his former manager of misappropriating funds.

The Rollers' *Ricochet* project collapsed. Album sales were laughable. The videos gathered dust. There was no point continuing. Faure went back to South Africa. It was the end for the Rollers.

"There was no money coming in," said Faure. "By the time I'd been there three and half years I hadn't seen a royalty cheque. There was no joy because we weren't getting any money. Things turned sour."

The other band members were stuck. They could not afford to continue to use the services of Martin Goldberg nor to pay for their legal costs. Their tax bills threatened to wipe them out. The case against Stephen Goldberg in London collapsed. The firm of Goldberg Ravden went on to represent many star names, such as George Michael, before the partnership of Stephen Goldberg and David Ravden ended and the company was dissolved in 1987. The band did get some money. They settled out of court with their American accountant Stephen Tenenbaum. He paid them a figure reputed to be close to $2 million. All the ALK Enterprises companies, including the band members' individual limited companies, were placed into liquidation, the most common form of bankruptcy. The publishing company, Bay City Music, that owned all the Rollers' song copyrights, was sold off in the liquidation sale for a reputed $1.5 million but the money went not to the band but to satisfy the bankruptcy courts, chiefly to pay for the tax still owing. What had happened to the tens of millions the band had generated from merchandising, record sales, touring and publishing would never now be completely or satisfactorily explained.

There was a confidentiality agreement attached to the settlement with Tenenbaum that involved much detail about the relationship between ALK, Arista and the band. Tenenbaum went on to advise Yoko Ono in the affairs of John Lennon and spend over 25 years as advisor to Apple Corps, the company that runs The Beatles' affairs. He also enjoyed a successful relationship of at least a decade with film director and movie star, Woody Allen, whom he currently manages. The contract Arista had with the now defunct ALK was rewritten with the band members simply placed into the existing framework instead of ALK. Arista owned all the band's recordings "in perpetuity", forever.

Faulkner, Wood, the Longmuirs and McKeown shared the $2 million settlement money. Sterling was strong and it translated to approximately £1 million. It was not enough to cover their individual tax bills – the band said they faced immediate demands of close to half a million pound each. McKeown wrote that he had managed to get a £180,000 payment out of the band.

"If I said we got £120,000 each for the whole period I'd be exaggerating," said Faulkner. "And we got a tax bill on millions."

"These people around us took everything," Faulkner added. "They eat you up and spit you out. They don't want to take some of your money. They want to take all of it, everything. Those business types don't give a damn about anybody, you're just a commodity to them."

"We got nothing," said McKeown. "It was fucked up so bad, you could employ a team of 100 experts and it would take years to unravel it."

CHAPTER 13

Humiliation

"[They are owed] tens of millions... probably more... with interest and merchandising. They have never been paid by their exclusive record label for all global earnings. The scale of this rip off is incredible. The band has been ill-treated but we will win every penny they are owed in the end."
— Mark St John.

McKeown and Faulkner were forced to bury their differences pretty quickly. The lure of money led to The Bay City Rollers reforming for a September 1982 matinee and early evening show at the Budokan in Tokyo. McKeown "feeling vulnerable and pretty desperate" was high on cocaine and dressed in plain denim jeans and denim jacket. Faulkner, who'd brokered the gig, was bulky in a sleeveless leather jacket and leather trousers. He seemed drunk.

Wood flew in from Los Angeles where he and Duncan Faure had formed a three-piece band called Karu. He was tanned and wearing a hideous towelling headband. The Longmuir brothers looked less like rock stars by the minute. They seemed bemused by life. Wood stayed on bass and Alan played second guitar. The reception from the crowd was a fillip. They had sold 20,000 tickets for the two shows. The band avoided fighting, mimed on several TV shows, took the money and promised to be back. The visit coincided with the release of a Japanese greatest hits package, *And Forever*, released by Nippon Phonogram, the country's new Arista licensee.

Back in Los Angeles, Wood and Faure were working with former Managing Director of Bay City Music, Colin Slater, who had become Karu's manager. "They had wanted to leave Scotland and England just to get away from the acrimony within the band," said Slater. "Woody could seriously not give me an answer why that was happening." The two musicians were the same age, just 25, and socialised with a hard-core crowd of former Roller groupies. Faure managed to buy a house in Granada Hills, San Fernando Valley, where Wood took up residence. There was much drinking and partying. Around four, sometimes more, young teenage women also lived at the house. There were orgies and much screaming and freaking out. Karu cut material for an album but could not get a major deal and struggled to make money, so one of the girls who lived at the house made a few adult films to pay the bills.

Former Bay City Roller Ian Mitchell had also made an adult film. After quitting Rosetta Stone he had pursued a solo career, fronting a pop rock outfit called the Ian Mitchell Band that toured Japan, where his attachment to the Rollers and Rosetta Stone guaranteed him a following. He was at best an average vocalist but he'd released two albums as the Ian Mitchell Band in Japan.

More recently he'd revamped and renamed the outfit, La Rox, and gone glam metal. He often played in drag, sometimes dressed as a schoolgirl. The band had a song called 'Jailbait'. La Rox played small venues in London, going nowhere but were notable for having Lindsay Honey, aka future porn superstar Ben Dover, on drums. Via Honey and his partner, porn star Linzi Drew, Mitchell had been drawn into the porn industry, the cover star of the video, *Rock & Roll Ransom,* released in 1982. Honey, who directed the porno, said he had learned to have sex in front of other people in La Rox's dressing rooms after shows. Mitchell was also said to be involved in the making of other porn videos.

By early 1983, he was aged 24, with long, backcombed hair and a penchant for leopard skin. He smoked and drank heavily and was fond of drugs. But he still, just, had the looks that had made him "the centre of attention" at Little Kellerstain. He was slight, only five foot six inches, and boyishly cute.

Faulkner, about to turn 30, now asked Mitchell to re-join The Bay City Rollers for a plan he was hatching. It got more bizarre. He was also recruiting guitarist Pat McGlynn, who had briefly replaced Mitchell in the Rollers before re-joining his brother's band, Wot's Up. They were a tight disco funk outfit, and had used McGlynn's Rollers fame to good effect too. Under the tutelage of songwriter/producer Miki Antony, a former Bell Records act, they signed to Japanese label King and were rebranded as Pat McGlynn's Scotties and then as the Pat McGlynn Band. Antony claimed two of the band's albums, released in 1977 and 1978, heavy with manufactured bubblegum pop, went platinum in Japan with sales of over 250,000. They'd made several visits to the country for concerts. It was all over by 1979, however, and since then, McGlynn's musical career had failed to reignite.

Living in Edinburgh, still slight and boyish-looking with a disconcerting hillbilly mullet, he was broke, having made nothing from the music business. McKeown, also back living in Edinburgh, knocked about with McGlynn. The two shared a passion for cocaine, and were seen often scoring at Tam Paton's Little Kellerstain home.

Faulkner had put together a new Rollers single, a cover version of the 1981 Bucks Fizz single, 'Piece Of The Action', for release in Japan on a new label Teichiku, a leading pop label in the country. The deal had nothing to do with Arista. For a man keen to establish credibility as a musician, covering Bucks Fizz was perverse to say the least. The Abba-esque Eurovision Song Contest winners had scored three number ones and become one of the top-selling British groups of the early eighties but they were taken even less seriously than the Rollers.

Their career had been overseen by RCA Records A&R boss, Bill Kimber, who had previously produced Bell Records pop act Hello (one time rivals to the Rollers) and Alan Longmuir's 1977 solo single, 'I'm Confessing'. Kimber was a pal of the Rollers' old and trusted musical director Colin Frechter and had a hand in Faulkner's plans. At the time Kimber was A&R-ing Eurythmics and was the brains behind Minipops, the kiddie group who covered the hits of the day, as part of the currently controversial Mike Mansfield Enterprises TV show of the same name. Critics had dubbed the TV show, where young kids often dressed in raunchy adult outfits and performed with adult suggestion, kiddie porn.

Huge concert dates were lined up for the seven-piece Rollers in Japan for July 1983 and there were plans to record a live album at the Budokan, also for release on Teichiku. Faulkner was advertising the dates and the new line-up as the 'Rollers Carnival', hence the new improved seven-piece line-up. They mimed the single 'Piece Of The Action' on a Japanese TV show, looking interesting as a four-guitar line-up. McGlynn and Mitchell's youth cleverly camouflaged the ageing band appearance (35-year-old Alan was at the back on keyboards) but the sound did not reflect the guitar-heavy line-up. It was lightweight, dominated by synth and processed synth bass.

The show travelled to major cities such as Sapporo and there were spotlight moments for each member with songs by McGlynn and McKeown/Ryder included in long sets that featured a mix of the Rollers' biggest hits plus more mature later material. The live album sold well.

The seven-piece Bay City Rollers tentatively played live in the UK at the two-day Futurama 5 Festival at the Queens Hall, Leeds, on September 17, 1983. They were a last minute replacement for proposed headliner Howard Devoto, formerly of Buzzcocks. For their first performance in the UK since 1977, they had two female backing vocalists. One was Janine Andrews, a former Page 3 model who had a role in the Bond film *Octopussy* and had dated Duran Duran's John Taylor. Faulkner was helping her explore a career in music.

The Smiths pulled out of the event at the last minute after learning the Rollers were Devoto's replacement, prompting a near riot. The Bay City Rollers, headlining on Saturday night, were bottled off despite there being a large contingent of their old fans present. They were a curious addition to a bill made up exclusively of leftfield post punk performers such as Danielle Dax and John Cooper Clarke. McKeown ended up in a fight with members of the audience. The police had to be called to restore order and McKeown was arrested.

They fared better in London where they had a sold-out show at the fashionable 2,000-capacity Lyceum theatre in late 1983. The Japanese activity had gone largely unnoticed in the UK and there was some media interest in the news that the Rollers had 'reformed' for the date.

They also announced they were making a new album, purportedly commissioned for an unnamed film project. In 1984 they began to cut new songs in Edinburgh's Planet Studios. Faulkner, initially, was upbeat. He had hopes for a song he'd co-written with Janine Andrews, 'This Could Be Love'. There were more sessions in Palladium Studios in the city with Faulkner acting as producer.

McKeown was now badly addicted to cocaine. He was also feeling suicidal and having therapy. He'd recently sold a house in Cornwall where his mum and dad lived to invest in a snooker hall with his brother Brian. He said his brother had ripped him off. He was not in good shape. One night he broke into the studio and destroyed the tapes of the album in the making. He said he didn't like the way the material was sounding.

Derek decided it was time to bail out and was soon followed by the equally disgruntled Alan. Faulkner also backed off. The film project fell through. McKeown and the equally cocaine-fuelled McGlynn, who had begun dating Janine Andrews, were left in charge of the recording. They co-wrote the majority of the songs on the finished product, recorded with session men in Matrix Studios in London. They had overseen a soulless body of ersatz jazz-funk synth pop in an attempt to sound contemporary alongside current pop hit acts Duran Duran and Level 42.

Wood contributed one song to the new album that was called *Breakout*. His band with Faure, Karu, had found some success in South Africa, where their single 'Where Is The Music' had reached number two, but had now run its course. Wood had abandoned Los Angeles and moved to South Africa. He introduced a new drummer, George Spencer, to the band to replace Derek.

There were a slew of dates booked for The Bay City Rollers in 1985 and Wood was keen to have Faure involved. He had been invited but was unable to take part in the Roller Carnival due to restrictions on South Africans travelling to Japan, thus denying the world an eight-piece Rollers line-up. Faure played live with the band in Edinburgh and did 12 shows with them in Dublin in the early summer of 1985. In Ireland McKeown recalled playing in working men's clubs on stages made of Formica tables held together with tape.

Faure could not continue with the group as they headed for gigs in Japan and Australia. The Rollers could no longer fill the 12,000-capacity Budokan in Tokyo and instead, in July 1985, played a 3,000-capacity amphitheatre in a park in the heart of Tokyo, near the Imperial Palace grounds. The show featured up to 60 minutes of the new album material with 30 minutes devoted to the old hits. The album, *Breakout*, and the lead single from it, 'When You Find Out', released under a new Japanese deal with Polydor, sold poorly. A briefcase full of the band's money was also reputedly stolen in Japan.

In Australia the new album was being released by Powderworks, the label that distributed Mute Records (home to Depeche Mode and Nick Cave) in the country. But the gigs, spread over an optimistic eight weeks, were all in pubs and clubs. It was an experience far removed from the hysteria McGlynn had witnessed here in late 1976 on his first tour with the group. Back then the Australia media feared someone would get killed during wild scenes at the 'astonishing and dangerous' concerts. Nine years on the band were ragged and beleaguered, a mixture of bare-chests, hair spray and over-sized tartan suits (with the sleeves rolled up). Janine Andrews and another female vocalist Karen Prosser were on the tour providing backing vocals.

Faulkner told the Australian *Woman's Weekly*: "We're here to say we're back together, we're deadly serious, we have a new album out and there is life after the hysteria. Our musical direction has changed a lot. The songs are a bit blacker, funkier and great to dance to."

The new act and album was not a success in Australia. The band was also disgruntled to find Arista had recently released a *Greatest Hits* album in the country without their knowledge. They were concerned that the label was not paying them record royalties on such releases.

The Australian tour was "a nightmare", said McKeown. "None of us had grown-up. We were still like children." The most shocking incident came when McGlynn head-butted Wood, leaving the 28-year-old bleeding heavily on the floor. "I broke Woody's nose in Australia," McGlynn told me. "I knocked him up and down the place. I gave him a right doing. I smashed him to bits."

There were many unresolved issues between the two. They had played together in a teen band before either had joined the Rollers. McGlynn, understandably, still had major difficulties with dealing with his experiences at the hands of Paton although he had yet to go public with his accusations of rape and sexual abuse. Wood, he felt, had not done enough to intervene. "Tam would call you to his room and as he would be telling you how bad it was to go with girls and how you'd be better with boys," said McGlynn. "Then he'd try to get you to drink and take drugs…"

"A lot of people who ended up at Little Kellerstain had a difficult time with Tam abusing them and feeding them up with drink and drugs," he surmised.

In Australia, the anger he'd felt spilled over. He felt Wood and Faulkner were putting up a wall of silence about Paton while he was keen to expose what went on behind the scenes. "If they, or Alan or Derek, had opened their mouths I'd have been able to get Tam Paton jailed for the things he put me through," he said.

McGlynn went further. He claimed members of the band were afraid to speak out because they were protecting themselves as they had been complicit in Paton's behaviour. "I knew what was going on. I saw it with my own eyes."

"I would go into a hotel room and Tam would be having sex," McGlynn said. "I'd have to sit there while he was having orgies and he'd try and get me to join in. He'd want me to wank someone off and suck his cock. They'd be in bed with each other, wanking each other off and sucking each other's knobs and shagging each other. I used to see them doing it and they'd try and get me involved. I'd say, 'Get to fuck, I'm not doing it. Suck your own dick.'"

In his autobiography, McKeown – in barely-concealed dream sequences – also makes reference to gay orgies involving Paton taking place during the band's heyday. He has a particularly lurid dream involving Paton, Faulkner and Wood.

McGlynn said he had re-joined the band for the money but also "so I could get back near Faulkner, Wood and [Derek] Longmuir to try and expose them. I wasn't interested in the Rollers, I was trying to get these guys locked up."

Faulkner, who'd been acting as band manager, quit the Australia tour with many dates still to play. He left with backing singer Karen Prosser. "She was a fan of the band," said McGlynn.

Police questioned Faulkner at the airport about $3,500 McKeown and McGlynn thought he was trying to steal from the band. They also soon quit the tour, leaving Wood, Mitchell and drummer Spencer to complete the dates. It was surely the end.

McKeown's coke habit was raging. In 1986 he earned £20,000 from a tabloid newspaper for a kiss-and-tell about his time with Britt Ekland. "I needed drugs, I was a junkie, that's why I sold the story," he said. He also squeezed one last payday out of the Rollers. In April 1986, he, McGlynn and Mitchell played a handful of dates in Japan as The Bay City Rollers. McKeown said Wood came along too and they used a drum machine rather than pay a drummer. It was a new low.

In London Faulkner worked with Karen Prosser, aka Kass, on a project initially called the Eric Faulkner Co-Operative. It quickly morphed into a band called The New Rollers. He and Kass ran a fan club from Faulkner's Chelsea home knocking out mail order tapes such as the (previously unreleased) *Burning Rubber* soundtrack and *Bay City Take Two*, ten versions of the old band hits by The New Rollers with Faulkner and Kass singing.

There was also a collection of Faulkner demos for sale and a chance to buy a collection of poems by him plus the first three chapters of an autobiography he was writing. Chapters were being sold separately. Prices ranged from between £25 for the album tapes to £7 for the poems. Faulkner also funded the making and release of a seven-inch EP by The New Rollers on his own label. The title track, 'Party Hardy' was co-penned with Kass.

He added backing musicians for gigs, with Kass sharing centre stage alongside him. Faulkner had grown weightier and his hair was an overblown mullet. He did not look good. He played a clutch of dates in America, where the band was billed as The New Bay City Rollers. They were filmed performing 'Saturday Night' and 'I Only Wanna Be With You' live on a Detroit daytime TV show. It was excruciatingly bad.

Over Christmas 1988 Faulkner and Kass recorded the album *Life Is A Wasteland* with only the help of a drum machine. It was another fan club tape. Under the revised name of the Rollers, they and their put-together band schlepped around the UK, picking up what work they could in in universities, pubs and clubs. There was very little else they could squeeze out of the name.

In 1989, Faulkner rescued a pensioner trying to drown himself at Bexhill-on-Sea in East Sussex. The press reported that he said to the man: "You think you've got problems – I used to play guitar with The Bay City Rollers."

Wood hooked up with Faulkner and Kass in 1989 for a tour of Australia. The band was billed as The Bay City Rollers. Wood had been playing in jazz/rock fusion band Neill Solomon & the Passengers in South Africa. The group had reached number five in the charts with a single 'Hold On' that Wood had co-written. They had also written the theme tune to TV series *Honeytown* and just released their debut album. "We were big fish in a very small pond," Wood said. They were painful to listen to. He was preparing to return to Scotland.

Alan Longmuir, who had briefly tried his hand at managing a Scottish band to little success, re-joined in 1990. He had just divorced his wife after five years of marriage and was drinking heavily. It was reported they had a child together. The hotel he owned and had run with his wife had gone bankrupt, and his farm in Dollar, near Stirling, was going as part of the divorce settlement.

Faulkner arranged more European gigs under the banner of The Bay City Rollers. Alan, Wood, Faulkner and Kass with a pick-up drummer played to an impressive crowd of 4,000 in Germany in August 1990. They were on the oldies circuit. But at least they could make money.

Faulkner was 37. He shrewdly bought back, from the liquidator, the Bay City Music publishing company that had gone bankrupt in 1981. In the intervening years it had been picked apart, all the major hits stripped from the company, but the majority of the minor Faulkner/ Wood songs from across the nine studio albums the band had made between 1974-1981 were now back under his ownership.

This line-up of the Rollers made several recordings available in the early nineties, often via the fan club. There was a live tape, a single on Faulkner's own label – a version of the unofficial Scottish national anthem 'Flower Of Scotland' – and two CDs. The first, called *Bye Bye Baby*, included a mix of new songs and re-recordings of old hits. The second was a *Greatest Hits* CD made up purely of re-workings of old hits. Kass, Faulkner and Wood shared vocals. These were low budget, poor quality affairs but met with some commercial success. The *Scottish Sun* gave away a CD with some of these tracks on them.

This version of The Bay City Rollers toured the UK, playing reasonable sized venues such as the King George's Hall in Blackburn, with the odd standout show such as playing with The Sweet to 18,000 in Chelmsford, Essex. They also made several appearances on TV, including a guest spot on *The Word*. Faulkner even filmed a commercial for Skol lager. "Buy me one and we'll cancel the comeback," was the line.

It was a living. "Being a Bay City Roller was the only job open to me," said Faulkner.

"People think we got paid millions when Rollermania was at its peak, but we didn't. That's why we had to keep touring, to survive. The bills didn't stop coming in, but the royalties did. If you only cover your old hits, you become a parody. But for years we had to do old stuff to survive."

There were more gigs planned for Europe, America, Japan and Canada. Then Alan had a heart attack while walking down the street in Stirling. He said he had actually "slipped away" in hospital and was brought back to life by a defibrillator. He described the experience as "incredibly scary". He spent three weeks in hospital.

After abandoning plans to open a fast food restaurant in London, McKeown had, in the late-eighties, briefly reinvigorated his solo career. In Germany he'd hooked up with writer/producer Dieter Bohlen, from the country's leading pop groups Modern Talking and Blue System, and their first single together 'She's A Lady' was a hit on the German charts. The success did not translate to any other territory.

Now 32, McKeown found himself miming the lightweight synth pop track on TV shows. He looked lost or out of it. One memorable German TV clip shows him bounding up to the stage and slipping over on steps leading up to it. As he struggled to his feet his vocals were already booming out on the backing track. He did get his act together, becoming increasingly polished and smartly turned out, but the material he made with Bohlen grew weaker – instantly forgettable Euro-pop. Nonetheless, in 1989, they had a run of five more minor hits in Germany capped by an album called *It's A Game* (the same title previously used for a Rollers album) that was also was released in Japan.

In early 1990, he made a return to the public eye in the UK attempting to represent Great Britain in the Eurovision Song Contest. He sang the song, 'Ball And Chain', live on BBC1 during the televised heats but came fifth. The song was co-written by guitarist Danny McIntosh who would soon marry Kate Bush.

In London he played small clubs with an act called The Fabulous Tartan Army during which he emerged from a coffin, wearing a crown, cape and flares, to sing a techno version of 'Bye Bye Baby'. The idea was that he was back from the dead. "It's fun, it's light," he said. "There's scope for new things."

McKeown had failed to get a grip on his cocaine consumption. He was also now mixing the drug with heroin and Ecstasy and had begun to booze heavily. Out of desperation and hunger for easy cash, he began to put together, with the help of Danny McIntosh, his own version of The Bay City Rollers, a rival act to the Faulkner, Wood, Alan and Kass version. He was booked to play the illustrious 2,000-capacity Town & Country in London as 'Les McKeown's Bay City Rollers'.

A week before the September 7, 1991 gig he received a solicitor's letter from Faulkner explaining that it was actually illegal, an infringement of copyright, for McKeown to use the name Bay City Rollers for the gig or any future gigs. This was followed by a High Court injunction. Faulkner, along with fellow directors Kass, Wood and the Longmuir brothers, owned a company called Bay City Rollers Ltd, which had trademarked the band name.

McKeown believed Faulkner was envious he could play a venue like the Town & Country while their version of the band could play only small clubs and pubs. Faulkner's injunction stated that McKeown was damaging the band's name, was trading on their market and it was confusing for the public. In a press interview Faulkner referred to McKeown as an unemployed van driver.

In February 1992 the High Court ruled that McKeown could continue to use The Bay City Rollers' name but only if he included a prefix of an historical description such as 'formerly of' or 'previously of' (and when in written form these descriptions or descriptive words should be of at least equal size and in the same colour and design as those of the remaining words). All told, it had cost Faulkner and Bay City Rollers Ltd an estimated £208,000 in legal fees. All the money they'd made from the Skol ad, gloated McKeown.

He now gleefully booked more gigs as 'Les McKeown's 70s Bay City Rollers' or 'Les McKeown's Legendary Bay City Rollers'. He felt the new band names were an improvement on 'Les McKeown's Bay City Rollers' and suggested his band was more original than Faulkner's version. As themed out of season weekends in holiday camps began to become more popular, the Butlins circuit opened up to him in the UK and in early 1992 he persuaded Ian Mitchell to join his Rollers for gigs in Germany and Europe. He bragged of playing to crowds of 5,000 and described the venture as "a nice little earner". Now, in his mid-thirties, he was on the oldies circuit too.

Alan recovered from his heart attack and re-joined The Bay City Rollers, often tagged as the Original Bay City Rollers, for a 1992 tour of Scandinavia. The following year they toured the UK, America and Japan. In America, an unemployed music fan stole their guitars and hid them in a derelict house. He later told a court he was trying to "save the world from The Bay City Rollers".

"We played in Tokyo to an audience whose ages ranged from 20 to 50, and we had an audience of 12,000 at Westchester, near New York," said Wood. In 1994 they released a tape, *Ruff Roughs*, of all new songs via their fan club and extensively toured Germany and the UK again, playing the college and festival circuit, and sometimes pubs.

Still drinking heavily, Alan suffered a second cardiac arrest in January 1995, spending time on a life support machine. The drinking, he admitted, had become "a problem". On re-joining the band he vowed to cut down. Following the release of a cheap German CD, *New Recordings*, which compiled their versions of the old hits, Kass left the band in 1996. None of the material she and Faulkner had written together had gone anywhere. Faulkner put out a final solo album of demos via the fan club before it folded. He had reputedly invested in a recording studio in Camden that had gone bankrupt. In June 1996, Alan was again rushed to hospital after collapsing hours before he was due on stage with Faulkner and Wood. He missed a string of dates but insisted the problem was "not as serious as the last time".

McKeown's band featuring, briefly, Terry Chimes, the original Clash drummer, and Mitchell, re-recorded the old Rollers' hits for cheap CD releases in Japan and in the UK. McKeown and Mitchell had no qualms about stepping back into the classic all-white, tartan-trimmed uniforms. They toured Japan and East Germany and, in early 1995, America. Mitchell, who had relocated to California and was selling himself as a "motivational speaker", ended up missing gigs due to excessive alcohol consumption and was hospitalised before the end of the tour.

Faulkner silently fumed over McKeown's version of the band. He found that often, especially in America and Germany, his version of the group was fighting over the same gig bookings with McKeown's. And promoters only wanted one Bay City Rollers. The animosity between the two groups was accentuated by a band of no more than 50 hard-core Rollers fans, predominantly American women who had been fans in their teens. McKeown claimed a late 1995 tour of Canada and an early 1996 tour of America were plagued by problems that had been stirred by Faulkner and his loyal group of fans, resulting in a string of cancelled gigs. McKeown, however, also had his own fervent group of female fans that he could manipulate.

The two versions of the group had split the hardcore fan base down the middle. The Internet made it easier for these fans to band together on chat rooms and their number was expanding all the time. There had been a fan gathering, a 'Rollerfest', in 1995 in Las Vegas [attended by McGlynn, Mitchell and Nobby Clark] and in 1996 three dedicated Bay City Rollers fan websites sprang up, two based in Germany. That year there were two fan gatherings, one in Japan and the other in Bay City, Michigan – the city the group was purportedly named after.

About 100 fans attended the Michigan event dubbed the 'Absolute Rollerfest 96'. They sang karaoke versions of the group's hits and there was a best costume winner as the fans, mainly middle-aged women, took the opportunity to wear the classic Roller gear again. They watched 30 hours of Bay City Rollers on video and saw an acoustic performance by Ian Mitchell. "I didn't know what to expect when I came here," Mitchell said. "But it is so cool. There is such an outpouring of love." His wife was involved in organising these Rollerfests. In August 1997 there was another in California. "We're all grown up now, but here, we can forget our problems and remember when times were simpler," said one of the organisers. It was the devotion of these fans that sustained the group.

There had been little communication between Arista Records and the Rollers since the band had settled with Stephen Tenenbaum in 1981 and signed the new contract with the label. After overseeing the sale of Arista to BMG, Clive Davis had seen the label slide dramatically, losing approximately $70 million in 1983. BMG had panicked and dumped a 50 per cent stake of Arista on to RCA for a sale price of zero. The supremacy of Davis as a record mogul seemed at an end. Then he discovered Whitney Houston who went on to become Arista's biggest selling artist of all time with sales of over 200 million. In the late eighties Davis made a label deal with La Face Records which brought Arista the huge girl group TLC. He was back on top. After a series of mergers, BMG ended up acquiring RCA Records for around $600 million, and took back control of Arista.

The individual Rollers were supposed to receive royalty statements every six months, detailing how many records the band had sold in that period and in total. They were also supposed to get royalty payments every six months, earnings based on a percentage of record sales. In the turmoil of the early eighties, a period when the band was not recouping their recording costs on album sales, the missing paperwork had been easy to overlook. But since then it had been a constant issue. The band members claimed they had repeatedly asked for but never received any accounts from Arista.

Meanwhile, the label had been releasing greatest hits type Bay City Rollers albums around the world, notably Australia, Germany and Japan. Since the late eighties the releases had been on the new compact disc format. The band knew from the sales on their own fan club type CD recordings that there was a strong appetite for their back catalogue. But they claimed, due to the lack of official figures, they did not know how many records Arista was selling, nor were they being paid royalties on the sales.

It was not just the band compilations. There had been scores of Best Of The 70s-type compilation albums that featured individual Rollers songs released over the past 15 years, perhaps as many as 200. The number had increased rapidly in the CD era, with Arista licensing various Rollers masters for at least 23 separate compilations in 1996, 34 in 1997, with 26 more instances in the first half of 1998 alone. The *Guardian* stated that between 1996 and 1998 Bay City Rollers hits were released on 118 albums worldwide. Arista also generated money from merchandising licenses and master synchronisation licenses (such as television, commercial and movie rights). In 1993 the band's track 'Saturday Night' featured prominently in the Mike Myers' film *So I Married An Axe Murderer*. The band said they had not received payments on any of this from Arista since 1981, thus in some part explaining their increasingly forlorn actions to generate cash.

In 1996 there were press reports of a total amount now said to be almost £3.5 million in royalties owing the band. Arista was purportedly holding the cash in an American bank account until an agreement with the band could be brokered. A spokesman for the label was quoted as saying there was such animosity between the individual band members "they can't agree on who should get what".

McKeown said it was the animosity between himself and Faulkner that had prevented Arista paying royalties to the band. Neither, he said, trusted the other to fairly divide the income. There appeared to be a dispute within the group, that Arista was aware of, about what amounts individual band members should get.

Furthermore, it was reported that Arista would release the money if the group reformed to promote a new best of compilation album, *Absolute Rollers*, planned for release in the UK and Europe. Arista was talking about advertising the release with a "megamix" single of four tracks backed by a major TV advertising campaign. There was suggestion of the band reforming for a fundraiser in the wake of the 1996 Dunblane School massacre in Stirling. Ultimately, there would be no reunion; the Roller's internal fissures were too great.

The promo plans for the compilation album were quickly scrapped. A spokesman for Arista Records said: "It would have been a nightmare to get them all together. Former lead singer Les McKeown was originally involved in the album release, but we soon decided against involving any of the band." Still the label had great hopes for the £15 album: "I think an album with every Bay City Rollers hit on it will do very well. After all, they were the Take That of their day. There have been several collections of Rollers songs before, but none of them have had all the greatest hits on the same album."

There was no satisfactory resolution to the question of the band's royalties. A disappointed McKeown said: "I don't believe there's £3.5 million there. But if there is what would be left for the Rollers if we tried to get it, by the time the agents, the lawyers and everybody else get their share? I'm not too bothered. If someone sends me a fat cheque, fine. But I'm not chasing after it. I'd rather we met just to sort our relationship out."

Faulkner, however, was bothered. The news of £3.5 million being owed the band had attracted widespread interest. He hired Mark St John to look at the situation. St John was an eccentric figure, with long hair and black leggings, who came with an illustrious pedigree of having worked for heavyweight Led Zeppelin manager Peter Grant and partnered Danny Sims, the Mob-connected former manager/producer of Bob Marley, whose estate he now helps run.

St John had a reputation for representing acts that had been short-changed by their record companies over unpaid royalties. "Right against might," the 43 year old called the struggle, describing himself as "the Robin Hood of rock'n'roll". In the early nineties he had taken on EMI on behalf of The Pretty Things and scored a significant victory: winning the band back all their master tapes, copyrights and an undisclosed sum of money as settlement. "I bite the legs of the bigger boys," he said, describing himself as a man "who sues record companies for a living".

St John immediately told the press that Arista owed the group more than the reported £3.5million. He suggested the Rollers were owed 'tens of millions... probably more... with interest and merchandising. They have never been paid by their exclusive record label for all global earnings. The scale of this rip off is incredible. The band has been ill-treated but we will win every penny they are owed in the end."

The two band factions went back to gigging. McKeown released another CD of his version of the band doing the Rollers' greatest hits as well as a solo hits collection. In February 1997, while drinking and watching the rugby at a pub, Alan had a stroke that temporarily left him with no feeling on his left side. The stroke, he said, was caused by a blood clot on the brain. He blamed stress. "I've had a lot on my mind," he said. "But that's me, I've always been a natural worrier. I've been going on stage for 30 years but each time I feel sick with nerves." He said he was now "determined not to worry about things so much". The Bay City Rollers, with just Wood and Faulkner as original members, toured America without him.

St John was aggressively pursuing Arista and in September 1997 he managed to squeeze a one-off payment of approximately £230,000 out of the label. In what he described as "a fractured dialogue of correspondence", Arista promised St John, "on many occasions", to pay the band in full. He was astonished that Arista had not provided the band with royalty statements for such a long period of time. The label argued they had been unable to release the money because they had requested and not yet received a change of address/payee letter signed by "each of the parties duly authorised to execute such modification". St John though this was a poor excuse.

"In 1981 when the band were put into the stead of ALK, they entered into an agreement [with Arista] and the agent for payment was set up as

Arrow, Edelstein & Laird, who were the band's then lawyers," he said. "They were based in New York and after 21 months, during which time they hadn't recovered a payment despite numerous requests, they moved to LA, informing all their clients and their agency payees of the new address. Additionally as Peter Shukat [a partner at the firm] was representing the band and Barry Manilow [Arista's main act pre-Whitney], the suggestion that they [Arista] couldn't know where the agents for payments and account recipients were is nonsense."

St John held several meetings with various members of Arista's legal team. At one point he recalled being told by an Arista representative that there "were no records available to create any past royalty accounts". St John began collecting all the various contracts, statements and legal documents held by the band. Faulkner had collected much of it, pestering Paton for paperwork. The band's former manager had been happy to comply. Paton's partner, Ray Cotter, had spent many afternoons faxing through to Faulkner any relevant documents and letters left at the Little Kellerstain office. He said Faulkner and Kass got "quite friendly" again with Paton who claimed Faulkner had even asked him to manage the band again.

"They were basically asking us to furnish them with photocopies of letters from Clive Davis and Arista," said Cotter. "Have you got this contract, that contract... funny enough a lot of contracts were in the office gathering dust." Cotter said Faulkner and Kass visited Little Kellerstain and looked through Paton's books and paperwork. Derek and Alan had done the same. "I was trying to assist them with any information they wanted," Paton said.

It was abundantly clear the paperwork was incomplete. It came as little surprise when, in 2006, a British bargain-hunter actually found a stack of the Rollers' financial documents under a potato masher in a £3 box of kitchenware she'd bought at a house clearance.

St John tried to simplify things. The Rollers had entered into two record deals. The first, with Bell Records, was struck in the early seventies. "We couldn't do anything about [any money owing on] that," said St John. "We were out of time on it [the maximum time after an event when legal proceedings may be initiated under the statute of limitation laws]." The second record deal was made with Arista in 1975. "Bell was signed under British law, Arista signed under New York State law with ALK acting for the band," said St John. "There was no connection between the agreements. They were two different agreements, two different companies, two different jurisdictions.

"When I came along I was able to maintain the case against Arista by getting them to acknowledge a debt against the Rollers. We were already out of time [the statute of limitations was set at six years in America] but I came along and kept up a barrage of letters and meetings at my own cost and eventually I got a letter from the head of legals [at Arista] that acknowledged the debt which got the clock running again, otherwise there would have been no case against Arista."

As far as the rest of the band's business, St John said he could find no accounts pertaining to merchandising money. He claimed the Rollers had sold more merchandising than any act barring The Beatles and Elvis and that the income from it should have been astronomical. "I can't even find where it went," he said. "It certainly did not go to the band members. I'm not saying the merchandisers didn't pay, everybody paid and it went into the machinery operated by the accountants and professionals." He estimated that including record royalties, publishing incomes, merchandising and touring, the band had during their peak "probably generated in excess of $1 billion in turnover and at least 25 per cent of that was profit".

St John blamed Paton for not keeping on top of business but did not think he had swindled the band. "He was not up to the task," St John said. "Tam was incredibly stupid. He was not up to managing a band that was a multinational success. I think he was totally blindsided by the big lawyers. If he went into an office and there was a lot of marble and pictures on the wall and people in Brook Brothers suits he was impressed. This is just a working-class guy who used to carry sacks of spuds around and liked to bugger people up the arse behind the van. He made some terrible deals for them."

Ultimately, though, it didn't matter where vast tranches of that money had gone. St John couldn't do anything about much of what had happened. All he could do was focus on fighting Arista to get the band the record royalties they were due. He was able to put a figure on it now: he told the press the "missing royalties" Arista actually owed the band stood at £35 million, and with interest, was "now estimated" at £200 million. He said that The Bay City Rollers had been "financially destroyed" by the situation and by their "huge past losses at the hands of certain of their past advisors". He talked in the media about a "rock'n'roll tragedy" and "pain and financial deprivation".

One issue that particularly aroused his curiosity pertained to the 1981 agreement Arista had made with the band, when the Rollers were substituted directly into the existing 1975 contract in ALK's place. "In 1975 it wasn't entirely unheard of to have a corporate structure deal where accountants sat in front of the band allowing the band some tax protection," said St John. "But in 1981, having removed the cumbersome entity of ALK, it would make much more sense for Arista in terms of payment and their accounts to set it up as a simple artist deal.

"ALK was a deliberately structured artifice to bring potential tax benefit but operated always by extremely specific professionals," he added. "With those professionals deliberately removed and the situation being deliberately simplified the natural thing to do would have been to sign the Rollers directly to the label and tear down the ALK arrangement. By keeping that structure in place, to just put the band instead of ALK, it meant that, essentially Woody becomes ALK. It's five blokes from Edinburgh with zero professional skills. They're not accountants. All sorts of things were required of them; operation of all the income, operation of the publishing companies, operation of the third party companies, of the producers."

St John even felt the 1981 agreement had been "potentially unlawful" as parts of it were "unenforceable". It was an extremely complex legal situation. The band, he said, didn't understand the contract when they signed it. They still didn't.

Although he claimed Arista could not supply him with statements from 1981-1995, St John had received royalty statements from Arista for 1996 and 1997. He claimed they were "unsatisfactory" and continued to demand that the company account, in full, for worldwide income generated by the group since February 28, 1979 [when St John had evidence the payments had ceased] "and payable to the group under the prevailing 1981 agreement".

The situation continued to attract press headlines. By October 1997 there were reports circulating that sources claimed Arista owed the band tens of millions, £60 million was commonly mentioned, so it was not surprising that Pat McGlynn came forward to say he wanted his share. "I helped make the band famous and I helped keep them at the top, and all I am looking for is my just rewards," he said. "My lawyer thinks I have an open and shut case but it looks like being a long legal battle." McGlynn was demanding £3 million, claiming it was his intervention that was now preventing Arista from paying the band.

Further complicating the issue was original singer Nobby Clark who also came forward to claim a share of the unpaid royalties. "Records are coming out and someone is making money," he said. "But it certainly isn't me." Clark, then 45, had sung on the band's first five singles, including the original version of 'Saturday Night'. These tracks often featured on band compilation albums from as early as 1978 and were often included on the more modern CD compilations. "I'm taking action to make sure that I won't be left out," he said. "I should get what is rightly mine." Clark claimed he had worked out he was owed about £1 million but "would settle for £300,000".

Although he had been approached specifically to negotiate with Arista, St John adopted the mantle of band manager and was soon talking about rebuilding the Rollers as a creative force. It would be a fragile process with "old, deep wounds" among the band members that needed repairing. He told the press he planned "to bring back major, worldwide focus" to the group "on the global stage".

St John insisted Faulkner and McKeown bury their differences and reform the two touring factions as one band. He also planned on including Derek so that the famous five would be reunited for live gigs for the first time since 1983. When he had left the group Derek said he wanted to get away from the "pretentiousness" of the scene and the "people we met' who he "never felt comfortable" around. He said he wanted to "live quietly" and had retrained as a nurse, and was now a senior staff psychiatric nurse at Edinburgh Royal Infirmary.

At their first meeting to discuss reforming, the band members looked at each other's beat-up old cars and sensed they should acquiesce to St John's reunion plans. An "uneasy flag of truce", St John called it. The classic line-up first reappeared in public, tentatively, for a one-off television special for a Japanese broadcaster in 1988. They were interviewed in the UK and travelled to Japan to play their breakthrough hit, 'Saturday Night', on a TV show. It was revealed the Rollers had sold 500,000 greatest hits CDs in Japan during 1998. The band claimed they received no record royalties from the sales.

St John also organised for the band to feature in two major TV documentaries: the BBC's *The Bay City Rollers – Remember* and VH1's *Behind The Music*. They would both be aired in 1999. This was the start of a new chapter for the Rollers and there was talk of major gigs in the pipeline and even a new album. Faulkner, 45, and St John discussed a glam, "pink satin" concept for the band's big comeback, and said the band had in its heyday attracted "a massive teen-gay" following that was only now coming to light. "There was a time when everyone involved with us was gay or bisexual," said Faulkner. "Nowadays, we have a big gay following, too." Faulkner had written a swathe of new songs including the tantalizing 'Gossamer Dream'.

"We've got to move our careers on," said Faulkner. "We're a man band now, not a boy band. George Michael had a second chance after Wham! and I hope we do, too. But the music scene is circular. Sit around long enough and we'll be back in vogue. Since punk, everything has been recycled – and we're on spin wash at the moment."

Wood said, musically, the reunion, was "not satisfying" but, "you feel that if people want to see you, you're in the world of entertainment, they've almost got a right." This was a man who had been schlepping round the world knocking out the old hits alongside Faulkner for most of the nineties. Wood, however, was beginning to build a second career as a producer and musician in his own Edinburgh studio. Beginning in 1996, under the name Celtic Spirit, he'd issued a series of five mood albums, themed as *Scottish Moods*. He described the work as Celtic Fusion Music, a combination of acoustic guitars, ambient keyboard sounds, choral backing vocals and traditional Scottish melodies. It was proving to be popular with much promise. He said he kept this name off the records because the media, especially in the UK, "did not regard the Rollers as musicians" and the records would have suffered by association.

He was also proudly leading a new healthy lifestyle and had recently married. Alan was his best man. Paton and Cotter had been guests at the evening celebration. St John had also been a guest and Paton had introduced himself. With barely disguised menace, Paton suggested St John would never get any money the Rollers were owed while Paton lived. St John suggested to the band Paton could be taken care of. "There are people I know," he said. "But there wasn't much take up."

With *Scottish Moods II* about to be released, Wood was in a good place. He had reputedly bought his mother and father a house worth an estimated half a million, and lived in the picturesque village suburbs south of Edinburgh close to a river and woodland. "I wanted to swap the darker colours in my life for much brighter ones," he told television sports presenter Hazel Irvine as part of the new BBC series, *Feeling Good*. His quest for a more peaceful existence had also not stopped him issuing a solo album, *In Different Skies*, in 1998. It had not been a great success. Similarly, the Gibraltar pubs in which he had invested had gone bankrupt.

McKeown just came right out and said he was doing it for the money. He thought Arista would release the new album and pay the band in line with the royalties they were owed. For the BBC 1 documentary, the 43 year old was interviewed sitting on a couch with his arm casually draped over Faulkner's shoulder. "This is something I thought I would never see," he said. "Without trying, we've just become friends like we used to be. All the animosity has gone and I don't hold any grudges. We wasted a lot of time being angry with each other." Faulkner said reuniting with McKeown had been "surprisingly painless" but "a very strange experience... We saw a chance to solve our differences. And I'm glad we did. It's time to forget the past and move on."

McKeown remained angry with Paton. "We got into this messy financial position through sheer bad management by Tam," he said. "We were idiots for listening to him. Tam was too busy creating stories for the newspapers to run our affairs properly. We didn't see any of our money. We reckon we've sold in excess of 120 million records worldwide but we've never been paid a penny. To say we're pissed off is an understatement."

Faulkner harboured hopes the band would be awarded some critical respect. "We were one of the few British bands to crack America," he said. "We had six gold albums over there. That's why all the legal problems over the money have been so difficult to solve, because we signed all our deals in the States." He did not blame Paton. "Some of it was down to us signing bad deals," he said. "We came out of Edinburgh and into the London music scene and were ripped to shreds. We were young boys and we didn't really even realise what was happening." He mentioned the song 'Money Honey', a massive 1976 hit single for the group that he and Wood had written. "How can you have a song that sells six million copies around the world and yet we never received a penny from it?" he asked. "When everything finally gets unearthed, this will be seen as one of the biggest rock'n'roll rip-offs ever. The merchandising situation alone was an absolute robbery."

Alan agreed. "It is incredible to think that with all our success we never made a penny," he said. "It seems impossible to do, but we did it." He was 50 and not fully recovered from his recent stroke. "We were just five working-class lads who knew nothing about the music business," Alan said. "We were just getting on with it, but there were people conning us left, right and centre. It's not surprising money has gone missing. We'd be getting ready to go on stage and someone would shove a contract in front of us and say, 'Sign it'. We didn't know half of what we were signing for."

He was optimistic for the reunion and looking forward to getting back on stage. There had been talk of replacing him with Duncan Faure while he convalesced. He had insisted he would be fine. It was Alan, along with Wood and Derek, who had kept Bay City Rollers Ltd afloat. Faulkner, who had formed the company, had let the limited company slide as his own life had in the late nineties. Faulkner kept his share in the company and the other three generously, perhaps foolishly, handed a share in the company to McKeown who replaced Kass in the set up.

It was not a voting share but McKeown was delighted. Wood was the principal director while Alan was also a director.

The band updated their image, posing for publicity shots wearing kilts and Doc Marten boots. "We wouldn't be The Bay City Rollers without tartan," said Faulkner. "I remember seeing Status Quo on TV once and they were wearing suits. It just wasn't the same seeing the band minus their denims."

The optimism was short-lived. Missing from the publicity shots was Derek whose Edinburgh apartment was raided on September 15, 1998, by serious crime squad officers from Lothian and Borders police acting on a tip off. Derek was charged with three counts of committing indecency with a youth under 18, the then homosexual age of consent. The offences had allegedly been committed since December 1997.

At the time of the raid Derek, 47, was in the apartment with 15-year-old Nelson Queiros, from Amadora near Lisbon. Queiros reportedly told officers that he loved Derek. He claimed he was there on holiday and was said to regularly spend weeks at a time at the flat. Derek, he said, also spent time in Amadora with Queiros and his family. Police officers found photos of a 14-year-old Queiros naked from the waist down during the raid.

Queiros was sent back to Portugal and Derek bailed, denying any improper relationship with him. Believing they would find child pornography at the apartment, the police seized 152 videotapes, two computers and a number of floppy disks. Once they had been examined, fresh charges were brought against Derek: making indecent photos of children and having indecent video recordings, films and photographs of children. He was also charged with possessing cannabis. The indecency charges were not pursued.

The publicity was horrendous. Derek withdrew from the band reunion but his arrest cast a dark cloud over the future plans of the Rollers, although both the BBC and VH1 went ahead with airing the documentaries in which he featured.

Derek had been working as full-time nurse since 1993. In 1991, while working as trainee nurse at Edinburgh Royal Infirmary, he'd given a rare interview to the *Star* newspaper. He said the shock of seeing former

Bay City Roller, Billy Lyall, to whom he'd been very close, die of AIDS in late 1989 had inspired him to help people like him. Derek also praised the turnaround in his life on his girlfriend, Janice Green, 38, a lab-technician at London's Hammersmith Hospital. "I quit the Rollers and did nothing for years," he explained. "But I was going crazy with boredom and the idea of helping my fellow human beings appealed to me. I was doing voluntary work at the Sick Children's hospital in Edinburgh when I met Janice. She suggested I became a trainee nurse, so here I am. It's hard, but very fulfilling. I find it as enjoyable as the music I loved."

"People in the music business don't understand why I am doing this," he told the *Star*. "They think I have gone absolutely mad." In March 1994 while working as a cardiac ward nurse at Edinburgh Royal Infirmary, he gave an interview to the *Nursing Times*. It would be his last meaningful exchange with a journalist. He said: "I've come to a stage in my life where I am very contented. I don't know if that's a mid-life thing or not, but I'm very happy in what I do. There's more to life than riding around in big limousines."

In the interview he admitted to still having his drums set up in the garage but he adamantly ruled out a comeback with the Rollers. He said the fun went out of the band for him when the accountants and lawyers moved in and the Rollers became big business. He had been glad to leave. "The money we generated was frightening, but we were not aware how much," he said. "We were so hyped up we signed anything... big business people lined their pockets. There are some vile characters in the music business. I don't know how they sleep at night."

The £125,000 penthouse apartment at Queens Park Court in central Edinburgh, which overlooked the Scottish Parliament on the edge of the beautiful Holyrood Park, where the raid had taken place, was not Derek's only property. Paton said that Derek owned six or seven flats in Edinburgh plus "a house which must be worth about a quarter of a million pounds". *The Sun* also reported that "bachelor Derek" owned a luxury flat and villa in Portugal.

On August 17, 1999, Derek denied the charges against him at Edinburgh Sheriff Court. The band's scheduled UK shows, for November and

December 1999, at 2,000-capacity venues such as the Manchester Apollo, Glasgow Barrowland and two nights at the Forum in London, were postponed and rescheduled for February 2000 before being abandoned altogether – a move said to have cost the band £80,000.

The angle the band used in the press to explain the failure of the reunion – and to deflect attention away from Derek – was that Alan needed to prioritise his health. They feared the stress of touring might cause Alan, bedridden with high blood pressure, to suffer a fatal heart attack. St John said: "Alan is a simple soul. The pressure has given him stress. And he was going to the pub rather more than he should have. It's the curse of the Rollers." Arista went ahead with the American release of a new compilation album, *The Definitive Collection*. There was already a new UK compilation album circulating called *Shang-A-Lang*. There was also talk of a film being made based on the band's story. Kurt Cobain's widow, actress and Hole front woman Courtney Love, was said to have paid more than £45,000 for the film rights to the book *Bye Bye Baby* by music journalist Caroline Sullivan. Published in September 1999, the critically acclaimed work chronicled Sullivan's "tragic" teen lust for the Rollers as she chased them across America during the rise and fall of their American stardom, eventually bedding Wood, although he wasn't named. Love said she'd raised £60 million to make the film, casting herself as Sullivan with Leonardo DiCaprio as Wood. Her former husband, Kurt Cobain, had once described his band Nirvana as sounding like "The Knack and The Bay City Rollers being molested by Black Flag and Black Sabbath".

The reformed Rollers, without Derek, did perform one live show – at the December 31, 1999 Millennium Hogmanay in their hometown of Edinburgh. Around 200,000 people attended the celebrations with the band playing to over 10,000 in the popular Princes Street Gardens. For the gig Faulkner draped a huge flag of Scotland around himself and painted his entire head and hair a matching blue with a giant white cross over his face. He also wore dark glasses. To say he looked odd among the kilted and groomed band was an understatement. He was unrecognisable and played guitar with a ferocious intensity, tearing through the band's short set.

St John also went ahead with the independent release he had planned for a live album recorded over two shows in 1977 at the Budokan Hall in Tokyo, Japan. Titled *Rollerworld*, it was found on an old reel of tape gathering dust in Faulkner's garage. When he'd first heard it, St John said: "I couldn't believe it. I thought other people made the music and they were just there." The series of shows the band played at the Budokan in 1977 set attendance records that had yet to be broken, 12,000 screaming teenagers at each. The excitement on the record was palpable and the cover shot of the band's limo almost invisible beneath a sea of fans was perfect.

They'd been a stripped down four-piece at the time and seven of the 15-song set were originals by Faulkner/Wood, including 'Don't Let The Music Die' from the *It's A Game* album, always popular in Japan. In fact almost all the material on the album had been recorded post the Rollermania years of 1974 and 1975. "I heard these four blokes playing phenomenal music," St John said. Wood said the album represented the band "as it really was... Not some manufactured unit but a real band that was a bit rough around the edges but had some grit and attitude." There was no promotion, and the album sold a disappointing 500 copies. It remains one of their best ever.

Plans to release newly-recorded material, however, were abandoned. "We were meant to record an album down in Manchester," said Alan. "But when we got there Les and Eric were both pointing at one another saying, 'I'm not recording his songs'. So I packed up my bags and said, 'I'm out of here.' I couldn't be bothered with it." McKeown claimed both he and Wood were disgruntled that Faulkner was demanding they cut only his songs. He said he was also uncomfortable with St John suggesting the band should be chasing "the pink pound". There was a "major blow-up", recalled McKeown, and he and Wood walked out. Wood kept quiet but McKeown said that like him, he had felt "used, bullied and treated with absolutely no respect".

McKeown was restless. Since St John came on the scene he said he'd been declining offers of 'retro' gigs because St John felt such shows would be detrimental to the band's reunion shows. Now McKeown was eager to start playing and earning again. He said he did not want St John managing him and questioned the 20 per cent management commission he was charging. McKeown claimed there had been an agreement where St John would take only 10 per cent of the 1997 interim payment from Arista.

St John was furious with McKeown's attitude. He said he had been asking the singer to supply crucial paperwork regarding the Arista royalties issue and McKeown had let him down. McKeown admitted he was still drinking and drugging. In 2000 he played a set at a fan gathering in Edinburgh and tactlessly dedicated one song to Derek, the recent Paul McCartney song 'Young Boy'. Paton claimed that McKeown had to be taken off a radio show in Scotland because he said that he wouldn't let Derek within six feet of his young son. In a 2003 interview McKeown did say: "I'm convinced Paton made Derek the way he is."

The Edinburgh fan gathering had attracted fans from Australia, Canada, America, the Netherlands and Denmark. Some told reporters they had got close to the Rollers in their heyday, had taken drugs and boozed with them. One talked of a risky, thrilling, *ménage a trois* with two band members. Gail Shackley, 37, who had organised the fan convention spoke out about Derek. "A lot of fans have very strong feelings about what has happened," she said. "They are disgusted." Autographed pictures of Derek, due to be auctioned at the event, were withdrawn.

Derek's trial began on March 2, 2000, garnering another round of devastating headlines. He pleaded guilty to two charges of having indecent photographs, videos and computer disks of children at his Edinburgh home. He insisted he was storing the pornography for an American friend who had bought it in Portugal and left it with him when he returned to America. He admitted he was aware of the indecent nature of the material when he was storing it. He also admitted making indecent photos of children at his home (in March 1998) by downloading them from the Internet. He had already fought and lost a legal appeal at Edinburgh High Court on this charge. Derek argued that downloading computer images amounted to possession rather than "making" them as stated in the charge, which carried a higher sentence of up to three years in jail.

Derek again blamed the American who had stayed with him in 1998, explaining how his friend had used the computer in the spare bedroom in private to visit child porn sites and to download child porn onto disks. Derek said he had not looked at the images and had no interest in child pornography. He said he'd locked the disks away so no one could access the material. He admitted that out of curiosity he had used the "history" option on the computer to retrieve the sites his pal had visited. His not guilty pleas to two charges of possessing cannabis were accepted.

The court heard that among the material taken from Derek's flat were 1,000 indecent images involving children, including 117 showing sex involving children, some as young as six, on 73 floppy disks, plus 22 child porn videos and six projector reels containing child porn. One computer they had taken from the flat contained another 6,000 images, 1,700 of which related to the charges. Detective Sergeant Alan Eadie, of Lothian and Borders Police, who led the investigation, said outside court: "I've had 21 years in the job and dealt with a large number of sex-abuse inquiries but this material was extremely obscene and some of the worst I have ever seen."

Derek made no comment as he left the court on bail wearing a cap pulled over his eyes. Most reports mentioned that he was balding, as if this was another charge. He'd been told he was facing up to three years in jail and was suspended from his job. The tabloids ate him up: this was only weeks after Gary Glitter was released from prison after serving two months for possessing hard-core child pornography.

Derek, the 'Porn Shame Star', reportedly fled Scotland for Portugal, the country where *The Sun* claimed "he had previously met a number of young boys" including the boy found at his flat, Nelson Queiros. *The Daily Record* said Queiros was "believed to have been introduced" to Derek when he was 12 by a man "known only as Michael". From her local authority flat in Lisbon, Queiros' mother said: "Nelson often goes to spend holidays in the UK. He visited Derek, but for only a few days." It was also revealed that in 1988 Derek had fostered another young Portuguese boy, 16-year-old Jorge Loureiro, who'd spent years living with him in Edinburgh.

Alan, hounded by the press, said his brother had "got a different lifestyle from me" but he had "no idea about his sexuality". Derek returned to Scotland to face sentencing at Edinburgh Sheriff Court on March 24, 2000. His lawyer, Robbie Burnett, pleaded for leniency: "There is no suggestion in any way that he was involved in these aspects of pornography [taking pictures or making simulated pornography]."

Burnett told the court that Derek's American friend had admitted ownership of the items and that all Derek had confessed to was downloading four indecent pictures from the Internet onto his computer and onto four disks that were then put away in a locked drawer. He said Derek was a dedicated nurse and his life would be "destroyed" if he lost his job. There were also other significant extraneous circumstances in the case, he claimed, a suggestion that Derek may have been framed. Burnett said a few days before the raid by police some of the floppy disks had been sent to Derek anonymously.

It was reported that Sheriff Isobel Poole fully accepted that six videos, four films and a computer found at the flat belonged to Derek's American friend and had noted other "substantial mitigatory" factors when she imposed a 300-hour community service order rather than jail. She also placed Derek on the sex offender register.

Campaigners went public in their attacks on the leniency of the sentence. Director of ChildLine Scotland, Anne Houston, said she was disappointed Derek was not jailed. Lyndsay McIntosh, Scottish Conservative law and order spokesman, said: "If you are looking to make an example of someone having the worst kind of child pornography, 300 hours' community service does not look at it."

Derek was dismissed from his post at Edinburgh Royal Infirmary after almost six years' service. In May 2000, the Portuguese boy Derek had fostered, Jorge Loureiro, now 28 and married with two children, broke his silence. He told the *Sunday Herald* that he'd met Derek when he was 15 and a glue-sniffing street child, surviving as a petty thief alongside prostitutes in the slums of Lisbon. For a year they had lived together in Derek's Lisbon flat while Derek did voluntary work for the Red Cross in the city. He said Derek paid for him to attend a private school and helped him beat his glue addiction. He had arranged to foster him with his mother's consent and Derek had brought him to Scotland for a better future. "He was the first person who ever cared about me," he said.

Loureiro told police Derek had been framed by an obsessed American fan whom he had befriended. "Detectives asked me at least five times in the course of two, two-hour interviews whether Derek and I ever had a sexual relationship," he said. "I kept on saying no, that it was never like that, but they just kept on coming back to that question."

The Sunday Herald insinuated Paton could have been involved in Derek's initial arrest. Paton denied it. "I wouldn't harm a hair on his head," he said. "We all had little secrets about each other we'd never disclose. He was always one of the quieter band members and never chased the girls like the others did." Prior to his arrest Derek and Paton had often been seen dining together. Derek now cut off contact with Paton who, it was suggested, had been desperate to derail the band's reunion plans.

The stigma of Derek's conviction stank out the band. Already they were routinely associated with child sex abuse following Paton's own early 1980s underage sex scandal, for example *The Sun* called them the "brainchild of child molester Tam Paton".

"People talk as if we were a cross between puppets and victims," McKeown had admitted. Faulkner said it was one of the first things people wanted to know when they came to interview him. "People have kept asking whether Tam abused me, but he didn't," he said.

The efforts of St John had begun to shift that perception but Derek's arrest and conviction seemed to slam the door on any further rehabilitation of their reputation.

The case had many troubling aspects but ultimately it shone a light on Derek's life that raised a whole raft of unanswered questions. Why would he have a friend who appeared to have an active sexual interest in children stay at his flat and agree to look after his stash of child pornography? What was a 15-year-old boy doing living at his flat and why did he have a photograph of the boy's genitals taken when he was 14? Why was he picking up street children in Lisbon, a city long suspected as being the hub of a paedophile network with links to similar rings across Europe and America?

In the spring of 2001, the press reported that the "Bay City pervert" Derek was still working as a nurse, having joined an English nursing agency and completed a night shift at Murrayfield private hospital in Edinburgh. A senior nurse, reportedly, said: "It's disgusting. He was looking after men and women and there could have been children brought to the ward as visitors. I don't know how he managed to slip through the net."

Bosses at the BUPA hospital called Longmuir's employment "regrettable" and said he had not been back. He appeared before a hearing held by the Nursing and Midwifery Council (NMC, the UK regulatory body for nursing) Conduct Committee in October 2001. Derek pleaded at the hearing: "Please understand that while nursing might be the only source of income for me, it's more than a job, it's my very being." He was found guilty of misconduct, handed a formal caution but retained his right to remain on the nursing register.

Mary Scanlon, the Conservative health spokesman, said the decision "made a mockery" of new regulations that meant every person working with children must be checked, monitored and registered.

CHAPTER 14

Litigation

"I hated him. He was a beast. He preyed on young people. He wanted to exploit them financially and sexually. He is the worst human being I know. Tam always said if it wasn't for him I'd still be working on a building site. But if it wasn't for me he'd still be humping potatoes."

— Les McKeown

St John had repeatedly advised the Rollers to enter into a formal litigation with Arista but, he said, the band members were nervous about taking such a step, as they were "all totally penniless and had never seen litigation result in any meaningful benefit for them". And, against all odds, he said the band were "seemingly mindful to believe Arista's continual assurances that they would get paid".

St John felt certain now that those assurances were "wholly false". But in October 2002 Paton told the press that a New York court had awarded him £750,000 for "commission" on the unpaid royalties. Paton said he would pocket about £600,000 after lawyers' fees. "I never thought I would see it," he told *The Scotsman*. "But in the end it came down to a point of principle and I knew I was in the right." It was put to him that the band members had still not seen a penny from all those hits. Paton crowed that they should have stuck with him and they too would be enjoying a similar windfall.

"He was doing it purely to rattle the band's cage," said Ray Cotter. "That's how childish and spiteful it got. Depending on what mood he was in he'd contact the press every so often and just make up a story: I've just settled with such and such when he wasn't really settled with anything at all. He dined out on that one for quite a few years."

The band thought Paton's story was true. It added to the confusion they felt about how best to handle the Arista situation. Their recordings continued to be exploited by the label. There'd been another CD compilation album *Saturday Night* released in 2001. In 2002, 'Saturday Night' was the year's most played song by a British artist on Japanese radio. In 2003, the Rollers 'Bye Bye Baby' featured prominently in the hit British film *Love Actually* and 'Saturday Night' was used in an American TV advert for Planters mixed nuts.

St John continued to negotiate with several senior Arista staff, chiefly the company's Director of Business and Legal Affairs, Glenn Delgado. Arista, he claimed, told him they had lost some of the band's historic royalty statements. There was no disputing the fact Arista had placed a 'hold' on all royalty payments due the Rollers "at least as far back as 1982" St John said. And the company appeared to be more than willing to pay these royalties to the Rollers with "statutory interest". The argument was simply over how much the band was owed. Getting access to accurate royalty statements was key.

There were small victories that backed St John's opinion that the band was owed far more than Arista was offering. He claimed he was now able to provide paperwork that showed Arista had, during the 1981 Tenenbaum settlement and the inking of a new contract with the band, conceded that the band was owed a significant amount of royalties prior to 1979. The figure was "multi-millions" St John said, even without interest. The fight went on.

In 2003 he organised for Channel 4 to make a documentary about the band's missing money, *Who Got The Rollers' Millions?* An in-house lawyer at Arista sent an e-mail to a television producer working on the documentary reiterating their position: Arista had "always stood ready to pay royalties whenever the Rollers were able to agree among themselves as to who were the appropriate payees" and "that they were holding royalties in a trust for the band until a long-standing dispute between members is resolved". And, they threatened to sue if the documentary makers took any other position. St John said he felt this was a "pretext intended to deprive the Rollers of the royalties to which they are entitled".

"It was the principal raft for their defence," he said. "Their main thing was they believed that there was dispute within the band as to who should get paid what and therefore they held up payment because they didn't want to pay the wrong person. It was a much more robust argument [than their earlier they didn't know where to send the money one] but doesn't cease or pause their contracted legal and absolute requirement to present the band with their accounts [royalty statements]."

The documentary came to no definitive conclusions about the "missing millions" but was memorable for a scene where an angry McKeown confronted Paton at Little Kellerstain. The more measured contributions by the other band members were left on the cutting room floor. McKeown showed Paton a copy of a 1976 US tax return purportedly showing the band's profit and losses for that year. Why, he wanted to know, had Paton earned almost $4 million that year, as much as the whole group put together?

"I wanted to stab him in the eye with the pen in my hand," said McKeown of the episode. "I hated him. He was a beast. He preyed on young people. He wanted to exploit them financially and sexually. He is the worst human being I know. Tam always said if it wasn't for him I'd still be working on a building site. But if it wasn't for me he'd still be humping potatoes."

Paton, of course, insisted he'd never seen the paperwork before and said there was no such payment. "I do not have any doubt that the band was ripped off," he said. "But I certainly didn't rip them off. I had my 15 per cent and that is all." He said the band "had a lot more than I ever had when I was sacked" and suggested McKeown had wasted his money on cocaine.

He advised McKeown: "This will screw you up inside. You can never be at peace with yourself, until you can forget all this stuff."

"The Rollers have spent half their life chasing money that is lost," he added. "I think they should get their heads out of their arseholes and start growing up. They are desperate men clutching at straws at the side of the river. Look what it's done to them – they have become bitter and twisted old men."

Since the collapse of the reunion McKeown had gone back to touring under the 'Les McKeown's Legendary Bay City Rollers' banner. In October 2003 he published his autobiography *Shang-A-Lang*, and came forward to publicly back Pat McGlynn who had finally made a well-publicised rape allegation against Paton who at the time had also been caught up in a separate child gang rape investigation. McKeown generated further column inches surrounding the release of the book with a variety of revelations about his time with the band.

He described how he'd smuggled drugs on tours by concealing them in the turn-ups of his trademark tartan trousers. He reiterated claims that Paton fed the band drugs, "various medications", so they could fulfil their heavy workload. "Pill-popping to keep us going was an everyday part of life," McKeown revealed.

McKeown also said he had never liked the rest of the band. "If it was legal I'd have shot every one of them dead, except for Alan," he stated. He said the band was just "me and session players" and "those guys were just muppets at the back." *Trainspotting* author Irvine Welsh had written the foreword for McKeown's book but the songs he and McKeown were purportedly working on failed to materialise. Welsh did, however, name the Rollers' 'Bye Bye Baby' as his favourite single of all time.

The St John-organised Channel 4 documentary, aired in 2004, coincided with the release of another Arista compilation, *The Very Best Of The Bay City Rollers*. It was a European release and the band's first top 20 in the UK since 1977, peaking at number 11 in May 2004. It proved the lasting power of their music, image and aura but also how little control they had over these things. The band had not been consulted on the release. "We imagine the company arbitrarily decided that it was a good time to release *The Very Best Of* type album," said St John. "They will pocket the profits from it but the Rollers will see nothing [while the dispute over record royalties continued]."

An Arista spokesman told *The Guardian* that the company had been unable to pay royalties because they did not have a copy of the initial band contract and that the band had been feuding so long that they are unable to agree who is owed what. The money remained on hold in an escrow account. "The company continues to work in good faith with representatives of The Bay City Rollers to resolve this matter," the spokesperson said.

The band members had taken down the gold and silver discs from around the world that had once lined the walls of their homes. Looking at them hurt too much. In 2004, Faulkner took delivery of a huge cache of such discs that had been unearthed in a dusty loft by a Scottish policeman. Apparently Faulkner had given him them for safekeeping in the late seventies and then forgotten.

Amid the stash were two gold discs for selling 500,000 copies in the UK of the singles 'Bye Bye Baby' and 'Give A Little Love'. There were two more gold discs to mark 250,000 UK album sales of the albums *Once Upon A Star* and *Rollin'*. And four silver disc for selling more than 250,000 copies in the UK of the singles 'All Of Me Loves All Of You', 'Shang-A-Lang', 'Remember' and 'Summerlove Sensation'. It was only a tiny snapshot of their career but there was upward of three million sales in the loft alone. Wood told the media Faulkner would be glad to get them back.

Faulkner had disappeared, often only in contact with St John. He had developed a habit of going off the radar for long periods. "Unlike most acts who think I've got a chance to talk about myself, great," said St John. "These guys are not like that. They don't want to talk. It's been knocked out of them by their history. That bit of delight... moving toward pensionable age talking about their pomp is not in them. Even the good things, so much blights it. My belief, based on my perception, is that some of the band members suffered abuse... physical abuse, both sexual and elements of violence, on a fairly regular occurrence. Les has gone on record talking about it. There's a lot of denial in the way people manage to cope with abuse particularly if it's back in a moment in your life you can't revisit... and it had a lasting effect on some of them while others keep it at bay with coping strategies that pretty much involve denial."

In July 2004 McKeown crashed his silver Volvo, first into a car and then into a traffic island, in Dalston, east London while twice the legal drink-driving limit. He tried to flee the scene. His lawyer said McKeown had panicked because the crash had brought back memories of a previous crash he'd been involved in when he'd knocked over and killed a woman at the height of his Rollers fame in 1975.

District judge Jackie Comyns, who heard how McKeown walked away from the scene of the Dalston crash and hailed a cab, ignoring the pleas of passers-by, said, "It doesn't sound like someone who panicked." McKeown, 48, was ordered to pay a court bill of nearly £2,000 and handed an 18-month ban after admitting driving with excess alcohol, failing to stop at the scene of an accident and driving without insurance.

Despite his increasingly severe drink and drug problems, he was the only Bay City Roller to capitalise on the band's past by playing live with any consistency. In 2005 his version of the band played large venues like Wembley Arena as part of a successful UK seventies package tour with The Osmonds and David Cassidy. Asked if there would be any other Rollers playing with him, he said: "Just me, the only one who matters."

He nevertheless found it difficult to stay out of trouble. In June 2005 McKeown was arrested at his London home for conspiring to supply cocaine and told he was facing a potential 10-year stretch. Pat McGlynn, also tied up in the case and charged with the same offence, was swooped on by the drugs squad in the car park of the Marriott Hotel, close to junction 26 on the M25, in Essex. He recalled having an officer's gun pressed down on the back of his head as he lay face down on the car park floor. "It was absolutely terrifying," he said.

McGlynn, who had almost died after crashing his motorbike into a tree in 1998 during the final lesson for his motorbike test the following day, spent six weeks in the category B Chelmsford Prison in Essex, where other prisoners thought it funny to sing 'Bye Bye Baby' every night, before he was released on £90,000 bail organised by his wife, Janine Andrews. McKeown had to sign on at police station twice a day.

After a highly publicised two-week trial, both of them were found not guilty at Basildon Crown Court. In court McGlynn explained how he had met with McKeown to discuss the possibility of joining him on tour. He said that at the time he was also looking for a new car and McKeown had put him in touch with "some friends of his".

He said he'd gone to the hotel car park to look at a Porsche and that was why he was carrying £30,000 in cash. The two men he met there were in a VW Golf and had half a kilo of high-grade cocaine in the car. McGlynn was said to have snorted a line. Once processed, the drug would have had a street value of around £110,000. The two men in the Golf were both arrested and admitted conspiring to supply cocaine.

It was suggested in court that McKeown had put the alleged drug deal together. While awaiting trial McGlynn said he had contemplated suicide and was on medication for depression. He said he no longer wished to associate with McKeown. "Les said he didn't know his mate was involved in things like that but he has known him for 20 years."

In the aftermath of the trial, McKeown was full of bravado. He raged against the "flimsy" evidence, protested he didn't take cocaine anymore, said that he had to cancel gigs in the US while facing the charge and would sue police for £280,000 in lost earnings. He did not.

Another Rollers compilation CD, *S-a-t-u-r-d-a-y Night*, was released in Europe by Arista in 2005. The company had finally begun sending St John twice-yearly royalty statements. He said this was as a direct result of the 2004 merger between BMG (who owned Arista Records) and Japanese global corporate powerhouse Sony.

St John hoped that with a new corporate structure in place the Rollers would finally be accounted to fully. Sony, after all, was a respected media company in the vanguard of the modern era. He was confident that the new management at Arista "would want to do the right thing" and that "the log jam might finally break". St John was to be disappointed. There would be no quick and easy end to this dispute. St John had met Sony's Head of Legal Affairs and come away astonished by "the sheer callousness" of Sony's "stance and position". Sony, he said, saw the dispute with the Rollers "as a war to win and not a wound to heal".

Clive Davis was still the main man at Arista. He had actually been removed as President of the label in 2000 during a highly publicised boardroom power play but the then 68-year-old had fought his corner ferociously, even after BMG handed him his own boutique label. When Sony merged with BMG, he was appointed CEO of the newly formed, BMG/Sony-owned, RCA Music Group. He was responsible for overseeing several labels in the new RCA stable, one of which happened to be Arista.

St John had always been curious about the level of his involvement in the Rollers' affairs. Davis had, after all, been the boss of the company when Arista made the deals with the band in 1975 and in 1981, had known all the principal American players involved in those deals, and had been at the helm all through the eighties and nineties.

"Alan Parsons and Ace Of Bass filed lawsuits against Arista," St John said. "So did others. It was not just the Rollers who had trouble with the label. But the thing is you have to look where the money is. My job was just to get them paid. So ultimately it didn't matter what had happened in the past. It's who can fix it. And that was Sony. They had an opportunity to do so cheaply and elegantly."

Finally, in 2006, the Rollers acknowledged the inevitable and St John hired one of the largest law firms in America, Holland & Knight, to represent the band, on a contingency basis, in a formal lawsuit against Arista/BMG/Sony. In the lawsuit, Faulkner, McKeown, Wood, the Longmuir brothers *and* Duncan Faure were named as plaintiffs. Faure was on a lesser percentage than the others but was included by dint of the fact he was named on the 1981 Arista contract that was at the centre of the case.

The choice of Holland & Knight was said to have been McKeown's not St John's. Wood and Derek had been talking to other lawyers and plenty were interested in taking the case on a contingency basis – charging a fee, calculated as a percentage of winnings, if the case was successful. Holland & Knight were said have approached the band via the barrister who represented McKeown during his recent cocaine trial. The firm, while acknowledged as one of the best in the world, were not specialists in the music industry. St John said he advised against hiring them. "It's like going fishing with a cricket bat," he said. McKeown, St John said, dug his heels in, demanding the firm get the job.

The lawsuit did not state how much money was involved, most media reports covering the news mentioned "tens of millions". Lead counsel for the group, Joshua Krumholz at Holland & Knight, was quoted as saying: "We know it's in the millions. The Rollers have had remarkable success and staying power over the last 30 years. To this day, Arista Records is still successfully exploiting their recordings in the US and around the world. Despite that success and Arista's many assurances over the years that it would pay the band, Arista has simply refused to do what its own contract requires it to do. Through this lawsuit, we intend to secure the royalties owed to the Rollers for the huge commercial success of their music. They have waited long enough."

In March 2007 the legal action against Arista/Sony was issued in a US District Court in the Southern District of New York. In it, the band claimed Arista had breached its contract and failed to provide any or adequate royalty statements for the period 1979 to 2004, were withholding royalties dating back to 1979, as well as a royalty sum owed for the period pre-1979, and had consistently acknowledged as such (in letters dating back to 1980). The band was also claiming substantial damages and wanted to take back ownership of its master recordings.

Two months later Arista filed a motion to dismiss the action, largely on the basis of the Statute of Limitations, which limits plaintiffs from recovering damages past six years in contract disputes. It was their main defence.

McKeown continued to disintegrate. In March 2007 he'd been involved in a violent affray in a pub in east London, ending up in hospital with an alleged fractured eye socket and some teeth knocked out. His wife was also allegedly punched and racially abused during the incident. The case went to court. The alleged attackers, a father and son combo, aged 59 and 22, were charged with GBH, ABH and racially aggravated assault. In court, they claimed McKeown had come at them with a 10-inch spanner. McKeown denied this but the pub landlord testified he had seen a spanner fall from the singer's pocket. When it was revealed a police blunder had resulted in the spanner being destroyed, the jury was ordered to return not guilty verdicts on charges against the father and son.

Professionally, McKeown also struggled. He was booed off stage in Fareham, Hampshire, after staggering on stage 90 minutes late and then reportedly forgetting lyrics. Fans who had paid £16.50 for tickets demanded their money back. He also admitted he'd also been "banned for life" from Butlins for baring his bottom to a fan during a gig. "I was completely out of control," he said.

It would take Judge Deborah Batts, appointed to oversee the lawsuit in New York, two years to rule on the motion to dismiss the case filed by Arista. During that time the media had nothing to report on the case of the 'missing millions' and The Bay City Rollers slipped back into obscurity.

The fans, however, remained loyal. In April 2007 at the Holiday Inn in Edinburgh North, a hard-core of just over 100 flew in from America, Canada and Australia for a weekend of entertainment that included a trip to Paton's parents' home in Prestonpans, a Rollers tribute band and an auction of original costumes donated by McKeown and Derek. Alan went along in person. "Our fans have been there over the years for us and this is our chance to give something back," he said. "They are the people who made us famous." The highlight of the weekend was an acoustic set from Eric Faulkner.

Less prolifically than McKeown, Faulkner had continued to gig, without Wood or Alan, as Eric Faulkner's Bay City Rollers, "still Rollin' with all the hits" ran the ads, since the band's reunion collapsed. More intriguingly, he had developed a parallel career as a folk artist performing Celtic-tinged solo acoustic sets at arts centres, folk clubs and specialist acoustic festivals. They were casual affairs with Faulkner mixing anecdotes and new original songs, often political, always reflective, with covers of songs by Pete Seeger and Ewan McColl.

He was, after all, the son of a Communist Party member and Scottish Trades Union Congress delegate. In the summer of 2007 Faulkner played a solo set featuring songs linked to the union movement at the 2007 Glastonbury Festival ahead of a speech by veteran left-wing political figure, Tony Benn. Faulkner said he had always wanted to be a protest singer. "Even when I was in The Bay City Rollers I used to talk about issues," he said. "But it didn't fit the agenda. The record company and management just wanted the boy-next-door thing."

Having moved out of London, he was also said to be running a small studio in Sussex near his Eastbourne farmhouse. He had produced an album by a promising local rock band Steadman who had ironically once been signed to Arista. There was talk of him recording a solo acoustic album. He guarded his privacy. There was speculation among fans that he had married Kass and they had a child together. Faulkner also reportedly had homes in the south of France and Scotland.

With his long grey hair, blue eyes, and laidback feel, he said he enjoyed fishing, a boyhood passion. He occasionally held guitar master classes and songwriting circles and undertook work as a session guitarist. He had been left deeply disappointed by the collapse of the Rollers' reunion plans, having spent "between 1998 and 2004 trying to make it happen. A waste of time," he said ruefully.

In a 2007 interview with a local paper in Morecambe, where he was performing his solo show, he said he had not entirely ruled out a band reunion. "Never say never," he said. "We were a great band. We're all doing our own thing now but who knows?"

"I don't wake up in the morning cut-up about things anymore," he added in the same interview. "The money thing is being dealt with by lawyers in America. It is being resolved. But I try to keep out of it; it interferes with me trying to record new songs. That was always the problem with the Rollers. Whenever we get together we spend more time talking about nonsense than we do about making an album and that always frustrated the hell out of me... now, we're on the same side of the fence for once [in the court case]. The media spin was always that Les McKeown and me didn't get along. But I don't have any ruck with Les. Whenever we sit down and talk it's like nothing bad ever happened. I argue more with Woody!"

In 2007 Wood released *Rollercoaster*, a DVD telling his life story. Sold via his independent company, Music Kitchen, it was a largely innocuous and shallow trawl through his life story with some rare footage, including himself as a 17 year old, lithe and bare-chested in tight cut-off denim shorts, on holiday in Jamaica with Paton and Derek in 1974.

He allowed other glimpses of what being a Roller had really been about. Jealous fans had hospitalised his girlfriend, he said, by putting rat poison in her tea. His mum suffered a nervous breakdown from fans gathering outside the family home in Marchmont, Edinburgh. Night after night, they'd be there, forcing his parents to eventually move home. The Scottish farmhouse that he said he co-owned with Faulkner, and where they'd lived together, Dykefoot Farm, had been repeatedly broken into by fans. Wood admitted he used to lock the Rollers' part of his life away and "not want to go there".

Ultimately, Wood said he found talking about the band "boring". By now he'd released over 50 records of Celtic-influenced music with titles such as *Bagpipe Magic* and *Voices From The Glen*. Since 2003 most had been released via the Music Kitchen label he co-owned with Gordon Campbell, a former accountant and songwriter. They were thriving in Scotland with releases such as *The Scottish Chillout Album* and the *Scottish Moods* series. One album, *The Lone Piper*, had sold well in America. He and Campbell were optimistic for the future of Music Kitchen.

Wood had also produced the successful debut album by the *X Factor* finalists The McDonald Brothers for Music Kitchen, and work by *Pop Idol* star Michelle McManus and Scottish singer Eddi Reader. He also lectured part-time at Glasgow's Stow College on music technology. He and his wife had a dog called Elvis but no children.

In the few interviews he did to promote the release of *Rollercoaster*, he was described as mid-mannered, unassuming and the "least controversial" Bay City Roller. He said he remained friendly with Alan, occasionally chatted to Derek and "kept in touch" with Faulkner. Wood acknowledged his relationship with McKeown was, however, "often fraught". "Everyone's different," he said. "I don't always agree with how some people go about things."

In November 2008 McKeown was paid to take part in a TV show called *Rehab* for the Living channel in the UK and filmed at the Passages rehabilitation clinic in Malibu. He admitted he had long struggled with depression and was drinking two bottles of Wild Turkey bourbon every day. He said he had been hospitalised regularly following booze binges and warned by his doctor he shouldn't expect to live beyond six months unless he dried out.

He said he had been drinking heavily since 2002. He also admitted to abusing cocaine: in his own words sticking "a fortune up his nose". McKeown also talked about spending three months in Thailand smoking opium and admitted he had contemplated suicide several times. Filmed while undergoing therapy, he also admitted to struggling with feelings of "self-loathing and worthlessness" following what he termed "a date rape" by an unnamed perpetrator when he was 17.

He said: "Date rape is the best way I can think of to explain how I was cajoled into a situation through drugs into having sex with another man. It happened in America in a hotel room. I was given Quaaludes, a drug for lowering your inhibitions and making you horny. If a girl took it she'd be all over you. I ended up taking part in things I would not have otherwise. Afterwards I felt really used and abused. I never told anybody about it, not even the other guys in the band, because I was ashamed. Maybe part of the shame was that I'd actually enjoyed it.

"Before that, I'd always thought I was straight, but what was happening to me was very erotic and I felt pleasure from it. Now I think a lot of the shame I've felt ever since has to do with the person who did that to me. I hated him. I tried to drink it away and push that memory into obscurity. The knock-on effect was that I found myself attracted to men, and now and again I've taken action on that."

Pressed to define "now and again", he reckoned "a couple of times a month" but later backtracked and admitted to a dozen gay partners in all. He said: "I've been a bit of a George Michael, meeting strangers for sex. I had a couple of regulars I'd see quite a lot of, but I didn't have what you would call a relationship with them. It was just meeting the same person for sex."

For the benefit of the cameras, his wife and son were flown in for McKeown to "confess" this to them. There were tears. His wife, McKeown said, had already forgiven him for his affairs with other women. He had described their relationship as "akin to what the Californians call an open marriage".

Wood, Paton and McKeown on a trampoline at Paton's Little Kellerstain home. The trampoline was a popular talking point.
ALLAN BALLARD/SCOPEFEATURES.COM

Paton with Ian Mitchell who joined the Bay City Rollers in April 1976. Mitchell, then 17, had lived at Little Kellerstain since he was 16.
PROFIMEDIA/ZUMA PRESS

Paton's commercial exploitation of the Rollers was unquenchable. They became heavily merchandised from chocolate bars and board games to shoes and even a Corgi car.

Gert Magnus was 15 when Paton discovered him and brought him to live at Little Kellerstain. He claimed Paton tried to sexually assault him.

A typical shot of a topless McKeown from American teen magazine *Tiger Beat*. McKeown later claimed Paton raped him.

The 1997 single, 'It's A Game' features a special message for Paton.

Pat McGlynn, 17, replaced Mitchell in November 1976 and would later claim Paton raped him.

Stuart Wood, posing nude bar scarf, joined the band when he had just turned 16.

Rosetta Stone, the Irish band featuring Ian Mitchell and the three McKee brothers that Paton managed from 1977. The youngest brother was 15.
BORIS SPREMO/TORONTO STAR VIA GETTY IMAGES

The band star, alongside puppets, in their own American weekly TV series in 1978.

Faulkner in a typically alluring band member solo pose. Such shots became increasingly sexualised.

New boy Pat McGlynn (far left) claimed Paton tried to rape him in Australia where this shot was taken. It is unclear why the band is offering up a Nazi salute, possibly in homage to their leader Paton (with baseball bat). ALLAN BALLARD/SCOPEFEATURES

New boy Duncan Faure (centre) joined the Rollers in November 1978 to replace McKeown as the band tried to project a post-tartan maturity. WARING ABBOTT/GETTY IMAGES

Paton posing in front of his Little Kellerstain home when he first bought it in 1975.

INSET
Paton (second from right) and Phil McNeil (centre) and some of the youngsters who lived at little Kellerstain. COURTESY OF RAY COTTER

Paton posing at gay club Fire Island with housekeeper Steven (left) and boyfriend Ray Cotter (right) in the late seventies.
COURTESY OF RAY COTTER

Paton and Cotter in the eighties. The pair were together for almost 27 years. COURTESY OF RAY COTTER

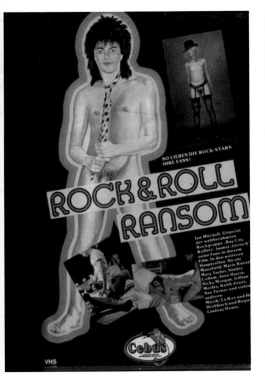

Ian Mitchell pictured on the cover of the 1982 porn movie he featured in.

Surprise Bay City Rollers reunion in 2015 with Alan, McKeown and Wood. After ugly arguments Wood quit.
KEN MCKAY/ITV/REX/SHUTTERSTOCK

The doomed turn of the century reunion. A recently arrested Derek absent from line-up. Faulkner's 'look' (far right) shocked the band.
MARIUS ALEXANDER/REX/SHUTTERSTOCK

Paton with one of his beloved dogs shortly before he died in April 2009. His weight had ballooned to almost 26-stone.

The two infamous caravans in the garden of Paton's Little Kellerstain home. COURTESY OF STEVEN

The media jumped on the story, putting McKeown back in the spotlight. He gave several interviews. 'My secret life as a Gay City Roller' was the *Daily Mail* headline while *The Sun* ran with: 'Rollers' Gay Confession: I Shang-A-Lang both ways'. McKeown said unburdening himself of the "dark secret" had saved him from suicide.

"When I agreed to do the TV series I didn't think I'd end up talking about things like this, but I feel relieved now it's out in the open," he said. "I think it will give me the opportunity to blossom a little bit." He admitted he'd "tried everything" during his time with the Rollers – "threesomes, foursomes, women, men, all the extremes… at one stage there were whole rooms of girls, but I got fed up with that. That was way too much action… it was exhausting."

Rehab was shown in February 2009. In the same month McKeown named Tam Paton as the man he claimed had date raped him. Then, after Paton's death just two months later, McKeown unloaded a further catalogue of accusations against his former manager, including violent physical abuse. He upgraded the date rape claim to straight rape, forcible sex.

To some, it looked as if McKeown was still unable to confront the sexual activity that actually went on between Paton and some band members. His version of his conversion to bisexuality via the date rape/rape incident at the hands of Paton would change over time. In 2013 he said he had realised he was bisexual before he was 18 while at school (he left aged 15).

Incredibly, on February 9, 2009, Derek's sex life became the subject of further frenzied media attention. Since his high-profile child porn conviction, he had been living quietly while working as a nurse looking after dementia patients in Edinburgh. Now *The Sun* had got hold of a sensational tape recording during which Derek had allegedly confessed to having sex with a 13-year-old.

"Bay City Rollers pervert Derek Longmuir was quizzed by cops over an alleged taped confession to child-sex abuse," reported *The Sun*. The newspaper ran the transcript of the taped conversation between Derek and Nelson Queiros, the 15-year-old boy found at Derek's flat when he'd been arrested on suspicion of committing indecency with a youth under 18. Those charges had been dropped at the time.

Queiros, now 26, said he had secretly taped the conversation on his mobile phone at Longmuir's Edinburgh home in October 2008. It 'proved', *The Sun* claimed, Derek had "preyed" on Queiros for more than 10 years and the abuse had started when Queiros was just 13 and sent to Scotland for "sex holidays". Several sections of the 90-minute transcript appeared to damn Derek. One section reproduced by *The Sun* had Queiros repeatedly asking Derek why he had had sex with him "since I was aged 13, 14, 15 up to 25". Derek, said to be heard sobbing at this point on the tape, allegedly responded: "At 16 my assumption was that you were participating". *The Sun* dubbed Derek "sleazy", "depraved" and a "snivelling paedophile". Queiros, now living permanently in North Berwick, East Lothian, claimed he had handed over the recording to *The Scottish Sun* after first approaching police who had questioned Derek but released him without charge. Queiros said: "I just want justice for what he did. That's why I went to his house to try to get evidence for the police... He is disgusting and is the lowest of the low. He took advantage of a 13-year-old boy and ruined my life."

Derek was questioned but never charged on these allegations. A unique feature of Scottish law is that at least two different and independent sources of evidence are required in support of each crucial fact before a defendant can be convicted of a crime.

It was also likely Queiros had been paid for the story by *The Sun*, throwing into question his motivation. The story, however, would cling to Derek. Had he really embarked on a 12-year relationship with a dirt-poor Portuguese boy who had apparently been forced into child prostitution? It also raised further questions about his relationship with his Portuguese foster son Loureiro, who appeared now to be having problems with his own personal life.

The lurid headlines generated by McKeown and Derek were amplified by those that followed Paton's passing in April 2009, specifically headlines linking Paton to child sex abuse networks. Overall it made for a disturbing picture of life within The Bay City Rollers: a real horror story was emerging.

In March 2009, an agonising two years after the lawsuit had been launched, Judge Batts decided in the band's favour and dismissed Arista's Statute of Limitations argument. It allowed the band's lawsuit to go forward without, said their counsel Krumholz, "any meaningful impediment".

"Although we are delighted, we are not surprised that the Court denied Arista's efforts to dismiss the Rollers' claims," he added. "This ruling is a highly significant victory for the Rollers and their efforts to recoup the millions owed to them by Arista Records in unpaid royalties. We now look forward to recovering in full the royalties that they have earned, but have been wrongly withheld from them, together with the interest and damages that is due to them for the many years that their money has been wrongfully withheld."

The case hadn't interrupted the steady flow of Rollers' compilation albums released by Arista: *Collections* in 2006, *Give A Little Love: The Best Of* in 2007 and *Rock N' Rollers: The Best Of* in 2009. There had also been a recent slew of *Best Of The 70s* type releases featuring the band's songs. In total, it was estimated that Arista had now failed to pay the band their royalties on about 600 album releases.

The band also continued to be denied their share of merchandising licenses and master synchronisation licenses (syncing the music with some kind of visual media output) by Arista. And with the modern music world progressing at a gallop, there were many other licensing revenue streams opening up from digital transmissions – downloads and streaming – that the band would be due a share of.

Sony now solely owned Arista Records. The Japanese conglomerate had bought out BMG in 2008 for a figure of $1.2 billion. Clive Davis was named Chief Creative Officer of Sony Music Entertainment. He was rated by many as one of the most respected and loved figure in the American music business. The famous, star-studded pre-Grammy Awards' curtain raiser party he had hosted for years, the Pre-Grammy Gala and Salute to Industry Icons to give it its full title, continued to be the most auspicious music business party in the calendar. He was the winner of five Grammy awards himself and also a member of the Rock and Roll Hall of Fame. His net worth was said to be around the $800 million mark.

Meanwhile, Alan Longmuir was back working as plumber. He'd completed an apprenticeship in the trade before going full-time with the Rollers. He described the work as driving his "wee van" around to "inspect people's boilers". He lived in a small semi-detached house at Bannockburn near Stirling, 35 miles from Edinburgh. He routinely rose at 5.30am to drive the 60 miles to work in the Scottish coastal city of Dundee, returning home for 7pm. He lived with his second wife, civil servant Eileen (11 years his junior), whom he had married in a private ceremony in the Caribbean island of St Lucia in 1998. She had nursed him through his heart attacks and strokes.

Alan's work colleagues called him 'Shang' and he still occasionally got together with pals in Bannockburn to make a little music. Visitors to Alan's home noted little in the way of flamboyant furnishings. "Everything's gone," he said. "I used to have gold discs, clothes, guitars but it's all away. I keep hearing about things being sold on eBay and I think was that mine and how did it end up there? I had a lot of stuff in storage then I found that people were pretty much helping themselves – there were folk taking stuff and going off to fancy dress parties dressed in my gear. Then I was told the roof had fallen in on the place where it was being stored and that everything was destroyed."

He suffered from severe depression alongside the long-standing drink problem. He said the band had ruined his life and how he wished he had never been a Roller. "I regret not having a more normal life," he'd said. "If I had the time over again, I'd definitely choose the life of a plumber, find myself a good wife and have three, maybe four kids. Yes, I think that would've made me a very happy man."

He said he still held out hope that the band would get their missing money. A "million pounds would be nice", he said. "I wouldn't mind if it was more. I'm not being greedy but I think it would be nice to have something to show for it all. The music business really stinks."

Asked about Paton, in the light of recent revelations, he said: "He was a good guy gone bad. He was living his own craving for fame through us. He was clever and he got our name out there. But he was a control freak." Alan said that before Paton had died he had not seen his former manager for 15 years. "I went around his home once and there were great slabs of cannabis on the table – and rent boys running about. I don't know how the police never caught him," he told the *Sunday Herald*. He acknowledged that Paton regularly "came on" to members of the band but he'd been "too old" for Paton to take much of an interest. "I'd say, go fuck yourself," he said. "I liked to go for a pint, I was like a man's man, so he didn't really bother me, to tell the truth."

In May 2009, Judge Batts recused herself (stood down) from the action, stating a conflict of interest, which was understood to involve Sony Music. Judge Loretta Preska, one of New York's most senior judicial figures, replaced her and immediately set a trial date for 1 March 2010.

Alan, 62, said he planned to travel to New York for the trial, what the press were now calling a "$110 million court battle". He told *The Scottish Sun*: "I just hope we will now at last get what is due to us and justice will be done."

On February 16, 2010, however, just two weeks before the trial was due to start, Judge Preska adjourned the case on the basis of fresh statements put forward by Arista/Sony. In March, she allowed their motion to file a Cross Motion for Summary Judgement. It meant instead of the time and expense of a trial, Judge Preska, not a jury, would decide the case. Arista/Sony's argument was that there was no dispute over the fact they owed the Rollers money – it was only a question of how much and that would be better judged on careful reading of paperwork rather than a trial. Both sides now were expected to present their best evidence.

In August 2010, Arista/Sony released another Rollers compilation, *The Greatest Hits. It* reached the UK top 20, peaking at number 12 and in early September *The Sun* announced the band was planning to reform for a world tour "once the band's legal fight to win £75 million in record royalties ends".

Alan told the tabloid he was keen to see the band back together. "I want to start the court case, get our money back, then go on tour," he said. "There are offers on the table, big offers, to do a world tour. I'm sure we would perform. I spoke to Les about it. I think we'd have a fantastic world tour."

He'd just come back from visiting a fan convention in America. "There were thousands there – all ages, but mainly 45 to 50-year-olds, our original fans who have stayed with us," said Alan. "I was mobbed. It was incredible." It was where he'd met with McKeown who was on a 32-gig tour of America and Canada with his own version of the Rollers. It was McKeown who had got him excited about the prospect of reforming the group.

McKeown, now 54, also began to talk up the band reunion in the press. He said he was now "a much nicer, better person" after being been dry for two years. He reckoned the band was due "over £120 million in royalties" and "the lawyers are saying it's not a case of if we get our money but when". While they were waiting "and before we get too old and decrepit" McKeown said, "perhaps we should get back on stage – it seems to be what our fans want".

He added: "The people who are interested in putting the money in for that want it to be the line-up it was when I joined originally – me, Woody, Eric, Derek and Alan. We're looking at an arena tour here and in the US. We want to revitalise ourselves, get on the road again and be a good band." He spoke about "closure over the fall-outs" and "no grudges" between the band members. "Things are even good between me and Eric," he said. "He's genuinely a nice guy and so are all the guys in the band."

An official press release from St John on September 24, 2010 put an end to the speculation. "There is no reunion of The Bay City Rollers planned or taking place at this time," he wrote. "The Bay City Rollers will not be performing or appearing together anywhere until further notice, any information to the contrary is incorrect and may not be relied upon as an accurate guide to the activities of The Bay City Rollers."

In the release, St John, who continued to act as manager to The Bay City Rollers but not to McKeown, listed the band members as Faulkner, Wood, the Longmuirs and Duncan Faure. The exclusion of McKeown was a reminder that there was still some residual resentment among the band that it was the singer alone still touring the world and earning money off the back of the band, its image and hits.

McKeown was currently selling a show called Rollermania, basically the 'Legendary Bay City Rollers' gig with anecdotes. "There's no post-fame depression or arguments involved in it at all, it's just a very positive show," he said. It seemed that unburdening himself of the dark secret involving Paton and his bisexuality had allowed him to find some peace in his life. Commenting on the situation regarding the other band members before a gig at the Cambridge Corn Exchange, he said that he had always been "a team player in The Bay City Rollers, no matter what you've read or seen".

He added: "It's difficult to keep the brand and the name in a positive light, and I've been able to do that over the years. I would've loved it if The Bay City Rollers were together and doing their thing. If they ever thought about reuniting, it'd be great for the fans, but I've had to look at the situation in real terms and think, Well, what's the possibility of that happening? It's pretty low, so get out there Les and do your thing."

Alan was left looking rather foolish by his premature declaration of a band reunion. "Me and Woody own the name but Les does stuff and [so does] Eric," he said. "I've known them for years and I'm not going to get in a fight about it." He fell seriously ill, with pneumonia and pleurisy, and was then made redundant. In December 2010 he also discovered a barber on Spain's Costa Blanca had stolen his identity and was dining out on tales of his days in the band, dropping hints the Rollers were about to reform and promising an appearance on the Costa Blanca any day now from McKeown

"There are some real weirdos out there," Alan told the *Edinburgh Evening News*, who were claiming the incident was further evidence of the "curse of The Bay City Rollers". "I've had them all – from one girl who used to post cornflakes through my letter box every morning so I'd have my breakfast, to people who just follow you around," Alan added. "But this is the first time I'm aware of anyone else actually pretending to be me. It's not like I'm loaded, living a fabulous lifestyle or that my name gets me anywhere. It's all a bit weird. To be honest, the guy in Spain is probably having a better time pretending to be me, than I'm having. It would be a better idea for me to adopt his identity, go and live in Spain and enjoy myself as him."

In May 2011, Judge Preska called a "mediation" meeting in New York between Arista/Sony and the Rollers' representatives in an attempt to resolve the long-running dispute. St John put forward an impassioned plea for a reasonable settlement in front of Wade Leak, Sony Music's new Head of Legal and Business Affairs.

St John estimated the band was owed a figure somewhere between £26 million to £90 million. According to St John, Arista/Sony suggested the amount was closer to £2 million. The mediation was doomed to failure, the disparity between the figures too wide to bridge. In August, Judge Preska set a new trial date – for July 1, 2012 but, disappointingly, that date was abandoned in late 2011 after Arista/Sony requested the ruling on the Cross Motion for Summary Judgement be reconsidered.

For the Rollers there were fresh complications in the case regarding former band members Nobby Clark, Pat McGlynn and now Ian Mitchell. Clark and McGlynn had not got anywhere with their efforts in the late nineties to include themselves in the lawsuit as band members. They had now joined forces with Mitchell and filed an intervention in New York in an attempt to be finally included in the Rollers' lawsuit against Arista and thus gain a share of any pay out.

Clark was now living in Dumbiedykes, an Edinburgh housing estate. After his solo career crashed, he'd battled alcoholism, gambling and drug addictions, been declared bankrupt, spent time living homeless and in a psychiatric hospital, and ultimately tried to kill himself.

Having fronted the group for seven years, he was, understandably, extremely bitter about not being included in the band's lawsuit. "It's my intention to make sure those guys don't get a penny," he said. "I will sue every single one of them. There is no money they could ever get that they could say I am not entitled to." He claimed in *The Sun* that, on the day after he quit the band, McKeown had gone on *Top Of The Pops* and mimed to his voice (on the hit single, 'Remember'). "Over the last 30 years there have been dozens of albums released with my voice on the songs," he said. "They have also used Pat and Ian's performances."

Now in his early 60s, Clark privately admitted regret at having to align himself with Mitchell and McGlynn, neither of whom had contributed to the band for any significant length of time. He was also disappointed to hear his old friend Alan calling him a "hanger-on". "I'm saddened by the whole thing," he said, "the way they turned their back on me and stabbed me in the back. We had been very close, especially Alan and I. It wasn't necessary and it was all done purely out of greed."

Mitchell, still living in America, had instigated the legal proceedings after striking a deal with an American lawyer who had already won him the right to continue to tour as 'Ian Mitchell's Bay City Rollers' (which he intermittently had). Mitchell admitted that he had done "the drugs and drink" and "got chewed, swallowed up and spat out by the industry". He was rumoured to continue to suffer from poor health. His wife was active among fans on social media.

The intervention sought by Clark, McGlynn and Mitchell was time-consuming, taking up almost a year of legal efforts. Wood, St John, Alan and Clark flew to New York in early 2012 to give their depositions (oral testimony of a witness taken under oath which will later be used in court). Faulkner, Derek and McKeown gave their depositions in London. Judge Preska ruled against Clark, Mitchell and McGlynn intervening in the Rollers' lawsuit against Sony/Arista because none of the three had been named in the 1981 Arista agreement but she said that they could sue both the Rollers for a share of any recovered royalties and Arista directly for unpaid royalties.

They followed her advice. Clark said he and McGlynn were persuaded to stump up another $10,000 each to cover the fees of Mitchell's American lawyer. Arista/Sony immediately tried but failed to have the Clark/Mitchell/McGlynn case against them thrown out using the Statute of Limitations defence. "We are just trying to get the money that we are entitled to," McGlynn told *The Sun*. "We have as much right as the other band members. We have been exploited for 30 years. It's time that our hard work and our contribution was rewarded."

McGlynn, 54, had cropped up in the news a few times since his high-profile 2005 cocaine trial. In 2008 he'd been up in court as the target of blackmailers following a big gambling win that saw him take ownership of a restaurant said to be worth half a million pounds. The contract transferring ownership of the restaurant to him was later found to be worthless. In 2010 he'd been in court again battling Edinburgh City Council over a £15,000 building bill he refused to pay. The same year he had suffered a heart attack and also been beaten up by a skinhead while he sat his car at traffic lights near his home in Liberton. "Some guy called me a poofy Bay City Rollers beast, screaming about paedophiles and perverts, and punched my teeth out," he said.

In January 2013, Judge Preska entirely dismissed the claims of Clark, McGlynn and Mitchell under the Statute of Frauds; stating that none of the three had contracts with either Arista or the Rollers. They appealed the decision, claiming their contributions to the band could be proved without need for any legal document. Appeal judges, however, upheld Judge Preska's decision, now also citing the Statue of Limitations. The contribution to the band of all three had occurred well over six years ago. It was the end for McGlynn, Mitchell and Clark.

"The other five objected to us, saying we weren't entitled to money because we weren't real members of the band," said McGlynn. Clark, particularly, felt badly done to. "I don't know how they could even argue that some of the money is not due to me," he said. In 2014 he published a painfully honest autobiography in which he detailed 26 recent Roller albums on which he felt his vocals had had been featured. His voice was certainly on the attractive CD box set released in Europe in 2013, featuring the band's first five albums plus bonus tracks.

Controversially, in the book he also claimed it was his voice on the version of 'Saturday Night' initially released in America, the single that had gone to number one and broken the band around the world. "Alan Longmuir phoned me from America to say you better get your lawyer because it's gone to number one with your voice on it," he told me.

"Dishonest and greedy are the two words I'd use to describe them," Clark said. He believed the band's protestations of being hard done to by Arista were overblown. Clark claimed that Paton had told him that the band had received close to £20 million (in advances set) against their record royalties while he'd been manager. "It's not about the royalties for me but I fight to get the truth out there," he said.

As their lawsuit against Arista entered its sixth year, the band members involved in the case were keen to bring the case to conclusion and get on with their lives. Judge Preska had reconsidered and now denied Arista/Sony's request to file the Cross Motion for Summary Judgement on the band's lawsuit and was preparing for trial. She requested to hear expert witness testimonies regarding the amount of royalties both sides felt were due and would rule on what evidence could be presented to a jury.

The band's legal team hired record company royalty auditing expert Wayne Coleman, the founder and CEO of the Royalty Compliance Organisation, which in the past had recovered more than $100 million in unpaid royalties for clients, including country music superstar Merle Haggard. "Record companies use questionable accounting tactics and contractual provisions to get away with unconscionable things," Coleman told the *Los Angeles Times*. "Of the thousands of royalty compliance audits I've conducted over the past 30 years, I can recall only one instance where the artist owed money to the company."

St John said that on May 3, 2013, just before the deadline to serve paperwork closed, Sony/Arista presented to Judge Preska a great bundle of it, relating to historic royalty information, including a 150,000-line spread sheet of sales data from overseas territories. St John was aghast: he said that Arista had constantly and repeatedly denied any such paperwork existed. Not only that but the band's position, as would imminently be placed before Preska by Coleman, was based on the paperwork that had been available before this late submission.

"From the day I came on board in 1996 and wrote my first major letter to Arista, their position was they had no records, no accounts, no history in order to provide me or anybody else with anything formal about the position of the Rollers," St John said. "That was very very strongly restated and reasserted or numerous occasions by [Glenn] Delgado and by Arista in direct correspondence with our lawyers when the action went formal in 2007."

In July 2013, Coleman testified to Judge Preska and was forced to admit that he had failed to review all of the recent documents produced by Arista. He said, however, that the documents he had examined prior to their late submission were "woefully incomplete and wholly unreliable" for purposes of calculating the royalties allegedly due the Rollers and "notably deficient" in areas such as overseas sales. He said there was an 11-year stretch with no royalty records at all. Coleman called the

Arista documentation "abysmal, useless, gap-ridden and meaningless". He brought up many errors including one on which a royalty balance of over $1million was crossed out by hand and never referred to again. He also claimed that Arista had failed to apply the correct royalty rates (the percentage due the band) to many releases over the years.

Coleman told Preska that based on his evaluation of the incomplete statements and accounts the band were owed a minimum of $8 million ($3 million with interest) but he felt that this was a "substantial under-representation". He said if the gaps in the paperwork were filled in the royalties owed to the band from 1979 through to 2012 actually amounted to almost $113million ($33 million plus interest). Coleman had used the "interpolation" method – a sound, acceptable mathematical formula – to fill in the gaps, using reliable data points to calculate missing figures. Coleman also presented a middling figure of $40 million ($11 million plus interest) worked out on a "release-based method", identifying record releases and assessing the number of sales and hence royalties due. There was no mention of the claims St John had made of an outstanding amount of record royalties owed the band by Arista prior to 1979.

Judge Preska then heard the testimony of Sony/Arista expert Tom Nilsen. He also had 30 years of experience in the music business and had, at one time, been manager in the domestic royalty accounting department of CBS Records (where Clive Davis had been President). For the past 12 years he had worked at Gelfand, Rennert & Feldman representing artists and publishers in royalty examinations. Nilsen protested that Arista's documentation was accurate and consistent and put forward a document he had constructed from available paperwork that recreated "a comprehensive and detailed statement summary of accounting and payments from Arista to The Bay City Rollers and their representatives for the 38-year period spanning July 1 1974 to June 30, 2012".

He said Arista had accounted for nearly $5.5 million (this figure is as stated and presumed to be an historical amount) in royalty earnings since the mid-seventies, consisting of $4.4 million (ditto) that Arista paid the band or their representatives from the mid-seventies through 1997 and almost $1 million in royalties from 1997 to the present that

Arista was holding. Nilsen strongly contested the methods Coleman had used to come to his conclusions. He said they ignored "almost all available historical documentation and data" and were founded on assumptions that he called "baseless" and "riddled with errors". Nilsen had calculated the royalty amount the band was owed to be just over $1 million – $1,042,203 to be precise.

In September 2013, the Rollers' filed a motion to exclude Nilsen's testimony from the trial and Arista/Sony filed a motion to exclude Wayne Coleman's expert witness testimony. Preska would decide. The Rollers' lawyers at Holland & Knight requested "a call" with her. They had recently discovered information that gave them reason to believe she may have a potential conflict of interest.

The Rollers' lawyers raised the issue that Preska's husband, Thomas Kavalar, a partner at Cahill Gordon, one of America's most profitable law firms, had strong links to Sony having acted as a high-profile defence lawyer for Sony Music in the past, at various times, and on similar cases to the one being brought against the company by the Rollers. In 2007 Preska had presided over high-profile litigation he had been involved in regarding an allegation Sony and four other major labels had collectively conspired to artificially fix the prices of digital music recordings. She had dismissed this digital music antitrust litigation.

Preska firmly denied any conflict and remained as the judge of record. She would take over a year to come to a decision on the testimonies of the respective royalty experts.

The band members were left in limbo. McKeown continued touring, as he had done consistently since 2010, routinely playing well over 50 shows a year while maintaining his sobriety and operating under what he described as "a new attitude to life", avoiding controversy and working hard. He said he'd bought "a few flats' as well as owning his Hackney townhouse. He toured as both 'Les McKeown's Legendary Bay City Rollers' and with a show he called 'The Bay City Rollers Story' which incorporated anecdotes and songs. Playing in America, Canada and the UK, he had established the act as a regular feature at small theatres and clubs. In 2013 he played a 50-plus-date headline tour of small English towns in the autumn months leading up to Christmas. The money added up nicely. He seemed to be bursting with energy.

McKeown was the Roller with the highest public profile by far, even accepting a booking as guest judge at the annual World Scotch Pie Championships. "I don't like him but I quite admire what he's done," said St John. "He just kept doing it. He was the only person, if you wanted a scoopful of Bay City Rollers nostalgia, you could get it from. It served him well and it became more valuable and that's how he's made some money."

For many McKeown *was* The Bay City Rollers. His website was professional and convincing. In the summer of 2014, as 'The Bay City Rollers starring Les McKeown', "The voice on all the original hits", he once again toured UK arenas, as part of a seventies package with David Essex, Showaddywaddy and The Osmonds. In the autumn he began another 50-plus-date headline UK tour. These gigs were jokey affairs, full of middle-aged women and much flirting from the stage, but regularly sold out. "I like putting a smile on people's faces," McKeown said. "All these years nobody was doing anything good with The Bay City Rollers but now it's coming good."

He said he would love to have a reunion with the other band members, although he was not on speaking terms with them. "I've had lots of great offers while I've been touring the world – offers I'm sure they would all be interested in," he said. "It's just a case of getting everyone on the same page." He suggested they should get back together and do a tour "maybe a world tour in 2016". There had been an "upsurge" in interest in the band, he claimed, and this was a "golden time" to get back together.

McKeown, now 59, also announced he was planning to release a Christmas single, 'Rock And Roll Christmas Time', a reworking of a long lost, unreleased, Rollers tune he claimed to have written circa Christmas 1975. It had been reworked by John McLaughlin who had written and produced hits for a string of manufactured bands such as Westlife, Blue and Liberty X. The eternal optimist, McKeown still felt a major comeback was possible. "If you look at someone like Tom Jones, there was a period where he was considered slightly naff," McKeown said. "Then he did songs like 'Kiss' and suddenly he was the bee's knees again. There is always a chance that something similar could happen [to me]."

He tried not to think about the lawsuit with Arista/Sony that kept "raising its very attractive financial head". "There are people that have invested millions of pounds in our court case, travelling all over the world to get royalty statements or to fly us to America," he said. "Knowing what I know about Americans makes me think they wouldn't do it if they weren't certain." Privately he was said to be haranguing Holland & Knight about their handling of the case, despite the fact it was his decision to hire them.

McKeown said he felt he had been given "a second chance" after his life-changing spell in rehab and believed he could help others by continuing to talk passionately and openly about his experiences of sexual abuse, alcoholism and drug addiction. He also suggested he was not the only band member to have suffered at the hands of "sexual predator" Paton. "I've been lucky enough to go through therapy and get it out of my system," he said. "I don't know how they are coping with that."

Such public proclamations plus the fact he was in the best shape financially of any former Roller caused resentment from the other band members who remained uneasy about his relentless cashing in on the band's name. There seemed to be particular animosity toward him from Wood who felt McKeown often abused the rights he held over the band's name via his limited company. Wood, however, appeared uninterested in putting a version of the band back on the road. Promoters in the UK had approached him with an offer of £70,000 for a four-date Rollers reunion, specifically requesting Duncan Faure as singer. In Japan there was a $40,000 offer for the same line-up to play three shows with a week's rehearsal all paid for. "They turned it down because of the lawsuit," said Faure.

The rift between McKeown and the other band members was sometimes played out on social media. Wood's wife was said to be particularly vocal, and aggressive, toward McKeown's activities. Hardcore fans devoted to one or the other faction could be relied on to stir up rumour and ill feeling. There was a lot of ugliness.

Wood and his wife had, for instance, caused a major ruckus about the July 2014 Rollerfest. They had not been happy to find Wood's name attached to the event alongside McKeown's. The Rollerfest was organised by DJ Dizzy who presented a weekly online radio show dedicated solely to the Rollers on Peterhead-based Buchan Community Radio. He had advertised it by declaring many of the original band members would be attending the event, including Mitchell, McGlynn and possibly Clark. Dizzy said Alan had agreed to come and then backed out. When St John stepped in to seek clarification of what exactly DJ Dizzy was selling the event as, Dizzy made public sections of the email. There was an undercurrent of bad feeling that the band was being exploited, even though all profits were intended for charity.

Wood was still active with his Music Kitchen company which continued to market its *Scottish Moods* and *Scottish Chillout* music, while mining other avenues of Scottish musical history. The company had hooked up with Scottish-based publishing company DC Thomson and begun issuing compilation albums of old fifties and sixties hits under the auspices of the Broons, the family at the heart of one of Scotland's most popular and longstanding comic strips. They did the same with Oor Willie, another famous cartoon strip character.

There was also jewellery, perfume, mugs, signed photos and T-shirts relating to the Rollers, some identified as 'Team Woody', available on Wood's personal website. It was not particularly classy. Faulkner was selling mugs, mouse mats and signed photos on his website as well as charging fans monthly or annual fees for exclusive content. He had two websites in fact, official and official fansite, both apparently run by his PA, Karin Ingram, a DJ on the Internet only community radio station TD1 based in Galshiels in the Borders region of Scotland. She had also been accused of stirring up trouble on social media between opposing factions of Rollers fans, purportedly fake profiles had been created to shore up hostility toward McKeown.

Faulkner, 61, attempted to dissociate himself from the on-going petty squabbles. "I stay away from it," he said. He still occasionally went out with a put-together band as 'Eric Faulkner's Bay City Rollers', chiefly for festivals, but was more often now seen playing intimate solo acoustic shows around the country. He often declined the demand to play old Rollers hits during the shows. In 2014, he toured Germany, Japan and Ireland. He was still working on his solo album, collaborating with Phil Cunningham from Scottish folk act Silly Wizard. Works in progress were up on his website. He'd kept his studio in south-west England but his relationship with long term partner Kass was said to be over and he often, with his long grey hair and lined face, appeared dishevelled.

He seemed angry about the lawsuit. Asked about a band reunion, he said: "I'm certainly not going to get together and sell a million CDs for Sony for Sony not to pay the band. I'm not going to get ripped off twice."

Alan didn't have a website. However, he was cashing in on The Bay City Rollers after an approach by Liam Rudden, entertainment editor at the *Edinburgh Evening News* and part-time playwright. Rudden was interested in writing a stage play based on Alan's story. Initially cautious, it was his wife Eileen who encouraged Alan to get involved. "She was sick of me just hanging around the house, getting in her way," he said.

The collaboration produced *And I Ran With The Gang,* a combination of drama, Rollers hits and a brief question and answer session with Alan. The show ran for almost three weeks at the 2014 Edinburgh Fringe Festival at the upmarket Le Monde venue space. It gave Alan the opportunity to get back up on the stage for the first time since Hogmanay 1999. "I'm absolutely buzzing," he told *Edinburgh News*. "It makes a change from just sitting at home. In fact, it's brilliant."

The show sold out and picked up good reviews. Alan was back in the spotlight. At the high-profile press night for musical *Jersey Boys* based around the story of New York's hit sixties group, The Four Seasons, at Edinburgh Playhouse, he was photographed alongside Judy Murray, Scottish tennis ace Andy's mum. She said she was "ridiculously excited" to meet Alan having named a Rollers tune as one of her Desert Island Discs.

Alan also put his name behind the *Edinburgh Evening News* appeal to raise money to install defibrillators in sports clubs across the region, reliving the terror of his own heart attacks in the press. Now 66, he looked well and conducted himself with a steady hand and with some still considerable panache, dressed offstage in dark denim jeans and chocolate brown leather bomber jacket.

Asked about the chances of reforming the Rollers, he remained cautious. "I'd like to, but there's too much politics involved," he said. McKeown had been the only member of The Bay City Rollers to attend *And I Ran With the Gang*. He'd even joined Alan on stage to sing 'Bye Bye Baby' and 'Shang-A-Lang'. Alan said "Woody and Eric" had been in touch, sending "nice messages" of support. "I stay friends with all of them," he said. The success of the play clearly had made him reconsider his musical life: "We've had our ups and downs but I couldn't change being a Roller for the world."

On September 15, 2014, Judge Preska ruled on the expert witness statements in the band's lawsuit with Arista. The band's motion to have the testimony of Sony/Arista expert Tom Nilsen excluded was denied. His calculation of the royalty amount owed the Rollers was reliable, Preska said. Arista/Sony's motion to have the testimony of the band's expert, Wayne Coleman, excluded, however, was granted – in part.

Coleman's calculations of the band being owed $110 million were deemed as "not reliable" and his testimony to that figure was excluded by Preska. He would however be allowed to testify to the minimum figure he had put forward – $8 million.

In the filed report, among the lengthy legalese it was possible to pick out why the ruling had gone against Coleman's $110 figure. Coleman had admitted relying on a partner at his firm, whom he'd called an "expert in math and computer science", to apply the "interpolation" method to come up with the figure. The method was not the problem. The figure was deemed unreliable because Coleman had not done the mathematic calculations himself. He therefore, the report stated, lacked "appropriate qualifications to present the interpolation method to the jury" – the necessary expertise in legal terms. It had been suggested that Coleman might bring his associate who could explain the method fully to court. The law was that only one expert witness be allowed.

The middle figure Coleman had presented, of $40 million was also ruled to be unreliable by Preska. The report explained that Coleman had rejected historical documents provided by Arista – presumably the ones presented at the eleventh hour – without sufficient analysis and failed to seek out further "source documents". The report added that the "release-based method" he had used to come up with the $40-million figure had myriad inconsistencies and that Coleman's analysis was improperly "aimed at achieving one result" and thus was unreliable.

Many of Coleman's opinions about the unreliability of the paperwork supplied by Arista Records were also excluded. After over seven years in the New York court system, the ruling by Preska instantly slashed the amount the Rollers could possibly walk away with; there would be no more talk of tens of millions. Sony's expert would argue the figure the band was owed in record royalties was as low as $1 million while Coleman had been set a limit of arguing for $8 million. It was a not insignificant win for Sony. Although the company's 2014 revenue was around the $40 billion mark with assets said to be worth approximately double that, they were well-known to be struggling to rebalance a net income loss of over $1 billion in the financial year.

For the Rollers it was a killer blow. There are no awards for costs in the American legal system and St John said the Rollers had run up at least $5 million in legal fees. The Rollers' lawyers would also take their contingency fee, estimated at 30 per cent, from of any amount awarded.

For St John the ruling was "obscene". He felt the US legal system had failed the band "completely". "As soon as Sony/Arista's sole core defence [the Statute of Limitation argument] had been ruled out, the lawsuit should have gone straight to jury trial," he said.

The mainstream media did not report on this latest development in the lawsuit. It did not look as if they would have their happy ending, no underdog victory, no easy copy, no giant slaying. Just dense legalise and more interminable waiting. St John told me the band would appeal the exclusion of Coleman's testimony to the higher figures.

ACT III

Death Of A Svengali

CHAPTER 15

Trade

"I may be an old poofter, but I'm not into children. Yes, I like attractive young men, but that doesn't make me a bad man. Some people say my lifestyle is bizarre. I would say it's eccentric. If anyone thinks we are running orgies here they're nuts. I am an old man who prefers to live with people so I'm not on my own."

— Tam Paton

On the day that he died, Wednesday, April 8, 2009, 26-stone multi-millionaire Tam Paton was alone in his private bedroom at Little Kellerstain, a property guarded by a 20-foot high perimeter wall topped with another six feet of barbed wire, huge wrought iron security gates, steel shutters, two armed men, two Rottweiler dogs, a Staffordshire Bull Terrier and a CCTV system watching its every corner.

The house — a modernist, white, single-storey, long rectangular-shaped, 300-square metre building — had recently been revamped to a standard that Paton bragged was "better than the Queen's". Cameras with night-vision, zoom and face-recognition were everywhere, all connected to a central computer and a split-screen monitor located in Paton's bedroom. The cameras watched not just the house but the private road leading to it, the long sweeping driveway, the vast courtyard and the large half-acre of gardens where two prominent and permanent mobile homes sat on raised concrete bases. There were several panic buttons and alarms around the house and, in the evenings, the entire area was patrolled by a private security company.

Paton spent much of his time alone in his bedroom, often watching movies on DVD or listening to CDs. It was at one end of 'LK', as insiders referred to the house, and almost an apartment in itself. Inside was an ensuite bathroom, steam room, walk-in wardrobe, two Adjustomatic chairs that cost £15,000 apiece and a plasma TV screen so big as to be a "conversation stopper".

It was his own personal retreat, away from whatever was going on elsewhere in the mansion he claimed was worth £2 million. The building's original impressively streamlined architectural design had not been entirely corrupted by the replacement of the original flat roof with a low-pitched terracotta tile one, and the addition of fussy wooden exterior door and window shutters and a bewildering hotchpotch of garden features. The south facing side of the building offered beautiful views of the nearby historic Pentland Hills and was still mostly glass with four separate sets of large double-sliding glass doors.

Three other men were currently in long-term permanent residence at LK, and the place could often get crowded or noisy, especially in the huge lounge or the luxury open-plan dining and kitchen area. The four spare bedrooms and the mobile homes were generally always occupied by tenants or guests and the house facilities – including the luxury wet room with shower, sauna, Jacuzzi and plunge pool and the many outdoor seating areas – could be hectic with visitors.

Paton was a sick man: 70 years old, morbidly obese and suffering from an almost crippling addiction to Valium. Invariably he stayed indoors, swathed in a big bell tent-like robe. When he ventured out he wore slippers rather than struggle to get his swollen feet into shoes, and the destination was usually no further than a nearby cash and carry wholesale warehouse where he bought food in bulk for himself or to sell on at a profit to his tenants and guests. Despite his vast wealth, he behaved parsimoniously.

On these outings one of his most-trusted live-in aides, a gun-toting 20-something with a heavy cocaine habit, would act as chauffeur behind the wheel of Paton's Range Rover with its custom number plate, P1B TON. The aide, slim and boyish, lived at LK and often had his wife to stay but he would occasionally share a bed with Paton who was desperately fond of him. He had become a central figure at LK and was suspected of being a gold-digger.

In his bedroom Paton furtively unwrapped a series of Cadbury's Star Bars, 32 of them in total, from a box bought at the cash and carry. Each bar, a mix of chocolate, peanuts and caramel, weighed 49 grammes, and using a sharp knife he chopped each one into bite size pieces. Sitting on the edge of his king-sized bed, he stuffed the pieces into his mouth, not stopping until the whole box of Star Bars was gone. Cadbury's Double Deckers – cereal, nougatine and chocolate – were also devoured this way, boxes and boxes of them.

Paton was secretive and obsessive with entrenched Machiavellian tendencies. "He let you know what you needed to know," said one long-time tenant at LK. He'd been addicted to prescription drugs for over 30 years, chiefly Valium but he'd also had long kicks on other strong sedatives such as Quaaludes and Tuinal. He kept a large stash of Valium and without it there loomed the spectre of even greater anxiety, irritation, cramps, heart palpitations, hallucinations and depression. He guarded these pills with even more ferocity than that which he reserved for his boxes of chocolates and sweets. If provoked, his temper could be brutal. In the past he had dished out beatings to some truly powerful men. The assaults on tenants, guests, lovers and aides were more often verbal but just as fierce – prolonged and venomous.

Although he had quit his 60-a-day cigarette habit and rarely drank alcohol, Paton's body was worn out from years of punishment. He had spent almost his entire lifetime in a constant state of drama and high levels of stress had become another addiction. He was a diagnosed diabetic, had suffered two strokes and doctors had repeatedly told him if he did not lose weight he would die, recommending surgery to replace a faulty heart valve. Alongside the sugar, stress and Valium he poured into himself, he went on prolonged laxative binges, misguidedly believing these pills would help combat his weight issues and food addictions. More hours were spent alone in his bedroom, often on the toilet.

Dark was falling now and Paton was expecting two bits of trade to be dropped off to help him pass the evening. One was a favourite with a burgeoning cocaine habit who would trade sex for the drug. The other was new and, he'd been told, stunningly good-looking. Paton may have been sick but his attraction to young men remained intoxicating.

Paton was still associating with 67-year-old John 'Sticky' Wilson, a former stable manager and horse-riding instructor who had reportedly turned Crown witness against him when they had been charged together in the high-profile eighties homosexual sex abuse scandal that had destroyed Paton's career in the music business.

Ever since, Paton had unstintingly been labelled a paedophile and a depraved pervert by the press. His long and continued protestations that he was neither seemed undermined by the presence of Wilson in his life.

In the January 1982 trial of the two men, Paton, then 43, had been sentenced to three years in prison after pleading guilty to: conducting himself in a shamelessly indecent manner toward 10 teenage boys "now aged 15 to 20" in separate incidents at Little Kellerstain between 1978 and 1980; acts of gross indecency with other teenage boys; showing the teenagers obscene and indecent films of sex acts; and supplying them with alcohol and controlled drugs, namely the Quaaludes that he admitted possessing. A month earlier, at the same High Court in Edinburgh, 'Sticky' Wilson had wept in the dock after being handed a four-month stretch. He pleading guilty to: committing an act of gross indecency with a 13-year-old; an act of gross indecency with a youth aged 17; attempting to procure the commission of an act of gross indecency with a 16-year-old and committing an act with him at his home and at Paton's house; and committing an act of gross indecency with a 15-year-old boy.

These incidents occurred in 1979 and 1980. Wilson had pleas of not guilty to eight other charges accepted and the leniency of his sentence was said to reflect his willingness to give evidence against Paton. The length of time he actually spent in jail, however, was complicated when it was reported that the then 40-year-old had later been sentenced to a further three years for threatening two men, aged 20 and 19, to give false evidence at his trial.

The court heard how Paton screened the "obscene films" and gave "beer, wine, whisky and vodka" and "intoxicating and stupefying drugs" to the teenagers with the likely intention to "deprave and corrupt" and to "seduce them to indecent practices and behaviour". There were an incredible 59 witnesses cited to give evidence, 22 offences and 23 youths involved.

Insiders claim the regular scenario involving Paton would unfold with the sauna in the wet room turned on and the lads, often teenagers, whose faces were usually the same, let loose on the infamous punchbowl full of booze in the kitchen and offered drugs, chiefly speed, marijuana, Seconal (aka 'reds', powerful barbiturates, normally used in the treatment of epilepsy and insomnia, with sedative and hypnotic properties) and Quaaludes.

The lads weren't rent boys or male prostitutes but seemed happy and willing, at least on the surface, to be flirtatious: they might accept a hand-job for £50 or its equivalent in hashish or cocaine. Others might be more sexually adventurous, keen to experiment, even attracted to older men. The wet room at LK featured a large TV on which pornographic videos would often be shown. Paton was frequently nude (conducting himself in a shamelessly indecent manner), possibly masturbating or encouraging others to. The gross indecency charges related to situations where the youths told the police touching had occurred (the term covers all homosexual acts except buggery, the legal term for anal intercourse). One of the regular lads at the parties was said to be the 18-year-old son of a senior police officer who had reacted badly to the news that his son was gay and frequenting Paton's place.

At the time, in Scotland, the homosexual age of consent was 21. Indeed, the homosexual act had only been decriminalised in the country two years prior, in 1980. Furthermore, it was claimed that a damning 8mm film confiscated from Paton's home, said to depict homosexual acts between young boys, and used as evidence against him, had never in fact been shown at LK and was not even Paton's property but belonged to a member of The Bay City Rollers who had all routinely stored items at the house.

In 2000, Paton, hoping to explain his behaviour, said everything that went on at LK was consensual. "The youngest boy was 15,' he said. "People have said he was 13 or 14, and shit like that, but that's just crap. There was one guy at 15, who actually just watched a movie called *Tina With The Big Tits* and we had a couple of lagers. I didn't lay a hand on him, nothing like that. And the rest of them were 16, 17 and 18. One of those chaps was actually the youngest soldier to serve in the Falkland Islands conflict, one of the marines. So it was all right for him to go and shoot some Argentineans at 17 or 18, but it was not all right to roll about with somebody who was 39 or 38 at the time."

If 15 had sent shivers of repulsion through the media ['Sordid Secrets Of Twisted Tam' and 'Tam's Night In The Sauna With The Boys' just two of the tabloid headlines from the time], 13 was a horror story – particular in regard to homosexual sex. This was the reputed age of one lad said to have been involved in the LK scene circa 1980. He was a handicapped boy commonly referred among those at LK as 'DD' (for deaf and dumb). He was not mentally impaired, and looked a lot older than his actual age; reputedly very muscular and almost six-feet tall. The charges Paton faced originally in 1980 had included 'Gross indecency against young boys *aged between 13 and 17*'. But by the time of the trial they were "now aged 15-20". The media reporting of the trial missed the subtle distinction and Paton subsequently exploited the confusion in all future media interviews. He talked of "hands on legs" in the sauna, "laddies in their late teens who didn't want to make complaints against me [to the police]" and a "a chap" who was "16, educated, a nice guy" and had arrived at LK in a taxi.

DD, it is said, wanted to be at LK and had lied about his age. Other lads at LK certainly lied about their age. Unbeknownst to Paton, there was another 13-year-old enjoying the party scene at Little Kellerstain in the late seventies. A resident at a small Boys Home called Ponton House in the Fountainbridge area of Edinburgh city centre he was initially taken out to the house by an 18-year-old male from the same care home. At LK he got enthusiastically stuck into the free booze and bought drugs, mainly hashish. When questioned he told Paton he was 16 and "I looked it". He acted it too and had already been involved in armed robbery.

Describing a typical late seventies' evening at Little Kellerstain with "at least 20 young guys" in party mode, he recalled being in the kitchen feeling "out of his head", although he'd not knowingly taken a drug that evening, and then his next memory, he said, was of slowly regaining consciousness in Paton's bedroom with Paton on top of him, breathing heavily, trying to kiss him. Although now awake, his body did not seem to be responding and he "could hardly move". His trousers were down and Paton was playing with his penis. "I'm 13," he managed to scream. Paton freaked, leaping off the bed and storming out. Next, he was bundled into the boot of a car. As the car moved off he thought perhaps that was going to be killed. Instead, after 10 minutes, the car stopped and he was let free in the centre of Edinburgh. Later he wondered what might have happened to him if he had not woken up.

Older guys in the care home, many of whom were regulars at Paton's parties, threatened him with violence not to say anything and he was soon back partying at LK. "A fancy house, money, drugs, drink… if you're a guy with nothing and someone's offering you all this when no one's ever been kind to you before."

When the police were compiling the charges against Paton, they accused the 13-year-old of being paid to take other boys out to Paton's. It was not true. They questioned him for hours, again and again. "Did he touch you?" they would repeatedly ask him. He always said no. They had him checked by a doctor. He had not been anally assaulted. He told them, again and again, nothing had happened. He said they called him a liar. Finally, aged 14, he was sent to a secure unit for children in Montrose, a remote coastal town 90 miles north of Edinburgh and one of the first such facilities established in the UK. He said friends of Paton's visited him there asking him to stay quiet while, in an attempt to get him to talk, the police beat him viciously. Often, he said, he was shackled. He did not testify against Paton. In fact, down the line, he moved back into LK and became one of Paton's key aides.

Another man who wished to remain anonymous said he was 15 when he first got involved with Paton and the Little Kellerstain scene in the late seventies. He was taken to the house by John Scambler, his mum's neighbour, after telling him he wanted to be a pop star. He was starry-eyed enough to believe Paton might turn him into one.

It was Scambler, he said, at one time married with kids, who first molested him. They were sat together watching a blue movie at LK. He was getting aroused. Paton was also in the room and fondling a 17-year-old Edinburgh club DJ (and future member of Paton-managed act, Rosetta Stone) who would later freely admit he was "gagging for it". The DJ said there was a family-size carton of pineapple-flavour hand cream involved in his initial encounter with Paton. "Rub that around your arse son," Paton had said to him. Then, hoisting the prostrate teenager's legs over his shoulders, "with no empathy or foreplay", Paton penetrated him and started "banging away". "Relax son," Paton said. "Play with yourself… play with yourself."

That evening, with the DJ and Paton squelching away on the shag-pile carpet and the blue movie continuing to arouse him, the confused 15-year-old felt Scambler fondling his penis. "What the fuck is going on here?" he thought. "I was really naïve and insecure. The next thing he had it out and he was sucking me off," he said.

"Scambler had his claws into me,' he added. "He used to entice me into his house. My mates were out playing football and I'd be getting done in his bedroom."

Paton began inviting him to stay over at LK on weekends. These visits passed without incident and then when he was 16 Paton offered him his own bedroom full-time. The teenager took it. He hoped it meant he could escape the attention of Scambler and he still dreamt of pop stardom, having put together a rudimentary four-piece band with other young men he met at Paton's. He dressed in tight leather trouser showing off "everything" and barely-there shirts – essentials, he said, if you wanted to be in a teen pop band. Paton was encouraging and hired a recording studio for the band in Edinburgh where they bashed away on old Bay City Rollers equipment. "We started off thinking we were going to happen but no…"

One night he was sat alone in the living room wearing a kimono Paton had given him. "Then he came through and gave me a pill, half a Mandrax, partly to relax me, and went back to his room. Half an hour later he came back and led me to his bedroom and that was it… from then on I'd regularly be spirited into his room. It went on and on and on. People say, 'Oh why did you not do anything?' but you have to be there. You don't want to tell anybody what was happening. Nobody would believe you. Tam used to invite my mum and dad for lunch. He had their confidence."

Paton told the 16-year-old he loved him and installed him as a housekeeper at LK, leaving him in charge of the house and the feeding of the dogs, two Dobermans at the time called Susie and Elsie, while he was away on business in Japan, London or America. The teenager was allowed "free food" but not paid. In fact, Paton charged him rent, taking a cut of his dole money. And he made sure the boy paid, one time driving him down to the dole office in his electric blue Rolls-Royce Silver Shadow.

Paton made him pose as his son while entertaining a Japanese music mogul at LK and he was a father figure to the 16-year-old, showing him the affection his own father never had. "There were two sides to Tam," he said. "He could be kind and he would talk to you knowledgeably about music and history. But he over-stepped the mark." It was not just sexual. Paton was often verbally abusive toward him. "It felt like the end of the world," he said of the attacks. "I wouldn't like to push him to the physical. Tam was a big strong guy. If he lost his temper you better watch out."

He did not see much of The Bay City Rollers during his two-year stay at LK although he had to leave the house for a week when Rollers guitarist Stuart Wood came to stay. "There was story in the paper that Woody claimed he'd had a nervous breakdown and disappeared," he said. "Nobody was supposed to know where he was. It was a big story at the time, 'Missing Roller' sort of thing. Well, he was sitting in Tam's house."

He also met Paton's family. He watched amused as Paton spiked the meal he was preparing for his elderly mother, Isabella, and elder brother, David, a Tory councillor (East Lothian District Council), and his wife. "He brought out this big block of hash and started grating this hash into a big pot of mince. He said I'm going to give them a dinner they'll remember."

471

Paton introduced him to Edinburgh's famous gay nightclub, Fire Island, and he came to know older Edinburgh men who were part of Paton's inner circle, men such as 'Sticky' Wilson. He recalled an occasion when two very young boys were brought to Little Kellerstain. "One was 14 and the other was 13," he said. "One was sitting on Tam's knee, teasing him, but Tam didn't want to get involved. Tam enjoyed the wee game the guy was playing but he didn't take it any further." Paton, he said, had a firm rule that he wouldn't get involved with anyone under 16. "He thought if it was okay for heterosexuals to have sex at 16 it was okay for him to have sex with 16-year-old boys."

Among the older men was Kevin Drumgoole who pretended to be Paton around Edinburgh in order to try and pick up guys. At LK he would leer at those present but Paton tried to keep him at a distance. In 1995, his defence counsel Robert Henderson QC described him as "a rather pathetic, lonely, insecure person" when the 56-year-old was sentenced to 18 months in prison after admitting six charges of sexual assault on teenage foreign tourists aged between 14 and 17. After plying lads with alcohol he filmed himself committing sex acts on them. Police confiscated 50 tapes from his flat, featuring more than 80 youngsters. He'd admitted to a further charge covering 20 incidents involving unknown youths.

Martin Frutin was an entirely different matter. He was popular, gregarious and charming, enjoyable to be around. Born into a well-known Glaswegian family that owned many theatres and cinemas in Scotland, Frutin came across Paton in the mid-sixties when they were both managing teenage Scottish beat groups. One early member of The Bay City Rollers claimed Frutin had tried to seduce him with Quaaludes and promises of riches in the early seventies. He made millions after starting up Frutin Travel, a late-booking travel centre in Edinburgh that went on to become the top independent travel agency in Scotland. Frutin invested in a holiday home in Pattaya, a notorious sex resort in Thailand.

In 1996, when he was 54, a raid on his Edinburgh home uncovered a collection of pictures and videos of sexual acts involving minors. He was fined £500 after admitting possessing indecent images of boys. He left Scotland, moving into the luxury mansion he'd had built in Pattaya. Frutin became a well-known face in Pattaya, driving a red Rolls-Royce and acting as a prominent member of the local Masonic Lodge. He died in 2009. The details of his child porn charges were absent from a prominent and lengthy obituary in *The Scotsman* newspaper.

Alongside characters such as Frutin, Drumgoole, Scambler and 'Sticky' Wilson, there was a list of other men who were regular visitors to LK, whose motives all seemed sexually driven. The regular parties at the house were infamous across Edinburgh and within showbusiness, particularly the debauched Saturday night soirées. They were a honeypot for a disparate bunch of men who enjoyed the company of reckless or starry-eyed youths. Remote, private and secure, there was a large covered barbeque area in the garden, plenty of booze and drugs and an air of celebrity glamour to proceedings.

Some of the men, prominent music industry figures or light entertainment stars, cannot be named for legal reasons. Others were known by nicknames or by their physical defects. The Edinburgh faces often brought rent boys picked up from the city's notorious Regent Road. Sometimes Paton might brag to the lads that these men were high-ranking police officers or in the Secret Intelligence Service. Alarmingly, many seemed involved in the care of youths or in work that that involved youths. All the older men, like Paton, could be characterised as 'chickenhawks', a gay slang term used to describe an older man sexually attracted to younger men roughly aged between 15 and 19, known as "chickens".

Paton was released from Edinburgh's Saughton Prison in time for Christmas 1984 after serving a year and a half of his sentence. The open house policy at LK was significantly tightened and the punch bowl was put away. In the southeast corner of the garden, a giant crater filled with thousands of empty booze bottles was symbolically covered in topsoil, the party days buried. The excesses were replaced by respectable dinners with old friends and their wives – some of the prison officers and warders he met at Saughton accepted invitations. Even high-ranking prison governors were seen at LK.

Paton also stayed friends with some of the inmates. These contacts would prove significant to a man with a conviction for underage sex offences and who was no longer able to pursue a career in respectable society. In prison Paton had earned their respect when he flattened a man who insulted him and spat on him. "The other prisoners expected an out-and-out poof, with high heels and a handbag by my side," he said. "I had a couple of fights in the exercise yard and managed to leave my mark."

In the bedroom things stayed pretty much the same. Paton simply became much more careful in verifying the age of any young visitors. He remained an outspoken critic regarding the age of homosexual consent [it would be 1994 before the age of consent for homosexual sex was lowed to 18. It became 16 in 2001]. "We can go fight for queen and country but we can't go to bed with who we want," he would say. "It's wrong."

For the remainder of the eighties and throughout the nineties, Paton rented out the spare rooms at Little Kellerstain to series of young men, often homeless or unemployed or at risk of falling into crime, many transient. "I let them stop here while they get a grip on their life," he said. His motives were not altogether altruistic. He took a cut of their benefits. Paton often abused their trust. If he had nothing better to do he would search their rooms when they were out. He enjoyed finding a person's weakness or darkest secret and exploiting it and them. Paton claimed not to be exploiting the lads at LK and was actually doing more good for the youngsters than any of the agencies who should be caring for them. This, among his old friends, was believed. The lads were not hidden away. Paton gave them jobs and seemed genuinely pleased if they got themselves together. He acted as a father figure to many.

Sometimes it was chaotic. Paton found himself under the spotlight again when it was reported that he'd been attacked in his bedroom by a sword-wielding assailant. Paton had apparently repulsed the attack and held an imitation Smith & Wesson to the man's head. It was later discovered his assailant was a paranoid schizophrenic who had murdered two other men. One young man slept in the wet room because he could not control his bladder at night and the room was easy to swill down.

Others would just come out to stay for weekends. Their backgrounds were never openly discussed, but sometimes they might offer snippets such as, "Oh, my dad's going to divorce my mum" but nothing too troubling to suggest they were terribly damaged. Most seemed blasé. One visitor in the mid-eighties observed Paton emerge from the sauna followed by a young guy who was "grinning like a Cheshire cat. Paton turned to another young man and said, 'Give him his bit.' The guy cut him a bit of hash and the deal was done."

Occasionally the rooms at LK were rented to young women and there were periods of calm. Paton's niece stayed for a while. He also took in, on/off, a 40-something female Bay City Rollers fan who appeared to have mental issues and was routinely laughed at by the others in the house.

The chickenhawks had not entirely flown the coop. A character called Phil McNeil took up residence in one of the caravans, acting as a handy man for Paton. McNeil, who at one time had shared a flat with John Scambler, lived at LK for a number of years and was sometimes a source of friction. It was alleged that because Paton was so possessive of the young men in his life, McNeil was forced to collect his own chickens.

The lurid newspaper headlines faded away over the years. Speculation and rumour about what was going on behind closed doors at LK (there was talk of suicides, overdoses and even murder) remained just that. Edinburgh taxi drivers told tales of regular trips out to Gogar ferrying young "druggy-looking" men back and forth.

This period of relatively low press attention ended in January 2003 when Paton was arrested over allegations that he was one of four men who had gang-raped a boy of 12 in the late seventies. The police revealed that a 39-year-old man had made a very detailed allegation about a "paedophile orgy". Two brothers, teenagers at time of the alleged incident, corroborated his allegation, claiming they had seen the assault. Police were also investigating claims that some of the boys' parents were at the party.

Paton and eight male lodgers were handcuffed in a high-profile raid at LK and computers, videos, diaries, mobile phones and bank statements were removed. Paton was taken to a police station at Berwick-upon-

Tweed for a nine-hour grilling. "They asked me if I'd had sex with my nephew because I had pictures of him," he said. "Of course I have pictures. He's my sister's son!"

In his cell, lying on a concrete slab, he tried to commit suicide. He had a £1 coin in his pocket. "I thought I can't go through this again, people believing I'm some kind of freak," he said. "I tried to choke myself, to lodge the coin in my throat. I was thinking about my mother and my father... my family reading all this crap. I tried to do it, but I got scared."

The alleged gang rape of the 12-year-old boy was said to have happened at the Surrey home of former BBC Radio 1 DJ Chris Denning who went on to work closely with Paton and The Bay City Rollers while Head of Promotions at Bell Records. The British police were actively looking to question the then 61-year-old in connection with the allegation and nine other alleged indecent assaults on children. Thought to be on the run in Eastern Europe, Denning had been found guilty of underage sex charges as early as 1974 when he was convicted of gross indecency and indecent assault at the Old Bailey. He had gone on to amass a long list of convictions relating to sexual behaviour with young boys including producing child pornography. He'd been sentenced to 18 months in 1985 for gross indecency with a child and three years in 1988 for indecent assault on a 13-year-old boy. Since then he had spent four years in prison in Prague and five years in prison in Slovakia for sexual offences against young boys. In 2014 he would admit to 40 charges of indecent assault and gross indecency on boys – some as young as nine – between 1967 and 1987 and was jailed for 13 years.

The whole investigation into the gang rape of the boy, it would transpire, had developed out of a 2002 Channel 4 TV documentary about hit maker, record producer and broadcaster Jonathan King, another former associate of Paton and the Rollers. Then 57 and a well-known media personality, King had been sensationally jailed for seven years for a series of sexual assaults against schoolboys aged 14 to 16. During King's high-profile trial Paton had spoken out in his defence, calling it a "fox hunt", alleging King had been targeted in the same way he had been in 1982 "because of his fame in the pop business" and because he was gay.

"Everyone wants to see the death of the fox," he said. "They would never have gone after us if we were heterosexual. But if you're a poof, my God."

The press tore Paton to pieces. All the rumours that had been building since the early eighties came tumbling out. They suggested that behind the doors of his "highly guarded mansion", his "fortress-like home", Paton answered to the name of Samantha and encouraged his young houseguests to dress up in high heels and stockings, a story that caused great hilarity inside LK. It was said he dished out cigarettes and sweets from a "tuck shop" and suggested that LK's extensive surveillance system was used to film sex acts surreptitiously. Paton was accused of travelling to places "like Bangkok" and hiring "whole families to do things for him".

One journalist wrote of being chased from the property by a young man armed with a crossbow. The Edinburgh *Evening News* said Little Kellerstain was better known as "the chicken ranch" and claimed it might house "as many as 20 youngsters at any one time", "always at least a dozen" in "cell-like rooms". A source, said to be close to Paton, was quoted as saying: "Paton and two other guys call themselves the sisters and they call the guys who live there the chickens. These guys are really vulnerable, either because they've been kicked out of their homes, or are homeless already. It's gross." Evenings, it was said, revolved around booze, drugs, sex, computer games and pornographic videos. Furthermore, it was claimed, when the young men at LK reached a certain age they were farmed out to flats (that Paton owned) in the west end of Edinburgh and put to work as rent boys.

Paton, now aged 65, went on an aggressive campaign to clear his name. He invited the *Daily Mirror* into LK and, wearing a pale blue Arabian dishdash robe, told them he had "nothing to hide". "I may be an old poofter, but I'm not into children," he said. "Yes, I like attractive young men, but that doesn't make me a bad man. Some people say my lifestyle is bizarre. I would say it's eccentric. If anyone thinks we are running orgies here they're nuts. I am an old man who prefers to live with people so I'm not on my own. A lot of the people who are here have had their parents come and visit. So there is no hanky panky going on here. People who stay here come and go as they please. We are one big happy family. People who know me know that's the way it's been here ever since I moved in."

Paton stated that he did not know the other men questioned in connection with the case, including record producer Stephen Jolley, 52, who had worked with acts such as Bananarama and Spandau Ballet.★ Paton did acknowledge knowing Jonathan King, but stated: "The implication by the police that I am involved in some big paedophile ring with other people is a load of rubbish. If it wasn't so serious, it would be laughable. It's about time the public separate paedophiles from men like me who live a different lifestyle. The police took away my computer, old photographs and other things but there is nothing in all those to incriminate me in anything bad."

It was an assured defence but privately Paton was in turmoil. He was being abused in the street and refused entry into restaurants. He hired expensive defence lawyers and private detectives and was consumed by the details of the case. His health suffered. "I'm supposed to have abused this boy in December 1978 or December 1979. My lawyers tell me that Chris Denning sold the house where this is supposed to have taken place in 1976. Also, I have been able to prove that I was abroad in December 1978. I can't wait for this to reach court because the case is so flimsy the police will be laughed out of the place."

Paton called for a change in the law, he wanted the statute of limitation to be introduced to stop people making allegations decades after events and also anonymity for men accused of sex crimes until they have been proven guilty in a court of law. "I have had all sorts of horrendous stories about me in the press and my reputation is in tatters," he said. "I can't walk down the street now without people sneering at me, growling at me, calling me a beast." His name appeared in a spate of unpleasant high-profile graffiti writing around Edinburgh city centre.

★ In 2001 Jolley was jailed for 18 months for indecently assaulting a 12-year-old boy and covertly filming the whole thing.

He was shouted at from passing cars. There had also been an incident in the city centre when a stranger had threatened him with physical assault. Paton had grabbed a plank of wood from a nearby building site and chased off the man.

A month after the allegations hit the headlines, Pat McGlynn went to the *News Of The World* with the news that Paton had tried to rape him on five separate occasions. McGlynn told the newspaper that his former manager had repeatedly tried to "touch him up" and had launched a sexual assault against him in a New York hotel room in 1977. He said he had been sacked from the band because he had threatened to expose Paton. McGlynn claimed he was promised £40,000 to "keep my mouth shut". All the band, he said, were "threatened to keep our mouths shut".

'Manager's Evil Lust For The Rollers' ran the *News Of The World* headline. "Absolute rubbish," responded Paton. McGlynn said he intended to contact the Surrey detectives who were investigating the gang rape allegations against Paton. Those allegations, however, were unravelling fast. In early March 2003, Paton was cleared. "Following consultation with the Crown Prosecution Service it has been decided that there is insufficient evidence to support the allegation," said a police spokesman.

"I am delighted," Paton told *The Scotsman*. "I am not a paedophile and have never been a paedophile." The allegations, he said, had been "outrageous", "ludicrous" and "sickening".

He swatted away McGlynn's claim of rape as "terrible and untrue" and was considering legal action. "There have been a lot of people coming out of the woodwork to make money on the back of this by making up ridiculous allegations against me," he said.

Les McKeown, however, backed McGlynn's rape claim. He recalled a specific incident in a Melbourne hotel, claiming he had arrived at the room he was sharing with McGlynn to find Paton on top of the guitarist. "I had to jump on Tam and get him round his neck and pull him off him," he said. "He's a dirty bastard. He tried to make out it was just a bit of fun, but if I hadn't gone back when I did Pat would have been raped."

He said Paton had threatened both McGlynn and himself with violence if they spoke out. McKeown even said he had feared for his life. He told a story of how one of Paton's dogs had attacked his father on command. McKeown claimed Paton had turned to him after the incident and said: "See, Les, nobody's safe." "Tam was very scary," he added. "I used to have palpitations just talking to him on the phone."

The quotes appeared in an interview that took place as McKeown promoted his autobiography. He claimed all the band were scared of Paton and among themselves referred to Paton's home as 'Beast Central' because every time they went there they saw "pretty young lads lying about in skimpy towels". He added that Paton "regularly" had sex with "children". "Paton tried it on with me," he added.

Having lodged an official allegation of attempted rape against Paton, McGlynn stated he had made around 15 previous attempts to tell police about the alleged ordeal but had been ignored. He and McKeown gave separate statements regarding the allegations to the police on October 9 and 10, 2003. Both branded Paton a paedophile, saying he should be behind bars. McKeown appealed for other victims to come forward. They said they would spearhead a campaign against those calling for a time limit on allegations of child abuse.

"Everybody knows that victims of abuse can take decades to get over the guilt they experience as a result of the abuse they have suffered, if in fact they ever do," McKeown said. "The only reason abusers want that [change of law] is because they think they can protect themselves and their kind. They mustn't be allowed to get away with it."

Paton called McGlynn and McKeown's claims "absurd" and said he planned to take legal action against the pair. "It's unbelievable what some people will do to sell a book," he said. He even claimed to have hired private investigators to try and clear his name. "I would love to get this into court," he said. "These people have had every opportunity to tell police about these claims and never have." He was interviewed under caution, fingerprinted and DNA-tested but never officially charged. The complaint however was not officially dismissed until August 2007, when the police finally concluded that there was "insufficient evidence" to substantiate the claim. Paton made his one and only admission of culpability with an apology: "I did make one terrible mistake and I'm greatly sorry for that," he said, referring to the 1982 case. "But they've said I have nothing to answer for and I'm happy with that."

McKeown continued to be a major irritant to Paton. Just three weeks before, on February 15, 2009, the singer had claimed in the *Scotland On Sunday* newspaper that Paton had raped him too. "There wasn't force, as such," he said. "There were drugs involved, and the next minute it was all going on." Paton was offered a chance to respond by *Scotland On Sunday*. They wrote that, "after his laughter had subsided", Paton called McKeown "deranged", and added: "I would say that I think Les is confused about his sexuality."

It was no laughing matter, however. McKeown's claims were highly detailed and not so easy to brush off. It added to a catalogue of problems that were crushing Paton, the stress almost unbearable at times. He had recently been arrested on high-profile drug charges and, privately, he had a 17-year-old transvestite who was demanding money from him. Paton had faced regular blackmail threats over the years. The teenager, a runaway who had fallen into the hands of older men at a very young age and been sexually abused and then introduced to working on gay sex chat lines, was a well-known face on Edinburgh's gay scene and bragged of being "a favourite" of Paton's. He told pals how a 16-year-old Turkish boy had been flown in especially for the pleasure of guests at one of Paton's recent "cocaine-fuelled" evenings. He saw Paton as his "big score" but was currently under police observation over claims he had extorted close to £90,000 out of several men, including a teacher, after luring them into talking about sex with children on a gay chat line he worked on.

"I'll tell you something," a reflective Paton told an interviewer in February 2009. "The more I know about human beings, the more I love my dogs." It would be his last ever press interview and summed up much about the man who seemed to have everything – the millions, the fame, the mansion and the sex – but was so desperately alone. He explained in the interview how one of his beloved Staffordshire Bull Terriers – "his children" he called the dogs – had recently been put down suffering from a brain tumour. Paton said he had spent hours cradling the little red Staffie's dead body tenderly, desolate, quietly sobbing.

It was pitiful, tragic: this fat, miserable and lost old man filling the vast emptiness in his life with trade and Star Bars.

CHAPTER 16

Rent

"In Edinburgh, The Bay City Rollers were such a big deal and everyone thought Tam was connected [to the showbiz world]. An awful lot of queens in Edinburgh used Tam's name inappropriately in order to satisfy their own ends. They either used to pose as Tam, or say, 'I'm a good friend of his' or 'I can take you up to his house'. Tam's name was being used from pillar to post.'

– Ray Cotter

The gate buzzer jolted Paton. An armed man went to the intercom and recognised Wilson. He pressed the button that opened the main gates. The arrangement was that 'Sticky' would drop off the two bits of trade and pick them up later.

Paton removed his ostentatious gold jewellery, the rings, chunky bracelets and necklace worth in total easily £30,000. There were two safes in the bedroom: one under the false floor and the other in the built-in wardrobe. Right now, he estimated, the one under the floor held approximately £900,000 in cash and close to £600,000 in drugs, chiefly marijuana but also a few kilos of cocaine. He opened the wardrobe and placed his gold in the safe there. Then he took out two kimonos from among the clothes.

He had been livid with 'Sticky' Wilson when he first came out of Staughton but that emotion had dulled over the years as other traumas overtook him and the two men slowly drifted back into one another's lives. Wilson had suffered too [in 2007, an 18-year-old male had stabbed him repeatedly in the back and arm at his home in a small town to the south of Edinburgh] and it was tempting to believe he had not turned grass on Paton as he insisted. Even in his late-sixties 'Sticky' retained much of his cheeky hillbilly charm. His wife [they had been a much talked about couple] was long gone but was still able to easily attract young men into his life. Paton's own powers of attraction, his once overwhelming charm, charisma and rugged sex appeal, had dwindled to virtually nothing. If he felt any emotion at all toward Wilson it was jealousy.

Paton left his bedroom and headed for the wet room On the way he passed his long abandoned office, its walls adorned with photos of The Bay City Rollers and of himself in his prime – at the controls of an aircraft, in a snazzy white suit in Jamaica, his arm around the singer, Lulu. He acknowledged the two-armed men sat in the kitchen smoking joints, both veterans of many such nights. One of them, high on cocaine, was involuntarily rocking backward and forward while holding a handgun.

Inside the wet room, Paton hung the two kimonos, one over a treadmill and the other over a step machine. Wilson had told him the new lad was straight. Inside the giant carcass, behind the gimlet eyes and hard-man act, beneath the unfathomable quagmire of emotional defences, multiple addictions and psychological disorders, overwhelming memories of great glory and scars of torturing regret, a pulse quickened. It had always been his kick, his turn-on: having sex with young men who on the surface seemed like well-adjusted heterosexuals, even if it meant offering them lots of drugs or lots of money.

The press estimated he was worth £10 million and intimated that much of it had been stolen from The Bay City Rollers. There had been almost as many headlines about the band's finances over the years as there had been about Paton's predilection for young men. The Rollers felt they had been ruthlessly exploited and Paton was an obvious target for the media. "Where's my fucking money?" an angry Les McKeown had infamously demanded of Paton in a confrontation between the two staged at LK for the 2004 Channel 4 documentary called *Who Got The Rollers' Millions?*

"I never stole a penny off them," he told the press repeatedly and with increasing frustration. That was not entirely true but during his 14-year rule as manager of the group he had been relatively honest, at least regarding the money. Paton blamed the band's financial woes on the professionals he had appointed in England and America.

He claimed that he had had trusted them and felt they had conspired against him, preyed on his lack of business acumen to entrap him; undermining his control of the band and stealing everyone's money. He was extremely sour about it and would spit out their names. Paton always felt he was as much a victim of the music industry as the band and that they had all been royally shafted. "I wasn't the brightest spark on the block at the time," he said. "The straw was coming out of my ears."

"Do you know how much I got from the Rollers?" he would ask journalists. "I was lucky if I got £300,000."

He was on 15 per cent of the band's gross earnings, another subtle indication of his honesty when many managers of the era took a higher percentage, and he should have come away with "at least £10 million". He had taken his eye off the band's finances, he said, because of the rancour among the band members. "We were too busy fighting and disputing and having to deal with five lawyers every time we wanted to do a tour," he said. "When I did get around to deal with all the accountants and all that I would have needed to be like an octopus, with about 22 arms... or 22 brains, dealing with everything, because it was an almost impossible monster to deal with."

At LK, Paton would play videos of Hitler speeches on a giant TV in the lounge. To whoever was listening he would name some of the music men he felt had exploited his naivety in business – all Jews. "Hitler had the right idea," Paton would say bitterly as he watched the speeches. Such anti-Semitic outbursts were reserved for just the men he felt had fleeced him. He was no neo-Nazi. He had long harboured, however, a fascination with Hitler and had actually channelled some of the Nazi party leader's characteristics – chiefly the frenzied impassioned nature of his oratory – in his ruthless manipulation of the Rollers. The intoxicating power he had held over the band and, through them, over millions of hysterical female fans, had caused him to further identify with the Nazi party leader.

Paton still suffered from megalomania. He'd been a notorious control freak as manager of the Rollers. Narcissism, ego and pride made it extremely difficult for him to admit to his managerial mistakes. The band had trusted him completely and it was he who had entrusted all their lives to theses accountants, lawyers and music moguls. It was his fault. He had been outmaneuvered. "I put everything into managing the Rollers," he said. "I did my best. But I was not the best manager in the world."

Few believed his bleating or knew how beleaguered Paton had been in his final years in the music business. Ray Cotter knew. He was the man who helped Paton pick up the pieces of his life and was closer than anyone to Paton. "He was very disillusioned and very mistrustful of anyone connected or involved in the music industry," said Cotter.

Paton and Cotter had met in London in 1978 when Cotter was 18 and a slim, handsome, outgoing gay man. At school he had starred in productions at the Old Vic youth theatre and his first job, at 16, was at Mike Mansfield's TV production office. Mansfield had directed the Bay City Rollers' own 1975 TV show, *Shang-A-Lang,* and was the director of several top ITV shows including *Supersonic* and the *Russell Harty Show.* Cotter said his boss had warned him about the 'not nice' people who frequented the London Weekend Television bar, meaning predatory men.

While working for Mansfield, Cotter came into close contact with Hilary Tipping, the former Bay City Rollers roadie who, in court, had put himself behind the trigger of the gun that had shot the teen fan outside Les McKeown's home. Tipping now worked for Mike Mansfield's company and could be seen sitting beside Mansfield on the segments of *Supersonic* that were filmed in the control room, when Mansfield would be filmed announcing, "Cue the music, or Cue the bubbles or Cue the Rollers etc." Mansfield and Tipping are still working together to this day.

Cotter went on to work in the post room at the Wardour Street offices of Anchor Records. There, he became friendly with a young A&R man, Barry Evangeli. In his early twenties, Evangeli knew Paton well and one evening, before taking Cotter to dinner, suggested they first swing by the Rollers' Heddon Street HQ to see him. "It was no big deal to walk into a reception full of gold and silver albums, I saw that on a daily basis," Cotter said. "I was meeting these people all the time, so it was just another person in the industry." Paton, he recalled, was extremely charming toward him, and they bumped into one another again over the next few months at swish music industry watering holes, restaurants, bars and discos such as Rags just off Berkeley Square and Monkberry's in Mayfair; places frequented by movers and shakers in the industry. "Not gay clubs," said Cotter.

In 1978, when Anchor's entire workforce was made redundant after the label's American parent company, ABC, was taken over by American record label MCA, Paton hired Evangeli to work for him and The Bay City Rollers and invited Cotter to visit him in Edinburgh.

Cotter, 20 years Paton's junior, went up to Little Kellerstain and never left. He had a thing for older men. The two enjoyed a whirlwind romance. "It all seemed very glamorous at first," Cotter said. There were Rollers fans from all over the world permanently camped outside the house. The band had just finished filming a major TV series in America and was touring Japan and Paton had just launched his new teen act, Rosetta Stone, featuring Ian Mitchell.

Their relationship was not sexually exclusive. Cotter recalled having a "fabulous time" one evening in one of the LK caravans after accepting a musician's opening gambit of, "Ray would you like a wank?" He mentioned having "a bit of fun" with another musician who had propositioned him twice and said he turned down offers from a well-known industry figure who was terrified their secret might come out. Cotter also recounted an occasion when Paton bedded three musicians "one after the other" while he waited in the front room. For a time the two shared a bedroom and the pursuit of their respective sex lives – Tam's "brazen sexual behaviour" – rarely caused argument. Cotter recalled just one incident when it did. "I had designs on the guy in there," he said. "I made it plainly obvious I fancied him. But the guy wanted the organ grinder not the monkey... I was furious at Tam."

LK was "palatial" and the lifestyle luxurious. Paton drove him around in the electric blue Rolls-Royce. The underground Edinburgh gay scene was among the most vibrant in the UK. Paton was a feted face in his home city and in London where he had the office on Heddon Street and a two-bedroom apartment in a block called the Fountains on Ballards Lane in West Finchley.

In London they partied amongst the high-living but as select and fashionable as these circles were, Cotter said Paton was appalled by some of the perfidious behaviour that went on. Paton was charismatic, often the life and soul of the party with a mischievous sense of humour. "He could charm the birds from the trees," said Cotter. He was a fabulous salesman. "Listening to him on the phone setting up world tours was impressive. He'd make the promoters think The Beatles were arriving in whatever country."

Paton bragged to Cotter of his famous musician conquests, who "loved it up the arse" and who had "huge" or "tiny" cocks. Paton was full of boasts. "One time we were in his flat in London and he said, 'Do you want to see me get the front page of all tomorrow's Sunday newspapers?'" said Cotter. "And he did. Next day in the *Sunday People, Sunday Mirror, News Of The World*... stories about basically how the band were all taking drugs together and did all these terrible debauched things."

'Pop Idols Who Lived A Lie' and 'Drug Confession By The Bay City Rollers' were two of the headlines that Sunday. The band was looking to shake their teenybop image and gain some rock credibility.

Paton took Cotter to Harrods and spent £70,000 on a sauna in the sports department before teasing a sales assistant on the floor below by turning up a Bang & Olufsen display stereo system to full blast. "He was dressed like a tramp," said Cotter. "Scruffy, rolled-up jeans..." Paton, after having his fun, bought the £20,000 display model.

It all seemed a little surreal. "There was one time we went away and when we got back some fans had got into the house," Cotter recalled. "They didn't take anything but left little notes all over the place, notes to Derek, notes to Les, notes to Alan... notes everywhere." Every

Valentine's Day, at Easter or Christmas, he said, the fans sent gifts for the band to LK from all over the world: mountains of soft toys, sweets, games, clothes, socks, underwear and endless supplies of chocolate. "So much chocolate you couldn't possibly eat it all."

LK was full of animals. As well as the Dobermans, there were two Rottweilers, Dusty and Lulu – "pets not guard dogs", Cotter insisted. There were also white doves nesting in the many dovecotes, an aviary full of brightly coloured lovebirds and parrots, a tank of piranhas and another full of tropical fish.

There was also drugs: Quaaludes, Diazepam [Valium] and Norries, slang for Temazepam, used to treat insomnia and another popular recreational tranquilliser and short-term hypnotic. There was also speed and marijuana and briefly a popular drug called Upjohn – Halcion sleeping pills manufactured by US firm Upjohn – which was abandoned after causing several instances of violence. Sometimes there were orgies as evenings unfolded. "You don't sit in a sauna with your clothes on," Cotter said. Paton was evidently unaware who was in his house half the time. "For a long time, ironically because the house had a lot of security to prevent the fans getting in, it was an open door at LK," said Cotter. "In Edinburgh The Bay City Rollers were such a big deal and everyone thought Tam was connected [to the showbiz world]. An awful lot of queens in Edinburgh used Tam's name inappropriately in order to satisfy their own ends. They either used to pose as Tam, or say, 'I'm a good friend of his' or 'I can take you up to his house'. Tam's name was being used from pillar to post."

Often though, Cotter said, life at the house was quiet, even drab. He had hoped to become a radio DJ and made tapes using Paton's equipment at LK. Paton did not encourage this. He was frequently away, usually on business. The domestic arrangements, although unusual, were stable: Cotter, the dogs and two other young men. One was the teenager who had been groomed by Scambler and taken in by Paton. "He seemed quite happy," Cotter said. Paton took him and Cotter to Fire Island and seemed to enjoy their grapple for his attention. The third young man was around 18 years of age. Paton had sex and cared for him too. He was a huge Bay City Rollers fan.

Cotter was with Paton the night The Bay City Rollers sacked him in April 1979. Paton had decided against accompanying the band on a short German tour and instead sent Barry Evangeli as a stand in. They had been out to Fire Island. The pioneering club was cooking. The Village People and Eartha Kitt had performed there and special buses brought punters from other cities such as Glasgow and Newcastle. "A fantastic place, really good fun," said Cotter.

There was just the two of them at LK. "I heard all this shouting in the kitchen and then he slammed the phone down," said Cotter. "I went through and said, 'What was that all about?'"

"I cannae believe it," said Paton. "That was the Rollers, they're all going mental because I'm not on the tour. They told me I was sacked unless I got my arse out there."

It was Woody and Alan Longmuir. "Obviously pissed," said Paton. "There was a lot of abuse."

"They called him a fat bastard," said Cotter. "You're sacked you lazy fat so-and-so..."

"What are you going to do?" Cotter asked.

"What can I do? That's me sacked."

Derek phoned the next morning to apologise; the pair had been drunk, didn't know what they were saying. Derek asked Paton to continue as band manager.

"No, I'm not interested," Paton replied.

He had made up his mind. "I'd really had enough," he told an interviewer. "There was nothing left there to manage. The monster had got out of control and was destroying itself." He felt an overwhelming sense of relief. "That day I just sat back and I thought, Jesus, thank God!" He said he'd never been as happy "in all my life. Thank God this monster has gone away and I can just get on with my life."

He thought he was a multi-millionaire, would cash in and relax, free of all the unpleasantness managing the Rollers had caused him. It wasn't just the band falling apart and the infighting. He was actively being pursued by the *News Of The World* who suspected Paton hid the true nature of his relationship with the Rollers and was involved with a wider cabal of homosexuals in the industry who preyed on young men.

Outing homosexuals was becoming a popular press pursuit, and few, if any, pop stars or men within the business would admit to being gay. It was seen as a career-killing admission. Paton had already been forced to pretend he was getting married, announcing a high-profile engagement to a pretty young student who had briefly been ensconced at LK. His apartment in West Finchley had recently been robbed and the *News Of The World* had linked it to a vice ring of homosexual teenagers who were targeting "top TV and showbiz celebrities". A series of burglaries were said to have netted the gang close to £500,000. A 17-year-old who admitted handling property stolen from Paton's flat said: "I have had sex with several well-known people." A 19-year-old, said to be behind the scam, was wanted for questioning.

Paton told the *News Of The World*: "My flat in London was cleaned out and I discovered that many showbiz colleagues who have been to clubs associated with gays have also been turned over. I have been completely open with the police. I have no doubt that several burglaries which took place are connected with a crowd of rent boys and gay hustlers whom I had the misfortune to meet."

Paton's retirement ideal did not go to plan. He could not get his hands on any of his Rollers' money. He had vicious arguments with the band's English accountant Stephen Goldberg in London. Goldberg was, at best, slow in providing paperwork. At worse, he seemed obstructive. When Paton received a demand from the Inland Revenue for approximately £800,000, he was not in a position to pay. "I hardly had two pennies to rub together," he said. In total he was told he owed close to £7million to Her Majesty's Revenue & Customs [HMRC] on what he was supposed to have earned from his management of the Rollers.

Paton was frantic: relentless phone calls, endless letters to Goldberg. He could never seem to get to the bottom of anything. "He just wanted to see if there was any physical evidence of income from sales or merchandise," said Cotter. Paton claimed Goldberg had skimmed off at least a couple of million pounds. He was supposed to be looking after and collecting record royalties but he wasn't, Paton said. Those figures were impossible to locate. Goldberg, he said, was only concentrating on getting money from live performances that he could skim.

The problem was further complicated by the situation in America. "They had been setting up companies here, there and everywhere," said Cotter. "Tam didn't even know half of what was going on." Now he was desperate to find out. In the meantime, he and Cotter went to meet with HMRC at an office in Holborn. "They said, 'You do realise we can take everything off you, the house, the flat, everything.' By the time we got back to Edinburgh there was a pending order on of all those things. Tam went, 'These guys are serious.'"

Paton got in touch with a financial adviser and within a week had agreed a £800,000 loan from the Newcastle Building Society "at some incredibly high interest rate", said Cotter, approximately 18 per cent. He had to pay off the Inland Revenue. LK was re-mortgaged and the flat in west Finchley up for sale, the Rolls-Royce too.

Paton borrowed money from his parents and flew to New York. He was, said Cotter, intent on getting his hands on his financial share of The Bay City Rollers, his due for 14 years of management of the band. What happened in America remains a mystery. Paton, Cotter recalled, returned with a lump sum that was shy of £500,000 and a long list of grievances. He would not directly benefit financially from the band ever again.

Back in Edinburgh he was depressed and could no longer raise any enthusiasm for the pop business. Rosetta Stone, particularly, suffered. Ian Mitchell had been sacked and replaced by another teen, Paul 'Flash' Lerwill, whose virginity Paton had taken. Their career had not hit the heights Paton had hoped for. He'd been thinking of putting a new singer, Christopher Hamill, into the group to revamp them. Hamill had approached Paton looking for management and Paton had liked his look. Now he couldn't be bothered with the hassle, the inevitable protest such a move would provoke within the band. It wasn't worth it. Hamill went on to become a star with his own band Kajagoogoo under the stage name Limahl. Billy Gaff became his manager.

Rosetta Stone left him, abandoning the Scottish cottage they had bought. One member said he feared violence. They had seen Paton recklessly drive his Rolls-Royce into female fans and even take a crowbar to the Rolls when he forgot the keys for the petrol cap. Barry Evangeli, who stayed in one of the LK caravans for a time, took over as their manager and briefly revived the band's career in Canada, utilising the songs of Bryan Adams, before they disbanded. Paton made a couple of threatening phone calls to him.

It was via a friend that Paton learned there was a property, a substantial double-fronted, four-storey town house with a basement that had been split into 17 bedsits, up for grabs in Edinburgh city centre. It was run-down but came with paying tenants and could easily be revamped and was going fairly cheap, £300,000, a steal. The money he had returned from America with could either go straight to the taxman or he could buy the property. Paton walked up the broad steps from the street, through the carved stone entranceway and decided to buy the property, 37 Palmerston Place, and opened up a whole new can of worms.

Although he had ostensibly retired from showbusiness, Paton's ego remained huge. He was flattered when a journalist calling himself Paul Hamilton asked about writing his biography. Paton invited him to stay in one of the spare bedrooms at Little Kellerstain. He had recently moved in two brothers, "extra skulls", on the pretence of, "It'd be nice if we had a bit more company," said Cotter. "Really he wanted to get more people into the house so they could pay rent." The new tenants were worth approximately £800 a month to Paton. One of the brothers, a resolute heterosexual, stayed for the next 30 years.

Cotter was immediately suspicious of Hamilton. There was "something shady about him", he said. After a few weeks Cotter went to his room, rifled through Hamilton's case and discovered prison letters "by the dozen". He was not an author. He was a con artist. Paton said Hamilton had only been interested in trying to get him to admit to sexual relations with the Rollers, a story he hoped would be worth £150,000. Hamilton had in fact been visiting some of the tenants at Paton's newly acquired Palmerston Place. "We'd inherited all the tenants when he bought the place," said Cotter. "And we had this elderly lady by the name of Nora, she was in her late sixties, had severe mental health issues and health issues too." Hamilton was suspected of bullying her into parting with money.

"His real name was not Paul Hamilton," said Cotter. After Cotter and Paton confronted him, he went to a bank on Edinburgh's George Street, handed over a note and tried to hold it up. The robbery was an abject failure and the guy got a long stretch in Saughton. Paton felt Hamilton may have told police exaggerated tales about the drugs and sexual activity inside LK. In prison Hamilton tried to pass himself off as Paton.

Soon the real Tam Paton would be in Saughton. He was now being investigated for the crimes that would result in him being jailed in 1982. Cotter had unwittingly opened the door, literally, on events at the very beginning of the whole debacle. He had starting DJ-ing, playing at birthdays or anniversary events in clubs, pubs and hotels. "Often I would come back to LK of an evening and find people dotted here, there and everywhere. I'd think, 'Oh right, they've had a good night tonight.'"

This particular evening he finished his DJ-ing and returned to LK about 2.30am and found two young men, aged "about 17 or 18", asleep on the couch in the living room. As he poured himself a drink the gate buzzer sounded. It was the police. He didn't see any reason to arouse Paton, there was nothing untoward on the property. At the door they told him the names of two people they were looking for and asked were they inside. Cotter said he would check. They marched past him.

What happened next is difficult to corroborate. It appeared the two young men had taken drugs at Paton's and under intense questioning at a police station admitted other activity. From here, the investigation into Paton began. It would last approximately 18 months. From the first two young men, it is presumed the police had extracted a list of other men seen at the house.

Month after month after month, friends of Paton's were summonsed to appear before the procurator fiscal [PF] in Edinburgh. In Scotland the PF conducts preliminary investigations, taking statements from witnesses, before presenting the case for prosecution. "The PF gave me one hell of a grilling," said Cotter. "He said to me, 'There's a hell of a lot you're not telling me.' I said it's the truth."

Paton was aggrieved. The way things were unfolding seemed insidious, he felt his private life was being looked into unfairly – and he felt that the authorities had it in for him. He believed that two young men the police had got to talk had been happy to go along with everything at LK, never once complaining. He hired a sizable defence team full of Scotland's best-known legal names.

People kept coming out to LK telling Paton how they'd been summoned to the PF's office to be questioned. The police were finding out a lot about John 'Sticky' Wilson but seemed interested in tying his activities to Paton. "Tam knew it, John knew it," said Cotter. "They wanted Tam, the ex-manager of The Bay City Rollers." Even if the young men had returned to LK of their own apparent free will on multiple occasions, they were still being pressured to testify. They had to give evidence.

A strong case against Paton was forming. Much of it was based on people saying the same thing about events at LK: the punchbowl of booze was often mentioned, also the availability of drugs, as well as Paton's habit of using a dresser drawer to secure his bedroom door if he was in there with someone.

"He thought they had it for him," said Cotter. "He said to me, 'I've had enough, I can't put up with all this. I'm going to plead guilty.'"

He did so on day three of his trial. He could take the shame of the evidence presented by witnesses no longer, his debauchery brought out in the open. The jury had also watched several hours of video and 8-millimetre films taken from Paton's house. "Whether such films are likely to deprave and corrupt is very much a matter for the individual," QC Donald Findlay told the court, acting for Paton. Findlay, then just 30, went on to become one of Scotland's most famous and highly-paid legal figures, widely regarded as the country's premier criminal law advocate. He said one film depicting homosexual acts between young boys was not Paton's property and was never shown to the boys. "It was very hardcore," Paton later told an interviewer. "They tried to make out they were homemade movies. They weren't. I'm not interested in making homemade movies with kids having sex."

Findlay added that there was no evidence to suggest that youths were compelled to watch any of the sex films. A whip was produced and photographs of Paton and young men. One was of Ian Mitchell sat on Paton's knee squeezing his cheek. Mitchell said he had several calls from "music biz people in state of panic" during Paton's trial.

Paton's home was said to be an attraction to "star-struck" young people, hoping to see Paton or bands he was associated with. Once there the boys were "caught up in sex sessions in bedrooms and a sauna". The house had become a meeting place for young men and women, some who had been friendly with Paton, others who had gone "to see what they could get out of him". It was "tragic that against his background he had succumbed to temptation", said Findlay.

Paton was described as a distraught and broken man, one who was no longer involved with the music business. Appealing for leniency in sentencing, it was stated that Paton had no previous convictions, there was no evidence of force or compulsion being used on the boys (none of them had been brought there by Paton), and, as manager of The Bay City Rollers, Paton had given generously of his time and money to charities, as a result of which he was an honorary captain of the New York Police Department. Paton was said to be, although not a millionaire, a man of substantial means who could afford to pay a large fine. The judge, Lord McDonald, said it was distressing to find a man in Paton's position facing such charges before handing down the three-year sentence. Paton immediately indicated he would appeal.

He had thought about suicide "on several occasions" during the trial. "I thought of hanging myself," he said. "My parents couldn't understand what I was [he had kept the fact he was gay a secret from them]; that was difficult, and I had to go through all that on my own and not one Bay City Roller ever got in touch with me."

He felt persecuted: others should have been in the dock beside him. "Society got their pound of flesh and that's what they wanted," Paton told the press.

Paton claimed he had a 200-page dossier containing damning evidence and photographs, claiming well-known TV personalities, plus lawyers and even policemen took part in sex parties at his home. "I'm talking about young male prostitutes and I'm talking about respectable people," he said. Cotter told me there was some truth in the claim and that Paton had had him write out parts of 'the dossier'. "Until I was charged my home was like an open hotel," Paton told *The Sun*. "A number of well-known people were frequent guests at parties and they accepted my hospitality gladly. But now these showbiz queens have crawled into the woodwork. Some are mincing around clubs in London pretending they've never heard of me. I don't believe I've done any harm to anyone. If I'm going [to prison], I'm not going alone."

"Tam is angry at a lot of people who deserve his place in jail," Cotter told the press at the time. "He's just small fry but the police were out to get him. One day the truth will come out and proof will be given about the nasty people in this affair."

Cotter claimed that some pornographic material shown in court had belonged to Rollers drummer, Derek Longmuir. "It was a genuine gripe of Tam's," he said. "Derek had been on a holiday somewhere and he left some material in Tam's house. Tam wasn't quite sure what it was... he had an office with all his business stuff, members of the band left bits and bobs there."

According to Cotter, Paton adapted quickly to prison life. "He went in a blaze of publicity which made him a sort of mini-celebrity," he said. "Tam had this very likeable nature and he was liked by the prison warders, prison officers and even the guys on the landings. He was like a chameleon. He just had this knack with people whatever their background." Paton said he was given "a job of trust working in the reception".

"I discovered that there were a lot of nice people in jail that understood everything that happened to me going right back to the Rollers," Paton said after his release from jail. "We were all equal. For years before that anyone who spoke to me or came near me always wanted something. Here I was and I couldn't give anyone a thing."

Once Paton was released from Saughton on parole, Cotter and Paton began, together, to rebuild his life. Young bands approached him asking if he'd consider managing them. But he'd had it with the music industry and always turned them down. Cotter tried to persuade him to give it a try. "I used to harp on about that for years after the Rollers," he said

"But because of his experiences within the music industry he thought it was way above his league, far too complicated. He had got to a point where it went right over his head, became far too complex for him. He would openly admit to me that was why he wouldn't consider it."

Paton did agree to take on one final job in the entertainment business. As a favour to a Scottish wrestler who had once acted as muscle for the Rollers, he and Cotter travelled to the United Arab Emirates [UAE] to promote professional wrestling tournaments. The wrestler had contacts with all the big British names of the time: Big Daddy, Giant Haystacks and Mick McManus. The plan was for the British stars to fight with wrestlers from the UAE in locally televised bouts. "Before you know it we were in Dubai and Sharjah promoting these pro wrestling tournaments," said Cotter. "A plane load of British wrestlers flew out and these tournaments were put on." Cotter said no one got properly paid but everyone enjoyed the hospitality of the host nation. It was a laugh. "Tam saw it as a few weeks in the sun," said Cotter. And it was. "It was gorgeous."

Back in Edinburgh they developed the Palmerston Place property. "We got a loan from the bank of £45,000. We spent that on decorating and painting... it was a hell of a lot of work," said Cotter. It was a dark, depressing place, and the tenants were mostly unemployed and had their rent paid by the Government. Some had been homeless previously. One visitor described the property as "like the Bates Motel in *Psycho*".

Paton rolled up his sleeves and got stuck in. He'd never been afraid of hard work. Many of the 17 bedsits were simply single rooms, others were double rooms and a few were a little bigger. The accommodation was basic at best. Over the next few years the decrepit pile noticeably improved. As the standards were raised Paton and Cotter were able to charge a higher rent and attract a better clientele. Ordinary but poor people moved in, couples, women, men. There remained, however, a significantly high percentage of unemployed people in Palmerston Place.

Paton proved his skills as a salesman were intact. "If you were renting a flat off him, he would have you believing by the end of the conversation that you were renting a luxury-serviced apartment," said Cotter. "And it was far from that." Cotter did the admin, keeping a close eye on the accounts of the business – which Paton named after himself, TDP Investments. "I kept him right on that level," said Cotter. "Everything was legitimate. There was nothing shady going on, I was quite vocal about that."

Paton slowly added to TDP's property portfolio. He wound up owning flats and bedsits in a variety of central Edinburgh buildings: on the famous Leith Walk close to Waverly Station, nearby in Leith Street, more close by in Union Street; on Torpichen Place near Haymarket; and in West Maitland Street in Leith. "They were simply flats," said Cotter. Again the accommodation was basic and the tenants were often unemployed or previously homeless. Paton found acquiring mortgages easy and the cash income was regular and handsome. LK also started to fill up with tenants.

As memories of the court case faded along with the wild parties at LK, Cotter and Paton re-evaluated their friendships. "We became regular visitors to Woody's mum and dad's in Oxgangs," said Cotter. "Woody bought that house for himself and moved his mum and dad in. Woody had a flat in a lovely part of Edinburgh and we'd go for dinner with Woody and [his partner] Denise." They also kept in contact and regularly saw Derek. Eric would call often, asking after old Rollers' contracts. Paton was happy to oblige.

Old business friends drifted back: Barry Evangeli visited LK. "There were endless amounts of people coming and going," he said. "It reminded me of Fagin's den, that scene in *Oliver* when they'd been out doing a day's work. These guys would come in with wads of money they collected from the rent on properties and they'd all sit around a table, I've collected this."

Australian TV director and producer Jack Strom also visited. He was a well-known figure in Australia's entertainment circles, close to celebrities such as Olivia Newton-John and Jason Donovan. He moved into music management in the nineties, striking gold with Vanessa Amorosi, a teenage sensation and major international star. At LK he was one just of the guys.

"I was bunking with other guys who would be on benefits and Tam was collecting a per cent of their benefits," he said. "Tam provided accommodation and meals. One night I woke up in middle of night and in the bed next to me there's this guy, Rocky, smelling of alcohol, blood all over his face. They were all devoted to Tam, they'd cook with him, look after his dogs, do the gardening. I never heard any of these guys say a bad word against Tam, they were not boyfriends, just guys who were renting rooms. Tam wasn't taking advantage; he treated them very respectfully. At LK, I never saw any pot, never smelled any. He and the boys were driving to buy cheap cigarettes from over the border…"

Paton was good company when he wanted to be. "Tam had the knack of being able to make people laugh, he was very witty at times," said Cotter. "He knew that. When he was in a good mood and was showing-off, which was a lot of the time, he just used to lark about and say daft things. He'd often say: 'Queens? They're all the fucking same; they're all so unreliable. The minute a bit of cock appears on the scene they're off.'"

Another of his favourites, when he was in a camp mood, was a corruption of the famous Miss Jean Brodie quote: "Give me a girl at an impressionable age and she is mine for life" which he would twist into, "Give me a boy at an impressionable age and he is mine for life." A wry sense of humour was one of his great strengths.

Paton and Cotter struck on the bright idea of renting their properties, particularly Palmerston Place, "exclusively to the pink pound". It was an era when landlords could discriminate against gay people, refuse to rent to them, and get away with it. Paton did the opposite. He turned away straight people. "We thought we'd honed in on a niche," said Cotter. Sometimes prospective tenants would ask if it was true that Paton used to manage the Rollers. "He would say somewhat reluctantly, 'Yeah, yeah, that was a few years ago but I used to manage them in their heyday,'" said Cotter.

Several incidents at Palmerston Place caused Paton and Cotter much distress. A man was found dead on the pavement outside after apparently falling from the window of one of the bedsits while supposedly high on drugs. There was a rumour he had been thrown out of the window, largely based upon the fact Paton owned the property. Another young man, from the nearby Ponton House care home, climbed to the top of a building and threw himself off. When a 37-year-old German man hung himself in another of the bedsits it was reported as "Rollers boss flat tragedy".

Another death at Palmerston Place was truly horrific. Rumours abounded. The victim was called Andy and he was gay. He had hooked up in a club and taken another man back to Palmerston Place. The man, said to be hiding a hatred for gays, split Andy open with a Stanley knife – from throat to groin. Gutted was how it was described. One of the most popular rumours was that Andy was working as a rent boy "in the courts" and had been selling sex to senior figures in Edinburgh's court system.

This rumour, of an ulterior motive for Andy's murder, gained some credence following a major national scandal that erupted following another shocking incident at Palmerston Place. It remains one of the most controversial scandals in recent Scottish history, one that still commands newspaper headlines.

In 1990, a 16-year-old boy from a children's home was allegedly drugged and repeatedly abused by a series of men over a period of 10 days in one of the bedsits at Palmerston Place. Police launched the infamous Operation Planet to investigate and initially brought 57 charges against 10 men.

The high-profile investigation was rumoured to implicate prominent establishment figures, including some from among the Edinburgh judiciary. It was further alleged that Palmerston Place was the hub of an Edinburgh rent boy network that was linked to a paedophile ring or circle, dubbed Edinburgh's 'Magic Circle', that including judges, sheriffs and lawyers. The Magic Circle was said to be involved in serious corruption within the Scottish justice system.

The case sparked a national outcry with names of senior judicial figures, prominent businessmen and secret societies heavily whispered in the press. Paton's named loomed large in the conversations. By dint of the fact he owned Palmerston Place, his past conviction and the rumours around his lifestyle, he was heavily suspected of running the rent boy network, overseeing the abuse and probably involved in it.

Edinburgh's gay scene revolved around a few key venues. The Laughing Duck bar, frequented by Paton and Cotter, was one of the most popular. Gossip about the ongoing case circulated. "We had already heard through the grapevine that QCs were up to things ... and then poor Andy, a lovely guy, was murdered," said Cotter. "We heard lots of bits of gossip but we never looked into it too deeply. Palmerston Place was just a business run by us. I would go round or Tam would go round every week to get the rents and that was it. We never got involved in the tenants' business because that's all they were: tenants."

As the case into the alleged gang rape of the 16-year-old progressed, some suspects were set free. It was reported that there now remained just 10 charges against five men. The police were said to be highly concerned with the final outcome of the case: with only one man jailed (for four years) over the rape of the boy.

The acquittal of so many suspects rang alarm bells among the media, contributing to the 'Magic Circle' scandal, variously known as the "sex for justice scandal" and "sex for judges scandal". Lord Nimmo Smith, then a highly regarded QC, was appointed to conduct a top level Government inquiry into allegations that members of the Scottish judiciary were liable to blackmail and to giving preferential treatment, including unusually lenient sentences, to homosexual criminals. Nimmo Smith delivered *Report On An Inquiry Into An Allegation Of A Conspiracy To Pervert The Course Of Justice In Scotland* to the House of Lords on 26 January 1993 having found no evidence of the existence of such a Magic Circle.

He concluded that Edinburgh QC Robert Henderson – one of Scotland's most admired and respected defence lawyers – was "one of the main instigators and perpetuators of the belief there was a document", or a file, implicating judges and other senior legal figures in homosexual activities and the Magic Circle.* Paton was not mentioned in the 101-page report, nor was he even interviewed during the report's long

---

* In September 2014, Henderson's daughter told the *Daily Mail* that her father (who had died in 2012) repeatedly sexual abused her when she was aged between four and 12. She claimed Sir Nicholas Fairburn, also dead, one time Solicitor General for Scotland and Conservative MP for Kinross, the location of the children's home Paton left money to in his will, was also involved in the abuse.

gestation. Nevertheless, directly after the Magic Circle affair, Paton and Cotter stopped renting to the pink pound. "We let various tenancies expire and we didn't renew them," said Cotter said. "He got rid of all the queens... far too much hassle." Nonetheless, the image of Paton, as some sort of pervert pimp persisted.

It was lesser discussed, and never publicly, that Paton was potentially an arsonist. In 1991 the razing of the grand historic country mansion Kellerstain House was the first in a series of fires in which he was suspected of being involved. Paton's Little Kellerstain was set among the many acres of beautiful countryside that formed part of Kellerstain House's vast estate that included a lodge and stables. Little Kellerstain, it is believed, was built in the estate's one time orchard – explaining the walls all around Paton's home and the fact Paton enjoyed fruit from an array of apple, pear and plum trees in his garden.

The rich, old couple that lived at Kellerstain House had complained fairly regularly about the disturbances emanating from Little Kellerstain: the teenage fans outside in the driveway, the loud parties and the yapping of the two Dobermans, Susie and Elsie. When the couple died, the mansion was bought by an architect and then sold to a developer who planned to turn the place into luxury flats. Tam had clashed with the developer and it was while the developer was in the process of renovating Kellerstain House that it caught fire.

In 1993, Paton's flats on Union Street burned down. Finally, there was a fire at Little Kellerstain itself. It tore through the whole house. Again this was seen as suspicious. Afterwards, Paton had the house revamped to a far higher standard than it had been previously. The redesign meant Little Kellerstain regained much if its wow factor. Paton had taste and some of the ornaments he collected were impressive, not least four Atlas globes of various sizes studded with gemstones. Paton entertained regularly, often on Sunday afternoons. He had kept in touch with many of his old band mates from The Crusaders. They, and their respective wives, all now in the sixties or seventies, would gather for dinner to reminisce about the old days. Paton also enjoyed visits from his brother, David, sitting for hours overs cups of tea and biscuits, recounting stories of their childhoods. Davie, as Paton called him, had taken over the family's potato business when their father grew too old to run it. He had managed it well and when it was finally sold, all the family, including Paton, had enjoyed a windfall. David, now a multi-millionaire, owned a house in Spain and several flats in Edinburgh that Cotter and Paton looked after. Paton often bragged to the press of a luxury villa on the Costa del Sol, "in the Fuengirola area". It was his brother's.

Paton had never come out to his family. "I think they just resigned themselves to the fact he was another nancy boy," said Cotter. "His brother Davie was accepting, but in a very conservative way. A lot of his relatives struggled to cope with Tam being gay." His mother Isabella (Bella) and father, Thomas, often visited the house. "They were very simple people," said Cotter. "His mum was really sweet, his dad could be a cranky old bugger." He was a drinker, still smoking well into his eighties and one time Cotter wondered if he might call a halt on the habit. "Don't fucking well tell me to stop smoking," he'd responded. "They were plain ordinary down to earth, lived in a little council house in Prestonpans, tottered away on the pension," said Cotter.

After Thomas passed away and Bella developed dementia and was moved to a care home (Paton visited her regularly there), the house in Prestonpans had to be cleared out. Thomas, like his son, had secrets. Cotter helped Paton sort through his parents' belongings. They found plastic supermarket bags full of money in cupboards and in the fireplaces upstairs and down. "Just notes," said Cotter. "Some of them had gone out of denomination, old pound notes, very old big ones, old fivers. It wasn't neatly kept, just stuffed in bags. There was tens of thousands of pounds.

Keeping secrets from everybody," Cotter said. "Tam got that from his dad."

If he had no guests, Sunday afternoons were turned over to music. Paton would crank up the volume and play his favourite hits. His tastes were old-fashioned. He was a great fan of Dionne Warwick but often returned to the same three songs: Bing Crosby's 'That's What Life Is All About', Stevie Wonder's 'A Place In The Sun' and Abba's 'Thank You For The Music'. "Tam said he would like those three songs played at his funeral," said Cotter.

504

Paton had a deeply sentimental side. Frequently, after reading a story in the Edinburgh *Evening News* about an elderly person being robbed or mugged, he would have Cotter call the newsdesk to try and find out the person's address. "He would send a cheque anonymously to them," said Cotter. "His accountant said you can't just go randomly writing cheques. Tam said, 'I don't want anyone finding out it was me.'"

The sexual relationship between Paton and Cotter had been slowly, over for years, replaced by a bond of close friendship and mutual support. They had bounced off each other combatively, playfully, for two decades. They knew how one another ticked and their routines had become predictable. Caesar, the blue-fronted amazon parrot kept in a huge cage inside LK, mimicked them.

"Tam swore an awful lot," Cotter said. "Caesar picked up the swear words. He would tell everyone to fuck off. Usually it was, 'fuck off Ray.'"

They had always been seen as a couple. When Kellerstain House was finally developed into three luxury apartments they were filled by well-off professionals. The doctors on the ground floor would invite Cotter and Paton to their New Year's Eve parties where the pair were gently ribbed for reminding people of Laurel & Hardy.

Paton had begun to balloon and was balding badly while Cotter was eerily thin, drawn-looking. Over the years he'd picked up his own bad habits, smoking marijuana heavily and bingeing on Valium and Norries. He was also drinking and often inexplicably depressed. Paton was also frequently ill having been hospitalised following a transient ischaemic attack in the mid-nineties, a mini stroke.

Paton and Cotter's relationship slowly disintegrated. Paton often talked about moving to Spain or Portugal for a more peaceful life. Cotter urged him to do so. It was bluff. He never left the UK not even on holiday. "Initially it was all novelty and let's go here, let's go there," said Cotter. "He bullied me pretty relentlessly. He'd shout and ball at me, bring me down in front of other people, thinking he was being clever."

A hard-core of young men, mostly in their late teens or early twenties, also lived at the house. They all had their uses, helping out with the upkeep of the properties for rent or fixing up Paton's many electronic gadgets. "He wasn't literally renting out the rooms," said Cotter. "He had people living there who gelled with one another. To an outsider it would look odd but when you're in the situation you don't question it. It was a family of sorts but a very dysfunctional one."

Cotter had his own deep-seated problems. His mother had killed herself, by hanging, in 1977, around Christmas time. That time of year was never good for him. Paton by contrast always made a big deal out of Christmas. He immersed himself in putting up multiple Christmas trees, decorations and lights. "On average I'd shove out 350 Christmas cards," said Cotter, now in a woozy, druggy alcoholic haze much of the time.

"It starts to get really grey and complicated," he said. "You realise you have people here who have issues of their own, whether it be family, marital, sexual, personal... then they're given drugs. I got lost in a haze of drugs for quite some time."

Life at LK could be disorientating even without drugs. Paton was addicted to the shopping channel QVC and he would buy from it regularly and spend hours and hours watching it. For a period Radio 1 DJ Tony Blackburn was a presenter on the channel and Paton would call in for a chat. "He would end up chatting with Tony live on TV," said Cotter. "And Tony would talk about the Rollers. Tam would roll out the same old stories: when this happened in Japan or in LA... and he would always add a little more to the story to make it sound more exciting than it actually was.

"He couldn't give up the past. He would constantly call up the newspapers, or be in the newspapers or this documentary or that documentary. There were film crews coming backward and forward from the house. He loved all that, recounting the Rollers story over and over again but missing out all the juicer bits. I said to him, 'Why can you not get your nose away from these bloody journalists, you're not managing a pop group anymore you're just managing flats and selling drugs? Why are you even entertaining the press?' He'd just tell me to shut up."

Fans of the Rollers would still show up at Little Kellerstain, often Japanese. The house was seen as a place of pilgrimage to many. Paton would sometime let them into the house before making himself scarce.

Paton still played host to young men who fulfilled his sexual desires, some regular faces. Many still seemed to come from care home backgrounds or were homeless or had problems of one sort or another. There was also a whole raft of other activity involving Paton and the men who lived in the house. One of them, who allowed Paton to have sex with him, drove Cotter to distraction. He was the new favourite and he worked that affection. He was in his early twenties and loved cocaine. Others in the house found him arrogant and he was an unpopular figure. It all got too much for Cotter. He finally moved into a new mobile home Paton had craned into the grounds at LK especially.

"I got pissed off with the people in the house," said Cotter. "I didn't want be involved in any nonsense he might be involved in. I made that clear. I want nothing to do with that. I said, 'Do whatever you want to do as long as you don't involve me.' That was a clear boundary."

Cotter was still DJ-ing and had progressed from playing anniversaries to club work. When it came to the property business Cotter had helped Paton build, there was an uneasy ˙stalemate. They attended private landlord forums together, arguing in favour of the newly introduced licencing for "houses of multiple occupancy" [HMOs] – houses that had been split into bedsits or flats. Paton bragged of owning "41 or 42" such flats. The raised standards needed to acquire a license, for instance the need for smoke detectors and fire doors, meant increased rents and the legitimisation of an area of the renting market often seen as slightly shifty. Failure to comply with the new licensing rules was a criminal offence.

"I was willing to help him with it but I was prepared to only go so far," said Cotter said. "I said, 'Put me on the payroll if you want me to do all these bits of paperwork and visit tenants', the boring stuff really. He wasn't willing to do that with me."

Paton took away Cotter's ability to sign the company cheques but still relied on him. "He had intercoms everywhere, the kitchen, living room, all the areas where people congregated, and he had them in the caravans. He'd shout, 'Ray! Ray! What are you doing? Get over here now. I'm needing this paperwork done!'"

Sometimes Cotter refused, so piles of letters that needed answering built up. "Tam was a very much here and now person, he'd want it dealt with," said Cotter. "Then I'd do a letter and present it to him and he'd say, 'No that's not the way I want it.' When four or five drafts later he still wasn't happy Cotter would tell him, 'Fuck you, do it yourself.'" They wouldn't speak for days. Paton might unplug the electricity supply to Cotter's caravan. "I would wait until he'd gone back in the house and then search for the fuse and put my electric back on. He'd say, 'Oh you're not dealing with this or that', and I'd go, 'No because you were a bastard'. So we were being as childish or as bloody-minded as one another."

Finally, in 2006, Paton moved Cotter out of Little Kellerstain and into one of his flats. He wanted to rent out the caravan. "It was Tam's greed for money," said Cotter. Paton bizarrely spoke to a newspaper about being "dumped" by his "toyboy". He spoke of being "suicidal", of his "heartbreak and devastation" in an article headlined: 'Rollers Boss Tam: My Lover's Left Me'. Plenty felt Paton only invoked Cotter as a long-term partner or boyfriend to prevent speculation over his deviant sex life.

"If I had been just an ordinary gay guy, I'd been allowed to go on with my life," he told one interviewer. "I was never into young boys or anything like that, as they're trying to make out now and all the kind of rubbish that goes along with it. I live with somebody and I've lived with him for 25 years."

He charged the man who had stuck by him for 27 years' rent of £160 a week, and then had him evicted by Sheriff's officers when he fell behind on it, making him homeless. They'd had a few runs in since then but were now talking again. But this was no time to think of Ray.

He chopped out the cocaine in the wet room and watched as the trade greedily hoovered it up. Sticky had not lied. The new one was gorgeous. Paton took hold of his penis and started to masturbate him.

CHAPTER 17

Drugs

"I've been spat at in the street. I go to the supermarket and people walk into doors they are so busy staring at me, they trip over trolleys. It's because I'm a peculiarity, I'm not normal and I don't live the normal life. I was never meant to be normal. I went to a restaurant recently and the owner came up and asked 'Are you Tam Paton? Then you'll have to leave, we don't want your type in here. Leave immediately'. That hurts me, it really does. I'm being judged by people, who are they to judge?"

– Tam Paton

For Paton the drug dealing began in earnest once he was released from prison. Some of the young men who had found themselves at LK over the years became his workers. They lived at the property like some weird kind of cult. They were known by odd sounding nicknames. Among the dogs at the property there were some equally loyal servants. Shona was mentioned as being particularly keen to protect Paton. The remoteness of Little Kellerstain and its heavy security system was another plus point.

One anonymous source spoke of his time working for Paton as an enforcer. There were several. His version of the events that unfolded at LK in the eighties and nineties rang true with several others interviewed for this book. Paton kept what he called a 'shop' inside his home but it was not the 'tuck shop' the *Daily Mirror* had reported on. From morning until 10 at night, the shops sold drugs. Mobile phones, secret stashes (in the grounds and at his other properties), dealers, buyers and suppliers; it was like a game to Paton, offering him the buzz he had been missing since leaving the music business. The profit, he found, was more attractive and there was less slipperiness involved: you knew where you stood with hashish, wads of cash and major underworld figures.

The source said Paton was a major player in Scotland's drug scene, a Mr Big of Edinburgh. It was not a role for the timorous. Twice, both times in the driveway at LK, Paton was seen fist-fighting with heavy players in the Edinburgh drug trade. The anonymous source said Paton progressed from ordering kilos of hashish – mainly soap bar – to tonnes [1,000 kilos] of the stuff and would routinely deal 200 kilos a week. He saw hundreds of thousands of pounds in cash being exchanged. Alongside the hashish, Ecstasy – the man saw hundreds of thousands of pills pass through Paton's hands – and speed were also on the menu. Cocaine was also being delivered to LK in bulk; in multiple kilos.

Les McKeown was seen to regularly visit LK to score cocaine while he stayed in Edinburgh at a house in nearby Corstorphine. He was often seen in Paton's room. Pat McGlynn was also seen at LK looking to score drugs.

The anonymous source said Paton demanded and commanded the utmost loyalty from his own key men, his lieutenants – Paton saw it all as a Mafia set-up. The man admitted that there were handguns and shotguns involved. Sometimes a hammer would suffice. Or a knife. "I would stab you as soon as look at you – quicker if Tam told me to do it," he said. Paton he said *had* made a pass at him but it had gone no further. The men he saw coming to LK to have sex with Paton were 16 or over and often Paton took the time to get to know their parents, although he seemed fonder of his dogs. There may have been hundreds of boys over the years, often from care home backgrounds, he said. There were often as many of six in the house, split between Paton and Phil McNeil out in his caravan. When it looked as if things were drifting toward sex, he said he went to his room, lit up a joint and put on headphones.

Over the years, incrementally, the scene at LK got heavier and heavier. An associate was shot dead in gangland activity and at one stage Paton was said to have met with the infamous Paul Ferris. Ferris was involved in one of Scotland's longest and costliest court cases in 1992, accused of the murder of several people and the attempted murder of 'The Godfather' of Glasgow, Arthur Thompson, with whom Ferris was said to have previously enjoyed a long career as an ultra-violent enforcer. Also accused of supplying heroin, cocaine and ecstasy, Ferris was acquitted of all charges but, after a two-year surveillance operation by MI5 and the Special Branch, was later jailed for seven years in the late nineties for offences relating to firearms and explosives.

It was said Ferris had an interest in taking over the Edinburgh drug market and that Paton had aggressively defended his territory. Word spread among his impressed men that Paton had told Ferris to fuck off.

Paton operated unfettered for almost two decades, through the eighties and nineties. There was one laughable raid on LK in 1999 following a tip-off. Forty officers descended on Paton's home but only found a tiny quantity of cannabis. They took away other 'substances' and a computer for analysis but no charges were brought against Paton. He received an apology from the Lothian & Borders' chief constable.

It was unclear who had tipped off the police. There were many visitors to LK and some were inevitably jealous of Paton's success or felt he had mistreated them in the past. One explanation as to why the raid had been an abject failure and why Paton had managed to get away with such large-scale drug dealing for so long was that he had a contact or contacts within the police. There was also speculation that Paton had turned police informant.

During the surprise search of his property (ordered by Surrey police), intended to uncover any links between Paton and the gang rape allegation, in January 2003, the police uncovered drugs said to be worth £30,000 including Ecstasy, amphetamines and cannabis. It was reported that 17 9 oz bars of cannabis (the equivalent of over 4 kilos) were recovered from the ensuite dressing room in Paton's bedroom, along with a tub containing another broken-up bar. He was immediately charged with various drug offences including supply.

Paton's bank accounts and assets were frozen due to the drug charges and his passport confiscated. The Crown contemplated an asset confiscation order. Paton insisted all his money came from property investments. "I had nothing when I came out of jail," he said. "Now I have 40 flats in Edinburgh's west end and a wonderful mansion. If the law tries to take away my wealth, they will have the biggest fight on their hands."

After consulting with lawyers, Paton, who had initially claimed he was looking after the cannabis for others, changed his story on the drugs found at LK: "Anything I had at the house was purely for personal use."

What happened next came as a surprise. There was another police raid on Little Kellerstain in March 2003 after Lothian & Borders' drug squads acting on a tip-off stopped a car leaving Paton's home at 2am. Inside they found crack cocaine worth over £10,000 and thousands of pounds in cash. Inside the house, Paton was caught holding four 9oz bars (the equivalent of a kilo) of cannabis and another two 9oz bars were discovered in a chair where he had been sitting. He claimed someone else living in the house had thrust the bars into his hands as the officers rushed in. An unspecified amount of cash was also recovered from the house. Paton was charged with further drug offences.

Nine months later, in December 2003, with Paton still not having stood trial, Little Kellerstain was sensationally raided again in what police described as an "intelligence-led" operation. Officers recovered £50,000 in cash, a small amount of cannabis, some sleeping tablets from Paton's bedroom and three air pistols. Paton was again cautioned.

A shocked Paton said: "I am being victimised. This is never ending. The police came here looking for drugs and took away three air pistols and my sleeping tablets. We were all handcuffed while they turned the house over. I can't believe this has happened again."

It did not stop there. In February 2004, 20 drugs squad police offices disguised in a Royal Mail van entered Little Kellerstain. They found two kilos of cannabis resin, a bag containing 300g of herbal cannabis, and £3,000 in cash in Paton's bedroom, plus two sets of weighing scales and a diary with notations in it and other drugs. Two visitors and five men renting rooms at the house were questioned.

Paton was not actually at home during this raid and was in fact attending a brief preliminary hearing into the January and March 2003 drug charges at Edinburgh High Court. He was chatting to his legal team outside the courtroom when uniformed officers moved in to arrest him on further drug charges: supplying cannabis and possession of cocaine and the tranquilliser diazepam.

Paton collapsed when he first appeared at Edinburgh High Court in April 2004, facing charges relating to the early 2003 raids including the supply of cannabis, trafficking in Ecstasy and cocaine. He was rushed by ambulance to hospital on a stretcher with an oxygen mask over his face. It was reported he may have suffered an angina attack. The trial date had to be postponed until reports on Paton's health were prepared. Paton insisted the episode was genuine, and was perhaps an anxiety attack. When finally the case did make it to court, Paton pleaded guilty to two charges of being concerned in the supply of cannabis. Paton was fined a then record £280,000. He was told his age and state of health along with his guilty pleas had saved him from being jailed. He told the press that the fine was "a lot" but "not a lot to me". He said he was worth £7.5 million with earnings of £30,000 a month from rent on his properties. Paton insisted he was starting legal proceedings to recover over £400,000 in cash he claimed the police had seized during the various drugs raids.

In November 2004, a trial for the second set of drug charges relating to the December 2003 and February 2004 raids was postponed after Paton was again rushed to hospital in an ambulance following a dramatic collapse. This time however Paton was beyond doubt precariously ill and had suffered a serious stroke. A blood clot had stopped the blood flow to his brain and Paton had collapsed at home. Doctors did not know if there would be any lasting damage. Common causes of a stroke are obesity and high blood pressure. In hospital the whole left side of his face was said to be totally unresponsive. Paton told the press that he blamed stress and police harassment. He stayed in hospital for five nights.

A month later, in December 2004 there was a remarkable fifth raid on Little Kellerstain. Two cars were stopped and searched near Paton's home on a Friday night and a total of £17,500 worth of cannabis was recovered. As part of the same operation, Paton's home was searched and a small amount of cannabis was recovered. Paton was not charged.

He said the police "came in like the Gestapo", cutting through metal gates and smashing through doors to gain entrance to his home. Paton said he had been handcuffed and held down on a sofa during the search. This, he pointed out, occurred just a month after his stroke. "I tried to explain that I had recently had a stroke but they wouldn't listen," he said. "They spent five-and-a-half hours searching my entire house and it was ripped apart."

His license to rent out bedsits at Palmerston Place was suspended by Edinburgh City Council's licensing committee. He also had permission to rent out rooms at LK removed. Paton said he would appeal the decision.

"In more than 30 years of having rented out accommodation, I have never had a complaint against me," he said. He claimed that two of the four people living at Little Kellerstain (the number had dwindled from 12 a year earlier) were carers who he needed to look after him following his stroke. "The council has got to tell me why I'm not a fit and proper person," he added. "Are they talking about my personal lifestyle? That's an infringement of human rights. If they are talking about neglecting people's safety, I have never had a major fire or lost a life at any of my properties. They are taking away roofs from over people's heads… putting people out on the streets."

Soon Paton no longer owned Palmerston Place. The "property tycoon" with a "property empire" was coming undone. He felt the pressure crushing down on him. But he did not crumble. He had presented a series of medical certificates over many months that kept stalling the start of his second trial on drug charges. The time limit on bringing the charges against him to court elapsed. It looked like he might walk free. In May 2005, however, with prosecutors describing it as an administrative error, a hastily arranged hearing was held and a retrospective extension was allowed. The indictment was re-raised.

"This has been a terrible strain on me, but I know that I am innocent and justice will prevail," Paton said. "I've been through sheer hell." He began to talk about heart attacks. He claimed to have had two already.

The trial began in June 2005. Paton pleaded not guilty to all charges. He told Edinburgh Sheriff court that in the instance of the February 2004 raid somebody must have dumped the drug in his home. He told the jury that he had rented out rooms to seven men at the time, some of who had been placed with him through Edinburgh City Council. He said the men had been homeless and used drugs including cannabis. "I did not leave cannabis in my bedroom," he stated. "I do not know how it got there. I do not know who put it there."

The notes in his diary found at the scene, he claimed, referred to cigarettes and money given to tenants. The scales the police found were for weighing his gold jewellery. He denied being concerned in the supply of cannabis and cannabis resin from his home between November 2003 and February 2004 while on bail. Although charges of possessing cocaine and diazepam, which Paton had also denied, had been dropped, he still faced a long stretch if found guilty. There were lengthy jail sentences for possession and supply of up to 14 years

At the end of a four-day trial the jury took just under an hour to return their majority verdict of not guilty. Talking to the press, Paton denied using cannabis, saying he had only once tried it in yoghurt. Inside LK, a jubilant Paton held his own court. He had won. He would often be heard waxing lyrical about the law, fancying himself as learned QC. He could quote passages of defence speeches made by the illustrious Sir Nicholas Fairburn QC. During these long riffs, Paton seemed to slip into another character and his hypnotic oratory was deeply convincing.

He continued to peddle drugs on an industrial scale. This seemed self-evident when a violent confrontation erupted at LK in October 2006. Five armed men from Liverpool held up Paton and five of his men and were said to have taken £100,000 in cash and £130,000 in gold and jewellery from one of the safes. During the confrontation Paton said he and his "friends" were attacked with knives and sprayed with CS gas. "They tried to kill me and would have if they had been able to," he said. One of his men suffered a broken leg and three broken ribs during the attack. Paton fought ferociously and released the dogs before fleeing to his Range Rover and speeding off.

Paton contacted the police and named one of the gang, a man he admitted knowing and willingly letting into LK. He later identified the other men involved at an identity parade. They had all been discussing a property deal, Paton said, and the talks had "got nasty".

The gang was variously charged with armed breach of the peace, supplying cannabis, assault and robbery and possession of an imitation firearm, namely a CS spray. They would receive sentences of between seven and thirteen-and-a-half months. Paton called the sentences lenient, the men "animals" and told police he was "quite disturbed and fearful for his safety". "I have been through a lot of things in my life and I can handle it, but that was terrifying," he said.

The press took the line Paton fed them and described the incident as a "property deal gone wrong". There was little investigative work done to suggest other factors were at play and that Paton was actually playing with fire. Only weeks after the incident at LK, one of the men from Liverpool, Phillip Woolley, was accused of being involved in the gangland slaying of Michael Wright. At Liverpool Crown Court he would receive a life sentence, with a minimum term of 24 years, for that murder.

Paton's notoriety as a drug lord was advanced when the £280,000 fine he had received for supply of cannabis was quashed and investigators were granted the power to look at Paton's financial dealings over the past six years under a Proceeds of Crime action. Crown prosecutors clearly felt Paton's substantial assets were the profits of drug dealing. In December 2006, at Edinburgh Crown Court, Paton was ordered to pay £240,000 under the action. He was also fined £40,000. The confiscation order under the Proceeds of Crime act was a significant black mark against his name although he insisted, to the press, that he could not prove his money was earned honestly only due to "bad book-keeping of many years".

Finally free of all pending drug charges, but aware the police were still watching him, Paton invited two prominent Scottish journalists into his home in January 2007. The idea was to show he had nothing to hide and maybe even garner a little sympathy. It was also a chance to show-off, a dangerous game in which the narcissist in him won out. After a life lived out in the press, he still craved publicity. He did not need to do this. It was almost a sickness.

'Welcome to Tam Paton's weird world' ran the *Edinburgh Evening News* feature in which Sandra Dick described "chunky gold and diamond jewellery" dripping from Paton's right hand and "£1,200 chandeliers" hanging from the sitting room ceiling. She wrote of being introduced to several men: Herman who "walks the dogs", Blockie, who does "all the electrical work" and Spam "who has been here nine years". One of them led away a "snarling, growling" Rottweiler. Massive TVs blared out in every room and there was a "faint whiff of cannabis lingering in the stale air".

"I've been spat at in the street," Paton told Dick. "I go to the supermarket and people walk into doors they are so busy staring at me, they trip over trolleys. It's because I'm a peculiarity, I'm not normal and I don't live the normal life. I was never meant to be normal. I went to a restaurant recently and the owner came up and asked 'Are you Tam Paton? Then you'll have to leave, we don't want your type in here. Leave immediately'. That hurts me, it really does. I'm being judged by people, who are they to judge?"

Talk turned to the drug charges. "I was raided five times, they got lucky twice," he said. "I'm not going to sit here and say I think cannabis is good. I know the effects it can have, paranoia, schizophrenia. I have always taken my cannabis in yoghurt, I have high blood pressure, it calms it down to the extent I sit and watch Mickey Mouse and think it's hilarious."

Dick described how the doorbell at Little Kellerstain chimed regularly with visitors coming and going, young men congregating in the kitchen just off a tiled "leisure suite". The men, "none seemed older than 30, some with shaven heads, others painfully thin", were said to sleep in four bedrooms lining the corridor leading to Paton's "cluttered master bedroom".

"People phone and say, 'Can you accommodate someone?'" said Paton. "There's Chris, he's 29, married, five kids. He was into heroin, he's on detox now. His mother and his wife didn't want anything to do with him. I fill that gap."

517

Dick noted how Herman wandered around "talking to himself" and how Spam had "the boyish looks of a teenager". Spam, she wrote, had arrived at Paton's after falling out with his parents. Paton had "taken him under his wing". Paton said: "I tell these lads to have a shave or get cleaned up. Maybe they are living off me but I don't want to be rattling around in this house all by myself."

He talked about his weakened heart and said he had drawn up a will leaving all his cash to the Canine Defence League, the Dog Trust plus "something for the dog and cat home at Seafield" and "a bit for the children's hospice at Kinross". "It'll be then that people will turn around and say, 'Oh he was okay after all, he wasn't the dirty old bugger that we thought he was,'" Paton predicted to Dick.

The second journalist was Matt Bendoris of the *Scottish Sun*. 'Sordid lifestyle of shamed Rollers' boss,' the headline. Bendoris would later describe Paton as "the most repulsive and sleaziest man I have ever met". During his visit to LK, he wrote how Paton was surrounded by several young men with skinheads and tattoos and that the two caravans at the bottom of the garden were "choc full of even more young men".

During the interview, Bendoris reported gleefully how Paton had mistakenly left his trouser zip undone. He was photographed this way, his vast girth to the fore as he sat on the couch with his arm around one of his dogs. Perhaps this said more about Bendoris than the obese old man in the picture. Why not tell him?

Bendoris did ask Paton if he was sleeping with the boys at his house. Tam insisted that "these laddies aren't gay". He boasted how hundreds of such "laddies" had stayed with him over the years. He went on to deny the allegations of rape made by McGlynn, which the police had not yet officially dismissed. "I never played with any of the Rollers," he said. "There wasn't one I fancied." He added that he loved to flaunt his wealth to taunt the band members who were reportedly penniless.

He also insisted that he was not a drug dealer. "Never have been. No heroin or cocaine are allowed in here."

After this interview was published, Ray Cotter got in contact with Bendoris and was reported as telling him: "Kellerstain is full of Tam's concubines. These young men do sexual favours for Tam in return for cocaine, cannabis or any drug of their choice. Tam is also a commercial drug dealer – not a social one. I used to live on my own in one of the static caravans. Whenever I told him that I was going to the police to expose him as a drug dealer he used to have me beaten up by his hired thugs, regularly – it was horrendous."

Paton responded to Cotter's claims. "He was a companion," he said. "He may have thought he was my partner but he was not. I kept him for about 22 years and he is struggling to accept our friendship's over. I want him out of my life. I wish he would just walk away. I'm nearly 70 and I am due to have heart surgery. I can't be doing with this type of thing. He is a poor soul with a mental problem who misguidedly thinks I owe him something. He is still a one-night stand who doesn't know how to walk away."

At the time Cotter, unemployed and depressed, was spending his nights at homeless accommodation in Edinburgh and dependent for food on charity-run soup kitchens. He had begun bombarding Paton with abusive phone calls and the pair clashed violently in a busy Edinburgh street. Cotter was arrested after ripping the windscreen wipers from Paton's Range Rover.

But Paton now really needed to stop thinking about Ray. He was breathing heavily already from the small exertion of wanking off the young man. He felt light-headed. He ought to stop. Paton was determined however to make him shoot his load. He wouldn't be happy until that happened. He redoubled his effort. He always had been a fighter, prepared to go that extra mile, to do what needed to be done – even when that meant stepping over the line. He smiled his last crooked smile. It was more a grimace.

The room was bathed in a grim reddish light and mould climbed the walls. Wet, dirty towels and rugs littered the floor. There was an unpleasant odour in the room that stuck in the nostrils like the faded glory still caught in Paton's clogged-up old arteries.

This great monster of a man, the sweat now falling off him as he wanked the boy feverishly, would never give up. Resolve and resilience; what else had kept him going during the battering he'd taken in the media over the past 30 years.

Even now, as the first searing pain shot through his chest, he was facing a fresh set of drug charges having been arrested just six months ago, in September 2008, in an Edinburgh car park following a month-long undercover police operation.

He stood accused of 12 charges including possession of herbal cannabis and cannabis resin, attempting to supply the Class C drug and being concerned in the supply of cannabis. The alleged offences were said to have taken place on two dates – in August 2008 and once again in September when he was arrested.

Paton had been forced to spend an uncomfortable 10 days in police custody before finally being bailed on appeal due to his ill health having made no plea or declaration. "I'm too old for all this," Paton said as *The Sun* headlined its story, 'Too Sick for Nick'.

Those charges would never be heard in court though. Paton was trying to say something now but couldn't get any words out. He buckled, gasping for breath. He felt himself contract violently. The heat filled his head and his vision started to blur. Another painful electric shock rifled through the left side of his body. He groaned out loudly.

The young man screamed. Paton's face looked hideous, twitching uncontrollably but with eyes frozen. Then he crashed heavily to the floor. The man ran from the wet room shouting for help as Paton's huge bulk slipped into the plunge pool. He was unconscious: in cardiac arrest after suffering a heart attack.

The two armed men, alerted by the man's screams, rushed to the wet room. Paton needed emergency CPR (cardiopulmonary resuscitation) – chest compressions and rescue breaths to keep blood and oxygen circulating in the body. The men panicked. Paton was enormous and they struggled with his body. One of them was not strong. The other was known as a bully. Both were greedy. Both were high. Their thoughts were confused. They could not easily remove Paton from the plunge pool.

The two bits of trade, both in shock, were told to go to one of the caravans and stay there. The contents of both safes in Tam's bedroom were then emptied – cash, jewellery and drugs and anything else of any value. There was over £1.5 million of stuff and it filled several black bin bags. The bags were hidden in the field opposite the house. It took several trips. There was a lot of notes.

Finally a paramedic arrived on the scene. He had travelled by motorbike. The Royal Edinburgh Hospital was less than 10km away. Paton was lying face down in the plunge pool. It was approximately 8.45pm. He was dead.

The official cause of death was a cardiac arrest. Whether efficient CPR could have saved Paton is unlikely to ever be known. There were no suspicious circumstances according to a spokeswoman for Lothian & Borders police. According to *The Sun*, the "sordid former boy band Svengali" had "checked out the way he would have liked, in a jacuzzi full of young men."

On being told the news by a Scottish newspaper, Pat McGlynn said simply: "Great. I hope he roasts in hell. Paton was a very bad guy but he had contacts in high places."

Les McKeown was equally forthright. On April 10, 2009, just 36 hours after Paton had died, *The Sun* published a major interview in which McKeown elaborated on his recent accusation that Paton had raped him. He said he was delighted Paton was dead.

"He was a drug dealer and rapist beast," said McKeown. "I'm sure all the Rollers were damaged by knowing Tam. Some of us were more badly affected than others. I was just a young boy when he raped me. Tam was an evil manipulator of young men. He used his power and drugs. Tam was great for plying the band with drugs to keep us working and under his control. He was always experimenting with new drugs. I dabbled with a bit of opium and it suited him – you don't understand what's happening to you. He was a really intimidating, big man. If he wanted something he forcibly got it."

McKeown said Paton had raped him when he was "18 or 19" and he had carried the burden of his "dark secret" ever since. He described how he'd been put off telling police after McGlynn's claims that Paton raped him were dismissed. "I did think about it but in all the recent court cases Tam seemed to get away with any allegation thrown at him," he said. "He was caught red handed with lots of cannabis in his house but just got a slap on the wrist. He was involved in a lot of seedy stuff in Edinburgh but he got away. It was almost like he was protected."

McKeown also reiterated his claims that he was fearful of what Paton might do to him if he went to the police. He claimed Paton had threatened to kill him once already if he did not stop accusing him of swindling The Bay City Rollers out of millions of pounds. "I was thinking I could be putting my wife and family in danger," he said. "I was that scared of him. He knew a lot of unsavoury people. People that are involved in drugs aren't very nice people. They shoot people, knife people and I just didn't want that around my front door. I have more or less been living in fear all these years. Every year he would send you a Christmas card and the whole purpose was him pointing out he knew where I lived. Any time I got a new telephone number he'd have someone ring up saying, 'Oh, sorry, I was trying to get a hold of Tam' yet I'd only had the number three days.

"The man was a monster and everyone knows it. I almost feel guilty for being so happy but I can't imagine a man nor beast who will be mourning his passing. It might sound a bit off celebrating a man's death, but he ruined a lot of peoples' lives including mine."

In *The Scotsman*, which had requested further comment, McKeown added: "The Scottish people can sleep well knowing the beast of Kellerstain is dead. The parents and children can feel safer as one more predator is off the streets. All the thousands [of] people that have been affected by his devastating reign of drugs, terror and abuse can breathe a sigh of relief. He can no longer directly affect our lives. The tyrant despot is dead; long may he remain so."

Elsewhere he called Paton, "a thug, a predator and a drug-dealing bastard" and said: "In the band we used to call Tam Paton, the Beast of Kellerstain. We knew even then there was something weird about him and that he was some sort of beast. I always found it very strange that Tam Paton should be singularly this different type of animal. He wasn't a gay person at all: he was a disgusting beast. I don't think he had any actual real relationships, he got his kicks from raping and pillaging. He was pillaging all our money and raping any young lad he could get on drugs basically."

The band had not routinely referred to Paton as the Beast of Kellerstain during the seventies. McKeown had been a drug addict and alcoholic for many years now and much of what he'd told the press in the past sat uneasily with the other band members. Many felt that having admitted he knew he was bisexual as a young teenager, any sexual encounters between him and Paton were more consensual.

Ian Mitchell was initially the only Bay City Roller to speak out positively about Paton. He said Paton was "like a father to me", adding: "He gave me an opportunity that comes only once in a lifetime. I will be forever in his debt. I truly loved Tam and I will miss him dearly. Thank you Tam, for if it wasn't for you, not *one* of The Bay City Rollers would be where we are today." McKeown said Mitchell was "in denial".

There were countless newspaper obituaries. *The Times* said Paton had "effectively invented" the "tartan-clad boy band". *The Guardian* said he was "scarred by a string of scandals involving sex offences with teenage boys, financial malfeasance and drug possession". *The Australian* called him a "master manipulator", while *The Independent* called him "disgraced". The *Irish Independent* wrote poetically of the "Svengali of the sugar-sweet Rollers" who had "seedy tastes" stating how Paton had "created a clean-cut image for the Scottish group, duping their fans – mostly screaming pre-pubescent girls – into believing that his charges preferred a glass of milk to sex and drugs". Liverpool's *Daily Post* wrote: "In the wheeling and dealing demi-monde of pop music promotion, there were few hustlers to match Tam Paton... there wasn't a word of truth [in what he said] as Paton tried to build up the band's squeaky-clean image."

The *Daily Mail* ran a hastily assembled but damning splash on April 11 with the headline 'The Sex Factor: He was the original boy band Svengali, yet Tam Paton ruined his reputation for ever with his lust for young men, drugs and money.'

Light on facts, its headline reflecting the popularity of *The X Factor* talent show, the *Daily Mail* called Paton a "rapist", "pederast", "criminal", "drug dealer", "police informant", "pervert", "thief" and "liar" who many – "including police sources" – claimed had made "most of his cash" as a cannabis kingpin.

The word pederast derives from the Greek "love of boys". Pederasty, broadly defined as a relationship between an adult male and adolescent male, generally 12-17, has a long history among many cultures. It is a widely accepted practice in English public schools. Cultural historians draw a line at anal sex. The legal status of pederasty in most countries is determined by whether or not the boy has reached the local age of consent, and as to whether such contact is considered abusive. There was no evidence that Paton had continued to practice pederasty beyond 1982. In fact most of his sexual partners at LK, all the trade, seemed to have been aged between 17 and their early twenties.

Also on April 11, just three days since his death, *The Scotsman* ran an article about Paton headlined: 'Rollers chief linked to sex abuse network'.

The main source was Dr Sarah Nelson, the same who would kindly supply the foreword for this book. She made a first plea for a full retrospective investigation into Paton. Nelson said that in 2004 she had carried out a study into adult male survivors of childhood sexual abuse on behalf of NHS Lothian and uncovered numerous allegations against Paton, many of them involving teenage boys who were afraid to go to the police at the time for "fear of repercussions".

"I think it is safe to say there are dozens of alleged victims," she said. Nelson said these were mainly very vulnerable teenagers, from a care background, who should have been under society's protection. "They were groups of severely damaged young men, offenders who were now in the criminal justice system, but who had eventually revealed being abused in some kind of network involving Mr Paton." Nelson asserted that there existed a network of flats in Edinburgh where the victims were "placed" and where "scenes of criminal activities took place". The flats belonged to Paton and the victims she said, were "men beholden" to him.

Nelson had recently concluded a further report into adult survivors of childhood sexual abuse, on behalf of the Scottish Government. She said more claims against Paton had been reported – usually reluctantly – to various workers, including those in the prison, criminal justice, housing and social work sectors.

Nelson's work in the area was being used by the Government to form a national strategy. She told *The Scotsman*: "Given that my own research report of February 2009 raised some very disquieting issues about apparently continuing risks to boys in care, especially those with a history of residential care and offending, I believe such an inquiry [into Paton] must be instigated in order to protect others and to learn lessons for protecting these boys in future."

The police *were* examining Paton but not in relation to sex abuse. It was reported that some of his fortune, estimated at between £8.5 and £12 million, could be seized under the Proceeds of Crime law. Much of the money, the Crown felt, had been made from Paton's drug dealing enterprises.

There was much speculation over Paton's money. Few believed his boasts while he was alive of leaving his fortune to charity, figuring it as a ruse to try and garner positive press coverage. He had rewritten his will at least once before he died. It was suggested one of young men who lived at LK had persuaded Paton to write out Ray Cotter who had, at one stage, been promised a large sum and some property. Cotter felt he had a legitimate claim to a share of Paton's wealth. There were plenty of others also eager to find out what they had been left.

Paton's brother, David, 79, who lived locally in the coastal town of Cockenzie, took control of his brother's funeral arrangements. Other family members, chiefly Paton's two sisters, were said to be on their way to Edinburgh to help deal with his affairs. One, Mary, had emigrated to America while the other, Jessie, lived in London with her French husband.

The body was said to be the subject of a post-mortem and the funeral set for April 24. In the meantime, a "devastated" Cotter went to *The Sun* claiming one of Paton's sisters Jessie had banned him from the funeral. "I don't know if he's left me any money and I really don't care about that," he said. "I just want my right to mourn the man I lived with and loved for 27 years." Cotter, despite Paton's cruelty toward him over the past few years, now defended Paton's shattered reputation. He cast particular doubt on Les McKeown's recent claims of rape. He also made it to the funeral. The coffin, he said, was "huge".

The Scotsman reported that "former stars of The Bay City Rollers", Alan Longmuir and Stuart 'Woody' Wood, were expected at Paton's funeral and, in an about-face, ran a lengthy two-part tribute to Paton's remarkable success in the pop world as "manager and mentor" to the Rollers. His "tireless work behind the scenes" and role as "image-maker" were picked out for particular praise.

The funeral was held at Edinburgh's stark, modernist Basil Spence-designed Mortonhall Crematorium. Paton had once said upon his death he fully expected, as the 'most hated man in Scotland', for baying crowds to push his coffin through the crematorium doors. In the event, around 250 family, friends, and business associates including many heavy faces from Scotland, Liverpool, Manchester, London and abroad, attended the respectable send-off. There was a subtle but noticeable undercover police presence with photographers using long lenses to take photographs of the mourners.

Phillipe Boussiere, Paton's nephew, his sister Jessie's son, led the family tributes. "A large number of articles in the public domain express opinions and recount events that bear no relationship to the man we knew," he said. "We have such love and respect for this man that despite all we have read, our gut instinct is this was a good man."

Boussierre also confirmed that Paton had left his entire fortune to charity. "I think he felt that if he had the ability to earn it, so did we," he said. "He chose to help those who were less fortunate."

'Rollers funeral snub for Paton' was *The Sun* headline the next day. Wood and Alan Longmuir (who told the *Sunday Herald* that Paton "did rip us off... and took our money") had not showed, nor had Derek Longmuir, Eric Faulkner, McGlynn or McKeown. One former Roller, however, had been there: Nobby Clark, singer with the band from 1965-1973. "I've got a long, long history with Tam and I just wanted to come along to remember the good times that we had," he said.

"For all his escapades, he was a likeable guy," Clark added. "He was the sort of person who was difficult not to like, despite what he got up to. Tam and I were friends; we stayed in touch. I met Tam when I was 15 and I was just thinking about the years we were on the road. He will be missed, regardless of what some people think about him. There was only one Tam Paton. He always said that he would leave all his money to charity but I never believed him."

Ray Cotter was in shock at not being remembered in Paton's will after standing by his side for 27 years. He told the *Daily Record*: "I believe he left his money to charity to ease his conscience. I've seen him do horrendous things, like putting drugs in people's drinks. He got away with it because people were scared of his criminal connections." Cotter said he was now planning to expose Paton's activities as a police informer, labelling him a "bully, drug dealer and grass".

"It still hurts to this day," Cotter later admitted. "He never left me a penny. It's an axe well and truly buried in my back. I should have got something." His attitude toward Paton, however, was now far more nuanced. Cotter said that much written about Paton posthumously made his "blood boil". "Tam wasn't a paedophile," he said. "He may have been a raving poofter but there were no children at LK. I'm not saying Tam was as white as the driven snow but who is?"

In July 2009 the police and Crown prosecutors gave up the battle to try and seize Paton's estate under Proceeds of Crime laws. It was not widely reported. Paton's lawyer Frank Moore said: "The Crown Office have removed all restrictions. The executors of his will should now be free to dispose of it." Documents, however, revealed Paton had been exaggerating his wealth to the press. His real worth was just over £3 million. Much of that was attached to property, with Little Kellerstain (valued at £1.3 million) and four central Edinburgh flats (valued at £600,000) all that was left of his portfolio. Paton also held over one million pounds in stocks and shares.

He had stipulated in his final will that he wanted his money to go to the Dogs Trust, World Wildlife Fund, Rachel House Children's Hospice in Kinross (who look after terminally ill children as part of Children's Hospice Association Scotland), the Scottish Society for the Prevention of Cruelty to Animals and cancer research charities. He had also given his executors permission to distribute funds to any charity of a similar nature to his five chosen groups.

Paton's old band-mates from his days as leader of The Crusaders organised a memorial concert for him at the Royal Golf Club in

Musselburgh with all proceeds donated to charity Chest, Heart and Stroke, Scotland. Paddy Dixon, one time drummer in The Crusaders, told the *East Lothian Courier*, the local paper that covered Prestopans, Musselburgh and Cockenzie: "I'm really sick of all the sleaze in the newspapers that has been written about him because I will remember him as a generous, courteous friend who would help anybody out." The Crusaders repeated their tribute to Paton, this time over three nights, in the same venue a year later in September 2010.

In September 2011, Little Kellerstain, described by *The Sun* as a "sleazy lair" and a "haven for teenage boys", was put on the market for a cut-price £800,000. The plunge pool where "the beast" Paton was said to have died had been "filled in" and concreted over amid fears it would put off buyers. By August 2012, the asking price was down to £540,000. Finally it was snapped up for £450,000 by an Edinburgh property developer. The proceeds from the sale went to the charities named in Paton's will. It was suggested, however, that some of the named benefactors had already refused Paton's donations.

In December 2013 Paton's bedroom and the "wet room" were bulldozed and a second floor added to Little Kellerstain. James Baillie, contracts director with Apex Developments, who were carrying out the renovations, told *The Sun*: "The master bedroom where Paton slept has already been demolished. It was seedy and we got rid of it because of its history. We wanted to erase the past. The sauna, where Tam Paton died, and the gym have also been knocked down for the same reason. The interior decor looked seedy, stuck in the seventies and eighties, and is being completely gutted."

He added: "There was a reluctance for people to buy the property because of its history and associations, but it was such a great deal and a great development opportunity we had no choice."

Pat McGlynn told the *Edinburgh News* in an article that ran on December 4, 2013 that he wished he could have demolished Paton's mansion himself. He also made fresh allegations against Paton, claiming how his former manager tried to sexually assault him in the bedroom of the mansion in 1976 after locking him inside. The 55-year-old said that his drink was spiked by Paton who sexually attacked him when he was just 18.

"The night I joined the band in 1976, Paton spiked my drink and assaulted me in the lounge," he said. "He also tried to assault me in his bedroom. He had a drawer that he would pull out which blocked the door. I had to fight him off. I was attacked by Paton three or four times in the house."

McGlynn said that he first reported the alleged attacks in 1977 but the police deemed there to be a lack of corroboration. He added: "Paton used to hold parties at the house where celebrities came up from London. There would be boys aged between 14 and 18 wandering around who would be abused. I was there, but I was too busy trying to protect myself to stop it. There was always a punch bowl in the lounge, which had been spiked with something. I didn't know much about drugs but there were sleeping tablets and cocaine around.

"With the police launching Operation Yewtree to investigate Jimmy Savile and others, I'm still hoping they investigate Tam Paton and his circle," added McGlynn. "Some of them were well-known names. I would be glad to give evidence. The full truth should come out. Paton still haunts me after all those years. I've suffered for 37 years and never got any justice. I phone the police every year to ask about whether anything has happened with the investigation, but nothing ever does."

McGlynn's fresh allegations resonated loudly in the current climate of suspicion and raised awareness caused by Operation Yewtree that had begun shortly after a controversial October 2012 ITV documentary about Sir Jimmy Savile, former BBC Radio 1 DJ and BBC TV presenter. The evidence against Savile, who had died in 2011, had amassed quickly (450 victims of rape and sexual abuse, most under 18, some under 10 were counted) and led to other celebrities being charged: Gary Glitter, Dave Lee Travis, Max Clifford, Rolf Harris and Chris Denning.★

★ Glitter, The Bay City Rollers' former label mate at Bell Records, was found guilty of historical child sex abuse in February 2015. One victim was eight. The 70-year-old was jailed for 16 years. Glitter had already been jailed for possessing child pornography and for committing obscene acts with girls aged 10 and 11.

There were links out of the norm between Paton and Savile, not just the whispers – dismissed by Cotter – that the two kept in touch via the telephone. It was also difficult, for instance, not to see Savile's hand behind the appearance of the Rollers at a free concert organised by Father Denis O'Connell in the grounds of the historic Colzium House estate, near Kilsyth, Lanarkshire in 1976. Father O'Connell ran the St Patrick's Church in Kilsyth with assistance from Father Keith O'Brien, who would go on to become Britain's most senior Catholic clergyman, and Father Thomas Mullen. Savile was a very good friend of Father O'Connell who had spent two years in London and worked at the BBC as a consultant on Catholic & Religious broadcasting during that time. Savile was regularly seen taking Mass at St Patrick's Church in Kilsyth, a small town of 10,000 in the lowlands of Scotland, between Glasgow and Edinburgh.

In 2013 Cardinal Keith O'Brien resigned as the head of the Scottish Catholic Church and as Archbishop of St Andrews and Edinburgh after a series of allegations of 'inappropriate acts' made by three priests and one former priest, with some incidents dating almost 30 years. He admitted improper sexual conduct throughout his career. Father Thomas Mullen was dismissed by the Vatican following accusations of child rape with one victim said to be aged nine at the time, and decades of sexual abuse allegations. Father O'Connell, who held popular youth Masses and organised many youth camps, games and events, died in 1997, aged 79.

In October 2014 Les Mckeown claimed in the *Daily Mail* that the now dead MP Sir Cyril Smith was a regular visitor to Little Kellerstain for "drink and drug-fuelled parties". "I saw him there half a dozen times in the late seventies, over a period of about two years," McKeown said. Smith was being posthumously investigated following a recorded 144 complaints of child sexual abuse against him from male victims as young as eight. Smith's name was heavily linked to the infamous homosexual brothel, the Elm Guest House in south west London, allegedly used by well-known establishment and celebrity figures, with a boy of 10 said to be a 'star attraction'. It was suggested that Smith was involved in a "high-level" paedophile ring that included other MPs, Cabinet members, senior police, judges and pop stars. There were calls now for Sir Nicholas Fairburn, among others, to be posthumously investigated. Fairburn's name was also linked to the Elm Guest House in several newspaper reports.

The *Scottish Daily Express* demanded that Paton be posthumously investigated and dubbed him the 'Scottish Savile'. The newspaper asked why Scottish Government had ignored the calls of "one of its own advisers" – Dr Sarah Nelson – to launch an investigation into a high-profile paedophile ring operating in Edinburgh. The *Express* said that ring was thought to have operated over several decades and to have included well-known TV personalities, lawyers and police officers. "In a chilling echo of the abuse scandal currently rocking Westminster, it now appears that a dossier of Scottish paedophiles with links to Paton was prepared in 1982 but never made public," the newspaper claimed.

Nelson told the newspaper: "I have heard longstanding claims that very vulnerable boys and young men were not only sexually abused by Tam Paton but also that there was a paedophile ring in existence. I also heard allegations that some homeless boys were placed in flats in Edinburgh for the purposes of prostitution. Both [my] studies involved young men in the criminal justice system who revealed over time they had been abused by Tam Paton and others. The feeling at the time was that this was so blatant and so obvious that there were suspicions Paton was being protected in high places. The boys were frightened, there was an atmosphere of fear around these boys of young men. It is not usually fear that holds them back it is embarrassment and shame, but these young men were frightened of retaliation." She added: "It is fair to say they were the most damaged young men I ever worked with."

The same national paper followed this with a fresh story from Pat McGlynn who claimed he had personally witnessed high-profile individuals from the diverse worlds of entertainment, law, genteel Edinburgh society and organised crime attend sex parties at Paton's secluded mansion. "This was 1976 to 1981 – there were lots of parties at Tam Paton's house and there were always young boys there, older men there. They used to dress the young boys up in women's clothes, and they'd be dancing in Paton's living room."

"The boys were anything from eight up to, well, after 17 or 18 they were too old for him [Paton]," McGlynn said. "A lot of them would come to see The Bay City Rollers and he'd get chatting to their parents and that's how Paton would get his hands on them. He was supplying the boys with drink and drugs. That's the only reason they were there. They weren't there because they liked Tam Paton. He would have a big punchbowl he would fill full of drugs – you wouldn't even know what you were taking. He got you in a trap, he got you addicted to drugs. I remember being in the band, I'd have a few drinks and I'd wake up with that man on top of me, having to fight him off. He was vile."

McGlynn suggested that drug addicts would willingly bring their children to Paton in exchange for a free high, while still more youngsters were flown in from abroad – sent to Scotland by their unwitting families with hopes of achieving pop stardom. "The police should really be investigating," he said. "The amount of people that I saw out at Little Kellerstain – there must be hundreds if not thousands of people that's been abused."

McGlynn may have been mistaken that that some boys had been as young as eight. No one else had claimed that during interviews for this book. Was he sure? "I'm talking about young boys, 12-16," he said. Twelve? "I was 18 at the time and they were a lot younger than me. I could tell by the way they were talking and their attitude... They were four or five years younger."

After Chris Denning was jailed for 13 years in November 2014 for multiple historic sex abuse of boys, some under 10, McGlynn told the *Daily Record* that Denning had been a regular at Little Kellerstain parties in the seventies "where young boys were drugged then molested". Most of the boys at the parties were 14 or 15 but some were just 10, McGlynn said. "Paton had drawers full of Quaaludes," he said. "There was cocaine and cannabis, almost everything. They would use sleeping tablets to spike kids' drinks. Chris Denning was always there. He would come up from London especially. Whenever he saw a kid who was in a bad way from the sleeping tablets he'd be straight across. Then he'd drag them into one of the bedrooms."

Denning was also said to have introduced boys to Jimmy Savile and been involved in a paedophile ring that operated from a youth disco in Walton-on-Thames, Surrey called the Walton Hop, where he had picked up some of his victims. When Jonathan King had been jailed for sexual assaults on schoolboys in 2001, the court heard he had picked up some of his victims at the same disco. Paton and The Bay City Rollers had visited the Walton Hop on multiple occasions.*

In December 2014, it was announced that a public inquiry on historical sex abuse in Scotland would go ahead following a number of scandals involving the abuse of children in care, including at institutions run by the Roman Catholic Church. The inquiry began in April 2015. Police quickly identified 37 VIPs "in the public eye" among more than 100 suspects. Tam Paton was one of 80 named suspects, 26 of whom were dead. Sir Nicholas Fairburn and Robert Henderson QC were also named. Abuse was said to have taken place in 45 institutions in Scotland. It is rumoured a member of The Bay City Rollers has been questioned as part of the inquiry.

There will, inevitably, be more to come from these various investigations and inquiries. Unnamed but heavily hinted at celebrities, actors, political and establishment figures, and pop stars are often suggested as being involved in sexual abuse.

What seems incredible is that Paton could be linked to so much of it, to so many different men convicted of abuse and alleged paedophile rings: Savile and the Catholic Church hierarchy; King, Denning and the Walton Hop; 'Sticky' Wilson, Kevin Drumgoole and potential abuse in Scottish care homes such as Ponton House; Cyril Smith and the Elm Guest House; Martin Frutin; Robert Henderson QC and the Magic Circle.

There were also the many other men, famous and not so, in Paton's circles who appeared to have uncommon, potentially abusive, sexual interests; milkmen, chauffeurs, DJs, TV stars, music promoters, managers

---

* In 2015, King was arrested, alongside two other men, aged 76 and 86, on suspicion of sexual offences against boys under the age of 16 at the Walton Hop disco in the seventies.

and producers, record shop owners and CID offices among them. This list of names would, of course, have to include The Bay City Rollers' drummer, Derek Longmuir.

Some of them may soon envy Paton's place in the grave. For he rests in peace, never truly believing he ever did anything wrong.

AFTERWORD

Reunion

Les McKeown planned to gig throughout 2015 as "Bay City Rollers starring Les McKeown". He began filming direct messages to his hundreds of female fans and used social media to post them. This became something of an addiction. He was soon posting messages "on TV", as he called it, daily, often while travelling. It allowed him to interact with the fans or "girlfriends", as he called them. He seemed preternaturally happy in many of the videos.

His single 'Rock And Roll Christmas Time' had not been a chart success but had notched up in excess of 24,000 hits on YouTube. He talked about his new album coming out in the summer and a new single called 'Boomerang'. The court case, he said was "not something I'm supposed to talk about". But, he admitted "it has turned out bad for the Rollers". "At one point we were supposed to be due £80 million... Now the settlement being quoted is a couple of million. I don't know what is going to happen but I have moved on from it."

The Rollers were briefly in the news in early 2015 when UK high street fashion chain, Topman, launched a fashion range inspired by the band's mid-seventies image. On the catwalk the models had the Rollers' 'tufty' haircuts, jeans in that unmistakable A-line shape, tight at the crotch, stopping wide and short above the ankle with exaggerated turn-ups, and wore figure-hugging tartan-trimmed jackets brightly embellished by sewn-on patches such as lightning bolts and slogans such as 'Max' or 'Jack'. There were also white one-piece outfits in the same shape with similar embellishment. Some of the models wore tartan scarves, hooped socks in loud clashing colours and approximations of the Roller's battered high-top Adidas trainers or baseball boots.

McKeown took his Rollers act to Japan, Latvia, Canada and Germany and booked a remarkable 80-plus date UK tour that would run over the final four months of 2015. Throughout the summer he kept busy playing one-off gigs in the UK, often at festivals. In Northern Ireland it was reported for one show he was paid £11,300. The new material was not released.

In June he was supposed to be the guest of honour at the 2015 Rollerfest held in Philadelphia. The organiser Susan Rostron, a Rollerfest veteran, had invited all the band members but only McKeown committed. Once again, however, as at the 2014 Rollerfest in Edinburgh, the Woods were not happy with the event. They had donated some items to be auctioned for charity but said they would not have participated if they knew McKeown was involved. There was consequently a spate of hostility on Facebook between fan factions. Some said they wouldn't come to the Rollerfest because McKeown was going.

In the event, McKeown did not make it to Philadelphia. He did spend more than an hour talking to the 200 women present via Skype. Rostron said the event had been more about the relationship between the women present than the band. "We've all been together about 20 years since we all first typed Bay City Rollers into the search engine," she said. "I found girls I used to write to when I was 12 as pen pals." Rostron followed the Rollerfest by organising a fan gathering in New York's Times Square on the 40th anniversary of the band's first American visit. A group of 40 or so fans in tartan outfits sang 'Saturday Night' and featured on the news.

McKeown did finally get to America in 2015. In August he flew in for a quick meet and greet in New Jersey that he'd organised. Forty fans paid $120 each to have a dinner and chat with him. He also put out a public request via social media to Eric Faulkner, Stuart Wood and Alan Longmuir to reunite the band – he said he didn't want to talk to "in between people". He asked them "to take advantage of the opportunities I've created". He talked of doing "a nice little swansong for a couple of years, making ourselves some proper money".

Faulkner played a few gigs as Eric Faulkner's Bay City Rollers over the summer, including a couple in Germany, but focused mainly on his solo acoustic work. He had fallen seriously ill in February after suffering a seizure that left him unconscious at his PA Karin Ingram's house. He was in intensive care for a week and remained in hospital for a further two. The diagnosis was a viral infection of the brain, Viral Encephalitis, which for most people results in lasting brain damage. Ingram posted on social media that Faulkner had made a complete recovery.

He was the only one of the famous five Bay City Rollers not take part in the filming of a new BBC Scotland TV documentary on the band. Even Derek was interviewed for *Rollermania: Britain's Biggest Boy Band* that was shot over the summer of 2015. It was anodyne stuff with only rare home footage, some featuring shots of Paton with his parents, providing anything new. There was no mention of Derek's or Paton's or McKeown's convictions. No dark stuff. It was little different from the 1999 BBC documentary on the band. It was shown, however at 9pm, on a Monday night on BBC Scotland in September, and provoked a fresh wave of celebratory articles about the band's heyday. Good promotion but for what?

Alan's play, *And I Ran With The Gang*, ran for three weeks at the Edinburgh Fringe Festival in August 2015. It was at the same venue as the 2014 run and did well again. The Le Monde Hotel space held between 100-450 people and tickets were £15. The show remained the same – some gentle acting, a lightweight live section followed by Q&As. Alan announced he'd be taking the show to Canada in 2016.

He still lived in the three-bed semi in Bannockburn, a town rich with Scottish history and not much else. It had been the scene in 1314 of a significant Scottish victory in the First War of Scottish Independence when a small army led by Robert the Bruce had defeated a far larger English force. Alan didn't seem ready to go into battle. He was 67, portly and balding.

But remarkably, in September, McKeown announced the Rollers were reforming for Christmas gigs with a new single in the pipeline. The manager of the reformed band was John McLaughlin, the man who had being working on McKeown's solo music. In Scotland the announcement was covered on the TV news. In America it was featured in *Billboard* magazine. The media largely ignored the fact that Faulkner and Derek were not involved, sidestepped the eighties and nineties, and broadly declared the Rollers were back after 40 years away. It was an exaggerated thumbs up, flashes of tartan and sips on glasses of milk by McKeown, Wood and Alan for promo pictures.

The late-December gigs at 2000-plus-capacity venues; four at Glasgow Barrowlands, two at Edinburgh Usher Hall, and others at Manchester Apollo and London Apollo, generated £400,000 worth of business on nearly 12,000 tickets sold. The Bay City Rollers were back.

The press surrounding the reunion – 'Grey City Rollers!' and 'Bay City Codgers!' were two British tabloid headlines – was also fillip for McKeown's own Rollers act that was in the middle of their own UK tour. It couldn't have come at a better time although tickets had already been selling well. There were half-hearted attempts to state that Wood and Alan would not be at these dates. He often filmed the shows live and transmitted them via social media. They were mostly pantomime.

The reformed Rollers played together for the first time at the Great Scot Awards in Glasgow in October. It was just a few numbers but a taste of what was to come: Alan and Woody with guitars either side of McKeown and his regular band. It was cabaret. They took the same harmless turn to the Scottish Music Awards in Glasgow in November where they were honoured with the 'Living Legends Award'.

There was talk of a new Bay City Rollers single, 'Boomerang' – the same song McKeown had been talking about releasing for months. McKeown was firmly in the driving seat of this reunion. There were plans for American dates in Los Angeles and at New York's iconic Madison Square Garden and a UK arena tour in 2016. McKeown admitted the band were back together for money. He was 60 and had got what he wanted. He was closest to Alan and they planned on travelling together to do more meet and greets with fans (for a price).

They, without Wood, were also booked for six February 2016 Japanese live dates in Tokyo and Osaka, including matinees (Alan was briefly hospitalised shortly after these dates). Wood, 58, must have simply bottled the recent animosity he and his wife had channelled toward McKeown for the successful Christmas shows. His website was now selling calendars, Roller T-shirts, bags and even chocolate bars.

There were vague suggestions that Eric Faulkner might re-join the band. I was told this would be unlikely but you only had to look at the history of the band to realise it could still happen. What about Derek? Alan insisted his brother was 'innocent' but that he would be an addition too far given the controversy surrounding him. "In Britain at least," added McKeown. Perhaps he planned to take the band to parts of the world where a conviction for possessing child porn and allegations of sex with a 13-year-old boy were less publicised. "He didn't do anything wrong," Alan said. "They weren't his pictures."

There was a hastily assembled cash-in Christmas album, *A Christmas Shang-A-Lang*, available on iTunes. It featured 'rollerised' versions of Christmas classics such as 'Jingle Bells' and 'White Christmas'. It was good, even if Alan and Wood were just passengers on the project. Wood talked of a 'proper' album in 2016.

McKeown eagerly promoted the Christmas album, the gigs and the future. Throughout 2015 there had been absolutely no mention in the media about the band's lawsuit with Sony and the band offered few clues as to what was going on in their reunion interviews. The *Daily Mail* reported that the band was still be 'at war' with Sony. "The fight will go on," McKeown said. In the same sentence he also suggested Sony might want to 'cut a deal' for the reformed band. It was confusing. Mark St John, who was not involved in this band reunion, promised to reveal all to me in the new year.

In early May 2016, I was told by a reliable source, that the band and Sony had settled out of court. St John had postponed a date to discuss the case with me several times earlier in the year. There had been no concrete developments in the lawsuit reported by the media. The settlement figure was rumoured to be $3.5 million and, in this version of events, the band members were said to have come away with just about £70,000 each. It seemed, following the judgements made on expert witness statements in late 2014, when limits were set for a band pay out of between $1 and $8 million, and considering the costs the band had incurred over the years plus the lack of any reported appeal, a believable, if rather limp, ending to their epic struggle with the record industry. After all, there had been a similar amount of money on offer from the label for many years. It had been tens of millions they had been chasing. Another reliable source stated that the rumoured settlement figures were not correct but did not elaborate. There was little disputing, however, the fact that there had been an out of court settlement brokered. Frustratingly, it almost certainly contained a confidentiality agreement. I wanted to ask St John about the figures, if what I had been told was true. It was also rumoured that, as a gesture, he had lowered his fees and that the band's American law firm had been persuaded to lower their contingency fee – otherwise the band would have got nothing. "Can't comment, sorry," was all St John could offer. Is that because he was not legally allowed to comment? "You'll have to draw your own conclusions," he said.

It seems we will now never know, conclusively, what the figures in the settlement are; how much the Rollers finally walked away with after over 30 years of confusion and acrimony, including a decade long, spirit-sapping court case. *Any* questions about court cases, money troubles, scandal, Derek and Paton, the dark stuff, were brushed away hastily by the band.

And that wasn't even the end of it, if there will ever be an end. In July 2016 Wood quit the reunion, claiming McKeown was more interested in promoting his own career than the reformed band. Wood's wife sent aggressive text messages to Alan's wife, Eileen, whom she claimed had assaulted her at a gig. Wood talked legal action. Alan suggested the band's lawsuit with Sony was not entirely 'resolved'. McKeown said he and Alan would continue as The Bay City Rollers. It was messy and confusing, as it always has been. As it always seems to be.

NOTES

Acknowledgements & Sources

The primary source of the factual material in this book is hundreds of hours of interviews conducted by the author. All of them, bar the few conducted off the record, were recorded. Some interviewees were interviewed over several days or weeks. The author spoke to close to 100 people in total, all who had detailed, direct knowledge of the inner workings of the Rollers. All interviews took place in 2015.

The book also relies on comprehensive, voluminous research conducted solely by the author. Alongside magazine and newspaper articles, the documentary material referenced includes TV footage, photographs, contracts, official press releases, private archives, radio broadcasts, books and several filed court documents.

Every interviewee was offered the transcript of their interview to check the statements they made. The documentary evidence was often used to resolve occasional conflicts in recollection between interviewees. Due consideration was also given to the reliability of the interviewee. If necessary further interviewing or correspondence via email to clarify facts was undertaken. As such, the author believes the assembled facts in this book are accurate.

The main text does not give specific citation to the source or sources of each written fact. Largely they are drawn from the first hand interviews.

The author can supply detailed attribution to quotations and facts that come from interviews not conducted with the author. Requests can be made in writing to the publisher.

The reconstructed dialogue does not represent the exact words used by the characters at the time but captures the flavour of the discussions. The conversation of historic cash figures into their current worth was intended to bring further clarity to the narrative. The conversion is open to dispute, depending on the many historic and current variables influencing cash worth, but the method used by the author was consistent and overall the figures remain a good, accurate indicator of the financial aspect of the band's affairs.

The hard work of many journalists, writers and fans were invaluable in compiling the book. The publications referenced include: *Tiger Beat*; *16*; *Bravo*; *Jackie*; *Pink*; *Sounds*; *Disc*; *Popswop*; *Melody Maker*; *Rolling Stone*; *Record Mirror*; *The Gazette*; *Teen Bag*; *New Musical Express*; *Supersonic*; *Fab208*; *Creem*; *Music Week*; *Billboard*; *Music Life*; *Story of Pop*; *Look-In*; *Music Star's*; *Vanity Fair*; *Mirabelle*; *Diana*; *Daily Record and its Sunday edition, Sunday Mail*; *The Scotsman and its Sunday edition, Scotland on Sunday*; *The Glasgow Herald and Sunday Herald*; *East Lothian Courier*; *Edinburgh Evening News*; *The Scottish Sun*; *The Evening Times*; *Stirling Observer*; *Scottish Express*; *The Times*; *The People*; *Tottenham and Wood Green Journal*; *Daily Express*; *London Evening Standard*; *Liverpool Echo*; *The Guardian*; *The Independent*; *Liverpool Daily Post*; *The Telegraph and Sunday Telegraph*; *Daily Mail*; *News of the World*; *The Week*; *Daily & Sunday Mirror*; *Leicestershire Chronicle*; *The Sun*; *The Morecambe Visitor*; *Daily Star*; *Newcastle Chronicle*; *The Birmingham Post*; *The Impartial Reporter*; *Harrogate Advertiser*; *Lancashire Evening Post*; *Hollywood Reporter*; *The Telegraph (Calcutta, India)*; *Irish Independent*; *The Australian*; *Newcastle Herald (Australia)*; *The Sydney Morning Herald*; *The National Law Review*; *Nashua Telegraph*; *The Pittsburgh Press*; *The Milwaukee Journal*; *The Dispatch*; *The Argus-Press*; *Schenectady Gazette*; *The Ledger*; *The Spokesman-Review*; *The Milwaukee Sentinel*; *Toledo Blade*; *Lakeland Ledger*; *Daytona Beach Morning Journal*; *The Deseret News*; *The Australian Women's Weekly*; *Edmonton Journal*; *The Sun-*

Herald; The Age; Daytona Beach Morning Journal; The Deseret News; The Bryan Times; Star-News; Reading Eagle; Regina Leader-Post; The Tuscaloosa News; The Southeast Missourian; Ottawa Citizen; St Petersburg Times; Sarasota Herald-Tribune; The Canberra Times; Observer-Reporter; The Village Voice; Gadsden Times; The Japan Times, Village Voice and Chicago Tribune.

The websites referenced include: baycityrollers-online.de; flashbak; uk420; theukcolumn; baycityrollers.weebly; digitalspy; deadline; wikipedia; pollstar; cannabisnews; communitycare; facebook; highbeam; spotlight; skynews; justicedenied; spiked; andrewdrummond; davidicke; freescotland; bilbomusic; bbcnews; baycityrollersgirls; baycityrollerspenpalreunion; neojapanisme; pagesix; cherryredtv; cathyfox; thescum; scottishreview; scottishlawreporter; desiringprogress; ozzienews; accountingweb; kentnews; justia; theneedle; theregister; discogs; aangirlfan; historyismadeatnight; glittersuits&platformboots; rockingscots; edinburghgigarchive; coffee-tablenotes; marycigarettes. wordpress; voyforums:theunofficialrickyfenderboard; bcr1.de; baycityrollerdcdsanddvds; 70steenpop.blogspot; rnrloveletters. blogspot; spencemusic.co.uk; bcrppr.blogspot; edinphoto.org; summerlovesensation.blogspot; twitter; huffingtonpost; thearmyoflove; erikfaulkner.org; redbullmusicacademy; members.shaw.ca/therollers; bloomberg.com; casetext; courtlistener; 45cat; e.watkins/musictv; radiorewind; prestoungrange.org; rubendefuentes; theimages.info; bcr40thusanniversaryfanfest.blogspot; tvpopdiaries; sjwood.miiduu; lesmckeown; bordersmusic.

The footage of the band performing on a variety of TV shows, including their own, was chiefly referenced via youtube. Also useful was the DVD, *Rollercoaster* (The Remarkable Life Story of Former Bay City Roller Stuart 'Woody' Wood, 2007), the TV programmes: *Behind The Music: Bay City Rollers* (VH1, 1999); *The Bay City Rollers – Remember* (BBC, 1999); *Who Got The Rollers' Millions?* (Ch4, 2004); *Rollermania: The Biggest boy band in the world* (BBC Scotland, 2015) and the radio programme, *Bay City Babylon,* presented by Mark Lamarr [BBC R2, 2008).

Bibliography

Allen, Ellis. *The Bay City Rollers* (Panther, 1975)

Beckett, Andy. *When The Lights Went Out: What Really Happened To Britain In The Seventies* (Faber & Faber, 2009)

Bernstein, Sid. *It's Sid Bernstein Calling* (Jonathan David, 2002)

Cassidy, David. *Could It Be Forever?: My Story* (Headline, 2007)

Clark, Nobby. *The Lost Roller* (Strategic, 2014)

Coleman, Bess. *Rollers In America* (Queen Anne, 1975)

Coy, Wayne. *Bay City Babylon: The Unbelievable But True Story Of The Bay City Rollers* (Hats Off, 2005)

Dannen, Fredric. *Hit Men* (Random House, 1991)

Davis, Clive. *The Soundtrack Of My Life* (Simon & Schuster, 2013)

Epstein, Brian. *A Cellarful Of Noise* (Souvenir Press, 2011)

Erickson, Hal . *Sid & Marty Krofft: A Critical Study Of Saturday Morning Children's Television, 1969-1993* (McFarland, 2007)

Falconer, Eric. *An Edinburgh Lad: A Collection Of Poetry And Prose* (self-published, 2015)

Golumb, David. *Bay City Rollers Picture Scrapbook* (Queen Anne, 1975)

Heilemann, Wolfgang (Bubi). *Live On Tour, At Home, Studio, Backstage* (Schwarzkopf & Schwarzkopf, 2004)

Hogg, Brian. *The History Of Scottish Rock And Pop: All That Ever Mattered* (Square One Books, 1993)

Irving, David. *Howff Tae Hip Hop : A Subjective History Of The Edinburgh Music Scene* (self-published)

Kielty, Martin. *Big Noise The Sound Of Scotland* (Black And White Publishing, 2006)

McClintick, David. *Indecent Exposure: A True Story Of Hollywood And Wall Street* (HarperBusiness, 2006)

McKeown, Les. *Shang-A-Lang: The Curse Of The Bay City Rollers* (Mainstream, 2006)

Rogan, Johnny. *Starmakers And Svengalis: The History of British Pop Management* (Macdonald Queen Anne Press, 1988)

Sullivan, Caroline. *Bye Bye Baby: My Tragic Love Affair With The Bay City Rollers* (Bloomsbury, 1999)

Wale, Michael. *The Bay City Rollers: Tam Paton's Inside Story Of Britain's No. 1 Pop Group* (Everest, 1975)

Wallace, Anne. *The Bay City Rollers On Tour* (World Distributors, 1975)

The Bay City Rollers Annuals of 1976 and 1977 and the band's official magazine were also referenced.

Acknowledgements

This book would not have been possible were in not for: Tony Roberts, Paddy Dixon, Frank Conner, Nobby Clark, David Golumb, Tony Calder, Stuart Hepburn, Jef Hanlon, Mark St John, Ray Cotter, Alan Walsh, John Gorman, Ron Fraser, Pat McGlynn, John Fogarty, Paul Pike, Jonathan King, Barry Evangeli, David Valentine, Phil Coulter, Alan Macleod, Ronnie Simpson, Colin Slater, Archie Marr, Gregory Ellison, Dr Sarah Nelson, Gert Magnus, Phil Wainman, Mike Pasternak, Beth Wernick, Steven, Jake Duncan, Harry Maslin, Robert S. Levinson, Jon Gillam, Brian Spence, Andrew Drummond, Mike Mansfield, Billy McGhee, Dick Leahy, Bob Gruen, Carol Klenfner, Scobie Ryder, Jimmy Ienner, Coco, Danny Fields, Derek Taxi, Martin Lee Goldberg, Bill Martin, Stephan Gelfas, Susan Rostron, Chris Charlesworth, Duncan Faure, Damian McKee, Muff Winwood, Jack Strom, Colin Frechter, Jeffrey 'Horshack' Grinstein and Rod Thear.

The above gave generously of their time in interviews that routinely lasted up to two hours. A special thanks to Tony Calder for the introductions, Carol Klenfner for the private paperwork, Ray Cotter for the radio show and the long interviews over the course of several months, David Valentine for the material and contacts, Billy McGhee for the photos, Betty Smith for helping with The Crusaders, Nobby Clark and Pat McGlynn for allowing me several interviews, Mark St John for the patience and continued assistance and Dr Sarah Nelson for the foreword. Final thanks to Katrina Gunasekera at Music Sales for legal advice and to Johnny Rogan for the spark, proof-read and index.

RIP: Neil Smith, Stephen Goldberg, Billy Lyall, Sid Bernstein, Neil Porteous, David Bridger, Marty Machat, Eric Kronfeld, Eupehemia Clunie, Joseph Beltrami, Robert Henderson, Mike Klenfner, Tam Smith, Davie Gold, Martin Frutin, Peter Ker, Muriel Young, Andy Truman, Peter Walsh, Bess Coleman, Barry Perkins, Ed Justin, Tam Paton, Tony Barrow.

Those who declined to be interviewed: Stephen Tenenbaum, Ian Mitchell, Barry Reiss, Glenn Delgado, Anne Baxter, David Sonenberg, David Ravden, Emio Zizza, Per Lyhne, Derek Longmuir.

This work comes to you via my agent Kevin Pocklington, Omnibus commissioning editor David Barraclough and the book's editor Chris Charlesworth.

Index

Singles releases are in roman type and albums are in italics. Persons listed in parentheses refer to the name of the recording or performing artistes of the particular song.